Library of America, a nonprofit organization,
champions our nation's cultural heritage
by publishing America's greatest writing in
authoritative new editions and providing resources
for readers to explore this rich, living legacy.

RECONSTRUCTION

RECONSTRUCTION

VOICES FROM AMERICA'S
FIRST GREAT STRUGGLE
FOR RACIAL EQUALITY

Brooks D. Simpson, *editor*

THE LIBRARY OF AMERICA

Published in the United States by Library of America.
Visit our website at www.loa.org.

Some of the material in this volume is reprinted
by permission of the holders of copyright and publication rights.
Every effort has been made to contact the copyright holders.
If an owner has been unintentionally omitted,
acknowledgment will gladly be made in future printings.
See Note on the Texts on page 688 for further information.

This paper meets the requirements of
ANSI/NISO Z39.48–1992 (Permanence of Paper).

Distributed to the trade in the United States
by Penguin Random House Inc.
and in Canada by Penguin Random House Canada Ltd.

Library of Congress Control Number: 2017939512
ISBN 978–1–59853–555–6

First Printing
The Library of America—303

Manufactured in the United States of America

Reconstruction:
Voices from America's First Great Struggle
for Racial Equality
is published with support from

WILLIAM R. BERKLEY
and
THE BERKLEY FAMILY FOUNDATION

Contents

CODA, 1879

Introduction

MOST Americans don't know very much about Reconstruction, and in many cases what they may think they know is wrong. This shortcoming is understandable. Sometimes passed over in traditional high school or college history courses, the period can also be marginalized as an unseemly interval between the heroic drama of the Civil War and the advent of the tremendous economic, social, and political changes set into motion by the late nineteenth-century triad of industrialization, urbanization, and immigration. Popular imagination of the era in the early twentieth century was captured in two famous films based on best-selling novels, *Birth of a Nation* (1915) and *Gone With the Wind* (1939), both of which offered vivid portrayals of the persistence and eventual triumph of southern whites over the forces of evil represented by a malevolent alliance of greedy carpetbaggers, treacherous scalawags, and ignorant freedmen. Although some scholars challenged this perspective—most notably, W.E.B. Du Bois in *Black Reconstruction* (1935)—only in the 1950s did a wave of revisionist reassessment, inspired in part by the civil rights movement, begin to present different perspectives as historians debated the meaning of Reconstruction and why it turned out as it did. These debates have yet to become part of our popular memory. There is no gripping PBS series on Reconstruction comparable to Ken Burns's *The Civil War*, no compelling one-volume narrative history for general readers such as James M. McPherson's *Battle Cry of Freedom*, and no vivid popular novel with the enduring appeal of Michael Shaara's *The Killer Angels*. For many Americans, Reconstruction is not an essential part of our national story, or fundamental to our sense of who we are today. The exception to this marginalization is to be found in the consciousness of black America, where the invocation of "forty acres and a mule" powerfully evokes memories of an era of promise and betrayal.

This volume aims to help redress that imbalance. It brings to life the words and deeds of Americans as they battled each other over what the Civil War did, and did not, achieve,

highlighting the struggle of African Americans to make freedom mean more than the absence of slavery, and recording
how other Americans resisted that struggle for equality. In the
twenty-first century too many Americans think of terrorism
as a recent phenomenon brought to our shores by outsiders,
erasing the fundamental role that merciless violence played in
the preservation of white supremacy. Much is made today of
the American promise, and yet during Reconstruction much
of that promise went unfulfilled in what historian Eric Foner
has termed an unfinished revolution.

A few words about the scope of this volume. Its aim is to collect contemporary writing by participants and observers that
records and illuminates our first national attempt to imagine
and build a biracial republic. The writings it presents focus on
the status of the freed people in the South after the Civil War,
on definitions of citizenship and the expansion of suffrage, on
the national political struggles that shaped the course of Reconstruction, and on the white supremacist terrorism that resisted
the movement toward equality. It is not intended to address
every aspect of American public life during the Reconstruction
era, and as a result does not encompass foreign policy, tariff
legislation and civil service reform, industrial expansion and labor unrest, or westward expansion and the accompanying wars
against the Indians. Moreover, while debates over reconstructing the republic began as far back as the secession winter of
1860–61, we have decided to start telling this story in 1865. A
range of writings about wartime reconstruction, including the
debate over emancipation and Lincoln's struggles with congressional Republicans over the framing of policy, are available
in the four-volume Library of America series *The Civil War
Told by Those Who Lived It* (2011–14). Finally, while a case can
be made that Reconstruction did not end in 1877, we have chosen to conclude our volume with the end of significant federal
efforts to maintain Republican state governments in the South
in the face of violence, intimidation, and the increasing desire
of many northerners for an end to civil strife.

By 1865 the war had destroyed slavery, yet no one knew what
a post-emancipation America would look like. Among those
trying to find a way forward was Abraham Lincoln. His efforts
to restore loyal state governments supported by white Unionists

in the South had been repeatedly frustrated by the stubborn determination of most white southerners to defend slavery and secession. Over the course of the war he moved from advocating gradual compensated emancipation, followed by the voluntary colonization of at least some of the freed people outside the United States, to emancipation as a war measure and the enlistment of 180,000 black soldiers, to support for the Thirteenth Amendment and, in what turned out to be his last speech, advocacy of limited black suffrage. Yet the sixteenth president never abandoned his desire for the rapid restoration of elected civilian governments in the South, and his vision for what emancipation would ultimately mean remained incomplete up to the day of his death. Many Republicans sought a more thoroughgoing revolution in southern society, envisioning a prolonged military occupation of the region, the confiscation of planter estates, and their redistribution to the very people who had worked them as enslaved labor. Others supported efforts to establish schools for the freed people and to set them on the path to citizenship and the franchise. While Lincoln may have seen emancipation as a means toward the end of preserving the republic, black leaders reversed those priorities and used the war for union to push for emancipation and equal citizenship. During the war African Americans, in ways large and small, helped undermine and then demolish the institution Confederate vice president Alexander H. Stephens had celebrated as the "corner-stone" of the Confederacy.

With the collapse of Confederate resistance in the spring of 1865, the imperatives that shaped wartime Reconstruction vanished, for there was no longer any slaveholding regime to subdue. The impending ratification of the Thirteenth Amendment made the destruction of slavery a permanent achievement, no longer subject to possible reversal by a Democratic president or a reactionary Supreme Court. Yet much remained to be done; as Lincoln said at a cabinet meeting on April 14, 1865, a scant five days after Robert E. Lee surrendered his army to Ulysses S. Grant at Appomattox Court House, Reconstruction "was the great question now before us, and we must soon begin to act." Lincoln's assassination meant that the exercise of executive initiative would be left to Andrew Johnson, an outspoken Tennessee Unionist who, in the words of his presidential private secretary, "at times exhibited a morbid distress and feeling against the negroes." Johnson's assumption of the presidency soon narrowed the boundaries of the possible. His pardon and amnesty proclamations in May 1865 put an end to the notion of widespread confiscation of planter lands, while he sought to restore white supremacist state governments under which the freed people would, at best, be second-class citizens, unable to vote in elections dominated by unrepentant secessionists. With the chance for more fundamental change thwarted, congressional Republicans settled for devising means within the framework of restored civil governments to protect black civil rights and curb the influence of former Confederates. They passed the first federal civil rights act, extended the life of the Freedmen's Bureau, and framed the Fourteenth Amendment. Johnson's repeated vetoes and ill-tempered public outbursts eroded his standing, and in 1867 Congress seized control of Reconstruction policy, restoring military rule in the South and insisting that black men be enfranchised and permitted to participate alongside whites in forming new state governments.

The refusal of most southern whites to accept emancipation and equality before the law as results of the war led to measures that were both revolutionary for their times and ultimately limited in their extent. Framed and proposed to the states by Congress in 1866 and ratified two years later, the Fourteenth Amendment fundamentally transformed the American republic, establishing national citizenship and guaranteeing due process and equal protection of the law to all persons. Yet it was uncertain what the impact of the amendment would be. Although its text gave Congress the power to enforce its provisions through appropriate legislation, it was unclear how enforcement would work in a nation historically averse to centralized power. And to the bitter frustration of the suffragist movement, neither Congress, the courts, nor the public at large would consider the status of women to have been changed by the amendment's adoption. Southern resistance to ratifying the Fourteenth Amendment helped push Congress to adopt the Reconstruction Acts in 1867, making male black voters in the South part of the political process. The struggle with Johnson over his attempts to interfere with the implementation of the Reconstruction Acts, which eventually led to his impeachment and near-conviction, exacted a toll on the Republicans and forced them to settle for measures that fell short of their intended goals. White supremacist violence escalated through the expansion of the Ku Klux Klan and other terrorist groups. Republicans struggled to institute black suffrage in the North as well as the South, a sign of the limits of white support for political equality and the power of the Democratic Party to obstruct change. Despite widespread violence and intimidation, in 1868 black men participated as voters in large numbers for the first time, with their ballots giving Ulysses S. Grant, the Republican presidential candidate, his margin of victory in the popular vote. (Absent a popular majority, Grant would have secured the presidency through the electoral college in any case.)

In accepting the 1868 Republican presidential nomination, Grant offered a deceptively simple rendering of his personal platform: "Let us have peace." The phrase could mean whatever one wanted it to mean: an end to violence against the freed people, an end to sectional rancor, an end to prolonged political bickering and conflict, and even an end to Reconstruction, so that the nation could move past the war. In arming black men with the ballot, Republicans could also claim that African Americans in the South were now empowered to defend themselves through the traditional political process, alleviating the need for continued federal intervention to protect them from white violence. The ratification of the Fifteenth Amendment in 1870 removed race as a barrier to voting, although states were still allowed to impose literacy tests, property qualifications, and poll taxes as long as they were applied on an ostensibly nonracial basis. Using the federal amendment process allowed Republicans in the North to enfranchise black men in their own states by a simple majority vote in their legislatures, bypassing the referenda often required to amend state constitutions. As one Pennsylvania Republican congressman put it, "Party expediency and exact justice coincide for once." Yet the amendment's passage also marked a turning point for many Republicans, who openly expressed doubt that the federal government could, or should, do anything further to secure the rights of the freed people. And, to the renewed frustration of the suffragist movement, the amendment did nothing to remove disenfranchisement on the basis of sex.

If Americans who voted for Grant thought his slogan "Let us have peace" signaled that he would bring an end to Reconstruction, they would find themselves sorely disappointed during the next eight years. Efforts to suppress black votes and topple Republican-controlled state governments in the South continued, forcing Republicans to pass a series of Enforcement Acts designed to give the federal government the power to protect the freed people from organized violence and electoral fraud. Although a vigorous application of federal military and judicial power broke the back of the Ku Klux Klan, white southerners found other ways to resist Reconstruction, and their use of terrorist tactics became more sophisticated. During the 1870s, in the wake of a devastating economic depression, more and more whites began to believe that nothing more could, or should, be done to protect the rights of southern blacks. Some northerners latched on to the corruption and factionalism of some southern Republicans as justification for washing their hands of the entire Reconstruction endeavor, while others lamented how the necessary means of enforcement, including expanded federal power and military intervention, went against American traditions of local rule and civilian government. A commitment to equality and freedom, never quite complete in the minds and hearts of many white people who had supported the war to preserve the Union, faltered, narrowing the limits of the possible through the erosion of public support for continued intervention. Additional civil rights legislation proved short-lived, although the debate over what became the Civil Rights Act of 1875 allowed the first African American representatives in the halls of Congress an opportunity to demonstrate their eloquence, idealism, and courage as they called upon their fellow Americans to make good on the promise of equality.

In the South the forces of white supremacy waged a skillful campaign to retake control of the region, displaying a commitment that had been lacking in the Confederacy's quest for independence. Whether Republicans conducted a retreat from Reconstruction or waged a fighting withdrawal, by the time of the nation's celebration of its centennial in 1876 it was clear that the few Republican state governments that remained in the South were in a precarious position that required federal support to persist, and such support would come to an end no matter who won the presidential contest that year. Once Republicans realized that they could maintain control of the presidency and the Senate without southern voters, they decided that the party's southern wing was a disastrous political liability. The resolution of the disputed Hayes-Tilden presidential contest through the series of agreements styled the Compromise of 1877 marked the end of an era in Reconstruction policy, while the restoration of home rule to white southerners paved the way for the era of disenfranchisement, Jim Crow segregation, and widespread lynching.

This collection focuses on our country's first great struggle for black freedom and equality. It is best understood as an introduction to Reconstruction, an effort to outline the perspectives of various participants in the historical drama that unfolded in the dozen years after Appomattox and a point of departure for readers who want to further explore the period. Like all volumes in the Library of America series, it is ultimately a story about Americans and their language—about how our fellow citizens have used the spoken and written word to make sense of their own experiences, to express their hopes and fears, to let posterity know what they believed to be right and wrong, and to tell us what ideals they thought our country should aspire to live up to. It is worth our while to listen to them.

Brooks D. Simpson

PRESIDENTIAL
RECONSTRUCTION
1865–1866

❧

As the American Civil War came to an end in the spring of 1865, all Americans, regardless of region or race, anxiously anticipated what would come next. Would former Confederates willingly accept their defeat and thus open the way to reconciliation and reunion? Would northerners welcome their former enemies back, or would they heed calls for the punishment of leading rebels and the confiscation of southern plantations? How would blacks—and whites—define what freedom and citizenship meant in a nation shorn of slavery? What, in short, had four years of fighting really achieved?

Different people viewed Reconstruction in different ways. Was it simply a process to provide for the reestablishment of loyal regimes in the former Confederate states as a prelude to the return of an antebellum order based on states' rights and a limited federal government? Or was it something more—an opportunity for a new birth of freedom that would remake former slaveholding states into more egalitarian societies? Was there any way to devise an approach that would provide both sectional reconciliation between American whites and equality and opportunity for African Americans, including the newly emancipated?

Abraham Lincoln struggled to answer those questions. While he hoped that what wartime reconstruction had achieved would not be undone, he knew that with the end of the war he would have to frame a policy more appropriate to new circumstances. An assassin's bullet cut short his opportunity to shape events. Taking his place in the White House was Andrew Johnson, a southerner who had maintained his allegiance to the Union during the war. Johnson's expressions of hatred toward the ruling planter class gave many observers cause to believe that he would pursue a harsher policy toward the defeated South than Lincoln's. Whether the Tennessean would demonstrate the same sort of commitment toward black freedom remained to be seen.

I

All eyes turned south to see how southerners, black and white, responded to emancipation. How would former slaves define and experience freedom? Would whites accept blacks as free laborers or would they seek to reimpose slavery in all but name? The decisions by freed people to reunite families, seek schooling, and control their own labor were cited by many whites as evidence that without coercion, blacks would not work. Observers from the North attempted to assess the willingness of former Confederates to accept the verdict of Appomattox. In turn many white southerners took their cues from Johnson, who seemed content with a restoration of the old order while setting aside or blocking African American aspirations. Having at first issued impassioned statements about punishing traitors, the new president soon retreated to requiring minimal concessions from white southerners in order for them to regain their place in the Union. Relieved that Johnson asked so little of them, white southerners squabbled over whether to accept even those requirements. Why ratify the Thirteenth Amendment abolishing slavery when one could simply accept the destruction of slavery as a consequence of military defeat? Why not seek compensation for lost property, including slaves? Was it really necessary to rescind the ordinances of secession adopted in 1860–61? If most southern whites begrudgingly accepted that slavery had become a casualty of the conflict, they were determined to confine blacks to a second-class status through legislation, intimidation, and violence. Most notable were the so-called Black Codes, a series of legislative acts adopted in the former slave states that restricted the legal rights and economic opportunities of African Americans. While their provisions varied, many of the codes prohibited black persons from bearing arms, serving on juries, or testifying against whites, and subjected them to harsher criminal punishments, including whipping. The crime of vagrancy was broadly defined and made punishable by forced labor in an effort to coerce freed people into signing year-long contracts as plantation workers. A sullen acquiescence in defeat accompanied a defiant resistance to black advancement that was aided by a president whose policy of pardon and amnesty cut short the possibility of widespread land confiscation. After all, reasoned Johnson, Reconstruction was nothing more than "restoration" of the prewar republic. His remarks to black veterans in October 1865 betrayed what his private secretary once characterized as "a morbid distress and feeling against the negroes." Appeals by African Americans for opportunity and protection fell on deaf ears at the White House.

Many northern Republicans expressed skepticism that the time was ripe for welcoming back white southerners. So long as the South remained in what the noted lawyer Richard Henry Dana called "the grasp of war," they reasoned, there was a chance for Congress to protect basic civil rights and promote opportunity for freed people. Thus, even as white southerners reassured Johnson that his policy of restoration was a smashing success, Republicans considered a different course, although many remained willing to work with the chief executive. But reports from the South of murderous violence being committed against blacks, white Unionists, and white northerners now living in the South, and of continued resistance to federal authorities, led northern Republicans to proceed cautiously, encouraged only by the president's characterization of his policy as "an experiment."

As the new Thirty-ninth Congress convened in December 1865, the president defended his policy. Republicans countered by refusing to seat congressmen and senators representing the former Confederate states, reasoning that work remained to be done to secure the fruits of northern victory, including emancipation. That meant striking down the Black Codes as well as providing protection for blacks against white violence and a southern civil court system that stacked the deck against the freed people. Johnson grew more defiant and defensive, engaging Frederick Douglass in a memorable interview that demonstrated that he still firmly embraced his assumptions about black inferiority and subordination. Nor would he look to assist black freedom. In early 1866 Congress sought to extend the life and expand the scope of the Bureau of Refugees, Freedmen, and Abandoned Lands, an organization established in 1865 under military management that offered food, shelter, and medical assistance to impoverished southerners, white and black. The Freedmen's Bureau assisted black advancement by founding schools, arbitrating disputes between black laborers and white landowners, and establishing a court system where black plaintiffs and defendants had a much better chance of obtaining justice than in the existing southern civil courts. Johnson, who had already curtailed the bureau's ability to help freed people secure their own land, would have nothing to do with legislation expanding its powers and issued a blistering veto message claiming that the bureau gave preferential treatment to blacks over whites, a charge that appealed to white supremacists North and South. Republicans failed to muster enough votes to override the veto, while the president denounced Radical Republican congressional leaders Charles Sumner and Thaddeus Stevens as traitors in an ill-tempered tirade delivered from the White House on Washington's birthday.

Ebullient in triumph, the president then overreached. Congressional Republicans, led by moderate Illinois Senator Lyman Trumbull, had framed the first ever federal civil rights legislation, intended to undo the damage caused by the Black Codes and the maladministration of justice in southern civil courts. The Civil Rights Bill would give freed people the right to make contracts, bring lawsuits, testify in court, and buy and sell property, and protect them from discriminatory legal punishments and penalties. Once more Johnson issued a scathing veto message. This time, however, Republicans managed to muster the votes to override it, marking the first time Congress had overturned a veto on a major piece of legislation. The proposal itself was moderate enough to attract broad support: it marked a retreat from the more ambitious plans of men like Sumner and Stevens that looked to secure the fruits of emancipation by revolutionizing the southern economic and political order and postponing full readmission of the former Confederate states. Henceforth the challenge for Republicans was to reach consensus on measures that could survive determined opposition from the White House.

Frederick Douglass: What the Black Man Wants

MR. PRESIDENT:

I came here, as I come always to the meetings in New England, as a listener, and not as a speaker; and one of the reasons why I have not been more frequently to the meetings of this society, has been because of the disposition on the part of some of my friends to call me out upon the platform, even when they knew that there was some difference of opinion and of feeling between those who rightfully belong to this platform and myself; and for fear of being misconstrued, as desiring to interrupt or disturb the proceedings of these meetings, I have usually kept away, and have thus been deprived of that educating influence, which I am always free to confess is of the highest order, descending from this platform. I have felt, since I have lived out West, that in going there I parted from a great deal that was valuable; and I feel, every time I come to these meetings, that I have lost a great deal by making my home west of Boston, west of Massachusetts; for, if anywhere in the country there is to be found the highest sense of justice, or the truest demands for my race, I look for it in the East, I look for it here. The ablest discussions of the whole question of our rights occur here, and to be deprived of the privilege of listening to those discussions is a great deprivation.

I do not know, from what has been said, that there is any difference of opinion as to the duty of abolitionists, at the present moment. How can we get up any difference at this point, or at any point, where we are so united, so agreed? I went especially, however, with that word of Mr. Phillips, which is the criticism of Gen. Banks and Gen. Banks's policy. I hold that that policy is our chief danger at the present moment; that it practically enslaves the negro, and makes the Proclamation of 1863 a mockery and delusion. What is freedom? It is the right to choose one's own employment. Certainly it means that, if it means any thing; and when any individual or combination of individuals, undertakes to decide for any man when he shall work, where he shall work, at what he shall work, and for what he shall work, he or they practically reduce him to slavery. [Applause.] He is a slave. That I understand Gen. Banks to do—to determine for the so-called freedman, when, and where, and at what, and for how much he shall work, when he shall be punished, and by whom punished. It is absolute slavery. It defeats the beneficent intentions of the Government, if it has beneficent intentions, in regard to the freedom of our people.

I have had but one idea for the last three years, to present to the American people, and the phraseology in which I clothe it is the old abolition phraseology. I am for the "immediate, unconditional, and universal" enfranchisement of the black man, in every State in the Union. [Loud applause.] Without this, his liberty is a mockery; without this, you might as well almost retain the old name of slavery for his condition; for, in fact, if he is not the slave of the individual master, he is the slave of society, and holds his liberty as a privilege, not as a right. He is at the mercy of the mob, and has no means of protecting himself.

It may be objected, however, that this pressing of the negro's right to suffrage is premature. Let us have slavery abolished, it may be said, let us have labor organized, and then, in the natural course of events, the right of suffrage will be extended to the negro. I do not agree with this. The constitution of the human mind is such, that if it once disregards the conviction forced upon it by a revelation of truth, it requires the exercise of a higher power to produce the same conviction afterwards. The American people are now in tears. The Shenandoah has run blood—the best blood of the North. All around Richmond, the blood of New England and of the North has been shed—of your sons, your brothers and your fathers. We all feel, in the existence of this Rebellion, that judgments terrible, wide-spread, far-reaching, overwhelming, are abroad in the land; and we feel, in view of these judgments, just now, a disposition to learn righteousness. This is the hour. Our streets are in mourning, tears are falling at every fireside, and under the chastisement of this Rebellion we have almost come up to the point of conceding this great, this all-important right of suffrage. I fear that if we fail to do it now, if abolitionists fail to press it now, we may not see, for centuries to come, the same disposition that exists at this moment. [Applause.] Hence, I say, now is the time to press this right.

It may be asked, "Why do you want it? Some men have got along very well without it. Women have not this right." Shall we justify one wrong by another? That is a sufficient answer. Shall we at this moment justify the deprivation of the negro of the right to vote, because some one else is deprived of that privilege? I hold that women, as well as men, have the right to vote [applause], and my heart and my voice go with the movement to extend suffrage to woman; but that question rests upon another basis than that on which our right rests. We may be asked, I say, why we want it. I will tell you why we want it. We want it because it is our *right*, first of all. [Applause.] No class of men can, without insulting their own nature, be content with any deprivation of their rights. We want it again, as a means for educating our race. Men are so constituted that they derive their conviction of their own possibilities largely from the estimate formed of them by others. If nothing is expected of a people, that people will find it difficult to contradict that expectation. By depriving us of suffrage, you affirm our incapacity to form an intelligent judgment respecting public men and public measures; you declare before the world that we are unfit to exercise the elective franchise, and by this means lead us to undervalue ourselves, to put a low estimate upon ourselves, and to feel that we have no possibilities like other men. Again, I want the elective franchise, for one, as a colored man, because ours is a peculiar government, based upon a peculiar idea, and that idea is universal suffrage. If I were in a monarchical government, or an autocratic or aristocratic government, where the few bore rule and the many were subject, there would be no special stigma resting upon me, because I did not exercise the elective franchise. It would do me no great violence. Mingling with the mass, I should partake of the strength of the mass; I should be supported by the mass, and I should have the same incentives to endeavor with the mass of my fellow-men; it would be no particular burden, no particular deprivation; but here, where universal suffrage is the rule, where that is the fundamental idea of the Government, to rule us out is to make us an exception, to brand us with the stigma of inferiority, and to invite to our heads the missiles of those about us; therefore, I want the franchise for the black man.

There are, however, other reasons, not derived from any consideration merely of our rights, but arising out of the conditions of the South, and of the country—considerations which have already been referred to by Mr. Phillips—considerations which must arrest the attention of statesmen. I believe that when the tall heads of this Rebellion shall have been swept down, as they will be swept down, when the Davises and Toombses and Stephenses, and others who are leading in this Rebellion shall have been blotted out, there will be this rank undergrowth of treason, to which reference has been made, growing up there, and interfering with, and thwarting the quiet operation of the Federal Government in those States. You will see those traitors handing down, from sire to son, the same malignant spirit which they have manifested, and which they are now exhibiting, with malicious hearts, broad blades, and bloody hands in the field, against our sons and brothers. That spirit will still remain; and whoever sees the Federal Government extended over those Southern States will see that Government in a strange land, and not only in a strange land, but in an enemy's land. A post-master of the United States in the South will find himself surrounded by a hostile spirit; a collector in a Southern port will find himself surrounded by a hostile spirit; a United States marshal or United States judge will be surrounded there by a hostile element. That enmity will not die out in a year, will not die out in an age. The Federal Government will be looked upon in those States precisely as the Governments of Austria and France are looked upon in Italy at the present moment. They will endeavor to circumvent, they will endeavor to destroy, the peaceful operation of this Government. Now, where will you find the strength to counterbalance this spirit, if you do not find it in the negroes of the South? They are your friends, and have always been your friends. They were your friends even when the Government did not regard them as such. They comprehended the genius of this war before you did. It is a significant fact, it is a marvellous fact, it seems almost to imply a direct interposition of Providence, that this war, which began in the interest of slavery on both sides, bids fair to end in the interest of liberty on both sides. [Applause.] It was begun, I say, in the interest of slavery on both sides. The South was fighting to take slavery out of the Union, and the North fighting to keep it in the Union; the South fighting to get it beyond the limits of the United-States Constitution, and the North fighting to retain it within those limits; the South fighting for new guarantees, and the North fighting for the old guarantees;—both despising the negro, both insulting the negro. Yet, the negro, apparently endowed with wisdom from on high, saw more clearly the end from the beginning than we did. When Seward said the status of no man in the country would be changed by the war, the negro did not believe him. [Applause.] When our generals sent their underlings in shoulder-straps to hunt the flying negro back from our lines into the jaws of slavery, from which he had escaped, the negroes thought that a mistake had been made, and that the intentions of the Government had not been rightly understood by our officers in shoulder-straps, and they continued to come into our lines, threading their way through bogs and fens, over briers and thorns, fording streams, swimming rivers, bringing us tidings as to the safe path to march, and pointing out the dangers that threatened us. They are our only friends in the South, and we should be true to them in this their trial hour, and see to it that they have the elective franchise.

I know that we are inferior to you in some things—virtually inferior. We walk about among you like dwarfs among giants. Our heads are scarcely seen above the great sea of humanity. The Germans are superior to us; the Irish are superior to us; the Yankees are superior to us [laughter]; they can do what we cannot, that is, what we have not hitherto been allowed to do. But while I make this admission, I utterly deny that we are originally, or naturally, or practically, or in any way, or in any important sense, inferior to anybody on this globe. [Loud applause.] This charge of inferiority is an old dodge. It has been made available for oppression on many occasions. It is only about six centuries since the blue-eyed and fair-haired Anglo-Saxons were considered inferior by the haughty Normans, who once trampled upon them. If you read the history of the Norman Conquest, you will find that this proud Anglo-Saxon was once looked upon as of coarser clay than his Norman master, and might be found in the highways and byways of old England laboring with a brass collar on his neck, and the name of his master marked upon it. *You* were down then! [Laughter and applause.] You are up now. I am glad you are up, and I want you to be glad to help us up also. [Applause.]

The story of our inferiority is an old dodge, as I have said; for wherever men oppress their fellows, wherever they enslave them, they will endeavor to find the needed apology for such enslavement and oppression in the character of the people oppressed and enslaved. When we wanted, a few years ago, a slice of Mexico, it was hinted that the Mexicans were an inferior race, that the old Castilian blood had become so weak that it would scarcely run down hill, and that Mexico needed the long, strong and beneficent arm of the Anglo-Saxon care extended over it. We said that it was necessary to its salvation, and a part of the "manifest destiny" of this Republic, to extend our arm over that dilapidated government. So, too, when Russia wanted to take possession of a part of the Ottoman Empire, the Turks were "an inferior race." So, too, when England wants to set the heel of her power more firmly in the quivering heart of old Ireland, the Celts are an "inferior race." So, too, the negro, when he is to be robbed of any right which is justly his, is an "inferior man." It is said that we are ignorant; I admit it. But if we know enough to be hung, we know enough to vote. If the negro knows enough to pay taxes to support the government, he knows enough to vote; taxation and representation should go together. If he knows enough to shoulder a musket and fight for the flag, fight for the government, he knows enough to vote. If he knows as much when he is sober as an Irishman knows when drunk, he knows enough to vote, on good American principles. [Laughter and applause.]

But I was saying that you needed a counterpoise in the persons of the slaves to the enmity that would exist at the South after the Rebellion is put down. I hold that the American people are bound, not only in self-defence, to extend this right to the freedmen of the South, but they are bound by their love of country, and by all their regard for the future safety of those Southern States, to do this—to do it as a measure essential to the preservation of peace there. But I will not dwell upon this. I put it to the American sense of honor. The honor of a nation is an important thing. It is said in the Scriptures, "What doth it profit a man if he gain the whole world, and lose his own soul?" It may be said, also, What doth it profit a nation if it gain the whole world, but lose its honor? I hold that the American government has taken upon itself a solemn obligation of honor, to see that this war—let it be long or let it be short, let it cost much or let it cost little—that this war shall not cease until every freedman at the South has the right to vote. [Applause.] It has bound itself to it. What have you asked the black men of the South, the black men of the whole country, to do? Why, you have asked them to incur the deadly enmity of their masters, in order to befriend you and to befriend this Government. You have asked us to call down, not only upon ourselves, but upon our children's children, the deadly hate of the entire Southern people. You have called upon us to turn our backs upon our masters, to abandon their cause and espouse yours; to turn against the South and in favor of the North; to shoot down the Confederacy and uphold the flag—the American flag. You have called upon us to expose ourselves to all the subtle machinations of their malignity for all time. And now, what do you propose to do when you come to make peace? To reward your enemies, and trample in the dust your friends? Do you intend to sacrifice the very men who have come to the rescue of your banner in the South, and incurred the lasting displeasure of their masters thereby? Do you intend to sacrifice them and reward your enemies? Do you mean to give your enemies the right to vote, and take it away from your friends? Is that wise policy? Is that honorable? Could American honor withstand such a blow? I do not believe you will do it. I think you will see to it that we have the right to vote. There is something too mean in looking upon the negro, when you are in trouble, as a citizen, and when you are free from trouble, as an alien. When this nation was in trouble, in its early struggles, it looked upon the negro as a citizen. In 1776 he was a citizen. At the time of the formation of the Constitution the negro had the right to vote in eleven States out of the old thirteen. In your trouble you have made us citizens. In 1812 Gen. Jackson addressed us as citizens—"fellow-citizens." He wanted us to fight. We were citizens then! And now, when you come to frame a conscription bill, the negro is a citizen again. He has been a citizen just three times in the history of this government, and it has always been in time of trouble. In time of trouble we are citizens. Shall we be citizens in war, and aliens in peace? Would that be just?

I ask my friends who are apologizing for not insisting upon this right, where can the black man look, in this country, for the assertion of this right, if he may not look to the Massachusetts Anti-Slavery Society? Where under the whole heavens can he look for sympathy, in asserting this right, if he may not look to this platform? Have you lifted us up to a certain height to see that we are men, and then are any disposed to leave us there, without seeing that we are put in possession of all our rights? We look naturally to this platform for the assertion of all our rights, and for this one especially. I understand the anti-slavery societies of this country to be based on two principles,—first, the freedom of the blacks of this country; and, second, the elevation of them. Let me not be misunderstood here. I am not asking for sympathy at the hands of abolitionists, sympathy at the hands of any. I think the American people are disposed often to be generous rather than just. I look over this country at the present time, and I see Educational Societies, Sanitary Commissions, Freedmen's Associations, and the like,—all very good: but in regard to the colored people there is always more that is benevolent, I perceive, than just, manifested towards us. What I ask for the negro is not benevolence, not pity, not sympathy, but simply *justice*. [Applause.] The American people have always been anxious to know what they shall do with us. Gen. Banks was distressed with solicitude as to what he should do with the negro. Everybody has asked the question, and they learned to ask it early of the abolitionists, "What shall we do with the negro?" I have had but one answer from the beginning. Do nothing with us! Your doing with us has already played the mischief with us. Do nothing with us! If the apples will not remain on the tree of their own strength, if they are worm-eaten at the core, if they are early ripe and disposed to fall, let them fall! I am not for tying or fastening them on the tree in any way, except by nature's plan, and if they will not stay there, let them fall. And if the negro cannot stand on his own legs, let him fall also. All I ask is, give him a chance to stand

on his own legs! Let him alone! If you see him on his way
to school, let him alone, don't disturb him! If you see him
going to the dinner-table at a hotel, let him go! If you see
him going to the ballot-box, let him alone, don't disturb him!
[Applause.] If you see him going into a work-shop, just let
him alone,—your interference is doing him a positive injury.
Gen. Banks's "preparation" is of a piece with this attempt to
prop up the negro. Let him fall if he cannot stand alone! If the
negro cannot live by the line of eternal justice, so beautifully
pictured to you in the illustration used by Mr. Phillips, the
fault will not be yours, it will be his who made the negro,
and established that line for his government. [Applause.]
Let him live or die by that. If you will only untie his hands,
and give him a chance, I think he will live. He will work as
readily for himself as the white man. A great many delusions
have been swept away by this war. One was, that the negro
would not work; he has proved his ability to work. Another
was, that the negro would not fight; that he possessed only
the most sheepish attributes of humanity; was a perfect lamb,
or an "Uncle Tom;" disposed to take off his coat whenever
required, fold his hands, and be whipped by anybody who
wanted to whip him. But the war has proved that there is a
great deal of human nature in the negro, and that "he will
fight," as Mr. Quincy, our President, said, in earlier days than
these, "when there is a reasonable probability of his whipping
anybody." [Laughter and applause.]

January 26, 1865

Abraham Lincoln: Speech on Reconstruction

WE MEET this evening, not in sorrow, but in gladness of heart. The evacuation of Petersburg and Richmond, and the surrender of the principal insurgent army, give hope of a righteous and speedy peace whose joyous expression can not be restrained. In the midst of this, however, He, from Whom all blessings flow, must not be forgotten. A call for a national thanksgiving is being prepared, and will be duly promulgated. Nor must those whose harder part gives us the cause of rejoicing, be overlooked. Their honors must not be parcelled out with others. I myself, was near the front, and had the high pleasure of transmitting much of the good news to you; but no part of the honor, for plan or execution, is mine. To Gen. Grant, his skilful officers, and brave men, all belongs. The gallant Navy stood ready, but was not in reach to take active part.

By these recent successes the re-inauguration of the national authority—reconstruction—which has had a large share of thought from the first, is pressed much more closely upon our attention. It is fraught with great difficulty. Unlike the case of a war between independent nations, there is no authorized organ for us to treat with. No one man has authority to give up the rebellion for any other man. We simply must begin with, and mould from, disorganized and discordant elements. Nor is it a small additional embarrassment that we, the loyal people, differ among ourselves as to the mode, manner, and means of reconstruction.

As a general rule, I abstain from reading the reports of attacks upon myself, wishing not to be provoked by that to which I can not properly offer an answer. In spite of this precaution, however, it comes to my knowledge that I am much censured for some supposed agency in setting up, and seeking to sustain, the new State Government of Louisiana. In this I have done just so much as, and no more than, the public knows. In the Annual Message of Dec. 1863 and accompanying Proclamation, I presented *a* plan of reconstruction (as the phrase goes) which, I promised, if adopted by any State, should be acceptable to, and sustained by, the Executive government of the nation. I distinctly stated that this was not the only plan which might possibly be acceptable; and I also distinctly protested that the Executive claimed no right to say when, or whether members should be admitted to seats in Congress from such States. This plan was, in advance, submitted to the then Cabinet, and distinctly approved by every member of it. One of them suggested that I should then, and in that connection, apply the Emancipation Proclamation to the theretofore excepted parts of Virginia and Louisiana; that I should drop the suggestion about apprenticeship for freed-people, and that I should omit the protest against my own power, in regard to the admission of members to Congress; but even he approved every part and parcel of the plan which has since been employed or touched by the action of Louisiana. The new constitution of Louisiana, declaring emancipation for the whole State, practically applies the Proclamation to the part previously excepted. It does not adopt apprenticeship for freed-people; and it is silent, as it could not well be otherwise, about the admission of members to Congress. So that, as it applies to Louisiana, every member of the Cabinet fully approved the plan. The Message went to Congress, and I received many commendations of the plan, written and verbal; and not a single objection to it, from any professed emancipationist, came to my knowledge, until after the news reached Washington that the people of Louisiana had begun to move in accordance with it. From about July 1862, I had corresponded with different persons, supposed to be interested, seeking a reconstruction of a State government for Louisiana. When the Message of 1863, with the plan before mentioned, reached New-Orleans, Gen. Banks wrote me that he was confident the people, with his military co-operation, would reconstruct, substantially on that plan. I wrote him, and some of them to try it; they tried it, and the result is known. Such only has been my agency in getting up the Louisiana government. As to sustaining it, my promise is out, as before stated. But, as bad promises are better broken than kept, I shall treat this as a bad promise, and break it, whenever I shall be convinced that keeping it is adverse to the public interest. But I have not yet been so convinced.

I have been shown a letter on this subject, supposed to be an able one, in which the writer expresses regret that my mind has not seemed to be definitely fixed on the question whether the seceded States, so called, are in the Union or out of it. It would perhaps, add astonishment to his regret, were he to learn that since I have found professed Union men endeavoring to make that question, I have *purposely* forborne any public expression upon it. As appears to me that question has not been, nor yet is, a practically material one, and that any discussion of it, while it thus remains practically immaterial, could have no effect other than the mischievous one of dividing our friends. As yet, whatever it may hereafter become, that question is bad, as the basis of a controversy, and good for nothing at all—a merely pernicious abstraction.

We all agree that the seceded States, so called, are out of their proper practical relation with the Union; and that the sole object of the government, civil and military, in regard to those States is to again get them into that proper practical relation. I believe it is not only possible, but in fact, easier, to do this, without deciding, or even considering, whether these states have even been out of the Union, than with it. Finding themselves safely at home, it would be utterly immaterial whether they had ever been abroad. Let us all join in doing the acts necessary to restoring the proper practical relations between these states and the Union; and each forever after, innocently indulge his own opinion whether, in doing the acts, he brought the States from without, into the Union, or only gave them proper assistance, they never having been out of it.

The amount of constituency, so to speak, on which the new Louisiana government rests, would be more satisfactory to all, if it contained fifty, thirty, or even twenty thousand, instead of only about twelve thousand, as it does. It is also unsatisfactory to some that the elective franchise is not given to the colored man. I would myself prefer that it were now conferred on the very intelligent, and on those who serve our cause as soldiers. Still the question is not whether the Louisiana government, as it stands, is quite all that is desirable. The question is "Will it be wiser to take it as it is, and help to improve it; or to reject, and disperse it?" "Can Louisiana be brought into proper practical relation with the Union *sooner* by *sustaining*, or by *discarding* her new State Government?"

Some twelve thousand voters in the heretofore slave-state of Louisiana have sworn allegiance to the Union, assumed to be the rightful political power of the State, held elections, organized a State government, adopted a free-state constitution, giving the benefit of public schools equally to black and white, and empowering the Legislature to confer the elective franchise upon the colored man. Their Legislature has already voted to ratify the constitutional amendment recently passed by Congress, abolishing slavery throughout the nation. These twelve thousand persons are thus fully committed to the Union, and to perpetual freedom in the state—committed to the very things, and nearly all the things the nation wants—and they ask the nations recognition, and it's assistance to make good their committal. Now, if we reject, and spurn them, we do our utmost to disorganize and disperse them. We in effect say to the white men "You are worthless, or worse—we will neither help you, nor be helped by you." To the blacks we say "This cup of liberty which these, your old masters, hold to your lips, we will dash from you, and leave you to the chances of gathering the spilled and scattered contents in some vague and undefined when, where, and how." If this course, discouraging and paralyzing both white and black, has any tendency to bring Louisiana into proper practical relations with the Union, I have, so far, been unable to perceive it. If, on the contrary, we recognize, and sustain the new government of Louisiana the converse of all this is made true. We encourage the hearts, and nerve the arms of the twelve thousand to adhere to their work, and argue for it, and proselyte for it, and fight for it, and feed it, and grow it, and ripen it to a complete success. The colored man too, in seeing all united for him, is inspired with vigilance, and energy, and daring, to the same end. Grant that he desires the elective franchise, will he not attain it sooner by saving the already advanced steps toward it, than by running backward over them? Concede that the new government of Louisiana is only to what it should be as the egg is to the fowl, we shall sooner have the fowl by hatching the egg than by smashing it? Again, if we reject Louisiana, we also reject one vote in favor of the proposed amendment to the national constitution. To meet this proposition, it has been argued that no more than three fourths of those States which have not attempted secession are necessary to validly ratify the amendment. I do not commit myself against this, further than to say that such a ratification would be questionable, and sure to be persistently questioned; while a ratification by three fourths of all the States would be unquestioned and unquestionable.

I repeat the question. "Can Louisiana be brought into proper practical relation with the Union *sooner* by *sustaining* or by *discarding* her new State Government?"

What has been said of Louisiana will apply generally to other States. And yet so great peculiarities pertain to each state; and such important and sudden changes occur in the same state; and, withal, so new and unprecedented is the whole case, that no exclusive, and inflexible plan can safely be prescribed as to details and colatterals. Such exclusive, and inflexible plan, would surely become a new entanglement. Important principles may, and must, be inflexible.

In the present "*situation*" as the phrase goes, it may be my duty to make some new announcement to the people of the South. I am considering, and shall not fail to act, when satisfied that action will be proper.

April 11, 1865

Springfield Republican:
Restoration of the Union

WE TALK of reconstruction, restoration and the re-admission of seceded States to the Union, and this loose habit of speech does no harm so long as we do not allow our ideas and acts to be hampered thereby. These phrases are inaccurate substitutes for a thought that cannot be expressed in a single word. What we want is to put the government machinery of the Southern States into loyal hands, and, whatever we may hold as to State rights, the general government must make sure of this, otherwise have the sacrifices of the war been in vain. Nominally the large majority of all the southern people have been disloyal. There are not enough men in the seceded States who have stood firm against the general defection to fill the State and local offices. It follows that we must accept as citizens those who renew their loyalty to the Union, or we must govern the entire South by satraps and armies for an entire generation. Which will we do? All questions of reconstruction resolve themselves at last into this single one. Under the wise foresight of the President the revival of the loyal State governments has kept pace with the progress of our arms, and with the fall of the military power of the rebellion all the States now controlled by disloyal governors and legislatures are put in a situation to undertake the same reconstructive work. Congress has provided no other mode, and the President's plan will be followed in all the States, with modifications adapted to the condition of things in each, perhaps with some general changes by his order.

The principle of the plan thus practically adopted is a sound one, notwithstanding the severe criticism it has provoked. The power rightfully belongs to the loyal men of the reclaimed States, and whether few or many they should constitute and control the government. Such as refuse to take the oath of allegiance have no claim to toleration upon the soil, much less to any rights as citizens. They are not to be counted into the number constituting the State.

Thus all the theories of reconstruction invented for the purpose of transforming a third of the States into territories or colonies, fall with the rebellion, as all sagacious men foresaw that they must. They have served only to distract loyal men and embarrass the government. They have fulfilled their mission, and their inventors will be glad to have them forgotten. We stand again on solid ground; the rebel is a citizen of the United States, to be forgiven and restored if he repents—to be excluded from all the rights of citizenship if he continues obdurate—to be punished as a traitor if the public safety require it. The rebel State is a State of the Union, to be recovered from disloyal and placed in loyal hands. This is the work we have been doing for four years, now almost accomplished. And now that the needful fighting has been done, all problems for the future are of easy solution, unless we willfully complicate them, for the narrow purposes of fraction or party, or by obstinate adhearance to crochety notions of policy. But of this there is little danger. The popular heart is sound, and the popular eye clear. We have not fought our way out upon the firm highway to be cheated of our object at last. The restoration of the Union is a simple and straightforward process, and it will be speedy and permanent. The heresy of secession perishes with the rebellion, and slavery ends with the war it provoked.

April 20, 1865

Andrew Johnson: Interview with Pennsylvania Delegation

May 3, 1865

MR. CHAIRMAN AND GENTLEMEN   I can only reply in general terms; perhaps as good a reply as I can make would be to refer to or repeat what I have already said to other delegations who have come for the purpose of encouraging and inspiring me with confidence on entering upon the discharge of duties so responsible—so perilous. All that I could now say would be but a reiteration of sentiments already indicated. The words you have spoken are most fully and cordially accepted and responded to by me. I, too, think the time has arrived when the people of this nation should understand that treason is a crime. When we turn to the catalogue of crime we find that most of those contained in it are understood, but the crime of treason has neither been generally understood nor generally appreciated, as I think it should be. And there has been an effort since this rebellion commenced to make the impression that it was a mere political struggle, or, as I see it thrown out in some of the papers, a struggle for ascendancy of certain principles from the dawn of the government to the present time, and now settled by the final triumph of the Federal arms. If this is to be a determined, settled idea and opinion the government is at an end, for no question can arise but they will make it a party issue, and then to whatever length they carry it the party defeated will be only a party defeated, and no crime attaches thereto. But, I say treason is a crime—the highest crime known to the law—and the people ought to understand it and be taught to know that unless it be so considered there can be no government. I do not say this to indicate a revengeful or improper spirit. It is simply the enunciation of deliberate consideration and temperate judgement. There are men who ought to suffer the penalties of their treason; but there are also some who have been engaged in this rebellion, who, while, technically speaking, are guilty of treason, yet are morally not. Thousands who have been drawn into it, involved

21

by various influences—by conscription, by dread, by force of public opinion in the localities in which they lived—these are not so responsible as those who led, deceived and forced them. To the unconscious, deceived, conscripted—in short, to the great mass of the misled—I would say mercy, clemency, reconciliation, and the restoration of their government. To those who have deceived—to the conscious, influential traitor, who attempted to destroy the life of a nation, I would say "On you be inflicted the severest penalties of your crime." [Applause.] I fully understand how easy it is to get up an impression in regard to the exercise of mercy; and, if I know myself and my own heart, there is in it as great a disposition to mercy as can be manifested on the part of any other individual. But mercy without justice is a crime. In the exercise of mercy there should be deliberate consideration, and a profound understanding of the case; and I am not prepared to say but what it should often be transferred to a higher court—a court where mercy and justice can best be united. In responding to the remarks of your chairman in reference to free government and the discharge of my duties, I can only say again that my past public life must be taken as the guide to what my future will be. My course has been unmistakable and well defined. I know it is easy to cry out "demagogue;" but let that be as it may. If I have spent the toil of youth and the vigor of my life for the elevation of the great masses of the people, why it was a work of my choosing and I will bear the loss. And if it is demagogism to please the people—if it is demagogism to strive for their welfare and amelioration—then I am a demagogue. I was always proud when my duties were so discharged that the people were pleased. A great monopoly—the remark of your chairman brings me to it—existed: that of slavery; and upon it rested an aristocracy. It is the work of freemen to put down monopolies. You have seen the attempt made by the monopoly of slavery to put down the government. But the making of the attempt, thereby to control and destroy the Government, you have seen the government put down the monopoly and destroy the institution. [Applause.] Institutions of any kind must be subordinate to the government or the government cannot stand. I do not care whether it be North or South. A government based upon popular judgment must be paramount to all institutions that spring up under that government; and if, when they attempt to control the government, the government does not put them down, they will put it down. Hence the main portion of my efforts have been devoted to the opposition of them. Hence I have ever opposed aristocracy—opposed it in any shape. But there is a kind of aristocracy that has always, that always will, command my respect and approbation—the aristocracy of talent, the aristocracy of virtue, the aristocracy of merit, or an aristocracy resting upon worth, the aristocracy of labor, resting upon honest industry, developing the industrial resources of the country—this commands my respect and admiration—my support in life. In regard to my future course in connection with this rebellion, nothing that I can say would be worth listening to. If my past is not sufficient guarantee, I can only add that I have never knowingly deceived the people, and never have betrayed a friend—[applause]—and, God willing, never will. [Applause.] Accept my profound and sincere thanks for the encouragement you have given me, and believe me when I say that your encouragement, countenance and confidence are a great aid and a great spur to the performance of my duties. Once more I thank you for this manifestation of your regard and respect.

Colored Men of North Carolina to Andrew Johnson

Newbern, May 10, 1865.

To His Excellency Andrew Johnson, President of the United States:—

We, the undersigned, your petitioners, are colored men of the State of North Carolina, of the age of twenty-one years and upwards; and we humbly come to you with our request, and yet in great confidence, because you are occupying a place so recently filled by a man who had proved himself indeed our friend, and it must be that some of his great and good spirit lingers to bless his successor; and then we are assured that you are a man who gives kind attention to all petitioners, and never turns a deaf ear to any one because he may be in poor or humble circumstances. In many respects we are poor and greatly despised by our fellow men; but we are rich in the possession of the liberty brought us and our wives and our little ones by your noble predecessor, secured to us by the armies of the United States and promised to be permanent by that victorious flag which now flies in triumph in every State of the Union. We accept this great boon of freedom with truly thankful hearts; and shall try by our lives to prove our worthiness. We always loved the old flag, and we have stood by it, and tried to help those who upheld it through all this rebellion; and now that it has brought us liberty, we love it more than ever, and in all future time we and our sons will be ready to defend it by our blood; and we may be permitted to say that such blood as that shed at Fort Wagner and Port Hudson is not altogether unworthy of such service. Some of us are soldiers, and have had the privilege of fighting for our country in this war. Since we have become freemen, and been permitted the honor of being soldiers, we begin to feel that we are men, and are anxious to show our countrymen that we can and will fit ourselves for the creditable discharge of the duties of citizenship. We want the privilege of voting. It seems to us that men who are willing on the field of danger to carry the muskets of republics, in the days of peace ought to be permitted to carry its ballots; and certainly we cannot understand the justice of denying the elective franchise to men who have been fighting for the country, while it is freely given to men who have just returned from four years fighting against it. As you were once a citizen of North Carolina, we need not remind you that up to the year 1835 free colored men voted in this State, and never, as we have heard, with any detriment to its interests. What we desire is that, preliminary to elections in the returning States, you would order the enrolment of all loyal men, without regard to color. But the whole question we humbly submit to your better judgment—and we submit it with full belief in your impartial integrity, and in the fond hope that the mantle of our murdered friend and father may have fallen upon your shoulders. May God bless and ever protect you and our beloved country from all assassins shall be the constant prayer of your faithful friends and humble petitioners.

Andrew Johnson: Reply to a Delegation of Colored Ministers

May 11, 1865

IN RESPONDING to what you have said on this occasion as the representative and organ of those colored men who stand about you, I presume it is hardly necessary for me to inform them as to what my course has been in reference to their condition. I imagine there is not a colored man within the reach of information but has to some extent been informed upon, and placed in possession of, a knowledge of the course I have pursued in the past in reference to their present condition.

Now I shall talk to them plainly. They know I have been born and raised in a slave State; that I have owned slaves, raised slaves, but I never sold one.

They know, I presume, that my slaves have been made free, and that there is a difference in the responsibility that persons have taken in reference to emancipation when living in or out of slave States. It is very easy for a man who lives beyond the borders to talk about the condition of colored men, when in fact they know little about it. They know they have some friends who feel as cordially toward them, and who live beyond the Southern lines. They know, too, there are men there who, though they have been masters, yet feel as deep an interest in and regard for them, and would do as much for their elevation and amelioration, as those who live anywhere else.

I feel it would be unnecessary for me to state what I have done in this great cause of emancipation. I have stood in their midst, met their taunts and jeers, and risked all in the shape of property, life, and limb—not that I would claim anything to myself in establishing, sustaining, and carrying out the great principle that man could not own property in man. I was the first that stood in a slave community and announced the great fact that the slaves of Tennessee were free upon the same principle as those who were assumed to own them.

I know it is easy to talk and proclaim sentiments upon paper, but it is one thing to have theories and another to reduce

26

them to practice; and I must say here, what I have no doubt is permanently fixed in your minds, and the impression deep, that there is one thing you ought to teach, and they should understand, that in a transition state, passing from bond to free, when the tyrant's rod has been bent and the yoke broken, we find too many—it is best to talk plain—there are, I say, too many in this transition state, passing from bondage to freedom, who feel as if they should have nothing to do, and fall back upon the Government for support; too many incline to become loafers and depend upon the Government to take care of them. They seem to think that with freedom every thing they need is to come like manna from heaven.

Now, I want to impress this upon your minds, that freedom simply means liberty to work and enjoy the product of your own hands. This is the correct definition of freedom, in the most extensive sense of the term.

There is another thing; and I have been surprised that people beyond the lines have not pressed upon you this important idea. It is easy in Congress and from the pulpit North and South to talk about polygamy, and Brigham Young, and debauchery of various kinds, but there is also one great fact, that four millions of people lived in open and notorious concubinage. The time has come when you must correct this thing. You know what I say is true, and you must do something to correct it by example as well as by words and professions.

It is not necessary for me to give you any assurance of what my future course will be in reference to your condition. Now, when the ordeal is passed, there can be no reason to think that I shall turn back in the great cause in which I have sacrificed much, and perilled all.

I can give you no assurance worth more than my course heretofore, and I shall continue to do all that I can for the elevation and amelioration of your condition; and I trust in God the time may soon come when you shall be gathered together, in a clime and country suited to you, should it be found that the two races cannot get along together.

I trust God will continue to conduct us till the great end shall be accomplished, and the work reach its great consummation.

Accept my thanks for this manifestation of your respect and regard.

Salmon P. Chase to Andrew Johnson

Charleston, May 12, 1865.

My dear Sir,

I wrote you briefly from Wilmington. I hope you have taken an opportunity to confer with General Dodge who bore my letter. I found the other two generals—Hawley who commands the District & Abbot who commands the post—ready in mind & heart to sustain your policy of enfranchisement and reorganization.

The white citizens may be divided into three classes; (1) the old conservatives who opposed secession and are now about and, in some cases, even more opposed to letting the black citizens vote; these would like to see slavery restored:—(2) the acquiescents who rather prefer the old order of things & would rather dislike to see blacks vote but want peace and means of living & revival of business above all things & will take any course the government may desire; this is the largest class:—(3) the progressives who see that Slavery is stone dead & are not sorry; who see too that the blacks made free must be citizens, &, being citizens must be allowed to vote; & who, seeing these things, have made up their minds to conform to the new condition & to lead in it. These are the men of brains and energy; but they are few, & few of the few have been hertofore conspicuous. In the end, however, they will control.

One of the best specimens of the first class I met in Wilmington was Mr. Moore. He is an able lawyer; a good citizen; a good man; thoroughly sincere & truly upright. He was a Whig of the Clay school; opposed secession earnestly & only submitted to it perforce. I promised to convey his views to you & will as well as I can.

They may be stated thus: (1) The best mode of reorganization in North Carolina is to reassemble the Legislature which was lately in session & require each member to take the oath of allegiance to the United States. He thinks nearly every member would take the oath & that this would be the severest

humiliation to them & the most impressive lesson to all others.
(2) The courts, Supreme, Superior, & Quarter Sessions should
be immediately required to resume the exercise of their respective jurisdictions; &, if this cannot be done, that the Courts
of Quarter Sessions, composed of the Justices of the Peace of
each county should at least be put in action. (3) If the Administration has decided not to recognize the Legislature, elected
while the State was in rebellion, then that the white loyal citizens shall be enrolled under order of the military commander
by Justices of the Quarter Sessions, selected by him, or by other
citizens where loyal Justices cannot be found to act; and that
the citizens enrolled should be invited to elect a Convention to
revise the Constitution & provide for the election of Governor
& Legislature; for the election or appointment of Judges; & for
the doing of such other things as may be necessary to restore
civil government & national relations. (4) That unrestricted
trade except in arms & powder within the state, with other
states & with foreign nations should be restored.

His first proposition is of course inadmissable. I think the
second equally so, except as to the Courts of Quarter Sessions:
perhaps these might well be authorized to resume their functions, each Justice taking the oath; but until complete state
restoration their action must necessarily be subject to military
supervision. The third seems right except that I would not restrict suffrage to whites. The fourth strikes me as altogether
expedient & just.

Nothing needs be said of the second class of citizens—the
acquiescents—except that its existence ensures the success of
any policy, right & just in itself & enforced with steady vigor,
which you may think best to adopt.

The third class includes the men of the future. I met several individuals of it. One of the best specimens at Wilmington
was Col. Baker, who was in the rebel service; made prisoner &
pardoned by President Lincoln. He seemed to comprehend
the new situation & was ready to take an active part in the
regeneration of North Carolina on the basis of universal suffrage. He is what you & I would call a young man—say thirty
five—active, ready, intelligent, ambitious, of popular manners.
Another individual a paroled Colonel from South Carolina was
described to me by Mr. Lowell, connected with the detective

service of the Treasury Department, who mixed freely with the people without being known to be of our party. They met at the Palmetto Hotel, where few of the northern men go. He declared himself fully satisfied that the Confederacy was gone up; that slavery was gone up with it; that the negroes must now be citizens & voters; &, for his part he was determined not to be behind the times.

This classification will give you with tolerable accuracy, I think, the sentiments of the several classes into which the southern whites may be divided; & will probably satisfy you that there is no course open, if we wish to promote, most efficiently, the interests of all classes, except to give suffrage to all. I see that the New York Herald, which, though rather unreliable as a supporter of anybody or anything, is a very fair barometer of opinion on measures, has come out for general suffrage. It never sustains a cause, which has been unpopular, until it is about to triumph.

At Wilmington, besides many white citizens, a colored deputation called on me. It was composed of four individuals. The spokesman was the minister of the 1st Presbyterian Church (Colored) in Philadelphia, who came down sometime ago at the instance of some benevolent association to look into the condition of the colored people & report upon it. Of the other three one was a carpenter, who many years ago bought himself & wife & two children. The whole family was conveyed to a white citizen, whose character was their only security against actual as well as legal slavery. Another also a carpenter had hired his time and had all the wages he could earn over the hire paid to his master. The third was a barber who had also bought himself, & then, like a sensible fellow, married a free woman & had himself conveyed to her. They wanted my advice in their present circumstances; were anxious to know whether or not they were to be allowed to vote, & whether they would be maintained in possession of the lands they had hired. I gave them the best advice I could; to be industrious, economical, orderly & respectful, proving by their conduct their worthiness to be free—as to the right of voting I could not tell whether they would have it immediately or not; but they would certainly have it in time if they showed themselves fit for it: I wd. give it at once if I had the right to decide; but the decision was

with you & you would decide according to your own judgment, with the best feeling towards all men of all classes. If they
should get it immediately they must not abuse it if they should
not they must be patient. As to the lands I said I did not doubt
that leases already made for this year would be maintained; but
that they could not expect to own the lands without paying for
them. They must work hard now; get & save all they could, &
await the future hopefully & patiently. They were well satisfied
with what I said & I hope it will meet your approval.

I could write a great deal more, but it would do no good.
While I am observing, you are doubtless resolving and acting.
I am sure you will follow out the great principles you have so
often announced & put the weight of your name and authority
on the side of justice and right. My most earnest wishes will be
satisfied, if you make your administration so beneficent & so
illustrious by great acts that the people will be as little willing
to spare Andrew Johnson from their *service* as to spare Andrew
Jackson. And it will be an exceedingly great pleasure to me if I
can in any way promote its complete success.

I shall try to write again from Hilton Head.

With the greatest respect & esteem

Yours truly S. P. Chase

P.S. If you can find time for writing me at New Orleans, where
I expect to be in two weeks I shall be glad. I am very desirous
to know from yourself, what you think of my observations &
suggestions & what you are doing & intending to do.

Joseph Noxon to Andrew Johnson

New York May 27/65

Andrew Johnson Prest.

You say you believe in democratic government, or *consent* of loyal people. Yet you *dare not* avow with practical effect the right of the colord man to vote. Are you honest?

You profess to protect loyal men & to punish traitors; yet you *refuse* the franchise to loyal colord people, the *only* means effectual for their protection or advancement. Are you honest?

You know rebels disappointed will wreak revenge on loyal blacks, & yet you refuse the franchise for their protection.

You say you have no right to grant it. You know in the first elections to be held to reorganize a seceded state *you* have the *power*, the *right*, & the *duty* to say who shall vote. Otherwise rebels will re-elect rebels, as witness Virginia.

You know by *prompt* & vigorous action *now*, the question of negro sufferage can be *settled* & *accepted* by the people as an *accomplished fact*. Why not settle it & take it *out* of political controversy.

Do you believe the *loyal* Union partys' success essential to the peace & prosperity of this country? Then dont refuse 850,000 *loyal votes* that are *always sure* for liberty & the Republic.

I am deprived of all I have by Rebels. I was formerly a resident of Tennessee but the rebs drove me from home. I was a scout for the Union army & lived in the mountains 11 months. I have some right that you hear me.

Yours truly Joseph Noxon

Delegation of Kentucky Colored People to Andrew Johnson

MR. PRESIDENT   Haveing been delegated by the colored People of Kentuckey to wait upon you and State their greiveances and the terrible uncertainty of their future, we beg to do so in as respectfull and concise a Manner as Posible. First then, we would call your attention to the fact that Kentuckey is the only Spot within all the bounds of these united States, where the People of colour have No rights *whatever* Either in Law or in fact—and were the Strong arm of Millitary power no longer to curb her—her Jails and workhouses would groan with the Numbers of our people immured within their walls.

Her Stattutes are disgraced by laws in regard to us, too barbarous Even for a community of Savages to have Perpetrated. Not one of those laws have Ever yet become obsolete. All have been Executed Promptly and Rigoursly up to the time the government intervened—and will be again Executed in the Most remorseless Manner and with four fold the Venom and Malignanty they were Ever heretofore Enforced—the Very Moment the government ceases to Shield us with the broad aegis of her Power.

Not only that—but the brutal instincts of the mob So Long restrained will Set no bounds to its ferocity but like an uncaged wild beast will rage fiercely among us—Evidence of which is the fact that a member of the present common council of the city of Louisville (who when formerly Provost Marshall of that city caused his guards to carry bull whips and upon Meeting colored Men, women or children in the Public high ways any time after dark to surround them and flay them alive in the public Streets) is allready a petitioner to *Genl. Palmer* to remove the Millitary Restrictions that he and others May again renew the brutaleties that Shocked humanity during that Sad Period. Therefore to Prevent all the horrible Calamities that would befall us and to shut out all the terrors that So fiercely Menace us in the immediate future—we Most humbly Petition and Pray you that you will not Remove Marshall Law from the State of Kentuckey Nor her Noble Millitary commander under whose Protection we have allmost learned to Realise the Blessings of a Home under the Safeguard and sancktion of law for in him and him alone do we find our Safety. We would Most Respectfully call your attention to a few of the laws that bear most cruelly upon Us.

1st we have No Oath

2nd we have no right of domicil

3rd we have no right of locomotion

4th we have No right of Self defence

5th a Stattute law of Kentuckey makes it a penal crime with imprisonment in the Penitentiary for one year for any free Man of colour under any Sircumstances whatever to pass into a free State Even although but for a Moment. Any free man Not a Native found within her Borders is Subject to the Same penalty and for the Second offence Shall be sold a slave for life.

The State of Kentuckey has contributed of her colored Sons over thirty thousand Soldiers who have illustrated their courage and devotion on Many battle fields and have Poured out their blood lavishly—in defence of their country and the country's flag and we confidently hope this Blood will be carried to our credit in any Political Settlement of our Native State. Yet if the government Should give up the State to the control of her civil authorities there is not one of these Soldiers who will not Suffer all the grinding oppression of her Most inhuman laws if not in their own persons yet in the persons of their wives their children And their mothers.

Therefore your Excellency we most Earnestly Petition and pray you that you will give us some security for the future or if that be impracticable at least give us timely warning that we may fly to other States where law and a christian Sentiment will Protect us and our little ones from Violence and wrong.

Chas. A Roxborough—chairman—
R M Johnson Thomas James
Jerry Meninettee Henry H. White
Wm. F. Butler Sec.

June 9, 1865

Charles C. Soule and Oliver O. Howard: An Exchange

Orangeburg, S.C., June 12[th.], 1865.
General: In accordance with the request embodied in your "Circular Letter" of the 16[th.] ult., I have the honor to tender the following report of the organization and operations of the Special Commission on Contracts with Freedmen, at Orangeburg, S.C.

Upon the occupation of this District by the U.S. troops, affairs were found to be in a very unsettled state. The "scouts" who had latterly enforced local order and preserved discipline upon the plantations, were disbanded; no civil magistrates had power to act; the planters, uncertain as to the wishes of the United States authorities, were afraid even to defend themselves against aggression and robbery;—while the negro laborers, who in this neighborhood outnumber the whites five to one, already excited by the prospect of freedom, were urged to lawlessness and acts of violence by the advice of many of the colored soldiers. Not only was there every prospect that the crops would be neglected, but it also seemed probable that the negroes would revenge themselves, by theft, insults, and violence, upon their former owners. To avert disorder and starvation, officers detailed for the purpose were sent into the country to explain to white and black alike their condition under the new state of affairs, and to induce the laborers, if possible, to resume work upon the crops,— which are now in the most critical stage. It was soon found, however, that uniformity was needed in these operations; and during the last week in May, Brevet Brigadier General Hartwell, commanding the Brigade, appointed a Special Commission to have charge over all the relations between proprietor and laborer; to supervise contracts, made under Brig. Gen'l. Hatch's orders, and to act also as Provost Judges in cases of disorder or crime upon the plantations. The commission originally consisted of four members; afterwards of five; and this number is at present reduced to two by the establishment of an auxiliary board in Columbia, S.C. The limits of jurisdiction are indefinite, and cases are frequently brought to our notice from remote districts of the State.

It is found that the office work alone,—merely answering questions, deciding disputes, and administering justice, occupies the attention of two officers and a clerk; while several officers are needed to visit the different sections of the neighboring country, to assemble the planters and the negroes at convenient points, and to explain,—to the former, the necessity of making equitable contracts with their workmen, of discontinuing corporal punishment, and of referring all cases of disorder and idleness to the military authorities:—to the latter, in plain and simple terms their new position as freedmen, their prospects, their duties, and their continued liability to punishment for faults and crimes. In the two weeks which have passed since the Commission was appointed, several hundred contracts have been approved, as many plantations visited, and probably two thousand whites and ten thousand blacks have been addressed. The officers engaged in this work have frequently ridden alone and unarmed twenty-five miles, or further, from the Post, and have almost invariably met with courteous and hospitable treatment at the hands of the planters,—most of whom seem desirous to comply in good faith with the wishes and orders of the Government, and to make the best of a system of labor in which, notwithstanding, they thoroughly disbelieve.

It is found very difficult to disabuse the negroes of the false and exaggerated ideas of freedom they have received, in a great measure, from our own colored troops. They have been led to expect that all the property of their former masters was to be divided out to them; and the most reasonable fancy which prevails, is that besides receiving their food, clothes, the free rent of houses and gardens, and the privilege of keeping their hogs and poultry, they are to take for themselves all day Saturday and Sunday, and to receive half the crops. Their long experience of slavery has made them so distrustful of all whites, that on many plantations they persist still in giving credit only to the rumors set afloat by people of their own color, and believe that the officers who have addressed them are rebels in disguise. Even where they are satisfied that the idea of freedom comprehends law, order, and hard labor, there are many whom the absence of the usual restraint and fear of punishment renders idle, insolent, vagrant and thievish. Owing to the entire want of cavalry in this Department, it has been found possible to investigate a few only of the cases brought before the board in its judicial capacity; and the members view with solicitude the alarming increase of vagrancy throughout the country, and the idleness, half-way-work, and turbulence of a large portion of the negro population,—which they are powerless to check, except in the immediate vicinity of a military force.

In the opinion of a majority of the Commission, little danger to the welfare of society, or of the country, need be apprehended from the former slaveowners, who appear generally desirous to become good citizens. It is the ignorance, the prejudice, the brutality, and the educated idleness,—if so it can be termed— of the freedmen,—all attributable, not so much to their race, as to the system of slavery under which they have lived,—that are mainly to be watched and placed under restraint. To supply the place of the rigid plantation discipline now suddenly done away with, some well digested code of laws and punishments, adapted to the peculiar position of affairs, should be applied throughout the entire South. The impossibility of attaching, in future, money value to the former slaves, will break up, in practice, as the Emancipation proclamation has done in theory, the system of slavery; and the interests of the capitalists and landowners of the South will lead them to make the best possible use of freed labor: but it will be more difficult to convince the freedmen themselves of their true position and prospects. Only actual suffering, starvation, and punishment will drive many of them to work. It is a general complaint on the part of the planters that although the laborers have had fair offers made to them of compensation, including a share of the crops, they nearly all have shortened their day's work several hours, and persist in taking to themselves every Saturday.

In districts remote from our posts of occupation the plantation discipline still prevails, and cases of flogging and shooting are continually brought to the notice of the Commission from places sixty or eighty miles from Orangeburg. Nor are the planters always to be blamed for such measures of self-defence. There must be some restraint in every community, and where there are but two classes, the one educated and intelligent, the other ignorant and degraded, it is preferable, if one class must govern, that it be the former. It is to be hoped, however, that civil or military authority will soon supplant such an exercise of irresponsible power, which is liable to great abuse.

A form for making contracts, adapted after consultation with a number of planters, is enclosed herewith. It was found, at the outset of our operations, that half the crop,—which General Hatch had recommended as fair compensation, was too much to give, if the laborers were also to be fed and clothed until the end of the year. At the wish of General Hartwell, therefore, the planters have been left to make their own proposals, the Commission reserving the right to disapprove such contracts as seemed unjust to the workmen. It has been found, however, that in almost every instance, the offers have been very liberal. It is usual to promise food, and as far as possible, clothing, to all the people on the plantations, both workers and dependents; and in addition, either a certain share of the crop, varying according to circumstances from one-tenth to one-half (the latter in very rare instances), to be divided among the laborers only;—or, so many bushels of corn to every "hand",—usually a year's supply. In consideration of the fact that only one third of the people supported, on the average, are laborers, and that General Sherman's armies have destroyed the fences, taken the stock, and devastated the whole region hereabouts, the Commission are of opinion that these contracts are very favorable to the workmen. It would appear that so low, uneducated and inefficient a class of laborers as these now suddenly freed, should not receive more pay than Northern farm laborers,—allowance being made for difference of circumstances. A day laborer at the North, with a large family, usually has to pay all his wages for food, clothing, and house-rent. If he can have his own little garden, and a stock of poultry and pigs,—as most of the freedmen have, he is fortunate; and if in addition to all this he gets a share of the crops—say a year's supply of food, over and above expenditures, he is prospering beyond most of his fellows. Were the freedmen to receive more, the relation between capital and labor would be disturbed, and an undue value placed upon the latter, to the prejudice and disadvantage, in the end, of the laborers themselves.

For the present year, a better condition of affairs than that now prevailing can hardly be looked for. An influx of immigrants from Europe and from the Northern States, increasing the proportion of the white inhabitants to the blacks, dividing into smaller farms the arable lands of the South, and introducing a system of money payments for labor, together with the gradual education of the negroes themselves, will, it is to be hoped, bring order out of this chaos. The plan adopted by the Commission is only meant to compose matters, as far as possible, in order that the crops may be tilled and reaped. It will give the members great satisfaction to be relieved by the adoption of some general plan, from duties which are very arduous and responsible, and in the discharge of which, through the want of a mounted police force, they cannot avoid disappointing many applicants, and neglecting a large number of cases which should properly demand their attention.

In addition to the form for contracts, is enclosed an address to the colored people of the District, which embodies all that the visiting officers include in their speeches. All the points upon which any doubt or question has arisen are touched upon and explained in the simplest and most familiar terms which can be used.

Awaiting instructions for the future, I have the honor, General, to remain Your obedient servant,

Charles C. Soule

To the Freed People of Orangeburg District.

You have heard many stories about your condition as freemen. You do not know what to believe: you are talking too much; wanting too much; asking for too much. If you can find out the truth about this matter, you will settle down quietly to your work. Listen, then, and try to understand just how you are situated.

You are now free, but you must know that the only difference you can feel yet, between slavery and freedom, is that neither you nor your children can be bought or sold. You may have a harder time this year than you have ever had before; it will be the price you pay for your freedom. You will have to work hard, and get very little to eat, and very few clothes to wear. If you get through this year alive and well, you should be thankful. Do not expect to save up anything, or to have much corn or provisions ahead at the end of the year. You must not ask for more pay than free people get at the North. There, a field hand is paid in money, but has to spend all his pay every week, in buying food and clothes for his family, and in paying rent for his house. You cannot be paid in money,—for there is no good money in the District,—nothing but Confederate paper. Then, what can you be paid with? Why, with food, with clothes, with the free use of your little houses and lots. You do not own a cent's worth except yourselves. The plantation you live on is not yours, nor the houses, nor the cattle, mules and horses; the seed you planted with was not yours, and the ploughs and hoes do not belong to you. Now you must get something to eat and something to wear, and houses to live in. How can you get these things? By hard work—and nothing else, and it will be a good thing for you if you get them until next year, for yourselves and for your families. You must remember that your children, your old people, and the cripples, belong to you to support now, and all that is given to them is so much pay to you for your work. If you ask for anything more; if you ask for a half of the crop, or even a third, you ask too much; you wish to get more than you could get if you had been free all your lives. Do not ask for Saturday either: free people everywhere else work Saturday, and you have no more right to the day than they have. If your employer is willing to give you part of the day, or to set a task that you can finish early, be thankful for the kindness, but do not think it is something you must have. When you work, work hard. Begin early—at sunrise, and do not take more than two hours at noon. Do not think, because you are free you can choose your own kind of work. Every man must work under orders. The soldiers, who are free, work under officers, the officers under the general, and the general under the president. There must be a head man everywhere, and on a plantation the head man, who gives all the orders, is the owner of the place. Whatever he tells you to do you must do at once, and cheerfully. Never give him a cross word or an impudent answer. If the work is hard, do not stop to talk about it, but do it first and rest afterwards. If you are told to go into the field and hoe, see who can go first and lead the row. If you are told to build a fence, build it better than any fence you know of. If you are told to drive the carriage Sunday, or to mind the cattle, do it, for necessary work must be done even on the Sabbath. Whatever the order is, try and obey it without a word.

There are different kinds of work. One man is a doctor, another is a minister, another a soldier. One black man may be a field hand, one a blacksmith, one a carpenter, and still another a house-servant. Every man has his own place, his own trade that he was brought up to, and he must stick to it. The house-servants must not want to go into the field, nor the field hands into the house. If a man works, no matter in what business, he is doing well. The only shame is to be idle and lazy.

You do not understand why some of the white people who used to own you, do not have to work in the field. It is because they are rich. If every man were poor, and worked in his own field, there would be no big farms, and very little cotton or corn raised to sell; there would be no money, and nothing to buy. Some people must be rich, to pay the others, and they have the right to do no work except to look out after their property. It is so everywhere, and perhaps by hard work some of you may by-and-by become rich yourselves.

Remember that all your working time belongs to the man who hires you: therefore you must not leave work without his leave not even to nurse a child, or to go and visit a wife or husband. When you wish to go off the place, get a pass as you used to, and then you will run no danger of being taken up by our soldiers. If you leave work for a day, or if you are sick, you cannot expect to be paid for what you do not do; and the man who hires you must pay less at the end of the year.

Do not think of leaving the plantation where you belong. If you try to go to Charleston, or any other city, you will find no work to do, and nothing to eat. You will starve, or fall sick and die. Stay where you are, in your own homes, even if you are suffering. There is no better place for you anywhere else.

You will want to know what to do when a husband and wife live on different places. Of course they ought to be together, but this year, they have their crops planted on their own places, and they must stay to work them. At the end of the year they can live together. Until then they must see each other only once in a while.

In every set of men there are some bad men and some fools; who have to be looked after and punished when they go wrong. The Government will punish grown people now, and punish them severely, if they steal, lie idle, or hang around a man's place when he does not want them there, or if they are impudent. You ought to be civil to one another, and to the man you work for. Watch folks who have always been free, and you will see that the best people are the most civil.

The children have to be punished more than those who are grown up, for they are full of mischief. Fathers and mothers should punish their own children, but if they happen to be off, or if a child is caught stealing or behaving badly about the big house, the owner of the plantation must switch him, just as he should his own children.

Do not grumble if you cannot get as much pay on your place as some one else, for on one place they have more children than on others, on one place the land is poor, on another it is rich; on one place, Sherman took everything, on another, perhaps, almost everything was left safe. One man can afford to pay more than another. Do not grumble, either, because, the meat is gone or the salt hard to get. Make the best of everything, and if there is anything which you think is wrong, or hard to bear, try to reason it out: if you cannot, ask leave to send one man to town to see an officer. Never stop work on any account, for the whole crop must be raised and got in, or we shall starve. The old men, and the men who mean to do right, must agree to keep order on every plantation. When they see a hand getting lazy or shiftless, they must talk to him, and if talk will do no good, they must take him to the owner of the plantation.

In short, do just about as the good men among you have always done. Remember that even if you are badly off, no one can buy or sell you: remember that if you help yourselves, GOD will help you, and trust hopefully that next year and the year after will bring some new blessing to you.

Washington D.C. June 21, 1865

Captain   Your report has been received and carefully read. I doubt not the Commission is to do all you can to secure harmony and good will in society, and that you must meet many difficulties. My views are set forth in the accompanying

Circulars. I do not expect to meet every difficulty arising under the new State of things. The belief on the part of old masters, that freedmen is impracticable, shows the existence of a prejudice, which time and experience alone can cure. The sophistries of planters are often insidious and hard to refute If they cannot get slavery, they try for a despotism next to it. Equality before the law is what we must aim at. I mean a black, red, yellow or white *thief* should have punishment for his theft without regard to the color of his skin. The same equitable rule applies with regard to rights of property. Under the guise of a desire to secure order the planter wishes United States Officers to put into his hands absolute power, or at the best he asks us to exercise that power. Now while we show the freedmen, how freemen support themselves at the North by labor, we ought to let him taste somewhat of the freemans privileges. The masters are prejudiced and mostly ignorant of the workings of free labor. you had better therefore draw up an address to them, also explaining their duties and obligations—

I have provided in my Circular No 5. for cases in dispute not taken cognizance of by military tribunals. Punishments are not prescribed. It will be necessary to call upon the military or police force for the execution of such punishment—An order No 102 of 1865 from the War Dept. will enable you to do this. Your form of contract is good. Genl Saxton is the Asst Commissioner for S.C. Please send reports to him or his Agent at Charleston,

O. O Howard

P.S. Why are wheat and rye excepted in the contract?

Richard Henry Dana: Speech at Boston

Mr. President,—It was hoped by those who have summoned us together this morning, that a voice might go out from Faneuil Hall, to which the people of the United States would listen, as in times past.

We deprecate, especially, anything like political agitation of the questions before us; but a calm consideration of them by the people, is a duty and a necessity. For, Mr. President and fellow-citizens, the questions pressing upon this country are the most vast and momentous that have ever presented themselves for solution by a free people.

We wish to know, I suppose, first, What are our powers. That is the first question—what are our just powers? Second—What ought we to do? Third—How ought we to do it? With your leave, I propose to attempt an answer to these three questions.

What are our just powers? Well, my friends, that depends upon the answer to one question—Have we been at war, or have we not? In what have we been engaged for the last four years?—has it been a war, or has it been something else and other than war? I take it upon myself to assert, that we have been in a condition of public and perfect war. It has been no mere suppression, by municipal powers, of an insurrection for the redress of grievances. It has been a perfect public war. The government has a right to exercise, at its discretion, every belligerent power. [Applause.] We are not bound to exercise them; the enemy can not compel us to do it; but, at our discretion, we may exercise every belligerent power. Do you doubt it? Does any man doubt it? [Voices—"No."]

I will tell you why you must not doubt it. In the first place, the Supreme Court of the United States has, by an unanimous decision, held that we are in a public war, and that the government can exercise every belligerent power. The court differed as to the time when we entered upon such a war, and whether recognition of war by Congress was necessary, but that we came to a war at last, was their unanimous decision. The

Prize Courts, like the Temple of Janus, are closed in peace, and open only in war. The Prize Courts have been thrown open, and every prize that has been condemned in this country has been condemned upon the principle of a public war. Congress gave us no rules for municipal condemnation, but left the Prize Courts to the rules which govern public international war. We have condemned the prizes upon the same rules, and no other, than those by which we condemned them in the war with Great Britain in 1812. This course of the Prize Courts has been sustained by the Supreme Court, acted upon by the Executive, and recognized by Congress. The statutes, too, have called it a war, in terms. The soldiers that are enlisted—what are they enlisted for? Why, they are enlisted "for the war," are they not? How is it at this moment? Is not the Executive holding those States by military occupation? Are we not holding them in the grasp of war? You cannot justify the great acts of our government for the last three years upon any other principle than the existence of war. You look in vain in the municipal rules of a constitution, to find authority for what we are doing now. You might as well look into the Constitution to find rules for sinking the Alabama in the British Channel,—to find rules for taking Richmond. You might as well look there to find rules for lighting General Grant's cigar. [Laughter.] No; we stand upon the ground of war, and we exercise the powers of war.

Now, my fellow-citizens, what are those powers and rights? What is a WAR? War is not an attempt to kill, to destroy; but it is *coërcion for a purpose*. When a nation goes into war, she does it to secure an end, and the war does not cease until the end is secured. A boxing match, a trial of strength or skill, is over when one party stops. A war is over, when its purpose is secured. It is a fatal mistake to hold that this war is over, because the fighting has ceased. [Applause.] This war is not over. We are in the attitude and in the *status* of war today. There is the solution of this question. Why, suppose a man has attacked your life, my friend, in the highway, at night, armed, and after a death-struggle, you get him down—what then? When he says he has done fighting, are you obliged to release him? Can you not hold him, until you have got some security against his weapons? [Applause.] Can you not hold him until you have searched him, and taken his weapons from him? Are you obliged to let him up to begin a new fight for your life? The same principle governs war between nations. When one nation has conquered another, in a war, the victorious nation does not retreat from the country and give up possession of it, because the fighting has ceased. No; it holds the conquered enemy in the grasp of war until it has secured whatever it has a right to require. [Applause.] I put that proposition fearlessly—*The conquering party may hold the other in the grasp of war, until it has secured whatever it has a right to require.*

But, what have we a right to require? We have no right to require our conquered foe to adopt all our notions, our opinions, our systems, however much we may be attached to them, however good we may think them; but we have a right to require whatever the public safety and public faith make necessary. [Applause.] That is the proposition. Then, we come to this:—*We have a right to hold the rebels in the grasp of war until we have obtained whatever the public safety and the public faith require.* [Applause and cries of "good."] Is not that a solid foundation to stand upon? Will it not bear examination? and are we not upon it today?

I take up my next question. We have settled what our just powers are. Need I ask an audience, in Faneuil Hall, what it is that the public safety and the public faith demand? Is there a man here who doubts? In the progress of this war, we found it necessary to proclaim the emancipation of every slave. [Applause.] On the first day of January, 1863, Abraham Lincoln, of blessed memory, declared the emancipation of every slave. It was a military act, not a civil act. Military acts depend upon military power, and the measure of military power is the length of the military arm. That proclamation of the first of January did not emancipate the slaves, but the military arm emancipated them, as it was stretched forth and made bare. [Applause.] District after district, region after region, State after State, have been brought within the grasp of the military arm, until at last, today, the whole rebel territory lies within and beneath the military arm. [Loud applause.] Therefore, in State after State, region after region, the slaves have been emancipated, until at last, over the whole country, every slave is emancipated. [Renewed applause.] I would undertake to maintain, before any impartial neutral tribunal in Christendom, the proposition that we have today an adequate military occupation of the whole rebel country, sufficient to effect the emancipation of every slave, by admitted laws of war. Whatever differences of opinion there may have been as to the *manner* in which the proclamation operated, there is no doubt left as to the result; because we have all the ground the slaves have stood upon within our military occupation.

The slaves are emancipated. In form, this is true. But the public faith stands pledged to them, that they and their posterity forever shall have a complete and perfect freedom. [Prolonged applause.] Not merely our safety; no, the PUBLIC FAITH is pledged that every man, woman and child of them, and their posterity forever, shall have a complete and perfect freedom. [Applause.] Do you mean to "palter with them in a double sense"? Are you willing that the great republic shall cheat these poor negroes, "keeping the word of promise to the ear, and breaking it to the hope"? Then, *how* shall we secure to them a complete and perfect freedom? The constitution of every slave State is cemented in slavery. Their statute-books are full of slavery. It is the corner-stone of every rebel State. If you allow them to come back at once, without condition, into the exercise of all their State functions, what guaranty have you for the complete freedom of the men you have emancipated. There must, therefore, not merely be an emancipation of the actual, living slaves, but there must be an abolition of the slave system. [Applause.] Every State must have the abolition of slavery in its constitution, or else we must have the amendment of the Constitution, ratified by three-fourths of the States. Yes, that little railroad-ridden republic, New Jersey, must be shamed into adopting the amendment to the Constitution. [Applause.] New Jersey, whose vote, seventy years ago, alone prevented the adoption of Jefferson's great ordinance, making subsequently acquired territories free, and which now stands alone among the free States against this proposition of amendment—must be shamed into its adoption. [Renewed applause.] Louisiana will adopt it before her; Kentucky, perhaps, may adopt it before her. They may come into the kingdom, when the children of the kingdom shut themselves out. [Applause.]

But, my fellow-citizens, is that enough? Is it enough that we have emancipation and abolition upon the statute books?

In some states of society, I should say yes. In ancient times,
when the slaves were of the same race with their masters, when
the slaves were poets, orators, scholars, ministers of state, merchants, and the mothers of kings,—if they were emancipated,
nature came to their aid, and they reached an equality with their
masters. Their children became patricians. But, my friends, this
is a slavery of race; it is a slavery which those white people have
been taught, for thirty years, is a divine institution. I ask you,
has the Southern heart been fired for thirty years for nothing?
Have these doctrines been sown, and no fruit reaped? Have
they been taught that the negro is not fit for freedom, have
they believed that, and are they converted in a day? Besides all
that, they look upon the negro as the cause of their defeat and
humiliation. I am afraid there is a feeling of hatred toward the
negro at the South today which has never existed before!

What are their laws? Why, their laws, many of them, do not
allow a free negro to live in their States. When we emancipated
the slaves, did we mean they should be banished—is that it?
[Voices—"No."] Is that keeping public faith with them? And
yet their laws declare so, and may declare it again.

That is not all! By their laws, a black man cannot testify in
court; by their laws he cannot hold land; by their laws he cannot vote. Now, we have got to choose between two results.
With these four millions of negroes, either you must have
four millions of disfranchised, disarmed, untaught, landless,
thriftless, non-producing, non-consuming, degraded men, or
else you must have four millions of land-holding, industrious,
arms-bearing and voting population. [Loud applause.] Choose
between these two! Which will you have? It has got to be decided pretty soon, which you will have. The corner-stone of
those institutions will not be slavery, in name, but their institutions will be built upon the mud-sills of a debased negro
population. Is that public safety? Is it public faith? Are those
republican ideas, or republican institutions? Some of these
negroes have shed their blood for us upon the public faith.
Ah! there are negro parents whose children have fallen in battle; there are children who lost fathers, and wives who lost
husbands, in our cause. Our covenant with the freedman is
sealed in blood! It bears the image and superscription of the

Republic! Their freedom is a tribute which we must pay, not only to Cæsar, but to God! [Applause.]

We have a right to require, my friends, that the freedmen of the South shall have the right to hold land. [Applause.] Have we not? We have a right to require that they shall be allowed to testify in the State courts. [Applause.] Have we not? We have a right to demand that they shall bear arms as soldiers in the militia. [Applause.] Have we not? We have a right to demand that there shall be an impartial ballot. [Great applause.]

Now, my friends, let us be frank with one another. On what ground are we going to put our demand for the ballot for freedmen? Some persons may say that they will put it upon the ground that every human being has an absolute and unconditional right to vote. There never was any such doctrine! We do not mean, now, to allow about one half the South to vote. [Applause.] Why not? Why, the public safety does not admit of it. [Applause.] We put the condition of loyalty on every vote. [Applause.] How have we done in this State? Half the people in this State are excluded from the ballot,—the better half, we are fond of calling them; no woman votes. We prescribe conditions for the men,—whatever conditions society sees fit; conditions of age; conditions of residence; conditions of tax-paying; and lately we have added, by a large popular majority, the further high condition, that they shall have intelligence enough to read and write. [Applause.] Of course there is no such doctrine as that every human being has a right to vote. Society must settle the right to a vote upon this principle—"The greatest good of the greatest number" must decide it. The greatest good of society must decide it. On what ground, then, do we put it? We put it upon the ground that the public safety and the public faith require that there shall be no distinction of color. [Applause.] That is the ground upon which it can stand.

To introduce the free negroes to the voting franchise is a revolution. *If we do not secure that now, in the time of revolution, it can never be secured, except by a new revolution.* [Loud applause.] Do you want, some years hence, to see a new revolution?—the poor, oppressed, degraded black man, bearing patiently his oppression, until he can endure it no longer, rising with arms for his rights—do you want to see that?

[Voices—"No."] Do you want to see them submit forever, and *not* rise for their rights? [Voices—"No."] No, neither, you say. Well, my friends, who cry "no," if either of those things happens, it is our fault. If they never get their rights, or get them by a new revolution, it will be, in either event, our fault. Do you wish to have that blame rest upon you? [Voices—"No."] No? Then "Now's the day, and now's the hour." [Loud applause.] They are in a condition of transition; a condition of revolution; seize the opportunity and make it thorough! [Renewed and hearty applause.]

This, then, fellow-citizens, is what we have a right to demand. Now comes my third question—How do you propose to accomplish it? We know our powers, we know what we want to do,—how do we propose to do it? First, the right to bear arms, fortunately, does not depend upon the decision of any State. That is a matter which, under the Constitution, depends upon the acts of Congress. Congress makes the militia, and Congress must see to it that the emancipated slaves have the privilege, the dignity and the power of an arms-bearing population. But the right to acquire a homestead, the right to testify in courts, the right to vote, by the Constitution, depend, not only in spirit but in the letter, upon the State constitutions. The right to vote in national elections depends on State constitutions. What are you going to do about it?

You find the answer in my first proposition. We are in a state of war. We are exercising war powers. We hold each State in the grasp of war until the State does what we have a right to require of her. [Applause.] Do you say this is coercion? Certainly it is. War is coercion, and this is part of the war. We have a military occupation. What is the effect of that? I appeal to the learned in the law of nations; I appeal to an authority that has spoken to you words of wisdom this morning [turning to Prof. Parsons], whether it is not a principle of war that when the conquering party has a military occupation of the country, the political relations of its citizens are suspended thereby? That is true; *suspended*, I do not say *destroyed*.

Let no man say that I overlook the distinction between a civil or domestic war and a war between recognized nations. My duties and studies and thoughts have kept my attention upon that. We have not been putting down an insurrection

of professed citizens. We have fought against an empire unlawfully established within the limits of this republic—a completed, *de facto* government, perfected in all its parts; and if we
had not destroyed it by war, it would have remained and stood
a completed government. It stood or fell, on the issues of war.
Nothing but war has destroyed it.

This *de facto* empire had possession of that whole country.
Why, from the Potomac to the Rio Grande, we had not one fort;
not one arsenal; not a court house, nor a custom house, nor a
light-house, nor a post-office, nor a single magistrate, or a spot
on which he could stand. They had forts, arsenals, light-houses,
custom-houses, courts, post-offices, magistrates, and were in
complete possession. It happened—it *happened*—that those
people preserved their State lines—did not obliterate them; but
they might have done so. It happened that they did not change
their constitutions, but they might have done it. They might
have resolved themselves into a consolidated republic, or a monarchy. They did as they chose. Under such circumstances, if the
parent government is not strong enough to hold possession of
the country, and a hostile, *de facto* government is established
upon it, the parent government proportionately loses its claims
to allegiance, for the time. Certainly it does—not absolutely, but
for the time.

What follows from all this? from a war fought over the continent and over every ocean,—their privateers vexing our commerce at the antipodes; we fighting the battles of the republic
in the mouth of the British Channel [applause]; and over this
whole vast republic, south of the Potomac and the Ohio,

> "Every turf beneath your feet
> Has been a soldier's sepulchre."

If such a war leaves this people just as they were before; if no
corresponding rights and powers have accrued to us, then I
say, it has been the most vast and bloody and cruel nullity that
the world ever saw. It is not so. We have a right now and a
duty to execute those powers which belong to the condition of
war. The political relations of these people to their State governments are suspended. Military occupation exists, and the
republic governs them by powers derived from war. You look
in vain to the Constitution to point out what shall be done.

The war is constitutional; but the consequences, powers and duties, arise out of *the nature of things*. The Constitution may distribute functions, but all the powers which the President or Congress hold, or both, and are exercising, are derived from the condition of war.

I ask, again, how shall we obtain what we have a right to require? The changes we require are changes of their constitutions, are they not? The changes must be fundamental. The people are remitted to their original powers. They must meet in conventions and form constitutions, and those constitutions must be satisfactory to the republic. [Loud applause.]

I desire at this point to say a word with reference to President Johnson and his course, to which I ask your special attention. When President Johnson called the people of North Carolina and one or two other States together, he did not call the blacks as well as the whites to the ballot. That was a question of process, which requires great discretion and wisdom. The President and his Cabinet know a great deal more about the details, and means, and probable results, than we do. I believe President Johnson has the same end in view that we have here today. [Applause.] He has his own mode of reaching it. Some may ask, why did he not ask the blacks to vote? I know nothing, personally, of his reasons; but I can easily see that two embarrassments might well beset him. They occur to us all, at once.

The people of those States are to vote for the purpose of making their organic law. President Johnson holds them by military power. Is it not a very serious thing, in a republican government, to dictate from the cannon's mouth the organic law for a great people? I do not ask what we have a right to do—that is not the question. The question is what ought we to do? I do not wonder that a man educated in republican principles hesitates to dictate, as military superior, who should vote in determining the organic law of a people. He took the voters as they stood before the war; he put the test of loyalty to them; he took securities against them; he went no further. That we may well suppose was one of his reasons.

We can easily suppose another. Take the whole black population. Shall I say to you, my friends, today, for the first time, that slavery is a beneficent, effective educational system? If I say it, will you believe it? Will you think me sane? Have we not all said, and thought, and fought because we believed that slavery degraded and brutalized its victims? If a man requires us to say that the four millions of slaves have not been debased and brutalized by slavery, he requires us to unsay all we have said and believed and fought for and prayed for, the last thirty years. Slavery has degraded the negroes. It has kept them ignorant and debased. It has not, thank God, destroyed them. The germ of moral and intellectual life has survived; and we mean to see to it that they are built up into a self-governing, voting, intelligent population. [Applause.] They are not that today. They will become so quicker than you think. They do not need half the care nor half the patronage we used to think they did. And the ballot is a part of our educating and elevating process.

There are various courses, all seeming to lead to one point. From these, President Johnson has chosen to make an experimental, tentative trial of one. On a question of means and processes, he has declined to clothe the negroes, by an exercise of military power, with the right to vote. True, he has by military power applied a test of loyalty to the voters. But that is a very mild and a necessary exercise of military power. No man, I believe, questions the necessity and fitness of that act. But it is a far different thing to speak a whole nation of voters into existence—not for temporary, but for permanent and fundamental objects—by a stroke of his pen, or rather, I should say, by the uplifted sword. His rule has not been to interfere as far as he could, but to accomplish his ends with the least possible interference.

One step further. Suppose the States do not do what we require—what then? I have not heard that question answered yet. Suppose President Johnson's experiment in North Carolina and Mississippi fails, and the white men are determined to keep the black men down—what then? Mr. President, I hope we shall never be called upon to answer, practically, that question. It remits us to an ultimate, and, you may say, a fearful proposition. But if we come to it, though I desire to consider myself the humblest of the persons here, I, for one, am prepared with an answer. I believe that if you come to the ultimate right of the thing, the ultimate law of the case, it is this: that this war— no, not the war, *the victory in the war*—places, not the person, not the life, not the private property of the rebels—they are governed by other considerations and rules—I do not speak of them—*but the political systems of the rebel States, at the discretion of the republic.* [Great applause.] Secession does not do this. Treason does not do this. The existence of civil war does not do this. It is the necessary result of conquest, with military occupation, in a war of such dimensions, such a character and such consequences as this.

You say that it is a fearful proposition. But, be not alarmed. Most political action is discretionary,—all that is fundamental and organic is so. Discretion has its laws, and even its necessities. Still, I know it is a fearful proposition. But is not war a fearful fact? If this is a fearful theory, is it not the legitimate fruit of a terrific fact, the war? If they have sown the wind, must they not expect to reap the whirlwind? War, my friends, is an appeal from the force of law, to the law of force. I declare it a proposition that does not admit of doubt in wars between nations, that when a conqueror has obtained military possession of his enemy's country, it is in his discretion whether he shall permit the political institutions to go on, and treat with them, or shall obliterate them and annex the country to his own dominions. That is the law of war between nations. Is it applicable to us? I think it is. [Applause.] I think, if you come to the ultimate right of the thing, we may, if we choose, take the position that *their political institutions are at the discretion of the republic.*

When a man accepts a challenge to a duel, what does he put at stake? He puts his life at stake, does he not? And is it not childish, after the fatal shot is fired, to exclaim, "O, death, and widowhood, and orphanage are fearful things!" They were all involved in that accepted challenge. When a nation allows itself to be at war, or when a people make war, they put at stake their national existence. [Applause.] That result seldom follows, because the nation that is getting the worst of the contest makes its peace in time; because the conquering nation does not always desire to incorporate hostile subjects in its dominions; because neutral nations intervene. The conqueror must choose between two courses—to permit the political institutions, the body politic, to go on, and treat with it, or obliterate it. We have destroyed and obliterated their central government. Its existence was treason. As to their States, we mean to adhere to the first course. We mean to say the States shall remain, with new constitutions, new systems. We do not mean to exercise sovereign civil jurisdiction over them in our Congress. Fellow-citizens, it is not merely out of tenderness to them; it would be the most dangerous possible course for us. Our system is a planetary system; each planet revolving round its orbit, and all round a common sun. This system is held together by a balance of powers—centripetal and centrifugal forces. We have established a wise balance of forces. Let not that balance be destroyed. If we should undertake to exercise sovereign civil jurisdiction over those States, it would be as great a peril to our system as it would be a hardship upon them. We must not, we will not undertake it, except as the last resort of the thinking and the good—as the ultimate final remedy, when all others have failed.

I know, fellow-citizens, it is much more popular to stir up the feelings of a public audience by violent language than it is to repress them; but on this subject we must think wisely. We have never been willing to try the experiment of a consolidated democratic republic. Our system is a system of States, with central power; and in that system is our safety. [Applause.] State rights, I maintain; State sovereignty, we have destroyed. [Applause.] Therefore, although I say that, if we are driven to the last resort, we may adopt this final remedy; yet wisdom, humanity, regard for democratic principles, common discretion, require that we should follow the course we are now following. Let the States make their own constitutions; but the constitutions must be satisfactory to the Republic [applause]; and—ending as I began—by a power which I think is beyond question, the Republic holds them in the grasp of war until they have made such constitutions. [Loud applause.]

June 21, 1865

Charles Sumner to Gideon Welles

Cotuit. Port—Mass.
4th July '65

My dear Sir,

Yr kind letter has followed me to this retreat by the sea-shore where I am for a few days with Mr Hooper.

What you say of the policy of the Administration, although not new to me, is indescribably painful. Of course, this policy, if carried out, inevitably breaks up the Republican party, & carries the President into the arms of the copperheads, who already praise him & lure him on to destruction. Can not the Cabinet save him & thus save the country?

Never since I have been in public life has there been any question on which public opinion was so prompt & spontaneous. The President had only to say the word, & he had the whole country at his back. All were ready to follow him in the path required by the Declaration of Independence. How he could go in the opposite direction is incomprehensible.

The question is naturally asked, where does the Presdt. get the power to re-organize a State? It would be difficult to say where. But, if he undertakes to exercise this power, he must proceed according to the requirements of the Declaration of Independence.

His present course in reviving the old Oligarchy of the skin & attempting to build *reformed* governments upon it is offensive (1) to the national safety which it endangers; (2) to national justice which it shocks; (3) to the Constitution, *which it sets aside* & (4) to God Almighty, Whom it insults.—

Seeing this policy thus, I can not recognize it as "within constitutional limits." It defies the highest principles of the Constitution, which are found in the national safety, national justice, & the requirements of a republican govt. *It openly sanctions a govt which is not founded on "the consent of the governed" &, therefore, cannot be republican in form.*

Nor can I consider such a policy as any thing but the worst

kind of "aggression." It is flagrantly "aggressive" on Human Rights.

Of course it utterly "incompatible with that harmony which it is desirable to maintain among those who have been faithful to the cause of the Union."

As to the power of the Federal Govt. over this subject in the rebel states, it is the same as the power to suppress the Rebellion, to carry on the war or to decree Emancipation, with that larger untried power superadded "to guarantee a Republican form of govt.," which at this moment it is bound to enforce in the rebel states.

It is because the difficulties of reorganizing the rebel states are so great, that the Govt. must proceed according to the rules of justice & the natural laws. We must have nature & God on our side.

There is no right reserved to any State, inconsistent with the national peace & security—especially can there be no right, according to the language of Burke, "to turn towards us the shameful parts of the Constitution," & insist that these—& these only—shall be recognized.

There is no question of "forfeiture," but simply *a question of fact. The old state govts. are vacated.* This is enough. Of course, *for the time being,* the power is with the Federal Govt., represented by Congress, which must proceed to set up republican govts.

The complications & antagonisms sure to come from this ill-considered policy are already apparent in the inability of the Provisional Governors to take the oath of office prescribed by Congress without perjury. It is idle to say that their office is not included within the Act of Congress. (1) It is a national office, under the national govt; paid by the National Treasury, (2) It is clearly within the spirit, if not the letter of the statute, (3) It is a notorious fact, that the object of Congress was to prevent any men who could not take that oath of office from having any thing to do with the great work of re-organization, *all of which must be put into the hands of men who have been loyal always.*

But I have faith in my country. The right will prevail. The present policy will come to shame & disaster; & the true principles will at last be recognized. I tremble to think how much of agitation, trouble & strife the country must pass through, in order to recover from the false move which has now been made.

I write to you plainly, as I have always been in the habit of speaking on public questions. The question is too serious for hesitation. *The discussion has begun, & it will not stop* until Human Rights are recognized & the Providence of God is vindicated.

Believe me, my dear Sir,

very sincerely Yours,   Charles Sumner

Wendell Phillips to the
National Anti-Slavery Standard

To the Editor of the Standard.

LET me call your attention and that of the country to the danger pointed out in the following extract from the letter of an acute and vigilant friend:

"President Johnson is rapidly issuing proclamations for the reorganization of all the Rebel States. The Governors appointed are old politicians who know all the ropes. Is it not their design, and will they not be able, before next December to make all their new Constitutions and elect new Governors and full Congressional delegations? Then what is to prevent those States from presenting themselves, fully accredited, on the floor of the *new* Congress, and participating in its organization. They will claim, as President Johnson does, that their States have never been out of the Union; that the government declares (as it will) the rebellion suppressed and military occupation withdrawn, and that they now resume their relations with the Federal Government, which have been only temporarily suspended. In this claim they will be backed by the whole power of the Administration, and this is the trap to be sprung on us. The Clerk of the House, you remember, presides until a new Speaker is elected. If he had firmness enough to refuse to receive the credentials of these rebel members, and to refuse to count their votes, this danger might be averted. But can we count on so much virtue in any politician? We may, perhaps, baffle this plan in the Senate. That body being always organized, no members can be admitted without the concurrence of the rest. But how long would even the Senate stand up against the action of the House of Representatives and enormous pressure of every other kind?

"I believe that this attempt will be made at the next meeting of Congress. Possibly South Carolina might be kept out, but even that is doubtful. I may exaggerate the importance of this matter, but that the attempt will be made there can be no doubt."

The importance of these suggestions cannot be over-estimated, and every means should be taken to avert this peril. We have been counting on the possibility of rallying a majority of the legally elected members of Congress to keep the members from Rebel States out of Congress, at least till they consented to certain conditions—ratifying the Anti-Slavery Amendment and other matters. Some sanguine friends believe they can be kept out until they agree to give the negro the right to vote. But, according to this rebel plot, the Southern members may enter Congress without agreeing to the Anti-Slavery Amendment or to any other conditions. Once inside the doors, they may take part in all the discussions and votes affecting themselves and their claims, and may checkmate the Anti-Slavery Amendment itself. In fact, our fate rests in the hands of the CLERK OF THE HOUSE OF REPRESENTATIVES. I know nothing about him; but how few men in the nation could be trusted to stand firm in such a post! The whole North should be roused to guard against this danger. If the Rebel States in their present mood, can, in any way, get inside Congress, and wield EIGHTY-FOUR VOTES there, and more especially if they can get there unpledged to any conditions and wield those votes, then truly the "South" will be as strong as ever, and the Negro almost as defenceless.

Yours,　　　　　　　　　　WENDELL PHILLIPS.

National Anti-Slavery Standard, July 8, 1865

Francis Preston Blair to Andrew Johnson

Silver Spring Augt. 1. 1865

My dear Mr. President

Having been in some degree associated with the leading men who have shaped the course of the liberal party during the last half century, & indulged in conferring with them in the measures proposed to advance its cause, I venture to express my views to you, now its champion, on a most important epoch, involving the fate of Republican Institutions throughout this continent and possibly beyond it.

Observe what vast questions already emerge from the rebellion. First—The policy of grafting the black race on the white race in the administration of the Government founded by the latter for its own behoof, involving in its result that of making it a hybrid Government to suit a motley hybrid race. Next—The policy of violating the rights of the States guarantied by the constitution, securing to them the regulation of the suffrage to provide for their municipal legislation as States, as well as for that of the nation, through the election of the President & Congress of the United States. And third—The policy of permitting the potentates of Europe to plant a monarchy in the midst of our Continent, thus to hold the key of the Isthmus—to open or shut the gate of the Oceans between our Atlantic & Pacific possessions and to array a great military Power on both flanks of our Republic wielded by a despot, prompt at any moment to strike it on the east or west of the Rocky mountains, to divide it or dissolve it entirely & partition it like Poland.

Now you have taken your stand on all the issues which have arisen from the rebellion, or rather which originated it, as they were all lurking in the Slavery which European monarchs imposed on our country & which their policy instigated Southern masters to employ to destroy our Government. The rebellion is crushed and with it the Slavery that animated it, but like the Hydra it puts out new heads—from the vines of the old trunk. It sprouts out with the bold front of negro equality.

Negro suffrage shouts out on one side with a political aspect and on the other we have the social aspect to emerge in the shape of amalgamation. What can come of this adulteration of our Anglo-Saxon race and Anglo-Saxon Government by Africanization, but the degradation of the free spirit & lofty aspirations which our race inherited from their ancestry and brought to this continent; and turn that whole portion of it engaged as manual Operatives into that class of mongrels which cannot but spring from the unnatural blending of the blacks & whites in one common class of laborers and giving to both an assimilation through that color, which has unhappily marked servitude during all generations from the days of Ham. The result would inevitably be to make a distinction in caste and put a brand on all our race associated in employment with people of color & crisped hair. It would not create equality between those thus associated and those engaged in professional & political pursuits. It would hasten the creation of a lower order—a serfdom—a foundation for an Aristocracy crowned with Royalty.

This is the real scope of all the enemies of our Government at home and abroad. To avoid such results our fathers constituted a Government in which the white race alone were invested with all the rights it conferred. That race have hitherto held it exclusively as their heritage. They were its sole Freeholders. It was the property of its creators and none can claim rights in it without their consent. It was for this reason that the popular Sovereignty exerted through the suffrages of the people was committed by the national constitution to the guardianship & control of the State Governments which are nearest to the people. But now that paramount power which was given to the states of the South as well as the North, the partizans of the negro race in the latter, insist must be stript from the former & in effect the rights of Government in the south conferred on the freedmen. This state of things would introduce the San Domingo problem in all the States of the South and the question of mastery between the races would be decided by the States of the North in declaring how many of the white race should remain under its ban of disfranchisement to subject it to the black race, all of which is enfranchised.

From the tenor of the Faneuil Hall appeal which comes to this issue, it would seem to be the purpose of those speaking for the party in New England, who look upon the result of the war as giving them the South as a conquest, that Congress is to vote out every representative who presents himself from a State which does not resign its constitutional right to regulate the suffrage of its people. This is simply an attempt at revolution, a breach of the Union by a vote of Congress.

The idea that suffrage will produce equality between the two races at the South is illusory. The black freedmen will find the prejudices of caste increased among the mass of white laborers by the new priviledge. They will become competitors with the superior race in that which touches their pride and it will be found more than was necessary to get under the wing of the master who hires them, for protection. They will be obliged to have white leaders at the polls as they had in the camps of both armies & those who hire them will control their ballot more absolutely than has ever been done by persons occupying similar relations because their safety will depend upon their employers in the exercise of their priviledge in the service of an increased prejudice & more powerful caste. It is absurd to suppose that the rich, educated, intelligent men will not command the suffrages of their negro hirelings if they venture to bring them to the polls to assert equality with the whites. The Indians although always a free race in this country & accustomed to Government, never could attain in the States in which they were embodied, the equality which a fraction of the North insist on giving the negroes in the south against the will of the mass of the whites in those States. The Indians melted away under that process of civilization now contemplated for the blacks. The result of the contact of races marked by nature to be distinct has induced all the great statesmen of our country to look to colonization & segregation as the means of saving the colored race & giving to them a Government of their own & with it the equality and independence they desire & deserve. The party who oppose this scheme, (yours as well as your predecessors), have no expectation of maintaining equality for the emancipated by suffrage. They assert it for them, some with a view to drive the whites from the Gulf States—others with the design of keeping those States out of the Union. To vote their members of congress out because those States refuse to obey the behests of other States as to the regulation of the right of suffrage, committed to them by the constitution, is to vote a dissolution of the Union—a subversion of the constitution. The pretense of establishing negro equality in a country which is compelled by the fist of the central Government to submit its suffrage to its control, makes the idea of equality with the arbitrary power asserting this superiority, absolutely absurd. If the Representatives of a state in one section are expelled because it does not surrender its constitutional rights, may not a state in another section be expelled because it will not surrender some of its rights at the dictation of a majority in congress? Why not expell the representatives from California & Oregon for refusing the suffrage to the Chinese & the whole group of the North eastern States for refusing it to free negroes? This movement against the south has its motive in the ambition which prompted Mr. Chase to say at the beginning of the rebellion, "Let the Seceding States go, they are not worth fighting for."

This issue to deny equality to the Southern States on the pretense of giving Equality to the negroes, is renewed by the Faneuil Hall programme—an Essex Junto of modern date, who have improved on the consolidation schemes of their prototypes. It was first made at the last session of congress against your predecessor by those calling themselves his friends. They carried a bill through congress to defeat his plan of giving the States the rights of which they were deprived by usurpation. He crushed the attempt by withholding his consent. They appealed to the people & sought to defeat his re-election but they were defeated and now in disregard of the verdict pronounced by the people they have renewed their efforts to compass their object. At the last congress the Democratic party sustained Mr. Lincoln, while opposed by his so called political friends. The people north & south who are at heart in favor of popular Sovereignty & of States rights to maintain it, will sustain you in your effort to accomplish the design of your predecessor, as they sustained him against the intriguers in his own cabinet and their abetters in congress.

Can you not lend your aid—at least give your countenance to those fighting your battle for the fundamental principles of

our federal system, against those in high places, who profess
party allegiance to you when in fact they are destroying that
party & intending to destroy you? Your position enables you
to help those struggling for the Country's cause by simply
adjusting the weights in the high stations around you, so as
to manifest your inclinations. Mr. Lincoln did not do this &
the weight of the members of his administration were found
in the scale against him. The men in congress most active in
carrying the vital measure against him were in the closest confidence with the highest cabinet officers and they used their
official patronage & commanding personal influence to thwart
the Presidents great scheme of adjusting the Union. Would it
be well now when a new epoch has arrived casting the whole
burden of reorganizing our disjointed fabric on your hands, to
work with the same instruments, that marred the wise patriotic
designs of your predecessor? Assistants that worked *con amore*
with the professing friends in Congress, ever ready to betray
him, not only voting against his leading measures openly, but
secretly intriguing to defeat his re-election. The principal men
to whom I here point are still in congress. They are still in co-
operation with those wielding your Departments and they are
still more inimical to your measures & to your re-election than
they were to Mr. Lincolns. Is it safe in such a boisterous time
to embark on a new voyage keeping them at the helm, to steer
your vessel through the currents of the approaching elections
& the coming Congress? If your administration is committed
by the same heads of Departments to the same hands in congressional committees—if they are to shape all movements of
the body & apply the influence controlled by the Secretaries
to array the rank and file under such leaders, will not your fate
be worse than Mr. Lincoln's, the accumulation of your burden
being greater & the preparation of your opponents to break
you down, being vastly increased; You can do nothing to appease the ambition of these aspiring men. They look beyond
you & rely on their measures to defeat you as the means of
compassing their own ends. You must appeal to the people and
rely upon the power of your principles to accomplish the general work you & they have at heart, to make you victorious. To
do this you have only to say "out upon this half-faced fellowship"—to have your Assistants in the great executive trust you

wield, like yourself outspoken—thorough—uncompromising in the maintenance of the constitutional cause now at stake & ready to hazard all in its defense. I have never doubted your purpose to take this stand. I think you intimated as much to me some months since & I write only to say that I think this is the accepted time. The motions of the coming elections are felt already in the great States of New York Ohio & Pennsylvania. The Democracy which gave such immense votes against Lincoln during a war that commanded even their approval at heart, are now in favor of all the objects you design to accomplish by it. You indeed make it their war by the consequences you bring from it, and those men who now seek to pervert those consequences into a defeat of the restoration of the Union, with equality among the States, deserve to forfeit the favor they gained by giving the war their countenance. The Democrats will nominate candidates pledged to support all your leading policy. Their opponents are already out in Massachusetts and other states with manifestos not only at war with your avowed policy but abhorrent to the constitution & tending to make Congress a revolutionary club—a convention of northern representatives bent on subjecting the south to their will and using negro enfranchisement as the means of the disfranchisement of our white brethren of that section, of their equality as citizens and states in the Union.

This issue was broadly made by the action of Mr. Lincolns enemies in the last congress & is now vehemently pressed by the same leaders who still seek to defeat the policy which you & he inaugurated to preserve the Republic. This makes the new epoch which is to take direction from your hand. Can you give it the impulse you desire with the forces in your Cabinet every way complicated, if not absolutely combined with the hostile elements against you in & out of congress? Your Cabinet have no strength or weight in the country except among those who are inimical to your policy and they have neither the desire or power to draw them to its aid, and is there no danger that the retention of these men who are without the confidence of the great body of the liberal Republicans and Democrats, who united alone support your policy, will lose you the confidence of the only men in the nation upon whom you can rely?

It appears to me that the change you contemplate ought to

be made at once, as new combinations of parties are forming throughout the country looking to coming elections, which will certainly produce new combinations in the already elected congress at its next Session. If you are to have a control in these combinations, it must come from the influence you exert over public opinion by the administration you propose & the men you select to make it manifest to the people & *give it the executive stamp.* If the present cabinet remain your attitude to the next congress will be much the same with that of Mr. Lincoln to the last, with the majority of those calling themselves his party friends hostile to his measures and to his succession and poisoning the feelings of the masses of the people, solicitous for the success of the cause for which he labored, by lack of confidence as to the means employed. By the selection of a new cabinet you not only get rid of the odium incurred by the Rump left to you, but you may constitute it of men who will bring to you an accession of strength from all parties who concur in your views of the re-organization which the late conflicts have made necessary. You will of course turn out no man who has not distinguished himself from first to last against all the principles at the bottom of the rebellion—& who has not given his whole strength in bringing out the glorious reform that has banished slavery from the continent. Conspicuous men of this kind may be found of Democratic antecedents—of Republican antecedents—of Whig antecedents, blending both—such you may draw into your administration able & honorable men of these original types ready to merge all minor differences of by gone parties in the great *Democratic Republican* ideas of Mr. Jefferson of the Union of States combined by the popular will under a national Executive & Legislature giving full life to the constitution.

This is your mission at this moment on entering the new Era of our history and let me entreat you to open the process of the new elections and of the creation of new parties in the approaching Congress with a new Cabinet strongly imbued with your opinions, entirely worthy of your confidence and of a caste calculated to win the confidence of men of all parties, who are willing to embrace the scheme of restoration to which you commit your administration in the nomination of the heads of its Departments.

The Democracy, I learn, north and South will make its nominations for National & State Representatives & for other functionaries of men of the type to which I have Just referred. The Republicans will be divided in their nominations, a portion going for the scheme of the Faneuil Hall manifesto derived from the movement which took the shape of the bill passed & presented to the President at the last congress to defeat his plan of re-Union. If you declare your design to the nation by the creation of a new cabinet to express & to execute it distinctly & patently, the party opposed to it who would go to the people & come into congress as the friends of the administration, but really to defeat its policy, will I believe be reduced to a faction. But if you allow them to proceed under the shadow of a great party name, & under prestige already acquired by them of swaying the Cabinet they will command in Congress as at the last session & through it may command the country unless overthrown by the Democracy which will take a stand against it and the Rump Cabinet.

Let me explain my view by supposing a practical illustration. We know that the States of New York & Pennsylvania were canvassed by the Republicans & Democrats in the last Presidential election under the disadvantage to the latter of an anti-war and anti-administration platform. The Democrats lost the election by some eight or ten thousand, where many hundred thousand votes were cast—the returning soldiers carrying it for the Republicans. The Democrats will present themselves at the approaching election on your programme. The candidates who will poll as Republicans on the programme presented in the bill of last Session to Mr. Lincoln to defeat his & your policy & which is now proclaimed at Faneuil Hall as the party test, will claim your support & that of Messrs Seward & Stanton, who as Cabinet ministers represent those states in your administration—suppose confidence in you personally and devotion to the plan of reconstruction you promise them should induce liberal Democrats and Republicans to coalesce so as to give the triumph to the tickets nominated in contravention of your policy, simply because they were called administration candidates. You would then have an appearance of an administration success but it would not be your success. It would be that of the Rump Parliament & Cabinet. It would establish the Faneuil Hall doctrine & defeat your policy. It would accomplish the objects of Messrs Seward & co. so far as their personal & party aims are concerned, but your power at this moment of vital interest would be paralized and your future put in "cold obstruction." If however you were at once to make a new Cabinet drawn from the different sections of the country and representing the various parties in it, yet agreeing to support your plan of reconstruction, on an issue so essential, it would be no matter what party organization returned members, men who gave in this adhesion would become identified with the administration. Their election would be your success and in this epoch of reconstruction would create a new party, embracing the whole Union, adverse to that of Faneuil Hall limited to a northern latitude and exulting in a revolutionary creed. If the old Cabinet be continued while this formation of parties is in progress it is to be apprehended that the organization which approved the existing Cabinet on the ground of its Bastile arrests—incarcerations without accusation and release upon payments of such money as the prisoner possessed or could command on the ground also of its leanings to France giving countenance to the invasion of our continent—on the ground of its demonstrations of hostility to England calculated to Justify the aristocracy there in acceding to the invitations of Napoleon to Join him in recognizing the confederacy & defy the feelings of the British commonalty in favor of our Government, will gain such strength as to induce it to look to the attainment of the control of the Government independently of the Executive head whose policy it adopts.

The vote of the south will be drawn almost as an unit to the side of that party which it finds in opposition to a ministry known to be hostile to its dearest rights in the Union & confederated with the scheme promulgated at Faneuil Hall, which would deprive its *States* of equality *as States*, would create a war of caste & a war of Sections a war of factions breaking up the ancient foundations of the constitution.

Nor is it to be supposed that France will withdraw from Mexico as long as a Minister is retained who has already conceded to her the right to remain there. Nor can it be hoped that men of character can be found in our Country who will risk themselves to raise a force to expel Maximilian from Mexico without involving the country in a foreign war, so long as France & her Puppet have a steadfast friend in the Secretary of State, whose appointee and instrument is still retained in the War Department. So long as they are retained the country may be pardoned even for distrusting your disposition to maintain the inviolability of our continent from the invasion of European Powers.

                                        Yo mo af fd F P. Blair

P.S. The appointment of a new cabinet with a firm aspect looking towards mexico, might, without giving offence to France, manifest a determination that would induce a Surrender of the Scheme of giving "the ascendancy to the latin race in the South american Continent."

Colored People of Mobile to Andrew J. Smith

Mobile August 2d 1865

Sir

We the colored people of Mobile laboring under a deep sense of gratitude to the Government of the United States and understanding that it is the Military Arm and not the civil who has been the instrumentality of giving to us and to our children the blessed boon of pure freedom.

Next to our heavenly Father we revere the good old Constitution of the United States, and now that it acknowledges our existance we are unanimous as a people to die in "its" defence.

We take this method of stating to you believing you to be a friend to our people and to freedom, believing that you do not countenance or sanction any act done in opposition or in Confliction with the policy of the government in relation to our people, and firmly believing that you will mete justice and not Southern Civil law to us. Therefore we take this method of laying before you the following resolutions.

Resolved that we the Colored people of Mobile and "its" vicinity are determined to work hand in hand with the Government and that we will state our grievances to that power who freed us from chains and slavery.

Resolved that the civil law, as administered to us, is in confliction with various acts and orders issued by the Military since the ocupation of Mobile as for Example.

General Orders No 6.

In all Courts and judicial proceedings in this district the testimony of freed or colored people will be received and admitted according to the same principles and rules of Evidence that apply to white persons.

By Order of Brevet Major Genl
C. C. Andrews

Resolved that we can *prove* facts showing where Mayor Slough departs wilfully and knowingly from above order, as in the case of Ferdinand Smith, Pastor of Zions Church who was fined on the morning of the 2d inst and was not permitted to appear even as a spectator in Court and was not called by his name but treated disrespectfully in said Mayors Court. Also, Case of Hugh McKeever (*white* man) who knocked down a Colored woman whose Evidence was not admitted in Said Court.

Resolved that we think shutting our people out of the Civil Courts of Mobile does not shut us out from the halls of Justice, for Justice and white winged mercy have forever fled from the Legislative halls of the South and particularly when men who *hate* our people are ocupying high seats in said halls of Southern Civil Legislation.

Resolved that aforesaid resolution will also apply to Senators, Congressmen, delegates for Conventions and all others who may make, frame, or cause to be framed, laws for our people and who do not or may not guide themselves according to the *Spirit* of the Constitution and all proclamations issued by our Lamented President Abraham Lincoln.

Resolved that we the Colored people of Mobile know and feel that we are free and while we bless the government that *freed* us we will also point out the derelections of officials who may be clothed with a little authority and who take a keen delight in yet keeping us in *Semibondage* for their own pecuniary advantage.

Resolved that if our testimony is not taken in Courts that corrupt officials will yet *grind* the face of the poor, and will also deprive widows and orphans and our people of their inheritance, as for example the step taken by the Methodists South (in this city of Mobile) to dispossess the members of the little Zion of their Zion (*unprecedented and audacious Robbery*) and numberless other wrongs too numerous here to mention.

Resolved that a committee of three (3) Colored men be appointed to wait on Genl Smith and tender to him respectfully above resolutions.

> A. Saxon
> C. Trainer } Committee
> F. D. Taylor

That reports come to us from all sources that our people are cruelly maltreated in the interior of this State of Alabama. That the planters will not yet let our people go but cruelly scourges them and shoots them if they remonstrate or plead for their freedom that numerous tales of untold horror have reached us in Mobile which eye witnesses can prove tales of terrible and heartrending atrocitys which if related not to a civilized and christian community but to the beasts of the forest to the rocks the trees and stones that at the recital of such wrongs those mute and inanimate things would be thrown into Confusion.

Colored People of Mobile

Jourdon Anderson to P. H. Anderson

LETTER FROM A FREEDMAN TO HIS OLD MASTER.

The following is a genuine document. It was *dictated* by the old servant, and contains his ideas and forms of expression.

[Cincinnati Commercial.

DAYTON, Ohio, August 7, 1865.

To my Old Master, Col. P. H. ANDERSON, *Big Spring, Tennessee.*

SIR: I got your letter and was glad to find that you had not forgotten Jordan, and that you wanted me to come back and live with you again, promising to do better for me than anybody else can. I have often felt uneasy about you. I thought the Yankees would have hung you long before this for harboring Rebs. they found at your house. I suppose they never heard about your going to Col. Martin's to kill the Union soldier that was left by his company in their stable. Although you shot at me twice before I left you, I did not want to hear of your being hurt, and am glad you are still living. It would do me good to go back to the dear old home again and see Miss Mary and Miss Martha and Aliea, Esther, Green and Lee. Give my love to them all, and tell them I hope we will meet in the better world, if not in this. I would have gone back to see you all when I was working in the Nashville Hospital, but one of the neighbors told me Henry intended to shoot me if he ever got a chance.

I want to know particularly what the good chance is you propose to give me. I am doing tolerably well here; I get $25 a month, with victuals and clothing; have a comfortable home for Mandy (the folks here call her Mrs. Anderson), and the children, Milly Jane and Grundy, go to school and are learning well; the teacher says Grundy has a head for a preacher. They go to Sunday-School, and Mandy and me attend church regularly. We are kindly treated; sometimes we overhear others saying, "Them colored people were slaves" down in Tennessee. The children feel hurt when they hear such remarks, but I tell them it was no disgrace in Tennessee to belong to Col. Anderson. Many darkies would have been proud, as I used to was, to call you master. Now, if you will write and say

74

what wages you will give me, I will be better able to decide whether it would be to my advantage to move back again.

As to my freedom, which you say I can have, there is nothing to be gained on that score, as I got my free-papers in 1864 from the Provost-Marshal-General of the Department at Nashville. Mandy says she would be afraid to go back without some proof that you are sincerely disposed to treat us justly and kindly—and we have concluded to test your sincerity by asking you to send us our wages for the time we served you. This will make us forget and forgive old sores, and rely on your justice and friendship in the future. I served you faithfully for thirty-two years, and Mandy twenty years, at $25 a month for me, and $2 a week for Mandy. Our earnings would amount to $11,680. Add to this the interest for the time our wages has been kept back and deduct what you paid for our clothing and three doctor's visits to me, and pulling a tooth for Mandy, and the balance will show what we are in justice entitled to. Please send the money by Adams Express, in care of V. Winters, esq., Dayton, Ohio. If you fail to pay us for faithful labors in the past we can have little faith in your promises in the future. We trust the good Maker has opened your eyes to the wrongs which you and your fathers have done to me and my fathers, in making us toil for you for generations without recompense. Here I draw my wages every Saturday night, but in Tennessee there was never any pay day for the negroes any more than for the horses and cows. Surely there will be a day of reckoning for those who defraud the laborer of his hire.

In answering this letter please state if there would be any safety for my Milly and Jane, who are now grown up and both good looking girls. You know how it was with poor Matilda and Catherine. I would rather stay here and starve and die if it come to that than have my girls brought to shame by the violence and wickedness of their young masters. You will also please state if there has been any schools opened for the colored children in your neighborhood, the great desire of my life now is to give my children an education, and have them form virtuous habits.

From your old servant,   JOURDON ANDERSON.

P. S.—Say howdy to George Carter, and thank him for taking the pistol from you when you were shooting at me.

Carl Schurz to Andrew Johnson

Vicksburg, Miss. Aug. 29th 1865.

To his Excellency Andrew Johnson,
President of the United States.

Sir,

In my report from Montgomery Ala. I laid before you the information I had gathered so far about the condition of things in Alabama. Since then I visited Selma and Demopolis. What I saw and learned there confirmed me in the opinion, that the civil authorities as far as they are or can be reestablished under present circumstances, are entirely incapable of restoring anything like public order and security. The demoralization of the people is frightful to behold in its manifestations. Murder, assault with intent to kill, theft and robbery are matters of every day occurrence. The people seem to have lost all conception of the rights of property. Travellers are frequently attacked on the public highways, cotton is stolen in enormous quantities, horses and mules are run off whenever they are not watched with the utmost care, and the perpetrators are almost never arrested and punished. Some cases of that kind happened almost under my own eyes while I was at Selma. I enclose a report furnished to me by the Provost Marshal at Selma, to which I beg leave to invite your particular attention.

At Demopolis I received information very much to the same effect, only that murders did not occur so frequently; the Assistant Superintendent of Freedmen at that place, Capt. A. C. Haptonstall, knew only of two bodies of negroes and one of a white soldier that had been thrown into the Black Warrior River and floated down, all three bodies with marks of violence upon them. As to theft and robbery as well as negro-whipping the same practices prevail, as far as I have been able to ascertain, all over the State.

I beg leave to repeat what I said in my former reports: It is absolutely indispensable that the country should be garrisoned with troops as thickly as possible. There ought to be a company

76

at least in every county. I have not seen Maj. Genl. Woods, comdg the Department of Alabama, so as to converse with him about the matter; I intend to go to Mobile from New. Orleans. I understand, however, that he does nothing with regard to the maintenance of order in the State without being called upon by the civil authorities. The result is apparent. It seems to me, Gov. Parsons, in undertaking to maintain order in the State by the machinery of the civil government, has undertaken a thing which he cannot carry through, and which, I have abundant reason to believe, a good many of his subordinate civil officers are not disposed to carry through. Governor Parson's own proclamation, of which I sent you a copy in my last, furnishes sufficient evidence of this fact. The Governor himself feels it, although he may not be willing openly to acknowledge it.

In my letter dated Montgomery Aug. 20th I stated that there was an abundance of troops in the State for all practical purposes, but since then I have learned that a considerable number of regiments is going to be mustered out. This may change the aspect of things. I would suggest that the Commanders of Departments be ordered to furnish the War Department an estimate of the number of troops necessary for garrisoning every county in their respective States and for keeping at the principal points a force adequate to any emergency that is likely to arise. In my opinion it is unsafe to deplete these States too rapidly. We may need more troops three months hence than we do now.

From Demopolis I went to Meridian and Jackson Miss. I regret to say that I did not succeed in reaching Jackson previous to the adjournment of the Convention. The action of that body is before you. It may be worth while to give you a glimpse of its secret history. In the Committee which was charged with recommending to the Convention some action to be taken with regard to the Ordinance of Secession, two propositions were taken into consideration: one to declare the Ordinance of Secession "repealed", thus, by implication, declaring the ordinance of secession a lawful act that might be done or undone by the people at pleasure;—and another to declare the Ordinance of Secession "null and void". The two propositions were discussed distinctly upon the issue of the legality or illegality of secession. The vote in the committee stood seven in favor of "repealing", and seven in favor of declaring the Secession Ordinance "null and void". The Chairman of the Committee, Mr. Amos R. Johnson, gave his casting vote in favor of declaring it "null and void" stating as his reason, that the State would not be readmitted if they did adopt another policy. In the Convention he delivered the following opinion: "If we do this, the President and the Copperhead party will be with us to defeat the Black Republicans."

Although the Convention had adjourned when I arrived at Jackson I still found some of its most influential members there, and from my conversations with them and with some gentlemen who had closely watched the proceedings of the Convention, I formed the opinion, that the conviction that the rejection of the Secession doctrine and the abolition of slavery in the State were indispensable to secure readmission, was the principal if not the only thing which secured the adoption of these two measures. You will have noticed that the Congressional Amendment to the Constitution was not adopted; the main reason urged against its adoption was that the second section of the Amendment was hostile to State rights.

It is evident that the action of the Convention with regard to the abolition of slavery is very incomplete in itself, and must necessarily be amplified by laws to be passed by the Legislature to be worth anything. As to the prospective action of the Legislature I abstain from expressing any opinion; that body will soon make a record for itself.

One important thing, however, I must not omit to state. Most of the members of the Convention were elected on their general merits as to intelligence and character without a full canvass of their opinions on distinct issues; there were but two or three among them that we would call thorough going Union men. Acting upon motives of policy which they appreciated but which the people did not appreciate, they did not dare to submit their action to the people for ratification. A motion to that effect was at once smothered in the Convention and not taken up again. Some of them explained this by saying, that they wanted to avoid all further agitation of the subject, but others confessed openly that they knew they did not represent the people.

My observations lead me to believe that this is the truth. The people of the State of Mississippi feel with regard to the main problems before them, especially the negro question, as the people of Alabama Georgia and South Carolina do. There is no difference worth mentioning. Some of the more enlightened men are gradually acquiring a more accurate idea of the things that will be required of them, and thus, obeying the impulse from abroad, show a certain progressive spirit. But so far they have not been able to modify or control the brutal instincts of the masses; nor have they shown much courage in boldly facing them. A member of the convention said to a friend of mine: "We dare not say to our people what I now tell you, but we may gradually bring them up to it if we get a chance. Just as soon as the Legislature meets we will try to give the negro the right to give evidence before the Courts etc. But we dare not now come before the people with that sentiment." If gentlemen like this member succeed again in smuggling themselves into the Legislature, the action of that body will be, if not quite satisfactory, at least to a certain extent progressive. But if the people succeed in securing a true representation, we must look for bad results.

There is far less disorder in this State than in Alabama. I enclose a list of capital offences that came to the notice of the Commander of the northern District of Mississippi, Genl. Osterhaus. From the two other Districts I have received no reports yet. Most of the cases on the list happened before the military occupation of the State was completed. At the present moment this State is more perfectly garrisoned than any of those that I have visited. The consequence is that order is more efficiently preserved, and that crime, even where it could not be prevented, is at least at once traced up and the offenders punished. There is a garrison in every county, and the machinery is in very fine working order. The promptness with which, whenever any crime is committed, the arrest of the perpetrators is effected, shows that the thing can be done if only those whose business it is, are honestly disposed to do it. In Alabama, where the matter is left to the sheriffs, hardly one offender in twenty is caught and brought to justice.

I enclose a letter addressed to me by Maj. Genl. Osterhaus, giving an account of the condition of things in his command.

I wish to call your particular attention to what he says about the four murders recently committed in Attala county. That county had been the theatre of gross outrages when the military occupation was effected; the garrison was successful in restoring tranquillity and order. About two weeks ago the regiment to which the garrison belonged, was mustered out, and no sooner was the garrison withdrawn when four murders happened in quick succession, two of white Union men and two of negroes. This fact proves, that a bad spirit was prevailing there, that the garrison succeeded in checking it, and that the withdrawal of the garrison was the signal for a fresh installment of murderous outbreaks. There is evidence at the same time of the spirit of the people and of the efficiency and the necessity of the garrison system.

You have been informed of Gov. Sharkey's attempt to reorganize the militia of the State, calling especially upon the young men who had distinguished themselves for gallantry in the rebel service, to take up arms. I have the honor to enclose Gen'l. Osterhaus' correspondence with Gov. Sharkey and with Department Headquarters about this matter; I enclose also Genl. Slocum's Genl. Order No. 22 having reference to the same subject. These documents contain so full an account of this whole business that I have but little to add.

I have made Gov. Sharkey's acquaintance and have come to the conclusion that he is a good, clever old gentleman, and probably a first class lawyer, but not in the least calculated for the discharge of duties so delicate and so responsible as those pertaining to his present position. He is continually surrounded by a set of old secessionists whom he considers it his duty to conciliate. These men are naturally very anxious to have our forces withdrawn from the State, so as to have it all their own way; and they being anxious, Gov. Sharkey is anxious also. In order to have the U. S. forces withdrawn it was considered advisable that the militia be organized. As a reason for ordering the organization of the militia some outrages committed between Jackson and Big Black are seized hold of, probably perpetrated by some of the same men who are very eager to see the militia organized. Gen. Osterhaus has since arrested some of them, and all the indications point that way. It would seem that, before venturing upon a step of such importance, Gov. Sharkey ought to have felt it his duty to consult with Gen. Slocum, the Commander of the Department, or at least with Gen.

Osterhaus, the Commander of the District who had his office in the same building with the Governor and is in daily communication with him. But the Governor did not give the least intimation of his design and suddenly issued his proclamation, a proclamation calling upon rebel soldiers to take matters into their hands because the Union troops had proved inefficient.

It would be wrong to suppose, however, that Gov. Sharkey is entirely unaware of the difficulties surrounding him; he admits that all the outrages that are committed, are perpetrated upon negroes and Union men; and he said to me in the presence of Genl. Osterhaus that, if the Union troops were withdrawn, the life of no Northern men in Mississippi would be safe. At the same time he is anxious to have the Union troops make room for his militia and told me, he expected to see our forces withdrawn in a very few weeks. Gen. Slocum's order, aside from repelling the insult thrown into the face of the U. S. forces in this Department by the Governors proclamation, is eminently calculated to restore order and prevent the perpetration of crime in every District of the State. While the organization of the returned rebel soldiers as a State militia would have been the terror of the Union men and negroes, Genl. Slocums policy as set forth in his order, can hardly fail to make Mississippi the quietest State in the South, and I have no doubt it would have a most excellent effect if the same policy were applied to Alabama and Georgia. As to Alabama especially I see no other remedy.

If it was your policy to place the Governments of the States lately in rebellion into the hands of the Union element of those States, I am sorry to say that this policy has been most completely disregarded in Mississippi. Leaving the union sentiments of Gov. Sharkey out of discussion, I have not been able to learn of a single thorough Union man in this State having been placed in office. But the contrary has been the case. One of the best and most consistent Union men in this State is Judge Houghton. He was one of the Probate Judges. While all the other Judges in the State were reinstated in their functions—I can not hear of a single exception,—Judge Houghton was dropped and in his place Gov. Sharkey appointed Mr. A. B. Smedes, the President of the rebel vigilance committee, whose principal business consisted in dragooning Union men into obedience or running them out of the State.

Thus, a Union man was virtually removed from office to make room for one of the most active and odious disloyalists. Gov. Sharkey was applied to by some prominent Union men of Vicksburg to correct this apparent mistake; but it turned out that Gov. Sharkey did not consider it a mistake. He replied that Judge Houghton was incompetent, while Judge Houghton had been elected by the people to the Probate Judgeship for three successive terms. This would seem to speak for his fitness.

The Secretary of State appointed by Gov. Sharkey as well as one of the Governors two Aids were rebel officers, and it seems generally that if any discrimination is made, it is made in favor of men of rebel antecedents. In his recommendations for appointments to federal offices the Governor seems to have been equally unfortunate. I understand that upon his recommendation Mr. Richard Barnett was appointed postmaster at this place. The same Mr. Barnett was sent out of our lines by Gen. Dana as one of the most prominent and notorious disloyalists of this city, and the members of his family made themselves so obnoxious by their ostentatious manifestations of hatred to the Union, that they were sent out of our lines by Gen. McPherson.—I understand also that on the Governors recommendation Col. Jones Hamilton was appointed United States Marshal for the Southern District. I am informed here by persons who have every opportunity of knowing, and whose statements are considered trustworthy at Department Headquarters, that Col. Hamilton served during the war as a Provost Marshal, a conscripting officer and an officer of the Cotton Bureau on the rebel side. If such men received federal appointments it was not because there were no true Union men in this State,—for I have seen here a sufficient number of gentlemen of unflinching loyalty, good intelligence and respectable standing in society—but because the Governor chose to recommend rebels in preference to Union men.

I presume it is the desire of the Administration to build up a Union party in the Southern States; but I apprehend this object cannot be attained if the power and patronage connected with federal offices are placed into the hands of late rebels to the discouragement of the true Union element. I have discussed this matter with Gen. Slocum, and the experience he has had in this Department leads him to be decidedly of the same opinion.

By what I have said I do not mean to impeach Gov. Sharkeys loyalty. I consider him a good, honest, but very weak man who permits himself to be moulded as to his views and policy by those who take hold of him with the greatest energy and assiduity. I do not see in him the right man in the right place. If the Government should choose to let him remain where he is until a Governor is regularly elected, I would respectfully suggest that he be advised to confine himself strictly within the sphere of duties assigned to him in the proclamation by which he was appointed.

While writing this report I was called upon by several Union men of this city, who informed me that they would find themselves obliged to sell out what interests they have here, and to leave the place if Genl. Slocum's order concerning the militia should not be sustained by the Government. I find this feeling to be quite general among the Union people and especially among those who came from the North to invest money and do business here. It seems to me very essential that Genl. Slocums order should be openly approved by the President and the Secretary of War. It would reassure the Union men and the colored people and show the unruly spirits in this region that the Government will not permit them to disturb the public peace with impunity.

I understand the Government has been memorialized for the withdrawal of the colored troops from this State principally on the ground that their presence is very obnoxious to the people. I have been very careful in forming an opinion as to the policy of garrisoning these States with colored soldiers, and the information I have gathered, leads me to the following conclusions:

There is one complaint brought against them which has some foundation in fact. Colored soldiers doing duty in the country are sometimes found to put queer notions into the heads of negroes working on the plantations; and their camps are apt to be a point of attraction for colored women. These complaints I heard urged especially in South Carolina. But these difficulties are easily overcome by keeping the soldiers in a strict state of discipline or, in particularly bad cases, by taking the obnoxious individuals out and placing them on duty in the larger depots. I understand, this remedy has worked well in South Carolina; in this State I heard no such complaints at all.

On the other hand I hear complaints from all quarters that white soldiers garrisoning the country, in a great many instances combine with the white population against the blacks and sometimes aid the former in inflicting cruel punishments on the latter. A good many cases of this description have come to my notice. But this is not all. I am reliably informed that much of the cotton stealing going on all over the country especially in Alabama, is effected not only with the passive connivance, but by the active aid and cooperation of white soldiers. The reports that have come to me, leave no doubt in my mind as to the truthfulness of this statement. Finally, white soldiers are generally tired of serving; they say that the war is over, that they were enlisted for the war, and that they want to go home. Their discipline is in a majority of cases rather lax, and they perform their duties with less spirit than the exigencies of their situation require.

The discipline of the black troops, on the contrary, is uniformly as good as their officers want to have it. They perform their duties with pride and a strict observance of their instructions. I have not heard of a single instance, nor even of a suspicion, that a colored soldier connived at any dishonest practices such as cotton stealing etc. In this State I have not heard a single officer complain of their conduct. Gen. Osterhaus who at present has none but colored troops in his District, tells me that he never saw any better behaved troops, and that, if the choice between a white and a black regiment was offered him for such duties as they have at present to perform, he would without hesitation choose the blacks.

That their presence is somewhat distasteful to former slaveowners, I have no reason to doubt, especially to those who like to whip a negro but do not like to pay him wages. But it seems to me, the garrisoning of this country with colored troops is apt to produce one important moral result. When discussing with men of liberal views the many atrocities perpetrated in the country, they almost uniformly tell me, apologizingly: "You see, it is so difficult for our people to realize that the negro is a free man." If this true—and no doubt it is—if the main cause of the horrible outrages committed almost daily, is the not-realizing on the part of the Southern people that the negro is a free man, there is no better remedy than to make the fact as evident as possible to all concerned. And there is nothing that will make it more evident than the bodily presence of a negro with a musket on his shoulder.

For these reasons it is my deliberate opinion that the negro troops now garrisoning the country ought not only not to be withdrawn, but that they are the best troops that can be put here for the duties now to be performed.

I am informed that Mr. William Porterfield of this city is an applicant for one of the most lucrative mail contracts in this part of the country, and that he has received encouraging assurances from the employees of the Post-office Department at Washington. Mr. Porterfield bases his claims upon a protection paper he received from Gen. Grant intended to cover his property. I learn from *the most reliable sources* that he is one of the most disreputable characters in this part of the country in every respect. He was several times indicted for felonies and the official records of the cases can be found in this city. Mr. G. L. Little, Treasury agent in this city, took up a copy of them together with other documents concerning Mr. Porterfield to Washington. Aside from his general character he has been one of the worst rebels in this place. If such a man received any favors at the hands of the Government, and if power is placed in the hands of such characters, the Union men have certainly a right to feel themselves aggrieved.

I would respectfully suggest that as to federal appointments in this State, Gen. Slocum be consulted. He has better means of information than anybody else.

> Very truly and respectfully
> Your obedt servant C. Schurz.

Enclosures: No. 1.   Letter of Maj. Houston, Prov. Mar. at Selma.
             No. 2. Letter of Gen. Osterhaus to C. Schurz
             No 3.   List of capital offenses committed in Northern District of Mississippi
             No 4.   Letters addressed by Gen. Osterhaus to Department

No. 5.   Headquarters.
No. 6.   Maj. Genl. Osterhaus to Gov. Sharkey
No. 7.   Gov. Sharkey to Maj. Genl. Osterhaus.
No. 8.   Genl. Slocums Genl. Order No. 22.
No. 9.   Gov. Sharkey to Col. Yorke
No. 10.   Lt. Col. Yorke to Genl. Davidson.

I would invite special attention to No. 9 and 10., two letters bearing upon the militia question.

C. S.

Christopher Memminger to Andrew Johnson

Flat Rock, Sep. 4, 1865.

EVERY SOUTHERN man is so deeply interested in the great questions of public policy which are now under your consideration, that it will scarcely be deemed officious in one of them to offer you some suggestions, if made solely with a view to the public good. Although I am not personally known to your Excellency, and at present am under the Ban of the Government, yet I feel assured that your judgment can easily discern the ring of truth, and will justly appreciate any effort to relieve the immense responsibilities which are now pressing upon you.

I take it for granted that the whole Southern Country accepts emancipation from Slavery as the condition of the African race; but neither the North nor the South have yet defined what is included in that emancipation. The boundaries are widely apart which mark on the one side, political equality with the white races, and on the other, a simple recognition of personal liberty. With our own race, ages have intervened between the advance from one of these boundaries to the other. No other people have been able to make equal progress, and many have not yet lost sight of the original point of starting. Great Britain has made the nearest approach; Russia has just started; and the other nations of Europe, after ages of struggle, are yet on the way from the one point to the other, none of them having yet advanced even to the position attained by England. The question now pending is, as to the station in this wide interval which shall be assigned to the African race. Does that race possess qualities, or does it exhibit any peculiar fitness which will dispense with the training which our own race has undergone, and authorize us at once to advance them to equal rights? It seems to me that this point has been decided already by the Laws of the free States. None of them have yet permitted equality, and the greater part assert this unfitness of the African by denying him any participation in political power.

The Country then seems prepared to assign to this race an inferior condition; but the precise nature of that condition is yet to be defined, and also the Government which shall regulate it. I observe that you have already decided (and I think wisely) that the adjustment of the right of suffrage belongs to the State Governments, and should be left there. But this, as well as most of the other questions on this subject, rest upon the decision which shall be made upon the mode of organizing the labor of the African race. The Northern people seem generally to suppose that the simple emancipation from slavery will elevate the African to the condition of the white laboring classes; and that contracts and competition will secure the proper distribution of labor. They see, on the one hand, the owner of land wanting laborers, and on the other, a multitude of landless laborers without employment; and they naturally conclude that the law of demand and supply will adjust the exchange in the same manner as it would do at the North. But they are not aware of the attending circumstances which will disappoint these calculations.

The laborer in the Southern States, with his whole family, occupies the houses of his employer, built upon plantations widely separate. The employment of a laborer involves the employment and support of his whole family. Should the employer be discontent with any laborers and desire to substitute others in their place, before he can effect that object, he must proceed to turn out the first with their entire families into the woods, so as to have houses for their successors. Then he must encounter the uncertainty and delay in procuring other laborers; and also the hostility of the laborers on his own plantation, which would probably exhibit itself in sympathy with the ejected families and combinations against himself. Should this occur at any critical period of the crop, its entire loss would ensue. Nor would his prospect of relief from other plantations be hopeful. On them arrangements will have been made for the year, and the abstraction of laborers from them would result in new disorganization. The employer would thus be wholly at the mercy of the laborer.

It may be asked why the laborer is more likely to fail in the performance of his contract than his employer. The reasons are obvious. The employer by the possession of property affords a guarantee by which the law can compel his performance. The laborer can offer no such guarantee, and nothing is left to control him but a sense of the obligation of the contract.

The force of this remedy depends upon the degree of conscientiousness and intelligence attained by the bulk of a people. It is well known that one of the latest and most important fruits of civilization is a perception of the obligation of contracts. Even in cultivated nations, the Law must be sharpened at all points to meet the efforts to escape from a contract which has become onerous; and nothing short of a high sense of commercial honor and integrity will secure its strict performance. It would be vain, under any circumstances, to count upon such performance from an ignorant and uneducated population. But where that population is from constitution or habit peculiarly subject to the vices of an inferior race, nothing short of years of education and training can bring about that state of moral rectitude and habitual self-constraint which would secure the regular performance of contracts. In the present case, to these general causes must be added the natural indolence of the African race, and the belief now universal among them that they are released from any obligation to labor. Under these circumstances the employer would have so little inducement to risk his Capital in the hands of the laborer, or to advance money for food and working animals in cultivating a Crop which, when reaped, would be at the mercy of the laborers, that he will certainly endeavor to make other arrangements. The effect will be the abandonment of the negro to his indolent habits, and the probable relapse of large portions of the Country into its original forest condition. The two races, instead of exchanging mutual good offices, will inflict mutual evil on each other; and the final result must be the destruction or removal of the inferior race.

The appropriate remedy for these evils evidently points to the necessity of training the inferior race; and we are naturally led to look to the means which would be employed by our own race for the same purpose. The African is virtually in the condition of the youth, whose inexperience and want of skill unfit him for the privileges of manhood. He is subjected to the guidance and control of one better informed. He is bound as an apprentice to be trained and directed; and is under restraint until he is capable of discharging the duties of manhood.

Such, it seems to me, is the proper instrumentality which should now be applied to the African race. The vast body are substantially in a state of minority. They have been all their lives subject to the control and direction of another; and at present are wholly incapable of self-government. Alongside of them are their former masters, fully capable of guiding and instructing them, needing their labor, and not yet alienated from them in feeling. The great point to be attained is the generous application by the one of his superior skill and resources, and their kindly reception by the other. This can be effected only by some relation of acknowledged dependence. Let the untrained and incapable African be placed under indentures of apprenticeship to his former master, under such regulations as will secure both parties from wrong; and whenever the apprentice shall have obtained the habits and knowledge requisite for discharging the duties of a citizen, let him then be advanced from youth to manhood and be placed in the exercise of a citizen's rights, and the enjoyment of the privileges attending such a change.

I have no means of procuring here a Copy of the Laws passed by the British Parliament on this subject, for the West India Colonies. They are founded upon this idea of apprenticeship. Such an adjustment of the relations of the two races would overcome many difficulties, and enable the emancipation experiment to be made under the most favorable circumstances. The experience of the British colonies would afford valuable means for improving the original plans; and no doubt the practical common sense of our people can, by amending their errors, devise the best possible solution of the problems and afford the largest amount of good to the African race.

The only question which would remain would be as to the Government which should enact and administer these Laws. Unquestionably the jurisdiction under the Constitution of the United States belongs to the States. This fact will most probably disincline the Congress to an early recognition of the Southern States upon their original footing under the Constitution, from the apprehension of harsh measures towards the former slaves. The difficulty would be obviated, if a satisfactory adjustment could be previously made of the footing upon which the two races are to stand. If by general agreement an apprentice system could be adopted in some form which would be satisfactory as well as obligatory, it seems to me that most of the evils now existing, or soon to arise, would be remedied; and that a fair start would be made in the proper direction. The details of the plan could be adjusted from the experience of the British Colonies; and if it should result in proving the capacity of the African race to stand upon the same platform with the white man, I doubt not but that the South will receive that conclusion with satisfaction fully equal to that of any other section.

C G Memminger.

Thaddeus Stevens: Speech at Lancaster

Fellow Citizens:

In compliance with your request, I have come to give my views of the present condition of the Rebel States—of the proper mode of reorganizing the Government, and the future prospects of the Republic. During the whole progress of the war, I never for a moment felt doubt or despondency. I knew that the loyal North would conquer the Rebel despots who sought to destroy freedom. But since that traitorous confederation has been subdued, and we have entered upon the work of "reconstruction" or "restoration," I cannot deny that my heart has become sad at the gloomy prospects before us.

Four years of bloody and expensive war, waged against the United States by eleven States, under a government called the "Confederate States of America," to which they acknowledged allegiance, have overthrown all governments within those States which could be acknowledged as legitimate by the Union. The armies of the Confederate States having been conquered and subdued, and their territory possessed by the United States, it becomes necessary to establish governments therein, which shall be republican in form and principles, and form a more "perfect Union" with the parent Government. It is desirable that such a course should be pursued as to exclude from those governments every vestige of human bondage, and render the same forever impossible in this nation; and to take care that no principles of self-destruction shall be incorporated therein. In effecting this, it is to be hoped that no provision of the Constitution will be infringed, and no principle of the law of nations disregarded. Especially must we take care that in rebuking this unjust and treasonable war, the authorities of the Union shall indulge in no acts of usurpation which may tend to impair the stability and permanency of the nation. Within these limitations, we hold it to be the duty of the Government to inflict condign punishment on the rebel belligerents, and so weaken their hands that they can never again endanger the Union; and so reform their municipal institutions as to make them republican in spirit as well as in name.

We especially insist that the property of the chief rebels should be seized and appropriated to the payment of the National debt, caused by the unjust and wicked war which they instigated.

How can such punishments be inflicted and such forfeitures produced without doing violence to established principles?

Two positions have been suggested.

First—To treat those States as never having been out of the Union, because the Constitution forbids secession, and therefore, a fact forbidden by law could not exist.

Second—To accept the position to which they placed themselves as severed from the Union; an independent government *de facto*, and an alien enemy to be dealt with according to the laws of war.

It seems to me that while we do not aver that the United States are bound to treat them as an alien enemy, yet they have a right to elect so to do if it be for the interests of the Nation; and that the "Confederate States" are estopped from denying that position. South Carolina, the leader and embodiment of the rebellion, in the month of January, 1861, passed the following resolution by the unanimous vote of her Legislature:

"Resolved, That the separation of South Carolina from the Federal Union *is final*, and she has no further interests in the Constitution of the United States; and that the only appropriate negotiations between her and the Federal Government are as to their mutual relations as *foreign* States."

The convention that formed the Government of the Confederate States, and all the eleven states that composed it, adopted the same declaration, and pledged their lives and fortunes to support it. That government raised large armies and by its formidable power compelled the nations of the civilized world as well as our own Government to acknowledge them as an independent belligerent, entitled by the law of nations to be considered as engaged in a public war, and not merely in an insurrection. It is idle to deny that we treated them as a belligerent, entitled to all the rights, and subject to all the liabilities of an alien enemy. We blockaded their ports, which is an undoubted belligerent right; the extent of coast blockaded marked the acknowledged extent of their territory—a territory criminally acquired but *de facto* theirs. We acknowledged their sea-rovers as privateers and not as pirates, by ordering their captive crews to be treated as prisoners of war. We acknowledged that a commission from the Confederate Government was sufficient to screen Semmes and his associates from the fate of lawless buccaneers. Who but an acknowledged government *de jure* or *de facto*, could have power to issue such a commission? The invaders of the loyal States were not treated as out-laws, but as soldiers of war, because they were commanded by officers holding commissions from that Government. The Confederate States were for four years what they claimed to be, an alien enemy, in all their rights and liabilities. To say that they were States under the protection of that constitution which they were rending, and within the Union which they were assaulting with bloody defeats, simply because they became belligerents through crime, is making theory overrule fact to an absurd degree. It will, I suppose, at least be conceded that the United States, if not obliged so to do, have a right to treat them as an alien enemy now conquered, and subject to all the liabilities of a vanquished foe.

If we are also at liberty to treat them as never having been out of the Union, and that their declarations and acts were all void because they contravened the Constitution, and therefore they were never engaged in a public war, but were merely insurgents, let us inquire which position is best for the United States. If they have never been otherwise than States in the Union, and we desire to try certain of the leaders for treason, the Constitution requires that they should be indicted and tried "*by an impartial jury of the State and district wherein the crime shall have been committed, which district shall have been previously ascertained by law.*"

The crime of treason can be committed only where the person is actually or potentially present. Jefferson Davis sitting in Richmond, counseling, or advising, or commanding an inroad into Pennsylvania, has committed no overt act in this State, and can be tried, if any where, only in the Richmond District. The doctrine of constructive presence, and constructive treason, will never, I hope, pollute our statutes, or judicial decisions. Select an *impartial* jury from Virginia, and it is obvious that no conviction could ever be had. Possibly a jury might be packed to convict, but that would not be an "impartial" jury. It would be judicial murder, and would rank in infamy with the trial of Lord Russell, except only that the one was the murder of an innocent man, the other of a traitor. The same difficulties would exist in attempting forfeitures, which can only follow conviction in States protected by the Constitution; and then it is said only for the life of the malefactor—Congress can pass no "bill of attainder."

Nor, under that theory, has Congress, much less the Executive, any power to interfere in remodelling those States upon reconstruction. What reconstruction is needed? Here are States which they say, have never been out of the Union, and which are consequently now in it without asking leave of any one. They are competent to send Senators and members to Congress. The state of war has broken no constitutional ligaments, for it was only an insurrection of individuals, not a public war waged by States. Such is the reasoning, notwithstanding every State acted in its municipal capacity; and the court in the prize cases (2 Black 673) say: "*Hence in organizing this rebellion they have acted as States.*" It is no loose unorganized rebellion, having no defined boundary or possession. It has a boundary, marked by lines of bayonets, and which can be crossed only by force—south of this line *is enemy's* territories, because it is claimed and held in possession by an "organized, hostile and belligerent power." What right has any one to direct a convention to be held in a sovereign State of this Union, to amend its constitution and prescribe the qualifications of voters? The sovereign power of the nation is lodged in Congress. Yet where is the warrant in the constitution for such sovereign power, much less the Executive, to intermeddle with the domestic institutions of a State, mould its laws, and regulate the elective franchise? It would be rank, dangerous and deplorable usurpation. In reconstruction, therefore, no reform can be effected in the Southern States if they have never left the Union. But reformation *must* be effected; the foundation of their institutions, both political, municipal and social, *must* be broken up and *relaid*, or all our blood and treasure have been spent in vain. This can only be done by treating and holding them as a conquered people. Then all things which we can desire to do, follow with logical and legitimate authority. As conquered territory, Congress would have full power to legislate for them; for the territories are not under the Constitution, except so far as the express power to govern them is given to Congress. They would be held in a territorial condition until they are fit to form State Constitutions, republican in fact, not in form only, and ask admission into the Union as new States. If Congress approve of their Constitutions, and think they have done works meet for repentance, they would be admitted as new States. If their Constitutions are not approved of, they would be sent back, until they have become wise enough so to purge their old laws as to eradicate every despotic and revolutionary principle—until they shall have learned to venerate the Declaration of Independence. I do not touch on the question of negro suffrage. If in the Union, the States have long ago regulated that, and for the Central Government to interfere with it would be mischievous impertinence. If they are to be admitted as new States they must form their own constitutions; and no enabling act could dictate its terms. Congress could prescribe the qualifications of voters while a Territory, or when proceeding to call a convention to form a State government. That is the extent of the power of Congress over the elective franchise, whether in a territorial or state condition. The President has not even this or any other power to meddle in the subject, except by advice to Congress—and they on territories. Congress, to be sure, has some sort of compulsory power by refusing the States admission until they shall have complied with its wishes over this subject. Whether those who have fought our battles should all be allowed to vote, or only those of a paler hue, I leave to be discussed in the future when Congress can take legitimate cognizance of it.

If capital punishments of the most guilty are deemed essential as examples, we have seen that, on the one theory, none of them can be convicted on fair trials—the complicity of the triers would defeat it. But, as a conquered enemy, they could not escape. Their trials would take place by courts-martial. I do not think they could thus be tried for treason; but they could be tried as belligerents, who had forfeited their lives, according to the laws of war. By the strict rights of war, as anciently practiced, the victor held the lives, the liberty and the property of the vanquished at his disposal. The taking of the life, or reduction to bondage of the captives, have long ceased to be practiced in case of ordinary wars; but the abstract right—the *summum jus*—is still recognized in exceptional cases where the cause of the war, or the character of the belligerent, or the safety of the victors justify its exercise. The same thing may be said of the seizure of property on land. Halleck (457) says some modern writers—Hautefeuille, for example—contends for the ancient rule, that private property on land may be subject to seizure. They are undoubtedly correct, with regard to the general abstract right, as deduced from "the law of nature and ancient practice." Vattel says: "When, therefore, he has subdued a hostile nation, he undeniably may, in the first place, do himself justice respecting the object which has given rise to the war, and *indemnify himself for the expenses and damages* which he has sustained by it." And at page 369: "A conqueror, who has taken up arms not only against the sovereign but against the nation herself, and whose intention it was to subdue a fierce and savage people, and once for all to reduce an obstinate enemy, such a conqueror may, with justice, lay burdens on the conquered nation, both as a compensation for the expenses of the war, and as a punishment."

I am happy to believe that the Government has come to this conclusion. I cannot otherwise see how Capt. Wirz can be tried by a Court Martial at Washington for acts done by him at Andersonville. He was in no way connected with our military organization, nor did he as a citizen connect himself with our Army so as to bring his case within any of the Acts of Congress. If he committed murder in Georgia, and Georgia was a State in the Union, then he should be tried according to her laws. The General Government has no jurisdiction over such crime, and the trial and execution of this wretch by a United States Military Court would be illegal. But if he was an officer of a belligerent enemy, making war as an independent people, now being conquered, it is a competent, holding them as a conquered foe, to try him for doing acts contrary to the laws of war, and if found guilty to execute or otherwise punish him. As I am sure the loyal man at the head of the Government will not involve the nation in illegal acts and thus set a precedent injurious to our national character, I am glad to believe that hereafter we shall treat the enemy as conquered, and remit their condition and reconstruction to the sovereign power of the nation.

In short, all writers agree that the victor may inflict punishment upon the vanquished enemy, even to the taking of his life, liberty, or the confiscation of all his property; but that this extreme right is never exercised except upon a cruel, barbarous, obstinate, or dangerous foe who has waged an unjust war.

Upon the character of the belligerent, and the justice of the war, and the manner of conducting it, depends our right to take the lives, liberty and property of the belligerent. This war had its origin in treason without one spark of justice. It was prosecuted before notice of it, by robbing our forts and armories, and our navy-yards; by stealing our money from the mints and depositories, and by surrendering our forts and navies by perjurers who had sworn to support the Constitution. In its progress our prisoners, by the authority of their government, were slaughtered in cold blood. Ask Fort Pillow and Fort Wagner. Sixty thousand of our prisoners have been deliberately starved to death because they would not enlist in the rebel armies. The graves at Andersonville have each an accusing tongue. The purpose and avowed object of the enemy "to found an empire whose corner-stone should be slavery," rendered its perpetuity or revival dangerous to human liberty.

Surely, these things are sufficient to justify the exercise of the extreme rights of war—"to execute, to imprison, to confiscate." How many captive enemies it would be proper to execute, as an example to nations, I leave others to judge. I am not fond of sanguinary punishments, but surely some victims must propitiate the manes of our starved, murdered, slaughtered martyrs. A court-martial could do justice according to law.

But we propose to confiscate all the estate of every rebel belligerent whose estate was worth $10,000, or whose land exceeded two hundred acres in quantity. Policy if not justice would require that the poor, the ignorant, and the coerced should be forgiven. They followed the example and teachings of their wealthy and intelligent neighbors. The rebellion would never have originated with them. Fortunately those who would thus escape form a large majority of the people, though possessing but a small portion of the wealth. The proportion of those exempt compared with the punished would be I believe about nine tenths.

There are about six millions of freedmen in the South. The number of acres of land is 465,000,000. Of this, those who own above two hundred acres each number about 70,000 persons, holding, in the aggregate, (together with the States,) about 394,000,000 acres, leaving for all the others below 200 each, about 71,000,000 acres. By thus forfeiting the estates of the leading rebels, the government would have 394,000,000 of acres, beside their town property, and yet nine-tenths of the people would remain untouched. Divide this land into convenient farms. Give, if you please, forty acres to each adult male freedman. Suppose there are one million of them. That would require 40,000,000 of acres, which, deducted from 394,000,000, leaves three hundred and fifty-four millions of acres for sale. Divide it into suitable farms, and sell it to the highest bidders. I think it, including town property, would average at least ten dollars per acre. That would produce $3,540,000,000—three billions five hundred and forty millions of dollars.

Let that be applied as follows to wit:

1. Invest $300,000,000 in six per cent government bonds, and add the interest semi-annually to the pensions of those who have become entitled by this villainous war.

2. Appropriate $200,000,000 to pay the damages done to loyal men, North and South, by the rebellion.

3. Pay the residue, being $3,040,000,000 towards the payment of the National debt.

What loyal man can object to this? Look around you, and every where behold your neighbors, some with an arm, some with a leg, some with an eye, carried away by rebel bullets. Others horribly mutilated in every form. And yet numerous others wearing the weeds which mark the death of those on whom they leaned for support. Contemplate these monuments of rebel perfidy, and of patriotic suffering, and then say if too much is asked for our valiant soldiers.

Look again, and see loyal men reduced to poverty by the confiscations by the Confederate States, and by the Rebel States—see Union men robbed of their property, and their dwellings laid in ashes by rebel raiders, and say if too much is asked for them. But above all, let us inquire whether imperative duty to the present generation and to posterity, does not command us to compel the wicked enemy to pay the expenses of this unjust war. In ordinary transaction he who raises a false clamor, and prosecutes an unfounded suit, is adjudged to pay the costs on his defeat. We have seen, that, by the law of nations, the vanquished in an unjust war must pay the expense.

Our war debt is estimated at from three to four billions of dollars. In my judgment, when all is funded, and the pensions capitalized, it will reach more than four billions.

The interest at 6 per cent., only (now much more)	$240,000,000
The ordinary expenses of our Government are	120,000,000
For some years the extraordinary expenses of our army and navy will be	110,000,000
Total	$470,000,000

Four hundred and seventy millions to be raised by taxation—our present heavy taxes will not, in ordinary years, produce but little more than half that sum. Can our people bear double their present taxation? He who unnecessarily causes it will be accursed from generation to generation. It is fashionable to belittle our public debt, lest the people should become alarmed, and political parties should suffer. I have never found it wise to deceive the people. They can always be trusted with the truth. Capitalists will not be affected, for they can not be deceived. Confide in the people, and you will avoid repudiation. Deceive them, and lead them into false measures, and you may produce it.

We pity the poor Englishmen whose national debt and burdensome taxation, we have heard deplored from our childhood. The debt of Great Britain is just about as much as ours, ($4,000,000,000) four billions. But in effect it is but half as large—it bears but three per cent. interest. The current year, the chancellor of the exchequer tells us, the interest was $131,806,990. Ours, when all shall be funded, will be nearly double.

The plan we have proposed would pay at least three-fourths of our debt. The balance could be managed with our present taxation. And yet to think that even that is to be perpetual is sickening. If it is to be doubled, as it must be, if "restoration" instead of "reconstruction" is to prevail, would to God the authors of it could see themselves as an execrating public and posterity will see them.

Our new Doctors of National law, who hold that the "Confederate States" were never out of the Union, but only insurgents and traitors, have become wiser than Grotius, and Puffendorf, and Rutherford, and Vattel, and all modern publicists down to Halleck and Phillimore. They all agree that such a state of things as has existed here for four years is *public war*, and constitutes the parties independent belligerents, subject to the same rules of war as the foreign nations engaged in open warfare.

The learned and able Professor at Law in the Cambridge University, Theophilus Parsons, lately said in a public speech—

"As we are victorious in war we have a right to impose upon the defeated party any terms necessary for our security. This right is perfect. It is not only in itself obvious, but it is asserted in every book on this subject, and is illustrated by all the wars of history. The rebels forced a war upon us; it was a long and costly and bloody war; and now that we have conquered them, we have all the rights which victory confers."

The only argument of the Restorationists is, that the States could not and did not go out of the Union because the Constitution forbids it. By the same reasoning you could prove that no crime ever existed. No man ever committed murder for the law forbids it! He is a shallow reasoner who could make theory overrule fact!

I prefer to believe the ancient and modern publicists, and the learned Professors of legal science, to the extemporized doctrines of modern Sciolists.

If "Restoration," as it is now properly christened, is to prevail over "Reconstruction," will some learned pundit of that school inform me in what condition Slavery and the Slave laws are? I assert that upon that theory not a Slave has been liberated, not a Slave law has been abrogated, but on the "Restoration" the whole Slave code is in legal force. Slavery was protected by our constitution in every State in the Union where it existed.

While they remained under that protection no power in the Federal Government could abolish Slavery. If, however, the Confederate States were admitted to be what they claimed, an independent belligerent *de facto*, then the war broke all treaties, compacts and ties between the parties, and slavery was left to its rights under the law of nations. These rights were none; for the law declares that "Man can hold no property in man." (Phillimore, page 316.) Then the laws of war enabled us to declare every bondman free, so long as we held them in military possession. And the conqueror, through Congress, may declare them forever emancipated. But if the States are "States in the Union," then when war ceases they resume their positions with all their privileges untouched. There can be no "mutilated" restoration. That would be the work of Congress alone, and would be "Reconstruction."

While I hear it said everywhere that slavery is dead, I cannot learn who killed it. No thoughtful man has pretended that Lincoln's proclamation, so noble in sentiment, liberated a single slave. It expressly excluded from its operation all those within our lines. No slave within any part of the rebel States in our possession, or in Tennessee, but only those beyond our limits and beyond our power were declared free. So Gen. Smith conquered Canada by a proclamation! The President did not pretend to abrogate the Slave laws of any of the States. "Restoration," therefore, will leave the "Union as it was,"—a hideous idea. I am aware that a very able and patriotic gentleman, and learned historian, Mr. Bancroft, has attempted to place their freedom on different grounds. He says, what is undoubtedly true, that the proclamation of freedom did not free a slave. But he liberates them on feudal principles. Under the feudal system, when a king conquered his enemy, he parceled out his lands and conquered *subjects* among his chief retainers; the lands and serfs were held on condition of fealty and rendering military service when required. If the subordinate chief rebelled, he broke the condition on which he held them, and the lands and serfs became forfeited to the lord paramount. But it did not free the serfs. They, with the manors, were bestowed on other favorites. But the analogy fails in another important respect. The American slave-holder does not hold, by virtue of any grant from any Lord paramount—least of all by a grant from the General Government. Slavery exists by no law of the Union, but simply by local laws, by the laws of the States. Rebellion against the National authority is a breach of no condition of their tenure. It were more analogous to say that rebellion against a State under whose laws they held, might work a forfeiture. But rebellion against neither government would *per se* have any such effect. On whom would the Lord paramount again bestow the slaves? The theory is plausible, but has no solid foundation.

The President says to the rebel States: "Before you can participate in the government you must abolish Slavery and reform your election laws." *That* is the command of a conqueror. *That* is Reconstruction, not Restoration—Reconstruction too by assuming the powers of Congress. This theory will lead to melancholy results. Nor can the constitutional amendment abolishing Slavery ever be ratified by three-fourths of the States, if *they* are States to be counted. Bogus Conventions of those States may vote for it. But no Convention honestly and fairly elected will ever do it. The frauds will not permanently avail. The cause of Liberty must rest on a firmer basis. Counterfeit governments, like the Virginia, Louisiana, Tennessee, Mississippi and Arkansas pretenses, will be disregarded by the sober sense of the people, by future law, and by the courts. "Restoration" is replanting the seeds of rebellion, which, within the next quarter of a century will germinate and produce the same bloody strife which has just ended.

But, it is said, by those who have more sympathy with rebel wives and children than for the widows and orphans of loyal men, that this stripping the rebels of their estates and driving them to exile or to honest labor, would be harsh and severe upon innocent women and children. It may be so; but that is the result of the necessary laws of war. But it is revolutionary, say they. This plan would, no doubt, work a radical reorganization in Southern institutions, habits and manners. It is intended to revolutionize their principles and feelings. This may startle feeble minds and shake weak nerves. So do all great improvements in the political and moral world. It requires a heavy impetus to drive forward a sluggish people. When it was first proposed to free the slaves and arm the blacks, did not half the nation tremble? The prim conservatives, the snobs, and the male waiting-maids in Congress, were in hysterics.

The whole fabric of southern society *must* be changed, and never can it be done if this opportunity is lost. Without this, this Government can never be, as it never has been, a true republic. Heretofore, it had more the features of aristocracy than of democracy. The Southern States have been despotisms, not governments of the people. It is impossible that any practical equality of rights can exist where a few thousand men monopolize the whole landed property. The larger the number of small proprietors the more safe and stable the government. As the landed interest must govern, the more it is subdivided and held by independent owners, the better. What would be the condition of the State of New York if it were not for her independent yeomanry? She would be overwhelmed and demoralized by the Jews, Milesians and vagabonds of licentious cities. How can republican institutions, free schools, free churches, free social intercourse, exist in a mingled community of nabobs and serfs; of the owners of twenty thousand acre manors with lordly palaces, and the occupants of narrow huts inhabited by "low white trash?" If the South is ever to be made a safe republic, let her lands be cultivated by the toil of the owners or the free labor of intelligent citizens. This must be done even though it drive her nobility into exile. If they go, all the better. It will be hard to persuade the owner of ten thousand acres of land, who drives a coach and four, that he is not degraded by sitting at the same table, or in the same pew, with the embrowned and hard-handed farmer who has himself cultivated his own thriving homestead of 150 acres. This subdivision of the lands will yield ten bales of cotton to one that is made now, and he who produced it will own it and *feel himself a man*.

It is far easier and more beneficial to exile 70,000 proud, bloated and defiant rebels, than to expatriate four millions of laborers, native to the soil and loyal to the Government. This latter scheme was a favorite plan of the Blairs, with which they had for awhile inoculated our late sainted President. But, a single experiment made him discard it and its advisers. Since I have mentioned the Blairs, I may say a word more of these persistent apologists of the South. For, when the virus of Slavery has once entered the veins of the slaveholder, no subsequent effort seems capable of wholly eradicating it. They are a family of considerable power, some merit, of admirable audacity and execrable selfishness. With impetuous alacrity they seize the White House, and hold possession of it, as in the late Administration, until shaken off by the overpowering force of public indignation. Their pernicious counsel had well nigh defeated the reelection of Abraham Lincoln; and if it should prevail with the present administration, pure and patriotic as President Johnson is admitted to be, it will render him the most unpopular Executive—save one—that ever occupied the Presidential chair. But there is no fear of that. He will soon say, as Mr. Lincoln did: "YOUR TIME HAS COME!"

This remodeling the institutions, and reforming the rooted habits of a proud aristocracy, is undoubtedly a formidable task, requiring the broad mind of enlarged statesmanship, and the firm nerve of the hero. But will not this mighty occasion produce—will not the God of Liberty and order give us—such men? Will not a Romulus, a Lycurgus, a Charlemagne, a Washington arise, whose expansive views will found a free empire, to endure till time shall be no more?

This doctrine of Restoration shocks me. We have a duty to perform which our fathers were incapable of, which will be required at our hands by God and our Country. When our ancestors found a "more perfect Union" necessary, they found it impossible to agree upon a Constitution without tolerating, nay, guaranteeing, Slavery. They were obliged to acquiesce, trusting to time to work a speedy cure, in which they were disappointed. *They* had some excuse, some justification. But we can have none if we do not thoroughly eradicate Slavery and render it forever impossible in this republic. The Slave power made war upon the nation. They declared the "more perfect Union" dissolved—solemnly declared themselves a foreign nation, alien to this republic; for four years were in fact what they claimed to be. We accepted the war which they tendered and treated them as a government capable of making war. We have conquered them, and as a conquered enemy we can give them laws; can abolish all their municipal institutions and form new ones. If we do not make those institutions fit to last through generations of freemen, a heavy curse will be on

us. Our glorious, but tainted republic has been born to new
life through bloody, agonizing pains. But this frightful "Restoration" has thrown it into "cold obstruction, and to death." If
the rebel States have never been out of the Union, any attempt
to reform their State institutions, either by Congress or the
President, is rank usurpation.

Is then all lost? Is this great conquest to be in vain? That will
depend upon the virtue and intelligence of the next Congress.
To Congress alone belongs the power of Reconstruction—of
giving law to the vanquished. This is expressly declared by
the Supreme Court of the United States in the Dorr case,
7th Howard, 42. The Court say, "Under this article of the
Constitution (the 4th) it rests with Congress to decide what
government is the established one in a State, for the United
States guarantees to each a republican form of government,"
et cetera. But we know how difficult it will be for a majority of
Congress to overcome preconceived opinions. Besides, before
Congress meets, things will be so inaugurated—precipitated—
it will be still more difficult to correct. If a majority of Congress
can be found wise and firm enough to declare the Confederate States a conquered enemy, Reconstruction will be easy
and legitimate; and the friends of freedom will long rule in the
Councils of the Nation. If Restoration prevails the prospect
is gloomy, and new "lords will make new laws." The Union
party will be overwhelmed. The Copperhead party has become
extinct with Secession. But with Secession it will revive. Under
"Restoration" every rebel State will send rebels to Congress;
and they, with their allies in the North, will control Congress,
and occupy the White House. Then restoration of laws and ancient Constitutions will be sure to follow, our public debt will
be repudiated, or the rebel National debt will be added to ours,
and the people be crushed beneath heavy burdens.

Let us forget all parties, and build on the broad platform of
"reconstructing" the government out of the conquered territory converted into new and free States, and admitted into
the Union by the sovereign power of Congress, with another
plank—"THE PROPERTY OF THE REBELS SHALL PAY
OUR NATIONAL DEBT, *and indemnify freed-men and loyal
sufferers*—and that under no circumstances will we suffer the
National debt to be repudiated, or the interest scaled below

the contract rates; nor permit any part of the rebel debt to be assumed by the nation."

Let all who approve of these principles rally with us. Let all others go with Copperheads and rebels. Those will be the opposing parties. Young men, this duty devolves on you. Would to God, if only for that, that I were still in the prime of life, that I might aid you to fight through this last and greatest battle of freedom!

September 6, 1865

Georges Clemenceau to Le Temps

September 28, 1865.   The political parties of the country are just now passing through an interesting phase. Republicans and Democrats vie with each other in expressing their friendship for Mr. Johnson, the Democrats seeking to win him over, and the Republicans to keep their claim on him. Both parties have held their conventions, in Albany, New York, and the copperheads praised Johnson to the skies, the same Johnson whom three short months ago they were calling "Dionysius the Tyrant," accusing of the murder of Mrs. Surratt, Booth's accomplice, and threatening with dire vengeance unless he made haste to drop from his cabinet Stanton, his Secretary of War.

Indeed a surprising change! At the bottom of it is the hope of the Democrats that they may harvest for their party's advantage the fruits of the policies which Johnson appears to be adopting. The vital question just now in American politics is that of negro suffrage. Johnson declares that he will allow each state to settle it independently, whereas the radical Republicans would like to have him assert his authority and settle it once for all. The moderate Republicans are undecided and disturbed about it. They do not wish to join issue openly with the President, and they are consoling themselves for his action in passing the problem of negro suffrage over to the former slave owners and rebels for solution, with the thought that, as Congress must ratify the new constitutions of the Southern states, the question of negro suffrage is simply deferred and will reappear sooner or later before the Federal legislative authority.

When this happens, however, it will be difficult to require the Southern states to give the negro freedmen all the rights of citizenship if the blacks do not yet enjoy these in the North. In order to avoid any possibility of such a situation, the Republicans are now busy amending the various constitutions of the Northern states, to guarantee to the blacks their electoral rights. In Massachusetts, Vermont, and New Hampshire, the negroes have been full citizens for a long time. In Connecticut,

where negroes cannot qualify as voters without being property holders, an assembly is to be held next month to decide
whether blacks and whites shall be put on the same footing.
The decision made in Connecticut will influence all New England. The present constitution of New York state, dating
from 1846, limits the negro voters to those who hold property
worth $250 a year.

In all the coming elections, popular feeling about negro suffrage will be voiced: on October 2, in Connecticut; on October 10, in Minnesota and Iowa; on October 7, in Wisconsin.
The Unionist convention of Minnesota passed a resolution to
the effect that "Political rights should not depend on religion,
place of birth, race, nor color, and it is foreign to the spirit of
our laws and institutions to permit any part of our population
to exist as a subject caste, taxed without representation by a
hostile government."

In all the discussions, I note that the question of universal
suffrage does not arise. Each state is to be left free to define its
voting qualifications for itself. The point is that, whatever regulation is made, no distinction shall exist between blacks and
whites. Even Horace Greeley, the editor of the *Tribune*, does
not claim universal suffrage for the negroes. A recent statement by him says: "We would readily consent to admitting to
the suffrage only those who can read and write, or those who
pay taxes, or are engaged in some trade. Any standard which
would limit the voting privilege to the competent and deserving, would be acceptable to us." But the rules and restrictions
relating to the suffrage should be applied to all on the same
basis, in his opinion. The Southern states contain many poor
whites, who are not better qualified to vote than the most ignorant and degraded negroes.

The question of negro suffrage took a most important place
also in the convention of Massachusetts Republicans, recently
held in Worcester. Charles Sumner, chairman of the convention, made a very long speech which was garbled to some extent in the telegraphic report. He emphasized the necessity
of giving the negroes the suffrage in order to create in the
Southern states a voting faction of unquestionable loyalty, to
prevent any reëstablishment of slavery in any form, and to
avoid putting a helpless race at the mercy of a dominant race,

with no political redress. He protested vigorously against Mr. Johnson's policies, and would like to withhold full exercise of their former rights from the Southerners until they have given positive guarantees to the Union. When once the Federal garrisons have been entirely withdrawn from the South, and the freedmen's bureau abolished, the blacks will have no protection whatever from their former masters. Mr. Sumner believes time to be an essential factor in the adjustment of political affairs, and Mr. Johnson's solutions appear to him over hasty. His own advice would be to go slow in every respect. He would prefer to continue the military occupation of the Southern states until all spirit of revolt has entirely died out, and to keep the freedmen's bureaux in operation. This would mean that the Southern states would not be self-governing, as in the past, until their new constitutions were formed and approved by Congress. He would prefer not to have the country leave the solution of all unsettled problems to the executive power, and believes that the legislative power should be entrusted with far more responsibility in these matters. This hasty summary of his speech is all I can give. It has influenced public opinion profoundly, as does every utterance of this distinguished, upright, and justly popular statesman.

I cannot deny that many progressive men have not been able to decide among the contradictory views concerning Southern Reconstruction, and are still without any convictions. Many who do not want to oppose Mr. Johnson openly, believing him sincerely devoted to the liberal and popular cause, still are afraid that his moderation and generosity, perhaps too expansive, will allow the Southern states to resume the share of power which they held so long, and that the spirit of compromise, which plunged the United States step by step into the Civil War will once again obscure the issues, veiling the appearance of the danger spots until they grow deep and ineradicable. There is a feeling that the South is now at the mercy of the North, and that for the first time the opportunity is at hand to quell definitely, once for all, the temper of oligarchical pride which worked such disaster to the Republic. There is a widespread feeling of pity for the blacks, who behaved so admirably during the war, committed no excesses nor cruelties, and shed their blood for the Union in the hope of becoming its citizens. Now they are being forced to bargain for, perhaps in the end to lose entirely, the rights which they have already purchased so dearly.

The real misfortune of the negro race is in owning no land of its own. There cannot be real emancipation for men who do not possess at least a small portion of the soil. We have had an example in Russia. In spite of the war, and the confiscation bills, which remain dead letters, every inch of land in the Southern states belongs to the former rebels. The population of free negroes has become a nomad population, congregated in the towns and suffering wretchedly there, destined to be driven back eventually by poverty into the country, where they will be forced to submit to the harshest terms imposed by their former masters. It would be too much to expect those masters of their own accord to conciliate the negroes by conceding them a little land in order to secure their coöperation. They are still too blinded by passion to see their own best interests.

Thus on every hand political and social difficulties arise. But the people of the United States have a peculiar faculty for adjusting themselves to circumstances and learning by experience, suddenly changing their course and thus nearly always disappointing prophets of disaster. The Americans will make mistakes but they will quickly find out how to remedy them. They will lose their way temporarily among the problems which beset them, trying out and abandoning unsatisfactory solutions, but in the end, when truth and justice have taken some kind of shape and revealed themselves to the eyes of the world, the people will seize upon them. So we must reserve our judgment for a time. For the present I will do no more than indicate the fluctuations of public opinion. The events of the last four years have taught me never to give up hope for this country.

The President has just set at liberty the rebel Senator Hunter who was imprisoned for some time in Fort Pulaski. Jefferson Davis, Clement Clay, and John Mitchel are still in Fort Monroe, but they are free to see each other and go about as they please. Jefferson Davis's trial has been delayed by the long drawn-out trial of Wirz, the warden of Andersonville Prison. The atrocities of Wirz are unimaginable. The most crushing testimony was given against him by a Confederate general, who was commissioned in 1862 to make a report on the prisons. This general, named Chandler, denounced the cruelty of Wirz in an official report addressed to the Richmond government, but Wirz was continued in his position. This is one of the most serious accusations against Jefferson Davis. Bear in mind that thousands of wounded soldiers died at Andersonville through ill treatment, and that Wirz openly boasted that he killed more Northerners than did General Lee in his battles.

General Lee has accepted the presidency of a college, and has written letters to the newspapers urging submission and obedience to the laws. Joe Johnston has done likewise. Magruder, Price, and Polk have gone to Mexico City with Maury, who was made Director of the Observatory there.

George L. Stearns:
Interview with President Johnson

Washington, D.C., Oct. 3, 1865—11 1/2 A.M.

I have just returned from an interview with President JOHNSON, in which he talked for an hour on the process of reconstruction of rebel States. His manner was as cordial, and his conversation as free, as in 1863, when I met him daily in Nashville.

His countenance is healthy, even more so than when I first knew him.

I remarked, that the people of the North were anxious that the process of reconstruction should be thorough, and they wished to support him in the arduous work, but their ideas were confused by the conflicting reports constantly circulated, and especially by the present position of the Democratic party. It is industriously circulated in the Democratic clubs that he was going over to them. He laughingly replied, "Major, have you never known a man who for many years had differed from your views because you were in advance of him, claim them as his own when he came up to your stand-point?"

I replied, I have often. He said so have I, and went on; the Democratic party finds its old position untenable, and is coming to ours; if it has come up to our position, I am glad of it. You and I need no preparation for this conversation; we can talk freely on this subject for the thoughts are familiar to us; we can be perfectly frank with each other. He then commenced with saying that, the States are in the Union which is whole and indivisible.

Individuals tried to carry them out, but did not succeed, as a man may try to cut his throat and be prevented by the bystanders; and you cannot say he cut his throat because he tried to do it.

Individuals may commit treason and be punished, and a large number of individuals may constitute a rebellion and be punished as traitors. Some States tried to get out of the

Union, and we opposed it, honestly, because we believed it to be wrong; and we have succeeded in putting down the rebellion. The power of those persons who made the attempt has been crushed, and now we want to reconstruct the State Governments and have the power to do it. The State institutions are prostrated, laid out on the ground, and they must be taken up and adapted to the progress of events. This cannot be done in a moment. We are making very rapid progress; so rapid I sometimes cannot realize it; it appears like a dream.

We must not be in too much of a hurry; it is better to let them reconstruct themselves than to force them to it; for if they go wrong, the power is in our hands and we can check them at any stage, to the end, and oblige them to correct their errors; we must be patient with them. I did not expect to keep out all who were excluded from the amnesty, or even a large number of them, but I intended they should sue for pardon, and so realize the enormity of the crime they had committed.

You could not have broached the subject of equal suffrage, at the North, seven years ago, and we must remember that the changes at the South have been more rapid, and they have been obliged to accept more unpalatable truth than the North has; we must give them time to digest a part, for we cannot expect such large affairs will be comprehended and digested at once. We must give them time to understand their new position.

I have nothing to conceal in these matters, and have no desire or willingness to take indirect courses to obtain what we want.

Our government is a grand and lofty structure; in searching for its foundation we find it rests on the broad basis of popular rights. The elective franchise is not a natural right, but a political right. I am opposed to giving the States too much power, and also to a great consolidation of power in the central government.

If I interfered with the vote in the rebel States, to dictate that the negro shall vote, I might do the same thing for my own purposes in Pennsylvania. Our only safety lies in allowing each State to control the right of voting by its own laws, and we have the power to control the rebel States if they go wrong. If they rebel we have the army, and can control them by it, and, if necessary by legislation also. If the General Government controls the right to vote in the States, it may establish such rules as will restrict the vote to a small number of persons, and thus create a central despotism.

My position here is different from what it would be if I was in Tennessee.

There I should try to introduce negro suffrage gradually; first those who had served in the army; those who could read and write, and perhaps a property qualification for others, say $200 or $250.

It will not do to let the negroes have universal suffrage now. It would breed a war of races.

There was a time in the Southern States when the slaves of large owners looked down upon non-slaveowners because they did not own slaves; the larger the number of slaves their masters owned, the prouder they were, and this has produced hostility between the mass of the whites and the negroes. The outrages are mostly from non-slaveholding whites against the negro, and from the negro upon the non-slaveholding whites.

The negro will vote with the late master whom he does not hate, rather than with the non-slaveholding white, whom he does hate. Universal suffrage would create another war, not against us, but a war of races.

Another thing. This Government is the freest and best on the earth, and I feel sure is destined to last; but to secure this, we must elevate and purify the ballot. I for many years contended at the South that slavery was a political weakness, but others said it was political strength; they thought we gained three-fifths representation by it; I contended that we lost two-fifths.

If we had no slaves, we should have had twelve representatives more, according to the then ratio of representation. Congress apportions representation by States, not districts, and the State apportions by districts.

Many years ago, I moved in the Legislature that the apportionment of Representatives to Congress, in Tennessee, should be by qualified voters.

The apportionment is now fixed until 1872; before that time we might change the basis of representation from population to qualified voters, North as well as South, and in due course of time, the States, without regard to color, might extend the elective franchise to all who possessed certain mental, moral, or such other qualifications, as might be determined by an enlightened public judgment.

Andrew Johnson: Speech to the 1st U.S. Colored Infantry, Washington, D.C.

October 10, 1865

My Friends:

My object in presenting myself before you on this occasion is simply to thank you, members of one of the colored regiments which have been in the service of the country, to sustain and carry its banners and its laws triumphantly in every part of this broad land. I repeat that I appear before you on the present occasion merely to tender you my thanks for the compliment you have paid me on your return home, to again be associated with your friends and your relations, and those you hold most sacred and dear. I repeat, I have but little to say. It being unusual in this government and in most of the other governments to have colored troops engaged in their service, you have gone forth, as events have shown, and served with patience and indurance in the cause of your country. This is your country as well as anybody else's country. [Cheers.] This is the country in which you expect to live, and in which you should expect to do something by your example in civil life as you have done in the field. This country is founded upon the principles of equality, and at the same time the standard by which persons are to be estimated is according to their merit and their worth; and you have observed, no doubt, that for him who does his duty faithfully and honestly, there is always a just public judgment that will appreciate and measure out to him his proper reward. I know that there is much well calculated in the government and since the late rebellion commenced, to excite the white against the black and the black against the white man. There are things you should all understand, and at the same time prepare yourself for what is before you. Upon the return of peace and the surrender of the enemies of the country, it should be the duty of every patriot and every one who calls himself a Christian to remember that with the termination of the war his resentments should cease, that angry feelings should subside, and that every man should

117

become calm and tranquil, and be prepared for what is before him. This is another part of your mission. You have been engaged in the effort to sustain your country in the past, but the future is more important to you than the period in which you have just been engaged. One great question has been settled in this government, and that is the question of slavery. The institution of slavery made war against the United States, and the United States has lifted its strong arm in vindication of the government and of free government; and in lifting that arm, and appealing to the God of Battles, it has been decided that the institution of slavery must go down. [Cheers.] This has been done; and the Goddess of Liberty, in bearing witness over many of our battle-fields since the struggle commenced, has made the loftiest flight, and proclaimed that true liberty has been established upon a more permanent and enduring basis than heretofore. [Applause.] But this is not all; and as you have paid me the compliment to call upon me, I shall take the privilege of saying one or two words, as I am before you. I repeat that it is not all. Now, when the sword is returned to its scabbard, when your arms are reversed, and the olive branch of peace is extended, as I remarked before, resentment and revenge should subside. Then what is to follow? You do understand, no doubt, and if you do not, you cannot understand too soon, that simple liberty does not mean the privilege of going into the battle-field, or into the service of the country as a soldier. It means other things as well; and now, when you have laid down your arms, there are other objects of equal importance before you. Now that the government has triumphantly passed through this rebellion, after the most gigantic battles the world ever saw, the problem is before you, and it is best that you should understand it; and, therefore, I speak simply and plainly. Will you now, when you have returned from the army of the United States, and take the position of the citizen; when you have returned to the associations of peace, will you give evidence to the world that you are capable and competent to govern yourselves? That is what you will have to do. Liberty is not a mere idea; a mere vagary. It is an idea or it is a reality; and when you come to examine this question of liberty, you will not be mistaken in a mere idea for the reality. It does not consist in idleness. Liberty does not consist in being worthless.

Liberty does not consist in doing all things as we please, and there can be no liberty without law. In a government of freedom and of liberty there must be law and there must be obedience and submission to the law, without regard to color. [Cheers.] Liberty (and may I not call you my countrymen) consists in the glorious privilege of work; of pursuing the ordinary avocations of peace with industry and with economy; and that being done, all those who have been industrious and economical are permitted to appropriate and enjoy the products of their own labor. [Cheers.] This is one of the great blessings of freedom; and hence we might ask the question, and answer it by stating that liberty means freedom to work and enjoy the products of your own labor. You will soon be mustered out of the ranks. It is for you to establish the great fact that you are fit and qualified to be free. Hence, freedom is not a mere idea, but is something that exists in fact. Freedom is not simply the privilege to live in idleness; liberty does not mean simply to resort to the low saloons and other places of disreputable character. Freedom and liberty do not mean that the people ought to live in licentiousness, but liberty means simply to be industrious, to be virtuous, to be upright in all our dealings and relations with men; and to those now before me, members of the first regiment of colored volunteers from the District of Columbia and the Capital of the United States, I have to say that a great deal depends upon yourselves. You must give evidence that you are competent for the rights that the government has guaranteed to you. Henceforth each and all of you must be measured according to your merit. If one man is more meritorious than the other, they cannot be equals; and he is the most exalted that is the most meritorious without regard to color. And the idea of having a law passed in the morning that will make a white man a black man before night, and a black man a white man before day, is absurd. That is not the standard. It is your own conduct; it is your own merit; it is the development of your own talents and of your own intellectuality and moral qualities. Let this then be your course: adopt a system of morality. Abstain from all licentiousness. And let me say one thing here, for I am going to talk plain. I have lived in a Southern State all my life and know what has too often been the case. There is one thing you should esteem higher and more supreme than almost all others; and that is the solemn contract with all the penalties in the association of married life. Men and women should abstain from those qualities and habits that too frequently follow a war. Inculcate among your children and among your associations, notwithstanding you are just back from the army of the United States, that virtue, that merit, that intelligence are the standards to be observed, and those which you are determined to maintain during your future lives. This is the way to make white men black and black men white. [Cheers.] He that is most meritorious and virtuous and intellectual and well-informed, must stand highest without regard to color. It is the very basis upon which heaven rests itself. Each individual takes his degree in the sublimer and more exalted regions in proportion to his merits and his virtue. Then I shall say to you on this occasion in returning to your homes and firesides after feeling conscious and proud of having faithfully discharged your duty, returning with the determination that you will perform your duty in the future as you have in the past, abstain from all those bickerings and jealousies and revengeful feelings which too often spring up between different races. There is a great problem before us, and I may as well allude to it here in this connection; and that is, whether this race can be incorporated and mixed with the people of the United States, to be made a harmonious and permanent ingredient in the population. This is a problem not yet settled, but we are in the right line to do so. Slavery raised its head against the government, and the government raised its strong arm and struck it to the ground. So that part of the problem is settled: the institution of slavery is overthrown. But another part remains to be solved, and that is, Can four millions of people, raised as they have been with all the prejudices of the whites, can they take their places in the community and be made to work harmoniously and congruously in our system? This is a problem to be considered. Are the digestive powers of the American Government sufficient to receive this element in a new shape, and digest and make it work healthfully upon the system that has incorporated it? This is the question to be determined. Let us make the experiment, and make it in good faith. If that cannot be done, there is another problem before us. If we have to become a separate and distinct people, (although I trust that the system can be made to work harmoniously, and the great problem will be settled without going any further) if it should be so that the two races cannot agree and live in peace and prosperity, and the laws of Providence require that they should be separated—in that event, looking to the far distant future and trusting that it may never come; if it should come, Providence, that works mysteriously but unerringly and certainly, will point out the way, and the mode, and the manner by which these people are to be separated, and to be taken to their lands of inheritance and promise; for such a one is before them. Hence we are making the experiment. Hence let me impress upon you the importance of controlling your passions, developing your intellect, and of applying your physical powers to the industrial interests of the country; and that is the true process by which this question can be settled. Be patient, persevering and forbearing, and you will help to solve the problem. Make for yourselves a reputation in this cause as you have won for yourselves a reputation in the cause in which you have been engaged. In speaking to the members of this regiment I want them to understand that so far as I am concerned, I do not assume or pretend that I am stronger than the laws, of course, of nature, or that I am wiser than Providence itself. It is our duty to try and discover what those great laws are which are at the foundation of all things, and, having discovered what they are, conform our actions and our conduct to them, and to the will of God who ruleth all things. He holds the destinies of nations in the palm of His hand; and He will solve the question and rescue these people from the difficulties that have so long surrounded them. Then let us be patient, industrious and persevering. Let us develop any intellectual and moral worth. I trust what I have said may be understood and appreciated. Go to your homes and lead peaceful, prosperous and happy lives, in peace with all men. Give utterance to no word that would cause dissensions; but do that which will be creditable to yourselves and to your country. To the officers who have led and so nobly commanded you in the field, I also return my thanks for the compliment you have conferred upon me.

Sarah Whittlesey to Andrew Johnson

Alexandria Oct. 12th. 1865

President of the United States:

I respectfully enclose a copy of an order issued by "the Major General commanding this department," believing from past proclamations, you are not aware of the astounding fact that one of your subordinates defies your authority. Years ago, I met you in the Senate, and subsequently in the State Department; and as a native of my own dear State; as an *honorable man*, and great head of this people, I come to you, as a child to a father, and ask you, with humble boldness, by all that is good and merciful to help us, or we shall be driven to desperation, by such men as the "General commanding this department."

Our town is overrun with negroes, and they are daily coming in by scores—they are a lying, lazy people, in their present ignorant state, who will not work so long as they can steal, be supported by the Government, and protected by Northern men, who treat them cruelly, except where kindness enables them to gratify their hate for Southern white men. They will not engage for service for less than an exorbitant sum, which our people in their poverty, which *abolition first* and *secession second* have wrought, are not able to pay; they rent rooms, and run off, between two days to avoid paying for them—they cry "poor white trash" in the streets; carry guns and pistols, and threaten white men at pleasure; and if the white man, in self-defense turns upon his assailant, he is arrested by the *military authorities* and committed to jail, while the negro is left free. You are a southern man, sir, and well know what is absolutely necessary for a negro—they cannot be left to run wild, and behave decently; we should get along smoothly together, if Northern men, who being "clothed with a little brief authority" are "playing such fantastic tricks before high heaven, as make the angels weep!", would not interfere with our civil authorities, and trample upon State laws; and that too, against *your* command! I am a well known loyalist, sir, together with my father and brother, and do not bring to you the complaints of a rebel and prejudiced heart; but I come to you as one who *knows* our people have been imposed upon, tormented and tortured by Yankee officials, for the last four years, who have professed to be fighting from *patriotism*, when their sordid small soul is in their *pocket*, until the word UNION has an unsavory smell to the most faithful Southern heart to the Government. Now that war is ended, and our Southern people are returning to their allegiance—and I assure you, sir, they are more reliable than those who wear the livery of the United States, and steal from its Treasury—shall our State laws be crushed under *military* heels, and our city authorities driven before *military* commands? We are in frequent dread of an insurrection among the negroes, they are so ignorant and easily led by those who *profess* to be their *best* friends, and if they are permitted to supply themselves with guns and pistols, another and worse war, we believe to be inevitable. The northern men we firmly believe will *secretly* lead them on to destroy the Southern people, and then *openly* turn and exterminate them (for in their hearts they hate the race)—and take full possession of the coveted Southland.

Last Summer, in Connecticut, I heard a Yankee say, who wears the prefix of Rev to his name: "Virginia has got to have her nose put to the grindstone, and then pay for the turning"—and "*we* must give the negroes the right to vote in order to *keep the Southern people down*." President Johnson, *you* are a *Southern man*; *I* am a *Southern woman*, and those remarks burned my brain like livid lightning! I found *that* was the spirit that prevailed wherever I went, and I did not remain there through the summer, as I contemplated. I left the State in disappointment and disgust. That same *Rev.* rejoiced at the assassination of President Lincoln because, he said "Andy would hang the rebels"—as you did not, he abused you in my presence. Sir, are such men "to keep the Southern people down," with the force of a *negro's* foot?

Pardon me for presuming to address you—I do it without the knowledge of any one, believing you will sympathize with a suffering people, and reward their oppressors according to their deeds, when you are appraised of their mischievous tendency. Your position is such that you cannot know all the torments to which our people are subjected by those in authority under you, without private information; and I know you have ever done justly when appealed to by an oppressed and almost despairing people.

Sarah J.C. Whittlesey

Edisto Island Freedmen to Andrew Johnson

Edisto Island S.C.   Oct 28th 1865

To the President of these United States.

We the freedmen of Edisto Island South Carolina have learned from you through Major General O O Howard commissioner of the Freedmans Bureau, with deep sorrow and painful hearts of the possibility of goverment restoring these lands to the former owners. We are well aware of the many perplexing and trying questions that burden your mind and do therefore pray to god (the preserver of all and who has through our Late and beloved President (Lincoln) proclamation and the war made us A free people) that he may guide you in making your decisions and give you that wisdom that cometh from above to settle these great and Important questions for the best interests of the country and the Colored race. Here is where secession was born and nurtured. Here is where we have toiled nearly all our lives as slaves and were treated like dumb Driven cattle. This is our home, we have made these lands what they are. We were the only true and Loyal people that were found in posession of these lands. We have been always ready to strike for liberty and humanity yea to fight if needs be to preserve this glorious union. Shall not we who are freedman and have been always true to this Union have the same rights as are enjoyed by others? Have we broken any Law of these United States? Have we forfieted our rights of property in Land? If not then! are not our rights as A free people and good citizens of these United States to be considered before the rights of those who were found in rebellion against this good and just Goverment (and now being conquered) come (as they seem) with penitent hearts and beg forgiveness for past offences and also ask if thier lands cannot be restored to them? Are these rebellious spirits to be reinstated in thier *possessions* and we who have been abused and oppressed for many long years not to be allowed the privilige of purchasing land But be subject to the will of these large Land owners? God fobid. Land monopoly is unjurious to the advancement of the course of freedom, and if Government does not make some provision by which we as freedmen can obtain A Homestead, we have not bettered our condition.

We have been encouraged by Government to take up these lands in small tracts, receiving certificates of the same. We have thus far taken sixteen thousand (16000) acres of Land here on this Island. We are ready to pay for this land when Government calls for it and now after what has been done will the good and just government take from us all this right and make us subject to the will of those who have cheated and oppressed us for many years? God Forbid!

We the freedmen of this Island and of the State of South Carolina—Do therefore petition to you as the President of these United States, that some provisions be made by which every colored man can purchase land, and hold it as his own. We wish to have A home if it be but A few acres. Without some provision is made our future is sad to look upon. Yes our situation is dangerous. We therefore look to you in this trying hour as A true friend of the poor and neglected race, for protection and Equal Rights, with the privilege of purchasing A Homestead—A Homestead right here in the heart of South Carolina.

We pray that God will direct your heart in making such provision for us as freedmen which will tend to unite these states together stronger than ever before. May God bless you in the administration of your duties as the President of these United States is the humble prayer of us all.

J. A. Williamson to Nathan A. M. Dudley

Memphis Tenn   Oct 30th 1865

Dear Sir   Learning that you are desirous of obtaining correct information with regard to the Freedmen in their new
relation to their former owners & present employers with a
view of adopting such measures as shall insure peace tranquility & prosperity—throughout your District, you will permit
me to respectfully submit a few facts & suggestions for your
consideration—and action if you should deem it necessary.
In the neighborhood of the little village of Bellmont in the
County of Fayette some twelve miles distant in a North West-
erly direction from Sommerville (the County seat)—a large
number of negroes have procured arms and are manifesting
such a spirit of insubordination & frequently making such
threats & demonstrations as are calculated to disturb the
peace & tranquility of the community and which may lead
to serious results if not speedily checked. I learn through my
brother-in-law Mr W. E. Stamback (who is now in charge
of the plantation of my late father L P Williamson)—that
this is particularly observable upon the farm of the late Dr
Howell some ten miles from Sommerville upon the road
leading from Sommerville to Covington—also upon the farm
of Genl Jos Williams—both of which places are at present
under the control of superintendents & not owners. Upon
the first mentioned place the old gentleman has recently died
and the negroes seem to think they have the best right to the
premises & are disposed to appropriate them to their use,
and the owner of the latter place resides in this city & the
negroes are consequently under scarcely any discipline or restraint. The community is impressed with the belief that this
unfortunate state of affairs has resulted chiefly from the want
of means in the hands of employers of enforcing discipline
& order upon the plantations (corporal punishment having
been abolished) and the secret agency & influence of bad
men who induce the poor ignorant blacks to believe that the

annihilition of the whites will put them permanently in possession of their lands & estates. The negro being by nature indolent & improvident—living only for to day & permitting tomorrow to take care of itself—not influenced to any extent by the hope of reward but chiefly moved by the fear of punishment and in view of the fact that corporal punishment has been prohibited we must look about for some other means by which we can exact an amount of labor sufficient to justify the employer in paying him wages and at the same time insure order & discipline upon the premises. To accomplish these most desirable objects I would respectfully suggest Genl— First the disarming of the freedmen in the country as has been done in this city   Second the appointment by the sub Agents in the different counties of a police guard of four or five of the most reliable negroes upon every farm, one of whom can be styled Captain   This guard *not to be armed* & recieving their instructions from the agent of the Bureau for the county would meet with no resistance in arresting any negro who might be creating a disturbance upon the place or failing to perform his duty and taking him before the Agt for correction. I learn that this plan is working admirably in Phillips County Arkansas and they have none of those unfortunate & deplorable conflicts between whites & blacks which we are called upon sometimes to regret. I would further suggest the calling of meetings of the freedmen at one or two public places in the Counties & let them be addressed by Government officials & made clearly (& *thus authoritatively*) to understand their true status—the relation they *sustain to their former owners in point of property* and the penalties annexed to any violation of the laws—especially in regard to demonstrations of an insurrectionary character. All of which is respectfully submitted by Your obt Svt

J A Williamson

P.S. I will merely add that Mr Stamback called with me upon you during his recent visit to this city & found you absent & requested me to place this matter before you—   Respectfully &c

J A W

Address of the Colored State Convention to the People of South Carolina

FELLOW CITIZENS:—We have assembled as delegates representing the colored people of the State of South Carolina, in the capacity of State Convention, to confer together and to deliberate upon our intellectual, moral, industrial, civil, and political condition as affected by the great changes which have taken place in this State and throughout this whole country, and to devise ways and means which may, through the blessing of God, tend to our improvement, elevation, and progress; fully believing that our cause is one which commends itself to all good men throughout the civilized world; that it is the sacred cause of truth and righteousness; that it particularly appeals to those professing to be governed by that religion which teaches to "do unto all men as you would have them do unto you."

These principles we conceive to embody the great duty of man to his fellow man; and, as *men*, we ask only to be included in a practical application of this principle.

We feel that the *justness* of our cause is a sufficient apology for our course at this time. Heretofore we have had no avenues opened to us or our children—we have had no firesides that we could call our own; none of those incentives to work for the development of our minds and the aggrandizement of our race in common with other people. The measures which have been adopted for the development of white men's children have been denied to us and ours. The laws which have made white men great, have degraded us, because we were colored, and because we were reduced to chattel slavery. But now that we are freemen, now that we have been lifted up by the providence of God to manhood, we have resolved to come forward, and, like MEN, speak and *act* for ourselves. We fully recognize the truth of the maxim that "God helps those who help themselves." In making this appeal to you, we adopt the language of the immortal Declaration of Independence, "that all men are created equal," and that "life, liberty, and the pursuit of happiness" are the right of all; that taxation and representation should go together; that governments are to protect, not to destroy the rights of mankind; that the Constitution of the United States was formed to establish justice, to promote the general welfare, and secure the blessings of liberty to all the people of this country; that resistance to tyrants is obedience to God—are American principles and maxims; and together they form the constructive elements of the American Government.

We think we fully comprehend and duly appreciate the principles and measures which compose this platform; and all that we desire or ask for is to be placed in a position that we could conscientiously and legitimately defend, with you, those principles against the surges of despotism to the last drop of our blood. We have not come together in battle array to assume a boastful attitude and to talk loudly of high-sounding principles or unmeaning platforms, nor do we pretend to any great boldness; for we know your wealth and greatness, and our poverty and weakness; and although we feel keenly our wrongs, still we come together, we trust, in a spirit of meekness and of patriotic good-will to all the people of the State. But yet it is some consolation to know (and it inspires us with hope when we reflect) that our cause is not alone the cause of five millions of colored men in this country, but we are intensely alive to the fact that it is also the cause of millions of oppressed men in other "parts of God's beautiful earth," who are now struggling to be free in the fullest sense of that word; and God and nature are pledged in its triumph. We are Americans by birth, and we assure you that we are Americans in feeling; and, in spite of all wrongs which we have long and silently endured in this country, we would still exclaim with a full heart, "O America! with all thy faults we love thee still."

> Breathes there a man with soul so dead
> Who never to himself hath said—
> "This is my own, my native land!"
> Whose heart hath ne'er within him burned
> As home his footsteps he hath turned,
> From wandering in a foreign strand?

Thus we would address you, not as enemies, but as friends and fellow-countrymen, who desire to dwell among you in peace, and whose destinies are interwoven, and linked with those of the American people, and hence must be fulfilled in this country. As descendants of a race feeble and long oppressed, we might with propriety appeal to a great and magnanimous people like Americans, for special favors and encouragement, on the principle that the strong should aid the weak, the learned should teach the unlearned.

But it is for no such purposes that we raise our voices to the people of South Carolina on this occasion. We ask for no special privileges or peculiar favors. We ask only for *even-handed Justice*, or for the removal of such positive obstructions and disabilities as past, and the recent Legislators have seen fit to throw in our way, and heap upon us.

Without any rational cause or provocation on our part, of which we are conscious, as a people, we, by the action of your Convention and Legislature, have been virtually, and with few exceptions excluded from, first, the rights of citizenship, which you cheerfully accord to strangers, but deny to us who have been born and reared in your midst, who were faithful while your greatest trials were upon you, and have done nothing since to merit your disapprobation.

We are denied the right of giving our testimony in like manner with that of our white fellow-citizens, in the courts of the State, by which our persons and property are subject to every species of violence, insult and fraud without redress.

We are also by the present laws, not only denied the right of citizenship, the inestimable right of voting for those who rule over us in the land of our birth, but by the so-called Black Code we are deprived the rights of the meanest profligate in the country—the right to engage in any legitimate business free from any restraints, save those which govern all other citizens of this State.

You have by your Legislative actions placed barriers in the way of our educational and mechanical improvement; you have given us little or no encouragement to pursue agricultural pursuits, by refusing to sell to us lands, but organize societies to bring foreigners to your country, and thrust us out or reduce us to a serfdom, intolerable to men born amid the progress of American genius and national development.

Your public journals charge the freedmen with destroying

the products of the country since they have been made free, when they know that the destruction of the products was brought about by the ravages of war of four years duration. How unjust, then, to charge upon the innocent and helpless, evils in which they had no hand, and which may be traced to where it properly belongs.

We simply desire that we shall be recognized as men; that we have no obstructions placed in our way; that the same laws which govern white men shall direct colored men; that we have the right of trial by a jury of our peers, that schools be opened or established for our children; that we be permitted to acquire homesteads for ourselves and children; that we be dealt with as others, in equity and justice.

We claim the confidence and good-will of all classes of men; we ask that the same chances be extended to us that freemen should demand at the hands of their fellow-citizens. We desire the prosperity and growth of this State and the well-being of all men, and shall be found ever struggling to elevate ourselves and add to the national character; and we trust the day will not be distant when you will acknowledge that by our rapid progress in moral, social, religious and intellectual development that you will cheerfully accord to us the high commendation that we are worthy, with you, to enjoy all political emoluments—when we shall realize the truth that "all men are endowed by their Creator with inalienable rights," and that on the American continent this is the right of all, whether he come from east, west, north or south; and, although complexions may differ, "a man's a man for a' that."

ZION CHURCH, Charleston, S. C.,
   November 24, 1865.

Andrew J. Hamilton to Andrew Johnson

Austin Texas, Novr 27. 1865.

Mr President:

I have already advised you, by telegram, that I had by Proclamation ordered an election, on the 8th of January, for delegates, to assemble in Convention, on the 7th of February next. I can well conceive, that you have thought me slow to move in this matter, and that you may have felt some impatience, at Texas, being so far behind the other Southern States, in this necessary work. I believe, I have in former communications, given you the reasons, why it could not be done earlier—and I could also give reasons, why it might have been better for Texas, to have delayed the call still longer. The great body of the people are quiet and orderly. They seem disposed to obey the laws, and are doubtless, glad to be once more under the protection of the government of the United States, and anxious to accept every benefit it confers. Still it must be confessed, that a great many, even of this class, have had their minds and hearts so perverted by past teachings, that they accept the favor of Government, as a matter of course, without feeling any corresponding obligation on their part, to make the slightest sacrifice to sustain the Government, or its policy. Even Union men throughout the war, never doubted but the emancipation of slavery would be the result, now that it has come, are some of them, sore and complaining. The sacred negro, (sacred only when a slave) could not be yielded up, without a struggle. Now all sensible men admit, that slavery is dead, but still, there seems to be a desire, and a hope, that some plan will be adopted, which will keep the negro, practically, in bondage. This, it must not be supposed, is either the expectation or wish of *all* of the late slave owners; but certainly of many of them. And even those who do not desire this, have not for the most part, progressed far enough in the lessons taught by the rebellion, to accord to the negro, equal rights, under the law. I speak, not of suffrage; but protection of life, liberty, and property. There is an evident improvement in the public mind upon this subject, steadily going forward: but the public press of the State, and the political teachers became, so utterly depraved during the rebellion, and committed themselves and the people to such extravagances, that they cannot, thus early, embrace and declare the truth; hence, the public mind is working slowly, but I believe steadily, in the right direction. Six months would bring it right. And I even hope, that Congress when it meets, will give such early indications of what is expected of the people of the South, that our Convention will be inclined to act, with more deliberation, and better matured judgment, than would control them, under other circumstances. I can only form my own opinion of what will be expected of the Convention. I have determined in my own mind what it ought to do.

1st   To declare the ordinance of Secession null and void from the beginning.

2nd   That there is no such Thing as a legal or Constitutional right in a State, to secede, or otherwise attempt, a disruption of the Union.

3rd   That slavery is extinguished by the Proclamation of the President, and the acts of Congress.

4th   That slavery shall never again exist, in the State.

5th   The ratification of the amendments to the U.S. Constitution, prohibiting slavery in all the States and Territories.

6th   That the freedom of the late slaves, shall be protected, by guarantees to life liberty and property, by equal laws, allowing to them, the benefit of their oaths, in the courts of the country, upon the same rules of admissability and credability that apply to others.

7th   That the debt of the State, created for the purpose of upholding the rebellion, and destroying the Government of the United States; is not, and cannot be binding upon the people of Texas; and cannot be paid, or recognized, without an implied endorsement, of the rebellion, not only unjust to the people of the State; but contumacious and insulting to the Government: and that the same, is not, and can never be, a charge upon the people of Texas. These, I think, are necessary, as Constitutional provisions, to put us in proper position, to assume our former relations to the Union. Less than this, I confess, I would not, myself, be satisfied with; and something like this, in my judgment, will be expected and demanded by the American people, through their representatives in Congress. The influences to be contended against in bringing about this desirable action, are manifold. It would be nearly impossible to enumerate them all: but among the most prominent are: 1st, The wounded pride, resulting from the failure of the rebellion, and the consequent exposure of the false prophesies of its leaders. 2nd The indulgence of that spirit, which causes men, to refuse to be reconciled, to those, whom they have deeply injured, without cause.

3rd   The false pride, of not acknowledging an error—together with the want of correct information: soreness at the loss of property—the desire to be again considered political oracles—envy and hatred of Union men—and last and worst; even Union men, who, in order to obtain present preferment, are willing to pander to all of the prejudices of the past—and are full of cant about the tyranny of Govt. &c. &c. To meet all these, I have but little help, from any quarter. The best men of the State, feel very much disinclined, to throw themselves into the breach, and give their active exertions to sweep away all of these hindrances, to right action. I have done what I could, and shall continue to labor to the last. I contemplate making a tour through the most populous portions of the State, before the election, to address the people. I shall plainly and frankly present the views I entertain, of their situation and their duty. This is much needed. The people want to know the truth, and seem to feel instinctively that their former teachers are not the men from whom they can learn it. I have every day calls upon me to go out and talk to them, but up to this time, I have not been able to leave here, even for one day, or an hour. But having organized the State, and got it to running smoothly, I think, I can better employ my time, for two or three weeks, by mingling with the people and giving them good advice, than by attending to the mere details of business in my office, which can be as well done, by my Secretary of State. It is a labor necessary to be performed, and if I dont perform it, so far as I can see, no one will. I could say to you, much more, as to the temper of the people, touching political questions; but it would be tedious. There have been, as was to be expected, many outrages committed upon the freedmen. I have done all in my power to prevent such, and to bring to punishment the guilty parties. But in sections of the State, remote from any Military force, I have not been able to accomplish much. You will perceive, that I felt it my duty, to issue an address to the freedmen, with a view of disabusing their minds of false notions, as to what the Government would do for them. There is no doubt, but that many of them, really believed, that about Christmas, they would be furnished with homes, and whatever else they might need. This was calculated to disincline them to hire, to labor for fair wages, and I had reason to fear that mid winter, would find them without homes or food, and that they would be compelled to go stealing, to preserve life, and then the whites, would have something more than a pretext, for killing them: and with a view, to prevent such a state of things, I issued the address to the freedmen: also, an authority to the Chief Justices of the Counties, to organize a Police force, to preserve order, and prevent violence—copies of which, I herewith enclose; as also a copy of my Proclamation for a Convention. I feel confident, that they will have the desired effect, and that the public peace will be maintained.

You will permit me now, Mr. President, to say a word, upon the subject of diminishing the Military force in Texas. I will not present you the reasons, at this time, for what I urge; beyond the statement which I deliberately make; that it will not be safe, to reduce it lower, than it now is. I do not mean that the United States would have anything to fear in a military point of view; but it would have much to lose, in the way of deferring the restoration of Society and Civil Government in Texas. There is no fear, of an organized force to openly defy the power of the Government, but there would, beyond doubt, be thousands of individual acts of insult and injury, to loyal citizens, by that class of men, who are bitter in their feelings towards the Government and its friends. They are not the majority, but there is so large a percentum of such men, as to enable them; in many localities, in the present demoralized condition of society, to defy the local civil law. The largest portion of the forces, now in the State, are on the Rio Grande, and this, I suppose, for obvious reasons, will continue to be the case; so that there is left for the whole of the immense territory of the State, where our people actually reside, not more than six or eight thousand troops. If this number should be distributed between such points in the State, as will afford reasonable aid to the Civil authorities, in keeping the public peace, they will be found hardly adequate to the task. As it now is, very much the largest portion of the State, in territory; and very much the largest portion of our people, have no such protection. Besides, the people on our Indian border, are suffering terribly, from the constant depredations of the Indians. So far, no permanent Posts, have been established on this border. If it is not soon done, the whole Northern frontier will be compelled to recede. It is now, in fact, daily receding. Our people have been patient. They know that they have not been blameless in producing this state of things. But it is sad, that the innocent, must suffer, for the wrongs of the guilty. I most respectfully urge upon your Excellency, that a force, be directed to occupy the Indian frontier and I at the same time, for the reasons given, would strongly recommend that no further diminution of the forces in Texas, be made.

They are needed, and will be, for many months to come, if we are to have order and security to life and property.

A J Hamilton　Provl. Govr. of Texas

Sidney Andrews:
from The South Since the War

SOME GENERAL CONCLUSIONS ON THE SITUATION
IN GEORGIA AND THE CAROLINAS.

ON SHIPBOARD, December 7, 1865.

If the representatives elect from the Southern States have been admitted to their seats in Congress, then has the South been victorious. But if the House has organized without their help, and if the whole reconstruction question is left open for general discussion in that body and in the public press, then indeed is there cause for most devout thanksgiving on this day set apart by the President.

My fourteen weeks' tour is at an end, and I am returning to New York. I have travelled over more than half the stage and railway routes in the States of North Carolina, South Carolina, and Georgia. I have been generally treated with civility and occasionally with courteous cordiality. I judge, from the stories told me by various persons, that my reception was, on the whole, something better than that accorded to the majority of Northern travellers.

I went South to study the political situation. I did not go to view the country, and consequently my letters have given but meagre information regarding the soil and climate and productions of the States visited. In pursuance of the plan marked out from the beginning, I sought conversation with all classes of Southerners,—my object being to gather information at first hand and to keep my reports free from the bias and prejudice of Northern sojourners. I was not obliged to write in the interest of any party or any person, and was not required to furnish arguments for upholding or breaking down any particular theory of reconstruction. In a word, my duty was that of a reporter. I meant to tell the truth, and I hoped to find the truth pleasant to tell.

Yet the conclusion of the whole matter is, that a very grave mistake, not to say a criminal blunder, has been committed, if the Southern representatives have been admitted into Congress.

It will not be safe to admit them to their seats at present. Some of them ought never to be admitted. They have no business in a Congress of the United States, for they are either of bitterly rebellious spirit or are encased in the poisonous bigotries of State supremacy. Against these the doors of our legislative halls should be forever closed. Other men there are of better disposition and larger views; but the time has not come for even their participation in the national counsels. If they are really fit for the places to which they have been chosen nothing will be lost if they prove anew that those also serve who stand and wait.

For it must be said that public sentiment is changing very rapidly in the South, and not wholly in the right direction. The President went to the extreme limit of magnanimity; but the more he gave the more was demanded. I have recently seen an article in one of the Southern papers in which the removal of Secretary Stanton is asked as a good-will offering to the people of the South; and a knot of gentlemen at the hotel in Augusta argued to me that the unconditional release of Jeff Davis was necessary to prove the kindly disposition of the North! So far as the people of Georgia and South Carolina, and a large proportion of those of North Carolina, are concerned, the indorsement of President Johnson, of which so much is said in their newspapers, is merely a grateful sense of favors to be received.

Possibly we were wrong to hope that one season could sow the grain of reconstruction and gather its fruitage of good order and fair respect for human rights. At least this season has not done that. I am sure the nation longs for nothing else so much as for honest and heroic peace; yet let not the representatives of the nation mistake this longing for weakness of faith or faintness of purpose in respect to the final triumph of justice.

It cannot be said that freedom of speech has been fully secured in either of the three States which I have visited. Personally, I have very little cause of complaint, for my *rôle* was rather that of a listener than of a talker; but I met many persons who kindly cautioned me, that at such and such places, and in such and such company, it would be advisable to refrain from conversation on certain topics. Among the members of the better class of people, resident in the cities and large towns, I found a fair degree of liberality of sentiment and courtesy of speech; but in travelling off the main railway lines, and among the average of the population, any man of Northern opinions must use much circumspection of language.

It follows, of course, that safety of person is not assured. Very likely one might travel through every county of either State without harm; but any Union man must expect to hear many insulting words; and any Northern man is sure to find his principles despised, his people contemned, and himself subjected to much disagreeable contumely; while any man holding and openly advocating even moderately radical sentiments on the negro question, stands an excellent chance, in many counties of Georgia and South Carolina, of being found dead some morning,—shot from behind, as is the custom of the country. Of course the war has not taught its full lesson till even Mr. Wendell Phillips can go into Georgia and proclaim "The South Victorious."

The leading men generally invite immigration, and are honest and sincere in their expression of desire for the influx of new life. They will, I am sure, do all they can to make the States safe and inviting for immigrants. In time even South Carolina will be as free as New York; but at present the masses of the people have little disposition of welcome for Northerners.

The late private soldiers of the Rebel army are the best class of citizens in the South. Generally speaking, they are disposed to go to work, though few of them know what work to do or to undertake. The bad classes are nearly all the women, who are as rebellious and as malignant as ever; most of the preachers, who are as hostile now as they were three years ago; many of the Rebel ex-officers who did n't see active service; and more than half the young men who managed in one way or another to keep out of the army.

I often had occasion to notice, both in Georgia and the Carolinas, the wide and pitiful difference between the residents of the cities and large towns and the residents of the country. There is no homogeneity, but everywhere a rigid spirit of caste. The longings of South Carolina are essentially monarchical rather than republican; even the common people have become so debauched in loyalty that very many of them would readily accept the creation of orders of nobility. In Georgia there is something less of this spirit; but the upper classes continually assert their right to rule, and the middle and lower classes have no ability to free themselves. The whole structure of society is full of separating walls; and it will sadden the heart of any Northern man, who travels in either of these three States, to see how poor and meagre and narrow a thing life is to all the country people. Even with the best class of townsfolk it lacks very much of the depth and breadth and fruitfulness of our Northern life, while with these others it is hardly less materialistic than that of their own mules and horses. Thus Charleston has much intelligence and considerable genuine culture; but go twenty miles away and you are in the land of the barbarians. So Raleigh is a city in which there is love of beauty and interest in education; but the common people of the county are, at least, forty years behind the same class of people in Vermont. Moreover, in Macon are many very fine residences, and the city may boast of its gentility and its respect for the nourishing elegances of life; but a dozen miles out are large neighborhoods not yet half civilized. The contrast between the inhabitants of the cities and those of the country is hardly less striking than that between the various classes constituting the body of the common people. Going from one county into another is frequently going into a foreign country. Travel continually brings novelty, but with that always came pain. Till all these hateful walls of caste are thrown down, we can have neither intelligent love of liberty, decent respect for justice, nor enlightened devotion to the idea of national unity. "Do men gather grapes of thorns, or figs of thistles?"

It has been the purpose of the ruling class apparently to build new barriers between themselves and the common people rather than tear away any of those already existing. I think no one can understand the actual condition of the mass of the whites of Georgia and the Carolinas, except by some daily contact with them. The injustice done to three fourths of them was hardly less than that done to all the blacks. There were two kinds of slavery, and negro slavery was only more wicked and debasing than white slavery. Nine of every ten white men in South Carolina had almost as little to do with even State affairs as the negroes had. Men talk of plans of reconstruction. That is the best plan which proposes to do most for the common people. Till civilization has been carried down into the homes and hearts of all classes, we shall have neither regard for humanity nor respect for the rights of the citizen.

Any plan of reconstruction is wrong that does not assure toleration of opinion and the elevation of the common people to the consciousness that ours is a republican form of government. Whether they are technically in the Union or out of the Union, it is the national duty to deal with these States in such manner as will most surely exalt the lower and middle classes of their inhabitants. The nation must teach them a knowledge of their own rights, while it also teaches them respect for its rights and the rights of man as man.

Stopping for two or three days in some back county, I was always seeming to have drifted away from the world which held Illinois and Ohio and Massachusetts. The difficulty in keeping connection with our civilization did not so much lie in the fact that the whole structure of daily life is unlike ours, nor in the other fact that I was forced to hear the Union and all loyal men reviled, as in the greater fact that the people are utterly without knowledge. There is everywhere a lack of intellectual activity; while as for schools, books, newspapers, why, one may almost say there are none outside the cities and towns!

Had schools abounded six years ago, I doubt if the masses of the South could have been forced into the war. "Why, d—n it," said an Americus man to me, "the Union never hurt me, but I was the hottest Secessionist I reckon you ever saw. Howell Cobb made me so." Talking with a Columbia gentleman about sectional characteristics he said, "We had one advantage over you: your people knew all about the war, while ours only knew they were fighting for their homes." I asked, "But could you have made your men fight at all if they had understood the whole question at issue?" He answered, "O, when I said we had the advantage, I spoke from a military stand-point."

In the important town of Charlotte, North Carolina, I found a white man who owned the comfortable house in which he lived, who had a wife and three half-grown children, and yet had never taken a newspaper in his life. He thought they were handy for wrapping purposes, but he could n't see why anybody wanted to bother with the reading of them. He knew some folks spent money for them, but he also knew a-many houses where none had ever been seen. In that State I found several persons—whites, and not of the "clay-eater" class either—who never had been inside a school-house, and who did n't mean to 'low their children to go inside one. In the upper part of South Carolina I stopped one night at the house of a moderately well-to-do farmer who never had owned any book but a Testament, and that was given to him. When I expressed some surprise at this fact, he assured me that he was as well off as some other people thereabouts. Between Augusta and Milledgeville I rode in a stage-coach in which were two of the delegates of the Georgia Convention. When I said that I hoped the day would soon come in which school-houses would be as numerous in Georgia as in Massachusetts, one of them answered, "Well, I hope it 'll never come; popular education is all a d—n humbug, in my judgment"; whereupon the other responded, "That 's my opinion too." These are exceptional cases, I am aware, but they truly index the situation of thousands of persons.

The Southern newspapers generally have a large advertising patronage, and appear to be prospering quite to the satisfaction of their proprietors. But they are all local in character, and most of them are intensely Southern in tone; while as sources of general information, and particularly of political information, they are beneath notice. The Southern colleges have mostly suspended operations on account of the war. Efforts are making to reopen them, and those in Georgia will probably be in working order by next spring. But that best fruit of modern civilization, so plentiful in the North,—the common-school house,—is almost wholly unknown in the Carolinas and Georgia. I have scarcely seen a dozen in my whole journey, while a trip of the same number of miles in New York and New England would probably show me five hundred. Underneath this one little fact lies the whole cause of the war.

The situation is horrible enough when the full force of this fact is comprehended; yet there is a still lower deep,—there is small desire, even feeble longing, for schools and books and newspapers. The chief end of man seems to have been "to own a nigger." The great majority of the common people know next to nothing, either of history or contemporaneous affairs; either of the principles of government or the acts of their own government; either of the work or thought of the present age; either of the desires or the purposes of nations. They get their information and their opinions mainly from the local office-seekers. It is therefore inevitable that the one should be meagre and the other narrow. It is this general ignorance, and this general indifference to knowledge, that make a Southern trip such wearisome work. You can touch the masses with few of the appeals by which we move our own people. There is very little aspiration for larger life; and, more than that, there is almost no opportunity for its attainment. That education is the stairway to a nobler existence is a fact which they either fail to comprehend or to which they are wholly indifferent.

Where there is such a spirit of caste, where the ruling class has a personal interest in fostering prejudice, where the masses are in such an inert condition, where ignorance so generally prevails, where there is so little ambition for betterment, where life is so hard and material in its tone, it is not strange to find much hatred and contempt. Ignorance is generally cruel and frequently brutal. The political leaders of this people have apparently indoctrinated them with the notion that they are superior to any other class in the country. Hence there is usually very little effort to conceal the prevalent scorn of the Yankee,— this term being applied to the citizen of any Northern State. Any plan of reconstruction is wrong that tends to leave these old leaders in power. A few of them give certain evidence of a change of heart,—by some means save these for the sore and troubled future; but for the others, the men who not only brought on the war, but ruined the mental and moral force of their people before unfurling the banner of Rebellion,—for these there should never any more be place or countenance among honest and humane and patriotic people. When the nation gives them life and a chance for its continuance, it shows all the magnanimity that humanity can in such case afford.

In North Carolina there is a great deal of something that calls itself Unionism; but I know nothing more like the apples of Sodom than most of this North Carolina Unionism. It is a cheat, a will-o'-the-wisp, and any man who trusts it will meet with overthrow. There may be in it the seed of loyalty, but woe to him who mistakes the germ for the ripened fruit.

In all sections of the State I found abundant hatred of some leading or local Secessionist; but how full of promise for the new era of national life is the Unionism which rests only on this foundation?

In South Carolina there is very little pretence of love for the Union, but everywhere a passionate devotion to the State; and the common sentiment holds that man guilty of treason who prefers the United States to South Carolina. There is no occasion to wonder at the admiration of the people for Wade Hampton, for he is the very exemplar of their spirit,—of their proud and narrow and domineering spirit. "It is our duty," he says, in a letter which he has recently addressed to the people of the State,—"it is our duty to support the President of the United States so long as he manifests a disposition to restore all our rights as a sovereign State." That sentence will forever stand as a model of cool arrogance, and yet it is in full accord with the spirit of the South-Carolinians. The war has taught them that the physical force of the nation cannot be resisted, and they will be obedient to the letter of the law; but the whole current of their lives flows in direct antagonism to its spirit.

In Georgia there is something worse than sham Unionism or cold acquiescence in the issue of battle: it is the universally prevalent doctrine of the supremacy of the State. In South Carolina, a few men stood up against the storm, but in Georgia that man is hopelessly dead who doubted or faltered. The common sense of all classes pushes the necessity of allegiance to the State into the domain of morals as well as into that of politics; and he who did not "go with the State" in the Rebellion is held to have committed the unpardonable sin. At Macon I met a man who was one of the leading Unionists in the winter of 1860–61. He told me how he suffered then for his hostility to secession, and yet he added, "I should have considered myself forever disgraced, if I had n't heartily gone with the State when she decided to fight." I believe it is the concurrent testimony of all careful travellers in Georgia, that there is everywhere only cold toleration for the idea of national sovereignty, and but little pride in the strength and glory and renown of the United States of America.

Much is said of the hypocrisy of the South. I found but little of it anywhere. The North-Carolinian calls himself a Unionist, but he makes no special pretence of love for the Union. He desires many favors, but he asks them generally on the ground that he hated the Secessionists. He expects the nation to recognize rare virtue in that hatred, and hopes it may win for his State the restoration of her political rights; but he wears his mask of nationality so lightly that there is no difficulty in removing it. The South-Carolinian demands only something less than he did in the days before the war, but he offers no plea of Unionism as a guaranty for the future. He rests his case on the assumption that he has fully acquiesced in the results of the war, and he honestly believes that he has so acquiesced. His confidence in South Carolina is so supreme that he fails to see how much the conflict meant. He walks by such light as he has, and cannot yet believe that destiny has decreed his State a secondary place in the Union. The Georgian began by believing that Rebellion in the interest of slavery was honorable, and the result of the war has not changed his opinion. He is anxious for readmission to fellowship with New York and Pennsylvania and Connecticut, but he supports his application by little claim of community of interest with other States. His spirit is hard and uncompromising; he demands rights, but does not ask favors; and he is confident that Georgia is fully as important to the United States as they are to Georgia.

The fact that such a large proportion of the offices in the gift of the people of these States have been filled with men who were officers in the Rebel army does not in itself furnish any argument against the good disposition of the people. The sentiment which voluntarily confers honor on a man who has shown personal bravery, who has been plucky and daring and gallant, is one we cannot afford to crush,—it is one of the strong moral forces of a nation, and deserves nurture rather than condemnation. Moreover, in not a few cases these ex-officers are of better will and purpose toward the government than any other men in their respective localities. It may not be pleasant to us to recognize this fact; but I am confident that we shall make sure progress toward securing domestic tranquillity and the general welfare just in proportion as we act upon it.

The other fact, that almost every candidate was defeated who did n't "go with the State" during the war is one of serious import. It indicates a spirit of defiance to the nation, of determined opposition to the principle of national unity. So long as this spirit prevails, we can hope for no sound peace. It will not again marshal armies in the field. Such a thing is utterly beyond the range of possibilities so far as this generation or the next is concerned. A few untamed fire-eaters will bluster, and local politicians will brag, but the leaders are wiser than they were, and the people have had enough of war. But there are things quite as bad as open war; and one of these is a sullen and relentless antagonism to the idea of national sovereignty,—from which will breed passionate devotion to local interests, unending persecution of the freedmen, never-ceasing clamor in behalf of State rights, and continual effort to break away from the solemn obligations of the national debt.

That is the true plan of reconstruction which makes haste very slowly. It does not comport with the character of our government to exact pledges of any State which are not exacted of all. The one sole needful condition is, that each State establish a government whereby all civil rights at least shall be assured in their fullest extent to every citizen. The Union is no Union, unless there is equality of privileges among the States. When Georgia and the Carolinas establish governments republican in fact as well as in form, they will have brought themselves into harmony with the national will, and may justly demand readmission to their former political relations in the Union. It is no time for passion or bitterness, and it does not become our manhood to do anything for revenge. Let us have peace and kindly feeling; yet, that our peace may be no sham or shallow affair, it is painfully essential that we keep these States awhile within national control, in order to aid the few wise and just men therein who are fighting the great fight with stubborn prejudice and hidebound custom. Any plan of reconstruction is wrong which accepts forced submission as genuine loyalty or even as cheerful acquiescence in the national desire and purpose.

Prior to the war we heard continually of the love of the master for his slave, and the love of the slave for his master. There was also much talk to the effect that the negro lived in the midst of pleasant surroundings, and had no desire to change his situation. It was asserted that he delighted in a state of dependence, and throve on the universal favor of the whites. Some of this language we conjectured might be extravagant; but to the single fact that there was universal good-will between the two classes every Southern white person bore evidence. So, too, during my trip through Georgia and the Carolinas they have generally seemed anxious to convince me that the blacks behaved well during the war,—kept at their old tasks, labored cheerfully and faithfully, did not show a disposition to be lawless, and were rarely guilty of acts of violence, even in sections where there were many women and children, and but few white men.

Yet I found everywhere now the most direct antagonism between the two classes. The whites charge generally that the negro is idle and at the bottom of all local disturbance, and credit him with most of the vices and very few of the virtues of humanity. The negroes charge that the whites are revengeful, and intend to cheat the laboring class at every opportunity, and credit them with neither good purposes nor kindly hearts. This present and positive hostility of each class to the other is a fact that will sorely perplex any Northern man travelling in either of these States. One would say, that, if there had formerly been such pleasant relations between them, there ought now to be mutual sympathy and forbearance, instead of mutual distrust and antagonism. One would say, too, that self-interest, the common interest of capital and labor, ought to keep them in harmony; while the fact is, that this very interest appears to put them in an attitude of partial defiance toward each other. I believe the most charitable traveller must come to the conclusion that the professed love of the whites for the blacks was mostly a monstrous sham or a downright false pretence. For myself, I judge that it was nothing less than an arrant humbug.

Individual cases of real attachment to individual servants were doubtless common enough before the war, and an honest observer finds not a few of them even now. But, having seen the present relations of the two classes, I wonder that I or any one else could ever have believed that the common white people, as a class, had any real love for the blacks as a race. Some of the better men are now willing to concede to them the minor rights of humanity, but not one man in five thousand proposes to give them all the rights of men and women, and scarcely one in twenty thousand would invest any of them with the rights of citizenship. To dream that any of these States will voluntarily grant the ballot to the negro during this generation seems to me to qualify yourself for the insane asylum. The plainest of all plain requirements is that the freed negro shall have the right to be heard in the courts; and the fierce and bitter opposition to meeting this requirement gives the sharp and unequivocal lie to all professions of love for him.

The negro is no model of virtue or manliness. He loves idleness, he has little conception of right and wrong, and he is improvident to the last degree of childishness. He is a creature,—as some of our own people will do well to keep carefully in mind,—he is a creature just forcibly released from slavery. The havoc of war has filled his heart with confused longings, and his ears with confused sounds of rights and privileges: it must be the nation's duty, for it cannot be left wholly to his late master, to help him to a clear understanding of those rights and privileges, and also to lay upon him a knowledge of his responsibilities. He is anxious to learn, and is very tractable in respect to minor matters; but we shall need almost infinite patience with him, for he comes very slowly to moral comprehensions.

Going into the States where I went,—and perhaps the fact is also true of the other Southern States,—going into Georgia and the Carolinas, and not keeping in mind the facts of yesterday, any man would almost be justified in concluding that the end and purpose in respect to this poor negro was his extermination. It is proclaimed everywhere that he will not work, that he cannot take care of himself, that he is a nuisance to society, that he lives by stealing, and that he is sure to die in a few months; and, truth to tell, the great body of the people, though one must not say, intentionally, are doing all they well can to make these assertions true. If it is not said that any considerable number wantonly abuse and outrage him, it must be said that they manifest a barbaric indifference to his fate which just as surely drives him on to destruction as open cruelty would.

There are some men and a few women—and perhaps the number of these is greater than we of the North generally suppose— who really desire that the negro should now have his full rights as a human being. With the same proportion of this class of persons in a community of Northern constitution, it might justly be concluded that the whole community would soon join or acquiesce in the effort to secure for him at least a fair share of those rights. Unfortunately, however, in these Southern communities the opinion of such persons cannot have the same weight it would in ours. The spirit of caste, of which I have already spoken, is an element figuring largely against them in any contest involving principle,—an element of whose practical workings we know very little. The walls between individuals and classes are so high and broad that the men and women who recognize the negro's rights and privileges as a freeman are almost as far from the masses as we of the North are. Moreover, that any opinion savors of the "Yankee"—in other words, is new to the South—is a fact that even prevents its consideration by the great body of the people. Their inherent antagonism to everything from the North—an antagonism fostered and cunningly cultured for half a century by the politicians in the interest of slavery—is something that no traveller can photograph, that no Northern man can understand, till he sees it with his own eyes, hears it with his own ears, and feels it by his own consciousness. That the full freedom of the negroes would be acknowledged at once is something we had no warrant for expecting. The old masters grant them nothing, except at the requirement of the nation, as a military or a political necessity; and any plan of reconstruction is wrong which proposes to at once or in the immediate future substitute free-will for this necessity.

Three fourths of the people assume that the negro will not labor except on compulsion; and the whole struggle between the whites on the one hand and the blacks on the other hand is a struggle for and against compulsion. The negro insists, very blindly perhaps, that he shall be free to come and go when he pleases; the white insists that he shall only come and go at the pleasure of his employer. The whites seem wholly unable to comprehend that freedom for the negro means the same thing as freedom for them. They readily enough admit that the government has made him free, but appear to believe that they still have the right to exercise over him the old control. It is partly their misfortune, and not wholly their fault, that they cannot understand the national intent as expressed in the Emancipation Proclamation and the Constitutional Amendment. I did not anywhere find a man who could see that laws should be applicable to all persons alike; and hence even the best men hold that each State must have a negro code. They acknowledge the overthrow of the special servitude of man to man, but seek through these codes to establish the general servitude of man to the Commonwealth. I had much talk with intelligent gentlemen in various sections, and particularly with such as I met during the Conventions at Columbia and Milledgeville, upon this subject, and found such a state of feeling as warrants little hope that the present generation of negroes will see the day in which their race shall be amenable only to such laws as apply to the whites.

I think the freedmen divide themselves into four classes: one fourth recognizing very clearly the necessity of work, and going about it with cheerful diligence and wise forethought; one fourth comprehending that there must be labor, but needing considerable encouragement to follow it steadily; one fourth preferring idleness, but not specially averse to doing some job work about the towns and cities; and one fourth avoiding labor as much as possible, and living by voluntary charity, persistent begging, or systematic pilfering. It is true that thousands of the aggregate body of this people appear to have hoped, and perhaps believed, that freedom meant idleness; true, too, that thousands are drifting about the country or loafing about the centres of population in a state of vagabondage. Yet of the hundreds with whom I talked, I found less than a score who seemed beyond hope of reformation. It is a cruel slander to say that the race will not work except on compulsion. I made much inquiry wherever I went, of great numbers of planters and other employers, and found but very few cases in which it appeared that they had refused to labor reasonably well when fairly treated and justly paid. Grudgingly admitted to any of the natural rights of man, despised alike by Unionists and Secessionists, wantonly outraged by many and meanly cheated by more of the old planters, receiving a hundred cuffs for one helping hand and a thousand curses for one kindly word, they bear themselves toward their former masters very much as white men and women would under the same circumstances. True, by such deportment they unquestionably harm themselves; but consider of how little value life is from their stand-point. They grope in the darkness of this transition period, and rarely find any sure stay for the weary arm and the fainting heart. Their souls are filled with a great but vague longing for freedom; they battle blindly with fate and circumstance for the unseen and uncomprehended, and seem to find every man's hand raised against them either for blows or reproaches. What wonder that they fill the land with restlessness!

However unfavorable this exhibit of the negroes in respect to labor may appear, it is quite as good as can be made for the whites. I everywhere found a condition of affairs in this regard that astounded me. Idleness, not occupation, seemed the normal state. It is the boast of men and women alike, that they have never done an hour's work. The public mind is thoroughly debauched, and the general conscience is lifeless as the grave. I met hundreds of hale and vigorous young men who unblushingly owned to me that they had not earned a penny since the war closed. Nine tenths of the people must be taught that labor is even not debasing. It was pitiful enough to find so much idleness, but it was more pitiful to observe that it was likely to continue indefinitely. The war will not have borne proper fruit if our peace does not speedily bring respect for labor as well as respect for man. When we have secured one of these things, we shall have gone far toward securing the other; and when we have secured both, then, indeed, shall we have noble cause for glorying in our country,—true warrant for exulting that our flag floats over no slave.

Meantime, while we patiently and helpfully wait for the day in which

> "All men's good shall
> Be each man's rule, and Universal Peace
> Lie like a shaft of light across the land,"

there are at least five things for the nation to do: make haste slowly in the work of reconstruction; temper justice with mercy, but see to it that justice is not overborne; keep military control of these lately rebellious States till they guarantee a republican form of government; scrutinize carefully the personal fitness of the men chosen therefrom as representatives in the Congress of the United States; and sustain therein some agency that shall stand between the whites and the blacks and aid each class in coming to a proper understanding of its privileges and responsibilities.

Carl Schurz: from Report on the Condition of the South

THAT THE result of the free labor experiment made under circumstances so extremely unfavorable should at once be a perfect success, no reasonable person would expect. Nevertheless, a large majority of the southern men with whom I came into contact announced their opinions with so positive an assurance as to produce the impression that their minds were fully made up. In at least nineteen cases of twenty the reply I received to my inquiry about their views on the new system was uniformly this: "You cannot make the negro work without physical compulsion." I heard this hundreds of times, heard it wherever I went, heard it in nearly the same words from so many different persons, that at last I came to the conclusion that this is the prevailing sentiment among the southern people. There are exceptions to this rule, but, as far as my information extends, far from enough to affect the rule. In the accompanying documents you will find an abundance of proof in support of this statement. There is hardly a paper relative to the negro question annexed to this report which does not, in some direct or indirect way, corroborate it.

Unfortunately the disorders necessarily growing out of the transition state continually furnished food for argument. I found but few people who were willing to make due allowance for the adverse influence of exceptional circumstances. By a large majority of those I came in contact with, and they mostly belonged to the more intelligent class, every irregularity that occurred was directly charged against the system of free labor. If negroes walked away from the plantations, it was conclusive proof of the incorrigible instability of the negro, and the impracticability of free negro labor. If some individual negroes violated the terms of their contract, it proved unanswerably that no negro had, or ever would have, a just conception of the binding force of a contract, and that this system of free negro labor was bound to be a failure. If some negroes shirked, or did not perform their task with sufficient alacrity, it was produced as irrefutable evidence to show that physical compulsion was actually indispensable to make the negro work. If negroes, idlers or refugees crawling about the towns, applied to the authorities for subsistence, it was quoted as incontestably establishing the point that the negro was too improvident to take care of himself, and must necessarily be consigned to the care of a master. I heard a Georgia planter argue most seriously that one of his negroes had shown himself certainly unfit for freedom because he impudently refused to submit to a whipping. I frequently went into an argument with those putting forth such general assertions, quoting instances in which negro laborers were working faithfully, and to the entire satisfaction of their employers, as the employers themselves had informed me. In a majority of cases the reply was that we northern people did not understand the negro, but that they (the southerners) did; that as to the particular instances I quoted I was probably mistaken; that I had not closely investigated the cases, or had been deceived by my informants; that they *knew* the negro would not work without compulsion, and that nobody could make them believe he would. Arguments like these naturally finished such discussions. It frequently struck me that persons who conversed about every other subject calmly and sensibly would lose their temper as soon as the negro question was touched.

———————

The south needs capital. But capital is notoriously timid and averse to risk itself, not only where there actually is trouble, but where there is serious and continual danger of trouble. Capitalists will be apt to consider—and they are by no means wrong in doing so—that no safe investments can be made in the south as long as southern society is liable to be convulsed by anarchical disorders. No greater encouragement can, therefore, be given to capital to transfer itself to the south than the assurance that the government will continue to control the development of the new social system in the late rebel States until such dangers are averted by a final settlement of things upon a thorough free-labor basis.

How long the national government should continue that

control depends upon contingencies. It ought to cease as soon as its objects are attained; and its objects will be attained sooner and with less difficulty if nobody is permitted to indulge in the delusion that it will cease *before* they are attained. This is one of the cases in which a determined policy can accomplish much, while a halfway policy is liable to spoil things already accomplished. The continuance of the national control in the south, although it may be for a short period only, will cause some inconvenience and expense; but if thereby destructive collisions and anarchical disorders can be prevented, justice secured to all men, and the return of peace and prosperity to all parts of this country hastened, it will be a paying investment. For the future of the republic, it is far less important that this business of reconstruction be done quickly than that it be well done. The matter well taken in hand, there is reason for hope that it will be well done, and quickly too. In days like these great changes are apt to operate themselves rapidly. At present the southern people assume that free negro labor will not work, and therefore they are not inclined to give it a fair trial. As soon as they find out that they must give it a fair trial, and that their whole future power and prosperity depend upon its success, they will also find out that it will work, at least far better than they have anticipated. Then their hostility to it will gradually disappear. This great result accomplished, posterity will not find fault with this administration for having delayed complete "reconstruction" one, two, or more years.

Although I am not called upon to discuss in this report the constitutional aspects of this question, I may be pardoned for one remark. The interference of the national government in the local concerns of the States lately in rebellion is argued against by many as inconsistent with the spirit of our federal institutions. Nothing is more foreign to my ways of thinking in political matters than a fondness for centralization or military government. Nobody can value the blessings of local self-government more highly than I do. But we are living under exceptional circumstances which require us, above all, to look at things from a practical point of view; and I believe it will prove far more dangerous for the integrity of local self-government if the national control in the south be discontinued—while by discontinuing it too soon, it may be rendered necessary again in the future—than if it be continued, when by continuing it but a limited time all such future necessity may be obviated. At present these acts of interference are but a part of that exceptional policy brought forth by the necessities into which the rebellion has plunged us. Although there will be some modifications in the relations between the States and the national government, yet these acts of direct interference in the details of State concerns will pass away with the exceptional circumstances which called them forth. But if the social revolution in the south be now abandoned in an unfinished state, and at some future period produce events provoking new and repeated acts of direct practical interference—and the contingency would by no means be unlikely to arise—such new and repeated acts would not pass over without most seriously affecting the political organism of the republic.

I may sum up all I have said in a few words. If nothing were necessary but to restore the machinery of government in the States lately in rebellion in point of form, the movements made to that end by the people of the south might be considered satisfactory. But if it is required that the southern people should also accommodate themselves to the results of the war in point of spirit, those movements fall far short of what must be insisted upon.

The loyalty of the masses and most of the leaders of the southern people, consists in submission to necessity. There is, except in individual instances, an entire absence of that national spirit which forms the basis of true loyalty and patriotism.

The emancipation of the slaves is submitted to only in so far as chattel slavery in the old form could not be kept up. But although the freedman is no longer considered the property of the individual master, he is considered the slave of society, and all independent State legislation will share the tendency to make him such. The ordinances abolishing slavery passed by the conventions under the pressure of circumstances, will not be looked upon as barring the establishment of a new form of servitude.

Practical attempts on the part of the southern people to deprive the negro of his rights as a freeman may result in bloody collisions, and will certainly plunge southern society into restless fluctuations and anarchical confusion. Such evils can be prevented only by continuing the control of the national government in the States lately in rebellion until free labor is fully developed and firmly established, and the advantages and blessings of the new order of things have disclosed themselves. This desirable result will be hastened by a firm declaration on the part of the government, that national control in the south will not cease until such results are secured. Only in this way can that security be established in the south which will render numerous immigration possible, and such immigration would materially aid a favorable development of things.

The solution of the problem would be very much facilitated by enabling all the loyal and free-labor elements in the south to exercise a healthy influence upon legislation. It will hardly be possible to secure the freedman against oppressive class legislation and private persecution, unless he be endowed with a certain measure of political power.

As to the future peace and harmony of the Union, it is of the highest importance that the people lately in rebellion be not permitted to build up another "peculiar institution" whose spirit is in conflict with the fundamental principles of our political system; for as long as they cherish interests peculiar to them in preference to those they have in common with the rest of the American people, their loyalty to the Union will always be uncertain.

I desire not to be understood as saying that there are no well-meaning men among those who were compromised in the rebellion. There are many, but neither their number nor their influence is strong enough to control the manifest tendency of the popular spirit. There are great reasons for hope that a determined policy on the part of the national government will produce innumerable and valuable conversions. This consideration counsels lenity as to persons, such as is demanded by the humane and enlightened spirit of our times, and vigor and firmness in the carrying out of principles, such as is demanded by the national sense of justice and the exigencies of our situation.

December 18, 1865

Ulysses S. Grant to Andrew Johnson

HEADQUARTERS ARMIES OF THE UNITED STATES,
Washington, D.C., December 18, 1865

SIR:

In reply to your note of the 16th instant, requesting a report from me giving such information as I may be possessed of coming within the scope of the inquiries made by the Senate of the United States in their resolution of the 12th instant, I have the honor to submit the following:

With your approval, and also that of the honorable Secretary of War, I left Washington city on the 27th of last month for the purpose of making a tour of inspection through some of the southern States, or States lately in rebellion, and to see what changes were necessary to be made in the disposition of the military forces of the country; how these forces could be reduced and expenses curtailed, &c.; and to learn, as far as possible, the feelings and intentions of the citizens of those States towards the general government.

The State of Virginia being so accessible to Washington city, and information from this quarter, therefore, being readily obtained, I hastened through the State without conversing or meeting with any of its citizens. In Raleigh, North Carolina, I spent one day; in Charleston, South Carolina, two days; Savannah and Augusta, Georgia, each one day. Both in travelling and whilst stopping I saw much and conversed freely with the citizens of those States as well as with officers of the army who have been stationed among them. The following are the conclusions come to by me.

I am satisfied that the mass of thinking men of the south accept the present situation of affairs in good faith. The questions which have heretofore divided the sentiment of the people of the two sections—slavery and State rights, or the right of a State to secede from the Union—they regard as having been settled forever by the highest tribunal—arms—that man can resort to. I was pleased to learn from the leading men whom I met that they not only accepted the decision arrived at as final, but, now that the smoke of battle has cleared away and time has been given for reflection, that this decision has been a fortunate one for the whole country, they receiving like benefits from it with those who opposed them in the field and in council.

Four years of war, during which law was executed only at the point of the bayonet throughout the States in rebellion, have left the people possibly in a condition not to yield that ready obedience to civil authority the American people have generally been in the habit of yielding. This would render the presence of small garrisons throughout those States necessary until such time as labor returns to its proper channel, and civil authority is fully established. I did not meet any one, either those holding places under the government or citizens of the southern States, who think it practicable to withdraw the military from the south at present. The white and the black mutually require the protection of the general government.

There is such universal acquiescence in the authority of the general government throughout the portions of country visited by me, that the mere presence of a military force, without regard to numbers, is sufficient to maintain order. The good of the country, and economy, require that the force kept in the interior, where there are many freedmen, (elsewhere in the southern States than at forts upon the seacoast no force is necessary,) should all be white troops. The reasons for this are obvious without mentioning many of them. The presence of black troops, lately slaves, demoralizes labor, both by their advice and by furnishing in their camps a resort for the freedmen for long distances around. White troops generally excite no opposition, and therefore a small number of them can maintain order in a given district. Colored troops must be kept in bodies sufficient to defend themselves. It is not the thinking man who would use violence towards any class of troops sent among them by the general government, but the ignorant in some places might; and the late slave seems to be imbued with the idea that the property of his late master should, by right, belong to him, or at least should have no protection from the colored soldier. There is danger of collisions being brought on by such causes.

My observations lead me to the conclusion that the citizens

of the southern States are anxious to return to self-government, within the Union, as soon as possible; that whilst reconstructing they want and require protection from the government; that they are in earnest in wishing to do what they think is required by the government, not humiliating to them as citizens, and that if such a course were pointed out they would pursue it in good faith. It is to be regretted that there cannot be a greater commingling, at this time, between the citizens of the two sections, and particularly of those intrusted with the law-making power.

I did not give the operations of the Freedmen's Bureau that attention I would have done if more time had been at my disposal. Conversations on the subject, however, with officers connected with the bureau, lead me to think that, in some of the States, its affairs have not been conducted with good judgment or economy, and that the belief, widely spread among the freedmen of the southern States, that the lands of their former owners will, at least in part, be divided among them, has come from the agents of this bureau. This belief is seriously interfering with the willingness of the freedmen to make contracts for the coming year. In some form the Freedmen's Bureau is an absolute necessity until civil law is established and enforced, securing to the freedmen their rights and full protection. At present, however, it is independent of the military establishment of the country, and seems to be operated by the different agents of the bureau according to their individual notions. Everywhere General Howard, the able head of the bureau, made friends by the just and fair instructions and advice he gave; but the complaint in South Carolina was that when he left, things went on as before. Many, perhaps the majority, of the agents of the Freedmen's Bureau advise the freedmen that by their own industry they must expect to live. To this end they endeavor to secure employment for them, and to see that both contracting parties comply with their engagements. In some instances, I am sorry to say, the freedman's mind does not seem to be disabused of the idea that a freedman has the right to live without care or provision for the future. The effect of the belief in division of lands is idleness and accumulation in camps, towns, and cities. In such cases I think it will be found that vice and disease will tend to the extermination or great reduction of the colored race. It cannot be expected that the opinions held by men at the south for years can be changed in a day, and therefore the freedmen require, for a few years, not only laws to protect them, but the fostering care of those who will give them good counsel, and on whom they rely.

The Freedmen's Bureau being separated from the military establishment of the country, requires all the expense of a separate organization. One does not necessarily know what the other is doing or what orders they are acting under. It seems to me this could be corrected by regarding every officer on duty with troops in the southern States as an agent of the Freedmen's Bureau, and then have all orders from the head of the bureau sent through department commanders. This would create a responsibility that would secure uniformity of action throughout all the south; would insure the orders and instructions from the head of the bureau being carried out, and would relieve from duty and pay a large number of employees of the government.

I have the honor to be, very respectfully,
your obedient servant,
U. S. Grant, Lieutenant General.

His Excellency Andrew Johnson,
President of the United States.

Lewis Hayden: from Caste among Masons

I WILL NOW speak of the character of the people—their seeming hopes and prospects. I regret to say that at Richmond they did not present so hopeful an aspect, so intellectual nor so dignified a character, as I found among the people of Petersburg and Charleston; for while at Richmond there seemed to be jealousies and bickerings, so that in the words of the Scriptures, like Ishmael of old, their hands are against every man, and every man's hand against them;—at Petersburg they had already formed land associations, building companies, &c.; and they appeared to be united and harmonious, under the leadership of such men as Eilbech, Scott, Colston, and others. The large brick building in which the Lodge is held, a four story building, is owned by themselves; while, at Richmond, we obtained a room in which to form the Lodge with great difficulty. I found in Charleston, S.C., a still higher class of people, even, than at Petersburg, as regards general education, the mechanical arts, and all the elements which tend to make a first-class society. In proof of this, I have brought with me a list of applications for initiations to their Lodge, the signers of which will compare favorably with the members of any Masonic Lodge, either white or black, in the United States—whether we take into consideration proficiency in the mechanical arts, or social and mental endowments. Of the people of Charleston, whether in the Order or not, I am constrained to say, that the many acts of kindness and the generous hospitality received at their hands, during my sojourn among them, have made an impression upon my heart, which neither time nor changing fortune can ever efface. I regret to add, that in each of the places I visited, there is evidently a deep and unalterable purpose in the hearts of the old oppressors to blast, or at least to crush out, the rising hopes and dawning prospects of their late bondmen. I rejoice, on the other hand, to be able to say that there is among our people that unwavering trust in God, and that abiding faith in the justice of their cause, which enable them to look to the future, not only with hope and confidence, but with exultation, feeling that—

> "Truth, crushed to earth, shall rise again;
> The eternal years of God are hers;
> But Error wounded, writhes in pain,
> And dies among his worshippers."

This, let me be understood, is the feeling of our people in the cities. With the dwellers in the country, it is different. Away from the cities and the seaboard, the condition of the colored man is deplorable enough to-day. Lacking the intelligence and opportunities of the freemen in the city,—never having enjoyed the same advantages,—he is still almost completely at the mercy of his old master. If the latter treats him kindly, it is well; but if ill-used and oppressed, in nine cases out of ten he has no remedy. There is no power under heaven to which he can appeal for redress. The United-States army can do nothing for him, for it has gone. If an agent of the Freedmen's Bureau happens along, no complaint can reach his ear till it has been forestalled by the story of the master and his interested attentions. The power of organized and concentrated effort, which may be available in the city, is denied to him. What then can he do? On what possible loop can he hang one solitary hope? God help him! for Andrew Johnson will not,—although he was to be our Moses to lead us to liberty and equality; instead of which, I fear he will prove to be the Pharaoh of our day. In this we ought not to be deceived; for it is plain that he who undertakes to be the friend of the black man in this land of negro haters, will not have the negro haters all over the country singing praises to him, as you see they are now doing to our said Moses; so much so, that the astonished people stand off amazed, and know not what to do or to say. First they look at him; then at Gettysburg; then at Pittsburg Landing; then at Milliken's Bend; then at Andersonville; and then at a murdered President. With all these things before them, and ere they have had time for reflection, they are startled by the perpetration of some new act of high-handed infidelity, which well serves his purpose to hide some former wrong. As an evidence of some of his new acts of infidelity, they beheld him, within three days after the murder of our ever-to-be-lamented President, Abraham

Lincoln, standing up before God, and in the presence of an outraged nation, solemnly declaring that he would make treason a crime, and punish the traitor. Has he done either? No. Then, what has he done? you ask. My answer is, that he has done much to make treason a virtue, by elevating traitors to offices of honor and trust,—to be paid for their services in such offices by the taxing of the widows and orphans, whose fathers and husbands their own hands have slain. By these acts he has honored and given new license to traitors to perpetrate outrages and crimes. Humanity revolts and refuses to believe that man, made in the image of God, could so debase and belie his nature as to be guilty of such wrong against his fellow-man. But did they not murder their slaves with impunity while they had a moneyed interest in them? If so, will they not slaughter the freedmen in whom they have no such interest, with such an one at the head of the nation fostering and honoring traitors? Were it not that we are forbidden to speak against those in authority, I should say, the Lord rebuke thee and deliver us from such a Moses.

December 27, 1865

Harriet Jacobs to The Freedman

SAVANNAH, Jan. 9, 1866.

From Harriet Jacobs.

Your letter with commission for teachers received, also three cases. At present I am well provided with clothing. The shoes have been the greatest comfort to the poor, shivering people. Just now it is bitter cold weather for this climate; Christmas day the thermometer was 82°, yesterday it was 31°, and it is freezing to-day. The change is so sudden the people feel it very much. They are turning most of the people from the plantations. It is a pitiful sight to go down to the Bluff where the poor creatures are landed. You will see crowds of them huddled around a few burning sticks, so ragged and filthy they scarce look like human beings. Some of these people are from Florida, some from Alabama, some from the upper country in South Carolina. They were carried to these places that they might be out of the reach of the Union army. Some of the river plantations that I visit are sending off all that will not make yearly contracts. The old men and women are not considered. Some of the conditions of these contracts are very unjust. They are not allowed to have a boat or musket. They are not allowed to own a horse, cow, or pig. Many of them already own them, but must sell them if they remain on the plantations. I was on one plantation where the master owns three hundred acres of rice land. He wants to employ thirty hands; make the contract for the year, at ten dollars per month; gives them rations and four dollars a month out of their wages. When the crop is laid by, the master has two-thirds, the laborer has one-third, *deducting the pay for the rations.* Many of the freed people are leaving this place. There was an interesting school established here, but it has been broken up.

HARRIET JACOBS.

The Freedman, February 1866

SAVANNAH, Jan. 19th, 1866.

From Harriet Jacobs.

We have a great deal to do here. In every direction the colored people are being turned from the plantations when unwilling to comply with the hard proposals of the planters. The contracts proposed are sometimes very severe and unjust. The freedmen are not allowed to hire land or work it on shares, but must work under their former overseers. They cannot own a horse, cow, pigs, or poultry, nor keep a boat; and they cannot leave the plantation without permission. If a friend calls to see them a fine is imposed of one dollar, and a second offence breaks the contract. They work for ten dollars and rations. They are very unwilling to be placed under the overseers who formerly treated them with cruelty. I have this week visited several plantations on both the Georgia and Carolina sides of the river. In these places the people are expecting the return of their old masters. Poor things! some are excited; others so dispirited that they cannot work. They say, "I can't eat, I can't sleep, for tinking of de hard time coming on me again; my heart 'pears to be all de time quiverin'; I knows 'tis trouble." I wrote in another letter of the poor people who are daily landing at the wharf to be scattered as they can find homes. The Bureau only assists them in making contracts.

A few days since I found a company on Ham Island in a starving condition. The children were crying for bread. I had thirteen dollars belonging to the Society, six dollars of which I spent at the Commissary to relieve their pressing needs. There were fifty women, fifty-six children, and twelve men. Among these I divided forty-six lbs. of salt pork and beef, twenty-five loaves of bread, and some salt. One old woman, too decrepid to walk, crawled to me to beg for food. The larger portion of the men were in the city, seeking work. The case must be presented to Colonel Sickles.

HARRIET JACOBS.

On the rice plantations that I have visited, the people are badly off. God pity them. I lose sight of their rags when I see how degraded and hard-hearted slavery has made them.

The Freedman, February 1866

Marcus S. Hopkins to James Johnson

Prince Wm Co. Va Brentsville Jan'y. 15″ 1866.
Sir: I have the honor to inform you that a dastardly outrage was committed in this place yesterday, (Sunday,) within
sight of my office, the circumstances of which are as follows.
A freedman named James Cook was conceived to be "impudent," by a white man named John Cornwell; whereupon the
whiteman cursed him and threatened him. The freedman, being alarmed, started away, and was followed and threatened
with "you d——d black yankee son of a b——h I will kill you";
and was fired upon with a pistol, the ball passing through his
clothes. He was then caught by the white man, and beaten
with the but of a revolver, and dragged to the door of the
Jail near where the affair occurred, where he was loosened and
escaped. He came to me soon after, bleeding from a deep cut
over the eye, and reported the above, which was substantiated
to me as fact by several witnesses. I have heard both sides of
the case fully, and the only charge that is brought against the
freedman is "impudence"; and while being pounced upon as a
"d——d Yankee," and cursed and called all manner of names,
this "impudence" consisted in the sole offense of saying, that
he had been in the union army and was proud of it. *No other
"impudence" was charged against him.* I know the freedman
well, and know him to be uncommonly intelligent, inoffensive,
and respectful. He is an old grey-headed man, and has been a
slave of the commonwealth attorney of this co. a long time. He
has the reputation I have given him among the citizens here,
and has rented a farm near here for the coming season. As an
evidence of his pacific disposition, he had a revolver which was
sold him by the Government, on his discharge from the army,
which he did not draw, or threaten to use during the assault;
choosing, in this instance at least, to suffer wrong rather than
to do wrong.

To show you the state of feeling here among *many* people,
(not all) in regard to such a transaction, Dr. C. H. Lambert,

the practicing physician of this place, followed the freedman to me, and said, that "Subdued and miserable as we are, we will not allow niggers to come among us and brag about having been in the yankee army. It is as much as we can do to tolerate it in white men." He thought "It would be a good lesson to the niggers" &c. &c. I have heard many similar, and some more violent remarks, on this, and other subjects connected with the freedmen. I would not convey the impression however, that there is the slightest danger to any *white* man, from these vile and cowardly devils. But where there are enough of them together, they glory in the conquest of a "nigger." They hold an insane malice against the freedman, from which he must be protected, or he is worse off than when he was a slave.

Marcus. S. Hopkins.

Andrew Johnson and Frederick Douglass: An Exchange
and
Reply of the Colored Delegation to President Johnson

Mr. George T. Downing then addressed the President as follows:

We present ourselves to your Excellency, to make known with pleasure the respect which we are glad to cherish for you—a respect which is your due, as our Chief Magistrate. It is our desire for you to know that we come feeling that we are friends meeting a friend. We should, however, have manifested our friendship by not coming to further tax your already much burdened and valuable time; but we have another object in calling. We are in a passage to equality before the law. God hath made it by opening a Red Sea. We would have your assistance through the same. We come to you in the name of the colored people of the United States. We are delegated to come by some who have unjustly worn iron manacles on their bodies—by some whose minds have been manacled by class legislation in States called free. The colored people of the States of Illinois, Wisconsin, Alabama, Mississippi, Florida, South Carolina, North Carolina, Virginia, Maryland, Pennsylvania, New York, New England States, and District of Columbia have specially delegated us to come.

Our coming is a marked circumstance, noting determined hope that we are not satisfied with an amendment prohibiting slavery, but that we wish it enforced with appropriate legislation. This is our desire. We ask for it intelligently, with the knowledge and conviction that the fathers of the Revolution intended freedom for every American; that they should be protected in their rights as citizens, and be equal before the law. We are Americans, native born Americans. We are citizens, we are glad to have it known to the world that you bear no doubtful record on this point. On this fact, and with confidence in the triumph of justice we base our hope. We see no recognition of color or race in the organic law of the land. It knows no privileged class, and therefore we cherish the hope that we may be fully enfranchised, not only here in this District, but throughout the land. We respectfully submit that rendering anything less than this will be rendering to us less than our just due; that granting anything less than our full rights will be a disregard of our just rights and of due respect for our feelings. If the powers that be do so it will be used as a license, as it were, or an apology for any community, or for individuals thus disposed, to outrage our rights and feelings. It has been shown in the present war that the Government may justly reach its strong arm into States, and demand for them, from those who owe it allegiance, their assistance and support. May it not reach out a like arm to secure and protect its subjects upon whom it has a claim?

Following upon Mr. Downing, Mr. Fred. Douglass advanced and addressed the President, saying:

Mr. President, we are not here to enlighten you, sir, as to your duties as the Chief Magistrate of this Republic, but to show our respect, and to present in brief the claims of our race to your favorable consideration. In the order of Divine Providence you are placed in a position where you have the power to save or destroy us, to bless or blast us. I mean our whole race. Your noble and humane predecessor placed in our hands the sword to assist in saving the nation, and we do hope that you, his able successor, will favorably regard the placing in our hands the ballot with which to save ourselves.

We shall submit no argument on that point. The fact that we are the subjects of Government, and subject to taxation, subject to volunteer in the service of the country, subject to being drafted, subject to bear the burdens of the State, makes it not improper that we should ask to share in the privileges of this condition.

I have no speech to make on this occasion. I simply submit these observations as a limited expression of the views and feelings of the delegation with which I have come.

RESPONSE OF THE PRESIDENT

In reply to some of your inquiries, not to make a speech about this thing, for it is always best to talk plainly and distinctly about such matters, I will say that if I have not given evidence in my course that I am a friend of humanity, and to that portion of it which constitutes the colored population, I can give no evidence here. Everything that I have had, both as regards life and property, has been perilled in that cause, and I feel and think that I understand—not to be egotistic—what should be the true direction of this question, and what course of policy would result in the melioration and ultimate elevation, not only of the colored, but of the great mass of the people of the United States. I say that if I have not given evidence that I am a friend of humanity, and especially the friend of the colored man, in my past conduct, there is nothing that I can now do that would. I repeat, all that I possessed, life, liberty, and property, have been put up in connection with that question; when I had every inducement held out to take the other course, by adopting which I would have accomplished perhaps all that the most ambitious might have desired. If I know myself, and the feelings of my own heart, they have been for the colored man. I have owned slaves and bought slaves, but I never sold one. I might say, however, that practically, so far as my connection with slaves has gone, I have been their slave instead of their being mine. Some have even followed me here, while others are occupying and enjoying my property with my consent. For the colored race my means, my time, my all has been perilled; and now at this late day, after giving evidence that is tangible, that is practical, I am free to say to you that I do not like to be arraigned by some who can get up handsomely rounded periods and deal in rhetoric, and talk about abstract ideas of liberty, who never perilled life, liberty, or property. This kind of theoretical, hollow, unpractical friendship amounts to but very little. While I say that I am a friend of the colored man, I do not want to adopt a policy that I believe will end in a contest between the races, which if persisted in will result in the extermination of one or the other. God forbid that I should be engaged in such a work!

Now, it is always best to talk about things practically and in a common sense way. Yes, I have said, and I repeat here, that if the colored man in the United States could find no other Moses, or any Moses that would be more able and efficient than myself, I would be his Moses to lead him from bondage to freedom; that I would pass him from a land where he had lived in slavery to a land (if it were in our reach) of freedom. Yes, I would be willing to pass with him through the Red sea to the Land of Promise—to the land of liberty; but I am not willing, under either circumstance, to adopt a policy which I believe will only result in the sacrifice of his life and the shedding of his blood. I think I know what I say. I feel what I say; and I feel well assured that if the policy urged by some be persisted in, it will result in great injury to the white as well as to the colored man. There is a great deal of talk about the sword in one hand accomplishing an end, and the ballot accomplishing another at the ballot-box.

These things all do very well, and sometimes have forcible application. We talk about justice; we talk about right; we say that the white man has been in the wrong in keeping the black man in slavery as long as he has. That is all true. Again, we talk about the Declaration of Independence and equality before the law. You understand all that, and know how to appreciate it. But, now, let us look each other in the face; let us go to the great mass of colored men throughout the slave States; let us take the condition in which they are at the present time—and it is bad enough, we all know—and suppose, by some magic touch you could say to every one, "You shall vote to-morrow," how much would that ameliorate their condition at this time?

Now, let us get closer up to this subject, and talk about it. [The President here approached very near to Mr. Douglass.] What relation has the colored man and the white man here-tofore occupied in the South? I opposed slavery upon two grounds. First, it was a great monopoly, enabling those who controlled and owned it to constitute an aristocracy, enabling the few to derive great profits and rule the many with an iron rod, as it were. And this is one great objection to it in a gov-ernment, it being a monopoly. I was opposed to it secondly upon the abstract principle of slavery. Hence, in getting clear of a monopoly, we are getting clear of slavery at the same time. So you see there were two right ends accomplished in the ac-complishment of the one.

Mr. Douglass. Mr. President, do you wish—

The President. I am not quite through yet.

Slavery has been abolished, a great national guarantee has been given, one that cannot be revoked. I was getting at the relation that subsisted between the white man and the colored men. A very small proportion of white persons compared with the whole number of such owned the colored people of the South. I might instance the State of Tennessee in illustration. There were there twenty-seven non-slaveholders to one slaveholder, and yet the slave power controlled the State. Let us talk about this matter as it is. Although the colored man was in slavery there, and owned as property in the sense and in the language of that locality and of that community, yet, in comparing his condition, and his position there with the non-slaveholder, he usually estimated his importance just in proportion to the number of slaves that his master owned, with the non-slaveholder.

Have you ever lived upon a plantation?

Mr. Douglass. I have, your Excellency.

The President. When you would look over and see a man who had a large family, struggling hard upon a poor piece of land, you thought a great deal less of him than you did of your own master's negro, didn't you?

Mr. Douglass. Not I!

The President. Well, I know such was the case with a large number of you in those sections. Where such is the case we know there is an enmity, we know there is a hate. The poor white man, on the other hand, was opposed to the slave and his master; for the colored man and his master, combined, kept him in slavery, by depriving him of a fair participation in the labor and productions of the rich land of the country.

Don't you know that a colored man, in going to hunt a master (as they call it) for the next year, preferred hiring to a man who owned slaves rather than to a man who did not? I know the fact, at all events. They did not consider it quite as respectable to hire to a man who did not own negroes as to one who did.

Mr. Douglass. Because he wouldn't be treated as well.

The President. Then that is another argument in favor of what I am going to say. It shows that the colored man appreciated the slave owner more highly than he did the man who didn't own slaves. Hence the enmity between the colored man and the non-slaveholders. The white man was permitted to vote before—Government was derived from him. He is a part and parcel of the political machinery.

Now by the rebellion or revolution—and when you come back to the objects of this war, you find that the abolition of slavery was not one of the objects; Congress and the President himself declared that it was waged on our part in order to suppress the rebellion—the abolition of slavery has come as an incident to the suppression of a great rebellion—as an incident, and as an incident we should give it the proper direction.

The colored man went into this rebellion a slave; by the operation of the rebellion he came out a freedman—equal to a freeman in any other portion of the country. Then there is a great deal done for him on this point. The non-slaveholder who was forced into the rebellion, who was as loyal as those that lived beyond the limits of the State, but who was carried into it, and his property, and in a number of instances, the lives of such were sacrificed, and he who has survived has come out of it with nothing gained but a great deal lost.

Now, upon the principle of justice, should they be placed in a condition different from what they were before? On the one hand, one has gained a great deal; on the other hand, one has lost a great deal, and, in a political point of view, scarcely stands where he did before.

Now, we are talking about where we are going to begin. We have got at the hate that existed between the two races. The query comes up whether these two races, situated as they were before, without preparation, without time for passion and excitement to be appeased, and without time for the slightest improvement, whether the one should be turned loose upon the other, and be thrown together at the ballot-box with this enmity and hate existing between them. The query comes up right there, whether we don't commence a war of races. I think I understand this thing, and especially is this the case when you force it upon a people without their consent.

You have spoken about government. Where is power derived from? We say it is derived from the people. Let us take it so and refer to the District of Columbia by way of illustration. Suppose, for instance, here, in this political community, which, to a certain extent must have government, must have laws, and putting it now upon the broadest basis you can put it—take into consideration the relation which the white has heretofore borne to the colored race—is it proper to force upon this community, without their consent, the elective franchise, without regard to color, making it universal?

Now, where do you begin? Government must have a controlling power; must have a lodgment. For instance, suppose Congress should pass a law authorizing an election to be held at which all over twenty-one years of age, without regard to color, should be allowed to vote, and a majority should decide at such election that the elective franchise should not be universal; what would you do about it? Who would settle it? Do you deny that first great principle of the right of the people to govern themselves? Will you resort to an arbitrary power, and say a majority of the people shall receive a state of things they are opposed to?

Mr. Douglass. That was said before the war.

The President. I am now talking about a principle; not what somebody else said.

Mr. Downing. Apply what you have said, Mr. President, to South Carolina, for instance, where a majority of the inhabitants are colored.

The President. Suppose you go to South Carolina; suppose you go to Ohio. That doesn't change the principle at all. The query to which I have referred still comes up when Government is undergoing a fundamental change. Government commenced upon this principle; it has existed upon it; and you propose now to incorporate into it an element that didn't exist before. I say the query comes up in undertaking this thing, whether we have a right to make a change in regard to the elective franchise in Ohio, for instance, whether we shall not let the people in that State decide the matter for themselves.

Each community is better prepared to determine the depository of its political power than anybody else, and it is for the Legislature, for the people of Ohio to say who shall vote, and not for the Congress of the United States. I might go down here to the ballot-box to-morrow and vote directly for universal suffrage; but if a great majority of the people said no, I should consider it would be tyrannical in me to attempt to force such upon them without their will. It is a fundamental tenet in my creed that the will of the people must be obeyed. Is there anything wrong or unfair in that?

Mr. Douglass (smiling.) A great deal that is wrong, Mr. President, with all respect.

The President. It is the people of the States that must for themselves determine this thing. I do not want to be engaged in a work that will commence a war of races. I want to begin the work of preparation, and the States, or the people in each community, if a man demeans himself well, and shows evidence that this new state of affairs will operate, will protect him in all his rights, and give him every possible advantage when they become reconciled socially and politically to this state of things. Then will this new order of things work harmoniously; but forced upon the people before they are prepared for it, it will be resisted, and work inharmoniously. I feel a conviction that driving this matter upon the people, upon the community, will result in the injury of both races, and the ruin of one or the other. God knows I have no desire but the good of the whole human race. I would it were so that all you advocate could be done in the twinkling of an eye; but it is not in the nature of things, and I do not assume or pretend to be wiser than Providence, or stronger than the laws of nature.

Let us now seek to discover the laws governing this thing. There is a great law controlling it; let us endeavor to find out what that law is, and conform our actions to it. All the details will then properly adjust themselves and work out well in the end.

God knows that anything I can do I will do. In the mighty process by which the great end is to be reached, anything I can do to elevate the races, to soften and ameliorate their condition I will do, and to be able to do so is the sincere desire of my heart.

I am glad to have met you, and thank you for the compliment you have paid me.

Mr. Douglass. I have to return to you our thanks, Mr. President, for so kindly granting us this interview. We did not come here expecting to argue this question with your Excellency, but simply to state what were our views and wishes in the premises. If we were disposed to argue the question, and you would grant us permission, of course we would endeavor to controvert some of the positions you have assumed.

Mr. Downing. Mr. Douglass, I take it that the President, by his kind expressions and his very full treatment of the subject, must have contemplated some reply to the views which he has advanced, and in which we certainly do not concur, and I say this with due respect.

The President. I thought you expected me to indicate to some extent what my views were on the subjects touched upon in your statement.

Mr. Downing. We are very happy, indeed, to have heard them.

Mr. Douglass. If the President will allow me, I would like to say one or two words in reply. You enfranchise your enemies and disfranchise your friends.

The President. All I have done is simply to indicate what my views are, as I supposed you expected me to, from your address.

Mr. Douglass. My own impression is that the very thing that your Excellency would avoid in the Southern States can only be avoided by the very measure that we propose, and I would state to my brother delegates that because I perceive the President has taken strong ground in favor of a given policy, and distrusting my own ability to remove any of those impressions which he has expressed, I thought we had better end the interview with the expression of thanks. (Addressing the President.) But if your Excellency will be pleased to hear, I would like to say a word or two in regard to that one matter of the enfranchisement of the blacks as a means of preventing the very thing which your Excellency seems to apprehend—that is a conflict of races.

The President. I repeat. I merely wanted to indicate my views in reply to your address, and not to enter into any general controversy, as I could not well do so under the circumstances.

Your statement was a very frank one, and I thought it was due to you to meet it in the same spirit.

Mr. Douglass. Thank you, sir.

The President. I think you will find, so far as the South is concerned, that if you will all inculcate there the idea in connection with the one you urge, that the colored people can live and advance in civilization to better advantage elsewhere than crowded right down there in the South, it would be better for them.

Mr. Douglass. But the masters have the making of the laws, and we cannot get away from the plantations.

The President. What prevents you?

Mr. Douglass. We have not the single right of locomotion through the Southern States now.

The President. Why not; the government furnishes you with every facility.

Mr. Douglass. There are six days in the year that the negro is free in the South now, and his master then decides for him where he shall go, where he shall work, how much he shall work—in fact, he is divested of all political power. He is absolutely in the hands of those men.

The President. If the master now controls him or his action, would he not control him in his vote?

Mr. Douglass. Let the negro once understand that he has an organic right to vote, and he will raise up a party in the Southern States among the poor, who will rally with him. There is this conflict that you speak of between the wealthy slaveholder and the poor man.

The President. You touch right upon the point there. There is this conflict, and hence I suggest emigration. If he cannot get employment in the South, he has it in his power to go where he can get it.

In parting, the President said that they were both desirous of accomplishing the same ends, but proposed to do so by following different roads.

Mr. Douglass, on turning to leave, remarked to his fellow delegates: "The President sends us to the people, and we go to the people."

The President. Yes, sir; I have great faith in the people. I believe they will do what is right.

February 7, 1866

———

Washington, February 7, 1866.

Mr. President:

In consideration of a delicate sense of propriety, as well as your own repeated intimations of indisposition to discuss or to listen to a reply to the views and opinions you were pleased to express to us in your elaborate speech to-day, the undersigned would respectfully take this method of replying thereto. Believing as we do that the views and opinions you expressed in that address are entirely unsound and prejudicial to the highest interests of our race as well as our country at large, we cannot do other than expose the same, and, as far as may be in our power, arrest their dangerous influence. It is not necessary at this time to call attention to more than two or three features of your remarkable address:

1. The first point to which we feel especially bound to take exception is your attempt to found a policy opposed to our enfranchisement, upon the alleged ground of an existing hostility on the part of the former slaves toward the poor white people of the South. We admit the existence of this hostility, and hold that it is entirely reciprocal. But you obviously commit an error by drawing an argument from an incident of a state of slavery, and making it a basis for a policy adapted to a state of freedom. The hostility between the whites and blacks of the South is easily explained. It has its root and sap in the relation of slavery, and was incited on both sides by the cunning of the slave masters. Those masters secured their ascendency over both the poor whites and the blacks by putting enmity between them.

They divided both to conquer each. There was no earthly reason why the blacks should not hate and dread the poor whites when in a state of slavery, for it was from this class that their masters received their slave-catchers, slave-drivers, and overseers. They were the men called in upon all occasions by the masters when any fiendish outrage was to be committed upon the slave. Now, sir, you cannot but perceive that, the cause of this hatred removed, the effect must be removed also. Slavery is abolished. The cause of antagonism is removed, and you must see that it is altogether illogical (and "putting new wine into old bottles," "mending new garments with old cloth") to legislate from slaveholding and slave-driving premises for a people whom you have repeatedly declared your purpose to maintain in freedom.

2. Besides, even if it were true, as you allege, that the hostility of the blacks toward the poor whites must necessarily project itself into a state of freedom, and that this enmity between the two races is even more intense in a state of freedom than in a state of slavery, in the name of Heaven, we reverently ask, how can you, in view of your professed desire to promote the welfare of the black man, deprive him of all means of defence, and clothe him whom you regard as his enemy in the panoply of political power? Can it be that you would recommend a policy

which would arm the strong and cast down the defenceless? Can you, by any possibility of reasoning, regard this as just, fair, or wise? Experience proves that those are oftenest abused who can be abused with the greatest impunity. Men are whipped oftenest who are whipped easiest. Peace between the races is not to be secured by degrading one race and exalting another, by giving power to one race and withholding it from another, but by maintaining a state of equal justice between all classes. First pure, then peaceable.

3. On the colonization theory you were pleased to broach very much could be said. It is impossible to suppose, in view of the usefulness of the black man in time of peace as a laborer in the South, and in time of war as a soldier at the North, and the growing respect for his rights among the people, and his increasing adaptation to a high state of civilization in this his native land, there can ever come a time when he can be removed from this country without a terrible shock to its prosperity and peace. Besides, the worst enemy of the nation could not cast upon its fair name a greater infamy than to suppose that negroes could be tolerated among them in a state of the most degrading slavery and oppression, and must be cast away, driven into exile, for no other cause than having been freed from their chains.

Joseph S. Fullerton to Andrew Johnson

Bureau of Refugees, Freedmen and Abandoned Lands.
Washington, February 9th 1866.
In reply to your verbal request I have the honor to submit the following objections to an Act now before Congress providing for the enlargement of the powers of the Freedmens Bureau.

1st. It is class legislation, conferring peculiar benefits on certain citizens, excluding or withholding the same from other citizens of the same locality.

2d. I believe its provisions if carried out will be injurious to the freedman in preventing him from acquiring a position as an independent citizen. This can only be done through his own exertions; by harmonizing his interests with those of the white people of the South; and by exercising such a spirit of forbearance and moderation as will overcome the prejudices that exist against him on the part of the white race of the South.

3d. There will be great danger of the organization becoming a political machine, thus destroying any usefulness it might otherwise have in the advancement of the interests of the freedman.

4th. The great expense to the government of conducting the Bureau.

5th. Objected to, because the contemplated organization is not necessary, as the interests of the freedman can be as well or better cared for by the military arm of the government, at a small expense additional to the necessary expense of supporting the Army.

The Act provides for the relief of "Freedmen and Loyal Refugees," which means that it provides for Freedmen only. There is now no such class as "Loyal Refugees." These are "catch" words which give to the Act the appearance of general legislation—Legislation for both the poor loyal whites and the blacks of the South. Had the intention been to furnish relief to the loyal whites, it would have been easy to insert

the words "for relief of Freedmen & Loyal whites." When the
Act, approved March 3d. 1865,—originally establishing the bureau, was passed there were a large number of persons in the
border States and within the lines of our Armies who on account of their loyalty to the government, had been driven or
forced to fly from their homes in the South. These persons,
generally being poor and without the necessities of life, were a
charge upon the Government, and such were contemplated in
the legislation for "Loyal Refugees." The war has ended; the
country is at peace, and all of such persons have been provided
for elsewhere, or have returned to their *former homes*, so that
now there is no class known as "Loyal Refugees." After the
surrender of the rebel armies, and until late in the following
fall many refugees were furnished by the Commissioner of this
Bureau with transportation to their homes, but none apply for
such assistance now. Under the construction of this expression,
the Agents of this Bureau have been instructed not to furnish
supplies to the poor whites of the South, even to those who
had been within the lines of our army and had returned to their
homes, for they were not then "refugees." The Act then is to
give relief only to "Freedmen." Commissary, Quarter master
and Medical supplies are to be furnished to this class of persons; public lands are to be set apart and reserved especially for
them; sights for schools and asylums, under certain conditions,
are to be purchased, and special courts or tribunals are to be
established for them by the Government. For the poor *loyal*
whites of the South, even those who have served in our Army,
there is nothing.

Aside from the fact of this being class legislation, it is such as
will intensify, on the part of the poor whites of the South, the
hatred that already exists between them and the blacks. This of
course will be more or less disastrous to the latter class. When
these poor whites realize that they have no special friends in
the Bureau Agents sent south by the Government; that certain
lands are not set apart for them; that Schools are not provided;
that Government stores are not furnished; and that the freedman even has his special tribunals, backed by military power,
where he can obtain very summary process, while they must
wait for the slow and uncertain action of Civil Courts, then
they will surely think that the Government intends to desert

and discriminate against them, instead of raising them up from the political subjection in which they also have been held by the ruling class of the South.

As slavery has been "constitutionally" abolished the old State slave codes are now null and void, and the military force of the Government in the South, if necessary, can prevent their execution. Congress also has power under the Constitutional Amendment abolishing slavery, to enforce said amendment by appropriate legislation. Would it not be better then for Congress to pass an Act declaring all slave codes, or state laws that abridge the personal liberty of the freedmen, inoperative, and give the Agents of the government power to enforce such Act, rather than to set up an immense civil or semi-military government, within a civil government, to be placed in the hands of, in many cases, inexperienced or bad men—strangers to the people—, for the protection of a certain class in the South?

The effect of establishing the Bureau upon the basis contemplated by this Act will be, I believe, to prevent the freedman, in a great measure, from acquiring that independence and self-reliance so necessary for his advancement. The Bureau as at present organized has been in existence for nearly ten months. During this time some damage and much good has been done by its agents. By some the freedman has been told that it is necessary for him, though free, to labor and work out his own salvation; by all he has been told that he is free. He knows now that he is free and with the tuition he has received he is now much better able to take care of himself, if let alone, than is generally supposed by his friends.

The bureau in its operations almost necessarily takes the place of a master. To it many of the freedmen look entirely for support, instruction and assistance. Even in those States where all civil rights have been conferred upon the freedman he does not go to the State Courts for a remedy, but to the bureau, for the process of civil law is too slow and the proceedings are not sufficiently convenient. The agents of the bureau decide for whom he shall work, for how much and when, and approve or disapprove all of his Contracts for labor. They have control in many places of his churches and schools, and some of them are endeavoring to control his finances. Special tribunals are to be organized in certain states for the trial of all cases where freedmen are concerned. Any system of Courts or Laws that look to the protection of a particular class must be objectionable and will be damaging in the end to such persons. It keeps them from endeavoring to gain admission to the state courts where they can obtain justice on the same footing as others. If we can judge from the past these courts will discriminate more against the white man than the State Courts can against the black. Some of these now in existence have been presided over by men inexperienced in law and evidence; men of strong prejudices in favor of the black men, who decide cases without reference to law, but the "right" as the right appears to them. Of course such justice is a farce, that pleases the black and exasperates the white. It is a bad plan by which to compell the people of the south to make just laws for the blacks: wholesome laws cannot be made under force. The longer these Courts remain in existence the harder it will be to give them up, and when given up the freedman, I fear, will be left in a worse condition than if they had not been established. The longer the offices of the bureau extend personal assistance to the freedman the less will he be prepared to take care of himself. Habitual dependence will prevent any class of people from making exertions for themselves.

By the too generous action of some agents of the bureau in furnishing rations & clothing many able bodied freedmen have been lost from the fields. It has been over eight months since the agents of this bureau commenced the "temporary" issue of rations. They are still issued. There appears to be no definite time when "temporary" issues shall cease, & this new act provides that such issues shall continue. There is work for all able bodied men in the South. But many will not engage in it as long as rations and clothing are furnished by the Government. The Asst. Commr. of the Bureau for North Carolina told me a few days ago that there are 3000 able bodied freedmen on Roanoke Island for whom he can get employment, but they will not take it. A short time ago he cut off the temporary issue of rations to these people. They then at once became "destitute & suffering freedmen" and again had to be fed to save them from starving. Some of the philanthropists interested in the freedmen complained of his bad treatment of these people in cutting off the rations. The aged and infirm must be taken care of until the State Governments in the South are able to take care of their own poor—but they will never be able—or show a willingness to do so as long as the general government provides it for them.

An immense number of agents will be required to carry out the provisions of this act. The Army will perhaps be called upon for a small number, the rest must be citizens. There are now on file in this Bureau hundreds of applications for such appointments. The most of these are from men of the North who profess to be philanthropists and wish to work for the good of the freedman, but none of them offer to work without pay, while some are very exorbitant in their demands. The class of men seeking such places are generally those who have strong prejudices in favor of the black and against the white man of the south, and many of them wish to go into the work to carry out some political theory or hobby. Instead of harmonizing capital & labor such men will keep the whites and blacks of the south in a chronic state of hostility. A few will be unprincipled enough to create disturbances in order to prove the existence of the bureau a necessity, so that they may be retained in position with pay. As it is now we have good reason to suppose that a few local agents of the bureau send startling accounts of outrages committed against the freedmen to the press of the country for the same reason or for a political purpose. Again some of the Agents will do as is now done by a few of those at present engaged in this work, i.e. take advantage of their positions to improve their finances;—such as renting plantations, and furnishing freedmen laborers to planters for a consideration.

It is true that the appointment of agents of the bureau must be made by your Excellency and the Commissioner. But it will be impossible for you to know much of the many applicants for position. When hundreds are to be appointed many bad men will slip in, and many who will come well recommended will not be able to stand the pecuniary & political temptations to which they will be subjected. It has been admitted to me by some of the warmest friends of the Act that the success of the bureau will depend entirely upon the character of its employees. The increase of its powers and agents is then a dangerous experiment. If the law has not inherent power to prevent evil some new law or remedy should be sought. I believe it to be impossible to have a majority of the agents—selected as they must be—good men. If then the Bureau is not a success it will be much worse for the freedman than if it had never been in existance.

It is almost certain that in certain localities the organization would become a political machine. Already there has been an example of this in the State of Louisiana, notwithstanding the Commissioner had given direct and positive orders against such an abuse of the institution. In such cases the true interest of the freedman would be neglected, to teach him political theories, at present impractical or impolitic, that will insure his enmity towards the white and the whites towards him—thus widening the breach that exists between them.

Another objection to the Act is the great expense that it will Entail upon the Government. Under the Act approved March 3d 1865, organizing the bureau, no appropriation of funds was made. Agents therefore had to be detailed from the Army, and the Hon. Secy. of War furnished all needful QrMaster & Commissary supplies. No person can complain that the freedman has not received sufficient attention and assistance from the bureau up to the present time. Yet it is proposed to increase the institution largely, and the expenses to an enormous amount. The estimate for funds made by the Commissioner for the coming year was not made for the expenses necessary under the Act now under consideration & is therefore not a criterion for the amt. that will be required.

In reference to confirming the posessary titles that the freedmen have to the Estates on the Sea Islands I have only to say that there are legal objections which will present themselves. I am sure that some of the good lawyers who voted in favor of the Act were aware of this fact, or they would have confirmed them forever—as Gen Shermans order provides—instead of for three years. There is no doubt but that the freedmen will remain, under this Act, in posession for three years, for it will take that length of time to bring the matter to a trial and decision in the U.S. Supreme Court. I believe it will be injurious to the freedmen to confirm their posession beyond the time for gathering their present crops, unless confirmed forever.

The freedmen can be better cared for, so far as the government should extend assistance, by the Military Authorities than in any other way: and this at a very small expense additional to the expense of supporting the troops in the south. If the head of the bureau, as at present, is in the War Department and issues orders and instructions from there, and then the officers and subalterns of the army are made ex-officio members of the bureau—or better, if its made part of their military duty to have general supervision of the freedmen, as they have of other persons where civil law is inoperative, the system would be much simplified, a large expense would be saved, and great good could be done. These military agents would be obliged to carry out the orders of the head of the bureau, and they would have the power to do so. They would have no political, selfish, or pecuniary designs to carry out. They would have no desire to promote strife between the whites and blacks, and both of these classes having confidence in them would advance in their interests and become reconciled to the situation. They will have no object to desire the continuance of the bureau longer than its existence is actually demanded in order that they may receive a support, for their offices would still continue.

The objection that some will offer to this proposition will be that the armies are being mustered out & there will not be material enough left for Agents of the bureau. But the Act in providing for a large number of Agents also provides, in Section 2., that the "President of the United States, through the War Department and the Commissioner, shall extend military jurisdiction and protection over all employees, agents and offices of this bureau in the exercise of the duties imposed or authorized by this act, or the act to which this is additional."

If there are enough officers & men in the Military service to extend such protection to the employees &c, surely there are enough to attend, as agents, to the requirements of the Bureau.

J. S. Fullerton   Bv. Brig. Genl. Vols.

Andrew Johnson: Veto of the Freedmen's Bureau Bill

Washington, February 19, 1866.

To the Senate of the United States

I have examined with care the bill, which originated in the Senate and has been passed by the two Houses of Congress, to amend an act entitled "An act to establish a bureau for the relief of freedmen and refugees," and for other purposes. Having with much regret come to the conclusion that it would not be consistent with the public welfare to give my approval to the measure, I return the bill to the Senate with my objections to its becoming a law.

I might call to mind in advance of these objections that there is no immediate necessity for the proposed measure. The act to establish a bureau for the relief of freedmen and refugees, which was approved in the month of March last, has not yet expired. It was thought stringent and extensive enough for the purpose in view in time of war. Before it ceases to have effect further experience may assist to guide us to a wise conclusion as to the policy to be adopted in time of peace.

I share with Congress the strongest desire to secure the freedmen the full enjoyment of their freedom and property and their entire independence and equality in making contracts for their labor, but the bill before me contains provisions which in my opinion are not warranted by the Constitution and are not well suited to accomplish the end in view.

The bill proposes to establish by authority of Congress military jurisdiction over all parts of the United States containing refugees and freedmen. It would by its very nature apply with most force to those parts of the United States in which the freedmen most abound, and it expressly extends the existing temporary jurisdiction of the Freedmen's Bureau, with greatly enlarged powers, over those States "in which the ordinary course of judicial proceedings has been interrupted by the rebellion." The source from which this military jurisdiction is to emanate is none other than the President of the United

States, acting through the War Department and the Commissioner of the Freedmen's Bureau. The agents to carry out this military jurisdiction are to be selected either from the Army or from civil life; the country is to be divided into districts and subdistricts, and the number of salaried agents to be employed may be equal to the number of counties or parishes in all the United States where freedmen and refugees are to be found.

The subjects over which this military jurisdiction is to extend in every part of the United States include protection to "all employees, agents, and officers of this bureau in the exercise of the duties imposed" upon them by the bill. In eleven States it is further to extend over all cases affecting freedmen and refugees discriminated against "by local law, custom, or prejudice." In those eleven States the bill subjects any white person who may be charged with depriving a freedman of "any civil rights or immunities belonging to white persons" to imprisonment or fine, or both, without, however, defining the "civil rights and immunities" which are thus to be secured to the freedmen by military law. This military jurisdiction also extends to all questions that may arise respecting contracts. The agent who is thus to exercise the office of a military judge may be a stranger, entirely ignorant of the laws of the place, and exposed to the errors of judgment to which all men are liable. The exercise of power over which there is no legal supervision by so vast a number of agents as is contemplated by the bill must, by the very nature of man, be attended by acts of caprice, injustice, and passion.

The trials having their origin under this bill are to take place without the intervention of a jury and without any fixed rules of law or evidence. The rules on which offenses are to be "heard and determined" by the numerous agents are such rules and regulations as the President, through the War Department, shall prescribe. No previous presentment is required nor any indictment charging the commission of a crime against the laws; but the trial must proceed on charges and specifications. The punishment will be, not what the law declares, but such as a court-martial may think proper; and from these arbitrary tribunals there lies no appeal, no writ of error to any of the courts in which the Constitution of the United States vests exclusively the judicial power of the country.

While the territory and the classes of actions and offenses that are made subject to this measure are so extensive, the bill itself, should it become a law, will have no limitation in point of time, but will form a part of the permanent legislation of the country. I can not reconcile a system of military jurisdiction of this kind with the words of the Constitution which declare that "no person shall be held to answer for a capital or otherwise infamous crime unless on a presentment or indictment of a grand jury, except in cases arising in the land or naval forces, or in the militia when in actual service in time of war or public danger," and that "in all criminal prosecutions the accused shall enjoy the right to a speedy and public trial by an impartial jury of the State and district wherein the crime shall have been committed." The safeguards which the experience and wisdom of ages taught our fathers to establish as securities for the protection of the innocent, the punishment of the guilty, and the equal administration of justice are to be set aside, and for the sake of a more vigorous interposition in behalf of justice we are to take the risks of the many acts of injustice that would necessarily follow from an almost countless number of agents established in every parish or county in nearly a third of the States of the Union, over whose decisions there is to be no supervision or control by the Federal courts. The power that would be thus placed in the hands of the President is such as in time of peace certainly ought never to be intrusted to any one man.

If it be asked whether the creation of such a tribunal within a State is warranted as a measure of war, the question immediately presents itself whether we are still engaged in war. Let us not unnecessarily disturb the commerce and credit and industry of the country by declaring to the American people and to the world that the United States are still in a condition of civil war. At present there is no part of our country in which the authority of the United States is disputed. Offenses that may be committed by individuals should not work a forfeiture of the rights of whole communities. The country has returned, or is returning, to a state of peace and industry, and the rebellion is in fact at an end. The measure, therefore, seems to be as inconsistent with the actual condition of the country as it is at variance with the Constitution of the United States.

If, passing from general considerations, we examine the bill in detail, it is open to weighty objections.

In time of war it was eminently proper that we should provide for those who were passing suddenly from a condition of bondage to a state of freedom. But this bill proposes to make the Freedmen's Bureau, established by the act of 1865 as one of many great and extraordinary military measures to suppress a formidable rebellion, a permanent branch of the public administration, with its powers greatly enlarged. I have no reason to suppose, and I do not understand it to be alleged, that the act of March, 1865, has proved deficient for the purpose for which it was passed, although at that time and for a considerable period thereafter the Government of the United States remained unacknowledged in most of the States whose inhabitants had been involved in the rebellion. The institution of slavery, for the military destruction of which the Freedmen's Bureau was called into existence as an auxiliary, has been already effectually and finally abrogated throughout the whole country by an amendment of the Constitution of the United States, and practically its eradication has received the assent and concurrence of most of those States in which it at any time had an existence. I am not, therefore, able to discern in the condition of the country anything to justify an apprehension that the powers and agencies of the Freedmen's Bureau, which were effective for the protection of freedmen and refugees during the actual continuance of hostilities and of African servitude, will now, in a time of peace and after the abolition of slavery, prove inadequate to the same proper ends. If I am correct in these views, there can be no necessity for the enlargement of the powers of the Bureau, for which provision is made in the bill.

The third section of the bill authorizes a general and unlimited grant of support to the destitute and suffering refugees and freedmen, their wives and children. Succeeding sections make provision for the rent or purchase of landed estates for freedmen, and for the erection for their benefit of suitable buildings for asylums and schools, the expenses to be defrayed from the Treasury of the whole people. The Congress of the United States has never heretofore thought itself empowered to establish asylums beyond the limits of the District of Columbia, except for the benefit of our disabled soldiers and sailors. It has never founded schools for any class of our own people, not even for the orphans of those who have fallen in the defense of the Union, but has left the care of education to the much more competent and efficient control of the States, of communities, of private associations, and of individuals. It has never deemed itself authorized to expend the public money for the rent or purchase of homes for the thousands, not to say millions, of the white race who are honestly toiling from day to day for their subsistence. A system for the support of indigent persons in the United States was never contemplated by the authors of the Constitution; nor can any good reason be advanced why, as a permanent establishment, it should be founded for one class or color of our people more than another. Pending the war many refugees and freedmen received support from the Government, but it was never intended that they should thenceforth be fed, clothed, educated, and sheltered by the United States. The idea on which the slaves were assisted to freedom was that on becoming free they would be a self-sustaining population. Any legislation that shall imply that they are not expected to attain a self-sustaining condition must have a tendency injurious alike to their character and their prospects.

The appointment of an agent for every county and parish will create an immense patronage, and the expense of the numerous officers and their clerks, to be appointed by the President, will be great in the beginning, with a tendency steadily to increase. The appropriations asked by the Freedmen's Bureau as now established, for the year 1866, amount to $11,745,000. It may be safely estimated that the cost to be incurred under the pending bill will require double that amount—more than the entire sum expended in any one year under the Administration of the second Adams. If the presence of agents in every parish and county is to be considered as a war measure, opposition, or even resistance, might be provoked; so that to give effect to their jurisdiction troops would have to be stationed within reach of every one of them, and thus a large standing force be rendered necessary. Large appropriations would therefore be required to sustain and enforce military jurisdiction in every county or parish from the Potomac to the Rio Grande. The condition of our fiscal affairs is encouraging, but in order to sustain the present measure of public confidence it is necessary that we practice not merely customary economy, but, as far as possible, severe retrenchment.

In addition to the objections already stated, the fifth section of the bill proposes to take away land from its former owners without any legal proceedings being first had, contrary to that provision of the Constitution which declares that no person shall "be deprived of life, liberty, or property without due process of law." It does not appear that a part of the lands to which this section refers may not be owned by minors or persons of unsound mind, or by those who have been faithful to all their obligations as citizens of the United States. If any portion of the land is held by such persons, it is not competent for any authority to deprive them of it. If, on the other hand, it be found that the property is liable to confiscation, even then it can not be appropriated to public purposes until by due process of law it shall have been declared forfeited to the Government.

There is still further objection to the bill, on grounds seriously affecting the class of persons to whom it is designed to bring relief. It will tend to keep the mind of the freedman in a state of uncertain expectation and restlessness, while to those among whom he lives it will be a source of constant and vague apprehension.

Undoubtedly the freedman should be protected, but he should be protected by the civil authorities, especially by the exercise of all the constitutional powers of the courts of the United States and of the States. His condition is not so exposed as may at first be imagined. He is in a portion of the country where his labor can not well be spared. Competition for his services from planters, from those who are constructing or repairing railroads, and from capitalists in his vicinage or from other States will enable him to command almost his own terms. He also possesses a perfect right to change his place of abode, and if, therefore, he does not find in one community or State a mode of life suited to his desires or proper remuneration for his labor, he can move to another where that labor is more esteemed and better rewarded. In truth, however, each State, induced by its own wants and interests, will do what is necessary and proper to retain within its borders all the labor that is needed for the development of its resources. The laws that regulate supply and demand will maintain their force, and the wages of the laborer will be regulated thereby. There is no danger that the exceedingly great demand for labor will not operate in favor of the laborer.

Neither is sufficient consideration given to the ability of the freedmen to protect and take care of themselves. It is no more than justice to them to believe that as they have received their freedom with moderation and forbearance, so they will distinguish themselves by their industry and thrift, and soon show the world that in a condition of freedom they are self-sustaining, capable of selecting their own employment and their own places of abode, of insisting for themselves on a proper remuneration, and of establishing and maintaining their own asylums and schools. It is earnestly hoped that instead of wasting away they will by their own efforts establish for themselves a condition of respectability and prosperity. It is certain that they can attain to that condition only through their own merits and exertions.

In this connection the query presents itself whether the system proposed by the bill will not, when put into complete operation, practically transfer the entire care, support, and control of 4,000,000 emancipated slaves to agents, overseers, or taskmasters, who, appointed at Washington, are to be located in every county and parish throughout the United States containing freedmen and refugees. Such a system would inevitably tend to a concentration of power in the Executive which would enable him, if so disposed, to control the action of this numerous class and use them for the attainment of his own political ends.

I can not but add another very grave objection to this bill. The Constitution imperatively declares, in connection with taxation, that each State *shall* have at least one Representative, and fixes the rule for the number to which, in future times, each State shall be entitled. It also provides that the Senate of the United States *shall* be composed of two Senators from each State, and adds with peculiar force "that no State, without its consent, shall be deprived of its equal suffrage in the Senate." The original act was necessarily passed in the absence of the States chiefly to be affected, because their people were then contumaciously engaged in the rebellion. Now the case is changed, and some, at least, of those States are attending Congress by loyal representatives, soliciting the allowance of the constitutional right for representation. At the time, however, of the consideration and the passing of this bill there was no Senator or Representative in Congress from the eleven States which are to be mainly affected by its provisions. The very fact that reports were and are made against the good disposition of the people of that portion of the country is an additional reason why they need and should have representatives of their own in Congress to explain their condition, reply to accusations, and assist by their local knowledge in the perfecting of measures immediately affecting themselves. While the liberty of deliberation would then be free and Congress would have full power to decide according to its judgment, there could be no objection urged that the States most interested had not been permitted to be heard. The principle is firmly fixed in the minds of the American people that there should be no taxation without representation. Great burdens have now to be borne by all the country, and we may best demand that they shall be borne without murmur when they are voted by a majority of the representatives of all the people. I would not interfere with the unquestionable right of Congress to judge, each House for itself, "of the elections, returns, and qualifications of its own members;" but that authority can not be construed as including the right to shut out in time of peace any State from the representation to which it is entitled by the Constitution. At present all the people of eleven States are excluded—those who were most faithful during the war not less than others. The State of Tennessee, for instance, whose authorities engaged in rebellion, was restored to all her constitutional relations to the Union by the patriotism and energy of her injured and betrayed people. Before the war was brought to a termination they had placed themselves in relations with the General Government, had established a State government of their own, and, as they were not included in the emancipation proclamation, they by their own act had amended their constitution so as to abolish slavery within the limits of their State. I know no reason why the State of Tennessee, for example, should not fully enjoy "all her constitutional relations to the United States."

The President of the United States stands toward the country in a somewhat different attitude from that of any member of Congress. Each member of Congress is chosen from a single district or State; the President is chosen by the people of all the States. As eleven States are not at this time represented in either branch of Congress, it would seem to be his duty on all proper occasions to present their just claims to Congress. There always will be differences of opinion in the community, and individuals may be guilty of transgressions of the law, but these do not constitute valid objections against the right of a State to representation. I would in no wise interfere with the discretion of Congress with regard to the qualifications of members; but I hold it my duty to recommend to you, in the interests of peace and the interests of union, the admission of every State to its share in public legislation when, however insubordinate, insurgent, or rebellious its people may have been, it presents itself, not only in an attitude of loyalty and harmony, but in the persons of representatives whose loyalty can not be questioned under any existing constitutional or legal test. It is plain that an indefinite or permanent exclusion of any part of the country from representation must be attended by a spirit of disquiet and complaint. It is unwise and dangerous to pursue a course of measures which will unite a very large section of the country against another section of the country, however much the latter may preponderate. The course of emigration, the development of industry and business, and natural causes will raise up at the South men as devoted to the Union as those of any other part of the land; but if they are all excluded from Congress, if in a permanent statute they are declared not to be in full constitutional relations to the country, they may think they have cause to become a unit in feeling and sentiment against the Government. Under the political education of the American people the idea is inherent and ineradicable that the consent of the majority of the whole people is necessary to secure a willing acquiescence in legislation.

The bill under consideration refers to certain of the States as though they had not "been fully restored in all their constitutional relations to the United States." If they have not, let us at once act together to secure that desirable end at the earliest possible moment. It is hardly necessary for me to inform Congress that in my own judgment most of those States, so far, at least, as depends upon their own action, have already been fully restored, and are to be deemed as entitled to enjoy their constitutional rights as members of the Union. Reasoning from the Constitution itself and from the actual situation of the country, I feel not only entitled but bound to assume that with the Federal courts restored and those of the several States in the full exercise of their functions the rights and interests of all classes of people will, with the aid of the military in cases of resistance to the laws, be essentially protected against unconstitutional infringement or violation. Should this expectation unhappily fail, which I do not anticipate, then the Executive is already fully armed with the powers conferred by the act of March, 1865, establishing the Freedmen's Bureau, and hereafter, as heretofore, he can employ the land and naval forces of the country to suppress insurrection or to overcome obstructions to the laws.

In accordance with the Constitution, I return the bill to the Senate, in the earnest hope that a measure involving questions and interests so important to the country will not become a law, unless upon deliberate consideration by the people it shall receive the sanction of an enlightened public judgment.

ANDREW JOHNSON.

Andrew Johnson: Speech on Washington's Birthday

Washington, Thursday, Feb. 22.

Fellow-citizens:

For I presume I have a right to address you as such, I come to tender to you my sincere thanks for the approbation expressed by your Committee in their personal address, and in the resolutions submitted by them, as having been adopted by the meeting which has been held in this city to-day. These resolutions, as I understand them, are complementary to the policy which has been adopted by the Administration, and which has been steadily pursued since it came into power. I am free to say to you on this occasion, that it is extremely gratifying to me to know that so large a portion of my fellow-citizens approve and indorse the policy which has been adopted, and which it is my intention shall be carried out. [Great applause.] That policy is one which is intended to restore all the States to their original relations to the Federal Government of the United States. [Renewed applause.] This seems to be a day peculiarly appropriate for such a manifestation. It is the day that gave birth to that man who, more perhaps, than any other, founded this Government. It is the day that gave birth to the Father of our Country. It is the day that gave birth to him who presided over that body which framed the Constitution under which all the States entered, and to this glorious Confederacy such a day is peculiarly appropriate for the indorsement of a policy whose object is the restoration of the union of the States as it was designed by the Father of his Country. [Applause.] WASHINGTON, whose name this city bears, is emblemed in the hearts of all who love free government. WASHINGTON, in the language of his eulogist, was first in war, first in peace and first in the hearts of his countrymen. No people can claim him, no nation can appropriate him. His reputation is commensurate with the civilized world, and his name is the common property of all those who love free government. To-day I had the pleasure of a visit from those persons who have been devoting their efforts to the completion of the monument which is being erected to his name. I was proud to meet them, and, so far as I could, to give them my influence and countenance in aid of the work they have undertaken. That monument, which is being erected to him whom I may say founded the Government, is almost within a stone's throw of the spot from which I address you. Let it be completed. [Applause.] Let those various blocks which the States and individuals and associations and corporations have put in that monument as pledges of their love for this Union be preserved, and let the work be accomplished. In this connection let me refer to the block from my own State, God bless her! [applause] which has struggled for the preservation of this Union, in the field and in the councils of the nation, and which is now struggling to renew her relations with this Government that were interrupted by a fearful rebellion. She is now struggling to renew these relations, and to take her stand where she had ever stood since 1796 until this rebellion broke out. [Great applause.] Let me repeat the sentiment that that State has inscribed upon the stone which she has deposited in that monument of freedom which is being raised in commemoration of Washington. She is struggling to get back into the Union, and to stand by the sentiment which is thereon inscribed, and she is willing to sustain it.

What is it? It is the sentiment which was enunciated by her distinguished son, the immortal, the illustrious JACKSON, "The Federal Union—it must be preserved." [Great applause.] If it were possible for that old man, whose statue stands before me and whose portrait is behind me, in the Executive Mansion, and whose sentiment is thus preserved in that monument in your vicinity to be called forth from the grave; or if it were possible to communicate with the spirit of the illustrious dead, and make him understand the progress of faction and of rebellion and treason, he would turn over in his coffin, and shaking off the habiliments of the tomb, would again stand erect, and reiterate that sentiment originally expressed by him on a memorable occasion, "The Federal Union, it must be preserved." [Great applause.] We have witnessed what has transpired since his day. In 1833, when treason and treachery, and infidelity to the Government and the Constitution of the United States, stalked forth in the land, it was his power and influence that crushed the serpent in its incipiency. The movement was then stopped, but only for a time. The same spirit of disaffection continued. There were men disaffected to the Government both in the North and in the South. There was in a portion of the Union a peculiar institution of which some complained, and to which others were attached. One portion of our countrymen in the South sustained that institution, while another portion in the North opposed it. The result was the formation of extreme parties, one especially in the South which reached a point at which it was prepared to dissolve the union of the States for the purpose, as was said, of securing and preserving that peculiar institution. There was another portion of our countrymen who were opposed to it, and who went to such an extreme that they were willing to break up the Government in order to get rid of that institution which was peculiar to the South. I say these things because I desire to talk plainly and in familiar phraseology. I assume nothing here to-day beyond the position of a citizen—one who has been pleading for his country and the preservation of the Constitution. [Immense cheering.] These two portions were arrayed against each other, and I stand here before you for the Union to-day, as I stood in the Senate of the United States for the Union in 1860 and 1861. I met there those who were making war upon the Constitution— those who wanted to break and destroy the Government—and I denounced them in my place, then and there, and exposed their true character. I said that these men who were engaged in the work of breaking up the Government, were traitors. I have never ceased on all proper occasions to repeat that sentiment, and, as far as my efforts could go, I have endeavored to carry it out. [Great applause.] I have just remarked that there were two parties, one of which was for destroying the Government and separating the Union in order to preserve Slavery and the other for breaking up the Government in order to destroy Slavery. True, the objects which they sought to accomplish were different, so far as Slavery was concerned, but they agreed in the desire to break up the Government, the thing to which I have always been opposed, and whether disunionists come from the South or from the North, I stand now, as I did then, vindicating the union of the States and the Constitution of my country. [Tremendous applause.] When rebellion and treason manifested themselves in the South I stood by the Government. I said then that I was for the Union with Slavery—or I was for the Union without Slavery. In either alternative I was for my Government and its Constitution. The Government has stretched forth its strong arm, and with its physical power it has put down treason in the field. The section of the country which then arrayed itself against the National Government has been put down by the strong arm. What did we say when this treason originated? We said, "No compromise." You yourselves in the South can settle this question in eight and forty hours. I said again and again, and I repeat it now—disband your armies in the South, acknowledge the supremacy of the Constitution of the United States, acknowledge the duty of obedience to the laws, and the whole question is settled. [Great applause.] What has been done since their armies have been disbanded, and they come forward now in a proper spirit and say, "We were mistaken; we made an effort to carry out the doctrine of secession and to dissolve this Union, and we have failed. We have carried this doctrine to its logical results, and we find that we were mistaken. We acknowledge the flag of our country, and are willing to obey the Constitution and to yield to the supremacy of the laws." [Great applause.] Coming in that spirit I say to them "When you have complied with the requirements of the Constitution, when you have yielded to the law, when you have acknowledged your allegiance to the Constitution, I will, so far as I can, open the door of the Union to those who had erred and strayed from the fold of their fathers for a time." [Great applause.] Who has suffered more by the rebellion than I have? I shall not repeat the story of the wrongs and sufferings inflicted upon me; but the spirit of revenge is not the spirit in which to deal with a whole people. I know there has been a great deal said about the exercise of the pardoning power. So far as your Executive is concerned there is no one who has labored with more earnestness than myself to have the principal, intelligent and conscious traitors brought to justice, the law vindicated, and the great fact judicially established that *treason is a crime.* [Applause.] But while anxious that leading and intelligent traitors should be punished, should whole communities and States and people be made to submit to the penalty of death? No, no. I have perhaps as much asperity and as much resentment in my nature as men ought to have; but we must reason in great matters of government about man as he is. We must conform our actions and our conduct to the example of Him who founded our holy religion. Not that I would make such a comparison on this occasion in any personal aspect. I came into this place under the Constitution of the country and by the approbation of the people, and what did I find? I found eight millions of people who were in fact condemned under the law, and the penalty was death. Was I to yield to the spirit of revenge and resentment, and declare that they should all be annihilated and destroyed? How different would this have been from the example set by the holy founder of our religion, the extreme points of whose divine arch rests upon the horizon, and whose span embraces the universe;—he who founded this great scheme came into the world and found man condemned under the law, and his sentence was death. What was his example? Instead of condemning the world or even a nation to death, he died upon the cross, attesting by his wounds and his blood that he died that mankind might live? Let those who have erred repent—let them acknowledge their allegiance—let them become loyal, willing supporters and defenders of our glorious stripes and stars, and of the Constitution of our country—let the leaders, the conscious, intelligent traitors, be punished and subjected to the penalties of the law; [applause;] but to the great mass, who have been forced into this rebellion, in many instances, and in others have been misled, I say extend leniency, kindness, trust and confidence. [Great applause.] My countrymen, when I look back over the history of the rebellion, I trust I am not vain when I ask you if I have not given as much evidence of my devotion to the Union as some who croak a great deal about it. When I look back over the battle-fields of the rebellion, I think of the many brave men in whose company I was. I cannot but recollect that I was some times in places where the contest was most difficult and the result most doubtful. But almost before the smoke has passed away, almost before the blood that has been shed has sunk into the earth—before the bodies of the slain have passed to their native dust—what do we now find? The rebellion has been put down by the strong arm of the Government in the field, but is that the only way in which you can have rebellion? One struggle was against an attempt to dissever the Union; but almost before the smoke of the battle-field has passed away—before our brave men have all returned to their homes, and renewed the ties of affection and love to their wives and their children, we find almost another rebellion inaugurated. We put down the former rebellion in order to prevent the separation of the States, to prevent them from flying off, and thereby changing the character of our Government and weakening its power. But when that struggle on our part has been successful, and that attempt has been put down, we find now an effort to concentrate all power in the hands of a few at the Federal head, and thereby bring about a consolidation of the Government, which is equally objectionable with a separation. [Vociferous applause.] We find that powers are assumed and attempted to be exercised of a most extraordinary character. It seems that Governments may be revolutionized—Governments at least may be changed without going through the strife of battle. I believe it is a fact attested in history that sometimes revolutions most disastrous to a people are effected without the shedding of blood. The substance of your Government may be taken away while the form and the shadow remain to you. What is now being proposed? We find that in point of fact nearly all the powers of the Government are assumed by an irresponsible central directory, which does not even consult the legislative or the executive departments of the Government. By resolutions reported from a committee in whom it seems that practically the legislative power of the Government is now vested, that great principle of the Constitution which authorizes and empowers each branch of the legislative department, the Senate and the House of Representatives, to judge for itself of the elections, returns and qualifications of its own members, has been virtually taken away from the two branches of the legislative department of the Government, and conferred upon a joint committee, who must report before either House can act under the Constitution as to accepting the members who are to take their seats as component parts of the respective bodies. By this rule it is assumed that there must be laws passed recognizing a State as being in the Union; or its practical relations to the Union as restored, before the respective Houses under the Constitution can judge of the elections, returns and qualifications of their own members. What a position is that! You struggled for four years to put down a rebellion. You denied in the beginning of the struggle that any State could go out of the Union. You said that it had neither the right nor the power to do so. The issue was made and it has been settled that the States had neither the right nor the power to go out of the Union. With what consistency, after it has been settled by the military arm of the Government and by the public judgment that the States had no right to go out of the Union, can any one now turn round and assume that they are out, and that they shall not come in? I am free to say to you as your Executive that I am not prepared to take any such position. [Great applause.] I said in the Senate in the very inception of this rebellion that the States had no right to go out. I asserted, too, that they had no power to go out. That question has been settled, and it being settled, I cannot turn around now and give the lie direct to all that I have professed, and all I have done for the last five years. [Applause.] When those who rebelled comply with the Constitution, when they give sufficient evidence of loyalty, when they show that they can be trusted, when they yield obedience to the law that you and I acknowledge, I say extend to them the right hand of fellowship, and let peace and union be restored. [Tremendous applause.] I fought traitors and treason in the South; I opposed the Davises, the Toombses, the Slidells, and a long list of others, which you can readily fill without my repeating the names. Now, when I turn round and at the other end of the line find men—I care not by what name you call them—who still stand opposed to the restoration of the Union of these States, I am free to say to you that I am still in the field. [Great applause.] I am still for the preservation of the Union. I am still in favor of this great Government of ours going on and filling out its destiny. [Great applause.]

VOICES—Give us three of these names at the other end.

THE PRESIDENT—I am called upon to name three at the other end of the line. I am talking to my friends and fellow-citizens who are interested with me in this Government, and I presume I am free to mention to you the names of those whom I look upon, as being opposed to the fundamental principles of this Government, and who are laboring to destroy it.

VOICES—"Name them—who are they?"

THE PRESIDENT—You ask me who they are? I say, THADDEUS STEVENS, of Pennsylvania, is one; I say Mr. SUMNER, of the Senate, is another, and WENDELL PHILLIPS is another. [Long continued applause.]

VOICES—"Give it to Forney."

THE PRESIDENT—In reply to that I will simply say I do not waste my ammunition upon dead ducks. [Great laughter and applause.] I stand for my country. I stand for the Constitution. There I have always placed myself from my advent in public life. They may traduce, they may slander, they may vituperate me, but let me say to you all this has no influence upon me. [Great applause.] Let me say further, that I do not intend to be overawed by real or pretended friends, nor do I mean to be bullied by my enemies. [Tremendous applause.] Honest conviction is my courage. The Constitution is my guide. I know, my countrymen, that it has been insinuated, it has been said directly in high places, that if such a usurpation of power as I am charged with had been exercised some 200 years ago, in a particular reign, it would have cost an individual his head. [Great laughter.] Of what usurpation has ANDREW JOHNSON been guilty? None; none. Is it a usurpation to stand between the people and the encroachments of power? Because, in a conversation with a fellow-citizen, who happened to be a Senator, I said that I thought amendments to the Constitution ought not to be so frequent; that if it was continually tampered with, it would lose its prestige and dignity, and the old instrument would be lost sight of altogether in a short time, and because in the same conversation I happened to say that if it were amended at all, such and such an amendment ought to be adopted, it was charged that I was guilty of an assumption of power that would have cost a king his head in a certain period of English history. [Great laughter.] From the same source the exclamation has gone forth that they were in the midst of earthquakes, that they were trembling and could not yield. [Laughter.] Yes, fellow-citizens, there is an earthquake coming; there is a grand swelling of popular judgment and indignation. [Great applause.] The American people will speak, and by their instinct, if not otherwise, they will know who are their friends and who are their enemies. I have endeavored to be true to the people in all the positions which I have occupied, and there is hardly a position in this Government which I have not at some time filled. I suppose it will be said that this is vanity; [laughter;] but I may say that I have been all of them, and I have been in both branches of the State Legislature.

A VOICE—You commenced a tailor.

THE PRESIDENT—A gentleman behind me says that I began
a tailor. Yes, I did begin a tailor [applause], and that suggestion
does not disturb me in the least, for when I was a tailor I had
the reputation of being a good one, and of making close fits.
[Laughter.] And I was always punctual to my customers and
did good work. [Applause.]

VOICES—We will patch up the Union yet.

THE PRESIDENT—No! I do not want any patchwork of it. I
want the original article restored. [Great applause.] But enough
of this raillery. I know it may be said, You are President, and
you must not talk about these things; but, my fellow-citizens,
I intend to talk the truth, and when principle is involved, when
the existence of my country is in peril, I hold it to be my duty
to speak what I think and what I feel, as I have always done on
former occasions. [Great applause.] I have said it has been declared elsewhere that I was guilty of usurpation which would
have cost a king his head, and in another place I have been
denounced for "whitewashing." When and where did I ever
whitewash anything or anybody? I have been an Alderman of a
town; I have been in both branches of the Legislature of my
State; I have been in both Houses of the National Congress; I
have been at the head of the Executive Department of my
State; I have been Vice-President of the United States; and I
am now in the position which I occupy before you, and during
all this time where is the man and where is any portion of the
people who can say that ANDREW JOHNSON ever made a pledge
which he did not redeem, or that he ever made a promise
which he violated. None! none! Point me to the man who can
say that ANDREW JOHNSON ever acted with infidelity to the
great mass of the people. [Great applause.] Men may talk about
beheading and about usurpation, but when I am beheaded I
want the American people to be the witness. I do not want it
done by innuendoes and indirect remarks, in high places to be
suggested to men who have assassination brooding in their bosoms. Others have exclaimed that the presidential obstacle
must be gotten out of the many. What is that but (I make use
of a strong word) inciting to assassination? Are the opponents
of the Government not yet satisfied? Are those who want to
destroy our institutions, and to change the character of the
Government, not yet satisfied with the quantity of blood that

has been shed? Are they not satisfied with one martyr in this place? Does not the blood of LINCOLN appease their vengeance and their wrath? Is their thirst still unsatisfed? Do they still want more blood? Have they not honor and courage enough to seek to obtain the end other wise than by the hand of an assassin? I am not afraid of an assassin attacking me where alone brave and courages men will attack another? I only dread him when in disguise and where his footsteps is noiseless. If they want blood let them have the courage to strike like men. I know they are "willing to wound yet afraid to strike." If my blood is to be shed because I vindicate the Union and insist on the preservation of this Government in its original purity, let it be shed out; let an altar to the Union be first erected and then, if necessary, take me and lay me upon it, and the blood that now warms and animates my existence shall be poured out as the last libation as a tribute to the union of the States. [Great applause.] But let the opponents of this Government remember when it is found out that the blood of the martyrs is the seed of the Church. This Union will grow and it will continue to increase in strength and power though it may be cemented and cleansed in blood. I have already spoken to you longer than I intended when I came out. ["Go on."] I merely intended to make my acknowledgments for the honor you have done me, but before I close allow me to say a word in regard to the question of amendings to the Constitution of the United States. Shortly after I reached Washington for the purpose of being inaugurated as Vice-President of the United States, I had a conversation with Mr. LINCOLN in regard to the condition of affairs; we talked particularly in reference to matters in my own State. I told him that we called a convention, that we had amended the Constitution; that we had abolished slavery in that State, which was not included in his Emancipation Proclamation. All these things met his approbation, and he gave me words of encouragement; we talked then about affairs generally, and upon the subject of amendments to the Constitution of the United States; he said to me "When the amendment of the Constitution now proposed is adopted by three-fourths of the States, I am pretty near done, or, indeed, quite done, in favor of amending the Constitution, if there was one other adopted." I asked him—"What is that, Mr. President?" He said—"I have labored to preserve this Union. I have toiled during the four years I have been subjected to calumny and misrepresentation. My great and sole desire has been to presume these States intact under the Constitution as they were before." I asked him again, Mr. President, what amendment is that which you would propose? Why, said he, it is that there should be an amendment added to the Constitution which would compel the States to send their Senators and Representatives to the Congress of the United States. [Great applause.] The idea was in his mind that as a part of the doctrine of secession, one of the means to break up this Government was that the States, if they saw fit, might withdraw their Senators and Representatives, or refuse to elect them. He wanted even to remove that difficulty by a constitutional amendment compelling the States to send Senators and Representatives to Congress. But what do we now find? The Constitution of the country, even that portion of it which allows amendment to the organic law, expressly provides that no State, without its consent, shall be deprived of its suffrage and it also provides that each State shall have at least one representative in the House of Representatives; but yet the position is taken that certain States cannot be represented. We impose taxes upon them, we send our tax gatherers into every region and portion of the States. The people are fit subjects of Government for the collection of taxes, but when they ask to participate in the legislation of the country they are met at the door and told, no you must pay taxes you must bear the burdens of Government but not participate in its legislation, that legislation which is to affect you through all time to come. Is this just? Is it fair? No! no!! I repeat, I am for the Union; I am for preserving all the States. I am for admitting into the counsels of the nation all their representatives *who are unmistakeably and unquestionably loyal.* A man who acknowledges allegiance to the Government and who swears to support the Constitution must necessarily be loyal. A man cannot take that oath in good faith unless he is loyal. A mere amplification of the oath makes no difference as to the principle. Whatever test is thought proper as evidence and as proof of loyalty is a mere matter of detail, about which I care nothing but let a man be unmistakeably and unquestionably loyal, let him acknowledge allegiance to the Constitution of the United States, and be willing to support the Government in its hour of peril and its hour of need and I am willing to trust him. [Applause.] I know that some do not attach as much importance to this point as I do, but I regard it as fundamental. One principle that carried us through the Revolution was that there should be no taxation without representation. I hold to that principle, which was laid down as fundamental by our fathers. If it was good then it is good now. If it was worth standing by then it is worth standing by now. It is fundamental, and should be observed as long as free government lasts. I am aware that in the midst of the rebellion it was said by some that the Constitution had been rolled up as a piece of parchment and laid away; that in time of war and rebellion there was no constitution. We know that sometimes in great necessities under great emergencies unconstitutional things must sometimes necessarily be done in order to preserve the Constitution itself. But if, while the rebellion was going on the Constitution was rolled up and laid away; if it was violated in some particulars in order to save the Government, and all may be excused and justified, because in saving the Government you really saved the Constitution; now that peace has come, now that the war is over, we want again the benefit of a written Constitution, and I say the time has come to take the Constitution down, to unroll it—to re-read it to understand its provisions thoroughly. And now, in order to save the Government, we must preserve the Constitution. Our only safety is in a strict adherence to and preservation of the Constitution of our fathers. It is now unfolded. It must now be read—it must now be digested and understood by the American people. I am here to-day, then, in making these remarks, to vindicate the Constitution and to save it, as I believe, for it does seem as if encroachment after encroachment is proposed upon it. As far as I can, I have ever resisted encroachments upon the Constitution, and I stand prepared to resist them to-day, and thereby to preserve the Constitution and Government of the United States. [Great applause.] It is now a time of peace, and let us have peace; let us enforce the Constitution; let us live under and according to its provisions. Let it be published and printed in blazing characters, as though it were in the heavens and punctuated by the stars, so that all can read and all can understand it. Let us consult that instrument and be guided by its provisions. Let us understand them, and understanding them abide by them.

I tell the opposers of this Government, I care not from what quarter they come, East or West, North or South, "You that are engaged in the work of breaking up the Government are mistaken. The Constitution of the United States and the principles of free Government are deeply rooted in the American heart, and all the powers combined cannot destroy that great instrument—that great chart of freedom." Their attempts, though they may seem to succeed for a time, will be futile. They might as well undertake to lock up the winds or chain the waves of the ocean and confine them within limits; they might as well undertake to repeal the Constitution, and, indeed, it seems now to be supposed that can be repealed by a concurrent resolution, [laughter;] but when the question is submitted to popular judgment and to the most of the people, these men will find that they might just as well introduce a resolution to repeal the law of gravitation; the attempt to keep this Union from being restored is just about as feasible as would be resistance to the great law of gravitation, which binds all to a common centre. The great law of political gravitation will bring back these States, and replace them in all their relations to the Federal Government. Cliques and cabals and conspiracies and machinations, North or South, cannot prevent this great consummation. [Tremendous applause.] All that is wanted is time. Let the American people get to understand what is going on, and they will soon manifest their determination. By way of exclamation, let me say that I would to God the whole American people could be assembled here to-day as you are. I wish there were a vast amphitheatre here capacious enough to sustain the whole thirty millions, and they could witness the great struggle going on to preserve the Constitution of their fathers. They would soon settle the question if they could once see how things are; if they could see the kind of spirit that is manifested in the effort to break up the real principles of free government. When they come to understand who was for them and who against them; who was for ameliorating their condition and who for elevating them by preserving their Government, if the combatants could stand before them, and there could be a regular set-to between the respective gladiators, in the first tilt that might be made you would find that the enemies of the country would be crushed, and the people would sustain its friends and the friends of Constitutional liberty. [Great cheering.] My fellow-citizens, I have detained you much longer than I intended. ["Go on, go on."] But we are in a great struggle, and I am your instrument, and I have thought it best to express myself frankly. When I ask you, have I usurped authority? Who is there in this country I have not toiled and labored for? Where is the man or the woman, either in private life or public life, that has not always received my attention and my time? Sometimes it has been said, Pardon me for being a little egotistical, but we are engaged in a friendly and familiar conversation. That that JOHNSON is a lucky man. [Laughter.] They can never defeat him. [Laughter.] Now I will tell you what constitutes my good luck. It is in doing right and being for the people. [Great applause.] The people somehow or other, although their sagacity and good judgment are very frequently underrated and underestimated, generally get to find out and understand who is for them and who is against them. They do it by instinct, if in no other way. They know who is the friend; they know in whom they can confide. So far, thank God, I can lay my hand upon my bosom, and state with heartfelt satisfaction that in all the positions in which I have been placed—and I have been placed in many that were as trying as any in which mortal man has ever been placed—I have never deserted them, nor do I believe they will desert me. [No, no, and applause.] Whom have I betrayed, what principle have I violated, what sentiment have I swerved from, can those who assail me put their finger upon any one. No, no; in all the speeches that have been made, no one has dared to put his finger upon a single principle I ever asserted from which I have deviated. Have you not heard some of them at some time attempt to quote my predecessor who fell a martyr to his country's cause, but they can give no sentiment of his that is in opposition or in contradiction to anything that I have done. The very policy that I am now pursuing was pursued by me under his administration—I having been appointed by him in a particular position for that very purpose. An inscrutable Providence saw proper to remove him from this to, I trust, a better world, and I came into his place, and there is not a principle of his in reference to the restoration of the Union from which I have departed. None. Then the war is not simply upon me, but it is upon my predecessor also. I have tried to do my duty. I know that some are envious and jealous, and speak of the White House as having attractions for the President. Let me say to you, the charms of the White House have as little influence upon me as upon any individual in this country, and much less upon me than upon those who are talking about it. The little that I eat and wear does not amount to much, and the difference between what is enough to sustain me and my little family. It is very small, for I am not kin to many folks by consanguinity, though by affinity I am akin to everybody. The difference between the little that suffices for my stomach and back, and more than enough, has no charms for me. The proud and conscious satisfaction of having performed my duty to my country, to my children and to the inner man is all the reward that I ask. [Great applause.]

In conclusion, let me ask this vast concourse here to-day, this sea of upturned faces, to come with me, or I will go with you, and stand around the Constitution of our country. It is again unfolded. The people are invited to read and understand, to sustain and maintain its provisions. Let us stand by the Constitution of our fathers, though the heavens themselves should fall, though faction should rage, though taunts and jeers may come, though abuse and vituperation may be poured out in the most virulent form. I mean to be found standing by the Constitution of my country. Stand by the Constitution as the chief ark of our safety, as the palladium of our civil and our religious liberty. Yes, let us cling to it as a mariner clings to the last plank when the night and the tempest close around him. Accept my thanks, my countrymen, for the indulgence you have extended to me while submitting to you extemporaneously and, perhaps, incoherently the remarks which I have now made. Let us go away forgetting the past and looking to the future, resolved to endeavor to restore our Government to its pristine purity, trusting in Him who is on high, but who controls all here below, that ere long our Union will be restored, and that we shall have peace not only with all the nations of the earth, but peace and good will among all parts of the people of the United States. I thank you for the respect you have manifested to me on this occasion, and if the time shall come during the period of my existence when this country is to be destroyed and its Government overturned, if you will look out you will find the humble individual who stands before you there with you endeavoring to avert its final destruction.

The President retired amidst a storm of applause.

1866

Andrew Johnson: Veto of the Civil Rights Bill

WASHINGTON, D. C., *March 27, 1866.*
To the Senate of the United States:

I regret that the bill, which has passed both Houses of Congress, entitled "An act to protect all persons in the United States in their civil rights and furnish the means of their vindication," contains provisions which I can not approve consistently with my sense of duty to the whole people and my obligations to the Constitution of the United States. I am therefore constrained to return it to the Senate, the House in which it originated, with my objections to its becoming a law.

By the first section of the bill all persons born in the United States and not subject to any foreign power, excluding Indians not taxed, are declared to be citizens of the United States. This provision comprehends the Chinese of the Pacific States, Indians subject to taxation, the people called gypsies, as well as the entire race designated as blacks, people of color, negroes, mulattoes, and persons of African blood. Every individual of these races born in the United States is by the bill made a citizen of the United States. It does not purport to declare or confer any other right of citizenship than Federal citizenship. It does not purport to give these classes of persons any status as citizens of States, except that which may result from their status as citizens of the United States. The power to confer the right of State citizenship is just as exclusively with the several States as the power to confer the right of Federal citizenship is with Congress.

The right of Federal citizenship thus to be conferred on the several excepted races before mentioned is now for the first time proposed to be given by law. If, as is claimed by many, all persons who are native born already are, by virtue of the Constitution, citizens of the United States, the passage of the pending bill can not be necessary to make them such. If, on the other hand, such persons are not citizens, as may be assumed from the proposed legislation to make them such, the grave question presents itself whether, when eleven of the thirty-six States are unrepresented in Congress at the present time, it is sound policy to make our entire colored population and all other excepted classes citizens of the United States. Four millions of them have just emerged from slavery into freedom. Can it be reasonably supposed that they possess the requisite qualifications to entitle them to all the privileges and immunities of citizens of the United States? Have the people of the several States expressed such a conviction? It may also be asked whether it is necessary that they should be declared citizens in order that they may be secured in the enjoyment of the civil rights proposed to be conferred by the bill. Those rights are, by Federal as well as State laws, secured to all domiciled aliens and foreigners, even before the completion of the process of naturalization; and it may safely be assumed that the same enactments are sufficient to give like protection and benefits to those for whom this bill provides special legislation. Besides, the policy of the Government from its origin to the present time seems to have been that persons who are strangers to and unfamiliar with our institutions and our laws should pass through a certain probation, at the end of which, before attaining the coveted prize, they must give evidence of their fitness to receive and to exercise the rights of citizens as contemplated by the Constitution of the United States. The bill in effect proposes a discrimination against large numbers of intelligent, worthy, and patriotic foreigners, and in favor of the negro, to whom, after long years of bondage, the avenues to freedom and intelligence have just now been suddenly opened. He must of necessity, from his previous unfortunate condition of servitude, be less informed as to the nature and character of our institutions than he who, coming from abroad, has, to some extent at least, familiarized himself with the principles of a Government to which he voluntarily intrusts "life, liberty, and the pursuit of happiness." Yet it is now proposed, by a single legislative enactment, to confer the rights of citizens upon all persons of African descent born within the extended limits of the United States, while persons of foreign birth who make our land their home must undergo a probation of five years, and can only then become citizens upon proof that they are "of good moral character, attached to the principles of the Constitution of the United States, and well disposed to the good order and happiness of the same."

The first section of the bill also contains an enumeration of the rights to be enjoyed by these classes so made citizens "in every State and Territory in the United States." These rights are "to make and enforce contracts; to sue, be parties, and give evidence; to inherit, purchase, lease, sell, hold, and convey real and personal property," and to have "full and equal benefit of all laws and proceedings for the security of person and property as is enjoyed by white citizens." So, too, they are made subject to the same punishment, pains, and penalties in common with white citizens, and to none other. Thus a perfect equality of the white and colored races is attempted to be fixed by Federal law in every State of the Union over the vast field of State jurisdiction covered by these enumerated rights. In no one of these can any State ever exercise any power of discrimination between the different races. In the exercise of State policy over matters exclusively affecting the people of each State it has frequently been thought expedient to discriminate between the two races. By the statutes of some of the States, Northern as well as Southern, it is enacted, for instance, that no white person shall intermarry with a negro or mulatto. Chancellor Kent says, speaking of the blacks, that—

> Marriages between them and the whites are forbidden in some of the States where slavery does not exist, and they are prohibited in all the slaveholding States; and when not absolutely contrary to law, they are revolting, and regarded as an offense against public decorum.

I do not say that this bill repeals State laws on the subject of marriage between the two races, for as the whites are forbidden to intermarry with the blacks, the blacks can only make such contracts as the whites themselves are allowed to make, and therefore can not under this bill enter into the marriage contract with the whites. I cite this discrimination, however, as an instance of the State policy as to discrimination, and to inquire whether if Congress can abrogate all State laws of discrimination between the two races in the matter of real estate, of suits, and of contracts generally Congress may not also repeal the State laws as to the contract of marriage between the two races. Hitherto every subject embraced in the enumeration of rights contained in this bill has been considered as exclusively belonging to the States. They all relate to the internal police and economy of the respective States. They are matters which in each State concern the domestic condition of its people, varying in each according to its own peculiar circumstances and the safety and well-being of its own citizens. I do not mean to say that upon all these subjects there are not Federal restraints—as, for instance, in the State power of legislation over contracts there is a Federal limitation that no State shall pass a law impairing the obligations of contracts; and, as to crimes, that no State shall pass an *ex post facto* law; and, as to money, that no State shall make anything but gold and silver a legal tender; but where can we find a Federal prohibition against the power of any State to discriminate, as do most of them, between aliens and citizens, between artificial persons, called corporations, and natural persons, in the right to hold real estate? If it be granted that Congress can repeal all State laws discriminating between whites and blacks in the subjects covered by this bill, why, it may be asked, may not Congress repeal in the same way all State laws discriminating between the two races on the subjects of suffrage and office? If Congress can declare by law who shall hold lands, who shall testify, who shall have capacity to make a contract in a State, then Congress can by law also declare who, without regard to color or race, shall have the right to sit as a juror or as a judge, to hold any office, and, finally, to vote "in every State and Territory of the United States." As respects the Territories, they come within the power of Congress, for as to them the lawmaking power is the Federal power; but as to the States no similar provision exists vesting in Congress the power "to make rules and regulations" for them.

The object of the second section of the bill is to afford discriminating protection to colored persons in the full enjoyment of all the rights secured to them by the preceding section. It declares—

> That any person who, under color of any law, statute, ordinance, regulation, or custom, shall subject, or cause to be subjected, any inhabitant of any State or Territory to the deprivation of any right secured or protected by this act, or to different punishment, pains, or penalties on account of such person having at any time been held in a condition of slavery

or involuntary servitude, except as a punishment for crime whereof the party shall have been duly convicted, or by reason of his color or race, than is prescribed for the punishment of white persons, shall be deemed guilty of a misdemeanor, and on conviction shall be punished by fine not exceeding $1,000, or imprisonment not exceeding one year, or both, in the discretion of the court.

This section seems to be designed to apply to some existing or future law of a State or Territory which may conflict with the provisions of the bill now under consideration. It provides for counteracting such forbidden legislation by imposing fine and imprisonment upon the legislators who may pass such conflicting laws, or upon the officers or agents who shall put or attempt to put them into execution. It means an official offense, not a common crime committed against law upon the persons or property of the black race. Such an act may deprive the black man of his property, but not of the *right* to hold property. It means a deprivation of the right itself, either by the State judiciary or the State legislature. It is therefore assumed that under this section members of State legislatures who should vote for laws conflicting with the provisions of the bill, that judges of the State courts who should render judgments in antagonism with its terms, and that marshals and sheriffs who should, as ministerial officers, execute processes sanctioned by State laws and issued by State judges in execution of their judgments could be brought before other tribunals and there subjected to fine and imprisonment for the performance of the duties which such State laws might impose. The legislation thus proposed invades the judicial power of the State. It says to every State court or judge, If you decide that this act is unconstitutional; if you refuse, under the prohibition of a State law, to allow a negro to testify; if you hold that over such a subject-matter the State law is paramount, and "under color" of a State law refuse the exercise of the right to the negro, your error of judgment, however conscientious, shall subject you to fine and imprisonment. I do not apprehend that the conflicting legislation which the bill seems to contemplate is so likely to occur as to render it necessary at this time to adopt a measure of such doubtful constitutionality.

In the next place, this provision of the bill seems to be unnecessary, as adequate judicial remedies could be adopted to secure the desired end without invading the immunities of legislators, always important to be preserved in the interest of public liberty; without assailing the independence of the judiciary, always essential to the preservation of individual rights; and without impairing the efficiency of ministerial officers, always necessary for the maintenance of public peace and order. The remedy proposed by this section seems to be in this respect not only anomalous, but unconstitutional; for the Constitution guarantees nothing with certainty if it does not insure to the several States the right of making and executing laws in regard to all matters arising within their jurisdiction, subject only to the restriction that in cases of conflict with the Constitution and constitutional laws of the United States the latter should be held to be the supreme law of the land.

The third section gives the district courts of the United States exclusive "cognizance of all crimes and offenses committed against the provisions of this act," and concurrent jurisdiction with the circuit courts of the United States of all civil and criminal cases "affecting persons who are denied or can not enforce in the courts or judicial tribunals of the State or locality where they may be any of the rights secured to them by the first section." The construction which I have given to the second section is strengthened by this third section, for it makes clear what kind of denial or deprivation of the rights secured by the first section was in contemplation. It is a denial or deprivation of such rights "in the courts or judicial tribunals of the State." It stands, therefore, clear of doubt that the offense and the penalties provided in the second section are intended for the State judge who, in the clear exercise of his functions as a judge, not acting ministerially but judicially, shall decide contrary to this Federal law. In other words, when a State judge, acting upon a question involving a conflict between a State law and a Federal law, and bound, according to his own judgment and responsibility, to give an impartial decision between the two, comes to the conclusion that the State law is valid and the Federal law is invalid, he must not follow the dictates of his own judgment, at the peril of fine and imprisonment. The legislative department of the Government of the United States thus takes from the judicial department of the States the sacred and exclusive duty of judicial decision, and converts the State judge into a mere ministerial officer, bound to decide according to the will of Congress.

It is clear that in States which deny to persons whose rights are secured by the first section of the bill any one of those rights all criminal and civil cases affecting them will, by the provisions of the third section, come under the exclusive cognizance of the Federal tribunals. It follows that if, in any State which denies to a colored person any one of all those rights, that person should commit a crime against the laws of a State—murder, arson, rape, or any other crime—all protection and punishment through the courts of the State are taken away, and he can only be tried and punished in the Federal courts. How is the criminal to be tried? If the offense is provided for and punished by Federal law, that law, and not the State law, is to govern. It is only when the offense does not happen to be within the purview of Federal law that the Federal courts are to try and punish him under any other law. Then resort is to be had to "the common law, as modified and changed" by State legislation, "so far as the same is not inconsistent with the Constitution and laws of the United States." So that over this vast domain of criminal jurisprudence provided by each State for the protection of its own citizens and for the punishment of all persons who violate its criminal laws, Federal law, whenever it can be made to apply, displaces State law. The question here naturally arises, from what source Congress derives the power to transfer to Federal tribunals certain classes of cases embraced in this section. The Constitution expressly declares that the judicial power of the United States "shall extend to all cases, in law and equity, arising under this Constitution, the laws of the United States, and treaties made or which shall be made under their authority; to all cases affecting ambassadors, other public ministers, and consuls; to all cases of admiralty and maritime jurisdiction; to controversies to which the United States shall be a party; to controversies between two or more States, between a State and citizens of another State, between citizens of different States, between citizens of the same State claiming lands under grants of different States, and between a State, or the citizens thereof, and foreign states, citizens, or subjects." Here the judicial power of the United States is expressly set forth and defined; and the act of September 24, 1789, establishing the judicial courts of the United States, in conferring upon the Federal courts jurisdiction over cases originating in State tribunals, is careful to confine them to the classes enumerated in the above-recited clause of the Constitution. This section of the bill undoubtedly comprehends cases and authorizes the exercise of powers that are not, by the Constitution, within the jurisdiction of the courts of the United States. To transfer them to those courts would be an exercise of authority well calculated to excite distrust and alarm on the part of all the States, for the bill applies alike to all of them—as well to those that have as to those that have not been engaged in rebellion.

It may be assumed that this authority is incident to the power granted to Congress by the Constitution, as recently amended, to enforce, by appropriate legislation, the article declaring that—

> Neither slavery nor involuntary servitude, except as a punishment for crime whereof the party shall have been duly convicted, shall exist within the United States or any place subject to their jurisdiction.

It can not, however, be justly claimed that, with a view to the enforcement of this article of the Constitution, there is at present any necessity for the exercise of all the powers which this bill confers. Slavery has been abolished, and at present nowhere exists within the jurisdiction of the United States; nor has there been, nor is it likely there will be, any attempt to revive it by the people or the States. If, however, any such attempt shall be made, it will then become the duty of the General Government to exercise any and all incidental powers necessary and proper to maintain inviolate this great constitutional law of freedom.

The fourth section of the bill provides that officers and agents of the Freedmen's Bureau shall be empowered to make arrests, and also that other officers may be specially commissioned for that purpose by the President of the United States. It also authorizes circuit courts of the United States and the superior courts of the Territories to appoint, without limitation, commissioners, who are to be charged with the performance of *quasi* judicial duties. The fifth section empowers the commissioners so to be selected by the courts to appoint in writing, under their hands, one or more suitable persons from time to time to execute warrants and other processes described by the bill. These numerous official agents are made to constitute a sort of police, in addition to the military, and are authorized to summon a *posse comitatus*, and even to call to their aid such portion of the land and naval forces of the United States, or of the militia, "as may be necessary to the performance of the duty with which they are charged." This extraordinary power is to be conferred upon agents irresponsible to the Government and to the people, to whose number the discretion of the commissioners is the only limit, and in whose hands such authority might be made a terrible engine of wrong, oppression, and fraud. The general statutes regulating the land and naval forces of the United States, the militia, and the execution of the laws are believed to be adequate for every emergency which can occur in time of peace. If it should prove otherwise, Congress can at any time amend those laws in such manner as, while subserving the public welfare, not to jeopard the rights, interests, and liberties of the people.

The seventh section provides that a fee of $10 shall be paid to each commissioner in every case brought before him, and a fee of $5 to his deputy or deputies "for each person he or they may arrest and take before any such commissioner," "with such other fees as may be deemed reasonable by such commissioner," "in general for performing such other duties as may be required in the premises." All these fees are to be "paid out of the Treasury of the United States," whether there is a conviction or not; but in case of conviction they are to be recoverable from the defendant. It seems to me that under the influence of such temptations bad men might convert any law, however beneficent, into an instrument of persecution and fraud.

By the eighth section of the bill the United States courts, which sit only in one place for white citizens, must migrate with the marshal and district attorney (and necessarily with the clerk, although he is not mentioned) to any part of the district upon the order of the President, and there hold a court, "for the purpose of the more speedy arrest and trial of persons charged with a violation of this act;" and there the judge and officers of the court must remain, upon the order of the President, "for the time therein designated."

The ninth section authorizes the President, or such person as he may empower for that purpose, "to employ such part of the land or naval forces of the United States, or of the militia, as shall be necessary to prevent the violation and enforce the due execution of this act." This language seems to imply a permanent military force, that is to be always at hand, and whose only business is to be the enforcement of this measure over the vast region where it is intended to operate.

I do not propose to consider the policy of this bill. To me the details of the bill seem fraught with evil. The white race and the black race of the South have hitherto lived together under the relation of master and slave—capital owning labor. Now, suddenly, that relation is changed, and as to ownership capital and labor are divorced. They stand now each master of itself. In this new relation, one being necessary to the other, there will be a new adjustment, which both are deeply interested in making harmonious. Each has equal power in settling the terms, and if left to the laws that regulate capital and labor it is confidently believed that they will satisfactorily work out the problem. Capital, it is true, has more intelligence, but labor is never so ignorant as not to understand its own interests, not to know its own value, and not to see that capital must pay that value.

This bill frustrates this adjustment. It intervenes between capital and labor and attempts to settle questions of political economy through the agency of numerous officials whose interest it will be to foment discord between the two races, for as the breach widens their employment will continue, and when it is closed their occupation will terminate.

In all our history, in all our experience as a people living under Federal and State law, no such system as that contemplated by the details of this bill has ever before been proposed or adopted. They establish for the security of the colored race safeguards which go infinitely beyond any that the General Government has ever provided for the white race. In fact, the distinction of race and color is by the bill made to operate in favor of the colored and against the white race. They interfere with the municipal legislation of the States, with the relations existing exclusively between a State and its citizens, or between inhabitants of the same State—an absorption and assumption of power by the General Government which, if acquiesced in, must sap and destroy our federative system of limited powers and break down the barriers which preserve the rights of the States. It is another step, or rather stride, toward centralization and the concentration of all legislative powers in the National Government. The tendency of the bill must be to resuscitate the spirit of rebellion and to arrest the progress of those influences which are more closely drawing around the States the bonds of union and peace.

My lamented predecessor, in his proclamation of the 1st of January, 1863, ordered and declared that all persons held as slaves within certain States and parts of States therein designated were and thenceforward should be free; and further, that the executive government of the United States, including the military and naval authorities thereof, would recognize and maintain the freedom of such persons. This guaranty has been rendered especially obligatory and sacred by the amendment of the Constitution abolishing slavery throughout the United States. I therefore fully recognize the obligation to protect and defend that class of our people whenever and wherever it shall become necessary, and to the full extent compatible with the Constitution of the United States.

Entertaining these sentiments, it only remains for me to say that I will cheerfully cooperate with Congress in any measure that may be necessary for the protection of the civil rights of the freedmen, as well as those of all other classes of persons throughout the United States, by judicial process, under equal and impartial laws, in conformity with the provisions of the Federal Constitution.

I now return the bill to the Senate, and regret that in considering the bills and joint resolutions—forty-two in number—which have been thus far submitted for my approval I am compelled to withhold my assent from a second measure that has received the sanction of both Houses of Congress.

ANDREW JOHNSON.

CONGRESSIONAL RECONSTRUCTION 1866–1869

※

In the spring of 1866 congressional Republicans took the lead in framing federal Reconstruction policy. Having overridden President Andrew Johnson's veto of the Civil Rights Bill, they now hammered out an approach marked by compromise and an increasing concern about presidential obstruction. That many people persist in labelling this period Radical Reconstruction overlooks the extent to which several measures associated with Radical Republicans—a prolonged military occupation of the former Confederacy, the confiscation and redistribution of land to the freed people, and the continuing exclusion of former Confederates from voting and holding office—faded from the realm of the politically possible. On the other hand, guarantees of equality before the law, the enfranchisement of black adult males in the South, and an increased federal role in establishing new state governments with the participation of southern freedmen seemed radical enough to those seeking to maintain a white supremacist America.

Events in the South demonstrated that federal protection was necessary. In May a white mob, led by local officials, attacked black veterans and their families in Memphis, killing forty-six African Americans. In July, a white mob in New Orleans targeted supporters of a new state constitution, killing thirty-four African Americans and three whites. At the same time, a white supremacist terrorist organization known as the Ku Klux Klan began to take root across the South. Johnson discounted such acts of violence or blamed them on his opponents; Republicans such as Indiana governor Oliver P. Morton warned that such violent acts represented an ominous revival of the spirit of rebellion.

The Republican effort at taking control of the Reconstruction process through the passage of the Fourteenth Amendment in June 1866, even as it bypassed the possibility of presidential veto, demonstrated that their efforts to refashion the American polity had its limits. Congress excluded women from the drive toward equality before the law, and most Republicans would not endorse women's suffrage. Moreover, should the former Confederate states follow the example of Tennessee and ratify the amendment, Reconstruction might come to an end. Once the former Confederate states were readmitted to representation in Congress, southern and northern Democrats could work together to diminish federal authority. The southern states could also choose not to enfranchise black men as long as they were willing to accept the reduced congressional and electoral college representation called for in the amendment's second section.

Determined to defeat his congressional foes during the midterm elections, Andrew Johnson embarked upon a speaking tour throughout the North in the summer of 1866. Dubbed "the Swing Around the Circle," the president's effort to rally support floundered as he engaged in ill-tempered exchanges with increasingly raucous crowds. Accompanying the president was General Ulysses S. Grant, who privately characterized the result as "a national disgrace," remarking that the effort reminded him of a man making speeches on the way to his own funeral. In the elections that fall, Republicans secured veto-proof majorities in both houses of Congress. When the remaining former Confederate states, encouraged by Johnson, failed to ratify the Fourteenth Amendment, congressional Republicans moved in early 1867 to enact legislation that provided for the framing of new southern state constitutions and governments under military supervision in a process that involved black men as voters, delegates, and officeholders. Sometimes called the Military Reconstruction Acts, this series of legislative enactments overrode Johnson's earlier attempts to restore state governments on a whites-only basis and promised revolutionary changes in the American polity.

The work of these state constitutional conventions and the governments they established represented significant change. Blacks and whites worked together to establish public schools, end discrimination in public facilities, and provide for individual rights. At the same time, however, the success of these conventions led many Republicans to believe that, armed with the ballot, blacks and their white allies could now defend themselves as well as shape their own futures, relieving the federal government of the need to use the military to protect and promote freedom in the South.

Seeking to hamstring Johnson's ability to oppose the implementation of its Reconstruction measures, Congress in March 1867 directed that orders issued by the president to military commanders had to be transmitted through Grant, the general-in-chief. It also passed the Tenure of Office Act, which required that the Senate concur in any presidential decision to remove civil officers appointed with Senate approval. The law deprived Johnson of the power to dismiss supporters of congressional initiatives (including cabinet members) from the executive branch, although supporters of the act were vague as to whether it also protected Lincoln appointees such as Secretary of War Edwin M. Stanton, a Democrat-turned-Republican who often opposed the president's policy.

Despite these measures, Andrew Johnson did his best to obstruct the implementation of congressional Reconstruction. He removed its supporters from positions of authority, resisted enforcement of legislation, and waged a relentless attack upon Republicans. Notable was his suspension in August 1867 of Secretary Stanton from his cabinet post, with Grant taking over on an ad interim basis, as well as the transfer of several generals who favored Republican policies from their commands established through the Reconstruction Acts. Emboldened by the results of the 1867 elections, which suggested that a majority of northern voters were reluctant to embrace black suffrage in their own states, Johnson attempted to seize control of the War Department after Grant bowed to the Senate's emphatic decision in January 1868 to restore Stanton to his position as secretary of war. Having earlier honored the letter if not the spirit of the Tenure of Office Act, Johnson now attempted to defy it by dismissing Stanton outright. Republicans in the House of Representatives saw their chance at last to muster a majority behind articles of impeachment. They did so on February 24, 1868.

In May 1868 Johnson barely escaped conviction by a single vote in the United States Senate. His survival owed much to the decision of Republicans to regain control of the presidency through the traditional means of electing a candidate. Ulysses

S. Grant's overwhelming popularity made him an ideal choice: his declaration of "Let us have peace" was flexible enough to appeal to voters with differing views on Reconstruction. In nominating former New York governor Horatio Seymour, the Democrats appeared determined to refight the issues of the war and Reconstruction, an impression confirmed when vice presidential candidate Frank Blair lashed out at Grant and promised to roll back Republican initiatives. With all but three of the former Confederate states having been restored to representation in Congress, the fall contest witnessed the first time black voters cast ballots in a presidential contest in large numbers.

Maria F. Chandler to Thaddeus Stevens

West Liberty, Ohio Co. West Va.
April 1st 1866

Mr. Thadeus Stephens, Pennsylvania

I know that every patriot's heart will thank the Giver of all good that *now* we have a Congress truly in unison with the sentiments expressed in the Declaration of Independence—a Congress in advance of all other Legislative Assemblies in the Nineteenth Century, and leading the Van of the Nations of the Earth in their progress toward Liberty, Justice and Equality.

Oh! be watchful! be vigilant, distrust the enemies of your country although they may appear in the form of an angel of light. They will try all the arts invented in the bottomless-pit to circumvent you. Beware of receiving them with "open arms" when they make a feint of coming over to your side—for the instant the reins of power are in their hands, they will throw their promises to the winds—violate all moral obligations, and ride rough-shod over prostrate humanity.

And now to pass to another subject—I thank you in the name of my sex for your advocacy of Woman Suffrage in Congress.

"Keep back no syllable of fire. Plunge deep the rowels of thy speech."

For years has Woman stood beside the ballot-box in her own native grace, dignity, and modesty, ballot in hand—hopefully awaiting that recognition of her political equality, guaranteed by a Republican form of Government.

Why is the Elective Franchise denied us? Will any sane person declare that we are "Not of sound mind"? If that is proved then never permit another female to attend the Public schools, close all the Female Seminaries, & Colleges—spend no more time, and money, in fruitless endeavor to educate idiots, or lunatics—but if female education is persisted in, do not insist on her occupation, with her cultivated talents, and enlarged mind, and capacities, the identical sphere and position, that her ancestors filled during the last age, or century.

Another view of the case present itself here—how extremely

229

absurd it appears in the light of reason, to allow men the Elective Franchise who can neither read, nor write, and withhold it from women of cultivated minds, and scholarly attainments.

It is obvious that woman under a Republican Government like ours educated at the expense of the state, has in consequence of her wider scope of mind—added responsibilities and duties which she cannot innocently ignore. These avenues lead in public and political directions, and invite her footsteps. With increased responsibility comes the necessity of enlarged rights, and privileges, it is therefore plain and self-evident, that if you would not cramp and stultify the minds of women, if you would not crush their aspirations after more enlarged spheres of thought and extended usefulness the only alternative is to allow to become members of the Body Politic and extend to them the Elective Franchise.

Very respectfully   M. F. Chandler.

Harper's Weekly:
Radicalism and Conservatism

IN EVERY political contest in a Constitutional system the names of Conservatism and Radicalism will be applied to the opposing policies, while the history of such governments shows that the policy which truly conserves the principle and spirit of a free system is that which is called Radicalism. In the conflict of opinion in England before our Revolution GEORGE III. and Dr. JOHNSON were the stiffest of Tory Conservatives, and saw in the doctrines and policy of EDMUND BURKE nothing but Radicalism and the overthrow of the monarchy. But BURKE was the true Conservative. His policy would have saved the empire upon its own principles.

In this country at this moment both Radicalism and Conservatism, as the names of a policy of national reorganization, are very easily defined and comprehended. Thus Radicalism holds that the late rebel States should not be suffered to take part in the government of the Union which they have so zealously striven to destroy except after searching inquiry into their condition, and upon terms which shall prevent any advantage having been gained by rebellion. By the result of the war the suffrage of a voter in South Carolina weighs as much as the vote of two voters in New York. Is that a desirable state of things? Would any fair-minded voter in South Carolina claim that he ought to have a preference in the Union because, however honestly, he has rebelled against it? Radicalism, therefore, favors an equalization of representation as a condition precedent to the full recognition of the disturbed States, and every citizen of those States who sincerely desires national unity and peace will favor it also.

Radicalism holds that equal civil rights before the law should be guaranteed by the United States to every citizen. It claims that the Government which commands the obedience of every citizen shall afford him protection, and that the freedom which the people of the United States have conferred the people of the United States shall maintain. Is that a perilous claim? Is any other course consistent with national safety or honor?

Once more: Radicalism asserts that, as the national welfare and permanent union can be established only upon justice, there should be no unreasonable political disfranchisement of any part of the people. It denies that complexion, or weight, or height are reasonable political qualifications, and it refers to the history of the country to show that they have not always been so regarded even in some of the late slave States, and remembers that both President JOHNSON and his predecessor were friends of impartial suffrage. Holding this faith, Radicalism urges that while we may honestly differ as to the wisest means of securing political equality, yet that all our efforts should constantly tend, with due respect for the proper and subordinate functions of the States in our constitutional system, to protect those equal rights of man with whose assertion our Government began, and in consequence of whose denial that Government has just escaped the most appalling fate.

This is Radicalism. Is it unfair? Is it unconstitutional? Is it anarchical or revolutionary? It denies no man's rights. It deprives no man of power or privilege. It claims for the National Government nothing which is not inseparable from the idea of such a Government. Does it demand any thing that every prudent and patriotic man ought not to be willing to concede? The views of Mr. THADDEUS STEVENS and of Mr. SUMNER, sincerely entertained and ingeniously defended as they are, are not the Radical policy. Mr. STEVENS holds that the disturbed States are conquered provinces in which the land should be confiscated, as that of Ireland has been three times over without giving Ireland peace. Does any body suppose that even the House, which respects Mr. STEVENS's sturdy fidelity to his own convictions, agrees with him, or that the National Union party holds his view? Mr. SUMNER holds that equal suffrage should be required of the absent States as a condition of representation, and in a Radical Senate which passed the Civil Rights Bill over the veto by a vote of 33 to 15, Mr. SUMNER's proposition obtained 8 votes. These gentlemen, of course, support the Radical policy, but they do not shape it. The opinions of the Union party are to be found, as President JOHNSON says, in the party platform. The policy of the Radicals is to be seen in the measures they adopt; and of the forty-two bills which at the time of the last veto they had presented to the President, he had signed forty.

In our present political situation Conservatism is the policy which declares that the late rebel States are already in a condition to resume their full functions in the Union, and which denounces Congress for presuming to inquire whether that opinion is well founded. It denies to Congress—that is, to the representatives of the loyal people who have maintained the Government—the authority to look behind the credentials of any man who comes from a State still panting with rebellion, and ascertain the origin and validity of the authority that issued the credentials. It objects to the legislation of Congress while eleven States are unrepresented, without reference to the reason of their absence, thus virtually maintaining the monstrous proposition that a combination of States, by refusing to be represented, may prohibit national legislation. It denies that the United States ought to protect the equal civil rights of citizens before the law, and would admit the absent States to Congress before requiring their assent to an amendment equalizing representation. Conservatism is the policy which, forgetting that the United States are bound by every moral obligation to secure the freedom which they have conferred, apparently believes that that freedom will be best maintained and the national peace most truly established by leaving those of every color who were heroically faithful to the Government during the rebellion to the exclusive mercy of those who sought to destroy it.

These are the distinctive points of the Conservative policy. Are they agreeable to an honorable and intelligent people? And of what is this policy conservative? If of the Constitution and Union, it will of course be earnestly supported by their true and tried friends. Is it so supported? Who are the present Conservatives? Who shout and sing and fire cannon and ring bells in jubilant exultation at every measure in supposed accordance with this policy? The reply is, unfortunately, unavoidable. The Conservative party, or the supporters of the policy we have described, is composed of the late rebels and of those who justified and palliated rebellion, with a few Republicans. And who oppose this policy? Who are the Radicals? The great multitude of those who believed in the war and supported it, whose children and brothers and friends lie buried in the battle-field in every rebel State, whose sentiments are now as they have been for five years expressed by the Union press of the country, and whose voice speaks in the vote of Union Legislatures and in the result of the spring elections.

It is useless for Conservatism to claim that conciliation is essential to reorganization. Nobody denies it. But the cardinal question is, not what will please the late insurgents, but what will secure the Government. If it be said that the Government can not be secured by alienating its late enemies, the reply is, that it certainly can not be secured by alienating its unwavering friends. If conciliation contemplates the filling of national offices in the South by known rebels to the disregard and exclusion of Union men, thereby rewarding rebellion and discrediting loyalty—if it proposes to leave freemen of the United States to the Black Codes of Mississippi and Carolina, and to recognize the fatal spirit of caste which has been our curse—then conciliation is simply a name for ignominy, and Conservatism may see its fate in that of Secession.

Radicalism has not a single vindictive feeling toward the late rebel States, but it does not propose to forget that there has been a rebellion. It has the sincerest wish, as it had the most undoubting expectation, of working with the President to secure for the country what the country has fairly won by the war, and that is, the equal right of every citizen before the law and the full resumption by the late insurgent States of their functions in the Union only upon such honorable and reasonable conditions as Congress might require. All reasonable men who support that policy will not lightly denounce those who differ with them. They will strive long for the harmony of those with whom during the war they have sympathized and acted. They will concede minor points of method, and bear patiently with impatient rhetoric leveled at themselves. But they will also bear steadily in mind the words of ANDREW JOHNSON when he accepted the nomination which has placed him where he is: "While society is in this disordered state and we are seeking security, let us fix the foundations of the Government on principles of eternal justice which will endure for all time." The Radical policy was never more tersely expressed; and it will unquestionably be maintained, for it is founded in the plainest common sense and the profoundest conviction of the loyal American people.

April 21, 1866

Thaddeus Stevens: Speech in Congress on the Fourteenth Amendment

Mr. STEVENS. The short time allowed by our resolution will suffice to introduce this debate. If unexpectedly there should be any objection to the proposed amendment to the Constitution I may ask the indulgence of the House to reply.

The committee are not ignorant of the fact that there has been some impatience at the delay in making this report; that it existed to some extent in the country as well as among a few members of the House. It originated in the suggestions of faction, no doubt, but naturally spread until it infected some good men. This is not to be wondered at or complained of. Very few could be informed of the necessity for such delay. Beside, we are not all endowed with patience; some men are naturally restive, especially if they have active minds and deep convictions.

But I beg gentlemen to consider the magnitude of the task which was imposed upon the committee. They were expected to suggest a plan for rebuilding a shattered nation—a nation which though not dissevered was yet shaken and riven by the gigantic and persistent efforts of six million able and ardent men; of bitter rebels striving through four years of bloody war. It cannot be denied that this terrible struggle sprang from the vicious principles incorporated into the institutions of our country. Our fathers had been compelled to postpone the principles of their great Declaration, and wait for their full establishment till a more propitious time. That time ought to be present now. But the public mind has been educated in error for a century. How difficult in a day to unlearn it. In rebuilding, it is necessary to clear away the rotten and defective portions of the old foundations, and to sink deep and found the repaired edifice upon the firm foundation of eternal justice. If, perchance, the accumulated quicksands render it impossible to reach in every part so firm a basis, then it becomes our duty to drive deep and solid the substituted piles on which to build. It would not be wise to prevent the raising of the structure because some corner of it might be founded upon materials subject to the inevitable laws of mortal decay. It were better to shelter the household and trust to the advancing progress of a higher morality and a purer and more intelligent principle to underpin the defective corner.

I would not for a moment inculcate the idea of surrendering a principle vital to justice. But if full justice could not be obtained at once I would not refuse to do what is possible. The commander of an army who should find his enemy intrenched on impregnable heights would act unwisely if he insisted on marching his troops full in the face of a destructive fire merely to show his courage. Would it not be better to flank the works and march round and round and besiege, and thus secure the surrender of the enemy, though it might cost time? The former course would show valor and folly; the latter moral and physical courage, as well as prudence and wisdom.

This proposition is not all that the committee desired. It falls far short of my wishes, but it fulfills my hopes. I believe it is all that can be obtained in the present state of public opinion. Not only Congress but the several States are to be consulted. Upon a careful survey of the whole ground, we did not believe that nineteen of the loyal States could be induced to ratify any proposition more stringent than this. I say nineteen, for I utterly repudiate and scorn the idea that any State not acting in the Union is to be counted on the question of ratification. It is absurd to suppose that any more than three fourths of the States that propose the amendment are required to make it valid; that States not here are to be counted as present. Believing, then, that this is the best proposition that can be made effectual, I accept it. I shall not be driven by clamor or denunciation to throw away a great good because it is not perfect. I will take all I can get in the cause of humanity and leave it to be perfected by better men in better times. It may be that that time will not come while I am here to enjoy the glorious triumph; but that it will come is as certain as that there is a just God.

The House should remember the great labor which the committee had to perform. They were charged to inquire into the condition of eleven States of great extent of territory. They sought, often in vain, to procure their organic laws and statutes.

They took the evidence of every class and condition of witness, from the rebel vice president and the commander-in-chief of their armies down to the humblest freedman. The sub-committees who were charged with that duty—of whom I was not one, and can therefore speak freely—exhibited a degree of patience and diligence which was never excelled. Considering their other duties, the mass of evidence taken may well be considered extraordinary. It must be remembered, also, that three months since, and more, the committee reported and the House adopted a proposed amendment fixing the basis of representation in such way as would surely have secured the enfranchisement of every citizen at no distant period. That, together with the amendment repudiating the rebel debt, which we also passed, would have gone far to curb the rebellious spirit of secession, and to have given to the oppressed race their rights. It went to the other end of the Capitol, and was there mortally wounded in the house of its friends.

After having received the careful examination and approbation of the committee, and having received the united Republican vote of one hundred and twenty Representatives of the people, it was denounced as "utterly reprehensible," and "unpardonable;" "to be encountered as a public enemy;" "positively endangering the peace of the country, and covering its name with dishonor." "A wickedness on a larger scale than the crime against Kansas or the fugitive slave law; gross, foul, outrageous; an incredible injustice against the whole African race;" with every other vulgar epithet which polished cultivation could command. It was slaughtered by a puerile and pedantic criticism, by a perversion of philological definition which, if when I taught school a lad who had studied Lindley Murray had assumed, I would have expelled him from the institution as unfit to waste education upon. But it is dead, and unless this (less efficient, I admit) shall pass, its death has postponed the protection of the colored race perhaps for ages. I confess my mortification at its defeat. I grieved especially because it almost closed the door of hope for the amelioration of the condition of the freedmen. But men in pursuit of justice must never despair. Let us again try and see whether we cannot devise some way to overcome the united forces of self-righteous

Republicans and unrighteous copperheads. It will not do for those who for thirty years have fought the beasts at Ephesus to be frightened by the fangs of modern catamounts.

Let us now refer to the provisions of the proposed amendment.

The first section prohibits the States from abridging the privileges and immunities of citizens of the United States, or unlawfully depriving them of life, liberty, or property, or of denying to any person within their jurisdiction the "equal" protection of the laws.

I can hardly believe that any person can be found who will not admit that every one of these provisions is just. They are all asserted, in some form or other, in our DECLARATION or organic law. But the Constitution limits only the action of Congress, and is not a limitation on the States. This amendment supplies that defect, and allows Congress to correct the unjust legislation of the States, so far that the law which operated upon one man shall operate *equally* upon all. Whatever law punishes a white man for a crime shall punish the black man precisely in the same way and to the same degree. Whatever law protects the white man shall afford "equal" protection to the black man. Whatever means of redress is afforded to one shall be afforded to all. Whatever law allows the white man to testify in court shall allow the man of color to do the same. These are great advantages over the present codes. Now different degrees of punishment are inflicted, not on account of the magnitude of the crime, but according to the color of the skin. Now color disqualifies a man from testifying in courts, or being tried in the same way as white men. I need not enumerate these partial and oppressive laws. Unless the Constitution should restrain them those States will all, I fear, keep up this discrimination, and crush to death the hated freedmen. Some answer, "Your civil rights bill secures the same things." That is partly true, but a law is repealable by a majority. And I need hardly say that the first time that the South with their copperhead allies obtain the command of Congress it will be repealed. The veto of the President and their votes on the bill are conclusive evidence of that. And yet I am amazed and alarmed at the impatience of certain well-meaning Republicans at the exclusion of the rebel States until the Constitution shall be so amended as to restrain their despotic desires.

This amendment once adopted cannot be annulled without two thirds of Congress. That they will hardly get. And yet certain of our distinguished friends propose to admit State after State before this becomes a part of the Constitution. What madness! Is their judgment misled by their kindness; or are they unconsciously drifting into the haven of power at the other end of the avenue? I do not suspect it, but others will.

The second section I consider the most important in the article. It fixes the basis of representation in Congress. If any State shall exclude any of her adult male citizens from the elective franchise, or abridge that right, she shall forfeit her right to representation in the same proportion. The effect of this provision will be either to compel the States to grant universal suffrage or so to shear them of their power as to keep them forever in a hopeless minority in the national Government, both legislative and executive. If they do not enfranchise the freedmen, it would give to the rebel States but thirty-seven Representatives. Thus shorn of their power, they would soon become restive. Southern pride would not long brook a hopeless minority. True it will take two, three, possibly five years before they conquer their prejudices sufficiently to allow their late slaves to become their equals at the polls. That short delay would not be injurious. In the mean time the freedmen would become more enlightened, and more fit to discharge the high duties of their new condition. In that time, too, the loyal Congress could mature their laws and so amend the Constitution as to secure the rights of every human being, and render disunion impossible. Heaven forbid that the southern States, or *any one of them*, should be represented on this floor until such muniments of freedom are built high and firm. Against our will they have been absent for four bloody years; against our will they must not come back until we are ready to receive them. Do not tell me that there are loyal representatives waiting for admission—until their States are loyal they can have no standing here. They would merely *mis*represent their constituents.

I admit that this article is not as good as the one we sent to death in the Senate. In my judgment, we shall not approach the measure of justice until we have given every adult freedman a homestead on the land where he was born and toiled and suffered. Forty acres of lands and a hut would be more valuable to him than the immediate right to vote. Unless we give them this we shall receive the censure of mankind and the curse of Heaven. That article referred to provided that if *one* of the injured race was excluded the State should forfeit the right to have any of them represented. That would have hastened their full enfranchisement. This section allows the States to discriminate among the same class, and receive proportionate credit in representation. This I dislike. But it is a short step forward. The large stride which we in vain proposed is dead; the murderers must answer to the suffering race. I would not have been the perpetrator. A load of misery must sit heavy on their souls.

The third section may encounter more difference of opinion here. Among the people I believe it will be the most popular of all the provisions; it prohibits rebels from voting for members of Congress and electors of President until 1870. My only objection to it is that it is too lenient. I know that there is a morbid sensibility, sometimes called mercy, which affects a few of all classes from the priest to the clown, which has more sympathy for the murderer on the gallows than for his victim. I hope I have a heart as capable of feeling for human woe as others. I have long since wished that capital punishment were abolished. But I never dreamed that all punishment could be dispensed with in human society. Anarchy, *treason*, and violence would reign triumphant. Here is the mildest of all punishments ever inflicted on traitors. I might not consent to the extreme severity denounced upon them by a provisional governor of Tennessee—I mean the late lamented Andrew Johnson of blessed memory—but I would have increased the severity of this section. I would be glad to see it extended to 1876, and to include all State and municipal as well as national elections. In my judgment we do not sufficiently protect the loyal men of the rebel States from the vindictive persecutions of their victorious rebel neighbors. Still I will move no amendment, nor vote for any, lest the whole fabric should tumble to pieces.

I need say nothing of the fourth section, for none dare object to it who is not himself a rebel. To the friend of justice, the friend of the Union, of the perpetuity of liberty, and the final triumph of the rights of man and their extension to every human being, let me say, sacrifice as we have done your peculiar views, and instead of vainly insisting upon the instantaneous operation of all that is right accept what is possible, and "all these things shall be added unto you."

I move to recommit the joint resolution to the committee on reconstruction.

May 8, 1866

Frances Ellen Watkins Harper: Speech at the National Woman's Rights Convention

I FEEL I am something of a novice upon this platform. Born of a race whose inheritance has been outrage and wrong, most of my life had been spent in battling against those wrongs. But I did not feel as keenly as others, that I had these rights, in common with other women, which are now demanded. About two years ago, I stood within the shadows of my home. A great sorrow had fallen upon my life. My husband had died suddenly, leaving me a widow, with four children, one my own, and the others stepchildren. I tried to keep my children together. But my husband died in debt; and before he had been in his grave three months, the administrator had swept the very milk-crocks and wash tubs from my hands. I was a farmer's wife and made butter for the Columbus market; but what could I do, when they had swept all away? They left me one thing—and that was a looking glass! Had I died instead of my husband, how different would have been the result! By this time he would have had another wife, it is likely; and no administrator would have gone into his house, broken up his home, and sold his bed, and taken away his means of support.

I took my children in my arms, and went out to seek my living. While I was gone; a neighbor to whom I had once lent five dollars, went before a magistrate and swore that he believed I was a non-resident, and laid an attachment on my very bed. And I went back to Ohio with my orphan children in my arms, without a single feather bed in this wide world, that was not in the custody of the law. I say, then, that justice is not fulfilled so long as woman is unequal before the law.

We are all bound up together in one great bundle of humanity, and society cannot trample on the weakest and feeblest of its members without receiving the curse in its own soul. You tried that in the case of the negro. You pressed him down for two centuries; and in so doing you crippled the moral strength and paralyzed the spiritual energies of the white men of the country.

When the hands of the black were fettered, white men were deprived of the liberty of speech and the freedom of the press. Society cannot afford to neglect the enlightenment of any class of its members. At the South, the legislation of the country was in behalf of the rich slaveholders, while the poor white man was neglected. What is the consequence to-day? From that very class of neglected poor white men, comes the man who stands to-day, with his hand upon the helm of the nation. He fails to catch the watchword of the hour, and throws himself, the incarnation of meanness, across the pathway of the nation. My objection to Andrew Johnson is not that he has been a poor white man; my objection is that he keeps "poor whits" all the way through. [Applause.] That is the trouble with him.

This grand and glorious revolution which has commenced, will fail to reach its climax of success, until throughout the length and breadth of the American Republic, the nation shall be so color-blind, as to know no man by the color of his skin or the curl of his hair. It will then have no privileged class, trampling upon and outraging the unprivileged classes, but will be then one great privileged nation, whose privilege will be to produce the loftiest manhood and womanhood that humanity can attain.

I do not believe that giving the woman the ballot is immediately going to cure all the ills of life. I do not believe that white women are dew-drops just exhaled from the skies. I think that like men they may be divided into three classes, the good, the bad, and the indifferent. The good would vote according to their convictions and principles; the bad, as dictated by prejudice or malice; and the indifferent will vote on the strongest side of the question, with the winning party.

You white women speak here of rights. I speak of wrongs. I, as a colored woman, have had in this country an education which has made me feel as if I were in the situation of Ishmael, my hand against every man, and every man's hand against me. Let me go to-morrow morning and take my seat in one of your street cars—I do not know that they will do it in New York, but they will in Philadelphia—and the conductor will put up his hand and stop the car rather than let me ride.

A Lady—They will not do that here.

Mrs. Harper—They do in Philadelphia. Going from Washington to Baltimore this Spring, they put me in the smoking car. [Loud Voices—"Shame."] Aye, in the capital of the nation, where the black man consecrated himself to the nation's defence, faithful when the white man was faithless, they put me in the smoking car! They did it once; but the next time they tried it, they failed; for I would not go in. I felt the fight in me; but I don't want to have to fight all the time. To-day I am puzzled where to make my home. I would like to make it in Philadelphia, near my own friends and relations. But if I want to ride in the streets of Philadelphia, they send me to ride on the platform with the driver. [Cries of "Shame."] Have women nothing to do with this? Not long since, a colored woman took her seat in an Eleventh Street car in Philadelphia, and the conductor stopped the car, and told the rest of the passengers to get out, and left the car with her in it alone, when they took it back to the station. One day I took my seat in a car, and the conductor came to me and told me to take another seat. I just screamed "murder." The man said if I was black I ought to behave myself. I knew that if he was white he was not behaving himself. Are there not wrongs to be righted?

In advocating the cause of the colored man, since the Dred Scott decision, I have sometimes said I thought the nation had touched bottom. But let me tell you there is a depth of infamy lower than that. It is when the nation, standing upon the threshold of a great peril, reached out its hands to a feebler race, and asked that race to help it, and when the peril was over, said, You are good enough for soldiers, but not good enough for citizens. When Judge Taney said that the men of my race had no rights which the white man was bound to respect, he had not seen the bones of the black man bleaching outside of Richmond. He had not seen the thinned ranks and the thickened graves of the Louisiana Second, a regiment which went into battle nine hundred strong, and came out with three hundred. He had not stood at Olustee and seen defeat and disaster crushing down the pride of our banner, until word was brought to Col. Hallowell, "The day is lost; go in and save it;" and black men stood in the gap, beat back the enemy, and saved your army. [Applause.]

We have a woman in our country who has received the name of "Moses," not by lying about it, but by acting it out [applause]—a woman who has gone down into the Egypt of slavery and brought out hundreds of our people into liberty. The last time I saw that woman, her hands were swollen. That woman who had led one of Montgomery's most successful expeditions, who was brave enough and secretive enough to act as a scout for the American army, had her hands all swollen from a conflict with a brutal conductor, who undertook to eject her from her place. That woman, whose courage and bravery won a recognition from our army and from every black man in the land, is excluded from every thoroughfare of travel. Talk of giving women the ballot-box? Go on. It is a normal school, and the white women of this country need it. While there exists this brutal element in society which tramples upon the feeble and treads down the weak, I tell you that if there is any class of people who need to be lifted out of their airy nothings and selfishness, it is the white women of America. [Applause.]

May 10, 1866

THE MEMPHIS RIOT: TENNESSEE, MAY 1866

George Stoneman to Ulysses S. Grant

(Received 12 o'clock, m.)
OFFICE U.S. MILITARY TELEGRAPH,
War Department, Washington, D. C., May 13, 1866
From HEADQUARTERS DEPARTMENT OF TENNESSEE,
Memphis, May 12, 1866

Lt. Gen. U. S. GRANT, *U. S. A*:

Your telegram of this date received.

The 3d colored artillery has been stationed here since its organization, and consequently were not under the best of discipline; large numbers of the men had what they call families living in South Memphis, contiguous to the fort in which the soldiers were stationed. These soldiers had been used as the instruments to execute the orders of government agents, such as provost marshal's, bureau agents, &c, and consequently had been more or less brought directly into contact with the law-breaking portion of the community and the police, which is far from being composed of the best class of residents here, and composed principally of Irishmen, who consider the negro as his competitor and natural enemy. Many negro soldiers have, from time to time, been arrested by the police, and many whites, including some of the police, have been arrested by the negro soldiers, and in both cases those arrested have not unfrequently been treated with a harshness altogether unnecessary. These remarks and hints will lead you to reflections which will explain and indicate to you the state of feeling which existed between the negro soldiers and their sympathizers and the lower class of whites and their sympathizers, in which last are included agitators, demagogues, and office-seekers. The testimony before the commission which I have assembled to investigate the circumstances connected with the riot shows, that about 4 o'clock Monday afternoon, April 30, four (4) policemen were walking down Cousey street and met three or four negroes; they jostled each other on the side-walk; an altercation occurred; one of the policemen struck a negro with a pistol, and was in return struck by another negro with a cane. There was no further trouble

246

though a good deal of excitement among the negroes during that night. Incident on this encounter, about 4 o'clock P. M., Tuesday, May 1, a crowd of from fifty to seventy-five negroes, mostly discharged soldiers, were congregated together near the corner of Main and South streets; the greater portion of these negroes were intoxicated. Six policemen approached the crowd and arrested two of the most boisterous of the negroes; the policemen proceeded to conduct these two negroes towards the station-house, being followed by the crowd of negroes, which increased as they proceeded, and who used very insulting and threatening language and accompanied their threats by firing pistols into the air; the police turned and fired upon the negroes, wounding one; one of the negro prisoners escaped, and the other was released by the police. The negroes returned the fire, wounding one of the police. The police force of the city, together with a large crowd of citizens, congregated together in the vicinity of South street, and being very much infuriated, proceeded to shoot, beat, and threaten every negro met with in that portion of the city. This was continued until about midnight on Tuesday night, when it was quelled by the interference of a small detachment of United States troops. Wednesday morning arrived, and found large crowds of people collected together in South Memphis, most of whom were armed; they remained there until about 1 o'clock P. M, when they were dispersed by a detachment of United States soldiers which had been employed during the day in keeping the discharged negro soldiers in and the white people out of the fort. During the day several negro shanties were burned down. About 10 o'clock Wednesday night a party of mounted men began to set fire to the negro school-houses, churches, and dwelling-houses. It is hoped that the investigation now being had will result in identifying the parties engaged. During Tuesday and Wednesday several inoffensive negroes were killed, and many maltreated and beaten in different parts of the city. The number killed and wounded in the riot, so far as can be ascertained by the commission, were one white man killed, shot by white man behind him; one white man wounded, shot by negroes. The number of negroes shot and beaten to death has not yet been ascertained. I will give you the information when procured. Frequent applications were made for arms and for permission to organize a militia force, all of which were refused, and Thursday I issued an order prohibiting any persons, under whatever pretext, from assembling anywhere armed or unarmed. Great fears were entertained that other buildings, such as the Freedmen's Bureau buildings of the Memphis post, would be burned down, but if any such intentions were had, the disposition made of the small force at my disposal prevented the realization. An attempt was made by some parties to gain possession of the muskets which a few days before had been turned in by the 3d colored artillery. Every officer and man here was on duty day and night during the riot. On the 4th they were relieved by a detachment I had ordered over from Nashville.

As before stated, the rioters were composed of the police, firemen, and the rabble and negro-haters in general, with a sprinkling of Yankee-haters, all led on and encouraged by demagogues and office hunters, and most of them under the influence of whiskey. It appears in evidence before the commission that John Creighton, recorder of the city, made a speech to the rioters, in which he said: "We are not prepared, but let us prepare to clean every negro son-of-a-bitch out of town." Very few paroled confederates were mixed up with the rioters on Tuesday and Wednesday, the large portion being registered voters. Who composed the incendiaries on Wednesday night remains to be developed.

GEORGE STONEMAN,
Major General Commanding.

May 12, 1866

The New York Times:
An Hour With Gen. Grant

HIS VIEWS UPON MEN AND MEASURES.

The editor of the Lewiston Falls *Journal*, now at Washington, recently spent an hour in the studio of the Maine artist SIM-MONS, in conversation with Gen. GRANT, and gives an interesting statement of the opinions expressed by him upon "men and measures." Some people will doubt whether the General would unbosom himself so fully to a stranger when he is habitually so reticent; but we give the story as we find it. The writer says:

"The General, who was dressed in a plain, black, civilian suit, had hardly removed his hat from his head before he took a cigar from his pocket, lighted it and began to puff out wreaths of smoke. 'I am breaking off from smoking,' remarked GRANT. 'When I was in the field I smoked eighteen or twenty cigars a day, but now I smoke only nine or ten!'

The conversation turned to the Virginia campaigns of 1864 and 1865. 'I notice,' remarked Gen. GRANT, 'that Mr. SWINTON has published a history of the campaigns in the Old Dominion, in which he takes the ground that I gained nothing, but, on the contrary, lost many valuable lives uselessly, by moving my army from the Rapidan direct toward Richmond, rather than by taking it around by water to the Peninsula, as McCLELLAN did. This,' observed the General, 'is a revival of the exploded theory [referring to the McClellan policy] of subduing the rebellion by peace measures. A half a million troops might have been kept within sight of Washington till doomsday, and the rebellion would have flourished more and more vigorously day by day. Fighting, hard knocks only, could have accomplished the work. The rebellion must be overcome, if overcome at all, by force; its resources destroyed, its fighting material obliterated, before peace could be obtained.'

'There were but two failures in the Virginia campaign of 1864 which ought to have been successes,' said GRANT, 'and those were the failure to capture Petersburg when we crossed the James and afterwards at the mine explosion. But,' added GRANT, 'it was all for the best that we failed in those two instances, for, had we succeeded at either time, LEE would have at once been obliged to abandon Richmond, and would have been able to secure a safe retreat into the interior of the South, where he would have prolonged the contest for years. Our failures then and the determination of the rebels to hold on to their Capital gave us time to extend our left southward, to bring up SHERMAN from Georgia, and thereby made it impossible for LEE to escape.'

In reply to a question as to whether he was not surprised as to the suddenness of the collapse of the rebellion, GRANT said that he was, although he had always supposed that when it would break down it would go all at once. 'I thought, however,' he remarked, 'that it would hold out another season, and I am not sure,' he added, 'but that it would have been better for the country if it had. There were some parts of the country where our armies had never trod, particularly Texas, which needed to feel the blighting effects of war to bring their people to a realizing sense of the enormity of their crime and the necessity of a thorough repentance. I find,' said he, 'that those parts of the South which have not felt the war, and particularly those which have been within our lines, and have therefore escaped the rebel conscription and taxes, are much less disposed to accept the situation in good faith than those portions which have been literally overrun with fire and sword.'

Referring to the temper of the Southern people, he remarked that they are much less disposed now to bring themselves to the proper frame of mind than they were one year since. 'A year ago,' said he, 'they were willing to do anything; now they regard themselves as masters of the situation. Some of the rebel generals,' he added, 'are behaving nobly and doing all they can to induce the people to throw aside their old prejudices and to conform their course to the changed condition of things. JOHNSTON and DICK TAYLOR particularly, are exercising a good influence; but,' he added, 'LEE is behaving badly. He is conducting himself very differently from what I had reason from what he said at the time of the surrender, to suppose he would. No man at the South is capable of exercising a tenth part of the influence for good that he is, but instead of using it he is setting an example of forced acquiescence so grudging and pernicious in its effects as to be hardly realized.'

'The men who were in the rebel armies,' said GRANT,

'acquiesce in the result much better than those who staid at home. The women are particularly bitter against the Union and Union men. Of course,' he added, 'there is some bitterness of feeling among all classes, but I am satisfied it would soon die out if their leading men had not somehow got the idea that treason, after all, was not very bad, and that the 'Southern cause,' as they phrase it, will yet triumph, not in war, but in politics. In my judgment,' said GRANT, 'the tone of certain men and certain papers at the North is such as to do incalculable mischief in making the late rebels believe that they are just as much entitled to rule as ever, and that if they will only stand by what they are pleased to call their "rights," they will have help from the North. This,' significantly added GRANT, 'is only playing over again the incipient stages of the rebellion.' He was confident that the large majority of the Southern people would smother their resentments and become good citizens, if these mischief-makers at the North (the Copperheads) would only let them alone. For himself, if he had the power, the first thing he would do would be to seize the New-York *News* and kindred sheets, which are giving the South so dangerous an idea of their own position and "rights."

'Troops,' said Gen. GRANT, 'must be kept in all the principal points in the South for some time to come. This will be necessary to repress the turbulence of a class of the South very dangerous to all well-disposed persons, and also to protect the rights of the freedmen, who are looked upon with deep hatred by a very large proportion of the people. I am in favor, however,' he added, 'of not retaining our volunteers for this duty, because they very naturally think that they fulfilled their engagement one year since.'

GRANT spoke in high terms of SHERMAN, SHERIDAN, HOWARD and other Generals, and referred to our Mexican difficulties, forcibly adding that he believed the French invasion of Mexico a part of the rebellion, and he should have been glad to have seen a detachment of our army sent there one year since. He would engage that SHERIDAN, with plenty of arms, and 2,000 American troops and a goodly number of American officers, would, with the aid of the Mexicans, clean MAXIMILIAN out of Mexico in six months."

The New York Times, May 24, 1866

Elihu B. Washburne to Thaddeus Stevens

Memphis, Tenn. May 24, 1866.

My Dear Sir,

We have got to work, and it is plain to see we have a long job before us. We are aided, however, very much by the examinations already made by Genl. Stoneman and the Freedmen's Bureau. From the partial investigations made by these commissions, it is evident that the country has no adequate conception of the true character and extent of the riotous proceedings. It was a mob organized substantially under the auspices of the city Government, and the butcheries and atrocities perpetrated scarcely have a parallel in all history. Forty persons were killed, including some women and children fifty-three wounded and eight maltreated and beaten. Seventy-eight houses, churches, and schoolhouses were burned, & ninety-three robberies committed. As Genl. Stoneman well says, it was no "negro riot," for the negroes had nothing to do with it but to be butchered. And yet no steps whatever have been taken to bring the murderers to justice.

The rebel spirit here is rampant, defiant, intolerant. The true Union, loyal feeling is weak, cowardly and pusillanimous. Instead of rebels being reconstructed as Union men, I find some of our late Union men re-constructed as very good rebels. So we go.

I intend to remain here till we get to the bottom of this business.

Please do not make this public in any way.

Yrs. Truly,   E B Washburne

Hon. Thaddeus Stevens

P.S. Further investigation shows as follows:

Houses burned	84
Robberies	99
Killed	46
Wounded	76
Maltreated	10
Property destroyed	from $60.000 to $100.000.

Cynthia Townsend: Testimony to House Select Committee

CYNTHIA TOWNSEND (colored) sworn and examined.

By the CHAIRMAN:

2207. Where do you live?   On Rayburn avenue, Memphis.

2208. How long have you been in Memphis?   About eighteen years.

2209. Have you been a slave?   Yes; but I worked and bought myself. I finished paying for myself a few days before they took this place.

2210. Were you here at the time of the riot; if so, state what you saw?   Yes. It was right before my door; I do not believe I could express what I saw. On Tuesday evening, the first of May, the riot began. I saw them shooting and firing. On Wednesday morning I saw a man by the name of Roach, a policeman, shoot a negro man; he was driving a dray. Mr. Roach ran up and shot him right in the side of his head. I saw Mr. Cash on Wednesday morning when he shot a man by the name of Charley Wallace. Charley ran down to the bayou; came back; and as he turned the corner of my house, Mr. Cash shot him in the back part of the head. They went up to him, turned him over, turned his pocket inside-out, and took out his pocket-book.

2211. Where were the policemen?   I do not know the policemen only by the star they wear. I know Mr. Cash. I did not see any other men killed. When the old man Pendergrast was burning up the houses there, I saw them shoot a young girl; I could not say who did it. She fell right between two houses standing close together, and the houses were burned down right over her. I saw the Pendergrasts burning and plundering until broad day-light. The colored people were trying to get out of the houses. They told them that if they came out they would kill them. They fired into one house at a woman. She said, "Please, master, let me out." He said, "If you don't go back I'll blow your damned brains out." She went back. They set the house on fire. She just broke right out, and they all fired at her as fast as they could. I saw Mr. Pendergrast's son Pat fire at her as soon as she came in sight. This girl Rachael who was shot and burned was a nice, smart girl; I could not tell you how old she was; she was quite a young woman.

2212. How many shots did they fire at this woman when she came out? I could not tell how many shots—a great many.

2213. Did you see them firing at other people who were coming out of the houses? Be sure and state only what you saw. Yes, sir; I am telling you the truth, and I know I have got to give an account of it. There were little children coming out of the houses, and they fired at them. I saw four or five come out at one time. Little children, old people, and women seemed to be all coming out together, and they just fired right at them. I did not see it, but they said they shot one little child's arm off.

2214. Where did these people go when they came out of the house? Some of them ran into my house. I do not know what has become of them since.

2215. Have you a husband? Yes. My husband and son are about seven miles in the country at work. I sent word to them not to come back until this fuss was over.

2216. Do you know the names of the family you saw come out of this house? No, sir; I do not. One woman came running up and said she liked to have been burned in her house. Mr. Pendergrast had shot at her. She said she got down on her knees and prayed the man to let her out; that she had a little son in there with her. He told her if she did not go back he would kill her. This man McGinn was in the crowd. He seemed to know this woman, and said, "That is a very good woman; it is a pity to burn her up; let her come out." She came out and her little boy with her. The boy had blue clothes on. They pushed him back, and said, "Go back, you damned son of a bitch." She fell on her knees and begged them to let the child out; that it was the only child she had. McGinn told her that she might take some of her things out, which she did; and I saw them take the things from her and burn them up. They let her little boy out afterwards. There was a man broke into my yard while they were shooting. They followed him and shot him down, right in my yard. His name is Dickerson. They did not kill him then. He was just as clever a man as ever I saw.

2217. Are you a member of the church? Yes; a member of the Baptist church. I saw Mr. Pendergrast go into his grocery, and give ammunition to a policeman to load his pistols with. Then they started out again, firing and shooting. They started a negro man, who ran up the bayou. They told him to come up to them. He came up, and one of them put his pistol to the man's mouth, and shot his tongue out, and killed him dead. His name was Lewis Robertson.

2218. Did you see that?   No, sir; but I saw him directly afterwards, when he was kicking and struggling in death. His tongue was out; they opened his mouth and said his tongue was shot off; they shot him twice, once through the head and once through the thigh. The lady who lives next door was looking out, and said, "Just look at that man, John Pendergrast, shooting and killing that negro;" and this Pendergrast was a man the colored folks thought so much of, too, and had done so much for him. I sent for the old man to ask him about it. He said, "Aunt Cynthia, I am the man that fetched this mob out here, and they will do just what I tell them; I know you are good old people here." I said, "Mr. Pender, will you please take my house and keep it for your own, and let me go away until this fuss is over?" He said he would not advise me to go away; that it was all done with now.

2219. Did they rob your house?   Yes; they took my clothes, and fifty dollars in money, but I did not consider that much. They came in my house and took what they pleased; they took out some quilts that I had, too, but I never said a word about it.

2220. Who did the money belong to?   It belonged to my son who was in the army, Frank King.

2221. Do you know of any violence being committed on the women in your neighborhood?   Yes, sir; I know of some very bad acts.

2222. State what you saw?   I could not tell you what I saw; I could have seen it if I had been a mind to.

2223. State the circumstances?   There is a woman who lives near me by the name of Harriet; Merriweather was her name before she was married; I do not know what her husband's name is. There were as many as three or four men at a time had connexion with her; she was lying there by herself. They all had connexion with her in turn around, and then one of them tried to use her mouth.

2224. Was this during the riot?   Yes, sir; it was on Monday evening.

2225. Did you see these men go in the house? Yes; I saw them going into the house and saw them coming out, and afterwards she came out and said they made her do what I told you they did; she has sometimes been a little deranged since then, her husband left her for it. When he came out of the fort, and found what had been done, he said he would not have anything to do with her any more. They drew their pistols before her and made her submit. There were white people right there who knew what was going on. One woman called me to go and look in and see what they were doing; that was when this thing was going on. She is the woman who came and made a complaint to Charley Smith; she is a very nice woman.

2226. Did she make complaint against Charley Smith for having a hand in this outrage? No; she complained to him; he was not in the house.

2227. What was the name of this woman? I cannot tell you; there are two of them who live on Webster street.

By Mr. BROOMALL:

2228. How many houses did you see burnt? I do not know that I could tell you; the first one I saw burnt was right close to my house. There was a square which had a school-house on it, and I could not tell you how many little cottages; I suppose there were as many as twenty cottages burned on that square.

By Mr. SHANKLIN:

2229. Did you see with your own eyes any portion of the difficulty on the evening of the first fight? Yes, sir; I did see a good deal; I saw a policeman shoot a soldier on Causey street. From that these black soldiers gathered, and a lieutenant at the fort shot the policeman who shot the soldier.

2230. Did you see colored soldiers shoot? Yes; I saw them shooting; I did not see them hit any one.

2231. How many colored soldiers were there shooting? I could not tell; they had given up their guns, and had nothing but their pistols.

2232. How many white men did you see engaged in shooting on Tuesday evening? I do not know; I never saw so many together, they gathered from every direction.

2233. Do you know the man who shot the policeman? He was a lieutenant in the colored regiment, a white man; I do not know his name.

2234. He was with the colored men shooting at the police, was he? Yes, sir; I do not know how the fuss began, though I was within two hundred yards of it when it began. I do not know that it amounted to anything, I only heard the report that the policeman was shot.

By the CHAIRMAN:

2235. Who was killed first, the colored man or the policeman? The colored man, one or two of them; then the soldiers came down South street, and went after the policemen as fast as they could.

May 30, 1866

Joint Resolution Proposing the Fourteenth Amendment

Joint Resolution proposing an Amendment to the Constitution of the United States.

Be it resolved by the Senate and House of Representatives of the United States of America in Congress assembled, (two thirds of both Houses concurring.) That the following article be proposed to the legislatures of the several States as an amendment to the Constitution of the United States, which, when ratified by three fourths of said legislatures, shall be valid as part of the Constitution, namely:—

ARTICLE XIV.

SEC. 1. All persons born or naturalized in the United States, and subject to the jurisdiction thereof, are citizens of the United States and of the State wherein they reside. No State shall make or enforce any law which shall abridge the privileges or immunities of citizens of the United States; nor shall any State deprive any person of life, liberty, or property, without due process of law, nor deny to any person within its jurisdiction the equal protection of the laws.

SEC. 2. Representatives shall be apportioned among the several States according to their respective numbers, counting the whole number of persons in each State, excluding Indians not taxed. But when the right to vote at any election for the choice of electors for President and Vice-President of the United States, representatives in Congress, the executive and judicial officers of a State, or the members of the legislature thereof, is denied to any of the male inhabitants of such State, being twenty-one years of age, and citizens of the United States, or in any way abridged, except for participation in rebellion or other crime, the basis of representation therein shall be reduced in the proportion which the number of such male citizens shall bear to the whole number of male citizens twenty-one years of age in such State.

SEC. 3. No person shall be a senator, or representative in Congress, or elector of President and Vice-President, or hold any office, civil or military, under the United States, or under any State, who having previously taken an oath, as a member of Congress, or as an officer of the United States, or as a member of any State legislature, or as an executive or judicial officer of any State, to support the Constitution of the United States, shall have engaged in insurrection or rebellion against the same, or given aid or comfort to the enemies thereof. But Congress may by a vote of two thirds of each house remove such disability.

SEC. 4. The validity of the public debt of the United States, authorized by law, including debts incurred for payment of pensions and bounties for services in suppressing insurrection or rebellion, shall not be questioned. But neither the United States nor any State shall assume or pay any debt or obligation incurred in aid of insurrection or rebellion against the United States, or any claim for the loss or emancipation of any slave; but all such debts, obligations, and claims shall be held illegal and void.

SEC. 5. The Congress shall have power to enforce, by appropriate legislation, the provisions of this article.

SCHUYLER COLFAX,
Speaker of the House of Representatives.
LA FAYETTE S. FOSTER,
President of the Senate pro tempore.

Attest: EDW. MCPHERSON,
Clerk of the House of Representatives.
J. W. FORNEY,
Secretary of the Senate.

Received at Department of State June 16, 1866.

June 13, 1866

Oliver P. Morton: from
Speech at Indianapolis

LADIES AND GENTLEMEN—If I were to consult prudence, the improvement of my health, I should not be here to-night, but I have a great desire to do whatever I can to promote the cause which is to be won or lost at the approaching election, and I have been desired by friends also, to deliver a short address before the people. In compliance with this desire of my own, and the wishes of others, I shall attempt to address you to-night upon some of the issues that are involved in the approaching campaign.

Since I have been here to-night my mind has been busy with the last five, now going on six years. I believe this is the first time I have been on this stage since the termination of the war, and I have been thinking over the times that I was on this stage during the dark hours of the rebellion, appealing to the people, calling for volunteers and exhorting the citizens of the State to stand by and support the Government.

The war is over—the rebellion has been suppressed—the victory has been won, and now the question is presented to us at the coming election, whether the fruits of victory shall be preserved or lost.

SPIRIT OF THE DEMOCRATIC PARTY.

It is beyond doubt that the temper of the Democratic party is not changed or improved since the termination of the war, but on the contrary it seems to have been greatly embittered by defeat in the field and at the ballot-box. Its sympathy with those who were lately in arms against the Government is more boldly avowed than ever, and it becomes argumentative and enthusiastic in behalf of the right of secession and righteousness of the rebellion. The true spirit of the Democratic party in Indiana has recently received a remarkable illustration that should command the solemn consideration of the people.

Some four or five weeks since a convention was held in the

city of Louisville, composed in large part of men who had been engaged in the rebel armies. These men assembled in convention, proclaimed themselves members of the National Democratic party, and declared their unfaltering devotion to its time-honored principles. They vindicated the righteousness of the rebellion and declared their stern purpose to maintain at the ballot box the sacred principles for which they had taken up arms. Prominent Indiana Democrats met with them in Convention; mingled their tears with those who wept over Southern heroes; uttered glowing eulogies upon the memory of Stonewall Jackson and John Morgan, and endorsed their most ultra and treasonable doctrines; and to show the complete identity between this assembly of traitors and the Democratic party of Indiana, the Indianapolis *Herald*, the organ of the party, in the broadest and most unqualified manner, earnestly and enthusiastically endorsed its proceedings, resolutions and speeches. The members of this convention did not disguise the fact that they were rebels and Northern Democratic leaders, believing that the time for punishing treason has gone by, now make haste to declare that they are and have been united with them in sympathy, sentiment and purpose, and that they will co-operate with them to the bitter end in restoring to them what they call their rights, and in repairing the damages done to them by the war. And to show that this malevolent and treasonable spirit is not confined to the Democratic leaders of Indiana, numerous meetings, resolutions, newspapers and declarations, in every part of the United States, may be referred to, and especially the votes and speeches of the Democratic members of Congress.

WHAT DEMOCRATIC LEADERS HAVE DONE.

The leaders who are now managing the Democratic party in this State, are the men who at the regular session of the Legislature in 1861, declared that, if an army went from Indiana to assist in putting down the then approaching rebellion it must first pass over their dead bodies.

They are the men who in the Democratic Convention on the 8th of January, 1862, gave aid and comfort to the rebellion, by resolving that the South had been provoked and driven into

the contest by the unconstitutional and wicked aggressions of
the people of the North.

They are the men, who, in speeches and resolutions proclaimed that "Southern defeats gave them no joy, and Northern
disasters no sorrows." They are the men who exerted their influence to prevent their Democratic friends from going into the
army, and who by their incessant and venomous slanders against
the Government checked the spirit of volunteering, and made
drafting a necessity. And when the draft had thus been forced
upon the country their wretched subordinates inspired by their
devilish teachings endeavored in many places by force of arms
and the murder of enrolling officers to prevent its execution.

They are the men who corresponded with the rebel leaders in
the South, giving them full information of our condition, and
assuring them that a revolution in public opinion was at hand,
and that they had but to persevere a few months longer and the
National Government would fall to pieces of its own weight.

They are the men who in the Legislature of 1863, attempted
to overturn the State Government and establish a Legislative
revolution by seizing the military power of the State and trans-
ferring it into the hands of four State officers, three of whom
were members of the treasonable society known as the "Sons
of Liberty."

They are the men, who, having failed to overturn the State
Government by seizing the military power, determined to defeat its operations and bring about anarchy, by locking up the
public treasure and thus withholding the money necessary to
carry on the Government.

They are the men who for the purpose of private speculation, and to discredit the State, before the world conspired
to prevent the payment of the interest on the public debt, by
withholding through a fraudulent lawsuit the money received
from taxes, paid for that very purpose. This lawsuit was fraud-
ulently smuggled through the Circuit Court and lodged in the
Supreme Court before the Minutes of the case had been read
and signed by the Circuit Judge, or he had been made acquainted with its character—and was hastily decided by the
Supreme Court against the credit of the State.

They are the men who introduced and organized in this
State that dangerous and wide-spread conspiracy first known

as the "Knights of the Golden Circle," and afterwards as the "Sons of Liberty," which had for its purpose the overthrow of the State and National Governments. Not all of them, it is true, belonged formerly to this infamous order, but such as stood on the outside had knowledge of its existence, purposes and plans, and carefully concealing their knowledge was ready to accept its work.

To accomplish the hellish work of this conspiracy, military officers were appointed, military organizations created, arms and ammunition purchased in immense quantities and smuggled into the State, correspondence opened with rebel commanders, and military combinations agreed upon, rebel officers and agents introduced into the capital and concealed in hotels and boarding houses, and it was deliberately planned and agreed that upon a day fixed, they would suddenly uprise and murder the Executive, seize the arsenal and its arms and ammunition, and releasing 9,000 rebel prisoners in Camp Morton, put arms into their hands, and with their combined forces effect a military and bloody revolution in the State. This dreadful scheme necessarily involved murder, conflagration, robbery, and the commission of every crime which makes black the chronicles of civil war, and yet its authors and abettors, with the proofs of their guilt piled mountain high, are again struggling for power and asking the people to put into their guilty hands the government and prosperity of the State. Some of these men who are high in favor and authority in their party, and are largely entrusted with its management, have heretofore occupied offices of great trust and responsibility in which they proved to be recreant and corrupt.

They are the men who, in the Legislature of Indiana bitterly opposed and denounced every effort to confer the right of suffrage upon soldiers in the field who could not come home to vote.

They are the men who wrote letters to soldiers in the army, urging them to desert, and assuring them of support and protection if they did.

They are the men who labored with devilish zeal to destroy the ability of the Government to carry on the war by depreciating its financial credit. They assured the people that "greenbacks" would die on their hands, and warned them solemnly against Government bonds, as a wicked device to rob them of their money.

They are the men who refused to contribute to the Sanitary Commission for the relief of sick and wounded soldiers, upon the lying and hypocritical pretence that the contributions were consumed by the officers of the army.

They are the men who excused themselves from contributing for the relief of soldiers' families at home by the infamous slander that they were living better than they had ever done, and by foul imputations on the chastity of soldiers' wives.

They are the men who declared in speeches, resolutions, and by their votes in Congress, that not another man nor another dollar should be voted to carry on a cruel war against their Southern brethren.

They are the men who in the midst of the last great campaign of 1864, at the time when Sherman was fighting his way, step by step, from Chattanooga to Atlanta, and Grant was forcing Lee back into the defenses of Richmond, in desperate and bloody battles from day to day; when the fate of the nation hung in the balance, and the world watched with breathless interest the gigantic struggle which was to settle the question of Republican Government, assembled in Convention in Chicago and resolved that the war was a failure; that our cause was unjust, and that we ought to lay down our arms and sue for peace. It was throwing a mountain into the Confederate scale to make the Union kick the beam. It was a bold and desperate interference in behalf of the rebellion, at the very crisis of the fight. It was an insult to the loyal armies of the nation, so vast, malignant and deadly that language can convey no adequate idea of its wickedness. And in future times the historian will record the fact with astonishment that the Government, at the most critical moment of its life, when a few hours, or a few days at the farthest, must determine whether it should live or die, could permit a large body of its enemies to meet upon its soil in peace and security, and publish a flagrant manifesto in behalf of the rebellion.

Now, I do not mean to say, that all the Democratic leaders have done all these things, but what I do say is this, that the men who have done these things are combined together, and constitute the real leaders of the Democratic party. The few moderate men of the party have been stripped of all power and influence, and are carried along with it merely for numbers and policy, while the living and aggressive element which controls it are the "Sons of Liberty" and those who acted in sympathy and concert with them.

They are the men who have perverted the word Democracy, from its once honorable meaning, to be a shield and cover for rebellion, and for every crime that attaches to a causeless and atrocious civil war.

WHO CALL THEMSELVES DEMOCRATS.

Every unregenerate rebel, lately in arms against his Government calls himself a Democrat.

Every "bounty jumper," every "deserter," every "sneak," who ran away from the draft, calls himself a Democrat. Bowles, Milligan, Walker, Dodd, Horsey and Humphreys call themselves Democrats. Every "Son of Liberty" who conspired to murder, burn, rob arsenals, and release rebel prisoners calls himself a Democrat. John Morgan, Sue Mundy, Champ Ferguson, Wirz, Payne and Booth proclaimed themselves Democrats. Every man who labored for the rebellion in the field, who murdered Union prisoners by cruelty and starvation, who conspired to bring about civil war in the loyal States, who invented dangerous compounds to burn steamboats and Northern cities, who contrived hellish schemes to introduce into Northern cities the wasting pestilence of yellow fever calls himself a Democrat. Every dishonest contractor who has been convicted of defrauding the Government—every dishonest paymaster or disbursing officer who has been convicted of squandering the public money at the gaming table or in gold gambling operations—every officer in the army who was dismissed for cowardice or disloyalty, calls himself a Democrat. Every wolf in sheep's clothing, who pretends to preach the gospel, but proclaims the righteousness of man-selling and slavery—every one who shoots down negros in the streets, burns negro school houses and meeting houses, and murders women and children by the light of their own flaming dwellings, calls himself a Democrat. Every New York rioter in 1863, who burned up little children in colored asylums—who robbed, ravished and murdered indiscriminately in the midst of a blazing city for three days and nights, called himself a Democrat. In short the Democratic party may be described as a common sewer and loathsome receptacle, into which is emptied every element of treason North and South, and every element of inhumanity and barbarism which has dishonored the age.

And this party, composed of the men and elements I have described, in defiance of truth and decency asserts itself as the special champion of the Constitution and the Union, which but a short sixteen months ago it was in arms to destroy; and proclaims to an astonished world that the only effect of vanquishing armed rebels in the field, is to return them to seats in Congress, and to restore them to political power. Having failed to destroy the Constitution by force, they seek to do it by construction, and assume to have made the remarkable discovery that rebels who fought to destroy the Constitution were its true friends, and that the men who shed their blood and gave their substance to preserve it were its only enemies.

DEMOCRATIC PURPOSES AND POLICY.

And now let us inquire what measures the Democratic party are for affirmatively. It is and has been opposed to whatever the Union party is in favor of, but it has also a positive and affirmative policy, which it is important that the people should understand. The great and leading measure of its policy is the immediate and unconditional admission of a full representation in both Houses of Congress from the rebel States; that the test oath shall be repealed; that there shall be no punishments; that there shall be no political or civil disabilities imposed upon any man who has been engaged in the rebellion; that there shall be no amendment to the Constitution to make it conform to the changed circumstances of the nation; that there shall be no legislation to prevent the recurrence of future rebellions; but that Union men and rebels, Union soldiers and rebel soldiers, shall be put upon a perfect equality before the law, and that no honors or rewards shall be extended to the one which are not equally bestowed upon the other. In proof of this last position, let me refer you to the notorious fact that, in their speeches and newspapers they bestow brilliant and glowing panegyrics upon the genius and virtues of General Lee, but are significantly silent about Grant, Sherman and Sheridan. They weep copiously over the memory of Stonewall Jackson, but have not a tear to shed for the untimely deaths of Lyon, Kearney, McPherson and Hackleman. They mourn from day to day over the fictitious sufferings of Jeff Davis, but have never yet expressed a regret for the murdered thousands at Andersonville and Salisbury.

These things point to their feelings and their policy with the unerring certainty of the needle to the pole, and leave the rational mind without a shadow of doubt as to what they would do should they again come into control of the Government. They are opposed to equalizing the representation North and South, because it would diminish the power of the rebels in the Government. They are opposed to prohibiting the assumption of the rebel war debt, for that would be to prevent them from doing just what they intend to do should they get the power.

We are able to predict with absolute certainty what would be their first measures should the great calamity happen that they come into power. They would assume the rebel war debt, and put the owners of it upon the same footing with the holders of the stocks of the United States; they would pension rebel soldiers and the families of rebel soldiers, bestowing upon them equal honors and emoluments with those who belonged to the loyal armies of the Nation; they would as nearly as possible reduce the freedmen of the South back to the condition of slavery by depriving them of all protection and civil rights. They would harrass and oppress Union men both North and South, by subjecting them to vindictive law suits, and to the brutal vengeance of rebels whom they had defeated in arms.

And most important of all, they would proclaim the right of secession, and bid the Southern States to go if they yet wished to do so, and tell the States of the Northwest to go in peace and form a Northwestern Confederacy, if such was their desire. There is not an active Democratic leader in the Northwest to-day who has not from the beginning of the war asserted that the people of the North were the aggressors, and that the people of the South were standing justly in defense of their constitutional rights.

COPPERHEAD INSULTS TO SOLDIERS.

While the war was in progress Copperhead politicians denounced Union soldiers as "Lincoln hirelings," as mercenaries, and as fighting for pay and plunder, and not for principle, and their treatment of Union soldiers now is precisely upon that theory. They appear to believe that the adherence of soldiers to the Union party, is for the sole purpose of getting office and official rewards, and if it happens that a soldier fails to receive a nomination for an office, an hundred Copperheads run after him and whisper treason in his ear, assert that he has been betrayed, and assure him that if he will but desert to his enemies, and join the ranks of those who fought against him, they will not only forgive the fact that he was a Union soldier, but will take him to their arms and cover him with rewards, just as the Devil offered our Savior, all the kingdoms of the world if he would but fall down and worship him, when in point of fact the lying old rascal was only a tenant at will himself and hadn't a foot of land to give. How the gallant soldier who periled his life for his country, and has returned maimed and shattered from the battle, must feel dishonored and humiliated when he finds himself treated as a mere mercenary, and is approached by Copperheads with arguments and temptations which stain his manhood and insult the memory of the dead who fell in battle by his side. Themselves regarding office getting, as the sole business of life, and that Governments were established only to provide hungry politicians with lucrative places, they are unable to conceive the idea of the patriot soldier, who loving his country more than wealth, luxury, and the comforts of home, laid all these together with his life, as a cheerful sacrifice upon the National altar.

A WORD TO YOUNG MEN.

And here let me address a word to the young men of Indiana. You are just starting in life, with the world all before you, where and how to choose. Beware how you connect your fortunes with a decayed and dishonored party, indelibly stained with treason, and upon whose tombstone the historian will write, "false to liberty, false to its country, and false to the age in which it lived." The Democratic party has committed a crime for which history has no pardon, and the memories of men no forgetfulness; whose colors grow darker from age to age, and for which the execrations of mankind become more bitter from generation to generation. It committed treason against liberty in behalf of slavery; against civilization in behalf of barbarism; and its chronicles will be written in the same volume which records the most dangerous and malignant factions that have ever afflicted government or retarded the progress of mankind. The rebellion was born of the Democratic party; cradled in its lap, nursed from its breast, and cherished and sustained by it, until it perished by the avenging sword of the nation, and it must soon be followed to the tomb by its guilty parent.

The Federal party opposed the war of 1812, and died from the effects of it in a few years. The Whig party opposed the Mexican war in 1846, and lived but six years longer; yet these parties meditated no treason, and when the conflict began did not sympathize with the enemy, or give him aid and comfort, but gave their earnest and hearty support to the government and the army. How, then, shall it be with the Democratic party? the parent of the rebellion, who, while the southern wing was in arms against the government, the northern wing gave to it material aid and comfort, and cheered it on in the deadly contest.

June 20, 1866

Philip H. Sheridan to Ulysses S. Grant

OFFICE UNITED STATES MILITARY TELEGRAPH,
Headquarters, War Department.
The following telegram received in cipher, 6.15 P. M. August
1, 1866, from New Orleans, Louisiana, August 1, 1866:
U. S. GRANT, *General*:

You are doubtless aware of the serious riot which occurred
in this city on the 30th. A political body styling themselves
the convention of 1864 met on the 30th for, as it is alleged,
the purpose of remodelling the present constitution of the
State. The leaders were political agitators and revolutionary
men, and the action of the convention was liable to produce
breaches of the public peace. I had made up my mind to arrest the head men, if the proceedings of the convention were
calculated to disturb the tranquillity of the department, but I
had no cause for action until they committed the overt act. In
the mean time official duty called me to Texas, and the mayor
of the city, during my absence, suppressed the convention by
the use of the police force, and in so doing attacked the members of the convention and a party of two hundred negroes
with fire-arms, clubs and knives, in a manner so unnecessary
and atrocious as to compel me to say that it was murder.
About forty whites and blacks were thus killed, and about
one hundred and sixty wounded. Everything is now quiet,
but I deem it best to maintain a military supremacy in the
city for a few days until the affair is fully investigated. I believe
the sentiment of the general community is great regret at this
unnecessary cruelty, and that the police could have made any
arrest they saw fit without sacrificing lives.

P. H. SHERIDAN,
Major General Commanding.

August 1, 1866

OFFICE UNITED STATES MILITARY TELEGRAPH,
Headquarters, War Department.

The following telegram received in cipher, 6 P. M. August 2, 1866, from New Orleans, Louisiana, August 2, 1866:

General U. S. GRANT, *Washington, D. C.*:

The more information I obtain of the affair of the 30th in this city the more revolting it becomes. It was no riot; it was an absolute massacre by the police, which was not excelled in murderous cruelty by that of Fort Pillow. It was a murder which the mayor and police of this city perpetrated without the shadow of a necessity; furthermore, I believe it was premeditated, and every indication points to this. I recommend the removing of this bad man. I believe it would be hailed with the sincerest gratification by two-thirds of the population of the city. There has been a feeling of insecurity on the part of the people here on account of this man, which is now so much increased that the safety of life and property does not rest with the civil authorities, but with the military.

P. H. SHERIDAN,
Major General Commanding.

August 2, 1866

Harper's Weekly:
The Massacre in New Orleans

THE late tragedy in New Orleans, terrible as it was, will be of the most salutary effect. Thirty years ago slavery shot LOVE-JOY in Alton for defending the right of free speech. Year after year slavery insulted, threatened, and mobbed Northern men for preaching the Declaration of Independence. For five and six years past slavery has exiled, tortured, hung, and burned Southern men for fidelity to the Union. But the sure mills of God grind slowly on, and slavery is abolished.

We have entered upon a new era. Already men are shot by stealth in the late slave States because they declare justice to be the best policy. Already school-houses are burned and teachers hunted away because they seek to enlighten the minds which slavery had darkened. Already the New York *World* and the other Northern lackeys of slavery denounce Southern men who were true to the Union through fire and flood as "cravens and cowards." In Memphis hatred of the principle of equal rights before the law massacres the most friendless and unfortunate part of the population; and in New Orleans the advocates of the same principle, meeting to discuss the subject, are ferociously murdered. But still the slow mills of God grind on. The seed of equal rights will be watered, not drowned, by the blood of the sowers. It will surely grow into a harvest which no storm can destroy. It will bear its natural fruit of national peace and prosperity; and in the happy day of its ripening those who sought to destroy the seed, whatever their station, whatever their temporary power, will be remembered only as the murderers of LOVE-JOY and the assassin of LINCOLN are remembered.

It is of no importance whether the members of the Louisiana Convention of 1864 were wise or unwise, fanatical or moderate. Any body of men, any where in the country, have the unquestionable right of assembling under any call whatever to consider public affairs. The desire of discussion is their authority. Any number of citizens of the State of New York may lawfully meet any where in the State to propose a new Constitution. One man alone may lawfully proclaim a new Constitution. There is no law against debate or against propositions of any kind, however sweeping or radical they may be. But when men proceed from debating to enforcing their propositions they become amenable to the law and must answer for their overt acts. The Secession Conventions of 1860–61 were properly tolerated as the disunion arguments of the abolitionists had been previously properly tolerated. The Fenian meetings to found an Irish republic were perfectly lawful. But when the secessionists passed from declarations to deeds, and fired upon the forts, and seized the navy-yards, and stole custom-houses; and when the Fenians attempted with arms to make war upon a peaceful neighbor, the United States justly interfered.

The President knew, as every body else knew, the inflamed condition of the city of New Orleans. He had read, as we had all read, the fiery speeches of both parties. He knew, unless he had chosen willfully to ignore, the smothered hatred of the late rebels toward the Union men of every color. He may have considered the "Conservatives" wise, humane, and peaceful. He may have thought the Radicals wild and foolish. He knew that the Mayor was a bitter rebel, whom he had pardoned into office. He knew that the courts had denounced the Convention, and he was expressly informed that they meant to indict the members. He could not affect ignorance of the imminent danger of rioting and bloodshed. Still, if, as he constantly asserts, Louisiana is rightfully in the same relation to the Union that New York is, he had no authority to say a word or to do an act in that State except "on application of the Legislature, or of the Executive when the Legislature can not be convened." Why did he presume, then, to judge of the authority of the Convention? What has the President of the United States to do with the manner in which delegates to a State Convention are selected? If his own assertion be correct as to the present relation of Louisiana to the Union, the President convicts himself of the most extraordinary and passionate act of executive usurpation and federal centralization recorded in our history.

If, however, he had any right whatever to intervene in the absence of a demand from the Legislature or the Governor, it was derived from the fact that Louisiana is held by the military power of the United States, in which case her present relation to the Union is *not* what the President declares it to be, and he has ample and absolute power to do in that State whatever is necessary to keep the peace. And he knew, as he knew his own existence, that a simple word to the military commander to preserve the peace at all hazards would prevent disorder and save lives. He did not speak that word. Assuming to plant himself upon the Constitution, which by his very act he violated, he telegraphed to the Attorney-General of the State. He threw his whole weight upon the side of those from whom he knew in the nature of things the disorder would proceed, and from whom it did proceed. He knew the city was tinder, and he threw in a spark. Every negro hater and every disloyal ruffian knew from the President's dispatch that the right of the citizens to assemble and declare their views would not be protected. The Mayor's proclamation was a covert but distinct invitation to riot. He announced to a city seething with passionate hatred of the Convention, that it would "receive no countenance from the President." It was simply saying, "The Convention is at your mercy."

And the mob so understood it. A procession of negroes carrying a United States flag was attacked. It defended itself; and the work which one word from the President would have stopped, and which he had the full authority to speak if he could speak at all, went on to its awful result. The rebel flag was again unfurled. The men who had bravely resisted it for four years were murdered under its encouragement, and while they were still lying warm in their blood the President telegraphed that they were "an unlawful assembly," and that "usurpation will not be tolerated"—words which he had no shadow of authority to utter except by the same right which empowered him to save all those lives; a right which he declined to exercise.

The President, who has undertaken by his own arbitrary will to settle every question of the war without consultation with the representatives of the people, says to the murdered men in New Orleans, "Why did you assume to act without obtaining the consent of the people?" The autumn elections will terribly echo that question. Surveying the Executive action of eighteen months, with its plain tendencies and apparent inspiration, seeing that it has left the President with no other party than the most vehement of the late rebels at the South, the Copperheads at the North, and the timid and trimming adherents of the Union party, while the great mass of sturdy Unionists in all parts of the country at the North and South still maintain the ground they have always held, those Union men will write upon the back of every ballot they cast at the coming elections, "Usurpation will not be tolerated;" and upon its face, "Why did you assume to act without obtaining the consent of the people?"

August 18, 1866

Andrew Johnson: Speech at St. Louis

FELLOW CITIZENS OF ST. LOUIS;

In being introduced to you to-night it is not for the purpose of making a speech. It is true I am proud to meet so many of my fellow citizens here on this occasion, and under the favorable circumstances that I do. [Cry, "how about our British subject?"] We will attend to John Bull after awhile so far as that is concerned. [Laughter and loud cheers.] I have just stated that I was not here for the purpose of making a speech, but after being introduced, simply to tender my cordial thanks for the welcome you have given to me in your midst. [A voice: "Ten thousand welcomes;" hurrahs and cheers.] Thank you sir. I wish it was in my power to address you under favorable circumstances upon some of the questions that agitate and distract the public mind at this time. Questions that have grown out of a fiery ordeal we have just passed through, and which I think as important as those we have just passed by. The time has come when it seems to me that all ought to be prepared for peace—the rebellion being suppressed, and the shedding of blood being stopped, the sacrifice of life being suspended and stayed, it seems that the time has arrived when we should have peace; when the bleeding arteries should be tied up. [A voice: "New Orleans"; "go on."]

Perhaps if you had a word or two on the subject of New Orleans, you might understand more about it than you do. [Laughter and cheers.] And if you will go back [cries for Seward]—if you will go back and ascertain the cause of the riot at New Orleans, perhaps you would not be so prompt in calling out New Orleans. If you will take up the riot at New Orleans and trace it back to its source, or to its immediate cause, you will find out who was responsible for the blood that was shed there.

If you will take up the riot at New Orleans and trace it back to the Radical Congress [great cheering and cries of "bully"], you will find that the riot at New Orleans was substantially planned—if you will take up the proceedings in their caucuses you will understand that they there knew [cheers] that a convention was to be called which was extinct, by its powers having expired; that it was said, and the intention was that a new Government was to be organized; and in the organization of that Government the intention was to enfranchise one portion of the population called the colored population, who had just been emancipated, and at the same time disfranchise white men. [Great cheering.] When you begin to talk about New Orleans [confusion] you ought to understand what you are talking about.

When you read the speeches that were made or take up the facts—on Friday and Saturday before that convention sat—you will there find that speeches were made incendiary in their character, exciting that portion of the population, the black population, to arm themselves and prepare for the shedding of blood. [A voice, "that's so!" and cheers.] You will also find that that convention did assemble in violation of law, and the intention of that convention was to supersede the recognized authorities in the State Government of Louisiana, which had been recognized by the Government of the United States, and every man engaged in that rebellion—in that convention, with the intention of superseding and upturning the civil government which had been recognized by the Government of the United States—I say that he was a traitor to the Constitution of the United States, [cheers,] and hence you find that another rebellion was commenced, having its origin in the Radical Congress. These men were to go there: a Government was to be organized, and the one in existence in Louisiana was to be superceded, set aside and overthrown. You talk to me about New Orleans! And then the question was to come up, when they had established their government—a question of political power—which of the two governments was to be recognized—a new government inaugurated under this defunct convention—set up in violation of law, and without the consent of the people. And then when they had established their government, and extended universal or impartial franchise, as they called it, to this colored population, then this Radical Congress was to determine that a government established on negro votes was to be the government of Louisiana. [Voices—"never," and cheers and "hurrah for Andy."]

So much for the New Orleans riot—and there was the cause and the origin of the blood that was shed, and every drop of blood that was shed is upon their skirts, and they are responsible for it. [Cheers.] I could trace this thing a little closer, but I will not do it here to night. But when you talk about New Orleans, and talk about the causes and consequences that resulted from proceedings of that kind, perhaps, as I have been introduced here, and you have provoked questions of this kind, though it don't provoke me, I will tell you a few wholesome things that *has* been done by this Radical Congress. [Cheers.]

In connection with New Orleans and the extension of the elective franchise, I know that I have been traduced and abused. I know it has come in advance of me here, as it has elsewhere, and that I have attempted to exercise an arbitrary power in resisting laws that *was* intended to be enforced on the Government. [Cheers, and cries of "hear."] Yes, that I had exercised the veto power, ["Bully for you,"] that I had abandoned the power that elected me, and that I was a *t-r-ai-tor* [cheers] because I exercised the veto power in attempting to, and did arrest for a time, a bill that was called a Freedmen's Bureau bill. [Cheers.] Yes, that I was a *t-r-ai-t-o-r*! And I have been traduced, I have been slandered, I have been maligned, I have been called Judas—Judas Iscariot, and all that. Now, my countrymen here to-night, it is very easy to indulge in epithets, it is very easy to call a man Judas, and cry out t-r-ai-t-o-r, but when he is called upon to give arguments and facts, he is very often found wanting.

Judaas, Judas Iscariot, Judaas! There was a Judas once, one of the twelve apostles. Oh! yes, and these twelve apostles had a Christ. [A voice, "and a Moses, too." Great laughter.] The twelve apostles had a Christ, and he couldn't have had a Judas unless he had had twelve apostles. If I have played the Judas, who has been my Christ that I have played the Judas with? Was it Thad. Stevens? Was it Wendell Phillips? Was it Charles Sumner? [Hisses and cheers.] Are these the men that set up and compare themselves with the Saviour of men, and everybody that differs with them in opinion, and try to stay and arrest their diabolical and nefarious policy, is to be denounced as a Judas? ["Hurrah for Andy," and cheers.]

In the days when there were twelve Apostles and when there ware a Christ, while there ware Judases, there ware unbelievers, too. Y-a-s; while there ware Judases there ware unbelievers. [Voices—"hear." "Three groans for Fletcher."] Yes, oh! yes! unbelievers in Christ: men who persecuted and slandered and brought him before Pontius Pilate and preferred charges and condemned and put him to death on the cross, to satisfy unbelievers. And this same persecuting, diabolical and nefarious clan to-day would persecute and shed the blood of innocent men to carry out their purposes. [Cheers.] But let me tell you—let me give you a few words here to-night—and but a short time since I heard some one say in the crowd that we had a Moses. [Laughter and cheers.] Yes, there was a Moses. And I know sometimes it has been said that I have said that I would be the Moses of the colored man. ["Never," and cheers.] Why, I have labored as much in the cause of emancipation as any other mortal man living. But while I have strived to emancipate the colored man, I have felt, and now feel, that we have a great many white men that want emancipation. [Laughter and cheers.] There is a set amongst you that have got shackles on their limbs, and are as much under the heel and control of their masters as the colored man that was emancipated. [Cheers.] I call upon you here to night, as freemen—as men who favor the emancipation of the white man as well as the colored ones. I have been in favor of emancipation. I have nothing to disguise about that. I have tried to do as much, and have done as much, and when they talk about Moses and the colored man being led into the promised land, where is the land that this clan proposes to lead them? [Cheers.] When we talk about taking them out from among the white population and sending them to other climes, what is it they propose? Why, it is to give us a Freedmen's Bureau. And after giving us a Freedmen's Bureau, what then? Why, here in the South it is not necessary for me to talk to you, where I have lived and you have lived, and understand the whole system, and how it operates; we know how the slaves have been worked heretofore. Their original owners bought the land and raised the negroes, or purchased them, as the case might be; paid all the expenses of carrying on the farm, and in the end, after producing tobacco, cotton, hemp and flax, and all the various products of the South, bringing them into the market, without any profit to them while these owners put it all into their own pockets. This was their condition before the emancipation. This was their condition before we talked about their "Moses." [Laughter.] Now what is the plan? I ask your attention. Come, as we have got to talking on this subject, give me your attention for a few minutes. I am addressing myself to your brains, and not to your prejudices; to your reason and not to your passions. And when reason and argument again resume their empire, this mist, this prejudice that has been incrusted upon the public mind must give way and reason become triumphant. [Cheers.] Now, my countrymen, let me call your attention to a single fact, the Freedmen's Bureau. [Laughter and hisses.]

Yes; slavery was an accursed institution till emancipation took place. It was an accursed institution while one set of men worked them and got the profits. But after emancipation took place they gave us the Freedmen's Bureau. They gave us these agents to go into every county, every township, and into every school district throughout the United States, and especially the Southern States. They gave us commissioners. They gave us $12,000,000 and placed the power in the hands of the Executive, who was to work this machinery, with the army brought to his aid, and to sustain it. Then let us run it, with $12,000,000 as a beginning, and, in the end, receive $50,000,000 or $60,000,000, as the case may be, and let us work the 4,000,000 of slaves. In fine, the Freedmen's Bureau was a simple proposition to transfer 4,000,000 of slaves in the United States from their original owners to a new set of taskmasters. [Voice: "Never," and cheers.] I have been laboring four years to emancipate them; and then I was opposed to seeing them transferred to a new set of taskmasters, to be worked with more rigor than they had been worked heretofore. [Cheers.] Yes, under this new system they would work the slaves, and call on the Government to bear all the expense, and if there was any profits left, why they would pocket them, [laughter and cheers,] while you, the people, must pay the expense of running the machine out of your own pockets, while they got the profits of it. So much for this question.

I simply intended to-night to tender you my sincere thanks. But as I go along, as we are talking about this Congress and these respected gentlemen, who contend that the President is wrong, because he vetoed the Freedmen's Bureau bill, and all this; because he chose to exercise the veto power, he committed a high offense, and, therefore, ought to be impeached. [Voice, "never."] *Y-e-s, y-e-s*; they are ready to impeach him. [Voice, "let them try it."] And if they were satisfied they had the next Congress by as decided a majority as this, upon some pretext or other—violating the Constitution—neglect of duty, or omitting to enforce some set of law, upon some pretext or other, they would vacate the Executive Department of the United States. [A voice, "too bad they don't impeach him."] *Wha-t?* As we talk about this Congress, let me call the soldiers' attention to this immaculate Congress. Let me call your attention. Oh! this Congress, that could make war upon the Executive because he stands upon the Constitution and vindicates the rights of the people, exercising the veto power in their behalf—because he dared to do this, they can clamor, and talk about impeachment. And by way of elevating themselves and increasing confidence with the soldiers, throughout the country, they talk about impeachments.

So far as the Fenians are concerned, upon this subject of Fenians, let me ask you very plainly here to-night, to go back into my history of legislation, and even when Governor of a State let me ask if there is a man here to-night, who, in the dark days of Knownothingism, stood and sacrificed more for their rights? [Voice, "good," and cheers.]

It has been my peculiar misfortune always to have fierce opposition, because I have always struck my blows direct, and fought with right and the Constitution on my side. [Cheers.] Yes, I will come back to the soldiers again in a moment. Yes, here was a neutrality law. I was sworn to support the Constitution and see that that law was faithfully executed. And because it was executed, then they raised a clamor and tried to make an appeal to the foreigners; and especially the Fenians. And what did they do? They introduced a bill to tickle and play with the fancy, pretending to repeal the law, and at the same time making it worse and then left the law just where it is. [Voice—"That's so."] They knew that whenever a law was presented to me, proper in its provisions, ameliorating and softening the rigors of the present law, that it would meet my hearty approbation. But as they were pretty well broken down and losing public

confidence, at the heels of the session they found they must
do something. And hence, what did they do? They pretended
to do something for the soldiers. Who has done more for the
soldiers than I have? Who has periled more in this struggle
than I have? [Cheers.] But then, to make them their peculiar
friends and favorites of the soldiers, they came forward with
a proposition to do what? Why, we will give the soldier $50
bounty—$50 bounty—your attention to this—if he has served
two years; and $100 if he has served three years. Now, mark
you, the colored man that served two years can get his $100
bounty. But, the white man must serve *three* before he can get
his. [Cheers.] But that is not the point. While they were tick-
ling and attempting to please the soldiers, by giving them $50
bounty for two years' service, they took it into their heads to
vote somebody else a bounty, [laughter] and they voted themselves not $50 for two years' service; your attention—I want to
make a lodgment in your minds of the facts, because I want
to put the nail in, and having put it in, I want to clinch it on
the other side. [Cheers.] The brave boys, the patriotic young
men, who followed his gallant officers, slept in the tented field,
and periled his life, and shed his blood, and left his limbs behind him and came home, mangled and maimed, can get $50
bounty, if he has served two years. But the members of Congress, who never smelt gunpowder, can get $4,000 extra pay.
[Loud cheering.]

This is a faint picture, my countrymen, of what has transpired. [A voice, "Stick to that question."] Fellow-citizens, you
are all familiar with the work of restoration. You know that
since the rebellion collapsed, since the armies were suppressed
in the field, that everything that could be done has been done
by the Executive Department of the Government for the restoration of the Government. Everything has been done, with
the exception of one thing, and that is the admission of members from the eleven States that went into the rebellion. And
after having accepted the terms of the Government, having
abolished slavery, having repudiated their debt, and sent loyal
representatives, everything has been done, excepting the admission of Representatives which all the States are constitutionally entitled to. [Cheers] When you turn and examine the
Constitution of the United States, you can find that you cannot

even amend that Constitution so as to deprive any State of its equal suffrage in the Senate. [A voice, "They have never been out."] It is said before me, "they have never been out." I say so, too. That is what I have always said. They have never been out, and they cannot go out. [Cheers.] That being the fact, under the Constitution they are entitled to equal suffrage in the Senate of the United States, and no power has the right to deprive them of it, without violating the Constitution. [Cheers.] And the same argument applies to the House of Representatives. How, then does the matter stand? It used to be one of the arguments, that if the States withdrew their Representatives and Senators, that that was secession—a peaceable breaking up of the Government. Now, the Radical power in this Government turn around and assume that the States are out of the Union, that they are not entitled to representation in Congress. [Cheers.] That is to say, they are dissolutionists, and their position now is to perpetuate a disruption of the Government, and that, too, while they are denying the States the right of representation, they impose taxation upon them, a principle upon which, in the revolution, you resisted the power of Great Britain. We deny the right of taxation without representation. That is one of our great principles. Let the Government be restored. Let peace be restored among the people. I have labored for it. Now I deny this doctrine of secession; come from what quarter it may, whether from the North or from the South. I am opposed to it. I am for the Union of the States. [Voices, "that's right," and cheers.] I am for the thirty-six stars, representing thirty-six States, remaining where they are, under the Constitution, as your fathers made it, and handed it down to you. And if it is altered, or amended, let it be done in the mode and manner pointed by that instrument itself, and in no other. [Cheers.] I am for the restoration of peace. Let me ask this people here to-night if we have not shed enough blood. Let me ask, are you prepared to go into another civil war. Let me ask this people here to-night are they prepared to set man upon man, and, in the name of God, lift his hand against the throat of his fellow. [Voice, "Never."] Are you prepared to see our fields laid waste again, our business and commerce suspended and all trade stopped. Are you prepared to see this land again drenched in our brothers' blood? Heaven avert it, is my prayer. [Cheers.] I am one of those who believe that man does sin, and having sinned, I believe he must repent. And, sometimes, having sinned and having repented makes him a better man than he was before. [Cheers.] I know it has been said that I have exercised the pardoning power. *Y-e-s*, I have. [Cheers and "what about Drake's Constitution?"] *Y-e-s*, I have, and don't you think it is to prevail? I reckon I have pardoned more men, turned more men loose and set them at liberty that were imprisoned, I imagine, than any other living man on God's habitable globe. [Voice, "bully for you," and cheers.] Yes, I turned forty-seven thousand of our men who engaged in this struggle, with the arms we captured with them, and who were then in prison, I turned them loose. [Voice, "bully for you, old fellow," and laughter.] Large numbers have applied for pardon, and I have granted them pardon. Yet there are some who condemn and hold me responsible for doing wrong. Yes, there are some who stayed at home, who did not go into the field on the other side, that can talk about others being traitors and being treacherous. There are some who can talk about blood, and vengeance, and crime, and everything to "make treason odious," and all that, who never smelt gunpowder on either side. [Cheers.] Yes, they can condemn others and recommend hanging and torture, and all that. If I have erred, I have erred on the side of mercy. Some of these croakers have dared to assume that they are better than was the Savior of men himself—a kind of over righteousness—better than everybody else, and always wanting to do Deity's work, thinking he cannot do it as well as they can. [Laughter and cheers.] Yes, the Savior of man came on the earth and found the human race condemned, and sentenced under the law. But when they repented and believed, he said, "Let them live." Instead of executing and putting the whole world to death, he went upon the cross and there was painfully nailed by these unbelievers that I have spoken of here to-night, and there shed his blood that you and I might live. [Cheers.] Think of it! To execute and hang, and put to death eight millions of people. [Voice, "never."] It is an absurdity, and such a thing is impracticable even if it were right. But it is the violation of all law, human and divine. [Voice, "hang Jeff. Davis."] You call on Judge Chase to hang Jeff. Davis, will you? [Great cheering.] I am not the Court, I am not the jury, nor the judge. [Voice, "nor the Moses."] Before the case comes to me, and all other cases, it would have to come on application as a case for pardon. That is the only way the case can get to me. Why don't Judge Chase—Judge Chase, the Chief Justice of the United States, in whose district he is—why don't he try him? [Loud cheers.] But, perhaps, I could answer the question; as sometimes persons want to be facetious and indulge in repartee, I might ask you a question, why don't you hang Thad. Stevens and Wendell Phillips? [Great cheering.] A traitor at one end of the line is as bad as a traitor at the other.

I know that there are some who have got their little pieces and sayings to repeat on public occasions, like parrots, that have been placed in their mouths by their superiors, who have not the courage and the manhood to come forward and tell them themselves, but have their understrappers to do their work for them. [Cheers.] I know there is some that talk about this universal elective franchise, upon which they wanted to upturn the Government of Louisiana and institute another; who contended that we must send men there to control, govern, and manage their slave population, because they are incompetent to do it themselves. And yet they turn round when they get there and say they are competent to go to Congress, and manage the affairs of State. [Cheers.] Before you commence throwing your stones, you ought to be sure you don't live in a glass house. Then, why all this clamor! Don't you see, my countrymen, it is a question of power; and being in power as they are, their object is to perpetuate their power? Hence, when you talk about turning any of them out of office, oh, they talk about "bread and butter." [Laughter.] Yes, these men are the most perfect and complete "bread and butter party" that has ever appeared in this government. [Great cheering.] When you make an effort, or struggle to take the nipple out of their mouths, how they clamor! They have staid at home here five or six years, held the offices, grown fat, and enjoyed all the emoluments of position; and now, when you talk about turning one of them out, "oh, it is proscription;" and hence they come forward and propose in Congress to do what? To pass laws to prevent the Executive from turning anybody out. [Voice, "Put 'em out."] Hence, don't you see what the policy was to be? I believe in the good old doctrine advocated by Washington,

Jefferson and Madison, of rotation in office. These people who have been enjoying these offices seem to have lost sight of this doctrine. I believe that when one set of men have enjoyed the emoluments of office long enough, they should let another portion of the people have a chance. [Cheers.] How are these men to be got out—[Voice, "Kick 'em out." Cheers and laughter] unless your Executive can put them out, unless you can reach them through the President? Congress says he shall not turn them out, and they are trying to pass laws to prevent it being done. Well, let me say to you, if you will stand by me in this action, [cheers,] if you will stand by me in trying to give the people a fair chance, soldiers and citizens, to participate in those offices, God being willing, I *will* "kick them out" just as fast as I can. [Great cheering.] Let me say to you in concluding, what I have said, and I intended to say but little, but was provoked into this rather than otherwise, I care not for the menaces, the taunts and the jeers. I care not for the threats; I do not intend to be bullied by my enemies nor overawed by my friends [cheers]; but, God willing, with your help, I will veto their measures whenever they come to me. [Cheers.] I place myself upon the ramparts of the Constitution, and when I see the enemy approaching, so long as I have eyes to see, or ears to hear, or a tongue to sound the alarm, so help me God, I will do it and call on the people to be my judges. [Cheers.] I tell you here to-night that the Constitution of the country is being encroached upon. I tell you here to-night that the citadel of liberty is being endangered. [A voice—"Go it, Andy."]

I say to you then, go to work; take the Constitution as your palladium of civil and religious liberty; take it as our chief ark of safety. Just let me ask you here to-night to cling to the Constitution in this great struggle for freedom, and for its preservation, as the ship wrecked mariner clings to the mast when the midnight tempest closes around him. [Cheers.] So far as my public life has been advanced, the people of Missouri, as well as other States, know that my efforts have been devoted in that direction which would ameliorate and elevate the interests of the great mass of the people. [Voice: "That's so."] Why, where's the speech, where's the vote to be got of mine, but what has always had a tendency to elevate the great working classes of this people? [Cheers.] When they talk about tyranny and despotism, where's one act of Andy Johnson's that ever encroached upon the rights of a freeman in this land? But because I have stood as a faithful sentinel upon the watch tower of freedom to sound the alarm, hence all this traduction and detraction that has been heaped upon me. ["Bully for Andy Johnson."] I now, then, in conclusion, my countrymen, hand over to you the flag of your country with thirty six stars upon it. I hand over to you your Constitution with the charge and responsibility of preserving it intact. I hand over to you to-night the Union of these States, the great magic circle which embraces them all. I hand them all over to you, the people, in whom I have always trusted in all great emergencies—questions which are of such vital interest—I hand them over to you as men who can rise above party, who can stand around the altar of a common country with their faces upturned to heaven, swearing by Him that lives forever and ever that the altar and all shall sink in the dust, but that the Constitution and the Union shall be preserved. Let us stand by the union of these States, let us fight enemies of the Government, come from what quarter they may. My stand has been taken. You understand what my position is, and in parting with you now, leave the Government in your hands, with the confidence I have always had that the people will ultimately redress all wrongs and set the Government right. Then, gentlemen, in conclusion, for the cordial welcome you have given me in this great city of the Northwest, whose destiny no one can foretell. Now, [Voice: "Three cheers for Johnson,"] then, in bidding you good night, I leave all in your charge, and thank you for the cordial welcome you have given me in this spontaneous outpouring of the people of your city.

September 8, 1866

Thaddeus Stevens: Speech at Lancaster

I COME NOT to make a speech, but for the want of one. When I left Washington I was somewhat worn down by labors and disease, and I was directed by my physician neither to think, to speak nor to read until the next session of Congress, or I should not regain my strength. I have followed the first injunction most religiously, for I believe I have not let an idea pass through my mind to trouble me since Congress adjourned. The second one, not to speak, I was seduced from keeping by some noble friends in the mountain districts of Pennsylvania, and I made a speech at Bedford, the only one I have made. The third one, not to read, I have followed almost literally. It is true I have amused myself with a little light frivolous reading. I have taken up the dailies and publications of that kind, and read things which would make no impression upon the mind. For instance, there was a serial account from day to day of a very remarkable circus that travelled through the country [laughter] from Washington to Chicago, and St. Louis and Louisville back to Washington. [Renewed laughter.] I read that with some interest, expecting to see in so celebrated an establishment—one which, from its heralding, was to beat Dan Rice and all the old circuses that ever went forth. I expected great wit from the celebrated character of its clowns. [Great laughter.] They were well provided with clowns; instead of one there were two, as the circus was to have a large circulation. One of these clowns was high in office and somewhat advanced in age; the other was a little less advanced in office, but older in years. They started out with a very respectable stock company. In order to attract attention they took with them, for instance, a celebrated general; they took with them an eminent naval officer, and they chained him to the rigging so that he could not get away, though he tried to do so once or twice. They announced the most respectable stock company that ever went forth with a manager or circus, though they had no very good man for the spring boards; but they took with them for a short distance a very good man, accustomed to ground and lofty tumbling, called Montgomery Blair. [Laughter.] And as they wanted to get up side-shows, as is always precedent where anything is to be made out of these concerns, they switched him off in various directions with a hand-organ and a monkey. [Laughter.] In the East they called his monkey Senator, Doolittle, because he looked so much like one. [Laughter.] Up through the mountain region, where I encountered them, Montgomery Blair was there, with Judge Kimmel, whom they called his monkey, as the two beasts looked and acted alike. But the circus went on all the time, giving performances at different points, sometimes one clown performing and sometimes the other. So far as I was able to judge the younger clown was the most vigorous, and had the most energy and malignity. The elder clown, owing to the wear and tear of age and suffering—you know he had his arm broken and his jaw broken, and his neck broken almost— [laughter] inducing a necessity for certain opiates, which had very much worn down his vigor—I looked upon his performance as rather silly; for instance the younger clown told them in the language of the ancient heroes who trod the stage, that he had it in his power, if he choose, to be Dictator. The elder clown pointed to the other one, and said to the people, "Will you have him for President, or will you take him for king?" [Laughter.] He left you but one alternative. You are obliged to take him for one or the other, either for President or king, if "My Policy" prevails. I am not following them all around. I shall not describe to you how sometimes they cut outside the circle and entered into street broils with common blackguards; how they fought at Cleveland and Indianapolis and other points. I shall not tell you; for is it not all written down in Colonel Forney's *Chronicle*? [Laughter and cheers.] But coming round, they told you, or one of them did, that he had been everything but one. He had been a tailor, I think he did not say drunken tailor; no, he had been a a tailor [laughter]—he had been a constable—[laughter]—he had been a city alderman— [renewed laughter]—he had been in the Legislature. God help that Legislature! [Great merriment.] He had been in Congress, and now he was President. He had been everything but one—he had never been hangman and he asked the leave to hang Thad Stevens. [Laughter.]

Now, I have given you badinage enough. As I stated that I would not make a speech, I will state one point of some substance. The great question between the President and Congress is not how we shall reconstruct the States, but who shall have the power. That is the great question for this nation to determine, and upon your decision depends the security or the despotism of this Government. When the Southern States went out of the Union, through rebellion, and all the ties that bound them to the Union were consumed in the hot fires of the war, they became conquered provinces under our armies. By the law of nations, the sovereign power of this nation was to fix their fate. Who is that sovereign power? [Cries of "Congress," "Congress."] If that power is the President, then he is right, and may go on reconstructing the States in his own way. But if Congress has the sovereign power, then the issue is in our favor. As I said, the sovereignty of the nation must fix the status of the new States and of conquered nations. By the Constitution of the United States, in a single sentence, the first paragraph of the first article in the Constitution says that all legislative power shall be vested in a Congress, which shall consist of a Senate and a House of Representatives. There is the whole legislative power of the nation. You cannot find a word in the Constitution which gives to any other branch of the Government one particle of legislative power. How, then, is it that the sovereign power rests in the President? In this country there is but one depository of sovereign power, of the sovereignty of the nation. It rests in the people, and nowhere else; and the people speak through Congress to all their servants. Therefore, it is you, the sovereigns of the nation, who are reconstructing these States. In no other branch of the government can you find a particle of sovereignty. The President cannot even erect a bureau. He cannot do a legislative act. He is the servant of the people as they order through Congress. Now, then, Congress is the sovereign power, because the people speak through them; and Andrew Johnson must learn that he is your servant, [cheers,] and that as Congress shall order he must obey. [Cheers.] There is no escape from it. God forbid that he should have one title of power except what he derives through Congress and the Constitution. [Cheers.] This is the whole question. The question of how our States shall be reconstructed is another one, to which I shall not now refer. I shall only apologize for having detained you.

Mr. Stevens here retired, but the calls for his reappearance were so prolonged that he again came forward, and, amid loud cheering, said:

I suppose you never fought chickens in your young days. [Laughter.] If you had you know there was a breed that they called the "Wheelers." They would fight awhile and then go back, and then turn and fight again. I must be a Wheeler, I suppose. [Cheers and laughter.] And since you have called me out, and I am able to speak, I will explain one single point, which I have been informed my friend Mr. Doolittle made particularly upon me, and which, I have no doubt, some of my Republican friends considered particularly well made to put me below the ticket. I cannot blame them in this. I shall not blame them for anything of the kind, but I shall be just as good friends with them as before.

But let me explain: He spoke of negro equality. Let me tell you exactly how it is. He, I understand, found fault with me, particularly because I advocated what he called negro equality. Under our law there is not a word said in either the civil-rights' bill or the new proposed amendment about color. It simply provides that the same law which punishes one man shall punish any other for the same offence; it simply provides that the law which gives a verdict to one man shall render the same verdict to another, whether he is Dutch, Irish or negro. [Cheers.] Is there anything wrong in that? [Voices, "No!" "No!"] That is the doctrine of negro equality. There is nothing which prohibits the negro from learning to read and write and say his prayers. There is nothing in it which says he shall have anything superior to another.

I admit that these Copperheads have some cause to complain that there is such a proviso, for there is great danger that those who find fault with this provision will find rivals among the colored race in business and in life. There is one thing, however, which I noticed Mr. Doolittle alluded to—a bill which I introduced for fixing the condition of the Southern States—and since I am here I will say one word in explanation of that. I introduced a bill into Congress for the purpose of enabling the rebel states, under certain conditions, to form loyal governments. They have no governments now except some counterfeits put up by Andy Johnson. ["Three cheers for Thad Stevens."]

I proposed in that bill that every one of those conquered States should be put upon the same footing with a territory: should elect delegates to a convention to form a republican constitution (not such as they have got now, with slavery in them), and in fixing the right of voters to elect those delegates I made it universal—I allowed the rebels, I allowed the black men, allowed every man to vote for delegates to the convention. When they came to form the constitution they should form it to suit themselves (not doing as Andy Johnson did, dictating what the terms of the constitution should be), and when they formed it, they should be allowed to refer it back to the people for ratification; and, if ratified, they might present it to Congress. Now, I did hope, in doing this, that our loyal friends, together with the loyal colored men, would carry the conventions and give negro suffrage. Every loyal Southern man came to me and asked me to put it in the bill. There was not a loyal man, from Governor Hamilton to Governor Holden, Chief Justice Powell and Governor Sherwood—there were twenty of these men driven from their homes—who dare not go back, for fear of being murdered. They came to help me to fabricate the bill. It was not the rebels that did it; it was the loyal men that said give us that bill; and the vote of the loyal white men added to that of the loyal black men, can carry every State but Virginia. I was in a caucus one night, when Gov. Hamilton told us "to give them that law; and although we are now in the minority, and I dare not go home, for I should be murdered—give us that bill, and we can carry Texas on the side of the Union by twenty-five thousand majority." Governor Holden told me the same, and so did everybody except the Virginians.

The noble men who went to Philadelphia after the traitors' convention, appointed a committee and passed resolutions asking that this very thing should be done by Congress, a copy of which they sent to me to strengthen my hands. This is confined to the rebel States alone; I am for it; first, because it is right; second, because it protects our brethren there; thirdly, because it prevents the States from going into the hands of the rebels, and thereby giving the President and Congress, for the next forty years, to rebel hands. I am for it, and I shall go for it when Congress meets with all my might.

Now, however, remember that I do not say, and never mean to, that when these amendments, which I now propose, are adopted the rebel States shall be allowed to come in until they present constitutions containing the essence of liberty; and when they do that I will let them in at any time.

With regard to the question of negro suffrage in the free States, every one knows that I am not afraid to express my opinion. Everybody has a right to vote and pay his taxes, and whoever is governed by the laws has a right to make them. I was in the Pennsylvania Convention that amended the constitution which put in the word white, and disfranchised a large number of voters. I voted against it, and while every other man put his name to the constitution that it might go down to posterity, I refused my name, and it is not among the signers, for I was not proud of the instrument and am not now. This question may be thought a little in advance of the age. What is this world but a world of progress? and what is the statesman worth who is afraid to fight in the front ranks? The liberty of the world is not yet effected. Half the world is yet in chains, half the world is yet under kingly government.

We must go ahead, and though I can do but little, I shall do what I can, and if, when I am dead, there sprouts any vigor from my bones and my grave to help forward posterity to proclaim the same doctrines of universal liberty and universal suffrage, and universal disenthrallment from kings, I shall be satisfied.

The Goddess of Liberty is represented in ancient statues as a very nice little goddess, but very small. I want her to grow—to put on the habiliments of mature age—until she can embrace within her folds every nation, and every tribe and every human being within God's canopy. [Loud cheers.] I care not what you say of negro equality; I care not what you say of radicalism; these are my principles, and with the help of God I shall die with them. I ask no epitaph, I shall have none; but I shall go with a pure consciousness of having tried to serve the whole human race, and never having injured a human being.

September 27, 1866

Frederick Douglass: Reconstruction

THE ASSEMBLING of the Second Session of the Thirty-ninth Congress may very properly be made the occasion of a few earnest words on the already much-worn topic of reconstruction.

Seldom has any legislative body been the subject of a solicitude more intense, or of aspirations more sincere and ardent. There are the best of reasons for this profound interest. Questions of vast moment, left undecided by the last session of Congress, must be manfully grappled with by this. No political skirmishing will avail. The occasion demands statesmanship.

Whether the tremendous war so heroically fought and so victoriously ended shall pass into history a miserable failure, barren of permanent results,—a scandalous and shocking waste of blood and treasure,—a strife for empire, as Earl Russell characterized it, of no value to liberty or civilization,—an attempt to re-establish a Union by force, which must be the merest mockery of a Union,—an effort to bring under Federal authority States into which no loyal man from the North may safely enter, and to bring men into the national councils who deliberate with daggers and vote with revolvers, and who do not even conceal their deadly hate of the country that conquered them; or whether, on the other hand, we shall, as the rightful reward of victory over treason, have a solid nation, entirely delivered from all contradictions and social antagonisms, based upon loyalty, liberty, and equality, must be determined one way or the other by the present session of Congress. The last session really did nothing which can be considered final as to these questions. The Civil Rights Bill and the Freedmen's Bureau Bill and the proposed constitutional amendments, with the amendment already adopted and recognized as the law of the land, do not reach the difficulty, and cannot, unless the whole structure of the government is changed from a government by States to something like a despotic central government, with power to control even the municipal regulations of States, and to make them conform to its own despotic will. While there remains such an idea as the right of each State to control its own local affairs,—an idea, by the way, more deeply rooted in the minds of men of all sections of the country than perhaps any one other political idea,—no general assertion of human rights can be of any practical value. To change the character of the government at this point is neither possible nor desirable. All that is necessary to be done is to make the government consistent with itself, and render the rights of the States compatible with the sacred rights of human nature.

The arm of the Federal government is long, but it is far too short to protect the rights of individuals in the interior of distant States. They must have the power to protect themselves, or they will go unprotected, spite of all the laws the Federal government can put upon the national statute-book.

Slavery, like all other great systems of wrong, founded in the depths of human selfishness, and existing for ages, has not neglected its own conservation. It has steadily exerted an influence upon all around it favorable to its own continuance. And to-day it is so strong that it could exist, not only without law, but even against law. Custom, manners, morals, religion, are all on its side everywhere in the South; and when you add the ignorance and servility of the ex-slave to the intelligence and accustomed authority of the master, you have the conditions, not out of which slavery will again grow, but under which it is impossible for the Federal government to wholly destroy it, unless the Federal government be armed with despotic power, to blot out State authority, and to station a Federal officer at every cross-road. This, of course, cannot be done, and ought not even if it could. The true way and the easiest way is to make our government entirely consistent with itself, and give to every loyal citizen the elective franchise,—a right and power which will be ever present, and will form a wall of fire for his protection.

One of the invaluable compensations of the late Rebellion is the highly instructive disclosure it made of the true source of danger to republican government. Whatever may be tolerated in monarchical and despotic governments, no republic is safe that tolerates a privileged class, or denies to any of its citizens equal rights and equal means to maintain them. What was theory before the war has been made fact by the war.

There is cause to be thankful even for rebellion. It is an impressive teacher, though a stern and terrible one. In both characters it has come to us, and it was perhaps needed in both. It is an instructor never a day before its time, for it comes only when all other means of progress and enlightenment have failed. Whether the oppressed and despairing bondman, no longer able to repress his deep yearnings for manhood, or the tyrant, in his pride and impatience, takes the initiative, and strikes the blow for a firmer hold and a longer lease of oppression, the result is the same,—society is instructed, or may be.

Such are the limitations of the common mind, and so thoroughly engrossing are the cares of common life, that only the few among men can discern through the glitter and dazzle of present prosperity the dark outlines of approaching disasters, even though they may have come up to our very gates, and are already within striking distance. The yawning seam and corroded bolt conceal their defects from the mariner until the storm calls all hands to the pumps. Prophets, indeed, were abundant before the war; but who cares for prophets while their predictions remain unfulfilled, and the calamities of which they tell are masked behind a blinding blaze of national prosperity?

It is asked, said Henry Clay, on a memorable occasion, Will slavery never come to an end? That question, said he, was asked fifty years ago, and it has been answered by fifty years of unprecedented prosperity. Spite of the eloquence of the earnest Abolitionists,—poured out against slavery during thirty years,—even they must confess, that, in all the probabilities of the case, that system of barbarism would have continued its horrors far beyond the limits of the nineteenth century but for the Rebellion, and perhaps only have disappeared at last in a fiery conflict, even more fierce and bloody than that which has now been suppressed.

It is no disparagement to truth, that it can only prevail where reason prevails. War begins where reason ends. The thing worse than rebellion is the thing that causes rebellion. What that thing is, we have been taught to our cost. It remains now to be seen whether we have the needed courage to have that cause entirely removed from the Republic. At any rate, to this grand work of national regeneration and entire purification Congress must now address itself, with full purpose that the work shall this time be thoroughly done. The deadly upas, root and branch, leaf and fibre, body and sap, must be utterly destroyed. The country is evidently not in a condition to listen patiently to pleas for post-ponement, however plausible, nor will it permit the responsibil-ity to be shifted to other shoulders. Authority and power are here commensurate with the duty imposed. There are no cloud-flung shadows to obscure the way. Truth shines with brighter light and intenser heat at every moment, and a country torn and rent and bleeding implores relief from its distress and agony.

If time was at first needed, Congress has now had time. All the requisite materials from which to form an intelligent judg-ment are now before it. Whether its members look at the ori-gin, the progress, the termination of the war, or at the mockery of a peace now existing, they will find only one unbroken chain of argument in favor of a radical policy of reconstruction. For the omissions of the last session, some excuses may be allowed. A treacherous President stood in the way; and it can be easily seen how reluctant good men might be to admit an apostasy which involved so much of baseness and ingratitude. It was natural that they should seek to save him by bending to him even when he leaned to the side of error. But all is changed now. Congress knows now that it must go on without his aid, and even against his machinations. The advantage of the pres-ent session over the last is immense. Where that investigated, this has the facts. Where that walked by faith, this may walk by sight. Where that halted, this must go forward, and where that failed, this must succeed, giving the country whole measures where that gave us half-measures, merely as a means of saving the elections in a few doubtful districts. That Congress saw what was right, but distrusted the enlightenment of the loyal masses; but what was forborne in distrust of the people must now be done with a full knowledge that the people expect and require it. The members go to Washington fresh from the inspiring presence of the people. In every considerable pub-lic meeting, and in almost every conceivable way, whether at court-house, school-house, or cross-roads, in doors and out, the subject has been discussed, and the people have emphati-cally pronounced in favor of a radical policy. Listening to the doctrines of expediency and compromise with pity, impatience, and disgust, they have everywhere broken into demonstrations of the wildest enthusiasm when a brave word has been spoken in favor of equal rights and impartial suffrage. Radicalism, so far from being odious, is now the popular passport to power. The men most bitterly charged with it go to Congress with the largest majorities, while the timid and doubtful are sent by lean majorities, or else left at home. The strange controversy between the President and Congress, at one time so threatening, is disposed of by the people. The high reconstructive powers which he so confidently, ostentatiously, and haughtily claimed, have been disallowed, denounced, and utterly repudiated; while those claimed by Congress have been confirmed.

Of the spirit and magnitude of the canvass nothing need be said. The appeal was to the people, and the verdict was worthy of the tribunal. Upon an occasion of his own selection, with the advice and approval of his astute Secretary, soon after the members of Congress had returned to their constituents, the President quitted the executive mansion, sandwiched himself between two recognized heroes,—men whom the whole country delighted to honor,—and, with all the advantage which such company could give him, stumped the country from the Atlantic to the Mississippi, advocating everywhere his policy as against that of Congress. It was a strange sight, and perhaps the most disgraceful exhibition ever made by any President; but, as no evil is entirely unmixed, good has come of this, as from many others. Ambitious, unscrupulous, energetic, indefatigable, voluble, and plausible,—a political gladiator, ready for a "set-to" in any crowd,—he is beaten in his own chosen field, and stands to-day before the country as a convicted usurper, a political criminal, guilty of a bold and persistent attempt to possess himself of the legislative powers solemnly secured to Congress by the Constitution. No vindication could be more complete, no condemnation could be more absolute and humiliating. Unless reopened by the sword, as recklessly threatened in some circles, this question is now closed for all time.

Without attempting to settle here the metaphysical and somewhat theological question (about which so much has already been said and written), whether once in the Union means always in the Union,—agreeably to the formula, Once in grace always in grace,—it is obvious to common sense that the rebellious States stand to-day, in point of law, precisely where they stood when, exhausted, beaten, conquered, they fell powerless at the feet of Federal authority. Their State governments were overthrown, and the lives and property of the leaders of the Rebellion were forfeited. In reconstructing the institutions of these shattered and overthrown States, Congress should begin with a clean slate, and make clean work of it. Let there be no hesitation. It would be a cowardly deference to a defeated and treacherous President, if any account were made of the illegitimate, one-sided, sham governments hurried into existence for a malign purpose in the absence of Congress. These pretended governments, which were never submitted to the people, and from participation in which four millions of the loyal people were excluded by Presidential order, should now be treated according to their true character, as shams and impositions, and supplanted by true and legitimate governments, in the formation of which loyal men, black and white, shall participate.

It is not, however, within the scope of this paper to point out the precise steps to be taken, and the means to be employed. The people are less concerned about these than the grand end to be attained. They demand such a reconstruction as shall put an end to the present anarchical state of things in the late rebellious States,—where frightful murders and wholesale massacres are perpetrated in the very presence of Federal soldiers. This horrible business they require shall cease. They want a reconstruction such as will protect loyal men, black and white, in their persons and property; such a one as will cause Northern industry, Northern capital, and Northern civilization to flow into the South, and make a man from New England as much at home in Carolina as elsewhere in the Republic. No Chinese wall can now be tolerated. The South must be opened to the light of law and liberty, and this session of Congress is relied upon to accomplish this important work.

The plain, common-sense way of doing this work, as intimated at the beginning, is simply to establish in the South one law, one government, one administration of justice, one condition to the exercise of the elective franchise, for men of all races and colors alike. This great measure is sought as earnestly by loyal white men as by loyal blacks, and is needed alike by both. Let sound political prescience but take the place of an unreasoning prejudice, and this will be done.

Men denounce the negro for his prominence in this discussion; but it is no fault of his that in peace as in war, that in conquering Rebel armies as in reconstructing the rebellious States, the right of the negro is the true solution of our national troubles. The stern logic of events, which goes directly to the point, disdaining all concern for the color or features of men, has determined the interests of the country as identical with and inseparable from those of the negro.

The policy that emancipated and armed the negro—now seen to have been wise and proper by the dullest—was not certainly more sternly demanded than is now the policy of enfranchisement. If with the negro was success in war, and without him failure, so in peace it will be found that the nation must fall or flourish with the negro.

Fortunately, the Constitution of the United States knows no distinction between citizens on account of color. Neither does it know any difference between a citizen of a State and a citizen of the United States. Citizenship evidently includes all the rights of citizens, whether State or national. If the Constitution knows none, it is clearly no part of the duty of a Republican Congress now to institute one. The mistake of the last session was the attempt to do this very thing, by a renunciation of its power to secure political rights to any class of citizens, with the obvious purpose to allow the rebellious States to disfranchise, if they should see fit, their colored citizens. This unfortunate blunder must now be retrieved, and the emasculated citizenship given to the negro supplanted by that contemplated in the Constitution of the United States, which declares that the citizens of each State shall enjoy all the rights and immunities of citizens of the several States,—so that a legal voter in any State shall be a legal voter in all the States.

December 1866

Thaddeus Stevens: Speech in Congress on Reconstruction

Mr. STEVENS. Mr. Speaker, I am very anxious that this bill should be proceeded with until finally acted upon. I desire that as early as possible, without curtailing debate, this House shall come to some conclusion as to what shall be done with the rebel States. This becomes more and more necessary every day; and the late decision of the Supreme Court of the United States has rendered immediate action by Congress upon the question of the establishment of governments in the rebel States absolutely indispensable.

That decision, although in terms perhaps not as infamous as the Dred Scott decision, is yet far more dangerous in its operation upon the lives and liberties of the loyal men of this country. That decision has taken away every protection in every one of these rebel States from every loyal man, black or white, who resides there. That decision has unsheathed the dagger of the assassin, and places the knife of the rebel at the throat of every man who dares proclaim himself to be now, or to have been heretofore, a loyal Union man. If the doctrine enunciated in that decision be true, never were the people of any country anywhere, or at any time, in such terrible peril as are our loyal brethren at the South, whether they be black or white, whether they go there from the North or are natives of the rebel States.

Now, Mr. Speaker, unless Congress proceeds at once to do something to protect these people from the barbarians who are now daily murdering them; who are murdering the loyal whites daily and daily putting into secret graves not only hundreds but thousands of the colored people of that country; unless Congress proceeds at once to adopt some means for their protection, I ask you and every man who loves liberty whether we will not be liable to the just censure of the world for our negligence or our cowardice or our want of ability to do so?

Now, sir, it is for these reasons that I insist on the passage of some such measure as this. This is a bill designed to enable loyal men, so far as I could discriminate them in these States, to form governments which shall be in loyal hands, that they may protect themselves from such outrages as I have mentioned. In States that have never been restored since the rebellion from a state of conquest, and which are this day held in captivity under the laws of war, the military authorities, under this decision and its extension into disloyal States, dare not order the commanders of departments to enforce the laws of the country. One of the most atrocious murderers that has ever been let loose upon any community has lately been liberated under this very decision, because the Government extended it, perhaps according to the proper construction, to the conquered States as well as to the loyal States.

A gentleman from Richmond, who had personal knowledge of the facts, told me the circumstances of the murder. A colored man, driving the family of his employer, drove his wagon against a wagon containing Watson and his family. The wagon of Watson was broken. The next day Watson went to the employer of the colored man and complained. The employer offered to pay Watson every dollar that he might assess for the damage that had been done. "No!" said he, "I claim the right to chastise the scoundrel." He followed the colored man, took out his revolver, and deliberately shot him dead in the presence of that community. No civil authority would prosecute him; and, when taken into custody by the military authority, he is discharged by order of the President under this most injurious and iniquitous decision.

Now, sir, if that decision be the law, then it becomes the more necessary that we should proceed to take care that such a construction as that shall not open the door to greater injuries than have already been sustained. Thus much I have said at the outset of my remarks, which shall not be very long.

The people have once more nobly done their duty. May I ask, without offense, will Congress have the courage to do its duty? Or will it be deterred by the clamor of ignorance, bigotry, and despotism from perfecting a revolution begun without their consent, but which ought not to be ended without their full participation and concurrence? Possibly the people would not have inaugurated this revolution to correct the palpable incongruities and despotic provisions of the Constitution; but having it forced upon them, will they be so unwise as to suffer it to subside without erecting this nation into a perfect Republic?

Since the surrender of the armies of the confederate States of America a little has been done toward establishing this Government upon the true principles of liberty and justice; and but a little if we stop here. We have broken the material shackles of four million slaves. We have unchained them from the stake so as to allow them locomotion, provided they do not walk in paths which are trod by white men. We have allowed them the unwonted privilege of attending church, if they can do so without offending the sight of their former masters. We have even given them that highest and most agreeable evidence of liberty as defined by the "great plebeian," the "right to work." But in what have we enlarged their liberty of thought? In what have we taught them the science and granted them the privilege of self-government? We have imposed upon them the privilege of fighting our battles, of dying in defense of freedom, and of bearing their equal portion of taxes; but where have we given them the privilege of ever participating in the formation of the laws for the government of their native land? By what civil weapon have we enabled them to defend themselves against oppression and injustice? Call you this liberty? Call you this a free Republic where four millions are subjects but not citizens? Then Persia, with her kings and satraps, was free; then Turkey is free! Their subjects had liberty of motion and of labor, but the laws were made without and against their will; but I must declare that, in my judgment, they were as really free governments as ours is to-day. I know they had fewer rulers and more subjects, but those rulers were no more despotic than ours, and their subjects had just as large privileges in governing the country as ours have. Think not I would slander my native land; I would reform it. Twenty years ago I denounced it as a despotism. Then, twenty million white men enchained four million black men. I pronounce it no nearer to a true Republic now when twenty-five million of a privileged class exclude five million from all participation in the rights of government.

The freedom of a Government does not depend upon the quality of its laws, but upon the power that has the right to enact them. During the dictatorship of Pericles his laws were just, but Greece was not free. During the last century Russia has been blessed with most remarkable emperors, who have generally decreed wise and just laws, but Russia is not free.

No Government can be free that does not allow all its citizens to participate in the formation and execution of her laws. There are degrees of tyranny. But every other government is a despotism. It has always been observed that the larger the number of the rulers the more cruel the treatment of the subject races. It were better for the black man if he were governed by one king than by twenty million.

What are the great questions which now divide the nation? In the midst of the political Babel which has been produced by the intermingling of secessionists, rebels, pardoned traitors, hissing Copperheads, and apostate Republicans, such a confusion of tongues is heard that it is difficult to understand either the questions that are asked or the answers that are given. Ask, what is the "President's policy?" and it is difficult to define it. Ask, what is the "policy of Congress?" and the answer is not always at hand.

A few moments may be profitably spent in seeking the meaning of each of these terms. Nearly six years ago a bloody war arose between different sections of the United States. Eleven States, possessing a very large extent of territory, and ten or twelve million people, aimed to sever their connection with the Union, and to form an independent empire, founded on the avowed principle of human slavery and excluding every free State from this confederacy. They did not claim to raise an insurrection to reform the Government of the country—a rebellion against the laws—but they asserted their entire independence of that Government and of all obligations to its laws. They were satisfied that the United States should maintain its old Constitution and laws. They formed an entirely new constitution; a new and distinct government, called the "confederate States of America." They passed their own laws, without regard to any former national connection. Their government became perfectly organized, both in its civil and military departments. Within the broad limits of those eleven States the "confederate States" had as perfect and absolute control as the United States had over the other twenty-five. The "confederate States" refused to negotiate with the United States, except upon the basis of independence—of perfect national equality. The two powers mutually prepared to settle the question by arms. They each raised more than half a million armed men. The war was acknowledged by other nations as a public war between independent belligerents. The parties acknowledged each other as such, and claimed to be governed by the law of nations and the laws of war in their treatment of each other. On the result of the war depended the fate and ulterior condition of the contending parties. No one then pretended that the eleven States had any rights under the Constitution of the United States, or any right to interfere in the legislation of the country. Whether they should ever have all men of both sections, without exception, agreed would depend on the will of Congress, if the United States were victorious. The confederate States claimed no rights unless they could conquer them by the contest of arms.

President Lincoln, Vice President Johnson, and both branches of Congress repeatedly declared that the belligerent States could never again intermeddle with the affairs of the Union, or claim any right as members of the United States Government until the legislative power of the Government should declare them entitled thereto. Of course the rebels claimed no such rights; for whether their States were out of the Union as they declared, or were disorganized and "out of their proper relations" to the Government, as some subtle metaphysicians contend, their rights under the Constitution had all been renounced and abjured under oath, and could not be resumed on their own mere motion. How far their liabilities remained there was more difference of opinion.

The Federal arms triumphed. The confederate armies and government surrendered unconditionally. The law of nations then fixed their condition. They were subject to the controlling power of the conquerors. No former laws, no former compacts or treaties existed to bind the belligerents. They had all been melted and consumed in the fierce fires of the terrible war. The United States, according to the usage of nations, appointed military provisional governors to regulate their municipal institutions until the law-making power of the conqueror should fix their condition and the law by which they should be permanently governed. True, some of those governors were illegally appointed, being civilians. No one then supposed that those States had any governments, except such as they had formed under their rebel organization. No sane man believed that they had any organic or municipal laws which the United States were bound to respect. Whoever had then asserted that those States had remained unfractured, and entitled to all the rights and privileges which they enjoyed before the rebellion, and were on a level with their loyal conquerors, would have been deemed a fool, and would have been found insane by any inquisition "*de lunatico inquirendo.*"

In monarchical Governments, where the sovereign power rests in the Crown, the king would have fixed the condition of the conquered provinces. He might have extended the laws of his empire over them, allowed them to retain portions of their old institutions, or, by conditions of peace, have fixed upon them new and exceptional laws.

In this country the whole sovereignty rests with the people, and is exercised through their Representatives in Congress assembled. The legislative power is the sole guardian of that sovereignty. No other branch of the Government, no other Department, no other officer of the Government, possesses one single particle of the sovereignty of the nation. No Government official, from the President and Chief Justice down, can do any one act which is not prescribed and directed by the legislative power. Suppose the Government were now to be organized for the first time under the Constitution, and the President had been elected and the judiciary appointed: what could either do until Congress passed laws to regulate their proceedings?

What power would the President have over any one subject of government until Congress had legislated on that subject? No State could order the election of members until Congress had ordered a census and made an apportionment. Any exception to this rule has been a work of grace in Congress by passing healing acts. The President could not even create bureaus or Departments to facilitate his executive operations. He must ask leave of Congress. Since, then, the President cannot enact, alter, or modify a single law; cannot even create a petty office within his own sphere of duties; if, in short, he is the mere servant of the people, who issue their commands to him through Congress, whence does he derive the constitutional power to create new States; to remodel old ones; to dictate organic laws; to fix the qualification of voters; to declare that States are republican and entitled to command Congress to admit their Representatives? To my mind it is either the most ignorant and shallow mistake of his duties, or the most brazen and impudent usurpation of power. It is claimed for him by some as the Commander-in-Chief of the Army and Navy. How absurd that a mere executive officer should claim creative powers! Though Commander-in-Chief by the Constitution, he would have nothing to command, either by land or water, until Congress raised both Army and Navy. Congress also prescribes the rules and regulations to govern the Army. Even that is not left to the Commander-in-Chief.

Though the President is Commander-in-Chief, Congress is his commander; and, God willing, he shall obey. He and his minions shall learn that this is not a Government of kings and satraps, but a Government of the people, and that Congress is the people. There is not one word in the Constitution that gives one particle of anything but judicial and executive power to any other department of Government but Congress. The veto power is no exception; it is merely a power to compel a reconsideration. What can be plainer?

"All legislative powers herein granted shall be vested in a Congress of the United States. Such shall consist of a Senate and House of Representatives."—*Constitution United States*, art. I, sec. I.

To reconstruct the nation, to admit new States, to guaranty republican governments to old States are all legislative acts. The President claims the right to exercise them. Congress denies it and asserts the right to belong to the legislative branch. They have determined to defend these rights against all usurpers. They have determined that while in their keeping the Constitution shall not be violated with impunity. This I take to be the great question between the President and Congress. He claims the right to reconstruct by his own power. Congress denies him all power in the matter, except those of advice, and has determined to maintain such denial. "My policy" asserts full power in the Executive. The policy of Congress forbids him to exercise any power therein.

Beyond this I do not agree that the "policy" of the parties are defined. To be sure many subordinate items of the policy of each may be easily sketched. The President is for exonerating the conquered rebels from all the expense and damages of the war, and for compelling the loyal citizens to pay the whole debt caused by the rebellion. He insists that those of our people who were plundered and their property burned or destroyed by rebel raiders shall not be indemnified, but shall bear their own loss, while the rebels shall retain their own property, most of which was declared forfeited by the Congress of the United States. He desires that the traitors (having sternly executed that most important leader, Rickety Weirze, as a high example) should be exempt from further fine, imprisonment, forfeiture, exile, or capital punishment, and be declared entitled to all the rights of loyal citizens. He desires that the States created by him shall be acknowledged as valid States, while at the same time he inconsistently declares that the old rebel States are in full existence, and always have been, and have equal rights with the loyal States. He opposes the amendment to the Constitution, which changes the base of representation, and desires the old slave States to have the benefit of their increase of freemen without increasing the number of votes; in short, he desires to make the vote of one rebel in South Carolina equal to the vote of three freemen in Pennsylvania or New York. He is determined to force a solid rebel delegation into Congress from the South, and, together with Northern Copperheads, could at once control Congress and elect all future Presidents.

In opposition to these things, a portion of Congress seems to desire that the conquered belligerent shall, according to the law of nations, pay at least a part of the expenses and damages of the war; and that especially the loyal people who were plundered and impoverished by rebel raiders shall be fully indemnified. A majority of Congress desires that treason shall be made odious, not by bloody executions, but by other adequate punishments.

Congress refuses to treat the States created by him as of any validity, and denies that the old rebel States have any existence which gives them any rights under the Constitution. Congress insists on changing the basis of representation so as to put white voters on an equality in both sections, and that such change shall precede the admission of any State. I deny that there is any understanding, expressed or implied, that upon the adoption of the amendment by any State, that such State may be admitted, (before the amendment becomes part of the Constitution.) Such a course would soon surrender the Government into the hands of rebels. Such a course would be senseless, inconsistent, and illogical. Congress denies that any State lately in rebellion has any government or constitution known to the Constitution of the United States, or which can be recognized as part of the Union. How, then, can such a State adopt the amendment? To allow it would be yielding the whole question and admitting the unimpaired rights of the seceded States. I know of no Republican who does not ridicule what Mr. Seward thought a cunning movement, in counting Virginia and other outlawed States among those which had adopted the constitutional amendment abolishing slavery.

It is to be regretted that inconsiderate and incautious Republicans should ever have supposed that the slight amendments already proposed to the Constitution, even when incorporated into that instrument, would satisfy the reforms necessary for the security of the Government. Unless the rebel States, before admission, should be made republican in spirit, and placed under the guardianship of loyal men, all our blood and treasure will have been spent in vain. I waive now the question of punishment which, if we are wise, will still be inflicted by moderate confiscations, both as a reproof and example. Having these States, as we all agree, entirely within the power of Congress, it is our duty to take care that no injustice shall remain in their organic laws. Holding them "like clay in the hands of the potter," we must see that no vessel is made for destruction. Having now no governments, they must have enabling acts. The law of last session with regard to Territories settled the principles of such acts. Impartial suffrage, both in electing the delegates and ratifying their proceedings, is now the fixed rule. There is more reason why colored voters should be admitted in the rebel States than in the Territories. In the States they form the great mass of the loyal men. Possibly with their aid loyal governments may be established in most of those States. Without it all are sure to be ruled by traitors; and loyal men, black and white, will be oppressed, exiled, or murdered. There are several good reasons for the passage of this bill. In the first place, it is just. I am now confining my arguments to negro suffrage in the rebel

States. Have not loyal blacks quite as good a right to choose rulers and make laws as rebel whites? In the second place, it is a necessity in order to protect the loyal white men in the seceded States. The white Union men are in a great minority in each of those States. With them the blacks would act in a body; and it is believed that in each of said States, except one, the two united would form a majority, control the States, and protect themselves. Now they are the victims of daily murder. They must suffer constant persecution or be exiled. The convention of southern loyalists, lately held in Philadelphia, almost unanimously agreed to such a bill as an absolute necessity.

Another good reason is, it would insure the ascendency of the Union party. Do you avow the party purpose? exclaims some horror-stricken demagogue. I do. For I believe, on my conscience, that on the continued ascendency of that party depends the safety of this great nation. If impartial suffrage is excluded in the rebel States then every one of them is sure to send a solid rebel representative delegation to Congress, and cast a solid rebel electoral vote. They, with their kindred Copperheads of the North, would always elect the President and control Congress. While slavery sat upon her defiant throne, and insulted and intimidated the trembling North, the South frequently divided on questions of policy between Whigs and Democrats, and gave victory alternately to the sections. Now, you must divide them between loyalists, without regard to color, and disloyalists, or you will be the perpetual vassals of the free-trade, irritated, revengeful South. For these, among other reasons, I am for negro suffrage in every rebel State. If it be just, it should not be denied; if it be necessary, it should be adopted; if it be a punishment to traitors, they deserve it.

But it will be said, as it has been said, "This is negro equality!" What is negro equality, about which so much is said by knaves, and some of which is believed by men who are not fools? It means, as understood by honest Republicans, just this much, and no more: every man, no matter what his race or color; every earthly being who has an immortal soul, has an equal right to justice, honesty, and fair play with every other man; and the law should secure him these rights. The same law which condemns or acquits an African should condemn or acquit a white man. The same law which gives a verdict in a white man's favor should give a verdict in a black man's favor on the same state of facts. Such is the law of God and such ought to be the law of man. This doctrine does not mean that a negro shall sit on the same seat or eat at the same table with a white man. That is a matter of taste which every man must decide for himself. The law has nothing to do with it. If there be any who are afraid of the rivalry of the black man in office or in business, I have only to advise them to try and beat their competitor in knowledge and business capacity, and there is no danger that his white neighbors will prefer his African rival to himself. I know there is between those who are influenced by this cry of "negro equality" and the opinion that there is still danger that the negro will be the smartest, for I never saw even a contraband slave that had not more sense than such men.

There are those who admit the justice and ultimate utility of granting impartial suffrage to all men, but they think it is impolitic. An ancient philosopher, whose antagonist admitted that what he required was just but deemed it impolitic, asked him: "Do you believe in Hades?" I would say to those above referred to, who admit the justice of human equality before the law but doubt its policy: "Do you believe in hell?"

How do you answer the principle inscribed in our political scripture, "That to secure these rights governments are instituted among men, deriving their just powers from the consent of the governed?" Without such consent government is a tyranny, and you exercising it are tyrants. Of course, this does not admit malefactors to power, or there would soon be no penal laws and society would become an anarchy. But this step forward is an assault upon ignorance and prejudice, and timid men shrink from it. Are such men fit to sit in the places of statesmen?

There are periods in the history of nations when statesmen can make themselves names for posterity; but such occasions are never improved by cowards. In the acquisition of true fame courage is just as necessary in the civilian as in the military hero. In the Reformation there were men engaged as able and perhaps more learned than Martin Luther. Melancthon and others were ripe scholars and sincere reformers, but none of them had his courage. He alone was willing to go where duty called though "devils were as thick as the tiles on the houses."

And Luther is the great luminary of the Reformation, around whom the others revolve as satellites and shine by his light. We may not aspire to fame. But great events fix the eye of history on small objects and magnify their meanness. Let us at least escape that condition.

January 3, 1867

Mobile Daily Advertiser and Register:
No Amendment—Stand Firm

DESOLATE IN heart, broken in fortunes, isolated in politics, and enduring all the trials and mortifications of a people subjugated by arms, the South has yet solemn duties to perform. It has temptations to avoid, the wiles of politicians to resist, and a noble fortitude to foster and cherish, in order to bear affliction with patience and hope and thus safely pass through the present, last and not the least of its many crises. We see danger in this Radical Constitutional Amendment, and we should be false to public duty did we not warn our countrymen of it. It is a Trojan horse sought to be introduced into our gates, with the difference that its armed enemies are not even concealed in its belly. There never was a clearer proposition to men whose visions are not darkened by apprehension, than that the excluded State owe it to themselves, to their heroic leaders, like Davis and Lee, to their fellow-Americans in the other States of the former Union, and to the genius of Constitutional Freedom, resolutely to decline to become parties, by consent, to this degrading amendment. Nothing worse could befall us from the most vindictive action of the present Congress; for granting that we get back into the Union, "so-called," at the price of this sacrifice of constitutional right, State character and honor, as a people, what do we gain but dead-sea fruit? We go back bound, hand and foot, and as much at the mercy of a Radical majority, whose sway will have been prolonged by our act, as we are now or could be under an act of territorialization. We go back with our heads hanging in shame, and our names blasted for all time to come, as a people who have sold their God-like Lee for thirty dirty pieces of silver. Do it not, men of the South! Let them not do the deed, women of the South! And as we have heretofore pleaded with you to count the cost of rashness before you leaped from the beetling verge into the dread abyss of civil war, and as when you had passed the Rubicon, we besought you by all your manhood and womanhood to make good, by sacrifice and valor, the step you had taken, we now implore you to stand firm in spurning self-degradation, to hold fast to the vantage ground of your present position, to be true to yourselves and the friends of liberty throughout this once free land, and show yourselves as faithful to principle and honor in defeat, as your dead and living soldiers were brave in war.

We deeply regret that Alabama should have been the first State to show signs of flinching where steadiness and nerve are demanded by duty and statesmanship. And if there should be danger that in the coming session the project should be revived with any prospect of success, it becomes the duty of the people in their several counties, where their representatives are hesitating, to meet in primary assemblies and command their servants not through cowardly apprehensions to surrender them to the indignities and injustice of this amendment. The wavering at Montgomery has already stimulated Radical energy to threaten and frighten us into a measure which is so important to them. The crazy resolutions and *projets* of laws with which Congress is being deluged are the evidences of this purpose. Let us be true to ourselves, stand firm and fear not. Radicalism is travelling a road that must come to a speedy end. They are driving the car of revolution with electric speed and a smash-up is inevitable unless the teachings of human history are all false, and the everlasting laws of cause and effect are to be suspended for Radical benefit. Congress is striving to concentrate all the powers of the Government in its own hands—the President's late message demonstrates this truth with unanswerable arguments. It remains to be seen whether the Executive and the Supreme Court will surrender the trusts and powers reposed in them as co-ordinate branches of the Government, and where the majority of the people of the country will be in such a struggle. Our policy is as clear as noon-day, to bide the time and wait and see. It certainly is *not* to help our enemies and the enemies of the Constitution of the United States.

Mobile Daily Advertiser & Register, January 9, 1867

Albion W. Tourgée: To the Voters of Guilford

Fellow Citizens:

Having been urgently solicited to become a candidate for the Constitutional Convention, and having consented to do so, I hereby offer for your suffrages, as the exponent of the following principles to the earnest and unflinching support of which, in the future as in the past, I am impelled by every incentive of justice, humanity and patriotism:

1st. Equality of civil and political rights to all citizens.

2nd. No property qualifications for jurymen.

3rd. Every voter eligible for election to any office of trust or emolument.

4th. All legislative, executive, and judicial officers of the state to be filled by the vote of the people.

5th. A criminal code humane and Christian, without whip or stocks.

6th. An ample system of public instruction reaching from the lowest primary school to the highest university course, free to the children of every citizen.

7th. A uniform ad valorum system of taxation upon property.

8th. The tax upon the poll (or more properly tax upon the value of labor) not to exceed three days' work upon the public highway or its equivalent.

9th. In addition to the provisions of Section 4th of the Constitutional Amendment, the assumption or payment by any county, city, or other political corporation, within the state of any debt, contracted in aid of rebellion, directly or indirectly, should be prohibited by Constitutional enactment.

10th. The rights of citizenship to be extended to the present excluded classes whenever the Congress of the United States shall see fit to remove their disabilities and not before.

These are the principles of equal and exact justice to all men, the marrow and essence of republican government. Incorporated in the Constitution they will order the new state a government of the people, by the people and for the people. Without them it will be government controlled and administered in the interests of the few.

Voters of Guilford, two courses are open before you. Shall the new State have an Oligarchy or a Republic? An Aristocracy or a Democracy? Shall its fundamental law respect the rights of the hundred thousand voters who do not own land enough to give to each a burial place, or consider only the interests of the fifteen hundred men who own two-thirds of the lands of the state? Shall the poor man's labor be taxed four or five percent and the rich man's property but one-third of one percent? Shall poverty be taxed higher than wealth? Shall the honest and capable, though landless voter, be allowed to hold offices of trust and emolument, or shall that privilege be granted only to "the lord of barren acres"? Shall the poor man be allowed a seat upon the jury, or is "red clay" necessary to give judgment and integrity? Shall capacity, honesty, and your suffrages be sufficient to entitle the voter to a seat in the assembly or shall the clayey Juggernaut set up his altar in the State House?

The aristocracy of slavery is dead. Shall we now build up an aristocracy of land? Shall we have a government of a few, by a few, and for a few? You have tried it once and the past seven years are its results—six hundred thousand dead are the glorious first fruits of aristocratic rule.

Poor men of Guilford & laboring men of Guilford, now is your golden moment! The tide is at the flood! Old things are passing away. Slavery, that fed daintily upon your lives, has ceased to ask its yearly hecatomb of men and women. Aristocracy, which would let "a thousand paupers die that our oligarch might live," is fighting its last battle with Democracy. Muscle is no longer bought and sold, nor brain made the subject of barter. Wealth is no longer the great I Am, nor manhood a political cipher. "The bone of contention" has become a constituent element of the Republic. "We, the people," has a new signification. Do you choose to govern yourselves or be ruled by those who still crave the name of "master"? Will you be free men or serfs? Will the "new people" have a "new" state, or the old one patched up, with its whip and stocks, its oppressive system of taxation and its tyrannic landed aristocracy!

Laborers of Guilford are you not as capable of self-government as those men who with the motto rule or ruin, did both rule and ruin all this glorious Southern land? Will you exercise and preserve the power which three hundred thousand martyrs died to place in your hands, or will you basely yield it *into the hands of our enemies*! But the cry is "Property must be protected!" That was the rallying cry of '61. "Our property! Our property! Great is Diana!" "The rich man's war and the poor man's fight" was the result. The contest which was meant to make every poor man a slave has made them free. Let then our battle cry be "Manhood, Equal Rights, Free Schools, Free Juries, Free Offices, Free Press, Free Speech, Free Men!"

For the purpose of more fully discussing the great issues which are upon us, I shall be happy to meet the citizens of the county wherever and whenever they may desire until the day of election.

> Very Respectfully,
> Your Obdt. Servant,
> A. W. Tourgee.
> Oct. 21, 1867.

Harper's Weekly: *Impeachment*

THE REPORT of the majority of the Judiciary Committee recommending impeachment of the President has unquestionably surprised and disappointed the country; nor are the temper and reasoning of that part of the report which has been published likely to inspire general confidence. In alluding to the subject some two months since, we said that "technically and verbally up to the present moment the President has not violated the law." We were reminded that he had issued an Amnesty Proclamation in defiance of the law which forbade him. But he held that his authority for such an act was derived from the Constitution, and that the law itself was in violation of that instrument. That is, his action was but another illustration of the difference of constitutional interpretation between himself and Congress. What we had in mind was that no law of undoubted constitutional sanction had been violated by him; and that however unwise, for example, his removal of SHERIDAN and SICKLES may have been, they were both acts strictly within the reconstruction law.

The charge of usurpation made by the majority of the Committee is, in a certain sense, valid. There is no doubt that the subject of reconstruction belongs properly to Congress; and we can all now see that it would have been better to assemble Congress before beginning the work. But there is equally no doubt that the action of the President was at the time justified by the country, for the reason that it was felt to be necessary to do something to restore civil government, and because it was supposed that his action was temporary and provisional. It was an assumption of power condoned by the conscious necessities of the situation. But it was not felt to be then, nor do we believe any large number of persons now suppose it to have been, a usurpation with treasonable or injurious intention. It was in no proper sense a high crime, or even a misdemeanor.

When Congress assembled and it became evident that the President meant to insist upon his theory of Reconstruction as final the hostility between him and Congress began. His theory was undoubtedly both false and foolish. But he maintained it within his Constitutional prerogative. His spirit was hateful as his understanding is mean. But when his theories were confuted and his Constitutional efforts through the veto were overborne; when the Freedmen's Bureau was continued; when the civil rights of the freedmen were declared; when the Reconstruction bill was passed; the President retained General HOWARD as chief of the Bureau; he did not formally resist the extension of civil rights, although he was morally guilty of the New Orleans massacre; and he appointed under the Reconstruction bill the very commanders who were most agreeable to its framers. He has opposed the whole Congressional policy of reconstruction; he has vituperated Congress and publicly insulted eminent citizens; he has in express terms denied the authority of Congress as now constituted; and his conduct has incalculably prolonged and deepened the difficulty of reconstruction. But while as a stump orator he has denied the authority of Congress, as President he has recognized it; and the encouragement which he has given to the spirit of disaffection is that which a President in opposition may always give to the party opposed to Congress.

The charge of usurpation is the only really grave charge, and that this was criminal can not be proved. The report of the majority has not revealed, so far as published, any thing new upon the point; and if there were any thing new of importance it would have been published in the abstract of the report. The vague charge of complicity in the assassination of President LINCOLN wholly disappears; and we do Mr. JOHNSON the justice of saying that we do not believe it was ever seriously believed by any body. Indeed we feel more strongly than ever that the impeachment project sprang from the hot impatience of those who felt that the President was an "obstruction" to the rapid success of their views of the true policy of reconstruction; and was not the result of a profound conviction that he was clearly guilty of impeachable offenses. Yet if Presidents are to be impeached because they obstruct or oppose the will of the Congressional majority, it is very evident that it will become an ordinary party measure.

As we have often said, there can be no doubt that in extreme cases, when the great powers of the Government come into conflict, Congress will prevail. However cunning a system of "checks and balances" and "co-ordinate powers" there may be, the supreme authority of every government resides somewhere, and extreme pressure will develop it. It is none the less true, however, that in our system the Executive is a well-contrived check upon the Legislative Department; while, if it transcends its restraining powers, it is submitted by the same system to trial and removal by the Legislature. The Legislature, however, is again and radically checked by the popular vote which elects it; and therefore its indictment and possible punishment of the Executive becomes also a question of expediency. To impeach and fail to convict would destroy the impeaching party. This consideration should not, of course, restrain any party when the positive guilt of the President is conspicuous and the national injury plain. But a party which believes that its possession of power is essential to the wise and permanent settlement of the most vital public questions ought to hesitate long before it impeaches the President under circumstances like those at present existing in the country.

It has been lately said with great vigor that a party must be plucky if it would succeed. Undoubtedly; but what is pluck in a party? It is invincible fidelity to principle. It is not obstinate tenacity of a measure merely because it is extreme. This kind of "pluck" in GEORGE III. lost England the American colonies. The same "pluck" in CHARLES X. of France lost him his crown; and in CHARLES I. of England his head. What principle is involved in the impeachment of a President upon doubtful grounds? What principle is involved in straining the interpretation of evidence to reach him? The principle by which the dominant party in this country is solemnly bound is equal rights; and the policy to which it is pledged is reconstruction upon that principle. It holds to that policy because it believes it to be of the highest expediency. But impeachment has never been more than the whim of a few. It has never been sanctioned by the intelligent judgment of the country to which all the facts are familiar; and we do not believe it will be sustained by Congress.

December 14, 1867

Albion W. Tourgée: The Reaction

To the Editor of the Standard:

It is an assertion constantly reiterated by men of almost every shade of political belief, that a political reaction has begun, and is now going on, in the minds of the American people. According to Conservative authority, the people are sickened of "nigger," "taxation," "equality," "loyal rule"; in short, justice applied to political questions. And to escape the omnipresent right and avoid commercial disaster, they are hurriedly crawfishing into the gaping maw of Democracy—that party which is never disturbed by questions of Right or Wrong, and whose acme of prosperity is only reached through the surges of financial ruin. To them it is a reaction from better to worse—from a higher to a lower political morality; a reaction which leads men to inquire upon every political question, not what is right, but what will best subserve the idea of government designed especially for the white man. In short a reaction which is to substitute prejudice for conscience.

The moderately inclined, constitutionally timid portion of the Republican party, men who are willing enough to be right if they are sure they can win thereby, who worship present success beyond all other gods, insist that their Congressional leaders have been too fast, too radical; that the Republican party has got ahead of the people, and that a movement to the rear is necessary, to prevent it from destruction. The party wire-pullers have sounded a retreat, and the puppets all over the country are advancing backward, each in his own peculiar manner, as circumstances or inclination dictates. Some bolt with such ready impetuosity as to outstrip their leaders and get into the very camp of Democracy, while they are yet dallying with the pickets. Others slowly and painfully drag themselves over the hindrances which time and their own efforts have placed in the backward pathway. Others, having burned their ships, have no recourse but to plunge boldly into the sea of inconsistency, only to be hopelessly choked by their own

utterances. The whippers-in of every aspirant for the Republican Presidential nomination, having the same theory of reaction in mind, are peculiarly anxious to establish the fact that
their man is moderate, or at least not offensively radical, insisting at the same time that the recent reaction (at the North, as
Southern trigger-workers are fond of saying) utterly forbids all
hope for the election of an ultra Radical. This reaction, then,
according to the timid Republicans, is of the same nature as is
claimed by the Conservatives, only a little less decided in its
character. Instead of substituting prejudice for conscience, they
only propose to make success the test in all political questions.

Upon this principle, a man who never expressed a political
belief in all his life, and one whose chief merits is, that the
most persistent quiz could never yet find out with which party
even his sympathies lay, and who cannot be proven by any set
or utterance to be good or bad, Radical or Conservative, man
or mouse, is claimed to be the most feasible candidate for the
Republican party in the coming struggle; and for the same
reasons the mouths of other candidates are closed, lest they
should utter some radical truth to interfere with their chances
of nomination. These moderate Republicans, who dream so
constantly of the horrors of reaction, whose timid souls can see
only defeat in the future, unless half the fruits of the past six
years of warfare is given up to the enemy, are very fond of saying, especially to colored men, and to our Southern Unionists,
when they are inclined to murmur at the chaff which is offered
to them, "You know our only hope is in the Republican party."
As if the people were not greater than the party! As if it were
not the party which was dependent upon them, rather than
they upon the party! The Republican theory of the "Reaction"
is, that the masses of the people, or at least of that party, have
pronounced against manhood suffrage and loyal reconstruction, and that now, in order to save the party from defeat, we
must perpetrate another Brobdingnagian lie. We must have a
candidate who shall be all things to all men, and a platform
which is ditto. To the newly enfranchised "brother of the African persuasion," in North Carolina, the Republican party must
stand forth still as the champion of "Liberty and Equality,"
the sanctified agency through which freedom came to those in
bondage, while to the jaundiced negrophobist in Ohio, it must

be represented as only having given a little to the colored man from necessity, and as very willing to revoke that little upon a reasonable opportunity. And this Janus-visaged party is now tried to be foisted on North and South alike, upon the special plea that the reaction in public sentiment at the North renders it imperatively necessary.

Now, the whole theory on which this outcry of "Reaction" is based is deceptive and false. There has been no reaction *among the people* in the reference to the great principles now at the issue. They gave their verdict, and sent it into the court of final appeal, sealed with the blood of hundreds of thousands of their sons. You might as well expect the tide of Niagara to reverse its flow, as to expect them to set aside that verdict. And as for us of the South, black or white, we had rather be killed than commit suicide. If our throats must be cut, we don't care about handling the cleaver. There is no reaction here, and will not be in our day, among the party of freedom and justice.

"But," says the objector, "there has been some change in the political world—you cannot deny that; for the elections show it unmistakably." Evidently there has been a change, and for lack of a better appreciation of its true character, it has been generally denominated a *reaction*. And because there could not possibly be any reaction or advance in the Conservative party, it being at the best only a sort of political backwater, it was at once concluded that it must of necessity be a retrograde movement among the rank and file of the Republican party.

Here is the mistake. What we see today is *not reaction, but the effects of reaction*, and the reaction itself is not of the present, but of the past, and was not a reaction in sentiment among the rank and file of the party, but a reaction in policy among its leaders. It began as soon as the business of the war was over, when Lee and Johnston had surrendered, and Abraham Lincoln had been borne to his prairie tomb. It was first fully developed—so far as the writer knows at least—at the Loyalist Convention in Philadelphia, in September, 1866, and was the result of the most egregious stupidity on the part of the recognized leaders of the Republican party. It is resulting now just as every clear-headed and sound-hearted Radical in that Convention prophecied that it would, either in the death or thorough reformation of the party.

The Republican party in 1861 was compelled to put itself in array against rebellion. Its very existence depended on the putting down of that war against the Union. The people were opposed to rebellion because it was a great wrong, and the consequences of a still greater wrong. The enormity of the crime of rebellion, the fearful wickedness on which it was based, was so apparent that its contemplation often made the boor a hero. To the leaders of the party its suppression was a political necessity, to the people a holy duty; and when it could no longer be hidden, but was evident to all that the deeply seared conscience of the people was at least touched, that they were determined to right the wrong of the past, that the long slumbering crater showed signs of life—*then* the Republican party, mindful for the first time of the maxim that "Honesty is the best policy," concluded to adopt the role of Peter the Hermit, and preach the crusade against rebellion, on the grounds of its justice and righteousness.

Its leaders approached the limits of the crater doubtfully, and began to stir the seething mass within very carefully. Nobody was to be hurt—nothing disturbed. Love for the "erring sisters" was too strong in their hearts to allow more than a big scare. The fire in the great crater flashed and flamed. They warmed to their work and patted one another gleefully, exclaiming, "See what a fire we have builded." By-and-by the flames grew hotter and began to burn the hay-straw hobby of the sanctity of slavery which some of them bestrode; and then some tried to put out the fire by blowing on it, as they would cool a plate of soup. But others saw that the sanctified hobby tried to hinder it. So they deserted the hobby, and as they had before cried, "Down with rebellion!" so they now cried, "Down with rebellion and slavery!" and they punched away at the seething mass within the crater, thinking all the time that the great flame which swept the length and breadth of our land and licked up the chaff with which the harvests of ninety years had cumbered the soil's threshing-floor, was a thing of their own creation.

Unconsciously to itself, the Republican party at the commencement of the war rose to the dignity of a party of right against wrong, of justice against expediency, of principle against policy. Accident offered it this character, and an overwhelming necessity compelled its acceptance. It was successful during the war simply because this was its character. It inaugurated a new school of political thought in our nation. "Right or wrong" was made the test question upon all political issues. The issues presented were mostly those of direct and apparent right against unmistakable wrong. The people supported the right because it was right and they were true. In so doing they supported the Republican party, because it happened to be on the side of right, and not right because it was on the side of the Republican party. This fact the leaders of that party have never yet apprehended. They regard that mighty exhibition of popular conscience which sustained and carried on the war, as a pleasant humbug, and its rallying cry—Justice, Liberty and Humanity— as one of the most successful tubs ever thrown to that great whale, the people. This was the miserable folly and mistake of the Republican leaders during the war. They thought that they, through the agency of the Republican party, had created the spirit which saved the country from destruction. The contemplation of this imaginary feat has so absorbed the energies of the party leaders, that the Republican members of Congress have had room for but little beside self-gratulation since the close of the war. They flatter themselves with the belief—comfortable, though false—that they are and have been, constantly "ahead of the people." Well does the writer recollect the quiet assumption with which, at the Philadelphia Convention, one of our well-fed M. C.'s folded his hands over his abdominal developments, and said to him, "We were ahead of the people. If we had not stirred up the people constantly the rebellion could never have been put down. The Republicans in Congress were the leaders of the people as the generals were of the army." The writer was one of the "people," and the smoke had scarcely settled about Sumter in 1861 before he had entered the service of the United States to put down rebellion. As he sat and talked with his sleek "leader of the people," he was a scarred and crippled veteran. He wondered if this "leader" thought that his listener was one of those whom he had stirred up, or who needed his stirring up. And yet he knew that the vast body of the people were as earnest upon this matter as himself, and this idea of being "ahead of the people" was an illusion very flattering to the vanity of our Radical Congressmen, but by no means complimentary to their discernment.

From this blindness sprung the only actual political reaction which has taken place since the war—a reaction not in the sentiments of the people, but in the policy of the leaders of the Republican party. Having no confidence in the conscience of the people, regarding the war itself as a sort of campaign document for the Republican party, when it was finally over, they adopted another policy. Before the war every party was Janus-faced, one visage gaping toward the North, the other facing towards the Gulf. It was supposed that the people only supported the right when carefully wheedled into so doing by some cunning policy. Many of the leaders of the Republican party were trained in this ante-war school and were no doubt skilled in the mystery of harmonizing the needs of slavery and freedom, in catering at once for North and South successfully. They are men who, having once become settled to one mode of action, can adopt no other. As soon, therefore, as the war was over, they considered that the special pleading of the Republican party was at an end. It would not do any longer to press any political measure because it was absolutely and essentially just, but the dose of righteousness must be sugared over with a coat of policy, or, in other words, covered with a lie. The Republican party had dealt with truths during the war, it must do so no more. The people must be deceived into its support. This was the *reaction*.

In accordance with this policy the political campaign of 1866 was built on that matchless lie, the Howard Amendment as a finality in reconstruction. Everyone knew that it must be either a shameless lie, or an absolute surrender and betrayal of all the rights of the colored men of the South, not excepting those who had fought against rebellion. This was the first fruit of the *reaction* which has periled the life of the Republican party. From that day to this it has lost ground. If they had taken the suffrage issue when first presented, and stood squarely upon it as a matter of intrinsic right, they would have been triumphantly sustained. The people would have accepted it as a right, but as a means of strengthening the Republican party they care nothing about it.

This change of policy, from What is Right to What will Win, at first puzzled the people. They could not understand why certain evidently just and proper measures did not meet the support of the Republican leaders. The fact has, however, at length forced itself upon very many of the most active and valuable men of the country, that our Republican Congressmen are more anxious about re-electing each other than about reconstructing the government, more concerned in the election of a President than in doing justice to all.

The latest exhibition of this anxiety is in reference to the Conventions now in session in the late rebel States. Even at this time a delegation of Republican lobbyists from Washington are said to be at Richmond to prevent the Virginia Constitution Convention doing anything which might prejudice the Republican party. It makes no difference what may be the needs of the people in these States, the Republican party and its interests are paramount. It must be saved though the liberties of the people are left unprotected. Much of the legislation which it thus sought to smother is not only very just and proper, but absolutely essential to the future people and prosperity of the states concerned.

Again the "reaction" cry, striking as it does the little remaining courage from the hearts of the thimble-riggers of the party, has developed a sudden and pressing necessity for relieving a large portion of the present excluded classes from disability. In so doing it is not proposed to afford specific relief to men who ought not to have been disfranchised at the first, but to offer a reward for party work in the matter of reconstruction. There are many men here who, according to the letter of the acts, are disfranchised, but who were as good Union men during the entire war as the South could show, yet after it was over honestly differed with the policy of Congress upon the matter of Reconstruction. These men were disfranchised upon the hypothesis that they had been disloyal to the United States, and in all cases where the reverse can be shown are of course entitled to relief from disabilities by Congress. These, however, are not the men whom it is proposed by "Reactionists" to relieve, but those who have done party-work, those who were shrewd enough to foresee the success of the party and ally themselves with it in good time. It is said these men "must be rewarded," that they have "condoned their offences," etc. As if work done for the Republican party, with the prospect of fat offices in view, could condone an offence against the government of the United States!

These are a few of the measures which, if persevered in for a while longer, if forced upon the Republican party to avoid the fancied terrors of "Reaction," will most certainly react upon the minds of all just and patriotic men and sound the knell of Republicanism.

The only way to save it alive, is to come back to the standard of Right and Wrong, stand squarely upon the principles of Justice, and select a Presidential candidate who shall represent them positively. A double-faced candidate will complete its ruin.

WINEGAR

National Anti-Slavery Standard, January 4, 1868

New-York Tribune: The President Must Be Impeached

WE DO NOT see how the House can refuse to arraign the President before the Senate for high crimes and misdemeanors. Impeachment is not a desirable proceeding. It is cumbersome and tedious. It may arrest legislation, and present a new issue to the country at a time when new issues are not wanted. It is not, perhaps, a wise precedent to make. It gives to power a temptation which passion cannot always resist. It is a high, solemn, sacred trust, only to be used, when absolutely necessary for the salvation of the country.

We believe the salvation of the country demands the impeachment of the President. We have all along felt that we might submit to Mr. Johnson's Administration, evil as it has been, rather than force an angry and doubtful question upon the country. With the Congress overwhelmingly Republican, there was no reason why we should not compel the President to pursue a wise policy. We reasoned upon the presumption that it was better to have impeachment held over him as a check than to begin a trial that might be as long as that of Warren Hastings. It was a debatable question. The evidence was far from being conclusive. Morally, there was no doubt that Mr. Johnson should be impeached. But impeachment is a question of law and evidence, not of moral belief. As a Republican, there were a hundred reasons why he should be removed. This would be a good plea in a Republican Convention, not before the Senate of the United States. Until impeachment became an inevitable, overwhelming necessity, without doubt as to the meaning of the law, and the force of the evidence, to enter upon it was only to give the President a chance to make himself a martyr before the country. Therefore we have constantly opposed impeachment, although at times we stood alone among the Republican press. There is no longer any doubt. The issue is as clear as it was when Gen. Beauregard opened his batteries upon Fort Sumter. Andrew Johnson, President of the United

States, tramples upon a law, defies the authority of Congress, and claims to exercise absolute and despotic power. *Congress must impeach him immediately.*

All other questions sink before the present. It would be difficult to have our course clearer. A law is passed, which defines it to be the duty of the President to consult with the Senate before removing a certain officer. This law may or may not be constitutional. The President has no business with that. It is constitutional until the Supreme Court decides otherwise. It is law until the Court interposes and invalidates it. The President's sworn duty is *to execute it*—to obey it—to see that it is carefully and studiously obeyed. He may not like it. But chief-magistrates have been compelled to execute laws they did not prefer. He may think it unconstitutional. That is of no more consequence than the opinion of any private citizen. His duty is not to execute laws which *he may think constitutional*, but to EXECUTE THE LAWS. If he had been clothed with judicatory power, if the founders of the Constitution had felt that it was wise to give the President any option in the matter, they would have so expressed it and declared that he might execute all laws only when the Supreme Court decided their constitutionality. If the President has the right to select his laws, and say "This act I will execute because it suits me, and the other I will not enforce because it strikes me to be unconstitutional," then Congress and the Supreme Court might as well adjourn without day. For the right to do as he pleases with any law, to assume to be its sole arbiter and judge, may become a tyranny more absolute than that of the Emperor of Russia. It is a comparatively small matter now. Apparently, it affects only the right of Mr. Stanton to hold the War-Office, and of the President to select his constitutional advisers. This is not the question, but only the merest incident of it. If the President has the right to remove Mr. Stanton in defiance of law, he may remove Mr. Chief-Justice Chase and Gen. Grant, and indeed the whole Senate. For the law by which Mr. Stanton holds his place is as much a law, as sacred and as binding, as that by which Mr. Chase presides over the Supreme Court, and Gen. Grant commands the army. If he may with impunity order Lorenzo Thomas to take possession of the War Department—a building which is not the property of Mr. Johnson, but of the

American people—he may also direct Mr. Coyle to open the next Supreme Court, and Gen. Hancock to assume command of the army. It may be said that there is a law which provides the form in which Mr. Chase may be removed, and another law which directs the manner for the removal of Gen. Grant. To this we reply that there is also a law which provides how Mr. Stanton may be removed, that one law is as binding as the other, and that if we permit the President to violate one, he may with impunity violate all.

There is no avoiding this conclusion. There is no explaining it away. There is no middle course. *The President has assumed the responsibility of breaking a law. Congress must assume the responsibility of impeaching him.* Not to do so in the face of this flagrant and insolent proceeding is to become a partner in the crime. It is no time to consider the party influence of impeachment, or its effect upon Presidential candidates. We would rather see the Republican party, candidates and all, driven into the deserts of Arabia than to have them tremble one moment in the presence of this high duty. Questions of expediency were all well enough so long as the President stood within the pale of the law. But now when he presumes to be the executive, legislative, and judicial power, when he claims to decide which laws Congress may pass, and what acts are constitutional, to hesitate a moment is criminal.

We are sure there will be no hesitation. The time has come to cease trifling with Andrew Johnson. This man, who reeled into the Presidency; who has debased his high office by unseemly and indecent demonstrations; who has surrounded himself with the worst members of the worst phase of Washington life; whose retinue consists of lobbyists, Rebels, and adventurers; who has polluted the public service by making espionage honorable, and treachery the means of advancement; who has deceived the party that elected him, as well as the party that created him; who has made his own morbid and overweening vanity the only rule of his administration; who has sought to entrap illustrious servants of the people into ignominious evasion of the law, and who now claims to break that law with impunity—this most infamous Chief-Magistrate should be swept out of office. LET HIM BE IMPEACHED! And let the Republican party show that it not only has the power to preserve the country from rebellion under Jefferson Davis, but also from treachery under Andrew Johnson.

THE FORBEARANCE OF CONGRESS.

Now that Andrew Johnson is about to be arraigned before the Senate for the crime of defying the laws, it may be profitable to look back at the action of Congress, especially upon the question of impeachment. We do this for the purpose of showing that the representatives of the people have acted with wisdom, prudence, and forbearance. Possibly they have forborne too long. We shall be told that we were all cowards for not impeaching the President before, and that if we had taken this step in the beginning there would be no trouble now.

Congress might, of course, have impeached Mr. Johnson at any time. The Republican party was in power. It had not only a majority, but enough votes to control a veto, and pass laws in spite of the Executive. It is difficult to imagine a greater power, or one more delicate to manage. The temptations of all great majorities is to tyrannize. Here was a party fresh from the great war, triumphant over rebellion, and eager to reap the fruits of victory by speedy reconstruction. Here was its President, so advanced in Radicalism that many prudent men were afraid he would execute all the Rebels within his reach. Surely, men said, this President has seen the South; he has been through the fiery furnace; he is scarred with the flames of rebellion, and he will give us a reconstruction that will be just, humane, and prompt. Congress was disappointed. Mr. Johnson had made himself Vice-President by pretending to be an extreme Radical. That was in war times. There were eleven States to return. In all probability they would be Democratic. He would insist upon their admission. He would be their champion and friend. He would ally himself with the Democratic party of the North, and then be elected President. We believe this has been Mr. Johnson's purpose since the beginning of his Administration. We believe he has always intended to betray the Republican party, and with it to betray Congress. For this he has labored with a tenacity which has no parallel in history—with an energy worthy of a better cause. During all the time that the President was planning, intriguing, arranging, backing and filling, saying one thing to-day and another to-morrow, Congress treated him with courtesy and patience. Not one word was said of dissent—impeachment was never breathed.

For the New-Orleans riots Mr. Johnson is responsible. No fair man can read the evidence without seeing that his hands are stained with the blood of loyal men. He is responsible for the great deficiency in the revenue. He debased that service to gratify his ambition. When it was necessary to construct a Philadelphia Convention, postmasters were removed by the hundred, and the collection of the revenues was transferred to those of his creatures who would accept the degrading office. Their needs were mainly pecuniary, and the surest way of supplying them was to have the gathering of the taxes. The result is that, under Mr. Johnson, corruption in the revenue service has been reduced to a science. We have men making fraud a profession, organizing it into a "ring," and boasting that with their money they can control his Administration. We believe that if this whisky-tax alone were made a matter of inquiry, enough would be found to warrant the impeachment of the President. For the failure of reconstruction he is preëminently responsible. Beginning his Administration by loudly proclaiming his intention to hang the Rebels, he speedily took to giving them offices. Clamorously insisting that his "policy" was to bring the States back to the Union, we find him directly interfering to keep Alabama out. Since he cannot make the South Democratic, he will produce anarchy. Everything must yield to his own selfish purpose. In nothing has the President been sincere and consistent except to secure his own reëlection to the Presidency.

—With Impeachment always at hand—with causes for impeachment as thick as autumn leaves—with every political passion aroused, and a war of bitterness raging—Congress has remained patient. Read, for instance, Mr. Johnson's last annual message. The Tudors in the splendor of their almost oriental power, the Stuarts in the days of their blindest arrogance, scarcely ventured to address such a message to an English Parliament. Our own feeling at that time was that Congress would be angered into impeaching the President who had put upon them such an insult. It seems almost as if Mr. Johnson has been trying to goad Congress to pass the resolutions which will most probably be adopted to-day. Possibly he may feel that this is his last chance of obtaining the nomination of the Democratic party, and has prepared a coup d'etat for the purpose of impressing Mr. Belmont and his friends with the vigor of which he has so often spoken. We do not care to dwell upon the President's motives, however. The main point is that Congress has acted with a wisdom and forbearance which deserves the highest praise. Subject to all the passions of a legislative body, it has shown in this impeachment business the serenity, the patience, and the dignity of a court of justice. Possibly His Excellency has presumed upon this, and supposed that because Congress was forbearing, it was cowardly, and would not dare to check him. He will find, we think, before many days are passed, how dreadfully he was mistaken.

MORAL CAUSES FOR IMPEACHMENT.

Although impeachment comes before the House to-day, because the President has violated a specific law of Congress—and there is little doubt that his trial will be confined to one specific point, namely, his refusal to obey the Tenure-of-Office law—yet there are moral causes for impeachment which the country will not fail to consider. The decision of the House to-day will form one of the most important pages in American History, and generations will discuss its wisdom.

The country cannot fail to see that Mr. Johnson is a man who cannot be measured by the ordinary moral tests. We do not honor a man for being a gentleman any more than we honor a lady for being virtuous. It is the duty of every man and woman so to live that their lives may be pure and their names unspotted. It is the duty of every public man to leave a name in history that future generations may regard as an example. It will be in the mind of every Christian to-day that there are a hundred reasons for impeachment in the case of President Johnson which will hold good in general esteem, if not in law. We all remember the scenes of his inauguration as Vice-President. He was elected to a high office. It was the triumph of an idea which was dear to the heart of every laboring man. He was the representative of a despised class. He had labored with his hands at one of the most unpretending of employments. He had no advantages of wealth, education, or social culture. At a time when most young men are about to leave college, full of the classics and mathematics, he was beginning to read. Surmounting these difficulties, he had risen from place to place until he was the second officer of the country. Every laboring man felt ennobled in the elevation, for it showed that in free America the highest stations were open to the humblest.

We do not repeat the history of that shameful day when Mr. Johnson not only insulted his audience, but the class from which he sprung, and gave the enemies of labor the opportunity of saying: "Look at your representative workingman, your exalted plebian, your Senatorial tailor. This is what comes of your Democratic institutions! A boor is always a boor. The quality of governing exists only in the blue veins of gentlemen like us, who come from the loins of kings. This is what Democracy brings you." We condoned that offense. But men buried it deep in their hearts, and Americans, proud of their country, and, above all, proud of the name of an American gentleman, blushed when they remembered that a drunken Vice-President had shaken his fist in the faces of the embassadors of foreign countries, and taunted them with their noble birth. They thought of it even more keenly when Mr. Johnson went "swinging around the circle." The story of that dreadful journey has never been fully told. The name of a dead statesman was degraded. We have heard, in ruder civilizations, of a people reveling around a coffin, and boisterously carousing over the dead body of a departed friend. But it remained for a President of the United States to dig from the grave, as it were, the body of the dead Douglas, and go junketing with it through the country. There may have been a hope that the memory of the great leader would bring followers to his cause: but, be that as it may, the dishonor put upon his memory, and upon the country, was humiliating. We saw the President bandying words with a mob in Cleveland, defending riot and murder in St. Louis, and making wild, incoherent speeches at every station. Men have told us that they read accounts of this journey, in foreign lands, with crimsoned cheeks, and tearful eyes, and hearts heavy with shame, and that they almost blushed at the name of an American citizen. Andrew Johnson is the first

Chief Magistrate of the country that ever disgraced his office by conduct unbecoming a gentleman.

Men will not fail to remember these things when the events of to-day are written in history. There are moral reasons for the impeachment of Andrew Johnson. Children will ask their parents what became of the man who thus dishonored his country, and the reply will be, he was driven from his office to obscurity, and was never afterward heard of beyond the tap-rooms of Greenville, where he lived to a green old age, making endless speeches about the Constitution and the Radicals, and what he would do when he was reëlected President of the United States. We owe something to the spirit of Christianity, to the moral law which every gentleman tries to obey and to teach to his children. The impeachment of Andrew Johnson will not merely be commended because he tried to evade the law, but because he degraded his high office, and brought his country to shame, and made it a scandal among the nations. Therefore, the moral sense of the country demands this impeachment. Congress should feel that every gentleman, that every Christian mother who has sons that she would see honored, that every American who is proud of his country, will stand by it in this solemn but unavoidable duty. There are moral laws as well as civil laws. While the tribunal of one is the present and palpable machinery of justice, the tribunal of the other is in the conscience and heart of all. Now that Andrew Johnson is about to appear before the civil law to answer for his misdemeanors, it is well to remember that, morally, he was long since tried by the common-sense of his countrymen, and condemned to the execration of the party which he betrayed, and to the contempt of that other party upon which he is now fawning.

February 24, 1868

Thaddeus Stevens: Speech in Congress on Impeachment

Mr. STEVENS, of Pennsylvania. Mr. Speaker, I agree with those gentlemen who have gone before me that this is a grave subject and should be gravely treated. It is important to the high official who is the subject of these charges, and it is important to a nation of forty million people, now free, and rapidly increasing to hundreds of millions. The official character of the Chief Executive of this great nation being thus involved, the charge, if falsely made, is a cruel wrong; if, on the other hand, the usurpations and misdemeanors charged against him are true he is guilty of as atrocious attempts to usurp the liberty and destroy the happiness of this nation as were ever perpetrated by the most detestable tyrant who ever oppressed his fellow-men. Let us, therefore, discuss these questions in no partisan spirit, but with legal accuracy and impartial justice. The people desire no victim and they will endure no usurper.

The charges, so far as I shall discuss them, are few and distinct. Andrew Johnson is charged with attempting to usurp the powers of other branches of the Government; with attempting to obstruct and resist the execution of the law; with misprision of bribery; and with the open violation of laws which declare his acts misdemeanors and subject him to fine and imprisonment; and with removing from office the Secretary of War during the session of the Senate without the advice or consent of the Senate; and with violating the sixth section of the act entitled "An act regulating the tenure of certain civil offices." There are other offenses charged in the papers referred to the committee, which I may consider more by themselves.

In order to sustain impeachment under our Constitution I do not hold that it is necessary to prove a crime as an indictable offense, or any act *malum in se.* I agree with the distinguished gentleman from Pennsylvania, on the other side of the House, who holds this to be a purely political proceeding. It is intended as a remedy for malfeasance in office and to prevent the continuance thereof. Beyond that, it is not intended as a personal punishment for past offenses or for future example.

Impeachment under our Constitution is very different from impeachment under the English law. The framers of our Constitution did not rely for safety upon the avenging dagger of a Brutus, but provided peaceful remedies which should prevent that necessity. England had two systems of jurisprudence; one for the trial and punishment of common offenders, and one for the trial of men in higher stations, whom it was found difficult to convict before the ordinary tribunals. This latter proceeding was by impeachment or by bills of attainder, generally practiced to punish official malefactors, but the system soon degenerated into political and personal persecution, and men were tried, condemned, and executed by this court from malignant motives. Such was the condition of the English laws when our Constitution was framed; and the Convention determined to provide against the abuse of that high power, so that revenge and punishment should not be inflicted upon political or personal enemies. Here the whole punishment was made to consist in removal from office, and bills of attainder were wholly prohibited. We are to treat this question, then, as wholly political, in which, if an officer of the Government abuse his trust or attempt to pervert it to improper purposes, whatever might be his motives, he becomes subject to impeachment and removal from office. The offense being indictable does not prevent impeachment, but is not necessary to sustain it. (See Story's Commentaries, Curtis on the Constitution, Madison, and others.) Such is the opinion of our elementary writers, nor can any case of impeachment tried in this country be found where any attempt was made to prove the offense criminal and indictable.

What, then, are the official misdemeanors of Andrew Johnson disclosed by the evidence? On the 2d day of March, 1867, Congress passed an act entitled "An act regulating the tenure of certain civil offices." Among other provisions it enacted that no officer who had been appointed by and with the advice and consent of the Senate should be removed from office without the consent of the Senate, and that, if during vacation a suspension should be made for cause, such cause should be reported to the Senate within twenty days after their next meeting. If the Senate should deem the reason of the suspension sufficient, then the officer should be removed and another appointed in his stead; but if the Senate should refuse to concur with the President, and declare the reasons insufficient, then the officer suspended should forthwith resume the functions of his office and the powers of the person performing its duties should cease. It is especially provided that the Secretary of War shall hold his office during the term of the President by whom he may have been appointed, and for one month thereafter unless removed by and with the consent of the Senate as aforesaid. On the 12th day of August, 1867, during the recess of the Senate, the President removed the Secretary of War, whose term of office had not expired, requiring him to surrender the office with the public property, and appointed General U.S. Grant Secretary of War *ad interim*.

When Andrew Johnson assumed the office of President he took the oath to obey the Constitution of the United States and to take care that the laws be faithfully executed. This was a solemn and enduring obligation, nor can he plead exemption from it on account of his condition at the time it was administered to him. An attempt to obstruct the execution of the law, not a mere omission amounting to negligence which would have been a misdemeanor, but a daring and bold conspiracy, was attempted by him to induce the General of the Army to aid him in defeating the operation of this law; and when he had suspended the Secretary of War he appointed General Grant Secretary *ad interim*, with the avowed purpose of preventing the operation of that law, if the Senate should decide in favor of the Secretary; and he says that the General did enter into such conspiracy to aid him in obstructing the return of the rejected Secretary notwithstanding the Senate might decide in his favor. This is denied by the General, and a question of veracity, rather angrily discussed, has arisen between them. Those gentlemen seem to consider that that question is one of importance to the public. In this they are mistaken. Which is the man of truth and which the man of falsehood is of no more public importance than if it arose between two obscure individuals. If Andrew Johnson tells the truth then he is guilty of a high official misdemeanor, for he avows his effort to prevent the execution of the law. If the General commanding tells the truth then the President is guilty of a high misdemeanor, for he declares the same thing of the President, denying only his own complicity. No argument can make this point plainer than the statement of the culprit. If he and the General told the truth then he committed willful perjury by refusing to take care that the laws should be duly executed.

To show the *animus* and guilty knowledge with which this law was violated we have only to turn to the proceedings of the Senate notifying him of his illegal and void conduct, and then to consider that he has since persevered in attempting to enforce it. Indeed, to show his utter disregard of the laws of his country, we have only to turn to his last annual message, in which he proclaims to the public that the laws of Congress are unconstitutional and not binding on the people. Who, after that, can say that such a man is fit to occupy the executive chair, whose duty it is to inculcate obedience to those very laws, and see that they are faithfully obeyed? Then the great beauty of this remedial and preventive process is clearly demonstrated. He is dull and blind who cannot see its necessity and the beneficial purposes of the trial by impeachment.

By the sixth section of the act referred to, it is provided:

"That every removal, appointment, or employment made, had, or exercised contrary to the provisions of this act, and the making, signing, sealing, countersigning, or issuing of any commission or letter of authority for in respect to any such appointment or employment, shall be deemed, and are hereby declared to be, high misdemeanors; and upon trial and conviction thereof every person guilty thereof shall be punished by a fine not exceeding $10,000 or by imprisonment not exceeding five years, or both said punishments, in the discretion of the court."

Now, in defiance of this law, Andrew Johnson, on the 21st day of February, 1868, issued his commission or letter of authority to one Lorenzo Thomas, appointing him Secretary of War *ad interim*, and commanded him to take possession of the Department of War and to eject the incumbent, E. M. Stanton, then in lawful possession of said office. Here, if this act stood alone, would be an undeniable official misdemeanor— not only a misdemeanor *per se*, but declared to be so by the act itself, and the party made indictable and punishable in a criminal proceeding. If Andrew Johnson escapes with bare removal from office, if he be not fined and incarcerated in the penitentiary afterward under criminal proceedings, he may thank the weakness or the clemency of Congress and not his own innocence.

We shall propose to prove on the trial that Andrew Johnson was guilty of misprision of bribery by offering to General Grant, if he would unite with him in his lawless violence, to assume in his stead the penalties and to endure the imprisonment denounced by the law. Bribery is one of the offenses specifically enumerated for which the President may be impeached and removed from office. By the Constitution, article two, section two, the President has power to nominate and, by and with the advice and consent of the Senate, to appoint all officers of the United States whose appointments are not therein otherwise provided for and which shall be established by law, and to fill up all vacancies that may happen during the recess of the Senate, by granting commissions which shall expire at the end of their next session. Nowhere, either in the Constitution or by statute, has the President power to create a vacancy during the session of the Senate and fill it without the advice and consent of the Senate, and yet, on the 21st day of February, 1868, while the Senate was in session, he notified the head of the War Department that he was removed from office and his successor *ad interim* appointed. Here is a plain, recorded violation of the Constitution and laws, which, if it stood alone, would make every honest and intelligent man give his vote for impeachment. The President had persevered in his lawless course through a long series of unjustifiable acts. When the so-called confederate States of America were conquered and had laid down their arms and surrendered their territory to the victorious Union the government and final disposition of the conquered country belonged to Congress alone, according to every principle of the law of nations.

Neither the Executive nor the judiciary had any right to interfere with it except so far as was necessary to control it by military rule until the sovereign power of the nation had provided for its civil administration. No power but Congress had any right to say whether ever or when they should be admitted to the Union as States and entitled to the privileges of the Constitution of the United States. And yet Andrew Johnson, with unblushing hardihood, undertook to rule them by his own power alone; to lead them into full communion with the Union; direct them what governments to erect and what constitutions to adopt, and to send Representatives and Senators to Congress according to his instructions. When admonished by express act of Congress, more than once repeated, he disregarded the warning and continued his lawless usurpation. He is since known to have obstructed the reëstablishment of those governments by the authority of Congress, and has advised the inhabitants to resist the legislation of Congress. In my judgment his conduct with regard to that transaction was a high-handed usurpation of power which ought long ago to have brought him to impeachment and trial and to have removed him from his position of great mischief. He has been lucky in thus far escaping through false logic and false law. But his then acts, which will on the trial be shown to be atrocious, are open evidence of his wicked determination to subvert the laws of his country.

I trust that when we come to vote upon this question we shall remember that although it is the duty of the President to see that the laws be executed the sovereign power of the nation rests in Congress, who have been placed around the Executive as muniments to defend his rights, and as watchmen to enforce his obedience to the law and the Constitution. His oath to obey the Constitution and our duty to compel him to do it are a tremendous obligation, heavier than was ever assumed by mortal rulers. We are to protect or to destroy the liberty and happiness of a mighty people, and to take care that they progress in civilization and defend themselves against every kind of tyranny. As we deal with the first great political malefactor so will be the result of our efforts to perpetuate the happiness and good government of the human race. The God of our fathers, who inspired them with the thought of universal freedom, will hold us responsible for the noble institutions which they projected and expected us to carry out. This is not to be the temporary triumph of a political party, but is to endure in its consequence until this whole continent shall be filled with a free and untrammeled people or shall be a nest of shrinking, cowardly slaves.

February 24, 1868

Bossier Banner: *White Men to the Rescue!*

IF YOU DON'T want negro equality forced upon you, go to the polls and vote against the proposed Constitution, framed by the social banditi, domestic bastards, catamites, scalawags, slubberdegullions, cow thieves and jay-hawkers of Louisiana.

If you don't want your State, District, Parish and Ward offices filled with negroes and white vagabonds, vote down the black vomit spewed up by the scrofulous vermin, late of the Mechanic's Institute.

If you don't want negro jurors, go to the polls and vote against the new constitution.

If you don't want to be ground down by taxes to educate negroes, go to the polls and vote against the new constitution.

If you don't want your wives and daughters to be insulted by insolent and depraved negro vagabonds, go to the polls and vote against the new constitution.

If you don't want negroes and Yankee thieves to be your masters and rulers, go to the polls and vote against the new constitution.

If you are opposed to amalgamation and miscegenation, vote against the new constitution.

If you wish the respect of all honest white men, go to the polls and vote against the new constitution.

If you prefer the Southern white man to the Northern thief as an office holder, go to the polls and vote down the infamous libel proposed as a constitution.

If you feel like stealing something, and wish to associate with negroes and white jayhawkers the balance of your life, go to the polls and vote FOR the new constitution.

If you want your children to go to the same school, eat at the same table, and sit in the same church pews with negro children, and wish to turn negro and jayhawker yourself, go to the polls and vote FOR the cow thieves' constitution.

March 28, 1868

The Nation: *The Result of the Trial*

THE vote on the verdict, even if it has not resulted in conviction, has abundantly justified the House in impeaching the President. When thirty-five out of fifty-four senators pronounce him guilty, it would be absurd as well as unjust to say that there was not "probable cause" for instituting the prosecution, and one may take this view of the matter even after making some allowance for the influence of party feeling and political excitement. The trial of a President by the Senate for offences committed in the course of a long quarrel with Congress touching the limits of his power under the Constitution cannot be a fair one in the sense in which we speak of a fair trial before an ordinary tribunal, where the accused and the judge have never previously had any relations whatever. The Senate, being a branch of the legislature, must have many imperfections as a court of justice; to expect that it will not, is to expect that senators will prove themselves more than men. All the public can ask of them is that they will make all possible efforts to rid their minds during the trial of pride, prejudice, and passion, and govern themselves to the best of their ability by the law and the evidence. That in the present instance they have done so we have never seen good reason to question, and we therefore think their action a sufficient vindication of the action of the House in preferring the charges. One may still doubt the policy of its course, but one cannot accuse it of mere vindictiveness, or mere subservience to party spirit in pursuing it.

The failure to convict is to be regretted for several reasons, but that it leaves Mr. Johnson in the Presidential chair we no longer include amongst the number. In the first place, it is not unlikely that during the remainder of his term he will behave well; in the second, even if he should desire to do mischief, his powers of mischief now, as we have already pointed out, are almost *nil*; and in the third, if he should commit fresh follies and extravagances, although the scandal will be great, it will be more than compensated for by the fact that they will help the Republican party during the coming campaign. His last follies helped it materially in 1866. Moreover, after the exhibition we have had during the last week or two of the taste and temper of the men who would in case of his deposition have had charge of the Government, it is difficult to believe that the country would have gained by the change, and it is quite certain that the party would have lost by it, for it would have had to bear the burden of their indiscretions.

But the acquittal, although the largeness of the vote for conviction may justify the House morally, is not likely to strengthen the confidence of the country in the judgment of the majority. Moreover, it has some tendency to create a certain amount of confidence in the President's judgment. It leaves him less hopelessly in the wrong than he seemed six months ago, and it leaves him in possession of the honors of the field. His escape, to be sure, has been very narrow, but in politics, as in war, an inch of a miss is as good as a mile. He was, before the trial, in the position of a man whom Congress might crush, but would not; now, he is in the position of a man whom Congress tried to crush, but could not. It is certainly not Congress that has gained by this change.

The House, too, did not shine on the trial. It was not well represented. It tried hard to have the case tried on high moral grounds, or on grounds of general expediency; and yet it put in the forefront of its battle a lawyer whose opinions on high moral questions, or questions of general expediency, nobody heeds, and whose forte lies in his sharpness as pleader in courts of law, and whose want of manners, or rather want of decency, throughout the case gave the President a constant advantage, which increased up to the very last day. Moreover, the Managers were overmatched throughout in learning and ability. There is no use now in passing this over without notice. The contrast was patent to everybody throughout the trial, and was a constant subject of comment. What the Managers wanted in law and logic they had to make up by warmth of language; but this, though useful in a short case, is not effective in a trial protracted over several weeks, and before a tribunal of elderly men hardened to rhetoric, and in whom the fires of enthusiasm have long died out.

What has made the effect of acquittal most injurious, however, has been the conduct of a portion of the Radical press and politicians towards those Republican members of the court who were not satisfied by the evidence and the arguments of the President's guilt. To fail to convict at all was rather mortifying, of course; but to fail after having spent a week in holding the most honored of the party leaders, its wisest heads and purest characters, up to execration as perjured villains, is more mortifying still. Happily the great body of the party, certainly all the intelligent portion of it, and all its most influential and respected newspapers, made a determined stand against this amazing burst of folly, and thus saved the party from damnation—and, let us add, from well-merited damnation. For a party which coolly informs the world that its most trusted, longest tried leaders and counsellors—men honored for their learning, ability, and integrity—have committed perjury while sitting as judges in the highest court known to the law, and have accepted bribes from the "whiskey ring" as the reward of their baseness—as the *Tribune* and some kindred sheets informed the public every day during the past week about Messrs. Trumbull, Fessenden, and others—of course ought not to exist any longer. To vote its ticket after such a revelation would be a degradation of the deepest kind. It would be useless for the *Tribune* to assure us that all the other politicians of the party were honest except these. Nobody could be deceived in this way. Fancy following Messrs. Butler, Stevens, Logan, and Horace Greeley with implicit confidence, after Trumbull, Fessenden, Grimes, Henderson, Fowler, and Van Winkle had turned out shameless and corrupt scoundrels. The party would have had to be broken up as an abomination. No men in it have given such guarantees of honor, and purity, and zeal as the so-called "traitors." If these be false, it is impudent to ask the country to trust any others the party can produce.

The more we look into this crusade against the fair fame of the dissentients, the more reason we find for feeling thankful that the main body of the party refused to share in it. As all our readers know, what brought impeachment down on Mr. Johnson was his violation of the Tenure-of-Office Act in removing Mr. Stanton and appointing General Thomas Secretary *ad interim* in his place. The other charges, including that of bad language in 1866, made in the articles, except the slender one of trying to seduce General Emory, were all brought before the House by the Impeachment Committee six months before the present articles were filed, were fully discussed, and it was solemnly declared by a large majority that they were insufficient to sustain a prosecution. When, however, he removed Mr. Stanton, the House agreed that he had at last done the deed which brought him within the meshes of the law, and voted for impeachment for *this act*, and in consequence of this act, and this only. Afterwards, and just before the filing of the articles, Thaddeus Stevens secured the addition of the eleventh article, which charged that the removal of Mr. Stanton was a high crime and misdemeanor, committed "*in pursuance of*" his declaration, made a year and a half previously, that "Congress was not the Congress of the United States, but only of a part of the States, thereby denying and intending to deny that its legislation was obligatory on him." The object of this article, therefore, was to connect the removal of Stanton in February, 1868, with a speech delivered in August, 1866; and this was an afterthought, too. It was not on this that impeachment was first voted; it was on the removal of Stanton taken by itself, as a violation in terms of a valid law of Congress. Now it is admitted that large numbers of the Republican senators would vote "not guilty" on the charge of violating the law in removing Stanton and appointing Thomas—that is, on the very charges which produced the impeachment. In fact, these charges, it now appears, are considered to have broken down in the course of the trial, so that a Republican senator may vote "not guilty" on them without laying himself open to the suspicion of corruption. Mr. Stevens, indeed, has declared that they have no weight; that the real weight is in his article; and his article was submitted first to the vote as the strongest and therefore the best test.

The position of Messrs. Trumbull and Fessenden's assailants, therefore, is just this. A Republican senator might say on his oath, and yet be an honest man, that the removal of Mr. Stanton and the appointment of General Thomas did not constitute a high crime or misdemeanor; and he might say on his oath, and yet be an honest man, that the wild speeches of 1866 did not constitute a high crime or misdemeanor; but if he says on his oath that he believes the removal of Mr. Stanton in February, 1868, was not done "in pursuance of" a plan formed by Mr. Johnson in 1866, and of which the only evidence is a fragment of a stump speech made in that year—popularly supposed to have been delivered under the influence of whiskey—although Mr. Johnson has ever since gone on acknowledging the validity of Congressional legislation day by day in the ordinary course of business, he must be a corrupt scoundrel—bribed to violate his oath by fraudulent distillers. His guilt is evident; he is not only to be driven out of the party, but to be held up to execration as a dishonorable man. This is a strictly correct statement of the case. This is the charge against the dissentient Republican senators, and the whole of it. There is not nearly as much reason for suspecting a man's good faith who refuses to convict on the eleventh article as on the second and third, on simple grounds of evidence. The reason why the eleventh article has been made a test of morals is the will of the extremists. They choose to consider it so, and "there's an end on 't." They say simply, "To this article we require your adhesion; on the others we give you your liberty. Vote it, or we blacken your character to the extent of our ability." We cast no imputation on anybody who voted guilty on that article; but we venture to say that the number of trained lawyers who could do so is small. Few, we venture to say, swallow it who have not worked themselves into the state of mental inflammation which seems to be endemic at Washington, and of which Mr. Boutwell offered such a striking symptom when he showed that Andrew Johnson's guilt was greater than that of Caius Verres by showing that the superficial area of the United States was greater than that of Sicily.

We believe, for our part, that the thanks of the country are due to Messrs. Trumbull, Fessenden, Grimes, Henderson, Fowler, Van Winkle, and Ross, not for voting for Johnson's acquittal, but for vindicating, we presume nobody but themselves knows at what cost, the dignity and purity of the court of which they formed a part, and the sacred rights of individual conscience. They have afforded American young men an example such as no politicians have ever afforded them in the whole course of American history, and at a time, too, when the tendency to put party claims above everything is rapidly increasing, and when we are adding to our voting population a vast body of persons on whom the great laws of morality sit only very lightly, and for whom party discipline has, of course, the attraction it has everywhere and always for those who have little other discipline to guide them.

The issue of the impeachment trial was no doubt important as regards the actual political situation; but the greatest of all questions for the American people is, whether amongst all the troubles and changes of this and coming ages the popular respect for the forms of law, for judicial purity and independence, can be maintained. As long as it can, all will go well, whatever storms blow; whenever the belief becomes general that a court of justice, and especially a "High Court," can be fairly used, whenever the majority please, as the instrument of their will, it will make little difference what its judgment will be or who fills the Presidential chair.

May 21, 1868

Frank P. Blair to James O. Broadhead

WASHINGTON, *June* 30, 1868.

Colonel JAMES O. BROADHEAD.

DEAR COLONEL: In reply to your inquiries, I beg leave to say, that I leave to you to determine, on consultation with my friends from Missouri, whether my name shall be presented to the Democratic Convention, and to submit the following as what I consider the real and only issue in this contest.

The reconstruction policy of the Radicals will be complete before the next election; the States so long excluded will have been admitted, negro suffrage established, and the carpet-baggers installed in their seats in both branches of Congress. There is no possibility of changing the political character of the Senate, even if the Democrats should elect their President and a majority of the popular branch of Congress. We cannot, therefore, undo the Radical plan of reconstruction by congressional action; the Senate will continue a bar to its repeal. Must we submit to it? How can it be overthrown? It can only be overthrown by the authority of the Executive, who is sworn to maintain the Constitution, and who will fail to do his duty if he allows the Constitution to perish under a series of congressional enactments which are in palpable violation of its fundamental principles.

If the President elected by the Democracy enforces or permits others to enforce these reconstruction acts, the Radicals, by the accession of twenty spurious Senators and fifty Representatives, will control both branches of Congress, and his administration will be as powerless as the present one of Mr. Johnson.

There is but one way to restore the Government and the Constitution, and that is for the President elect to declare these acts null and void, compel the army to undo its usurpations at the South, disperse the carpet-bag State governments, allow the white people to reorganize their own governments, and elect Senators and Representatives. The House of Representatives will contain a majority of Democrats from the North, and they will admit the Representatives elected by the white people of the South, and, with the co-operation of the President, it will not be difficult to compel the Senate to submit once more to the obligations of the Constitution. It will not be able to withstand the public judgment, if distinctly invoked and clearly expressed on this fundamental issue, and it is the sure way to avoid all future strife to put the issue plainly to the country.

I repeat, that this is the real and only question which we should allow to control us: Shall we submit to the usurpations by which the Government has been overthrown; or shall we exert ourselves for its full and complete restoration? It is idle to talk of bonds, greenbacks, gold, the public faith, and the public credit. What can a Democratic President do in regard to any of these, with a Congress in both branches controlled by the carpet-baggers and their allies? He will be powerless to stop the supplies by which idle negroes are organized into political clubs—by which an army is maintained to protect these vagabonds in their outrages upon the ballot. These, and things like these, eat up the revenues and resources of the Government and destroy its credit—make the difference between gold and greenbacks. We must restore the Constitution before we can restore the finances, and to do this we must have a President who will execute the will of the people by trampling into dust the usurpations of Congress known as the reconstruction acts. I wish to stand before the convention upon this issue, but it is one which embraces everything else that is of value in its large and comprehensive results. It is the one thing that includes all that is worth a contest, and without it there is nothing that gives dignity, honor, or value to the struggle.   Your friend,   FRANK P. BLAIR.

Frederick Douglass: The Work Before Us

It is eminently creditable to the sagacity, if not to the honesty, of the Democratic leaders that they prefer to limit discussion of the merits of their party, in the present canvass, strictly to the platform adopted in New York by their Fourth of July National Convention. For very obvious reasons, they are "dead" against dead issues. There is as much shrewdness as apparent resignation in their willingness to let "bygones be bygones." In this prompt, business-like course there would be much to commend, if one did not see lurking behind it a very ugly fact which it is designed to conceal. In the effort to withdraw the war record of the Democratic party there is either a sense of its criminality or a conviction of its present odiousness. Their policy evidently is to attack, not to defend; and in this they are wise. They are smart men, and largely gifted with powers of utterance; but the task of defending the policy of their party during the war would leave time for little else, were they once to enter upon it. They therefore cast it aside altogether. They know that, like Lord Granby's character, there are some things which can only pass without censure, as they pass without observation. No men more readily than they perceive the effect which time and events have wrought in the minds of men. Deeds which were once done with impunity, and even gloried in at the time of their perpetration, by a slight change in the varying current of events, assume an aspect too revolting for defense. It is now much easier to assail the Republican party for its awkward management of public affairs than to defend the efforts of Governor Seymour and his friends to resist the drafts and other necessary measures for the preservation of the Union. So far as the endeavor to divert attention from the position occupied by the Democratic party during the war may be taken as a confession, it is at least valuable to outsiders. It is always a decided gain to the cause of justice to have even an implied admission of guilt on the part of the culprit. Excellent, however, as confession is, it does very little good to anybody unless coupled with an honest purpose to forsake the evil way, and an earnest effort to reform.

Of course, nothing of this sort is a part of the purpose of the Democratic leaders. No men know better than themselves that their party cannot afford to repent. A party without voters is among the most worthless of all worthless things. What the Democratic party now most of all wants is voters—members. These are to be had mainly from those classes of the American people who are proud of their contempt for humanity—who scout benevolence and brotherly kindness as the weakest nonsense. The party can only thrive where pride of race and narrow selfishness would appropriate to a class the rights which belong to the whole human family. To renounce this meanness would be to renounce its existence. Its mission is to keep alive all the malice which the Negro's loyalty and his limited freedom have kindled against him. This is the necessity of the party. The country is divided; and, when it is impossible for a party to receive support from one part, it must seek it in another. Abuse of the Negro is not, therefore, always to be taken as a matter of choice on the part of Democratic editors and speakers; but rather as a necessity of the party to which they belong.

How much the Democratic party might gain were it, merely with a view to its own strength, to endeavor to lead a new life is a speculation upon which I need not enter. The little effort made in that direction with Mr. Chase is thought to have done the party more harm than good. The party is strongest with those who stand no nonsense of this decent sort. They want no smooth-faced concessions to virtue. They want the genuine pungent article of the Negro, with two "*gg's*." Besides, nobody could well believe in it were the party to declare a change of heart and purpose. With a confessed trickster and falsifier as its standard-bearer (a man who, if the reports of his associates can be relied upon, secured his nomination by a course of cunning, duplicity, lying, treachery, and bribery unparalleled in the history of party politics), people would be slow to accept the professions of such a party.

But let us not be deceived nor diverted from the real work we have in hand. The contest to which all good and true men are summoned in the present canvass is no new one. It is, in fact but a continuation of the mighty struggle of a great nation to shake off an old and worn-out system of barbarism, with all its natural concomitants of evil. It is a part of our thirty years' effort to place the country in harmony with the age, and to make her what she ought to be—a leader, and not a mere follower, in the pathway of civilization. Rebellion has been subdued, slavery abolished, and peace proclaimed; and yet our work is not done. The Democratic party has changed the whole face of affairs. The foe is the same, though we are to meet him on a different field and under different leaders. In the ranks of Seymour and Blair is the rebel army, without its arms. Let not the connection of the present with the past be ignored nor forgotten. We are face to face with the same old enemy of liberty and progress that has planted agony at a million hearthstones in our land. There has been no change in the character or in the general purpose of the Democratic party. It is for peace or for war, or against either, precisely as it can be made to serve the great privileged class at the South, to which it belongs. The party that annexed Texas; that began and prosecuted the inglorious war against a neighboring Republic, thus setting the bad example subsequently followed by France and Austria—the strong against the weak; that hunted down the humane Seminoles with bloodhounds, because they gave shelter to slaves running away from Georgia; that avowed its purpose to suppress freedom of speech and of the press in time of peace in the interest of slavery; that repealed the Missouri Compromise, and opened the blackened tide of bondage upon the virgin soil of Kansas; that, from the beginning to the end of the late war against slavery in arms, uniformly sided with the rebels and against the loyal North—is the same party from footsole to crown, unchanged and unchangeable. Its character is not better known to loyal men than to the defeated rebels. It is neither strange nor surprising that the latter flock to it as the last resort of their Lost Cause.

We have had many issues with the slave power during the past thirty years, but we have never had but one *cause*; and the same is true of the slave power. Indeed, the same is always true in all countries and in all times. The world has always been in some way divided essentially as parties are now divided in our country. Men change; principles are eternal. Holland—whether pleading her ancient charters; asking the removal of oppressive, dissolute, mercenary Spanish troops from her borders; opposing the establishment of new bishoprics; humbly appealing for the removal of the gifted but cruel and treacherous Cardinal Granville; or boldly resisting that grand aggregation of human horrors, the Inquisition—was all the while serving only one cause. The sacred liberty of conscience; the right of a man to form his own opinions upon all matters of religion—this was the cause of freedom then. While popery, on the other side, whether dealing in fair words or fierce blows, whether entangling its victims in cunningly-devised sophistries or torturing them with cord and steel, rack and fire, had but the same old cause—religious slavery. Think as we command, or die! As in our day men claim the right to dispose of the bodies of men, so they of Mother Church claimed the right to dispose of both soul and body. As stood the sturdy old Hollanders three centuries ago, so we stand to-day. Times change and new issues arise; men appear and disappear; but evermore the same old principles of good and evil, right and wrong, liberty and slavery, summon their respective votaries to the contest. The slaveholding rebels, struck down by Gen. Grant as by a thunderbolt, scarcely recover from the terrific shock before they stagger off to the Democratic party. There they go—stricken generals of the rebel army—Henry A. Wise and Wade Hampton, Toombs and Cobb, Forrest and Beauregard. The evil spirits cast out of the man among the tombs take refuge in the herd of swine. We shall see with what consequences to the poor animals in November, and to themselves.

The policy, but not the purpose, of the rebels is changed. Names are nothing. It matters little to them by what name the thing for which they strive is called; and equally indifferent are they as to the means they employ. Success is the main consideration.

Secession and rebellion were undertaken for one purpose, and one purpose alone—and that was to secure to the slaveholding class permanent control over the black laborers of the South. It was to give to white capital a firmer hold and a tighter grip upon the throat of the Negro. They believed in the Divine appointment of slavery. What they believed then they believe now; what they meant then they mean now. Here and there in the rebel states there may be found a man who has honestly renounced his ancient faith, and accepted the true doctrine of liberty and the great principle of *Equal Rights*; but the mass of Southern white men and women are in heart and purpose the same as when they confronted the free North on the battle-field. You may send General Lee a million of dollars for his rebel college; but, while Arlington Heights is the resting-place of our loyal dead, you will get no sign of a hearty renunciation of the malign purpose for which he drew his rebel sword.

The South to-day is a field of blood. Murder runs riot in Texas, Tennessee, Mississippi, and Louisiana. Assassination has taken the place of insurrection. Armed bands of rebels stalk abroad at midnight with blackened faces, and thus disguised go forth to shoot, stab, and murder their loyal neighbors.

It is impossible to exaggerate the solemn character of the crisis. While Andrew Johnson remains in the presidential chair, and the Democratic party, with Seymour and Blair, are in the field, feeding the rebel imagination with a prospect of regaining through politics what they lost by the sword, the South must continue the scene of war she is. The work to which every loyal man and woman in the country is now called is to employ every possible honorable means, between now and November, to defeat and scatter the Democratic party. Our one work now is to elect Grant and Colfax—and that by a vote so pronounced and overwhelming as to extinguish every ray of hope to the rebel cause.

The Independent, August 27, 1868

Elizabeth Cady Stanton:
Gerrit Smith on Petitions

PETERBORO, Dec. 30th, 1868.

MY DEAR SUSAN B. ANTHONY: I this evening receive your earnest letter. It pains me to be obliged to disappoint you. But I cannot sign the Petition you send me. Cheerfully, gladly can I sign a Petition for the enfranchisement of women. But I cannot sign a paper against the enfranchisement of the negro man, unless at the same time woman shall be enfranchised. The removal of the political disabilities of race is my first desire,—of sex, my second. If put on the same level and urged in the same connection neither will be soon accomplished. The former will very soon be, if untrammelled by the other, and its success will prepare the way for the accomplishment of the other.

With great regard your friend,

GERRIT SMITH.

To the Senate and House of Representatives, in Congress Assembled:

The undersigned, citizens of the State of —— earnestly but respectfully request, that, in any change or amendment of the Constitution you may propose to extend or regulate Suffrage, there shall be no distinctions made between men and women.

The above is the petition to which our friend Gerrit Smith, as an abolitionist, cannot conscientiously put his name, while republicans and democrats are signing it all over the country. He does not clearly read the signs of the times, or he would see that there is to be no reconstruction of this nation, except on the basis of Universal Suffrage, as the natural, inalienable right of every citizen to its exercise is the only logical ground on which to base an argument. The uprising of the women on both continents, in France, England, Russia, Switzerland, and the United States all show that advancing civilization demands a new element in the government of nations.

As the aristocracy in this country is the "male sex," and as Mr. Smith belongs to the privileged order, he naturally considers it important, for the best interests of the nation, that every type and shade of degraded, ignorant manhood should be enfranchised, before even the higher classes of womanhood should be admitted to the polls.

This does not surprise us! Men always judge more wisely of objective wrongs and oppressions, than of those in which they are themselves involved. Tyranny on a southern plantation is far more easily seen by white men at the north than the wrongs of the women of their own households.

Then again, when men have devoted their lives to one reform, there is a natural feeling of pride, as well as an earnest principle, in seeing that one thing accomplished. Hence in criticising such good and noble men as Gerrit Smith and Wendell Phillips for their apathy on Woman's enfranchisement at this hour, it is not because we think their course at all remarkable, nor that we have the least hope of influencing *them*, but simply to rouse the women of the country to the fact that they must not look to these men for their champions at this hour. But what does surprise us in this cry of "manhood suffrage" is, that every *woman* does not see in it national suicide, and her own destruction. In view of the present demoralization of our government, bribery and corruption alike in the legislative, the executive and the judicial branches, drunkenness in the White House, Congress, and every state legislature; votes and officers bought and sold like cattle in the market, what thinking mind can look for any improvement, in extending suffrage still further to the very class that have produced this state of things.

While philosophy and science alike point to woman, as the new power destined to redeem the world, how can Mr. Smith fail to see that it is just this we need to restore honor and virtue in the government. When society in California and Oregon was chiefly male and rapidly tending to savageism, ship loads of women went out, and restored order and decency to life. Would black men have availed anything among those white savages? There is sex in the spiritual as well as the physical, and what we need to-day in government, in the world of morals and thought, is the recognition of the feminine element, as it is this alone that can hold the masculine in check.

Again: Mr. Smith refuses to sign the petition, because he

thinks to press the broader question of "Universal Suffrage" would defeat the partial one of "Manhood Suffrage;" in other words, to demand protection for woman against her oppressors, would jeopardize the black man's chance, of securing protection against his oppressors. If it is a question of precedence merely, on what principle of justice or courtesy should woman yield her right of enfranchisement to the negro? If men cannot be trusted to legislate for their own sex, how can they legislate for the opposite sex, of whose wants and needs they know nothing! It has always been considered good philosophy in pressing any measure to claim the uttermost in order to get something. Being in Ireland at the time of the Repeal excitement, we asked Daniel O'Connell one day if he expected to secure a Repeal of the Union. "Oh! no," said he, "but I claim everything that I may be sure of getting something." Henry Ward Beecher advised abolitionists, right after the war, to demand "Universal Suffrage" if they wished to secure the ballot for the new made freedmen. "Bait your hooks," said he, "with a woman and perhaps you will catch a negro." But their intense interest in the negro blinded them, and they forsook principle for policy, and in giving woman the cold shoulder, they raised a more deadly opposition to the negro than any we had yet encountered, creating an antagonism between him, and the very element most needed, especially at the south, to be propitiated in his behalf. It was this feeling that defeated "negro suffrage" in Kansas.

The natural pride and jealousy of woman against all assumed power and superiority, heightened by the fact that black men stumped the state against "Woman's Suffrage," steadily infused into the minds of the men at every hearthstone a determined opposition to the measure, hence although that state always gives large republican majorities and "negro suffrage" was a party measure, politicians, party, press, were alike powerless, before the deep-settled indignation of the women at the proposition to place the negro above their heads.

Such was their feeling in the matter, that the mass of the men everywhere pledged them that if the women were not enfranchised neither should the negro be. The result was, that the vote for woman's suffrage, without party, press, or thorough canvass of the state, lacked but a few hundred of the vote of the great republican party for negro suffrage. Had republicans and abolitionists advocated both propositions, they would have been triumphantly carried. What is true in Kansas will prove equally true in every state in this Union; there can be no reconstruction of this government on any basis but universal suffrage. There is no other ground on which to debate the question. Every argument for the negro is an argument for woman and no logician can escape it.

But Mr. Smith abandons the principle clearly involved, and entrenches himself on policy. He would undoubtedly plead the necessity of the ballot for the negro at the south for his protection, and point us to innumerable acts of cruelty he suffers to-day. But all these things fall as heavily on the women of the black race, yea far more so, for no man can ever know the deep, the damning degradation to which woman is subject in her youth, helplessness and poverty. The enfranchisement of the men of her race, Mr. Smith would say, is her protection.

Our Saxon men have held the ballot in this country for a century, and what honest man can claim that it has been used for woman's protection? Alas! we have given the very hey day of our life to undoing the cruel and unjust laws that the men of New York had made for their own mothers, wives and daughters. Have Saxon women no wrongs to right, and will they be better protected when negroes are their rulers? Remember that all woman needs protection against to-day, is man, read the following:

SUPPOSED INFANTICIDE.

A young girl named Abson, who has for the past three months been an inmate of the Hudson County Almshouse, at Snake Hill, gave birth, four days ago, to a child of negro parentage, which was found dead in a bed yesterday morning, supposed to have been smothered by its mother. The circumstances of the case are somewhat singular. About eight years ago one Abson and his wife were living on a small farm in the lower part of Bergen, N. J. Suddenly the wife died by poison. The husband was arrested for the murder, and while lying in the Hudson County Jail, awaiting trial, committed suicide by cutting his throat. One child, a little girl six years of age, was left an orphan by the double tragedy. About a year ago, at which

time she was fourteen years of age, the girl was sent to work on
a farm at Rockaway, N. J. During the absence of her employer's
family, a negro on the farm effected her ruin, which, being discovered, and she being enceinte, she was sent back to Bergen,
and thence to the Almshouse, where the child was born, and
killed as stated. Coroner Warren will hold an inquest.

With judges and jurors of negroes: remembering the generations of wrong and injustice their daughters have suffered at
the white man's hands: how will Saxon girls fare in their courts
for crimes like this?

How do they fare in our own courts to-day, tried by Saxon
fathers, husbands, brothers, sons? Hester Vaughan, a young
English girl, under sentence of death for the alleged crime
of Infanticide, which could not be proved against her, has
dragged the weary days of a whole year away in the solitude
and gloom of a Pennsylvania prison, while he who betrayed her
walks this green earth in freedom, enjoying alike the sunshine
and the dews of Heaven. And this girl sits alone in her cell
to-day, weeping for friends and native land, while such men
as Generals Cole and Sickles, who shot their wives' paramours
dead before many witnesses in broad day-light, are feasted and
toasted by the press and the people.

Such is "manhood suffrage." Shall we prolong and perpetuate injustice like this, and increase its power by adding more
ignorance and brutality, and thus risk worse oppressions for
ourselves and daughters? Society, as organized to-day under
the man power, is one grand rape on womanhood, on the
highways, in our jails, prisons, asylums, in our homes, alike
in the world of fashion and of work; hence, discord, war, violence, crime, the blind, the deaf, the dumb, the idiot, the
lunatic, the drunkard, all things inverted and must be so, until
the mother of the race is made dictator in the social realm.
To this end we need every power to lift her up, and teach
mankind that in all God's universe there is nothing so holy
and sacred as womanhood. Do such men as Gerrit Smith and
Wendell Phillips teach this lesson to the lower orders of men
who learn truth and justice from their lips, when they tell
the most noble, virtuous, educated matrons of this republic,
to stand back, until all the sons of Adam are crowned with

citizenship? Do they teach woman self-respect, when they tell her to hold her claims to virtue, honor and dignity, in abeyance to those of *manhood*?

They who do aught to lessen woman's self-respect, or to lower her in the estimation of ignorant men, are responsible for the long train of evils, that must forever flow, in the subordination of moral power, to brute force. All this talk about woman's waiting for the negro is most invidious, and dangerous too, for while it paralyzes woman it infuses a conceit into the negro that makes him most offensive at the very time he needs wisdom and policy. As to the "rights of races," on which so much stress is laid just now, we have listened to debates in anti-slavery conventions, for twenty years or more, and we never heard Gerrit Smith plead the negroes cause on any lower ground than his manhood; his individual, inalienable right to freedom and equality; and thus, we conjure every thoughtful man to plead woman's cause to-day. Politicians will find, when they come to test this question of "negro supremacy" in the several states, that there is a far stronger feeling among the women of the nation than they supposed. We doubt whether a constitutional amendment securing "Manhood Suffrage" alone could be fairly passed in a single state in this Union. Women everywhere are waking up to their own God-given rights, to their true dignity as citizens of a republic, as mothers of the race.

Although those who demand "Woman's Suffrage" on principle are few, those who would oppose "Negro Suffrage" from prejudice are many, hence the only way to secure the latter, is to end all this talk of class legislation, bury the negro in the citizen, and claim the suffrage for all men and women, as a natural, inalienable right. The friends of the negro never made a greater blunder, than when, at the close of the war, they timidly refused to lead the nation, in demanding suffrage for all. If even Wendell Phillips and Gerrit Smith, the very apostles of liberty on this continent, failed at that point, how can we wonder at the vacillation and confusion of politicians at this hour. We had hoped that the elections of '67, with their overwhelming majorities in every state against Negro Suffrage, would have proved to all alike, how futile is compromise, how short-sighted is policy. We have pressed these considerations so often on Mr. Phillips and Mr. Smith, during the last four years, that we fear we have entirely forfeited the friendship of the one, and diminished the confidence of the other in our good judgment; but time, that rights all wrongs, will surely bring them back to the standpoint of principle.   E. C. S.

The Revolution, January 14, 1869

Joint Resolution Proposing the Fifteenth Amendment

A Resolution proposing an Amendment to the Constitution of the United States.

Resolved by the Senate and House of Representatives of the United States of America in Congress assembled, (*two thirds of both houses concurring,*) That the following article be proposed to the legislatures of the several States as an amendment to the Constitution of the United States, which, when ratified by three fourths of said legislatures, shall be valid as part of the Constitution, namely:

ARTICLE XV.

SECTION 1. The right of citizens of the United States to vote shall not be denied or abridged by the United States or by any State on account of race, color, or previous condition of servitude.

SEC. 2. The Congress shall have power to enforce this article by appropriate legislation.

SCHUYLER COLFAX,
Speaker of the House of Representatives.
B. F. WADE,
President of the Senate pro tempore.

Attest:

EDWD. MCPHERSON,
Clerk of House of Representatives.
GEO. C. GORHAM,
Sec'y of Senate U. S.

Received at Department of State February 27, 1869.

"LET US HAVE PEACE"
1869–1873

❦

When Ulysses S. Grant became president in 1869, Republicans breathed a sigh of relief. They hoped that with an ally in the White House, they could bring Reconstruction to a successful conclusion. The ratification of the Fifteenth Amendment in February 1870 seemed to secure black male suffrage across the nation. It evaded the difficult process of amending northern state constitutions through measures subject to popular referendums while seemingly preventing southern states from committing future acts of disenfranchisement should they again fall under Democratic control. The readmission of Texas, Virginia, and Mississippi to congressional representation in early 1870 promised to bring an end to congressional Reconstruction, although the decision to remand Georgia to congressional supervision after the state legislature expelled its black members served as a reminder of the depths of white resistance to biracial democracy. That the Fifteenth Amendment did not address women's suffrage continued to be a source of contention with those who did not want to limit Reconstruction to issues of race and reconciliation but sought an even broader restructuring of the republic. It was a reminder that Reconstruction, while revolutionary in the minds of many observers, had failed to go far enough to please other activists.

In his inaugural address Grant called for the nation to come together, accept the results of the war, and move forward. In March 1870 he celebrated the ratification of the Fifteenth Amendment as a sign that Americans had repudiated the legacy of the Dred Scott decision. All that remained was to treat the freed people as American citizens who were equal before the law. Yet it soon became apparent that such was not to be the case. Even as northern Democrats weighed the possibility of a "New Departure" that would allow the party to put the war and Reconstruction behind it, southern Democrats embraced terrorism as a tactic to help overthrow Republican state governments. This upsurge in violence challenged the notion that Reconstruction at the federal level had ended with the restoration of civil government throughout the South. Republicans divided over how to respond to terrorism in a debate that included South Carolina representatives Robert Brown Elliott and Joseph H. Rainey, two of the first African Americans to sit in Congress. That committed emancipationists such as Ohio congressman James Garfield and Missouri senator Carl Schurz now opposed additional federal measures to protect voters from violence helped demonstrate the limits of what was politically possible to achieve. Their concerns regarding the proper constitutional balance between the federal government and the states failed to impress black congressmen, who knew firsthand the threat posed by terrorist violence to any hopes of establishing a biracial democracy. Congress eventually passed the Enforcement Act of 1871, sometimes called the Third Force Act or the Ku Klux Klan Act, which gave the president the power to suspend the privilege of the writ of habeas corpus and employ military force to suppress "unlawful combinations." The act required offenders to be tried in federal court, while limiting the duration of the president's power to suspend habeas corpus to the end of the second session of the Forty-second Congress (June 1872). Prosecutions under the act in Mississippi and South Carolina dealt a significant blow to the Klan in 1871–72, but failed to prevent the emergence of other white supremacist terrorist groups.

President Grant made his share of enemies during his first term, and not all of them were Democrats. Some Republicans questioned his approach to Reconstruction; others disagreed with his stance on a host of issues, ranging from foreign and economic policy to civil service reform. A few raised questions about his handling of patronage or found allegations of corruption troubling. By the end of 1871, dissident Republicans were forging a coalition designed to block his reelection. What became known as the Liberal Republican movement reached its climax at Cincinnati in May 1872. The decision of the Liberal Republican convention to nominate New York newspaper editor Horace Greeley, who was later endorsed by the Democrats, proved disastrous. Greeley's plea for sectional reconciliation overlooked evidence of continuing violence and resistance by white southerners; in the fall contest Grant won reelection overwhelmingly. While the president interpreted his triumph as a personal vindication, it remained to be seen if it was also an endorsement of his Reconstruction policy.

Ulysses S. Grant: First Inaugural Address

Citizens of the United States:

Your suffrages having elected me to the office of President of the United States, I have, in conformity to the Constitution of our country, taken the oath of office prescribed therein. I have taken this oath without mental reservation and with the determination to do to the best of my ability all that is required of me. The responsibilities of the position I feel, but accept them without fear. The office has come to me unsought; I commence its duties untrammeled. I bring to it a conscious desire and determination to fill it to the best of my ability to the satisfaction of the people.

On all leading questions agitating the public mind I will always express my views to Congress and urge them according to my judgment, and when I think it advisable will exercise the constitutional privilege of interposing a veto to defeat measures which I oppose; but all laws will be faithfully executed, whether they meet my approval or not.

I shall on all subjects have a policy to recommend, but none to enforce against the will of the people. Laws are to govern all alike—those opposed as well as those who favor them. I know no method to secure the repeal of bad or obnoxious laws so effective as their stringent execution.

The country having just emerged from a great rebellion, many questions will come before it for settlement in the next four years which preceding Administrations have never had to deal with. In meeting these it is desirable that they should be approached calmly, without prejudice, hate, or sectional pride, remembering that the greatest good to the greatest number is the object to be attained.

This requires security of person, property, and free religious and political opinion in every part of our common country, without regard to local prejudice. All laws to secure these ends will receive my best efforts for their enforcement.

A great debt has been contracted in securing to us and our posterity the Union. The payment of this, principal and interest, as well as the return to a specie basis as soon as it can be accomplished without material detriment to the debtor class or to the country at large, must be provided for. To protect the national honor, every dollar of Government indebtedness should be paid in gold, unless otherwise expressly stipulated in the contract. Let it be understood that no repudiator of one farthing of our public debt will be trusted in public place, and it will go far toward strengthening a credit which ought to be the best in the world, and will ultimately enable us to replace the debt with bonds bearing less interest than we now pay. To this should be added a faithful collection of the revenue, a strict accountability to the Treasury for every dollar collected, and the greatest practicable retrenchment in expenditure in every department of Government.

When we compare the paying capacity of the country now, with the ten States in poverty from the effects of war, but soon to emerge, I trust, into greater prosperity than ever before, with its paying capacity twenty-five years ago, and calculate what it probably will be twenty-five years hence, who can doubt the feasibility of paying every dollar then with more ease than we now pay for useless luxuries? Why, it looks as though Providence had bestowed upon us a strong box in the precious metals locked up in the sterile mountains of the far West, and which we are now forging the key to unlock, to meet the very contingency that is now upon us.

Ultimately it may be necessary to insure the facilities to reach these riches, and it may be necessary also that the General Government should give its aid to secure this access; but that should only be when a dollar of obligation to pay secures precisely the same sort of dollar to use now, and not before. Whilst the question of specie payments is in abeyance the prudent business man is careful about contracting debts payable in the distant future. The nation should follow the same rule. A prostrate commerce is to be rebuilt and all industries encouraged.

The young men of the country—those who from their age must be its rulers twenty-five years hence—have a peculiar interest in maintaining the national honor. A moment's reflection as to what will be our commanding influence among the nations of the earth in their day, if they are only true to themselves, should inspire them with national pride.

All divisions—geographical, political, and religious—can join in this common sentiment. How the public debt is to be paid or specie payments resumed is not so important as that a plan should be adopted and acquiesced in. A united determination to do is worth more than divided counsels upon the method of doing. Legislation upon this subject may not be necessary now, nor even advisable, but it will be when the civil law is more fully restored in all parts of the country and trade resumes its wonted channels.

It will be my endeavor to execute all laws in good faith, to collect all revenues assessed, and to have them properly accounted for and economically disbursed. I will to the best of my ability appoint to office those only who will carry out this design.

In regard to foreign policy, I would deal with nations as equitable law requires individuals to deal with each other, and I would protect the law-abiding citizen, whether of native or foreign birth, wherever his rights are jeopardized or the flag of our country floats. I would respect the rights of all nations, demanding equal respect for our own. If others depart from this rule in their dealings with us, we may be compelled to follow their precedent.

The proper treatment of the original occupants of this land—the Indians—is one deserving of careful study. I will favor any course toward them which tends to their civilization and ultimate citizenship.

The question of suffrage is one which is likely to agitate the public so long as a portion of the citizens of the nation are excluded from its privileges in any State. It seems to me very desirable that this question should be settled now, and I entertain the hope and express the desire that it may be by the ratification of the fifteenth article of amendment to the Constitution.

In conclusion I ask patient forbearance one toward another throughout the land, and a determined effort on the part of every citizen to do his share toward cementing a happy union; and I ask the prayers of the nation to Almighty God in behalf of this consummation.

March 4, 1869.

Frederick Douglass and Susan B. Anthony: Exchange on Suffrage

THIS GENTLEMAN commenced to speak in a low voice, when Miss Anthony said to the audience: Mr. Douglass has a weak voice in debate and he is not used to public speaking. [Laughter.]

Mr. Douglass—I came here more as a listener than to speak, and I listened with a great deal of pleasure to the eloquent address of the Rev. Mr. Frothingham and the splendid address of the President. There is no name greater than that of Elizabeth Cady Stanton in the matter of Woman's Rights and Equal Rights, but my sentiments are tinged a little against the *Revolution*. There was in the address to which I allude a sentiment in reference to employment and certain names, such as "Sambo," and the gardener and the bootblack and the daughter of Jefferson and Washington, and all the rest that I cannot coincide with. I have asked what difference there is between the daughters of Jefferson and Washington and other daughters. [Laughter.] I must say that I do not see how any one can pretend that there is the same urgency in giving the ballot to the woman as to the negro. With us, the matter is a question of life or death. It is a matter of existence, at least, in fifteen States of the Union. When women, because they are women, are hunted down through the cities of New York and New Orleans; when they are dragged from their houses and hung upon lamp-posts; when their children are torn from their arms, and their brains dashed out upon the pavement; when she is an object of insult and outrage at every turn; when they are in danger of having their homes burnt down over their heads; when their children are not allowed to enter schools, then she will have an urgency to obtain the ballot equal to our own. [Great applause.]

A voice—Is that not all true about black women?

Mr. Douglass—Yes, yes, yes, it is true of the black woman, but not because she is a woman but because she is black. [Applause.]

Julia Ward Howe at the conclusion of her great speech delivered at the convention in Boston last year, said, "I am willing
that the negro shall get in before me." [Applause.] Woman! why
she has ten thousand modes of grappling with her difficulties.
I believe that all the virtue of the world can take care of all the
evil. I believe that all the intelligence can take care of all the ignorance. [Applause.] I am in favor of woman's suffrage in order
that we shall have all the virtue and all the vice confronted. Let
me tell you that when there were few houses in which the black
man could have put his head, this woolley head of mine found
a refuge in the house of Mrs. Elizabeth Cady Stanton, and if I
had been blacker than sixteen midnights, without a single star,
it have been the same. [Applause.]

Miss Susan B Anthony said: The question of precedence has
no place on an equal rights platform. The only reason why it
ever found a place here was that there were some who insisted
that woman must stand back & wait until another class should
be enfranchised. In answer to that, my friend Mrs Stanton &
others of us have said, If you will not give the whole loaf of
justice to the entire people, if you are determined to give it,
piece by piece, then give it first to women, to the most intelligent & capable portion of the women at least, because in
the present state of government it is intelligence, it is morality
which is needed. We have never brought the question upon
the platform, whether women should be enfranchised first or
last. I remember having a long discussion with Tilton, Powell, & Phillips on this very question, when we were about to
carry up our petitions to the Constitutional Convention. We
took the name of an Equal Rights association, & were thinking of making another person president. I remember then that
Mr Tilton said to me that we should urge the amendment to
our Constitution to strike out the word "white" as the thing
to be accomplished by that Convention, & he added, "The
question of striking out the word 'male' we shall of course, as
an Equal Rights association, urge as an intellectual theory, but
we cannot demand it as a practical thing to be accomplished
at this Convention." Mr Phillips acceded to that, & I think all
the *men* acceded to that, all over the State. But there was one
woman there who did not. My friend Mrs Stanton kept very
good natured in the discussion; but I was boiling over with

wrath; so much so that my friend Tilton noticed it & said, "What ails Susan? I never saw her behave so badly before." I will tell you what ailed Susan. It was the downright insolence of those two men, when I had canvassed the entire State from one end to the other, county by county, with petitions in my hand asking for woman suffrage,—if those two men, among the most advanced & glorious men of the nation, that they should dare to look me in the face & speak of this great earnest purpose of mine as an "intellectual theory" but not to be practised, or for us to hope to attain. [Applause.]

If Mr Douglass had noticed who clapped him when he said "black men first, & white women afterwards," he would have seen that they were all men. The women did not clap him. The fact is that the men cannot understand us women. They think of us as some of the slaveholders used to think of their slaves, all love & compassion, with no malice in their hearts, but they thought "The negro is a poor lovable creature, kind, docile, unable to take care of himself, & dependent on our compassion to keep them"; & so they consented to do it for the good of the slaves. Men feel the same today. Douglass, Tilton, & Phillips, think that women are perfectly contented to let men earn the money & dole it out to us. We feel with Alexander Hamilton, "Give a man power over my substance, & he has power over my whole being." There is not a woman born, whose bread is earned by another, it does not matter whether that other is husband, brother, father, or friend, not one who consents to eat the bread earned by other hands, but her whole moral being is in the power of that person. [Applause.]

When Mr Douglass tells us today that the case of the black man is so perilous, I tell him that wronged & outraged as they are by this hateful & mean prejudice against color, he would not today exchange his sex & color, wronged as he is, with Elizabeth Cady Stanton.

Mr Douglass. Will you allow me a question?

Miss Anthony. Yes; anything for a fight today.

Mr Douglass. I want to inquire whether granting to woman the right of suffrage will change anything in respect to the nature of our sexes.

Miss Anthony. It will change the nature of one thing very much, & that is the pecuniary position of woman. It will place her in a position in which she can earn her own bread, so that she can go out into the world an equal competitor in the struggle for life; so that she shall not be compelled to take such positions as men choose to accord to her & then take such pay as men choose to give her. In our working women's meetings it was proposed that the question of the decrease of marriages in this country should be taken into consideration, & Mr Croly (of the "World,") said, "I should like to know what you working women are up to; what has the increase or decrease of marriages to do with working women?" I replied, Send your reporters next Wednesday evening & we will show you. Men say that all women are to be married & supported by men, & the laws & customs & public sentiment are all based on that assumption. Wherever there is a woman loose—for we have sometimes women loose, as they had negroes loose, in slavery, & we have fugitive wives as they had fugitive slaves—whenever there is a woman loose or a fugitive wife, thrown out upon the world for support, she is an interloper, & she is paid but one half or one third the price that men receive. When a woman therefore is thrown upon her own resources, she has to choose one of two things, marriage or prostitution. Then it is getting to be a common saying among men all over the country, "Marriage is too expensive a luxury; men cannot afford it." There is the explanation. What we demand is that woman shall have the ballot, for she will never get her other rights until she demands them with the ballot in her hand. It is not a question of precedence between women & black men. Neither has a claim to precedence upon an Equal Rights platform. But the business of this association is to demand for every man black or white, & for every woman, black or white, that they shall be this instant enfranchised & admitted into the body politic with equal rights & privileges.

May 12, 1869

Mark Twain: Only a Nigger

A DISPATCH from Memphis mentions that, of two negroes lately sentenced to death for murder in that vicinity, one named Woods has just confessed to having ravished a young lady during the war, for which deed another negro was hung at the time by an avenging mob, the evidence that doomed the guiltless wretch being a hat which Woods now relates that he stole from its owner and left behind, for the purpose of misleading. Ah, well! Too bad, to be sure! A little blunder in the administration of justice by Southern mob-law, but nothing to speak of. Only "a nigger" killed by mistake—that is all. Of course, every high toned gentleman whose chivalric impulses were so unfortunately misled in this affair, by the cunning of the miscreant Woods, is as sorry about it as a high toned gentleman can be expected to be sorry about the unlucky fate of "a nigger." But mistakes will happen, even in the conduct of the best regulated and most high toned mobs, and surely there is no good reason why Southern gentlemen should worry themselves with useless regrets, so long as only an innocent "nigger" is hanged, or roasted or knouted to death, now and then. What if the blunder of lynching the wrong man does happen once in four or five cases? Is that any fair argument against the cultivation and indulgence of those fine chivalric passions and that noble Southern spirit which will not brook the slow and cold formalities of regular law, when outraged white womanhood appeals for vengeance? Perish the thought so unworthy of a Southern soul! Leave it to the sentimentalism and humanitarianism of a cold-blooded Yankee civilization! What are the lives of a few "niggers" in comparison with the preservation of the impetuous instincts of a proud and fiery race? Keep ready the halter, therefore, oh chivalry of Memphis! Keep the lash knotted; keep the brand and the faggots in waiting, for prompt work with the next "nigger" who may be suspected of any damnable crime! Wreak a swift vengeance upon him, for the satisfaction of the noble impulses that animate knightly hearts, and then leave time and accident to discover, if they will, whether he was guilty or no.

Buffalo Express, August 26, 1869

Georges Clemenceau to Le Temps

November 3, 1869. The blacks must henceforth work to better themselves. They have the right to education, they must learn; they have the right to work, they must work; lastly, they have civil and political rights which are effective and powerful weapons, they must use them in their own defense. They must gird up their loins, and struggle for their existence, in Darwin's phrase, for their physical as well as their moral existence. In a word, they must become men.

Given prosperity, to inspire or strengthen in the individual a sentiment of dignity and power, the result of the comfort it assures and the gratitude it arouses in conscientious souls; given also education, to develop the legitimate degree of refinement which it always produces—in spite of all that these can do, men must still follow the path their fate decrees. Can our aspirations for the blacks be realized? Is it possible that a race which, left to itself, has never contributed to history even rudimentary traces of civilization, can profit sufficiently by contact with a progressive race to pass over at one bound all the intermediary stages which separate it from the latter, and take a place at its side in marching toward the future? Can the African, with his natural indolence, compete successfully with white labor? There are many questions which it would be childish to try to solve *a priori*, of which the future holds and hides the answers.

In this ruthless struggle for existence carried on by human society, those who are weaker physically, intellectually or morally must in the end yield to the stronger. The law is hard, but there is no use in rebelling. European socialists who complain, not without reason, that some men are too well armed for this struggle, and others too ill, will not have modified the struggle itself, nor its causes, nor its conditions, nor its results, when, if ever, they succeed in putting nearly equal weapons into the hands of everyone. The conditions under which man lives can no doubt be changed, but not man himself, for he cannot be divided from his own passions, evil and good, nor from his self-interest, which is always the mainspring of his individual activity.

If, then, the black man cannot successfully compete with the white man, he is fated to be the victim of that natural selection which is constantly operating under our eyes in spite of everything, and he must eventually go under, in the more or less distant future.

It must be added that the Americans are now making the most laudable efforts to arouse the newly freed slaves to a sense of the dignity of their present condition. The South is sprinkled with schools, and since the end of the war a whole army of teachers, both men and women, has invaded it. All are at work, and time alone can show of what the black race is capable. As for the Republican party, which has done so much for the negroes in so short a time, considering the strength of the prejudices it had to combat, it will remain in power as long as its work is threatened, as long as the solution it has evolved for the question is not universally accepted by the conscience of the country. Once this result has been accomplished, its rôle will be over and there will be another transformation in the two great parties which rule the American Republic.

The New York Times:
Reconstruction Nationalized

HITHERTO THE Republican policy of Reconstruction has been essentially sectional. It has been the means employed by the major power in the Union to extinguish the last signs of the rebellion, and to reëstablish order and authority in the Southern States, in accordance with the principles and purposes which triumphed in the war. The measures employed for the attainment of this object were necessarily exceptional in their nature, and resulted in a reorganization of States on a basis fundamentally different from that which previously existed. The change, though arbitrary, was not unjust,—though radical, it was not illogical. The fact of resistance to the National Government was a sufficient reason for exacting guarantees against the recurrence of conflict. The fact of emancipation introduced a new element into citizenship, imposed upon a race new obligations, and entitled them to new privileges, and rendered inevitable the measures necessary to protect them in the exercise of the power conferred upon them. The proceedings incident to this policy may sometimes have looked harsh and objectionable. But the harshness, wherever it appeared, was simply the exercise of an absolute authority in a case which had resisted milder methods of treatment. And the features most objected to have really been the natural developments of a revolution begun in hostility to the Union, and ending, practically, in the revision of some of its conditions, and the consolidation of its power.

The Fourteenth Amendment invested the colored man with citizenship, and the Reconstruction acts gave him his share of political power. The citizenship was national,—the suffrage was restricted to the States to which those laws applied. Thus the anomaly was presented of a race enfranchised in certain States by virtue of Federal authority, and disfranchised in others by reason of local law. A prejudice begotten of slavery, after having been set at naught in States which once were devoted to its maintenance, was perpetuated in the States which had decreed emancipation, and invested the Southern negro with almost controlling power. The Fifteenth Amendment therefore became necessary, not only to harmonize the conditions of suffrage throughout the Union with the conditions imposed upon the South, but to guarantee those at the South who had coöperated with the National Government against possible political vicissitudes in their own States. The Amendment does this without impairing the control of States over the question of suffrage. It neither enacts universal suffrage, nor forbids the application of tests, whether of education or property, as qualifications for voters. It simply forbids unjust discrimination in the enforcement of tests. In providing that "the right of citizens of the United States to vote shall not be denied or abridged by the United States, or by any State, on account of race, color, or previous condition of servitude,"—it secures political equality. The measure was the completion of the work of which emancipation was the commencement. It purges the Union of the last taint of slavery, and makes Reconstruction national.

February 21, 1870

William W. Holden to Ulysses S. Grant

EXECUTIVE DEPARTMENT OF NORTH CAROLINA,
Raleigh, March 10, 1870.

SIR: I have felt it to be my duty to declare the county of Alamance, in this State, in a state of insurrection.

The copy of my proclamation, herewith inclosed, of date March 7, 1870, contains some of the reasons for this step.

There exists in this State a secret, oath-bound, armed organization, which is hostile to the State government, and to the Government of the United States. Bands of these armed men ride at night through various neighborhoods, whipping and maltreating peaceable citizens, hanging some, burning churches, and breaking up schools which have been established for the colored people. These outrages are almost invariably committed on persons, white and colored, who are most devoted in their feelings and conduct to the Government of the United States.

I cannot rely upon the militia to repress these outrages, for the reason that in the localities in which these outrages occur white militia of the proper character cannot be obtained, and it would but aggravate the evil to employ colored militia. Besides, the expense of calling out the militia would be greater than our people could well bear in their present impoverished condition. Federal troops inspire terror among evildoers, and they have the confidence and respect of a majority of our people. We therefore look to, and rely on, the Federal Government to aid us in repressing these outrages and in restoring peace and good order.

If Congress would authorize the suspension by the President of the writ of habeas corpus in certain localities, and if criminals could be arrested and tried before military tribunals and shot, we should soon have peace and order throughout all this country. The remedy would be a sharp and bloody one, but it is as indispensable as was the suppression of the rebellion.

I trust, sir, that you will issue to the commanding general of this department as stringent orders in this matter as the present laws will allow. The commanding general has been prompt to respond to the extent of the power which he has, but I fear this power will not be adequate to effect the desired result.

I have the honor to inclose a copy of the State law under which my proclamation was issued. Also, a pamphlet containing the testimony of witnesses in the preliminary examination of the Lenoir County prisoners, which will afford some idea of the organization and objects of the Ku-Klux Klan.

I have the honor to be, with great respect, your obedient servant,

W. W. HOLDEN, *Governor.*

Ulysses S. Grant: Message to Congress on the Fifteenth Amendment

EXECUTIVE MANSION, *March 30, 1870.*
To the Senate and House of Representatives:

It is unusual to notify the two Houses of Congress by message of the promulgation, by proclamation of the Secretary of State, of the ratification of a constitutional amendment. In view, however, of the vast importance of the fifteenth amendment to the Constitution, this day declared a part of that revered instrument, I deem a departure from the usual custom justifiable. A measure which makes at once 4,000,000 people voters who were heretofore declared by the highest tribunal in the land not citizens of the United States, nor eligible to become so (with the assertion that "at the time of the Declaration of Independence the opinion was fixed and universal in the civilized portion of the white race, regarded as an axiom in morals as well as in politics, that black men had no rights which the white man was bound to respect"), is indeed a measure of grander importance than any other one act of the kind from the foundation of our free Government to the present day.

Institutions like ours, in which all power is derived directly from the people, must depend mainly upon their intelligence, patriotism, and industry. I call the attention, therefore, of the newly enfranchised race to the importance of their striving in every honorable manner to make themselves worthy of their new privilege. To the race more favored heretofore by our laws I would say, Withhold no legal privilege of advancement to the new citizen. The framers of our Constitution firmly believed that a republican government could not endure without intelligence and education generally diffused among the people. The Father of his Country, in his Farewell Address, uses this language:

> Promote, then, as an object of primary importance, institutions for the general diffusion of knowledge. In proportion as

383

the structure of a government gives force to public opinion, it is essential that public opinion should be enlightened.

In his first annual message to Congress the same views are forcibly presented, and are again urged in his eighth message.

I repeat that the adoption of the fifteenth amendment to the Constitution completes the greatest civil change and constitutes the most important event that has occurred since the nation came into life. The change will be beneficial in proportion to the heed that is given to the urgent recommendations of Washington. If these recommendations were important then, with a population of but a few millions, how much more important now, with a population of 40,000,000, and increasing in a rapid ratio. I would therefore call upon Congress to take all the means within their constitutional powers to promote and encourage popular education throughout the country, and upon the people everywhere to see to it that all who possess and exercise political rights shall have the opportunity to acquire the knowledge which will make their share in the Government a blessing and not a danger. By such means only can the benefits contemplated by this amendment to the Constitution be secured.

U. S. GRANT.

Albion W. Tourgée to Joseph C. Abbott

Greensboro, May 24, 1870.

My Dear General,

It is my mournful duty to inform you that our friend John W. Stephens, State Senator from Caswell, is dead. He was foully murdered by the Ku-Klux in the Grand Jury room of the Court House on Saturday or Saturday night last. The circumstances attending his murder have not yet fully come to light there. So far as I can learn, I judge these to have been the circumstances: He was one of the Justices of the Peace in that township, and was accustomed to hold court in that room on Saturdays. It is evident that he was set upon by someone while holding this court, or immediately after its close, and disabled by a sudden attack, otherwise there would have been a very sharp resistance, as he was a man, and always went armed to the teeth. He was stabbed five or six times, and then hanged on a hook in the Grand Jury room, where he was found on Sunday morning. Another brave, honest Republican citizen has met his fate at the hands of these fiends. Warned of his danger, and fully cognizant of the terrible risk which surrounded him, he still manfully refused to quit the field. Against the advice of his friends, against the entreaties of his family, he constantly refused to leave those who had stood by him in the day of his disgrace and peril. He was accustomed to say that 3,000 poor, ignorant, colored Republican voters in that county had stood by him and elected him, at the risk of persecution and starvation, and that he had no idea of abandoning them to the Ku-Klux. He was determined to stay with them, and either put an end to these outrages, or die with the other victims of Rebel hate and national apathy. Nearly six months ago I declared my belief that before the election in August next the Ku-Klux would have killed more men in the State than there would be members to be elected to the Legislature. A good beginning has been made toward the fulfillment of this prophecy.

The following counties have already filled, or nearly so, their respective "quotas:" Jones County, quota full, excess 1; Orange

County, quota full, excess, 1; Caswell County, quota full, excess, 2; Alamance County, quota full, excess, 1; Chatham County, quota nearly full. Or, to state the matter differently, there have been twelve murders in five counties of the district during the past eighteen months by bands of disguised villains. In addition to this, from the best information I can derive, I am of the opinion that in this district alone there have been 1,000 outrages of a less serious nature perpetrated by the same masked fiends. Of course this estimate is not made from any absolute record, nor is it possible to ascertain with accuracy the entire number of beatings and other outrages which have been perpetrated. The uselessness, the utter futility of complaint from the lack of ability in the laws to punish is fully known to all. The danger of making such complaint is also well understood. It is therefore not unfrequently by accident that the outrage is found out, and unquestionably it is frequently absolutely concealed. Thus, a respectable, hard working white carpenter was working for a neighbor, when accidentally his shirt was torn, and disclosed his back scarred and beaten. The poor fellow begged for the sake of his wife and children that nothing might be said about it, as the Ku-Klux had threatened to kill him if he disclosed how he had been outraged. Hundreds of cases have come to my notice and that of my solicitor, in which we have hardly ascertained the names of the parties suffering violence.

Men and women come scarred, mangled, and bruised, and say: "The Ku-Klux came to my house last night and beat me almost to death, and my old woman right smart, and shot into the house, 'bust' the door down, and told me they would kill me if I made complaint," and the bloody mangled forms attest the truth of their declarations. On being asked if any one knew any of the party it will be ascertained that there was no recognition, or only the most uncertain and doubtful one. In such cases as these nothing can be done by the court. We have not been accustomed to enter them on record. A man of the best standing in Chatham told me that he could count up 200 and upward in that county. In Alamance County, a citizen in conversation one evening enumerated upward of 50 cases which had occurred within his own knowledge, and in one section of the county. He gave it as his opinion that there had been 200 cases in that county. I have no idea that he exceeded the proper estimate. That was six months ago, and I am satisfied that another hundred would not cover the work done in that time.

These crimes have been of every character imaginable. Perhaps the most usual has been the dragging of men and women from their beds, and beating their naked bodies with hickory switches, or as witnesses in an examination the other day said, "sticks" between a "switch" and a "club." From 50 to 100 blows is the usual allowance, sometimes 200 and 300 blows are administered. Occasionally an instrument of torture is owned. Thus in one case two women, one 74 years old, were taken out, stripped naked, and beaten with a paddle, with several holes bored through it. The paddle was about 30 inches long, 3 or 4 inches wide, and 1/4 of an inch thick, of Oak. Their bodies were so bruised and beaten that they were sickening to behold. They were white women and of good character until the younger was seduced, and swore her child to its father. Previous to that and so far as others were concerned her character was good.

Again, there is sometimes a fiendish malignity and cunning displayed in the form and character of the outrages. For instance, a colored man was placed astride of a log, and an iron staple driven through his person into the log. In another case, after a band of them had in turn violated a young negro girl, she was forced into bed with a colored man, their bodies were bound together face to face, and the fire from the hearth piled upon them. The K.K.K. rode off and left them, with shouts of laughter. Of course the bed was soon in flames, and somehow they managed to crawl out, though terribly burned and scarred. The house was burned.

I could give other incidents of cruelty, such as hanging up a boy of nine years old until he was nearly dead, to make him tell where his father was hidden, and beating an old negress of 103 years old with garden partings because she would not own that she was afraid of the Ku-Klux. But it is unnecessary to go into further detail. In this district I estimate their offenses as follows, in the past ten months: Twelve murders, 9 rapes, 11 arsons, 7 mutilations, ascertained and most of them on record. In some no identification could be made.

Four thousand or 5,000 houses have been broken open, and property or persons taken out. In all cases all arms are taken and destroyed. Seven hundred or 800 persons have been beaten or otherwise maltreated. These of course are partly persons living in the houses which were broken into.

And yet the Government sleeps. The poor disarmed nurses of the Republican party—those men by whose ballots the Republican party holds power—who took their lives in their hands when they cast their ballots for U. S. Grant and other officials—all of us who happen to be beyond the pale of the governmental regard—must be sacrificed, murdered, scourged, mangled, because some contemptible party scheme might be foiled by doing us justice. I could stand it very well to fight for Uncle Sam, and was never known to refuse an invitation on such an occasion, but this lying down, tied hand and foot with the shackles of the law, to be killed by the very dregs of the rebellion, the scum of the earth, and not allowed either the consolation of fighting or the satisfaction that our "fall" will be noted by the Government, and protection given to others thereby, is somewhat too hard. I am ashamed of the nation that will let its citizens be slain by scores, and scourged by thousands, and offer no remedy or protection. I am ashamed of a State which has not sufficient strength to protect its own officers in the discharge of their duties, nor guarantee the safety of any man's domicile throughout its length and breadth. I am ashamed of a party which, with the reins of power in its hands, has not nerve or decision enough to arm its own adherents, or to protect them from assassinations at the hands of their opponents. A General who in time of war would permit 2,000 or 3,000 of his men to be bushwhacked and destroyed by private treachery even in an enemy's country without any one being punished for it would be worthy of universal execration, and would get it, too. How much more worthy of detestation is a Government which in time of peace will permit such wholesale slaughter of its citizens? It is simple cowardice, inertness, and wholesale demoralization. The wholesale slaughter of the war has dulled our Nation's sense of horror at the shedding of blood, and the habit of regarding the South as simply a laboratory, where every demagogue may carry on his reconstructionary experiments at will, and not as an integral party of the Nation itself, has led our Government to shut its eyes to the atrocities of these times. Unless these evils are speedily remedied, I tell you, General, the Republican Party has signed its death warrant. It is a party of cowards or idiots—I don't care which alternative is chosen. The remedy is in our hands, and we are afraid or too dull to bestir ourselves and use it.

But you will tell me that Congress is ready and willing to act if it only knew what to do. Like the old Irish woman it wrings its hands and cries, "O Lawk, O Lawk, if I only knew which way." And yet this same Congress has the control of the militia and can organize its own force in every county in the United States, and arm more or less of it. This same Congress has the undoubted right to guarantee and provide a republican government, and protect every citizen in "life, liberty, and the pursuit of happiness," as well as the power conferred by the XVth Amendment. And yet we suffer and die in peace and murderers walk abroad with the blood yet fresh upon their garments, unharmed, unquestioned and unchecked. Fifty thousand dollars given to good detectives would secure, if well used, a complete knowledge of all this gigantic organization of murderers. In connection with an organized and armed militia, it would result in the apprehension of any number of these thugs *en masque* and with blood on their hands. What then is the remedy?

First: Let Congress give to the U.S. Courts, or to Courts of the States under its own laws, cognizance of this class of crimes, as crimes against the Nation, and let it provide that this legislation be enforced. Why not, for instance, make going armed and masked or disguised, or masked or disguised in the night time, an act of insurrection or sedition? *Second*: Organize militia, National—State militia is a nuisance—and arm as many as may be necessary in each county to enforce its laws. *Third*: Put detectives at work to get hold of this whole organization. Its ultimate aim is unquestionably to revolutionize the Government. If we have not pluck enough for this, why then let us just offer our throats to the knife, emasculate ourselves, and be a nation of self-subjugated slaves at once.

And now, Abbott, I have but one thing to say to you. I have very little doubt that I shall be one of the next victims. My steps have been dogged for months, and only a good opportunity has been wanting to secure to me the fate which Stephens has just met, and I speak earnestly upon this matter. I feel that

I have a right to do so, and a right to be heard as well, and with this conviction I say to you plainly that any member of Congress who, especially if from the South, does not support, advocate, and urge immediate, active, and thorough measures to put an end to these outrages, and make citizenship a privilege, is a coward, a traitor, or a fool. The time for action has come, and the man who has now only speeches to make over some Constitutional scarecrow, deserves to be damned.

Yours respectfully,
A. W. Tourgee

Robert K. Scott to Ulysses S. Grant

We have just passed through an Election which for rancour and virulence on the part of the opposition has never been excelled in any civilized community—The Republican Administration has been charged with every crime in the catalogue, and although these charges have been deliberately made and circulated throughout the entire State by nearly if not all of the outspoken champions of the Reform Party, yet no attempt has been made to substantiate a single one of them or to furnish a single particle of proof—The people of the State have had these charges before them, and by an overwhelming majority even in counties where the white population are largely in the ascendency, have decided that there was no foundation whatever for them: and by their votes have shown that the whole tissue of falsehoods was only devised for political capital—Unusual quietness characterised the day of Election throughout the State, and but little disturbance was experienced in any quarter which may be attributable to the presence of detachments of United States troops at the localities where they were most apprehended—In the upper or more northern counties where the white population predominated, fears were entertained that intruders from North Carolina and Georgia would interfere and cause trouble; but it appears from subsequent events that the programme was changed to an attack upon the ballot boxes and, by destroying them, to vitiate the Election. Reliable information has reached this Department that an organized force has appeared at Laurens Court House, assailed the State Constabulary driving them from their position, and killing and wounding several of them, together with a number of private citizens. These desperados seized upon the arms on deposit belonging to the State and drove many of the peaceful inhabitants from their homes creating a general reign of terror and lawlessness. Colored men and women have been dragged from their homes at the dead hour of night and most cruelly and brutally scourged for the sole reason that they dared to exercise their own opinions upon political subjects—For four years the National Government conducted a war for the perpetuity of the Union and the establishment and preservation of the Liberty of the people and those who were its opponents throughout that desperate struggle are the same class of men who now resist its policy and defy the constituted authorities, in their efforts to conform the State Government to the new order of things. In the struggle for National existence the United States Government made citizens of four millions of human beings, who had previously been kept in ignorance and poverty, and thus assumed the responsibility of their education and protection; & and if the state is powerless to secure these people their natural rights the duty clearly devolves upon the National Government to throw around them its arms of protection and the shield of its authority. The Republican party at the recent Election carried nearly every county in the State; even those where the white population were largely in the majority. The respectable portion of the community desire peace and tranquility, and are willing to abide the results of the late war; but this portion of the community is powerless to prevent the inhuman and brutal outrages that are continually being perpetrated in the name and by the authority of those calling themselves democrats. I have within a few moments witnessed in my own office a spectacle that has chilled my blood with horror. Four peaceable and unoffending citizens of Spartanburg county were at the dead hour of night dragged from their homes and lashed on their bare backs until the flayed flesh hung dripping in shreds, and seams were gaping in their mangled bodies large enough to lay my finger in. After this torture they were subjected to nameless indignities too gross and disgusting to be even remotely alluded to, when these fiends in human shape, exhausted by their own atrocities desisted from further torture. A humane gentleman brought these victims of political hate, to this city and quite a number of persons examined their wounds in my office. United States Senator Robertson and Col Patterson vice President of the Greenville & Columbia R. R. were present and will fully corroborate my statement. From the information of these gentlemen your Excellency will also learn the condition of things in this State and the necessities of the occasion, and will perceive the absolute necessity of military assistance on the part of the General Government. Our state militia are but imperfectly drilled, and are necessarily employed in their daily avocations as laborers, and it would be impracticable to continue them continuously in service, so as to be constantly prepared to arrest and punish the attempts at violence and crime while their opponents are largely composed of those who were engaged in the Confederate Armies, accustomed to the use of fire-arms, thoroughly drilled and armed with the most improved weapons, and would consequently possess many advantages over their antagonists. Humanity therefore as well as every sound principle of policy would dictate that regular troops should be employed in this service.

October 22, 1870

Horace Greeley and Robert Brown Elliott: Exchange on Amnesty

AMNESTY—PERSONAL SECURITY.

THE VOTES already taken indicate a decided majority in the House for a sweeping measure of Amnesty, while the deliberations in caucus indicate an equally decisive preponderance of those who insist on the efficient protection of life and liberty at the South. These majorities are very differently constituted, but they are both essentially right. It is expedient that the disabilities imposed for complicity in the Rebellion of six to ten years ago should be removed; it is essential that the rebels of 1871 shall be suppressed and their outrages punished. There is no conflict between these two propositions. Men who are now deporting themselves as good citizens should not be denied the common rights of citizens because they were wrong long ago; while men who do wrong now should be made to desist at whatever cost. A wise and strong government may well overlook bygone errors, while it is imperatively bound to give present protection and security to its loyal and peaceful supporters.

Mr. Elliott, one of South Carolina's new representatives, asserted on Tuesday that the Ku-Klux disturbers of the South are "the very class of men whom it is proposed to relieve of their political disabilities." In the absence of proof, probabilities are entitled to weight; and Mr. E.'s naked assertion does not suffice to prove that the midnight riders and raiders in masks and multiform disguises by whom the South is now disturbed are the ex-colonels, ex-legislators and ex-magistrates of the old slave-holding regime who are alone excluded from office by existing disabilities. If Mr. E. had asserted that pears and watermelons are generally stolen by clergymen and deacons fifty to eighty years old, his mistake would not be more obvious than it now is.

The truth of the matter tells against Mr. Elliott's position. The Ku-Klux are generally wild youngsters, badly trained and naturally reckless of moral and legal restraints, but often sons, or nephews, or cousins, of those who are excluded from office by their part in the Rebellion. This exclusion is a part of the raiders' excuse for their crimes. They see those whom they most respect and honor proscribed for acts which they esteem righteous and patriotic; and they are impelled thereby to revenge themselves on those whom they regard as the abettors and upholders of this injustice. Mr. Elliott's speech will confirm many in this malevolent and mischievous impression. "These niggers around us," they will say, "profess all manner of good will and kindly feeling toward their White neighbors; but that fellow in Congress betrays their real *animus*. Only give them power, and they would disfranchise all who are not Black." Mr. Elliott, we doubt not, is well-meaning; but he has done his race lasting harm by his first demonstration in the House. His allusion to Gen. Farnsworth as a sympathiser with the Rebellion was exceedingly injudicious and unfortunate.

Congress ought not to adjourn without passing a generous measure of Amnesty and an efficient Ku-Klux suppression act. Each is needed and would prove signally beneficent. But, if Amnesty must still be waited for, the need of legislation aimed at the Ku-Klux becomes still more urgent and imperative. Amnesty would do somewhat toward disarming and dissolving the Ku-Klux; its failure will embitter thousands, and thus inflame the spirit which keeps that organization alive, active, and formidable. We entreat Congress not to adjourn without having accorded all the security that repressive laws can give to the imperiled loyalists of the South.

New-York Tribune, March 16, 1871

MR. ELLIOTT ON THE KU-KLUX OUTRAGES.
To the Editor of The Tribune.

Sir: In your issue of yesterday, you were pleased to bring under review, my brief remarks made in the House of Representatives last Tuesday, on the bill to relieve certain classes of persons of their political disabilities, introduced by Mr. Beck of Kentucky. The editorial, to which I refer, contains many errors of fact and reasoning, and as I feel assured that you intended to be just in your criticism, I respectfully request the privilege of your columns for a response.

I did not assert that "the Ku-Klux disturbers of the South are the very class of men whom it is proposed to relieve of their political disabilities." My views upon this point are embodied in the following extract from the speech to which you refer, as it appears, unamended by me, in *The Congressional Globe* of the 15th inst.:

> "The gentleman from Illinois, in his argument, was pleased to ask this question, which he proposed to answer himself: Are these men who are disfranchised, and prohibited from holding office, the men who commit the murders and outrages of which complaint is made? And his answer to that question was that they are not. But permit me to say to that gentleman that those men are responsible for every murder, responsible for every species of outrage, that is committed in the South. They are men who, in their evil example, by their denunciations of Congress, by their abuse of the President of the United States, and of all connected with this Government, have encouraged, aided, and abetted the men who commit these deeds. They contribute to this state of things by their social influence, by their money and the money sent from the Northern States— money furnished by Tammany Hall for the purpose of keeping up these outrages in order to insure a Democratic triumph in the South in 1872."

In proof that I was warranted in expressing the opinion that the armed bands who murder unoffending citizens because of their political opinions in the Southern States, derive more aid and comfort from the so-called "respectable" portion of the section in which they act, I submit the following letter which appeared in *The Columbia* (S. C.) *Daily Union* on last Tuesday, the very day on which that opinion was uttered.

WINNSBORO, Monday, March 13, 1871.
To the Editor of The Daily Union:
Information has just been received here that two members of Capt. Jacob Moore's company of militia, Hilliard Ellison and Thomas Johnson by names, were attacked in their houses yesterday morning, before day, by the Ku-Klux, and Hilliard Ellison was shot through the back and mortally wounded, and

Thomas Johnson had his thigh shattered. There is no hope whatever of Hilliard Ellison. And it may be but proper to state that there are men of influence and wealth in this county, who are well known, who are in full sympathy with these deeds of violence, that are getting to be of nightly occurrence, and that have so disgraced the up-country of late. This took place about seven miles west of this place.

Permit me to add, upon this point, that your own admission, in the editorial above referred to, fully justifies the opinion that has made me obnoxious to your harsh criticism, for you state: "The Ku-Klux are *often sons, or nephews, or cousins*, of those who are excluded from office by their part in the Rebellion." Surely, then, it was not a very violent presumption that these gentlemen should sympathize with their kindred, and give them a moral, and, if need be, a material support?

You state further, in speaking of the Ku-Klux: "They see those whom they most respect and honor proscribed for acts which they esteem righteous and patriotic, and they are impelled thereby to revenge themselves on those whom they regard as abettors and upholders of this injustice." I must say, Mr. Editor, that this language would better befit the lips of an advocate endeavoring to "make the worse appear the better cause" in a defense of these masked murderers before a petit jury than the pages of THE NEW-YORK TRIBUNE. Your argument proves too much, and therefore proves nothing. If to continue the political disabilities imposed by the XIVth Amendment upon certain classes in the South is to "embitter thousands, and thus inflame the spirit which keeps that organization" (the Ku-Klux) "alive, active, and formidable," then the adoption of that amendment, which THE TRIBUNE advocated so earnestly, was itself a grave mistake. Those who advocated the evacuation of Fort Sumter by the Union forces, and subsequently urged our Government to recognize the independence of the so-called Confederate States, in the "interest of peace," fortified their opinions by a similar train of reasoning. Doubtless this is the true humanitarian mode of dealing with this matter. Doubtless, Congress should conform its legislation to the tender sensibilities of those who murder American citizens for their "opinion's sake;" yet it would seem to be decent and proper that the Government should withhold its act of grace and amnesty to the murderer until the grass springs upon the graves of the murdered.

Those loyal men who dwell among the scenes of violence now being enacted in South Carolina, in momentary expectation of murder, exile, or the lash, will deem amnesty an untimely grace, while the path of duty is the path of danger to the Southern Republican. Your editorial will not brighten the hopes or fortify the resolution of the loyal citizen of South Carolina, who is today,

> "A hunted seeker of the Truth,
> Oppressed for conscience sake."

Possibly, Mr. Editor, your graciousness to recalcitrant Confederates, would be somewhat modified if you lived, as I do, within the theater of their operations. The law of safe distances frequently molds our judgments in regard to men and their acts. Men often bear the misfortunes of their neighbors with great equanimity, and are ready most graciously to forgive wrongs to which they cannot be personally subjected. Thus the philosopher Seneca, seated in his magnificent villa, surrounded by symbols of opulence, wrote upon tablets of gold, his famous "Essay on the Beauties and Advantages of Poverty." You reason, Mr. Editor, upon the Ku-Klux in the abstract, while I view them as living realities, who show no mercy and, therefore, deserve none.

You are also mistaken in your statement that I made an "allusion to Gen. Farnsworth as a sympathizer with the Rebellion." On the contrary, I spoke of him as "a man whom I have been taught long to regard as one of those who are unflinching in their devotion to the cause of liberty and the preservation and maintenance of this great Government." I know Gen. Farnsworth as a Republican too well, and appreciate his services to the country and to my own race too highly, to cast the aspersion of "sympathizing with the Rebellion" upon him; nor do I believe that he so understood me. When, however, he presented an argument in favor of the bill then under discussion, drawing a parallel between the former master now disfranchised, and the former slave now enfranchised, I stated that he sympathized with the first in his present disfranchisement.

In this, I differed from him, for I deem it safer for this Republican to intrust the ballot to ignorant loyalty rather than to cultivated treason. I am, Sir, very respectfully, your obedient servant,

ROBERT B. ELLIOTT.

Washington, D. C., March 17, 1871.

New-York Tribune, March 21, 1871

Joseph H. Rainey: Speech in Congress on the Enforcement Bill

MR. SPEAKER, in approaching the subject now under consideration I do so with a deep sense of its magnitude and importance, and in full recognition of the fact that a remedy is needed to meet the evil now existing in most of the southern States, but especially in that one which I have the honor to represent in part, the State of South Carolina. The enormity of the crimes constantly perpetrated there finds no parallel in the history of this Republic in her very darkest days. There was a time when the early settlers of New England were compelled to enter the fields, their homes, even the very sanctuary itself, armed to the full extent of their means. While the people were offering their worship to God within those humble walls their voices kept time with the tread of the sentry outside. But, sir, it must be borne in mind that at the time referred to civilization had but just begun its work upon this continent. The surroundings were unpropitious, and as yet the grand capabilities of this fair land lay dormant under the fierce tread of the red man. But as civilization advanced with its steady and resistless sway it drove back those wild cohorts and compelled them to give way to the march of improvement. In course of time superior intelligence made its impress and established its dominion upon this continent. That intelligence, with an influence like that of the sun rising in the east and spreading its broad rays like a garment of light, gave life and gladness to the dark and barbaric land of America.

Surely, sir, it were but reasonable to hope that this sacred influence should never have been overshadowed, and that in the history of other nations, no less than in our own past, we might find beacon-lights for our guidance. In part this has been realized, and might have reached the height of our expectations if it had not been for the blasting effects of slavery, whose deadly pall has so long spread its folds over this nation, to the destruction of peace, union, and concord. Most particularly has its baneful influence been felt in the South, causing the people to be at once restless and discontented. Even now, sir, after the great conflict between slavery and freedom, after the triumph achieved at such a cost, we can yet see the traces of the disastrous strife and the remains of disease in the body-politic of the South. In proof of this witness the frequent outrages perpetrated upon our loyal men. The prevailing spirit of the Southron is either to rule or to ruin. Voters must perforce succumb to their wishes or else risk life itself in the attempt to maintain a simple right of common manhood.

The suggestions of the shrewdest Democratic papers have proved unavailing in controlling the votes of the loyal whites and blacks of the South. Their innuendoes have been evaded. The people emphatically decline to dispose of their rights for a mess of pottage. In this particular the Democracy of the North found themselves foiled and their money needless. But with a spirit more demon-like than that of a Nero or a Caligula, there has been concocted another plan, destructive, ay, diabolical in its character, worthy only of hearts without regard for God or man, fit for such deeds as those deserving the name of men would shudder to perform. Is it asked, what are those deeds? Let those who liberally contributed to the supply of arms and ammunition in the late rebellious States answer the question. Soon after the close of the war there had grown up in the South a very widely-spread willingness to comply with the requirements of the law. But as the clemency and magnanimity of the General Government became manifest once again did the monster rebellion lift its hydra head in renewed defiance, cruel and cowardly, fearing the light of day, hiding itself under the shadow of the night as more befitting its bloody and accursed work.

I need not, Mr. Speaker, recite here the murderous deeds committed both in North and South Carolina. I could touch the feelings of this House by the story of widows and orphans now wandering amid the ravines of the rural counties of my native State seeking protection and maintenance from others who are yet unable, on account of their own poverty, to grant them aid. I could dwell upon the sorrows of poor women, with their helpless infants, cast upon the world, homeless and destitute, deprived of their natural protectors by the red hand of the midnight assassin. I could appeal to you, members upon this floor, as husbands and fathers, to picture to yourselves the desolation of your own happy firesides should you be suddenly snatched away from your loved ones. Think of gray-haired men, whose fourscore years are almost numbered, the venerated heads of peaceful households, without warning murdered for political opinion's sake. In proof I send to the desk the following article and ask the Clerk to read. It is taken from the Spartanburg (South Carolina) Republican, March 29, 1871.

The Clerk read as follows:

"*Horrible Attempt at Murder by Disguised Men.*—One of the most cowardly and inhuman attempts at murder known in the annals of crime was made last Wednesday night, the 22d instant, by a band of disguised men upon the person of Dr. J. Winsmith at his home about twelve miles from town. The doctor, a man nearly seventy years of age, had been to town during the day and was seen and talked with by many of our citizens. Returning home late, he soon afterward retired, worn out and exhausted by the labors of the day. A little after midnight he was aroused by some one knocking violently at his front door. The knocking was soon afterward repeated at his chamber door, which opens immediately upon the front yard. The doctor arose, opened the door, and saw two men in disguise standing before him. As soon as he appeared one of the men cried out, 'Come on, boys! Here's the damned old rascal.' The doctor immediately stepped back into the room, picked up two single-barreled pistols lying upon the bureau, and returned to the open door. At his reappearance the men retreated behind some cedar trees standing in the yard. The doctor, in his night clothes, boldly stepped out into the yard and followed them. On reaching the trees he fired, but with what effect he does not know. He continued to advance, when twenty or thirty shots were fired at him by men crouched behind an orange hedge. He fired his remaining pistol and then attempted to return to the house. Before reaching it, however, he sank upon the ground exhausted by the loss of blood, and pain, occasioned by seven wounds which he had received in various parts of his body. As soon as he fell the assassins mounted their horses and rode away.

"The doctor was carried into the house upon a quilt, borne by his wife and some colored female servants. The colored men on the premises fled on the approach of the murderers, and the colored women being afraid to venture out, Mrs. Winsmith herself was obliged to walk three quarters of a mile to the house of her nephew, Dr. William Smith, for assistance. The physician has been with Dr. Winsmith day and night since the difficulty occurred, and thinks, we learn, that there is a possible chance of the doctor's recovery.

"The occasion of this terrible outrage can be only the fact that Dr. Winsmith is a Republican. One of the largest land-holders and tax-payers in the county, courteous in manner, kind in disposition, and upright and just in all his dealings with his fellow-men, he has ever been regarded as one of the leading citizens of the county. For many years prior to the war he represented the people in the Legislature, and immediately after the war he was sent to the senate. Because he has dared become a Republican, believing that in the doctrines of true republicanism only can the State and country find lasting peace and prosperity, he has become the doomed victim of the murderous Ku Klux Klan.

"The tragedy has cast a gloom over the entire community, and while we are glad to say that it has generally been condemned, yet we regret to state that no step has yet been taken to trace out and punish the perpetrators of the act. The judge of this circuit is sitting on his bench; the machinery of justice is in working order; but there can be found no hand bold enough to set it in motion. The courts of justice seem paralyzed when they have to meet such issues as this. Daily reports come to us of men throughout the country being whipped; of school-houses for colored children being closed, and of parties being driven from their houses and their families. Even here in town there are some who fear to sleep at their own homes and in their own beds. The law affords no protection for life and property in this county, and the sooner the country knows it and finds a remedy for it, the better it will be. Better a thousand times the rule of the bayonet than the humiliating lash of the Ku Klux and the murderous bullet of the midnight assassin."

Mr. RAINEY. The gentleman to whom reference is made in the article read, is certainly one of the most inoffensive individuals I have ever known. He is a gentleman of refinement, culture, and sterling worth, a Carolinian of the old school, an associate of the late Hon. John C. Calhoun, being neither a pauper nor a pensioner, but living in comparative affluence and ease upon his own possessions, respected by all fair-minded and unprejudiced citizens who knew him. Accepting the situation, he joined the Republican party in the fall of 1870; and for this alliance, and this alone, he has been vehemently assailed and murderously assaulted. By all the warm and kindly sympathies of our common humanity, I implore you to do something for this suffering people, and stand not upon the order of your doing. Could I exhume the murdered men and women of the South, Mr. Speaker, and array their ghastly forms before your eyes, I should not need remove the mantle from them, because their very presence would appeal, in tones of plaintive eloquence, which would be louder than a million tongues. They could indeed—

> "A tale unfold whose lightest word
> Would harrow up thy soul."

It has been asserted that protection for the colored people only has been demanded; and in this there is a certain degree of truth, because they are noted for their steadfastness to the Union and the cause of liberty as guarantied by the Constitution. But, on the other hand, this protection is equally desired for those loyal whites, some to the manner born, others who, in the exercise of their natural rights as American citizens, have seen fit to remove thither from other sections of the States, and who are now undergoing persecution simply on account of their activity in carrying out Union principles and loyal sentiments in the South. Their efforts have contributed largely to further reconstruction and the restoration of the southern States to the old fellowship of the Federal compact. It is indeed hard that their reward for their well-meant earnestness should be that of being violently treated, and even forced to flee from the homes of their choice. It will be a foul stain upon the escutcheon of our land if such atrocities be tamely suffered longer to continue.

In the dawn of our freedom our young Republic was widely recognized and proudly proclaimed to the world the refuge, the safe asylum of the oppressed of all lands. Shall it be said that at this day, through mere indifference and culpable neglect, this grand boast of ours is become a mere form of words, an utter fraud? I earnestly hope not! And yet, if we stand with folded arms and idle hands, while the cries of our oppressed brethren sound in our ears, what will it be but a proof to all men that we are utterly unfit for our glorious mission, unworthy our noble privileges, as the greatest of republics, the champions of freedom for all men? I would that every individual man in this whole nation could be aroused to a sense of his own part and duty in this great question. When we call to mind the fact that this persecution is waged against men for the simple reason that they dare to vote with the party which has saved the Union intact by the lavish expenditure of blood and treasure, and has borne the nation safely through the fearful crisis of these last few years, our hearts swell with an overwhelming indignation.

The question is sometimes asked, Why do not the courts of law afford redress? Why the necessity of appealing to Congress? We answer that the courts are in many instances under the control of those who are wholly inimical to the impartial administration of law and equity. What benefit would result from appeal to tribunals whose officers are secretly in sympathy with the very evil against which we are striving?

But to return to the point in question. If the negroes, numbering one-eighth of the population of these United States, would only cast their votes in the interest of the Democratic party, all open measures against them would be immediately suspended, and their rights, as American citizens, recognized. But as to the real results of such a state of affairs, and speaking in behalf of those with whom I am conversant, I can only say that we love freedom more, vastly more, than slavery; consequently we hope to keep clear of the Democrats!

In most of the arguments to which I have listened the positions taken are predicated upon the ground of the unconstitutionality of the bill introduced by the gentleman from Ohio, [Mr. SHELLABARGER.] For my part, I am not prepared, Mr. Speaker, to argue this question from a constitutional standpoint alone. I take the ground that, in my opinion, lies far above the interpretation put upon the provisions of the Constitution. I stand upon the broad plane of right; I look to the urgent, the importunate demands of the present emergency; and while I am far from advocating any step not in harmony with that sacred law of our land, while I would not violate the lightest word of that chart which has so well guided us in the past, yet I desire that so broad and liberal a construction be placed upon its provisions as will insure protection to the humblest citizen, without regard to rank, creed, or color. Tell me nothing of a constitution which fails to shelter beneath its rightful power the people of a country!

I believe when the fathers of our country framed the Constitution they made the provisions so broad that the humblest, as well as the loftiest citizen, could be protected in his inalienable rights. It was designed to be, and is, the bulwark of freedom, and the strong tower of defense, against foreign invasion and domestic violence. I desire to direct your attention to what is imbodied in the preamble, and would observe that it was adopted after a liberal and protracted discussion on every article composing the great American Magna Charta. And like a keystone to an arch it made the work complete. Here is what it declares:

> "We, the people of the United States, in order to form a more perfect Union, establish justice, insure domestic tranquillity, provide for the common defense, promote the general welfare, and secure the blessings of liberty to ourselves and our posterity, do ordain and establish this Constitution for the United States of America."

If the Constitution which we uphold and support as the fundamental law of the United States is inadequate to afford security to life, liberty, and property—if, I say, this inadequacy is proven, then its work is done, then it should no longer be recognized as the Magna Charta of a great and free people; the sooner it is set aside the better for the liberties of the nation. It has been asserted on this floor that the Republican party is answerable for the existing state of affairs in the South. I am here to deny this, and to illustrate, I will say that in the State of South Carolina there is no disturbance of an alarming character in any one of the counties in which the Republicans have a majority. The troubles are usually in those sections in which the Democrats have a predominance in power, and, not content with this, desire to be supreme.

I say to the gentlemen of the Opposition, and to the entire membership of the Democratic party, that upon your hands rests the blood of the loyal men of the South. Disclaim it as you will the stain is there to prove your criminality before God and the world in the day of retribution which will surely come.

I pity the man or party of men who would seek to ride into power over the dead body of a legitimate opponent.

It has been further stated that peace reigned in the rebellious States from 1865 until the enactment of the reconstruction laws. The reason of this is obvious. Previous to that time they felt themselves regarded as condemned traitors, subject to the penalties of the law. They stood awaiting the sentence of the nation to be expressed by Congress. Subsequently the enactments of that body, framed with a spirit of magnanimity worthy a great and noble nation, proved that, far from a vindictive course, they desired to deal with them with clemency and kindness. This merciful plan of action proved to be a mistake, for cowardice, emboldened by the line of policy of the President, began to feel that judgment long delayed meant forgiveness without repentance. Their tactics were changed, and again a warlike attitude was assumed, not indeed directly against the General Government, but against those who upon southern soil were yet the staunch supporters of its powers. Thus is it evident that if only the props which support such a fabric could be removed the structure must necessarily fall, to be built again by other hands. This is the animus of the Ku Klux Klan, which is now spreading devastation through the once fair and tranquil South.

If the country there is impoverished it has certainly not been caused by the fault of those who love the Union, but it is simply the result of a disastrous war madly waged against the best Government known to the world. The murder of unarmed men and the maltreating of helpless women can never make restitution for the losses which are the simply inevitable consequence of the rebellion. The faithfulness of my race during the entire war, in supporting and protecting the families of their masters, speaks volumes in their behalf as to the real kindliness of their feelings toward the white people of the South.

In conclusion, sir, I would say that it is in no spirit of bitterness against the southern people that I have spoken to-day. There are many among them for whom I entertain a profound regard, having known them in former and brighter days of their history. I have always felt a pride in the prestige of my native State, noted as she has been for her noble sons, with their lofty intellect or tried statesmanship. But it is not possible for me to speak in quiet and studied words of those unworthy her ancient and honorable name, who at this very day are doing all they can do to deface her fair records of the past and bring the old State into disrepute.

I can say for my people that we ardently desire peace for ourselves and for the whole nation. Come what will, we are fully determined to stand by the Republican party and the Government. As to our fate, "we are not wood, we are not stone," but men, with feelings and sensibilities like other men whose skin is of a lighter hue.

When myself and colleagues shall leave these Halls and turn our footsteps toward our southern homes we know not but that the assassin may await our coming, as marked for his vengeance. Should this befall, we would bid Congress and our country to remember that 'twas—

"Bloody treason flourish'd over us."

Be it as it may, we have resolved to be loyal and firm, "and if we perish, we perish!" I earnestly hope the bill will pass.

April 1, 1871

James A. Garfield: from Speech in Congress on the Enforcement Bill

Mr. SPEAKER: I am not able to understand the mental organization of the man who can consider this bill, and the subject of which it treats, as free from very great difficulties. He must be a man of very moderate abilities, whose ignorance is bliss, or a man of transcendent genius whom no difficulties can daunt and whose clear vision no cloud can obscure.

The distinguished gentleman [Mr. SHELLABARGER] who introduced the bill from the committee very appropriately said that it requires us to enter upon unexplored territory. That territory, Mr. Speaker, is the neutral ground of all political philosophy; the neutral ground for which rival theories have been struggling in all ages. There are two ideas so utterly antagonistic that when, in any nation, either has gained absolute and complete possession of that neutral ground, the ruin of that nation has invariably followed. The one is that despotism which swallows and absorbs all power in a single-central, government; the other is that extreme doctrine of local sovereignty which makes nationality impossible and resolves a general government into anarchy and chaos. It makes but little difference as to the final result which of these ideas drives the other from the field; in either case, ruin follows.

The result exhibited by the one, was seen in the Amphictyonic and Achæan leagues of ancient Greece, of which Madison, in the twentieth number of the Federalist, says:

> "The inevitable result of all was imbecility in the government, discord among the provinces, foreign influences and indignities, a precarious existence in peace and peculiar calamities in war."

This is a fitting description of all nations who have carried the doctrine of local self-government so far as to exclude the doctrine of nationality. They were not nations, but mere leagues bound together by common consent, ready to fall to pieces at the demand of any refractory member. The opposing idea was never better illustrated than when Louis XIV entered the French Assembly, booted and spurred, and girded with the sword of ancestral kings, and said to the deputies of France, "The State! I am the State!"

Between these opposite and extreme theories of government, the people have been tossed from century to century; and it has been only when these ideas have been in reasonable equipoise, when this neutral ground has been held in joint occupancy, and usurped by neither, that popular liberty and national life have been possible. How many striking illustrations of this do we see in the history of France! The despotism of Louis XIV, followed by reign of terror, when liberty had run mad and France was a vast scene of blood and ruin! We see it again in our day. Only a few years ago the theory of personal government had placed into the hands of Napoleon III absolute and irresponsible power. The communes of France were crushed, and local liberty existed no longer. Then followed Sedan and the rest. On the 1st day of last month, when France was trying to rebuild her ruined Government, when the Prussian cannon had scarcely ceased thundering against the walls of Paris, a deputy of France rose in the National Assembly and moved as the first step toward the safety of his country, that a committee of thirty should be chosen, to be called the Committee of Decentralization. But it was too late to save France from the fearful reaction from despotism. The news comes to us, under the sea, that on Saturday last the cry was ringing through France, "Death to the priests, and death to the rich!" and the swords of the citizens of that new republic are now wet with each other's blood.

EQUIPOISE OF OUR GOVERNMENT.

The records of time show no nobler or wiser work done by human hands than that of our fathers when they framed this Republic. Beginning in a wilderness world, they wrought unfettered by precedent, untrammeled by custom, unawed by kings or dynasties. With the history of other nations before them, they surveyed the new field. In the progress of their work they encountered these antagonistic ideas to which I have referred. They attempted to trace through that neutral ground the boundary line across which neither force should pass. The result of their labors is our Constitution and frame of government. I never contemplate the result without feeling that there was more than mortal wisdom in the men who produced it. It has seemed to me that they borrowed their thought from Him who constructed the universe and put it in motion. For nothing that more aptly describes the character of our Republic than the solar system, launched into space by the hand of the Creator, where the central sun is the great power around which revolve all the planets in their appointed orbits. But while the sun holds in the grasp of its attractive power the whole system, and imparts its light and heat to all, yet each individual planet is under the sway of laws peculiar to itself.

Under the sway of terrestrial laws, winds blow, waters flow, and all the tenantries of the planet live and move. So, sir, the States move on in their orbits of duty and obedience, bound to the central Government by this Constitution, which is their supreme law; while each State is making laws and regulations of its own, developing its own energies, maintaining its own industries, managing its local affairs in its own way, subject only to the supreme but beneficent control of the Union. When State rights run mad, put on the form of secession, and attempted to drag the States out of the Union, we saw the grand lesson taught, in all the battles of the late war, that a State could no more be hurled from the Union without ruin to the nation, than could a planet be thrown from its orbit without dragging after it, to chaos and ruin, the whole solar universe.

Sir, the great war for the Union has vindicated the centripetal power of the nation, and has exploded, forever I trust, the disorganizing theory of State sovereignty which slavery attempted to impose upon this country. But we should never forget that there is danger in the opposite direction. The destruction or serious crippling of the principle of local government would be as fatal to liberty as secession would have been fatal to the Union.

The first experiment which our fathers tried in government-making after the War of Independence was a failure, because the central power conferred in the Articles of Confederation was not strong enough. The second, though nobly conceived, became almost a failure because slavery attempted so to interpret the Constitution as to reduce the nation again to a confederacy, a mere league between sovereign States. But we have now vindicated and secured the centripetal power; let us see that the centrifugal force is not destroyed, but that the grand and beautiful equipoise may be maintained.

———————

But, sir, the President has informed us in his recent message, that in some portions of the Republic wrongs and outrages are now being perpetrated, under circumstances which lead him to doubt his power to suppress them by means of existing laws. That new situation confronts us. I deeply regret that we were not able to explore the length, breadth, and depth of this new danger before we undertook to provide a legislative remedy. The subject is so obscured by passion that it is hardly possible for Congress, with the materials now in our possession, to know the truth of the case, to understand fully the causes of this new trouble, and to provide wisely and intelligently the safest and most certain remedy.

But enough is known to demand some action on our part. To state the case in the most moderate terms, it appears that in some of the southern States there exists a wide-spread secret organization, whose members are bound together by solemn oaths to prevent certain classes of citizens of the United States from enjoying these new rights conferred upon them by the Constitution and laws; that they are putting into execution their design of preventing such citizens from enjoying the free right of the ballot-box and other privileges and immunities of citizens, and from enjoying the equal protection of the laws. Mr. Speaker, I have no doubt of the power of Congress to provide for meeting this new danger, and to do so without trenching upon those great and beneficent powers of local self-government lodged in the States and with the people. To reach this result is the demand of the hour upon the statesmanship of this country. This brings me to the consideration of the pending bill.

BILL TO ENFORCE THE FOURTEENTH AMENDMENT.

The first section provides, in substance, that any person who, under color of any State law, ordinance, or custom, shall deprive any person of any rights, privileges, or immunities secured by the Constitution, the offender shall be liable to an action at law, or other proper proceeding, for redress in the several district or circuit courts of the United States. This is a wise and salutary provision, and plainly within the power of Congress.

But the chief complaint is not that the laws of the State are unequal, but that even where the laws are just and equal on their face, yet, by a systematic maladministration of them, or a neglect or refusal to enforce their provisions, a portion of the people are denied equal protection under them. Whenever such a state of facts is clearly made out, I believe the last clause of the first section empowers Congress to step in and provide for doing justice to those persons who are thus denied equal protection.

Now if the second section of the pending bill can be so amended that it shall clearly define this offense, as I have described it, and shall employ no terms which assert the power of Congress to take jurisdiction of the subject until such denial be clearly made, and shall not in any way assume the original jurisdiction of the rights of private persons and of property within the States—with these conditions clearly expressed in the section, I shall give it my hearty support. These limitations will not impair the efficiency of the section, but will remove the serious objections that are entertained by many gentlemen to the section as it now stands.

I have made these criticisms, not merely for the purpose of securing such an amendment to the section, but because I am unwilling that the interpretation which some gentlemen have given of the constitutional powers of Congress shall stand as the uncontradicted history of this legislation. Amendments have been prepared which will remove the difficulties to which I have alluded; and I trust that my colleague [Mr. SHELLABARGER] and his committee will themselves accept and offer these amendments. I am sure my colleague will understand that I share all his anxiety for the passage of a proper bill. It is against a dangerous and unwarranted interpretation of the recent amendments to the Constitution that I feel bound to enter my protest.

Now, Mr. Speaker, I call the attention of the House to the third section of the bill. I am not clear as to the intention of the committee, but if I understand the language correctly, this section proposes to punish citizens of the United States for violating State laws. If this be the meaning of the provision, then whenever any person violates a State law the United States may assume jurisdiction of his offense. This would virtually abolish the administration of justice under State law. In so far as this section punishes persons who under color of any State law shall deny or refuse to others the equal protection of the laws, I give it my cheerful support; but when we provide by congressional enactment to punish a mere violation of a State law, we pass the line of constitutional authority.

SUSPENSION OF THE PRIVILEGES OF HABEAS CORPUS.

But, Mr. Speaker, there is one provision in the fourth section which appears to me both unwise and unnecessary. It is proposed not only to authorize the suspension of the privileges of the writ of *habeas corpus*, but to authorize the declaration of martial law in the disturbed districts.

I do not deny, but I affirm the right of Congress to authorize the suspension of the privileges of the writ of *habeas corpus* whenever in cases of rebellion or invasion the public safety may require it. Such action has been and may again be necessary to the safety of the Republic; but I call the attention of the House to the fact that never but once in the history of this Government has Congress suspended the great privileges of this writ, and then it was not done until after two years of war had closed all the ordinary tribunals of justice in the rebellious districts, and the great armies of the Union, extending from Maryland to the Mexican line, were engaged in a death-struggle with the armies of the rebellion. It was not until the 3d day of March, 1863, that the Congress of the United States found the situation so full of peril as to make it their duty to suspend this greatest privilege enjoyed by Anglo-Saxon people. Are we ready to say that an equal peril confronts us to-day?

My objection to authorizing this suspension implies no distrust of the wisdom or patriotism of the President. I do not believe he would employ this power were we to confer it upon him; and if he did employ it, I do not doubt he would use it with justice and wisdom. But what we do on this occasion will be quoted as a precedent hereafter, when other men with other purposes may desire to confer this power on another President for purposes that may not aid in securing public liberty and public peace.

But this section provides no safeguard for citizens who may be arrested during the suspension of the writ. There is no limit to the time during which men may be held as prisoners. Nothing in the section requires them to be delivered over to the courts. Nothing in it gives them any other protection than the will of the commander who orders their arrest.

The law of March 3, 1863, provided that whenever the privileges of the writ were suspended all persons arrested, other than prisoners of war, should be brought before the grand jury of some district or circuit court of the United States, and if no indictment should be found against them they must, on the discharge of the grand jury, be immediately discharged from arrest; and the officer who should detain any unindicted person beyond that limit was liable to fine and imprisonment.

Mr. SHELLABARGER. The bill refers it to the very law the gentleman cites; gives it to the operation of that law.

Mr. GARFIELD, of Ohio. My colleague is mistaken; the law of March 3, 1863, was a temporary act and expired with the rebellion. It is not contained in Brightly's Digest, and is no longer in force. Should the writ be suspended, I shall ask the House to reënact the second section of the law of 1863.

MARTIAL LAW.

But, sir, this fourth section goes a hundred bowshots further than any similar legislation of Congress during the wildest days of the rebellion. It authorizes the declaration of martial law. We are called upon to provide by law for the suspension of all law! Do gentlemen remember what martial law is? Refer to the digest of opinions of the Judge Advocate General of the United States, and you will find a terse definition which gleams like the flash of a sword-blade. The Judge Advocate says: "Martial law is the will of the general who commands the army." And Congress is here asked to declare martial law. Why, sir, it is the pride and boast of England that martial law has not existed in that country since the Petition of Right in the thirty-first year

of Charles II. Three years ago the lord chief justice of England
came down from the high court over which he was presiding
to review the charge of another judge to a grand jury, and he
there announced that the power to declare martial law no longer existed in England. In 1867, the same judge, in the case of
The Queen *vs.* Nelson, uttered this sentence:

> "There is no such law in existence as martial law, and no
> power in the Crown to proclaim it."

In a recent treatise entitled The Nation, a work of great
power and research, the author, Mr. Mulford, says:

> "The declaration of martial law, or the suspension of the
> *habeas corpus*, is the intermission of the ordinary course of
> law, and of the tribunals to which all appeal may be made. It
> places the locality included in its operations no longer under
> the government of law. It interrupts the process of rights and
> the procedure of courts and restricts the independence of civil
> administration. There is substituted for these the intention of
> the individual. To this there is in the civil order no formal lim-
> itation. In its immediate action it allows beyond itself no ob-
> ligation and acknowledges no responsibility. Its command or
> its decree is the only law; its movement may be secret, and its
> decisions are open to the inquiry of no judge and the investi-
> gation of no tribunal. There is no positive power which may
> act, or be called upon to act, to stay its caprice or to check its
> arbitrary career since judgment and execution are in its own
> command, and the normal action and administration is sus-
> pended and the organized force of the whole is subordinate to
> it."—*Pages* 185–6.

The Supreme Court, in *ex parte* Milligan, (4 Wallace, 124)
examined the doctrine that in time of war the commander of
an armed force has power within the lines of the military district to suspend all civil rights, and subject citizens as well as
soldiers to the rule of his will.

Mr. Justice Davis, who delivered the opinion of the court,
said:

> "If this position is sound to the extent claimed, then, when
> war exists, foreign or domestic, and the country is subdivided
> into military departments for mere convenience, the com-
> mander of one of them can, if he chooses, within his limits,

on the plea of necessity, with the approval of the Executive, substitute military force for and to the exclusion of the laws, and punish all persons as he thinks right and proper, without fixed or certain rules.

"The statement of this proposition shows its importance; for, if true, republican government is a failure, and there is an end of liberty regulated by law. Martial law established on such a basis destroys every guarantee of the Constitution, and effectually renders the 'military independent of and superior to the civil power;' the attempt to do which by the king of Great Britain was deemed by our fathers such an offense that they assigned it to the world as one of the causes which impelled them to declare their independence. Civil liberty and this kind of martial law cannot endure together; the antagonism is irreconcilable; and, in the conflict, one or the other must perish."

* * * * *

"Martial law cannot arise from a threatened invasion. The necessity must be actual and present; the invasion real, such as effectually closes the courts and deposes the civil administration."

* * * * *

"Martial rule can never exist where the courts are open and in the proper and unobstructed exercise of their jurisdiction. It is also confined to the locality of actual war."

The court was unanimous in the decree which was made in this case, though four of the judges dissented from some of the opinions expressed by the court. Yet these dissenting judges united in a declaration that martial law can only be authorized in time of war, and for the purpose of punishing crimes against the security and safety of the national forces. But no member of the court gave the least support to the proposition that martial law could be declared to punish citizens of the United States where the courts of the United States were open, and where war, by its flaming presence, has not made the administrations of justice difficult or impossible. The Chief Justice, who delivered the dissenting opinion, and in which all the dissenting judges concurred, said:

"Martial law proper is called into action by Congress, or temporarily, when the action of Congress cannot be invited, and in the case of justifying or excusing peril, by the President, in times of insurrection or invasion, or of civil or foreign war, within districts or localities, where ordinary law no longer adequately secures public safety and private rights.

"We think that the power of Congress, in such times and in such localities to authorize trial for crimes against the security and safety of the national forces, may be derived from its constitutional authority to raise and support armies and to declare war, if not from its constitutional authority to provide for governing the national forces."

I have quoted not only the opinion of the court, but that of the dissenting judges, for the purpose of exhibiting the unanimity of the court on the main questions relating to martial law. I cannot think that this House will, at this time, take such an extreme and unprecedented measure.

Sir, this provision means war, or it means nothing; and I ask this House whether we are now ready to take this step? Shall we "cry havoc and let slip the dogs of war?"

I have taken a humble part in one war, and I hope I shall always be ready to do any duty that the necessities of the country may require of me; but I am not willing to talk war or to declare war in advance of the terrible necessity. Are there no measures within our reach which may aid in preventing war? When a savage war lately threatened our western frontiers we sent out commissioners of peace in the hope of avoiding war. Have we done all in our power to avoid that which this section contemplates? I hope the committee will bring in a companion measure that looks toward peace and enable us to send the olive branch with the sword.

I hope this House will grant general amnesty to all except to those who held high official trust under the United States, and then breaking their oaths went into rebellion. We should enlist both the pride and the selfishness of the people on the side of good order and peace. But I remind gentlemen that we have not even an indication or suggestion from the President that such a remedy as this is needed; and yet we are called upon to authorize the suspension, not only of the great writ, but of all laws, and that, too, in advance of any actual necessity for it.

April 4, 1871

Maria Carter: Testimony to the Joint Select Committee

ATLANTA, GEORGIA, *October* 21, 1871.
MARIA CARTER (colored) sworn and examined.
By the CHAIRMAN:

Question. How old are you, where were you born, and where do you now live?

Answer. I will be twenty-eight years old on the 4th day of next March: I was born in South Carolina; and I live in Haralson County now.

Question. Are you married or single?

Answer. I am married.

Question. What is your husband's name?

Answer. Jasper Carter.

Question. Where were you on the night that John Walthall was shot?

Answer. In my house, next to his house; not more than one hundred yards from his house.

Question. Did any persons come to your house that night?

Answer. Yes, sir, lots of them; I expect about forty or fifty of them.

Question. What did they do at your house?

Answer. They just came there and called; we did not get up when they first called. We heard them talking as they got over the fence. They came hollering and knocking at the door, and they scared my husband so bad he could not speak when they first came. I answered them. They hollered, "Open the door." I said, "Yes, sir." They were at the other door, and they said, "Kindle a light." My husband went to kindle a light, and they busted both doors open and ran in—two in one door and two in the other. I heard the others coming on behind them, jumping over the fence in the yard. One put his gun down to him and said, "Is this John Walthall?" They had been hunting him a long time. They had gone to my brother-in-law's hunting him, and had whipped one of my sisters-in-law powerfully and two more men on account of him. They said they were going to kill him when they got hold of him. They asked my husband if he was John Walthall. He was so scared he could not say anything. I said, "No." I never got up at all. They asked where he was, and we told them he was up to the next house. They jerked my husband up and said that he had to go up there. I heard them up there hollering "Open the door," and I heard them break the door down. While they were talking about our house, just before they broke open our door, I heard a chair fall over in John Walthall's house. He raised a plank then and tried to get under the house. A parcel of them ran ahead and broke the door down and jerked his wife out of the bed. I did not see them, for I was afraid to go out of doors. They knocked his wife about powerfully. I heard them cursing her. She commenced hollering, and I heard some of them say, "God damn her, shoot her." They struck her over the head with a pistol. The house looked next morning as if somebody had been killing hogs there. Some of them said, "Fetch a light here, quick;" and some of them said to her, "Hold a light." They said she held it, and they put their guns down on him and shot him. I heard him holler, and some of them said, "Pull him out, pull him out." When they pulled him out the hole was too small, and I heard them jerk a plank part off the house and I heard it fly back. At that time four men came in my house and drew a gun on me; I was sitting in my bed and the baby was yelling. They asked, "Where is John Walthall?" I said, "Up yonder." They said, "Who lives here?" I said, "Jasper Carter." They said, "Where is John Walthall?" I said, "Them folks have got him." They said, "What folks?" I said, "Them folks up there." They came in and out all the time. I heard John holler when they commenced whipping him. They said, "Don't holler, or we'll kill you in a minute." I undertook to try and count, but they scared me so bad that I stopped counting; but I think they hit him about three hundred licks after they shot him. I heard them clear down to our house ask him if he felt like sleeping with some more white women; and they said, "You steal, too, God damn you." John said, "No, sir." They said, "Hush your mouth, God damn your eyes, you do steal." I heard them talking, but that was all I heard plain. They beat him powerfully. She said they made her put her arms around his neck and then they whipped them both together. I saw where they struck her head with a pistol and bumped her head against the house, and the blood is there yet. They asked me where my husband's gun was; I said he had no gun, and they said I was a damned liar. One of them had a sort of gown on, and he put his gun in my face and I pushed it up. The other said, "Don't you shoot her." He then went and looked in a trunk among the things. I allowed they were hunting for a pistol. My husband had had one, but he sold it. Another said, "Let's go away from here." They brought in old Uncle Charlie and sat him down there. They had a light at the time, and I got to see some of them good. I knew two of them, but the others I could not tell. There was a very large light in the house, and they went to the fire and I saw them. They came there at about 12 o'clock and staid there until 1. They went on back to old Uncle Charley's then, to whip his girls and his wife. They did not whip her any to hurt her at all. They jabbed me on the head with a gun, and I heard the trigger pop. It scared me and I throwed my hand up. He put it back again, and I pushed it away again.

Question. How old was your baby?

Answer. Not quite three weeks old.

Question. You were still in bed?

Answer. Yes, sir; I never got up at all.

Question. Did they interrupt your husband in any way?

Answer. Yes, sir; they whipped him mightily; I do not know how much. They took him away up the road, over a quarter, I expect. I saw the blood running down when he came back. Old Uncle Charley was in there. They did not carry him back home. They said, "Old man, you don't steal." He said, "No." They sat him down and said to him, "You just stay here." Just as my husband got back to one door and stepped in, three men came in the other door. They left a man at John's house while they were ripping around. As they came back by the house they said, "By God, goodbye, hallelujah!" I was scared nearly to death, and my husband tried to keep it hid from me. I asked him if he had been whipped much. He said, "No." I saw his clothes were bloody, and the next morning they stuck to him, and his shoulder was almost like jelly.

Question. Did you know this man who drew his gun on you?

Answer. Yes, sir.

Question. Who was he?

Answer. Mr. Finch.

Question. Where does he live?

Answer. I reckon about three miles off. I was satisfied I knew him and Mr. Booker.

Question. Were they considered men of standing and property in that country?

Answer. Yes, sir; Mr. Finch is married into a pretty well-off family. He is a good liver, but he is not well off himself.

Question. How is it with Mr. Booker?

Answer. I do not know so much about him. He is not very well off.

Question. How with the Monroes?

Answer. They are pretty well-off folks, about as well off as there are in Haralson. They have a mill.

By Mr. BAYARD:

Question. You said they had been looking a long time for John Walthall?

Answer. Yes, sir.

Question. Had they been charging John with sleeping with white women?

Answer. Yes, sir; and the people where he staid had charged him with it. He had been charged with it ever since the second year after I came to Haralson. I have been there four years this coming Christmas.

Question. That was the cause of their going after him and making this disturbance?

Answer. Yes, sir; that was it. We all knew he was warned to leave them long before he was married. His wife did not know anything about it. When he first came there he was staying among some white women down there.

Question. Do you mean living with them and sleeping with them?

Answer. He was staying in the house where they were.

Question. White women?

Answer. Yes, sir.

Question. Were they women of bad character?

Answer. Yes, sir; worst kind.

Question. What were their names?

Answer. They were named Keyes.

Question. How many were there?

Answer. There were four sisters of them, and one of them was old man Martin's wife.

Question. Were they low white people?

Answer. Yes, sir.

Question. Had John lived with them for a long while?

Answer. Yes, sir. They had threatened him and been there after him. They had gone there several times to run them off. My house was not very far from them, and I heard them down there throwing rocks.

Question. Was it well known among you that John had been living with these low white women?

Answer. Yes, sir.

Question. Did he keep it up after he was married?

Answer. No, sir; he quit before he was married. I heard that a white woman said he came along there several times last year and said he could not get rid of them to save his life.

Question. Did John go with any other white women?

Answer. No, sir; not that I know of.

Question. Was he accused by the Ku-Klux of going with any of them?

Answer. They did not tell him write down their names. I heard them say, "Do you feel like sleeping with any more white women?" and I knew who they were.

By the CHAIRMAN:

Question. These women, you say, were a low-down class of persons?

Answer. Yes, sir; not counted at all.

Question. Did white men associate with them?

Answer. It was said they did.

Question. Did respectable white men go there?

Answer. Some of them did. Mr. Stokes did before he went to Texas, and several of the others around there. I do not know many men in Georgia any way; I have not been about much. I have heard a heap of names of those who used to go there. I came by there one night, and I saw three men there myself.

Question. You say John Walthall had been going there a good while?

Answer. Yes, sir; that is what they say.

Question. How long had he quit before they killed him?

Answer. A year before last, a while before Christmas. He

was still staying at old man Martin's. I staid last year close to Carroll, and when I came back he had quit.

Question. Did he go with them any more after he married?

Answer. No, sir; he staid with his wife all the time. He lived next to me.

Question. How long had he been married before he was killed?

Answer. They married six weeks before Christmas, and he was killed on the 22d of April.

Question. Did they charge your husband with going after any white women?

Answer. No, sir; I never heard them say anything to him at all. The next morning I asked him what they whipped him for. He said they told him that he stole corn from old man Monroe. He staid at Monroe's a year and a half—so I was told; I do not know. People said that Monroe never paid him anything.

Question. How long before this was he living at old man Monroe's?

Answer. We have been married four years, and it was before we were married. I think it was the second year after he was free.

Question. Were any of these men along that night who had been going to see these low women?

Answer. I do not know; I heard that Mr. Murphy's sister said that he was in the crowd that night—his little sister—and I know he used to go there.

Question. Is he one of those who have gone to Texas?

Answer. No, sir.

By Mr. BAYARD:

Question. You know that because somebody told you so?

Answer. Yes, sir; that much. I do not know it myself; I heard some one else say it.

Horace Greeley: Reply to Committee of the Liberal Republican Convention

NEW YORK, May 20, 1872.

Gentlemen: I have chosen not to acknowledge your letter of the 3d inst. until I could learn how the work of your Convention was received in all parts of our great country, and judge whether that work was approved and ratified by the mass of our fellow-citizens. Their response has from day to day reached me through telegrams, letters, and the comments of journalists independent of official patronage, and indifferent to the smiles or frowns of power. The number and character of these unconstrained, unpurchased, unsolicited utterances satisfy me that the movement which found expression at Cincinnati has received stamp of public approval, and been hailed by a majority of our countrymen as the harbinger of a better day for the Republic.

I do not misinterpret this approval as especially complimentary to myself, nor even to the chivalrous and justly esteemed gentleman with whose name I thank your Convention for associating mine. I receive and welcome it as a spontaneous and deserved tribute to that admirable Platform of principles, wherein your Convention so tersely, so lucidly, so forcibly, set forth the convictions which impelled, and the purposes which guided its course—a Platform which, casting behind it the wreck and rubbish of worn-out contentions and by-gone feuds, embodies in fit and few words the needs and aspirations of To-Day. Though thousands stand ready to condemn your every act, hardly a syllable of criticism or cavil has been aimed at your Platform, of which the substance may be fairly epitomized as follows:

I. All the political rights and franchises which have been acquired through our late bloody convulsion must and shall be guaranteed, maintained, enjoyed, respected, evermore.

II. All the political rights and franchises which have been lost through that convulsion should and must be promptly restored and reestablished, so that there shall be henceforth no proscribed class and no disfranchised caste within the limits of our Union, whose long estranged people shall reunite and fraternize upon the broad basis of Universal Amnesty with Impartial Suffrage.

III. That, subject to our solemn constitutional obligation to maintain the equal rights of all citizens, our policy should aim at local self-government, and not at centralization; that the civil authority should be supreme over the military; that the writ of habeas corpus should be jealously upheld as the safeguard of personal freedom; that the individual citizen should enjoy the largest liberty consistent with public order; and that there shall be no Federal subversion of the internal polity of the several States and municipalities, but that each shall be left free to enforce the rights and promote the well-being of its inhabitants by such means as the judgment of its own people shall prescribe.

IV. There shall be a real and not merely a simulated Reform in the Civil Service of the Republic; to which end it is indispensable that the chief dispenser of its vast official patronage shall be shielded from the main temptation to use his power selfishly by a rule inexorably forbidding and precluding his re-election.

V. That the raising of Revenue, whether by Tariff or otherwise, shall be recognized and treated as the People's immediate business, to be shaped and directed by them through their Representatives in Congress, whose action thereon the President must neither overrule by his veto, attempt to dictate, nor presume to punish, by bestowing office only on those who agree with him, or withdrawing it from those who do not.

VI. That the Public Lands must be sacredly reserved for occupation and acquisition by cultivators, and not recklessly squandered on the projectors of Railroads for which our people have no present need, and the premature construction of which is annually plunging us into deeper and deeper abysses of foreign indebtedness.

VII. That the achievement of these grand purposes of universal beneficence is expected and sought at the hands of all who approve them, irrespective of past affiliations.

VIII. That the public faith must at all hazards be maintained, and the National credit preserved.

IX. That the patriotic devotedness and inestimable services of our fellow-citizens who, as soldiers or sailors, upheld the flag and maintained the unity of the Republic shall ever be gratefully remembered and honorably requited.

These propositions, so ably and forcibly presented in the Platform of your Convention, have already fixed the attention and commanded the assent of a large majority of our countrymen, who joyfully adopt them, as I do, as the bases of a true, beneficent National Reconstruction—of a New Departure from jealousies, strifes, and hates, which have no longer adequate motive or even plausible pretext, into an atmosphere of Peace, Fraternity, and Mutual Good Will. In vain do the drill-sergeants of decaying organizations flourish menacingly their truncheons and angrily insist that the files shall be closed and straightened; in vain do the whippers-in of parties once vital, because rooted in the vital needs of the hour, protest against straying and bolting, denounce men nowise their inferiors as traitors and renegades, and threaten them with infamy and ruin. I am confident that the American People have already made your cause their own, fully resolved that their brave hearts and strong arms shall bear it on to triumph. In this faith, and with the distinct understanding that, if elected, I shall be the President, not of a party, but of the whole People, I accept your nomination, in the confident trust that the masses of our countrymen, North and South, are eager to clasp hands across the bloody chasm which has too long divided them, forgetting that they have been enemies in the joyful consciousness that they are and must henceforth remain brethren.

> Yours, gratefully,
> HORACE GREELEY.

Frederick Douglass:
Speech at New York City

Frederick Douglass was next introduced, and spoke as follows:

FELLOW-CITIZENS: For the first time in the history of this Republic, the whole body of colored citizens will have the right to vote for a President of the United States in November. They are not only men but freemen, not only freemen but citizens of the Republic and men among men.

The people of this country are composed of different nations and races, but no race in the United States have as much at stake in the present election as we who have been so recently invested with the rights of manhood and citizenship. The rights of all others have been secured and confirmed by time and practice. No power in the country is tempted to interfere with or in any manner abridge such rights. With us the case is different. We are still a hated caste, and motives stand thick through all the land for compassing our degradation. The master class at the South is not yet reconciled, and there are many in the North who sympathize with them. Hence, though we are now free and legally enfranchised, though we are equal before the law with all other citizens, we have reasons for special vigilance and exertion in order to hold and exercise the rights so recently secured to us as a class.

As a general rule, I deprecate all appeals to classes for political purposes. The time is not distant when all classes will be merged in a common citizenship, and when to be an American citizen will be sufficient to insure respect in every part of the country and among all classes of the American people; but that time has not yet come, and until it does come, we are almost compelled to act as a class to exert our proper influence. We are, in some measure, on trial before our country and the world, and thoughtful men are everywhere watching and studying our deportment in the exercise of the high trust with which we are now invested.

It was once said that the negro does not know enough to vote, and this was the only decent ground upon which our right to vote was denied and withheld.

I am sorry to say that some of our number—only a very few—men who have more learning than common sense, have been making concessions to this degrading idea. They have been writing to Mr. Sumner and sundry other white gentlemen in different parts of the country to tell them how to vote.

Now, if we colored people are so destitute of sense and political sagacity as to ask the white people how we shall vote, it might be well to confine all voting to the white people, and thus save the trouble and expense of counting our votes at all.

Now, gentlemen, if any of our people are confused and bewildered, and do not know how to vote in the approaching election, or if any class of the American people have doubts of our ability to form intelligent opinions of public men, parties, principles, and measures, I hope the proceedings of this meeting may be made useful to them. The colored citizens of New-England have already spoken in Faneuil Hall, and their word has gone over the whole country. The colored citizens of New-York will have a not less universal hearing, nor be less potent in point of right influence.

Fellow-citizens, while we are deeply interested in maintaining the present financial and foreign policy of the Government which has given to our country credit, prosperity and peace; while we are touched by the humanity of the Administration toward the Indians, and commend its wisdom; while we, in common with other citizens, desire light taxation and an honest administration of the Government, the chief and all commanding interest which all feel in the contest, is found in its bearing upon the great questions of human liberty and equality. Here it touches us deeply, and is a matter of supreme concern. To the millions of our color at the South it is vastly more important than to us. It is, in effect, a thing of peace and war, of order and disorder, of life and death, if not of liberty and slavery. It, in fact, involves the maintenance of all the progress made during the last dozen years, and the inauguration of a process of reaction, which may land our race into a condition only a little better than the bondage and degradation of ages from which we have just begun to emerge.

I know that this statement of the issues involved is stoutly denied by one party to this canvass, and no doubt honestly denied, but you and I know that there is such a thing as being honestly wrong. Hell is said to be paved with good intentions.

The political canvass before us is indeed a very peculiar one. There is nothing like it in the past, and I hope there may never be anything like it in the future. To outward seeming we have two political parties seeking to possess the Government, while professing substantially the same principles and commending their candidates for the same noble qualities and dispositions. Two parties and one platform. It is this seeming agreement which leads to confusion, and would almost deceive the very elect. We have no longer an honest fight between armies under their own respective colors, battling for their own honestly-cherished objects, but a war under the same flags, between armies in the same uniforms, and professing the same objects.

The best illustration of the political contest now proceeding is found in our late war for the Union. You will remember that neither party to that conflict was willing to declare its true object. The South said it was not fighting for slavery, and the North said it was not fighting against slavery; and yet they were fighting hard and everybody who had any brains knew at the time that the two were really fighting about slavery, and that one was for it and the other was against it.

If we were left to find the path of duty simply by the light of professions and platforms, and by the men we find on the one side and on the other, we might possibly be misled; but happily we are dependent upon no such deceptive guides. There is such a thing as history, and the parties to this canvass have their respective histories. All the present rests upon all the past. You cannot divorce today from yesterday, nor this year from last year. In front of us today we have the same old enemy, the same old snake in a new skin, the same old Democratic Party, thinly veneered by a scale torn off the Republican Party. The wolf is all the more dangerous because of his white coat.

It is said that they have changed, that they have reformed; and yet you learn here to-night, from the words of the leading traitor of the South, that he is not ashamed of the lost cause. There is great talk about reconciliation; it is said that we must forget and forgive. We have heard a great deal of religion preached lately about our Southern brethren and the Democratic Party. It is said to have been converted. [Laughter.] But I am a little incredulous—some would say sceptical—about this matter. Conversion is a great fact, even in the individual, but when 2,900,000 men are suddenly converted, a fact of that kind, it seems to me, requires a good deal of evidence to support it. The largest number I ever heard of being converted in a single day was three thousand, and that was on the day of Pentecost. [Applause and laughter.] For my part, I have learned this in the case of individuals: They usually remember the time when and the place where their dungeon shook; when their feet were taken out of the mire and clay and set upon a rock; but thus far the Democratic Party have been unable to tell me when, where, how, and under whose preaching this great conversion has taken place. Where I have been they were talking of the Prodigal Son, but here in New-York, perhaps, they don't care much about the Prodigal Son. [Laughter.] Between the two—between the Democratic Party and the Prodigal Son—there are certainly some points of resemblance. For instance: He was hungry. [Loud laughter and applause.] He seems to have been from home for about twelve years, and to have had little or nothing to eat all the time, so that he would even fain have filled himself with the husks that the swine did eat. But when he saw his father he said: "Father, I have sinned before heaven and in thy sight, and am no more worthy to be called thy servant." Now, this was humility, and it is there that the parallel ceases. [Applause.] He did not come home to drive out the elder son, but only wanted to be made a servant in his father's house. It is here, as I said, that the analogy ceases. The Democratic Party does not come home in that spirit, after having spent our substance, wasted our wealth, piled up a mountain of debt. Well, I did not come here to argue or to expound. I have doubts about the sincerity of this Democratic conversion. For one, I don't think it will be safe to trust to that conversion just yet. I am willing to receive the Prodigal Son, but I would keep him in a subordinate position for a little time longer. Let us imitate the wisdom of our Methodist brethren and take the Democrats on probation. [Applause and laughter.] I have an appeal to make to you on behalf of my race. There are millions of them who are to-night like chickens under a fence when the scream of the hawk is heard in the air. In this anxious state they are afraid of the shadow—of the adumbration of a possibility of the reinstatement of the old master class to power in the Southern States, and I am here to-night to ask you for four years more of the beneficent rule of the Republican Party, and four years more of the steady, unimpassioned, eagle-eyed, clear, steady, firm-nerved little man—Ulysses S. Grant. [Enthusiastic applause.] When you felt the earth crumbling beneath your feet, when the fate of the Republic trembled in the balance, oh, then, in your extremity you called upon the black man to reach out his black, iron arm. [Applause.] Also they came 200,000 strong; and from that hour the tide of battle turned. We don't say we put down the rebellion, but we helped to put it down, and so incurred the heavy displeasure of the master-class at the South. And that displeasure is not now passed. We are unable to meet it without your help. The only thing that stops the bloody arm of the Kuklux to-night is Ulysses S. Grant. [Loud applause.] Keep him there. [Voices—We will.] I am not here to abuse Horace Greeley. I have known him well and long, and have loved him much, but he is in very bad company. My friends say, Why, Mr. Douglass, are you going to desert Horace Greeley? I answer, No, but Horace Greeley has deserted us. It is like the story of Paddy when he landed in the United States and first resolved to ride a mule. He knew nothing of the use of a saddle and still less of that of the stirrups. Well, he mounted the mule, but disdained to use the stirrups. Using a stick, he made the mule begin to gallop, and as the animal dashed along the stirrups struck his sides and caused him to rush madly on, nearly unseating Paddy. By and by the mule got one of his hind legs in the stirrup, which being observed by Paddy, he shouted: "Be jabers, if yez is going to get on, it is time for me to get off." [Laughter.] Now, as the Democratic Party has begun to mount Horace, it is time for me to get off Horace. [Loud applause.] It is a remarkable evidence of the intelligent instincts of the colored people of the South, and shows how wisely they have selected in this matter, when it is known that, notwithstanding all the blandishments, they can see that with Horace Greeley in power the old master is again brought back into power, while with Grant in power liberty and equality prevails throughout the land. [Loud applause.]

But I have spoken of the Democratic platform as in substance the same as the Republican platform. In this I have been too liberal to our adversaries, and less than just to our friends. The Democratic platform was doubtless intended to bear a Republican construction, and to seem like the genuine article, but it is, in fact and in effect, as opposed to it as freedom is to slavery. There are three or four little words in it, put in for a purpose which makes it a political document of the most dangerous and destructive kind. As on a railroad, you have only to move the switch a single inch, and the train is taken from the true track and hurled over the embankment, killing and maiming the passengers. So here we have one or two little words which change the whole direction of the country from safety to ruin, and from liberty to slavery. The Cincinnati Democratic platform declares itself opposed to reopening the questions settled by the Thirteenth, Fourteenth and Fifteenth Amendments. In another place it declares for "local self-government with impartial suffrage," as against national protection and universal suffrage.

Now, first: I object to the word "settled." It leaves room for certain men to deny, as Mr. Black, of Pennsylvania, does deny, that anything was settled by those amendments. Nothing is, or can be settled by fraud; and the Democratic party has again and again declared these amendments frauds and unconstitutional. But the most objectionable and most dangerous feature of this Democratic platform is its denial of the right of the National Government to protect the liberties of its citizens in the States, and its declaration in favor of impartial suffrage against universal suffrage. Under these two doctrines the whole body of liberty as contained in the several amendments of the Constitution may be undermined, subverted and destroyed. They point out the two ways in which those amendments may be evaded and made of non-effect. By the one they may limit suffrage, and by the other they may strip the freedmen and their friends of national protection.

But we are told by our friends of the Greeley persuasion that our fears are groundless; that the Thirteenth, Fourteenth and

Fifteenth Amendments are now a part of the Constitution, and there is no power to take them out of the Constitution.

Alas! this assurance is little better than a mockery: constitutions do not execute themselves. We have had justice enough in our Constitution from the beginning to have made slavery impossible. The trouble never was in the Constitution, but in the administration of the Constitution. All experience shows that laws are of little value in the hands of those unfriendly to their objects.

Besides, the very essence of the Thirteenth, Fourteenth, and Fifteenth Amendments is in the grant of power to Congress to enforce them by "appropriate legislation." Without legislation these provisions may be evaded and practically rendered null and void. Now, what hope have we that a Democratic Congress will enforce these provisions by appropriate legislation?

But let us look at the workings of the Constitution. Under that instrument it would appear that oppression of an American citizen would be impossible in any of the States; that the citizen of New-York would be as safe in South Carolina as in New-York; yet we well know that until within the last few years the free liberty of a Northern man was impossible in the South. I, therefore, as a black man first, as a man next, and as a newly-born citizen of the United States—a citizenship beyond all others on the globe—as such a citizen I ask you, one and all, to exert every faculty to retain in power that party which has made the country glorious before the world, if you want the country prosperous. I now ask you, if you desire success, to give three hearty, rousing cheers for Ulysses S. Grant, and if you wish to do so, follow me. Hip, hip, hip. [As he thus spoke he waved his handkerchief three times, each wave eliciting a thundering cheer that made the walls ring. At the end of the last, three additional cheers were given for Douglass.]

The Chairman then announced that the meeting stood adjourned until next Wednesday, when other speakers would be present, and by which time Horace Greeley would furnish them plenty of new texts to speak upon.

September 25, 1872

James S. Pike: South Carolina Prostrate

THE STATE UNDER A NEGRO GOVERNMENT.

A BLACK LEGISLATURE—HUMILIATION OF THE WHITES
—THEIR SUBJECTION COMPLETE AND HOPELESS.

[FROM AN OCCASIONAL CORRESPONDENT OF THE TRIBUNE.]

COLUMBIA, S. C., Feb. 20.—This town, the capital of South Carolina, is charmingly situated in the heart of the upland country, near the geographical center of the State. It has broad, open streets, regularly laid out, and fine, shady residences, in and about the town. The opportunity for rides and drives can hardly be surpassed. There are good animals and good turn-outs to be seen on the streets at all times, and now, in midwinter, the weather invites to such displays. It seems there was a little real Winter here at Christmas and New Year's, when the whole country suffered such an excess of sudden cold. There was even skating and sleighing for a week. But now there is no frost, and the recollection of it is dispelled by the genial Spring weather that prevails.

Yesterday about 4 P. M. the assembled wisdom of the State, whose achievements are illustrated on that theater, issued forth from the State-house. About three-quarters of the crowd belonged to the African race. They were of every hue from the light octoroon to the deep black. They were such a looking body of men as might pour out of a market-house or a court-house at random in any Southern State. Every negro type and physiognomy were here to be seen, from the genteel serving man to the rough-hewn customer from the rice or cotton field. Their dress was as varied as their countenances. There was the second-hand black frock coat of infirm gentility, glossy and threadbare. There was the stove-pipe hat of many ironings and departed styles. There was also to be seen a total disregard of the proprieties of costume in the coarse and dirty garments of the field; the slub jackets and slouch hats of soiling labor. In some instances, rough woolen comforters embraced the neck and hid the absence of linen. Heavy brogans and short, torn trowsers it was impossible to hide. The dusky tide flowed out into the littered and barren grounds, and, issuing through the coarse wooden fence of the inclosure, melted away into the street beyond. These were the legislators of South Carolina.

A CULTURED SOCIETY OVERTURNED.

In conspicuous bas-relief over the door of exit, on the panels of the stately edifice, the marble visages of George McDuffie and Robert Y. Hayne overlooked the scene. Could they veritably witness it from their dread abode? What then? "I tremble," said Jefferson, in the opening scenes of American Independence, "I tremble when I reflect that God is just." But did any of that old band of Southern revolutionary patriots who wrestled in their souls with the curse of Slavery ever contemplate such a descent into barbarism as this spectacle implied and typified? "My God, look at this!" was the unbidden ejaculation of a low-country planter, clad in homespun, as he leaned over the rail inside the House, gazing excitedly upon the body in session. "This is the first time I have been here. I thought I knew what we were doing when we consented to emancipation. I knew the negro and I predicted much that has happened, but I never thought it would come to this. Let me go."

Here then is the outcome, the ripe, perfected fruit of the boasted civilization of the South, after two hundred years of experience. A white community, that had gradually risen from small beginnings, till it grew into wealth, culture, and refinement, and became accomplished in all the arts of civilization; that successfully asserted its resistance to a foreign tyranny by deeds of conspicuous valor; which achieved liberty and independence through the fire and tempest of civil war, and illustrated itself in the councils of the nation by orators and statesmen worthy of any age or nation; such a community is then reduced to this. It lies prostrate in the dust, ruled over by this strange conglomerate, gathered from the ranks of its own servile population. It is the spectacle of a society suddenly turned bottom side up. The wealth, the intelligence, the culture, the wisdom of the State, have broken through the crust of that social volcano on which they were contentedly reposing, and have sunk out of sight, consumed by the subterranean fires they had with such temerity braved and defied.

THE BLACK HOUSE IN SESSION.

In the place of this old aristocratic society stands the rude form of the most ignorant democracy that mankind ever saw, invested with the functions of government. It is the dregs of the population habilitated in the robes of their intelligent pre-decessors, and asserting over them the rule of ignorance and corruption, through the inexorable machinery of a majority of numbers. It is barbarism overwhelming civilization by physical force. It is the slave rioting in the halls of his master, and put-ting that master under his feet. And though it is done without malice and without vengeance, it is nevertheless none the less completely and absolutely done. Let us approach nearer and take a closer view. We will enter the House of Representatives. Here sit 124 members. Of these, 23 are white men, represent-ing the remains of the old civilization. These are good-looking, substantial citizens. They are men of weight and standing in the communities they represent. They are all from the hill country. The frosts of sixty and seventy Winters whiten the heads of some among them. There they sit, grim and silent. They feel themselves to be but loose stones, thrown in to partially ob-struct a current they are powerless to resist. They say little and do little as the days go by. They simply watch the rising tide, and mark the progressive steps of the inundation. They hold their places reluctantly. They feel themselves to be in some sort martyrs, bound stoically to suffer in behalf of that still great element in the State whose prostrate fortunes are becoming the sport of an unpitying fate. Grouped in a corner of the commodious and well-furnished chamber, they stolidly survey the noisy riot that goes on in the great black Left and Center, where the business and debates of the House are conducted, and where sit the strange and extraordinary guides of the for-tunes of a once proud and haughty State. In this crucial trial of his pride, his manhood, his prejudices, his spirit, it must be said of the Southern Bourbon of the Legislature that he comports himself with a dignity, a reserve, and a decorum that command admiration. He feels that the iron hand of destiny is upon him. He is gloomy, disconsolate, hopeless. The gray heads of this generation openly profess that they look for no relief. They see no way of escape. The recovery of influence, of position, of control in the State, is by them felt to be impossible. They accept their position with a stoicism that promises no reward here or hereafter. They are the types of a conquered race. They staked all and lost all. Their lives remain, their property and their children do not. War, emancipation, and grinding taxation have consumed them. Their struggle now is against complete confiscation. They endure and wait for the night.

This dense negro crowd they confront, do the debating, the squabbling, the law-making, and create all the clamor and disorder of the body. These 23 white men are but the observers, the enforced auditors of the dull and clumsy imitation of a deliberative body, whose appearance in their present capacity is at once a wonder and a shame to modern civilization.

THE LOOKS OF THE MEMBERS.

Deducting the 23 members referred to, who comprise the entire strength of the opposition, we find 101 remaining. Of this 101, 94 are colored, and seven are their white allies. Thus the blacks outnumber the whole body of whites in the House more than three to one. On the mere basis of numbers in the State the injustice of this disproportion is manifest, since the black population in the State is relatively four to three of the whites. A just rectification of the disproportion, on the basis of population merely, would give 54 whites to 70 black members. And the line of race very nearly marks the line of hostile politics. As things stand, the body is almost literally a Black Parliament, and it is the only one on the face of the earth that is the representative of a white constituency and the professed exponent of an advanced type of modern civilization. But the reader will find almost any portraiture inadequate to give a vivid idea of the body and enable him to comprehend the complete metamorphosis of the South Carolina Legislature without observing its details. The Speaker is black, the Clerk is black, the doorkeepers are black, the little pages are black, the chairman of the Ways and Means is black, and the chaplain is coal black. At some of the desks sit colored men whose types it would be hard to find outside of Congo; whose costume, visages, attitudes, and expression only befit the forecastle of a buccaneer. It must be remembered also that this whole body of men, with not more than half a dozen exceptions, were themselves slaves, and their ancestors have been slaves for generations. Recollecting the report of the famous schooner Wanderer, fitted out by a Southern slaveholder twelve or fifteen years ago, in ostentatious defiance of the laws against the slave trade, and whose owner and master boasted of having brought a cargo of slaves from Africa and safely landed them in South Carolina and Georgia, one thinks it must be true, and that some of these representatives are the very men then stolen from their African homes. If this be so, we will not now quarrel over their presence. It would be one of those extraordinary coincidences that would of itself almost seem to justify the belief of the direct interference of the hand of Providence in the affairs of men.

J. S. P.

New-York Tribune, March 29, 1873

Ulysses S. Grant:
Second Inaugural Address

FELLOW-CITIZENS: Under Providence I have been called a second time to act as Executive over this great nation. It has been my endeavor in the past to maintain all the laws, and, so far as lay in my power, to act for the best interests of the whole people. My best efforts will be given in the same direction in the future, aided, I trust, by my four years' experience in the office.

When my first term of the office of Chief Executive began, the country had not recovered from the effects of a great internal revolution, and three of the former States of the Union had not been restored to their Federal relations.

It seemed to me wise that no new questions should be raised so long as that condition of affairs existed. Therefore the past four years, so far as I could control events, have been consumed in the effort to restore harmony, public credit, commerce, and all the arts of peace and progress. It is my firm conviction that the civilized world is tending toward republicanism, or government by the people through their chosen representatives, and that our own great Republic is destined to be the guiding star to all others.

Under our Republic we support an army less than that of any European power of any standing and a navy less than that of either of at least five of them. There could be no extension of territory on the continent which would call for an increase of this force, but rather might such extension enable us to diminish it.

The theory of government changes with general progress. Now that the telegraph is made available for communicating thought, together with rapid transit by steam, all parts of a continent are made contiguous for all purposes of government, and communication between the extreme limits of the country made easier than it was throughout the old thirteen States at the beginning of our national existence.

The effects of the late civil strife have been to free the slave and make him a citizen. Yet he is not possessed of the civil rights which citizenship should carry with it. This is wrong,

440

and should be corrected. To this correction I stand committed, so far as Executive influence can avail.

Social equality is not a subject to be legislated upon, nor shall I ask that anything be done to advance the social status of the colored man, except to give him a fair chance to develop what there is good in him, give him access to the schools, and when he travels let him feel assured that his conduct will regulate the treatment and fare he will receive.

The States lately at war with the General Government are now happily rehabilitated, and no Executive control is exercised in any one of them that would not be exercised in any other State under like circumstances.

In the first year of the past Administration the proposition came up for the admission of Santo Domingo as a Territory of the Union. It was not a question of my seeking, but was a proposition from the people of Santo Domingo, and which I entertained. I believe now, as I did then, that it was for the best interest of this country, for the people of Santo Domingo, and all concerned that the proposition should be received favorably. It was, however, rejected constitutionally, and therefore the subject was never brought up again by me.

In future, while I hold my present office, the subject of acquisition of territory must have the support of the people before I will recommend any proposition looking to such acquisition. I say here, however, that I do not share in the apprehension held by many as to the danger of governments becoming weakened and destroyed by reason of their extension of territory. Commerce, education, and rapid transit of thought and matter by telegraph and steam have changed all this. Rather do I believe that our Great Maker is preparing the world, in His own good time, to become one nation, speaking one language, and when armies and navies will be no longer required.

My efforts in the future will be directed to the restoration of good feeling between the different sections of our common country; to the restoration of our currency to a fixed value as compared with the world's standard of values—gold—and, if possible, to a par with it; to the construction of cheap routes of transit throughout the land, to the end that the products of all may find a market and leave a living remuneration to the producer; to the maintenance of friendly relations with all our neighbors and with distant nations; to the reestablishment of our commerce and share in the carrying trade upon the ocean; to the encouragement of such manufacturing industries as can be economically pursued in this country, to the end that the exports of home products and industries may pay for our imports—the only sure method of returning to and permanently maintaining a specie basis; to the elevation of labor; and, by a humane course, to bring the aborigines of the country under the benign influences of education and civilization. It is either this or war of extermination. Wars of extermination, engaged in by people pursuing commerce and all industrial pursuits, are expensive even against the weakest people, and are demoralizing and wicked. Our superiority of strength and advantages of civilization should make us lenient toward the Indian. The wrong inflicted upon him should be taken into account and the balance placed to his credit. The moral view of the question should be considered and the question asked, Can not the Indian be made a useful and productive member of society by proper teaching and treatment? If the effort is made in good faith, we will stand better before the civilized nations of the earth and in our own consciences for having made it.

All these things are not to be accomplished by one individual, but they will receive my support and such recommendations to Congress as will in my judgment best serve to carry them into effect. I beg your support and encouragement.

It has been, and is, my earnest desire to correct abuses that have grown up in the civil service of the country. To secure this reformation rules regulating methods of appointment and promotions were established and have been tried. My efforts for such reformation shall be continued to the best of my judgment. The spirit of the rules adopted will be maintained.

I acknowledge before this assemblage, representing, as it does, every section of our country, the obligation I am under to my countrymen for the great honor they have conferred on me by returning me to the highest office within their gift, and the further obligation resting on me to render to them the best services within my power. This I promise, looking forward with the greatest anxiety to the day when I shall be released from responsibilities that at times are almost overwhelming, and from which I have scarcely had a respite since the eventful firing upon Fort Sumter, in April, 1861, to the present day. My services were then tendered and accepted under the first call for troops growing out of that event.

I did not ask for place or position, and was entirely without influence or the acquaintance of persons of influence, but was resolved to perform my part in a struggle threatening the very existence of the nation. I performed a conscientious duty, without asking promotion or command, and without a revengeful feeling toward any section or individual.

Notwithstanding this, throughout the war, and from my candidacy for my present office in 1868 to the close of the last Presidential campaign, I have been the subject of abuse and slander scarcely ever equaled in political history, which to-day I feel that I can afford to disregard in view of your verdict, which I gratefully accept as my vindication.

March 4, 1873

THE END OF
RECONSTRUCTION
1873–1877

❦

Grant's reelection proved at best to be a temporary respite from the challenges posed by Reconstruction. While the fall contest itself was fairly peaceful, disputes over election returns in Louisiana and Arkansas plagued Republicans and promised renewed violence, with the most vivid example happening on Easter Sunday, April 13, 1873, in Colfax, Louisiana, where at least seventy-one African Americans were slaughtered in cold blood by a white supremacist militia. Congressional corruption scandals tainted the Republican triumph and distracted lawmakers from their duties, while in September 1873 a major financial panic led to a severe economic depression that persisted for years.

Nor was the news any better the following year. Violence escalated throughout the South in 1874, bringing down Republican regimes in several states. A federal circuit court decision in the Colfax massacre case, *U.S. v. Cruikshank*, held key provisions of federal enforcement legislation to be unconstitutional, crippling the Grant administration's ability to prosecute terrorists. Opponents of Reconstruction did not limit their efforts to the ballot box: between September 1874 and January 1875, Louisiana Democrats tried to overthrow the Republican governor and legislature by force in a series of unsuccessful efforts at executing a coup d'état. Voters in the North were weary of Reconstruction and held Republicans accountable for the economic downturn; in the South the continuing depression angered whites, who lost faith in Republican economic initiatives while denouncing government spending that allegedly taxed whites to serve black interests. The Democrats claimed victory in the 1874 midterm elections, seizing control of the House of Representatives and thus dooming the passage of future federal Reconstruction legislation.

Ulysses S. Grant railed against southern terrorism and northern apathy in a series of public messages to Congress. His blunt language and impassioned protests provided vivid indictments of Reconstruction's opponents, but did little to halt the deterioration of support for federal intervention in southern affairs. While black congressmen offered powerful arguments in favor of the passage of new civil rights legislation forbidding racial discrimination in public transportation, schools, and accommodations, the resulting Civil Rights Act of 1875 (passed by a lame-duck Republican Congress) excluded public schools, proved difficult to enforce, and would be ruled unconstitutional by the Supreme Court in 1883. Mississippi Democrats plotted to retake control of their state in 1875, "peaceably if we can, forcibly if we must," and the resulting Mississippi Plan used violence and intimidation in such a carefully calibrated way as to evade a federal response. When the state's Republican governor, Adelbert Ames, requested federal intervention, Grant speculated that such action no longer enjoyed public support in the North. Attorney General Edwards Pierrepont then seized upon the president's hesitation and took it upon himself to direct Ames to rely upon his own resources. Many northern Republicans, afraid that continued federal intervention would hurt the party in northern state elections, especially in Ohio, breathed a sigh of relief when the administration failed to act; so did Mississippi's Democrats, who claimed victory that fall. Convinced that they had to abandon the South in order to secure the party's survival in the North, Republicans watched as state after state in the South was "redeemed" by Democratic victories.

By the time the nation celebrated the centennial of its independence in 1876, many white Americans, North and South, were ready to abandon Reconstruction. Supreme Court decisions that March in *Cruikshank* and in *U.S. v. Reese*, a Kentucky voting rights case, dealt death blows to existing enforcement legislation. Only three southern states—South Carolina, Louisiana, and Florida—remained under increasingly tenuous Republican rule. That fall Samuel J. Tilden, the Democratic governor of New York, captured a majority of the popular vote in a presidential contest shaped by violence and voter suppression. Convinced that they would have won in a free and fair election, Republicans realized that should disputed returns in South Carolina, Louisiana, and Florida result in victories for their candidate, Ohio governor Rutherford B. Hayes, the party could still claim victory in the Electoral College. With Grant in the White House ready to thwart any Democratic attempt to seize power through violence while pressing for a peaceful resolution of the dispute, Congress hammered out legislation creating an electoral commission. Composed of five congressmen, five senators, and five Supreme Court justices, the commission was charged with sorting through the disputed returns and determining a winner. When the original fifteenth member of the commission, the nominally neutral Supreme Court Justice David Davis, declined to serve in the wake of his election as an independent to the United States Senate from Illinois, it fell to Davis's replacement, Justice Joseph P. Bradley, a Grant appointee who had spearheaded the Court's overturning of Reconstruction legislation in the *Cruikshank* case, to cast the deciding vote. In a series of 8–7 rulings that reflected the partisan affiliations of its members, the commission awarded all of the disputed electoral votes to Hayes, giving him an electoral majority of one. Behind-the-scenes negotiations prevented a Democratic filibuster that would have kept Congress from accepting the commission's decision, although the degree to which Republicans and Democrats exchanged favors and promises in a so-called Compromise of 1877 remains in dispute.

Regardless of the negotiations surrounding the resolution of the disputed election, it had always been Hayes's intention to adopt a new approach to Reconstruction that shelved federal intervention in favor of encouraging cooperation between southern whites and blacks. This optimistic vision proved a flat failure. Democrats regained control of South Carolina, Louisiana, and Florida while retaining their hold on other southern states with nearly no interruption for decades to come. The smothering of black equality in favor of disfranchisement, subordination, and segregation became a cornerstone of the "Redeemed South," while racial discrimination remained pervasive throughout the nation. As Reconstruction ended, Republicans pondered whether alternate courses of action would have yielded success, or whether the entire enterprise of securing black freedom was doomed to failure from the beginning. African Americans refused to abandon their struggle for equality, but it would take a long time for the nation as a whole to realize that there remained many wrongs to address, a challenge that remains to this day.

Levi Nelson and Benjamin Brim: Testimony in the Colfax Massacre Trial

TRIAL IN THE UNITED STATES CIRCUIT COURT.

Fifth day's proceedings in the trial of J. P. Hadnot and others, charged with conspiracy and murder in Grant parish, in April of last year:

Levi Nelson, sworn—Live at New Hope plantation, Grant parish; was a slave in Grant parish before the war; belonged to old Mr. Calhoun; was in Colfax last April; went to Colfax, as I understood Hadnot's men were going there to take the courthouse; we remained at the courthouse; old man Hadnot and his sons, Luke, Gilly and Johnny, were there; the men were armed; I was close to them; did not know the other men with them; remained in Colfax ten or twenty days; at one time I saw ———— armed men at Colfax; there were 300 colored men at the courthouse; one-half the colored men had no arms; they assembled at the courthouse because they were too frightened to remain home; saw A. Tillman there; on the evening of the fight saw him about three o'clock; that was Easter Sunday; the first white man I saw that day was old man Hadnot; he was within 300 yards of the courthouse; he had men with him; the colored men were lying down when the shooting began; shooting began about 6 A.M.; bullets struck where I was lying; one hit my hat, and one my shoulder; they were firing at us three hours before we got up; some of the colored men fired back; twenty-five colored men were outside the fort; the white men first put their cannon on a pair of cart wheels; they fired at us six times from the first place where they located it on the bank; the bullet was a slug of iron; this one in court is not like those I saw; the slugs struck the courthouse; knew some of the white men at the cannon; John Green was at it; Bill Irwin was there; Bill Cruikshanks and his brother also; this one was there; they kept up the fight

449

all day; they told us to stack our arms and they wouldn't hurt us, and for us to march out; Shack White held up a white leaf, and asked them not to kill him; Irwin shot him down; the colored people stayed in the fort, laying down; we left the fort because we did not dare to remain; some went into the courthouse and some ran away; the first thing the white men did was to shoot the gun at us; after we went inside the courthouse they shot at us through the windows; then they set the courthouse on fire; I was inside then; when I got a chance to run off I made an attempt, but a man was about to shoot me, when another man saved me, telling me to save a burning building; I did as directed, and when through I asked if I might go; he cursed me, saying he did not come 400 miles to kill niggers for nothing; did not know him; they made me go among the prisoners; the white men then took the colored men around the corner of a coffeehouse and shot them; there were thirty-seven prisoners there with me; the white men said they had a good mess of beeves and would have a good time of it; Nash said it would not do to take prisoners and then kill them; Hickman said to Nash, "Unless these niggers are killed we will kill you;" they stopped killing colored men then to wait for night; Dr. Compton, Clement Penn, Oscar Given, Prudhomme Lemoine, Bill Cruikshanks, Bill Irwin, John Hadnot, Clement Penn, Denis Lemoine, Tom Hickman, all now in court, and George Marsh, Willy Marsh, M. Roberts, ——— Sloan, Ben Ballet, Jr., D. Hickman, William Hickman, James Hickman and J. Buckland were in the killing party; they kept me prisoner until midnight; they took me and another man out to shoot us; one bullet struck me in my neck, stunning and dropping me; the other man was killed; they shot him five times; one man told somebody to shoot me again, saying that I was not dead; they did not shoot me again; laid on the ground until morning, fearing to move; dead men all around me; heard the men talking about killing niggers; I crawled off the field, not daring to get on my feet; I finally stood up and walked off, after seeing that the men had gone off; this is the scar made by the bullet which struck my neck; when they first came up with their cannon they halted about 300 yards from the courthouse; one of us tore off a shirt sleeve as a white flag, and shook in the window; firing did not cease then, but colored men were shot down as they left the courthouse, after the white flag was shown; it took me an hour to pull down the burning gutter; there were 300 white men around there then; some of the colored men fired from the courthouse; saw the white men try to set the courthouse on fire; they fired something from the cannon, which was burning; it was a mop with oil on it; the north end was set on fire; they made a colored man set the building on fire; A. Tillman was killed by the white men after the surrender; one man, inside the courthouse was shot and disemboweled, and he was burned up alive in the courthouse; his name was Allen; I know the names of several persons who were in the courthouse; the colored people assembled at Colfax for safety, as they had been told that they would be hurt; I was a voter.

Counsel for defense took a commission to cross-examine witness, but did not meet with more success than partly confusing witness. Had witness been in free command of language it may be that the counsel would have been confused. It was evident that Levi knew exactly what he was saying, although he had a halting way of expressing himself. Questions as to distance, time, locations, numbers and such would prove difficult for almost any one to answer under the circumstances; when a man's life is in great danger his mind is not likely to closely observe things generally, so as to fix circumstances in his brain to make him a fluent witness.

CROSS-EXAMINATION

—Two of the Hickman brothers look very much alike; think Tom is the oldest; heard a man say that it was best to kill the niggers at once; saw William Cruikshank before sundown; there was a small shower at dusk; saw both brothers (Cruikshank) there at one time, and think I can't be mistaken; saw Prudhomme Lemoine after I was taken prisoner; saw him about five o'clock; didn't see him after that; he had a gun; saw him guarding prisoners; he had a double-barreled gun on his shoulder; saw Denis Lemoine there; of these prisoners here I saw only Bill Cruikshank and his brother; did not see Mr. Lewis there at all; Nash spoke to Denis Hickman when he talked of not killing the niggers; Nash said that to Hickman; the man who took me out at midnight was a stranger to me; the man who was taken out with me to be killed was Mac Brown; he and I were side by side; the man who shot at us stood about fifteen feet from us; he said he was going to shoot us through our heads; when he fired we both fell, I on my face; laid there until daylight; when I crawled off did not feel of Mac Brown's body; can't say what time it was when I crawled off; the bullet that wounded me cut my neck, glancing off, stunning me; I did not stir all night, but remained on my face. Mac Brown yelled after he fell, and the man shot him five times after that; when I got home no one was there, but my wife got in an hour afterward; I had nothing to do with making the gas pipe gun; Gilly and Luke Hadnot had repeating rifles.

New Orleans Republican, February 28, 1874

TRIAL IN THE UNITED STATES CIRCUIT COURT.

Eighth day's proceedings in the trial of W. J. Cruikshank and others, charged with conspiracy and murder last April in Grant parish:

Benjamin Brim sworn—Last April was living about seven miles below Colfax; I was in Colfax, about the time Jesse Mc-Kinney was killed, to see about it, and to be among the people; was afraid to remain at home; our people in Colfax talked of the scary times; was in Colfax Easter Sunday, and saw the fight. [This witness described the situation of things Sunday morning just the same as other witnesses have.] Heard Shack White call to Bill Irwin and say that we surrendered; none of our people were shooting then, on account of the fire; firing outside had ceased for the time; some one told us to stack our arms; we went to the door, having laid down our guns; when our people went out the white men commenced shooting at us; I saw our men falling, and I fell, though not wounded;

a man saw I was not hurt, and told me to get up and go to a tree where prisoners were placed; remained there fifteen or twenty minutes; a man asked me if there were no more men in the courthouse; he told me to go in and get them out; they were under the floor; all left except one, and we went back prisoners; one man under the floor said he would as soon be burned as shot down; the prisoners were marched into a field and ordered to sit down; there were many dead men near the courthouse; we remained under guard until dusk; one of the guards said to Captain Nash, "Here are your prisoners, what are we to do with them?" Nash told him to take us down to the boardinghouse; the wounded were also taken there; there were eight or nine wounded men; we sat in the yard until after dark; there were twenty-eight prisoners; kept us in the yard during the rain; the wounded were permitted to lie on a gallery; Nash came and said he would send us home if we would go home to our cotton and sugar; another man said, "Nash, have you no better sense than to send them old niggers home? You won't live to see two weeks;" Nash went to the river with a large crowd of men; after that a stout man asked me where that yellow fellow was who had been with me; it was William Williams; "I want you and G. Nelson; I want two, and if you run I will shoot hell out of you;" Williams and Nelson said they did not intend to run; he told them to march on before him; Nelson said he would ride behind him, but the man told him no; the stout man said to others to get their own men and let them walk side by side; so all the prisoners were taken away; the stout man, when all was ready, asked if all the beeves were yoked up, and then said march off; my partner was Baptiste Mills; the foremost men did not go more than fifty or sixty yards, when I heard shooting; when I heard the firing I stopped; the man who had me said he was to carry me to the sugar house, and that he was not going to shoot me; I stopped again, and my captor cocked his pistol; I turned around to look at him and the bullet struck my nose close to my eyes just as I turned; I fell and laid there some time; Baptiste Mills fell as I fell; I was shot afterward as I was on the ground; the bullet entered my back and passed out of my side; Mills was not wounded; we finally got up and left; a man who had charge of the wounded said he could not mind them all; some one told him to shoot them; a good part of the wounded men escaped; when the whites were hunting them I was on the ground, my nose full of blood, and as I blew it out they heard me and shot me again, saying, "That will do him," and then they left; after everybody was gone I got up and tried to walk, but could not stand; I bled freely, but finally I began to crawl, twenty feet at a time; I was all night going two hundred yards; got to a road as day was breaking and tried to walk, but failed; crawled into a ditch among weeds and remained there all day; at night I went about five hundred yards, to a house; the rain helped me; Mike Brannon lived in the house; remained there a long time; when I first went out of the courthouse saw Bill Irwin, Dennis Lemoine, Prudhomme Lemoine, D. Hickman, Willy and George Marsh, Hopkins, Oscar Lacour and Gus Lacour. [Witness pointed out the first three confidently.] When I and my partner were called out there were many white men in sight; when I got out of the ditch where I had been hiding, I saw some men driving mules and horses off toward the sugar house; the men were armed and mounted; they did not see me; Alex Tillman was not among the prisoners; saw John Carter as he lay dead; he was one of us in the line; a yellow woman, Matilda, nursed me; do not know the man who shot me the second time; there were several white men shooting; I felt sure they intended to shoot me when they took me out, although the man told me not; know none of the men who were shooting in the morning, only those I named; saw no wounded white men; heard Nash say: "Cease firing men, you are shooting our own men;" heard one of them yell; did not see the man who yelled; he said, "Men save me, I am shot;" saw no wounded white men; am sure Tillman was not among the prisoners; saw no flag of truce; was in a little room in the courthouse; when we surrendered we dropped our arms.

CROSS-EXAMINATION

—At Colfax I had my gun and ammunition, which were taken from me when a prisoner; I did not fire a shot; did not give any ammunition away; do not know who the man was outside who was yelling; the people in the courthouse did not fire a shot inside after the surrender, I think; did not see Mr. Lewis at Colfax that day; the stout man who shot me was about thirty-five or forty years old, good beard and full face; never saw him before; do not know that Shaw was held a prisoner by the colored people.

New Orleans Republican, March 4, 1874

Robert Brown Elliott:
Speech in Congress on the Civil Rights Bill

WHILE I am sincerely grateful for this high mark of courtesy that has been accorded to me by this House, it is a matter of regret to me that it is necessary at this day that I should rise in the presence of an American Congress to advocate a bill which simply asserts equal rights and equal public privileges for all classes of American citizens. I regret, sir, that the dark hue of my skin may lend a color to the imputation that I am controlled by motives personal to myself in my advocacy of this great measure of national justice. Sir, the motive that impels me is restricted by no such narrow boundary, but is as broad as your Constitution. I advocate it, sir, because it is right. The bill, however, not only appeals to your justice, but it demands a response from your gratitude.

In the events that led to the achievement of American Independence the negro was not an inactive or unconcerned spectator. He bore his part bravely upon many battle-fields, although uncheered by that certain hope of political elevation which victory would secure to the white man. The tall granite shaft, which a grateful State has reared above its sons who fell in defending Fort Griswold against the attack of Benedict Arnold, bears the name of Jordan, Freeman, and other brave men of the African race who there cemented with their blood the corner-stone of the Republic. In the State which I have the honor in part to represent the rifle of the black man rang out against the troops of the British crown in the darkest days of the American Revolution. Said General Greene, who has been justly termed the Washington of the North, in a letter written by him to Alexander Hamilton, on the 10th day of January, 1781, from the vicinity of Camden, South Carolina:

> There is no such thing as national character or national sentiment. The inhabitants are numerous, but they would be rather formidable abroad than at home. There is a great spirit of enterprise among the black people, and those that come out as volunteers are not a little formidable to the enemy.

At the battle of New Orleans, under the immortal Jackson, a colored regiment held the extreme right of the American line unflinchingly, and drove back the British column that pressed upon them, at the point of the bayonet. So marked was their valor on that occasion that it evoked from their great commander the warmest encomiums, as will be seen from his dispatch announcing the brilliant victory.

As the gentleman from Kentucky, [Mr. BECK,] who seems to be the leading exponent on this floor of the party that is arrayed against the principle of this bill, has been pleased, in season and out of season, to cast odium upon the negro and to vaunt the chivalry of his State, I may be pardoned for calling attention to another portion of the same dispatch. Referring to the various regiments under his command, and their conduct on that field which terminated the second war of American Independence, General Jackson says:

> At the very moment when the entire discomfiture of the enemy was looked for with a confidence amounting to certainty, the Kentucky re-enforcements, in whom so much reliance had been placed, ingloriously fled.

In quoting this indisputable piece of history, I do so only by way of admonition and not to question the well-attested gallantry of the true Kentuckian, and to suggest to the gentleman that it would be well that he should not flaunt his heraldry so proudly while he bears this bar-sinister on the military escutcheon of his State—a State which answered the call of the Republic in 1861, when treason thundered at the very gates of the capital, by coldly declaring her neutrality in the impending struggle. The negro, true to that patriotism and love of country that have ever characterized and marked his history on this continent, came to the aid of the Government in its efforts to maintain the Constitution. To that Government he now appeals; that Constitution he now invokes for protection against outrage and unjust prejudices founded upon caste.

But, sir, we are told by the distinguished gentleman from Georgia [Mr. STEPHENS] that Congress has no power under the Constitution to pass such a law, and that the passage of such an act is in direct contravention of the rights of the States. I cannot assent to any such proposition. The constitution of a free government ought always to be construed in favor of human rights. Indeed, the thirteenth, fourteenth, and fifteenth amendments, in positive words, invest Congress with the power to protect the citizen in his civil and political rights. Now, sir, what are civil rights? Rights natural, modified by civil society. Mr. Lieber says:

> By civil liberty is meant, not only the absence of individual restraint, but liberty within the social system and political organism—a combination of principles and laws which acknowledge, protect, and favor the dignity of man. * * * Civil liberty is the result of man's two-fold character as an individual and social being, so soon as both are equally respected.—*Lieber on Civil Liberty*, page 25.

Alexander Hamilton, the right-hand man of Washington in the perilous days of the then infant Republic, the great interpreter and expounder of the Constitution, says:

> Natural liberty is a gift of the beneficent Creator to the whole human race; civil liberty is founded on it; civil liberty is only natural liberty modified and secured by civil society.—*Hamilton's History of the American Republic*, vol. I, page 70.

In the French constitution of June, 1793, we find this grand and noble declaration:

> Government is instituted to insure to man the free use of his natural and inalienable rights. These rights are equality, liberty, security, property. All men are equal by nature and before the law. * * * Law is the same for all, be it protective or penal. Freedom is the power by which man can do what does not interfere with the rights of another; its basis is nature, its standard is justice, its protection is law, its moral boundary is the maxim: "Do not unto others what you do not wish they should do unto you."

Are we then, sir, with the amendments to our Constitution staring us in the face; with these grand truths of history before our eyes; with innumerable wrongs daily inflicted upon five million citizens demanding redress, to commit this question to the diversity of State legislation? In the words of Hamilton—

> Is it the interest of the Government to sacrifice individual rights to the preservation of the rights of an artificial being,

called States? There can be no truer principle than this, that every individual of the community at large has an equal right to the protection of Government. Can this be a free Government if partial distinctions are tolerated or maintained?

The rights contended for in this bill are among "the sacred rights of mankind, which are not to be rummaged for among old parchments or musty records; they are written as with a sunbeam, in the whole volume of human nature, by the hand of the Divinity itself, and can never be erased or obscured by mortal power."

But the Slaughter-house cases!—the Slaughter-house cases!

The honorable gentleman from Kentucky, always swift to sustain the failing and dishonored cause of proscription, rushes forward and flaunts in our faces the decision of the Supreme Court of the United States in the Slaughter-house cases, and in that act he has been willingly aided by the gentleman from Georgia. Hitherto, in the contests which have marked the progress of the cause of equal civil rights, our opponents have appealed sometimes to custom, sometimes to prejudice, more often to pride of race, but they have never sought to shield themselves behind the Supreme Court. But now, for the first time, we are told that we are barred by a decision of that court, from which there is no appeal. If this be true we must stay our hands. The cause of equal civil rights must pause at the command of a power whose edicts must be obeyed till the fundamental law of our country is changed.

Has the honorable gentleman from Kentucky considered well the claim he now advances? If it were not disrespectful I would ask, has he ever read the decision which he now tells us is an insuperable barrier to the adoption of this great measure of justice?

In the consideration of this subject, has not the judgment of the gentleman from Georgia been warped by the ghost of the dead doctrines of State-rights? Has he been altogether free from prejudices engendered by long training in that school of politics that wellnigh destroyed this Government?

Mr. Speaker, I venture to say here in the presence of the gentleman from Kentucky, and the gentleman from Georgia, and in the presence of the whole country, that there is not a line or word, not a thought or dictum even, in the decision of the Supreme Court in the great Slaughter-house cases which casts a shadow of doubt on the right of Congress to pass the pending bill, or to adopt such other legislation as it may judge proper and necessary to secure perfect equality before the law to every citizen of the Republic. Sir, I protest against the dishonor now cast upon our Supreme Court by both the gentleman from Kentucky and the gentleman from Georgia. In other days, when the whole country was bowing beneath the yoke of slavery, when press, pulpit, platform, Congress, and courts felt the fatal power of the slave oligarchy, I remember a decision of that court which no American now reads without shame and humiliation. But those days are past. The Supreme Court of to-day is a tribunal as true to freedom as any department of this Government, and I am honored with the opportunity of repelling a deep disgrace which the gentleman from Kentucky, backed and sustained as he is by the gentleman from Georgia, seeks to put upon it.

What were these Slaughter-house cases? The gentleman should be aware that a decision of any court should be examined in the light of the exact question which is brought before it for decision. That is all that gives authority to any decision.

The State of Louisiana, by act of her Legislature, had conferred on certain persons the exclusive right to maintain stock-landings and slaughter-houses within the city of New Orleans, or the parishes of Orleans, Jefferson, and Saint Bernard, in that State. The corporation which was thereby chartered were invested with the sole and exclusive privilege of conducting and carrying on the live-stock, landing, and slaughter-house business within the limits designated.

The supreme court of Louisiana sustained the validity of the act conferring these exclusive privileges, and the plaintiffs in error brought the case before the Supreme Court of the United States for review. The plaintiffs in error contended that the act in question was void, because, first, it established a monopoly which was in derogation of common right and in contravention of the common law; and, second, that the grant of such exclusive privileges was in violation of the thirteenth and fourteenth amendments of the Constitution of the United States.

It thus appears from a simple statement of the case that the question which was before the court was not whether a State law which denied to a particular portion of her citizens the rights conferred on her citizens generally, on account of race, color, or previous condition of servitude, was unconstitutional because in conflict with the recent amendments, but whether an act which conferred on certain citizens exclusive privileges for police purposes was in conflict therewith, because imposing an involuntary servitude forbidden by the thirteenth amendment, or abridging the rights and immunities of citizens of the United States, or denying the equal protection of the laws, prohibited by the fourteenth amendment.

On the part of the defendants in error it was maintained that the act was the exercise of the ordinary and unquestionable power of the State to make regulation for the health and comfort of society—the exercise of the police power of the State, defined by Chancellor Kent to be "the right to interdict unwholesome trades, slaughter-houses, operations offensive to the senses, the deposit of powder, the application of steam-power to propel cars, the building with combustible materials, and the burial of the dead in the midst of dense masses of population, on the general and rational principle that every person ought so to use his own property as not to injure his neighbors, and that private interests must be made subservient to the general interests of the community."

The decision of the Supreme Court is to be found in the 16th volume of Wallace's Reports, and was delivered by Associate Justice Miller. The court hold, first, that the act in question is a legitimate and warrantable exercise of the police power of the State in regulating the business of stock-landing and slaughtering in the city of New Orleans and the territory immediately contiguous. Having held this, the court proceeds to discuss the question whether the conferring of exclusive privileges, such as those conferred by the act in question, is the imposing of an involuntary servitude, the abridging of the rights and immunities of citizens of the United States, or the denial to any person within the jurisdiction of the State of the equal protection of the laws.

That the act is not the imposition of an involuntary servitude the court hold to be clear, and they next proceed to examine the remaining questions arising under the fourteenth amendment.

Upon this question the court hold that the leading and comprehensive purpose of the thirteenth, fourteenth, and fifteenth amendments was to secure the complete freedom of the race, which, by the events of the war, had been wrested from the unwilling grasp of their owners. I know no finer or more just picture, albeit painted in the neutral tints of true judicial impartiality, of the motives and events which led to these amendments. Has the gentleman from Kentucky read these passages which I now quote? Or has the gentleman from Georgia considered well the force of the language therein used? Says the court on page 70:

> The process of restoring to their proper relations with the Federal Government and with the other States those which had sided with the rebellion, undertaken under the proclamation of President Johnson in 1865, and before the assembling of Congress, developed the fact that, notwithstanding the formal recognition by those States of the abolition of slavery, the condition of the slave race would, without further protection of the Federal Government, be almost as bad as it was before. Among the first acts of legislation adopted by several of the States in the legislative bodies which claimed to be in their normal relations with the Federal Government, were laws which imposed upon the colored race onerous disabilities and burdens, and curtailed their rights in the pursuit of life, liberty, and property to such an extent that their freedom was of little value, while they had lost the protection which they had received from their former owners from motives both of interest and humanity.
>
> They were in some States forbidden to appear in the towns in any other character than menial servants. They were required to reside on and cultivate the soil, without the right to purchase or own it. They were excluded from any occupations of gain, and were not permitted to give testimony in the courts in any case where a white man was a party. It was said that their lives were at the mercy of bad men, either because the laws for their protection were insufficient or were not enforced.
>
> These circumstances, whatever of falsehood or misconception may have been mingled with their presentation, forced upon the statesmen who had conducted the Federal Government in safety through the crisis of the rebellion, and who supposed that by the thirteenth article of amendment they had secured the result of their labors, the conviction that something more was necessary in the way of constitutional protection to

the unfortunate race who had suffered so much. They accordingly passed through Congress the proposition for the fourteenth amendment, and they declined to treat as restored to their full participation in the Government of the Union the States which had been in insurrection until they ratified that article by a formal vote of their legislative bodies.

Before we proceed to examine more critically the provisions of this amendment, on which the plaintiffs in error rely, let us complete and dismiss the history of the recent amendments, as that history relates to the general purpose which pervades them all. A few years' experience satisfied the thoughtful men who had been the authors of the other two amendments that, notwithstanding the restraints of those articles on the States and the laws passed under the additional powers granted to Congress, these were inadequate for the protection of life, liberty, and property, without which freedom to the slave was no boon. They were in all those States denied the right of suffrage. The laws were administered by the white man alone. It was urged that a race of men distinctively marked as was the negro, living in the midst of another and dominant race, could never be fully secured in their person and their property without the right of suffrage.

Hence the fifteenth amendment, which declares that "the right of a citizen of the United States to vote shall not be denied or abridged by any State on account of race, color, or previous condition of servitude." The negro having, by the fourteenth amendment, been declared to be a citizen of the United States, is thus made a voter in every State of the Union.

We repeat, then, in the light of this recapitulation of events almost too recent to be called history, but which are familiar to us all, and on the most casual examination of the language of these amendments, no one can fail to be impressed with the one pervading purpose found in them all, lying at the foundation of each, and without which none of them would have been even suggested: we mean the freedom of the slave race, the security and firm establishment of that freedom, and the protection of the newly-made freeman and citizen from the oppressions of those who had formerly exercised unlimited dominion over him. It is true that only the fifteenth amendment in terms mentions the negro by speaking of his color and his slavery. But it is just as true that each of the other articles was addressed to the grievances of that race, and designed to remedy them, as the fifteenth.

These amendments, one and all, are thus declared to have as their all-pervading design and end the security to the recently enslaved race, not only their nominal freedom, but their complete protection from those who had formerly exercised unlimited dominion over them. It is in this broad light that all these amendments must be read, the purpose to secure the perfect equality before the law of all citizens of the United States. What you give to one class you must give to all; what you deny to one class you shall deny to all, unless in the exercise of the common and universal police power of the State you find it needful to confer exclusive privileges on certain citizens, to be held and exercised still for the common good of all.

Such are the doctrines of the Slaughter-house cases— doctrines worthy of the Republic, worthy of the age, worthy of the great tribunal which thus loftily and impressively enunciates them. Do they—I put it to any man, be he lawyer or not; I put it to the gentleman from Georgia—do they give color even to the claim that this Congress may not now legislate against a plain discrimination made by State laws or State customs against that very race for whose complete freedom and protection these great amendments were elaborated and adopted? Is it pretended, I ask the honorable gentleman from Kentucky or the honorable gentleman from Georgia—is it pretended anywhere that the evils of which we complain, our exclusion from the public inn, from the saloon and table of the steamboat, from the sleeping-coach on the railway, from the right of sepulture in the public burial-ground, are an exercise of the police power of the State? Is such oppression and injustice nothing but the exercise by the State of the right to make regulations for the health, comfort, and security of all her citizens? Is it merely enacting that one man shall so use his own as not to injure another's? Are the colored race to be assimilated to an unwholesome trade or to combustible materials, to be interdicted, to be shut up within prescribed limits? Let the gentleman from Kentucky or the gentleman from Georgia answer. Let the country know to what extent even the audacious prejudice of the gentleman from Kentucky will drive him, and how far even the gentleman from Georgia will permit himself to be led captive by the unrighteous teachings of a false political faith.

If we are to be likened in legal view to "unwholesome

trades," to "large and offensive collections of animals," to "nox-
ious slaughter-houses," to "the offal and stench which attend
on certain manufactures," let it be avowed. If that is still the
doctrine of the political party to which the gentlemen belong,
let it be put upon record. If State laws which deny us the common rights and privileges of other citizens, upon no possible or
conceivable ground save one of prejudice, or of "taste," as the
gentleman from Texas termed it, and as I suppose the gentlemen will prefer to call it, are to be placed under the protection
of a decision which affirms the right of a State to regulate the
police of her great cities, then the decision is in conflict with
the bill before us. No man will dare maintain such a doctrine.
It is as shocking to the legal mind as it is offensive to the heart
and conscience of all who love justice or respect manhood. I
am astonished that the gentleman from Kentucky or the gentleman from Georgia should have been so grossly misled as to
rise here and assert that the decision of the Supreme Court in
these cases was a denial to Congress of the power to legislate
against discriminations on account of race, color, or previous
condition of servitude, because that court has decided that exclusive privileges conferred for the common protection of the
lives and health of the whole community are not in violation
of the recent amendments. The only ground upon which the
grant of exclusive privileges to a portion of the community is
ever defended is that the substantial good of all is promoted;
that in truth it is for the welfare of the whole community that
certain persons should alone pursue certain occupations. It is
not the special benefit conferred on the few that moves the legislature, but the ultimate and real benefit of all, even of those
who are denied the right to pursue those specified occupations.
Does the gentleman from Kentucky say that my good is promoted when I am excluded from the public inn? Is the health
or safety of the community promoted? Doubtless his prejudice
is gratified. Doubtless his democratic instincts are pleased; but
will he or his able coadjutor say that such exclusion is a lawful
exercise of the police power of the State, or that it is not a
denial to me of the equal protection of the laws? They will not
so say.

But each of these gentlemen quote at some length from
the decision of the court to show that the court recognizes a

difference between citizenship of the United States and citizenship of the States. That is true, and no man here who supports this bill questions or overlooks the difference. There are privileges and immunities which belong to me as a citizen of the United States, and there are other privileges and immunities which belong to me as a citizen of my State. The former are under the protection of the Constitution and laws of the United States, and the latter are under the protection of the constitution and laws of my State. But what of that? Are the rights which I now claim—the right to enjoy the common public conveniences of travel on public highways, of rest and refreshment at public inns, of education in public schools, of burial in public cemeteries—rights which I hold as a citizen of the United States or of my State? Or, to state the question more exactly, is not the denial of such privileges to me a denial to me of the equal protection of the laws? For it is under this clause of the fourteenth amendment that we place the present bill, no State shall "deny to any person within its jurisdiction the equal protection of the laws." No matter, therefore, whether his rights are held under the United States or under his particular State, he is equally protected by this amendment. He is always and everywhere entitled to the equal protection of the laws. All discrimination is forbidden; and while the rights of citizens of a State as such are not defined or conferred by the Constitution of the United States, yet all discrimination, all denial of equality before the law, all denial of the equal protection of the laws, whether State or national laws, is forbidden.

The distinction between the two kinds of citizenship is clear, and the Supreme Court have clearly pointed out this distinction, but they have nowhere written a word or line which denies to Congress the power to prevent a denial of equality of rights, whether those rights exist by virtue of citizenship of the United States or of a State. Let honorable members mark well this distinction. There are rights which are conferred on us by the United States. There are other rights conferred on us by the States of which we are individually the citizens. The fourteenth amendment does not forbid a State to deny to all its citizens any of those rights which the State itself has conferred, with certain exceptions, which are pointed out in the decision which we are examining. What it does forbid is inequality, is discrimination, or, to use the words of the amendment itself, is the denial "to any person within its jurisdiction the equal protection of the laws." If a State denies to me rights which are common to all her other citizens, she violates this amendment, unless she can show, as was shown in the Slaughter-house cases, that she does it in the legitimate exercise of her police power. If she abridges the rights of all her citizens equally, unless those rights are specially guarded by the Constitution of the United States, she does not violate this amendment. This is not to put the rights which I hold by virtue of my citizenship of South Carolina under the protection of the national Government; it is not to blot out or overlook in the slightest particular the distinction between rights held under the United States and rights held under the States; but it seeks to secure equality, to prevent discrimination, to confer as complete and ample protection on the humblest as on the highest.

The gentleman from Kentucky, in the course of the speech to which I am now replying, made a reference to the State of Massachusetts which betrays again the confusion which exists in his mind on this precise point. He tells us that Massachusetts excludes from the ballot-box all who cannot read and write, and points to that fact as the exercise of a right which this bill would abridge or impair. The honorable gentleman from Massachusetts [Mr. DAWES] answered him truly and well, but I submit that he did not make the best reply. Why did he not ask the gentleman from Kentucky if Massachusetts had ever discriminated against any of her citizens on account of color, or race, or previous condition of servitude? When did Massachusetts sully her proud record by placing on her statute-book any law which admitted to the ballot the white man and shut out the black man? She has never done it; she will not do it; she cannot do it so long as we have a Supreme Court which reads the Constitution of our country with the eyes of justice; nor can Massachusetts or Kentucky deny to any man, on account of his race, color, or previous condition of servitude, that perfect equality of protection under the laws so long as Congress shall exercise the power to enforce, by appropriate legislation, the great and unquestionable securities embodied in the fourteenth amendment to the Constitution.

But, sir, a few words more as to the suffrage regulation of Massachusetts.

It is true that Massachusetts in 1857, finding that her illiterate population was being constantly augmented by the continual influx of ignorant emigrants, placed in her constitution the least possible limitation consistent with manhood suffrage to stay this tide of foreign ignorance. Its benefit has been fully demonstrated in the intelligent character of the voters of that honored Commonwealth, reflected so conspicuously in the able Representatives she has to-day upon this floor. But neither is the inference of the gentleman from Kentucky legitimate, nor do the statistics of the census of 1870, drawn from his own State, sustain his astounding assumption. According to the statistics we find the whole white population of that State is 1,098,692; the whole colored population 222,210. Of the whole white population who cannot write we find 201,077; of the whole colored population who cannot write, 126,048; giving us, as will be seen, 96,162 colored persons who can write to 897,615 white persons who can write. Now, the ratio of the colored population to the white is as 1 to 5, and the ratio of the illiterate colored population to the whole colored population is as 1 to 2; the ratio of the illiterate white population is to the whole white population as 1 is to 5. Reducing this, we have only a preponderance of three-tenths in favor of the whites as to literacy, notwithstanding the advantages which they have always enjoyed and do now enjoy of free-school privileges, and this, too, taking solely into account the single item of being unable to write; for with regard to the inability to read, there is no discrimination in the statistics between the white and colored population. There is, moreover, a peculiar felicity in these statistics with regard to the State of Kentucky, quoted so opportunely for me by the honorable gentleman; for I find that the population of that State, both with regard to its white and colored populations, bears the same relative rank in regard to the white and colored populations of the United States; and, therefore, while one negro would be disfranchised were the limitation of Massachusetts put in force, nearly three white men would at the same time be deprived of the right of suffrage—a consummation which I think would be far more acceptable to the colored people of that State than to the whites.

Now, sir, having spoken as to the intention of the prohibition imposed by Massachusetts, I may be pardoned for a slight inquiry as to the effect of this prohibition. First, it did not in any way abridge or curtail the exercise of the suffrage by any person who at that time enjoyed such right. Nor did it discriminate between the illiterate native and the illiterate foreigner. Being enacted for the good of the entire Commonwealth, like all just laws, its obligations fell equally and impartially upon all its citizens. And as a justification for such a measure, it is a fact too well known almost for mention here that Massachusetts had, from the beginning of her history, recognized the inestimable value of an educated ballot, by not only maintaining a system of free schools, but also enforcing an attendance thereupon, as one of the safeguards for the preservation of a real republican form of government. Recurring then, sir, to the possible contingency alluded to by the gentleman from Kentucky, should the State of Kentucky, having first established a system of common schools whose doors shall swing open freely to all, as contemplated by the provisions of this bill, adopt a provision similar to that of Massachusetts, no one would have cause justly to complain. And if in the coming years the result of such legislation should produce a constituency rivaling that of the old Bay State, no one would be more highly gratified than I.

Mr. Speaker, I have neither the time nor the inclination to notice the many illogical and forced conclusions, the numerous transfers of terms, or the vulgar insinuations which further incumber the argument of the gentleman from Kentucky. Reason and argument are worse than wasted upon those who meet every demand for political and civil liberty by such ribaldry as this—extracted from the speech of the gentleman from Kentucky:

> I suppose there are gentlemen on this floor who would arrest, imprison, and fine a young woman in any State of the South if she were to refuse to marry a negro man on account of color, race, or previous condition of servitude, in the event of his making her a proposal of marriage, and her refusing on that ground. That would be depriving him of a right he had under the amendment, and Congress would be asked to take it up and say, "This insolent white woman must be taught to know that it is a misdemeanor to deny a man marriage because of race,

color, or previous condition of servitude;" and Congress will
be urged to say after a while that that sort of thing must be put
a stop to, and your conventions of colored men will come here
asking you to enforce that right.

Now, sir, recurring to the venerable and distinguished gentleman from Georgia, [Mr. STEPHENS,] who has added his remonstrance against the passage of this bill, permit me to say
that I share in the feeling of high personal regard for that gentleman which pervades this House. His years, his ability, and
his long experience in public affairs entitle him to the measure
of consideration which has been accorded to him on this floor.
But in this discussion I cannot and I will not forget that the
welfare and rights of my whole race in this country are involved.
When, therefore, the honorable gentleman from Georgia lends
his voice and influence to defeat this measure, I do not shrink
from saying that it is not from him that the American House
of Representatives should take lessons in matters touching human rights or the joint relations of the State and national governments. While the honorable gentleman contented himself
with harmless speculations in his study, or in the columns of a
newspaper, we might well smile at the impotence of his efforts
to turn back the advancing tide of opinion and progress; but,
when he comes again upon this national arena, and throws
himself with all his power and influence across the path which
leads to the full enfranchisement of my race, I meet him only as
an adversary; nor shall age or any other consideration restrain
me from saying that he now offers this Government, which
he has done his utmost to destroy, a very poor return for its
magnanimous treatment, to come here and seek to continue,
by the assertion of doctrines obnoxious to the true principles
of our Government, the burdens and oppressions which rest
upon five millions of his countrymen who never failed to lift
their earnest prayers for the success of this Government when
the gentleman was seeking to break up the Union of these
States and to blot the American Republic from the galaxy of
nations. [Loud applause.]

Sir, it is scarcely twelve years since that gentleman shocked
the civilized world by announcing the birth of a government
which rested on human slavery as its corner-stone. The progress

of events has swept away that *pseudo*-government which rested on greed, pride, and tyranny; and the race whom he then ruthlessly spurned and trampled on are here to meet him in debate, and to demand that the rights which are enjoyed by their former oppressors—who vainly sought to overthrow a Government which they could not prostitute to the base uses of slavery—shall be accorded to those who even in the darkness of slavery kept their allegiance true to freedom and the Union. Sir, the gentleman from Georgia has learned much since 1861; but he is still a laggard. Let him put away entirely the false and fatal theories which have so greatly marred an otherwise enviable record. Let him accept, in its fullness and beneficence, the great doctrine that American citizenship carries with it every civil and political right which manhood can confer. Let him lend his influence, with all his masterly ability, to complete the proud structure of legislation which makes this nation worthy of the great declaration which heralded its birth, and he will have done that which will most nearly redeem his reputation in the eyes of the world, and best vindicate the wisdom of that policy which has permitted him to regain his seat upon this floor.

To the diatribe of the gentleman from Virginia, [Mr. HAR-RIS,] who spoke on yesterday, and who so far transcended the limits of decency and propriety as to announce upon this floor that his remarks were addressed to white men alone, I shall have no word of reply. Let him feel that a negro was not only too magnanimous to smite him in his weakness, but was even charitable enough to grant him the mercy of his silence. [Laughter and applause on the floor and in the galleries.] I shall, sir, leave to others less charitable the unenviable and fatiguing task of sifting out of that mass of chaff the few grains of sense that may, perchance, deserve notice. Assuring the gentleman that the negro in this country aims at a higher degree of intellect than that exhibited by him in this debate, I cheerfully commend him to the commiseration of all intelligent men the world over—black men as well as white men.

Sir, equality before the law is now the broad, universal, glorious rule and mandate of the Republic. No State can violate that. Kentucky and Georgia may crowd their statute-books with retrograde and barbarous legislation; they may rejoice in the odious eminence of their consistent hostility to all the great steps of human progress which have marked our national history since slavery tore down the stars and stripes on Fort Sumter; but, if Congress shall do its duty, if Congress shall enforce the great guarantees which the Supreme Court has declared to be the one pervading purpose of all the recent amendments, then their unwise and unenlightened conduct will fall with the same weight upon the gentlemen from those States who now lend their influence to defeat this bill, as upon the poorest slave who once had no rights which the honorable gentlemen were bound to respect.

But, sir, not only does the decision in the Slaughter-house cases contain nothing which suggests a doubt of the power of Congress to pass the pending bill, but it contains an express recognition and affirmance of such power. I quote now from page 81 of the volume:

> "Nor shall any State deny to any person within its jurisdiction the equal protection of the laws."
>
> In the light of the history of these amendments, and the pervading purpose of them, which we have already discussed, it is not difficult to give a meaning to this clause. The existence of laws in the States where the newly emancipated negroes resided, which discriminated with gross injustice and hardship against them as a class, was the evil to be remedied by this clause, and by it such laws are forbidden.
>
> If, however, the States did not conform their laws to its requirements, then, by the fifth section of the article of amendment, Congress was authorized to enforce it by suitable legislation. We doubt very much whether any action of a State not directed by way of discrimination against the negroes as a class, or on account of their race, will ever be held to come within the purview of this provision. It is so clearly a provision for that race and that emergency, that a strong case would be necessary for its application to any other. But as it is a State that is to be dealt with, and not alone the validity of its laws, we may safely leave that matter until Congress shall have exercised its power, or some case of State oppression, by denial of equal justice in its courts shall, have claimed a decision at our hands.

No language could convey a more complete assertion of the power of Congress over the subject embraced in the present bill than is here expressed. If the States do not conform to the requirements of this clause, if they continue to deny to any person within their jurisdiction the equal protection of the laws, or as the Supreme Court had said, "deny equal justice in its courts," then Congress is here said to have power to enforce the constitutional guarantee by appropriate legislation. That is the power which this bill now seeks to put in exercise. It proposes to enforce the constitutional guarantee against inequality and discrimination by appropriate legislation. It does not seek to confer new rights, nor to place rights conferred by State citizenship under the protection of the United States, but simply to prevent and forbid inequality and discrimination on account of race, color, or previous condition of servitude. Never was there a bill more completely within the constitutional power of Congress. Never was there a bill which appealed for support more strongly to that sense of justice and fair-play which has been said, and in the main with justice, to be a characteristic of the Anglo-Saxon race. The Constitution warrants it; the Supreme Court sanctions it; justice demands it.

Sir, I have replied to the extent of my ability to the arguments which have been presented by the opponents of this measure. I have replied also to some of the legal propositions advanced by gentlemen on the other side; and now that I am about to conclude, I am deeply sensible of the imperfect manner in which I have performed the task. Technically, this bill is to decide upon the civil status of the colored American citizen; a point disputed at the very formation of our present Government, when by a short-sighted policy, a policy repugnant to true republican government, one negro counted as three-fifths of a man. The logical result of this mistake of the framers of the Constitution strengthened the cancer of slavery, which finally spread its poisonous tentacles over the southern portion of the body-politic. To arrest its growth and save the nation we have passed through the harrowing operation of intestine war, dreaded at all times, resorted to at the last extremity, like the surgeon's knife, but absolutely necessary to extirpate the disease which threatened with the life of the nation the overthrow of civil and political liberty on this continent. In that dire extremity the members of the race which I have the honor in part to represent—the race which pleads for justice at your hands to-day, forgetful of their inhuman and brutalizing servitude at the South, their degradation and ostracism at the North—flew willingly and gallantly to the support of the national Government. Their sufferings, assistance, privations, and trials in the swamps and in the rice-fields, their valor on the land and on the sea, is a part of the ever-glorious record which makes up the history of a nation preserved, and might, should I urge the claim, incline you to respect and guarantee their rights and privileges as citizens of our common Republic. But I remember that valor, devotion, and loyalty are not always rewarded according to their just deserts, and that after the battle some who have borne the brunt of the fray may, through neglect or contempt, be assigned to a subordinate place, while the enemies in war may be preferred to the sufferers.

The results of the war, as seen in reconstruction, have settled forever the political status of my race. The passage of this bill will determine the civil status, not only of the negro, but of any other class of citizens who may feel themselves discriminated against. It will form the cap-stone of that temple of liberty, begun on this continent under discouraging circumstances, carried on in spite of the sneers of monarchists and the cavils of pretended friends of freedom, until at last it stands in all its beautiful symmetry and proportions, a building the grandest which the world has ever seen, realizing the most sanguine expectations and the highest hopes of those who, in the name of equal, impartial, and universal liberty, laid the foundation stones.

The Holy Scriptures tell us of an humble hand-maiden who long, faithfully and patiently gleaned in the rich fields of her wealthy kinsman; and we are told further that at last, in spite of her humble antecedents, she found complete favor in his sight. For over two centuries our race has "reaped down your fields." The cries and woes which we have uttered have "entered into the ears of the Lord of Sabaoth," and we are at last politically free. The last vestiture only is needed—civil rights. Having gained this, we may, with hearts overflowing with gratitude, and thankful that our prayer has been granted, repeat the prayer of Ruth: "Entreat me not to leave thee, or to return from following after thee; for whither thou goest, I will go; and where thou lodgest, I will lodge; thy people shall be my people, and thy God my God; where thou diest, will I die, and there will I be buried; the Lord do so to me, and more also, if aught but death part thee and me." [Great applause.]

January 6, 1874

New York Herald:
General Grant's New Departure

GENERAL GRANT'S NEW DEPARTURE—NOTICE TO
THE REPUBLICAN PARTY AND ITS MONSTROSITIES.

General Grant is reported to have said on Friday last to some prominent republicans who called upon him at the White House:—"I begin to think it is time for the republican party to unload. There has been too much dead weight carried by it. The success of our arms during the rebellion and the confidence that the republican party was strong enough to hold up any burden have imposed all the disaffection in the Gulf States on the administration. I am tired of this nonsense. Let Louisiana take care of herself as Texas will have to do. I don't want any quarrel about Mississippi State matters to be referred to me. This nursing of monstrosities has nearly exhausted the life of the party. I am done with them, and they will have to take care of themselves." These words from such a speaker are of the sort to "give us pause." There is, of course, no doubt that they were spoken as indicated, and in the absence of definite statement to the contrary it is to be supposed they were remembered by some one of the prominent republicans referred to and repeated outside with substantial accuracy. The authenticity of the words being thus reasonably clear of doubt, we are of opinion that none of General Grant's famous utterances will prove more memorable than this one. From the time when Grant informed a rebel commander that he proposed "to move immediately on his works"—when the country first became clearly acquainted with his name—the few words of this silent man have had a greater effect upon the popular mind than the orators, with all their speeches. His accidental expressions have been caught up and conned over, and have generally been found to cover the whole case they dealt with in that rapid yet complete way that is almost national with us; and the secret of the success of Grant's phrases is precisely in the fact that they are an exaggeration of the practical spirit in speech of a people that hates to waste words and wants what is said to be thoroughly to the point. They are neat statements of thoughts that find general acceptance because of the keen perception they indicate, or because of their apt relation to existing circumstances. And the utterance given above is in character with those heard before, and will have equal influence in giving definite direction to a wide and vague public opinion on the subject it handles. It is a summary of the condition of the dominant political party, and it indicates the most threatening symptom and the practical remedy, and deals with the subject, too, in a tone of resolute impatience that is in sympathy with the feelings of the people.

From a potential source, therefore, we have these points: —That the republican party has been "nursing monstrosities," and that these have nearly exhausted its life; that in future these monstrosities, which are reconstruction difficulties, "must take care of themselves," as the official head of the party means to cut them loose; that the party has been carrying a great deal of dead weight—that is to say, that it has been playing false with its supporters by foisting into the party purposes and programmes various issues and facts, that had no relation whatever to those principles which alone the people supposed they were supporting when they voted republican tickets; that the leader is of opinion the party ought to unload this dead weight and turn honest; that Louisiana, as well as Texas, "must" govern herself; and, finally, greatest point of all, that General Grant is "tired of this nonsense." The phrase "nursing monstrosities" describes accurately the general activity of the republican party. If that party addresses itself to the subject of reconstruction it solves no vexed problem, pacifies no excitement, lays the foundation of no useful progress; it only nurses some monstrosity conceived by profligate wretches eager to utilize for their own advantage public misfortune or national ruin. If it turns to the subject of great national enterprises, urged by the needs of communication with the Pacific Coast, it does not stimulate and encourage a healthy material progress; it nurses the Credit Mobilier monstrosity. And so through the category. One cannot touch a topic of public interest but the action of the republican party in regard to it resolves itself at once into the mere nursing of some monstrosity instead of the honest performance of some legitimate function. Neither need one go far into the measures with which the party is identified to find the dead weight that threatens to carry it down. Indeed, it is difficult to say what is not dead weight—to indicate any one purpose which the party advocates now earnestly urge that may fairly be called a vital, throbbing portion of the party principle. All the financial policy is dead weight, because the party principle would require a strict economy and the administration of the Treasury in the interest of the people. But it is all done in the interest of jobbers. All the nominations are dead weight, for they are bargains. Reconstruction, the carpet-baggers, the usurpation of power supported by troops—all this is dead weight, a millstone, that if not speedily disengaged will carry republicanism to the bottom. Was there ever in the history of politics a party whose leaders had so crippled it with gratuitous loads of issues not related to its principles and outrageously offensive to the people?

But General Grant, being "tired of this nonsense," thoroughly disgusted with the antics of the party leaders, is not the man patiently to countenance and assist a policy whose inevitably ruinous consequences he clearly perceives; and he indicates the tendency of his revolt against the enormities that are loosening the hold of his party on the people. He intends to separate himself entirely from the Congressional policy and to inaugurate a policy of his own, at the risk of any probable issue with the leaders in Congress; to cut away the dead weight and carry the party nearer to the popular impulse. It is a project that, if wisely acted upon and successfully carried out, will add to his laurels as a soldier the fame of a great political leader, without which fame his name will be impressed on the history of the time like that of many others, as a brave and skilful soldier, but with which his name will eventually stand alone in the history of the great American crisis. An issue between Grant and the leaders in Congress is the imminent fact of the day, and his resolution to have a Chief Justice of his own choosing has already shown how easily such an issue may be made. Should General Grant's endeavor to free his party from the burdens that it unprofitably bears receive the co-operation of any considerable portion of the party leaders success in the admirable project proposed would be certain and easy; but it is far more likely that he will awaken the hostility and meet the furious opposition of the party leaders, and then his ultimate success will be gained in a struggle that may make its triumphs all the more precious to the public. It is clear why the party leaders will oppose him. They are no longer interested in the successes of the party, but only in the net result that such successes may secure to them individually—that is to say, they are more interested in the dead weights than in the legitimate party vitality; and the proposition to cut away all the grand schemes of plunder and all that corrupt system of administration that is the ruin of the party North and South is simply a proposition to cut away that which they hold more precious than all beside. Any new departure in this direction, therefore, they will oppose with characteristic ferocity, and they will, of course, endeavor to assimilate the course of the President to that of Andrew Johnson. But the result will be an exposure of their motives and the public exhibition of the fact that the leaders care nothing for the purposes that the people have at heart in party victories. This will be fatal to their standing in popular esteem, and we may see almost as marvellous a political mortality as we saw in 1860. Inevitably such a disintegration would result in the formation of a middle party; for which, indeed, on altogether different reasons, the time is ripe. All the legitimate purposes of the original republican party are gained, and its dismemberment must follow the loss of its objective unless it changes ground, and the only ground it can take is to move a little nearer the opposition, dropping its extreme on one hand as the democrats drop theirs on the other. This would be to repeat the liberal movement of the last campaign, or the frame of that movement; but the animating spirit would be different, for here the impulse would not be captious or personal. This would not be an intrigue of candidates, but would be inspired by the generous patriotic purposes of the need of good government. And in the machinery of this new party General Grant could dictate the succession, and he would have the glory of restoring and reinvigorating with fresh purpose the party that has saved the country from armed foes and may yet save it from the assault of insidious plunderers.

New York Herald, January 20, 1874

Richard Harvey Cain:
Speech in Congress on the Civil Rights Bill

MR. SPEAKER, I had supposed "this cruel war was over," and that we had entered upon an era of peace, prosperity, and future success as a nation. I had supposed that after the sad experience of more than five years, after we had sought to heal the wounds the war had made, after we had passed amnesty bills, and, as we thought, had entered upon the smooth, quiet road of future prosperity, we would meet on a common level in the halls of Congress, and that no longer would we brood over the past; that we would strike out a new line of policy, a new national course, and thus succeed in laying broad and deep the foundations of the future welfare of this country; that every man, of every race, of every section of this country, might strike hands and go forward in national progress.

I regret, however, that it again becomes my lot to answer a member from a neighboring State—North Carolina. It was my misfortune a few Saturdays ago to have to answer a gentleman from the same State [Mr. VANCE] in relation to strictures upon my race. I regret that it becomes my duty again, simply in defense of what I regard as a right—in defense of the race to which I belong—to meet the arguments of another gentleman from North Carolina, [Mr. ROBBINS,] to show, if I can, their fallacy, and to prove they are not correct.

The gentleman starts out by saying that if we pass the pending civil-rights bill it may indeed seem pleasant to the northern people, but to his section, and to the South, it will be death. I do not think he is correct, for the reason that they have in the South suffered a great many more terrible things than civil rights, and still live. I think if so harmless a measure as the civil-rights bill, guaranteeing to every man of the African race equal rights with other men, would bring death to the South, then certainly that noble march of Sherman to the sea would have fixed them long ago. [Laughter.]

I desire to answer a few of the strictures which the gentleman

479

has been pleased to place upon us. He states that the civil-rights bill will be death to that section. I cannot see it in that light. We lived together before the war—four millions of colored men, women, and children, with the whites of the South—and there was no special antagonism then. There might have been some friction in some places and in some cases, [great laughter,] but no special antagonism between the two races in the South. I fail, therefore, to see the force of the gentleman's argument. I would like to ask why, in all conscience, after the measures of education, these noble efforts to educate these "barbarians," as he terms us, for two hundred years or more—after all the earnest efforts on their part, with their superior civilization, and all the appliances which the gentleman from North Carolina [Mr. Robbins] claims were brought to bear on these "barbarians"—I ask why there was no such antagonism then, but just at this time? Why, sir, if it be true, as the gentleman says, that such philanthropic efforts have been put forth for the education and improvement of the black race, there would be no occasion for antagonism. It is, I believe, a law of education to assimilate, to bring together, to harmonize discordant elements, to bring about oneness of feeling and sentiment, to develop similarity of thought, similarity of action, and thus tend to carry forward the people harmoniously. That does not seem to have been the case, if the argument of the gentleman from North Carolina is correct. Now, look at the fallacy of the gentleman's argument. This race of barbarians, in spite of all their disadvantages, had been educated to such an extent that the white community of the South were not afraid of them after their emancipation. Is not that singular?

The gentleman further states that the negro race is the world's stage actor—the comic dancer all over the land; that he laughs and he dances. Sir, well he may; there are more reasons for his laughing and dancing now than ever before. [Laughter.] There are more substantial reasons why he should be happy now than during all the two hundred years prior to this time. Now he dances as an African; then he crouched as a slave. [Laughter and applause.]

The gentleman further states that not more than eighteen hundred negroes were killed during the four years of the war. The gentleman forgets some battles; he forgets Vicksburgh;

I presume he does not remember Petersburgh; he does not know anything of Fort Pillow. He knows nothing about all the great achievements of the black men while Sherman's army was moving on to victory. He forgets who entered Charleston first; he forgets who entered Richmond first; he forgets all this in the blindness of his prejudice against a race of men who have vindicated themselves so nobly on the battle-field. But I will grant the gentleman the charity of dwelling no longer on that point.

Mr. Speaker, the gentleman states that during the struggle for freedom four millions of negroes lifted no hand to liberate themselves; that no stroke was made by them to deliver themselves from their thralldom; yet a few moments afterward he makes the statement that their kind-heartedness prevented them from rising up and destroying the wives and children of the rebel soldiers who were at the front. I accept the admission. Sir, there dwells in the black man's heart too much nobleness and too much charity to strike down helpless women and children when he has a chance to do so. No; though the liberty of our race was dear to us, we would not purchase it at such a dastard price as the slaying of helpless women and children, while their husbands and fathers were away. I would scorn the men of my race forever if they had lifted their hands at such a period as that against helpless women and children, who were waiting in silent anxiety the return of their natural and lawful protectors. Our strong black arms might have destroyed every vestige of their homes; our torches might have kindled a fire that would have lighted up the whole South, so that every southern man fighting in the army would have hastened back to find his home in ashes. But our race had such nobleness of heart as to forbear in an hour of such extremity, and leave those men their wives and children.

Sir, I mean no disrespect to the gentleman, but I think the facts will bear me out in the statement that on every occasion on the battle-field where the black man met the white man of the South there was no flinching, no turning back, on the part of the black man. He bravely accepted his part in the struggle for liberty or death.

The gentleman says he still looks upon the whites as the superior race. That may be the case in some respects; but, sir, if they educated us they certainly should not find fault with us if we follow out what they have taught, and show ourselves obedient servants.

But, Mr. Speaker, there is another point. The gentleman states that we would make no movement to achieve our liberty. Why, sir, the education which those gentlemen gave the southern slaves was of a peculiar kind. What school-house in all the South was open to the colored race? Point to one. Name the academy where you educated black men and black women as lawyers or doctors, or in any other department of science or art. Point out the county. Give us the name of the district. Tell the name of the school commissioner. Name the teacher. I will name one. Her name was Missa Douglas. And for the attempt to educate those of our race she was incarcerated in prison, and remained there for five years. That is the only instance, so far as I remember, of the education of the colored people of the South.

Examine the laws of the South, and you will find that it was a penal offense for any one to educate the colored people there. Yet these gentlemen come here and upbraid us with our ignorance and our stupidity. Yet you robbed us for two hundred years. During all that time we toiled for you. We have raised your cotton, your rice, your corn. We have attended your wives and your children. We have made wealth for your support and your education, while we were slaves, toiling without pay, without the means of education, and hardly of sustenance. And yet you upbraid us for being ignorant; call us a horde of barbarians! Why, sir, it is ill-becoming in the gentleman to tell us of our barbarism, after he and his have been educating us for two hundred years. If New England charity and benevolence had not accomplished more than your education has done we would still be in that condition. I thank the North for the charity and nobleness with which it has come to our relief. The North has sent forth those leading ideas, which have spread like lightning over the land; and the negro was not so dumb and not so obtuse that he could not catch the light, and embrace its blessings and enjoy them. Sir, I hurl back with contempt all the aspersions of the gentleman on the other side against my race. There is but very little difference, even now, between the condition of the whites of the South and the condition of the blacks of the South. I have given some attention to the statistics of education in the Southern States.

I find this pregnant fact, that there is about 12 per cent. more ignorance existing among the whites in the South than there is among the colored people in the South, notwithstanding the slavery of the colored race. I wish I had the reports here, that I might show the gentleman how the facts stand in reference to his own State especially, because, if I remember correctly, his State shows there is a preponderating aggregate of ignorance in the State of North Carolina, amounting to 60 per cent. and upward, compared with the entire number of the inhabitants in that State.

Tell us of our ignorance—the ignorance of the colored race! Why, Mr. Speaker, it appears to me to be presumption on the part of the gentleman to state that we—we whom they have wronged, whom they have outraged, whom they have robbed, whose sweat and toil they have had the benefit of for two hundred years; whose labor, whose wives, whose children, have been at their beck and call—I say it ill-becomes them to taunt us now with our barbarism and our ignorance. Sir, if he will open to us the school-house, give us some chance, we would not have to measure arms with him now. But even now, Mr. Speaker, although there is such disparity between us and him so far as relates to education and resources, even now we fear not a comparison in the condition of education in the last eight years between the whites and the blacks of North Carolina.

The gentleman, moreover, states that the reason why they did not educate the colored race was that the colored man was not ready. Not ready, Mr. Speaker; if I had that gentleman upon the floor, with my foot upon his neck, and holding a lash over him, with his hands tied, with him bound hand and foot, would he expect that I should boast over him and tell him "You are a coward, you are a traitor, because you do not resist me!" Would he expect me to tell him that when I had him down under my foot, with his hands tied and the lash in my hand lashing his back? Would he tell me that, in conscience, I would be doing justice to him? Oh, no, no! And yet such was the condition in which he had my race. Why, sir, the whipping-post, the thumb-screw, and the lash, were the great means of education in the South. These were the school-houses, these were the academies, these were the great instruments of education, of which the gentleman boasts, for the purpose of bringing these barbarians into civilization. [Applause.] When men boast, they ought to have something to boast of. When I boast, Mr. Speaker, I shall boast of some noble deed. I will boast not of the wrongs inflicted upon the weak; I will boast not of the outrages inflicted upon the indigent; I will not boast, Mr. Speaker, of lashing the weak and trampling under foot any class of people who ought to have my sympathy, nor will I reproach them for being ignorant, when they have been kept away from every means to educate them.

He says we are not ready for it. How long would it have taken us to get ready under their kind of teaching? How long, O Lord, how long! [Laughter and applause.] How long would it have taken to educate us under the thumb-screw, to educate us with the whip, to educate us with the lash, with instruments of torture, to educate us without a home? How long would it have taken to educate us under their system? We had no wives; we had no children; they belonged to the gentleman and his class. We were homeless, we were friendless, although those stars and stripes hanging over your head, Mr. Speaker, ought to have been our protection. That emblem of the Declaration of Independence, initiated by the fathers of the Republic, that all men are born free and equal, ought to have been our protection. Yet they were to us no stars of hope, and the stripes were only stripes of our condemnation.

The gentleman talked something, I believe, about buzzards or crows taking the place of our brave eagle. Sir, the crow would, I think, more beautifully represent the condition of the South now—the croaking bird, you know. They have been croaking ever since the rebellion came on, and they have been croaking against emancipation and the Constitution ever since. They are a nation of croakers, so to speak. Like the crow they are cawing, cawing, cawing, eternally cawing. [Great laughter.] Mr. Speaker, you will pardon me, for I did not expect to speak this morning.

The gentleman says the negro has done less for himself than any other race of men on earth; and he instances the German, the Irishman, the Scotchman, the Englishman, and the Frenchman, as having done something. But he forgets the men of those nationalities come from stations which are the proud, educated, refined, noble, advancing nations of the earth. He forgets that those nations of which he speaks, from which those men have sprung, have given, and are still giving, to the world some of the brightest minds that ever adorned the galaxy of human intellect.

But he tells us that the negroes never produced anything. Well, sir, it may be that in the gentleman's opinion negroes have never produced anything. I wonder if the gentleman ever read history. Did he ever hear tell of any persons of the name of Hannibal, of Hanno, of Hamilcar, of Euclid—all great men of ancient times—of Æsop, and others? No, sir; no; for that kind of literature does not come to North Carolina. [Great laughter.] It grows, it flourishes, on the free mountain peaks and in the academies of the North. That kind of literature comes to such men as Wendell Phillips, as Lloyd Garrison, as Charles Sumner, as Benjamin Butler, and other distinguished men, men of the North, men that are thinkers, men that do not croak, but let the eagle ever soar high in the conception of high ideas. They are ideas that belong to a free people; they are not consistent with or consonant with slavery. No, sir; they do not tell the negro of Euclid, the man that in his joy cried out "Eureka, I have found it;" no, that is not the language for the slave. No; that is not the language they teach by the whip and the thumb-screw; no, sir; it is not that.

But I must pass on. The gentleman says that the black men in the South, since emancipation and enfranchisement, have put bad men into office. Well, sir, that may be true, and I regret that we have put so many bad men in office. No one regrets it more than I do, but they were not colored men after all. [Great laughter.] They were not black men, those bad men in office, who have done so much to deteriorate the value of the country. Not at all. Why, sir, they did not elect our distinguished friend [Mr. VANCE] from North Carolina by black votes. They did not elect Mr. Holman, or a gentleman of some such name, in North Carolina. They did not run the State in debt. They were not the men who took the cash; they were simply mudsills who did the voting, while another class of individuals did the stealing. That is the difference.

Well, Mr. Speaker, I beg to say that we did the best we could; and one of the results of our education was that we had been taught to trust white men in the South. We trusted them, and if they did wrong it was no fault of ours; not at all. I presume the gentleman who addressed the House to-day had some colored constituents who voted for him and sent him here. I will not dare to say, however, that he is a bad man. He may be one of the very best of men; but I think he has some very bad ideas, so far as my race is concerned. [Applause.]

The gentleman says that this is a white man's land and government. He says it has been committed to them in a sacred relationship. I ask in all conscience what becomes of our black men and women and children, to the number of five millions; have we no rights? Ought we to have no privileges; ought we not to have the protection of the law? We did not ask any more. The gentleman harps upon the idea of social equality. Well, sir, he has not had so much experience of that as I have had, or as my race have had. We have some objections to social equality ourselves, very grave ones. [Applause.] For even now, though freedom has come, it is a hard matter, a very hard matter, to keep sacredly guarded the precincts of our sacred homes. But I will not dwell upon that. The gentleman knows more about that than I do. [Laughter.]

The gentleman wishes that we should prepare ourselves to go to Africa, or to the West Indies, or somewhere else. I want to enunciate this doctrine upon this floor—you have brought us here, and here we are going to stay. [Applause.] We are not going one foot or one inch from this land. Our mothers and our fathers and our grandfathers and great-grandfathers have died here. Here we have sweated. Here we have toiled. Here we have made this country great and rich by our labor and toil. It is mean in you now to want to drive us away, after having taken all our toil for two hundred years. Just think of the magnitude of these gentlemen's hearts. After having taken all our toil for two hundred years; after having sold our wives and children like so many cattle in the shambles; after having reared the throne of great king cotton on our labors; after we have made their rice-fields wave with luxuriant harvests while they were fighting against the Government and keeping us in bondage—now we are free they want us to go away. Shame on you! [Applause.]

Now, Mr. Speaker, we are not going away. We are going to stay here. We propose to stay here and work out this problem. We believe that God Almighty has made of one blood all the nations upon the face of the earth. We believe we are made just

like white men are. [Laughter.] Look; I stretch out my arms.
See; I have two of them, as you have. Look at your ears; I have
two of them. I have two eyes, two nostrils, one mouth, two feet.
I stand erect like you. I am clothed with humanity like you. I
think, I reason, I talk, I express my views, as you do. Is there any
difference between us? Not so far as our manhood is concerned,
unless it be in this: that our opinions differ, and mine are a little
higher up than yours. [Laughter.]

The gentleman states that this idea of all men being created equal is a fallacy, announced some years ago by Thomas
Jefferson, that old fool-hardy man, who announced so many
ideas that have been woven into the woof of the nation, who
announced so many foolish things that have made this nation
strong, and great, and powerful. Sir, if he was in error, I accept
the error with pleasure. If he was a foolish man, I would to
God that North Carolina had been baptized in that foolishness
about two hundred years ago. [Great laughter.]

The gentleman also states that if you pass this bill your power
over the South will pass away; that the power of the republican
party in the South will pass away. Sir, let me tell the gentleman
that behind this bill are nine hundred thousand voters; that,
like the warriors of the tribe of Benjamin, every one of them
is left-handed and can "sling a stone at a hair's breadth;" that
each will come up stronger and mightier and more infused
with power than ever before when you pass this bill giving
them their rights, as other men have them. They will come up
as never before to the support of the republican party, and they
will make the South a source of joy and gladness.

The gentleman also talks about the colored people deteri-
orating. Sir, who tills your lands now? Who plants your corn?
Who raises your cotton? I have been in the South during the
last ten years. I have traveled over the Southern States, and
have seen who did this work. Going along I saw the white men
do the smoking, chewing tobacco, riding horses, playing cards,
spending money, while the colored men are tilling the soil, and
bringing the cotton, rice, and other products to market.

Sir, I do not believe the gentleman from North Carolina
wants us to go to Africa; I do not believe it. It was a slip of the
tongue; he does not mean that the black people should leave
North Carolina; not a bit of it. If they did you would see such
an exodus of white people from that State as you never saw

before, for they would follow them wherever they might go. [Laughter.]

Sir, we feel that we are part and parcel of this great nation; and as such, as I said before, we propose to stay here and solve this problem of whether the black race and the white race can live together in this country. I make the statement that I regard it as essential to their welfare and interests that they should live together in this country. Why not? I can see no reason why not, if they contribute their quota to the advancement of progress and civilization. Sir, the mechanics of the South are almost altogether colored people. The carpenters, the machinists, the engineers—nearly all the mechanics in the Southern States are colored people. Why can we not stay here and work out this problem?

I ask Congress to pass this bill for the reason that it would settle this question, once and forever. The gentleman says that he does not desire that the colored people shall be crowded into the schools of the white people. Well, I do not think that they would be harmed by it; some few of them might be. But experience has taught us that it is not true that great harm will come from any such measure. I think, therefore, that if we pass this bill we will be doing a great act of justice, we will settle for all time the question of the rights of all people. And until that question is settled there cannot be that peace and harmony in the country that is necessary to its success.

The gentleman says the colored people and the white people are living together now in North Carolina in amicable relations. I am glad for that admission, for he rounded off all that he had said before by that last sentence. He said that the two races could not live together, and yet at the close of his speech he says that the whites and blacks are now living in North Carolina in amicable relations. Sir, if they are so living now, why not hereafter? Will peace and good order be destroyed because all are to have their rights? Sir, I do not think so.

I close with this thought: I believe the time is coming when the Congress of the United States, when the whole nation, will recognize the importance of the passage of this bill in order to settle this question once and forever. I regard the interests of the black man in this country as identical with the interests of the white man. I would have that set forth so clearly and unmistakably that there should be no antagonism between the races, no friction that should destroy their peace and prosperity. I believe Almighty God has placed both races on this broad theater of activity, where thoughts and opinions are freely expressed, where we may grasp every idea of manhood, where we may take hold of every truth and develop every art and science that can advance the prosperity of the nation. I believe God designed us to live here together on this continent, and in no other place, to develop this great idea that all men are the children of one Father. We are here to work out the grand experiment of the homogeneity of nations, the grand outburst of the greatness of humanity, by the development in us of the rights that belong to us, and the performance of the duties that we owe each other.

Our interests are bound up in this country. Here we intend to stay and work out the problem of progress and education and civilization. I say to the gentleman from North Carolina, [Mr. ROBBINS,] and to the gentleman from Virginia, [Mr. HARRIS,] and to the gentleman from New York, [Mr. COX,] who discussed civil rights the other day, and to gentlemen from the other States, that we are going to remain in this country side by side with the white race. We desire to share in your prosperity and to stand by you in adversity. In advancing the progress of the nation we will take our part; and if the country should again be involved in the devastation of war, we will do our part in the struggle. We propose to identify ourselves with this nation, which has done more than any other on earth to illustrate the great idea that all races of men may dwell together in harmony, working out together the problem of advancement and civilization and liberty.

Mr. Speaker, we will drive the buzzard away; we will scare the crow back to North Carolina. We will take the eagle as the emblem of liberty; we will take that honored flag which has been borne through the heat of a thousand battles. Under its folds Anglo-Saxon and Africo-American can together work out a common destiny, until universal liberty, as announced by this nation, shall be known throughout the world.

January 24, 1874

James T. Rapier:
Speech in Congress on the Civil Rights Bill

MR. SPEAKER, I had hoped there would be no protracted discussion on the civil-rights bill. It has been debated all over the country for the last seven years; twice it has done duty in our national political campaigns; and in every minor election during that time it has been pressed into service for the purpose of intimidating the weak white men who are inclined to support the republican ticket. I was certain until now that most persons were acquainted with its provisions, that they understood its meaning; therefore it was no longer to them the monster it had been depicted, that was to break down all social barriers, and compel one man to recognize another socially, whether agreeable to him or not.

I must confess it is somewhat embarrassing for a colored man to urge the passage of this bill, because if he exhibit an earnestness in the matter and express a desire for its immediate passage, straightway he is charged with a desire for social equality, as explained by the demagogue and understood by the ignorant white man. But then it is just as embarrassing for him not to do so, for, if he remain silent while the struggle is being carried on around, and for him, he is liable to be charged with a want of interest in a matter that concerns him more than any one else, which is enough to make his friends desert his cause. So in steering away from Scylla I may run upon Charybdis. But the anomalous, and I may add the supremely ridiculous, position of the negro at this time, in this country, compel me to say something. Here his condition is without a comparison, parallel alone to itself. Just think that the law recognizes my right upon this floor as a law-maker, but that there is no law to secure to me any accommodations whatever while traveling here to discharge my duties as a Representative of a large and wealthy constituency. Here I am the peer of the proudest, but on a steamboat or car I am not equal to the most degraded. Is not this most anomalous and ridiculous?

What little I shall say will be more in the way of stating the case than otherwise, for I am certain I can add nothing to the arguments already made in behalf of the bill. If in the course of my remarks I should use language that may be considered inelegant, I have only to say that it shall be as elegant as that used by the opposition in discussing this measure; if undignified, it shall not be more so than my subject; if ridiculous, I enter the plea that the example has been set by the democratic side of the House, which claims the right to set examples. I wish to say in justice to myself that no one regrets more than I do the necessity that compels one to the manner born to come in these Halls with hat in hand (so to speak) to ask at the hands of his political peers the same public rights they enjoy. And I shall feel ashamed for my country if there be any foreigners present, who have been lured to our shores by the popular but untruthful declaration that this land is the asylum of the oppressed, to hear a member of the highest legislative body in the world declare from his place, upon his responsibility as a Representative, that notwithstanding his political position he has no civil rights that another class is bound to respect. Here a foreigner can learn what he cannot learn in any other country, that it is possible for a man to be half free and half slave, or, in other words, he will see that it is possible for a man to enjoy political rights while he is denied civil ones; here he will see a man legislating for a free people, while his own chains of civil slavery hang about him, and are far more galling than any the foreigner left behind him; here will see what is not to be seen elsewhere, that position is no mantle of protection in our "land of the free and home of the brave;" for I am subjected to far more outrages and indignities in coming to and going from this capital in discharge of my public duties than any criminal in the country providing he be white. Instead of my position shielding me from insult, it too often invites it.

Let me cite a case. Not many months ago Mr. Cardozo, treasurer of the State of South Carolina, was on his way home from the West. His route lay through Atlanta. There he made request for a sleeping-berth. Not only was he refused this, but was denied a seat in a first-class carriage, and the parties went so far as to threaten to take his life because he insisted upon his rights as a traveler. He was compelled, a most elegant and accomplished gentleman, to take a seat in a dirty smoking-car, along with the traveling rabble, or else be left, to the detriment of his public duties.

I affirm, without the fear of contradiction, that any white ex-convict (I care not what may have been his crime, nor whether the hair on the shaven side of his head has had time to grow out or not) may start with me to-day to Montgomery, that all the way down he will be treated as a gentleman, while I will be treated as the convict. He will be allowed a berth in a sleeping-car with all its comforts, while I will be forced into a dirty, rough box with the drunkards, apple-sellers, railroad hands, and next to any dead that may be in transit, regardless of how far decomposition may have progressed. Sentinels are placed at the doors of the better coaches, with positive instructions to keep persons of color out; and I must do them the justice to say that they guard these sacred portals with a vigilance that would have done credit to the flaming swords at the gates of Eden. Tender, pure, intelligent young ladies are forced to travel in this way if they are guilty of the crime of color, the only unpardonable sin known in our Christian and Bible lands, where sinning against the Holy Ghost (whatever that may be) sinks into insignificance when compared with the sin of color. If from any cause we are compelled to lay over, the best bed in the hotel is his if he can pay for it, while I am invariably turned away, hungry and cold, to stand around the railway station until the departure of the next train, it matters not how long, thereby endangering my health, while my life and property are at the mercy of any highwayman who may wish to murder and rob me.

And I state without the fear of being gainsaid, the statement of the gentleman from Tennessee to the contrary notwithstanding, that there is not an inn between Washington and Montgomery, a distance of more than a thousand miles, that will accommodate me to a bed or meal. Now, then, is there a man upon this floor who is so heartless, whose breast is so void of the better feelings, as to say that this brutal custom needs no regulation? I hold that it does and that Congress is the body to regulate it. Authority for its action is found not only in the fourteenth amendment to the Constitution, but by virtue of that amendment (which makes all persons born here citizens,) authority is found in article 4, section 2 of the Federal

Constitution, which declares in positive language "that the citizens of each State shall have the same rights as the citizens of the several States." Let me read Mr. Brightly's comment upon this clause; he is considered good authority, I believe. In describing the several rights he says they may be all comprehended under the following general heads: "Protection by the Government; the enjoyment of life and liberty, with the right to acquire and possess property of every kind, and to pursue and obtain happiness and safety; the right of a citizen of one State to pass through or to reside in any other State for purposes of trade, agriculture, professional pursuits, or otherwise."

It is very clear that the right of locomotion without hinderance and everything pertaining thereto is embraced in this clause; and every lawyer knows if any white man in *ante bellum* times had been refused first-class passage in a steamboat or car, who was free from any contagious disease, and was compelled to go on deck of a boat or into a baggage-car, and any accident had happened to him while he occupied that place, a lawsuit would have followed and damages would have been given by any jury to the plaintiff; and whether any accident had happened or not in the case I have referred to, a suit would have been brought for a denial of rights, and no one doubts what would have been the verdict. White men had rights then that common carriers were compelled to respect, and I demand the same for the colored men now.

Mr. Speaker, whether this deduction from the clause of the Constitution just read was applicable to the negro prior to the adoption of the several late amendments to our organic law is not now a question, but that it does apply to him in his new relations no intelligent man will dispute. Therefore I come to the national, instead of going to the local Legislatures for relief, as has been suggested, because the grievance is national and not local; because Congress is the law-making power of the General Government, whose duty it is to see that there be no unjust and odious discriminations made between its citizens. I look to the Government in the place of the several States, because it claims my first allegiance, exacts at my hands strict obedience to its laws, and because it promises in the implied contract between every citizen and the Government to protect my life and property. I have fulfilled my part of the contract to the extent I have been called upon, and I demand that the Government, through Congress do likewise. Every day my life and property are exposed, are left to the mercy of others, and will be so as long as every hotel-keeper, railroad conductor, and steamboat captain can refuse me with impunity the accommodations common to other travelers. I hold further, if the Government cannot secure to a citizen his guaranteed rights it ought not to call upon him to perform the same duties that are performed by another class of citizens who are in the free and full enjoyment of every civil and political right.

Sir, I submit that I am degraded as long as I am denied the public privileges common to other men, and that the members of this House are correspondingly degraded by recognizing my political equality while I occupy such a humiliating position. What a singular attitude for law-makers of this great nation to assume, rather come down to me than allow me to go up to them. Sir, did you ever reflect that this is the only Christian country where poor, finite man is held responsible for the crimes of the infinite God whom you profess to worship? But it is; I am held to answer for the crime of color, when I was not consulted in the matter. Had I been consulted, and my future fully described, I think I should have objected to being born in this gospel land. The excuse offered for all this inhuman treatment is that they consider the negro inferior to the white man, intellectually and morally. This reason might have been offered and probably accepted as truth some years ago, but no one now believes him incapable of a high order of culture, except some one who is himself below the average of mankind in natural endowments. This is not the reason as I shall show before I have done.

Sir, there is a cowardly propensity in the human heart that delights in oppressing somebody else, and in the gratification of this base desire we always select a victim that can be outraged with safety. As a general thing the Jew has been the subject in most parts of the world; but here the negro is the most available for this purpose; for this reason in part he was seized upon, and not because he is naturally inferior to any one else. Instead of his enemies believing him to be incapable of a high order of mental culture, they have shown that they believe the reverse to be true, by taking the most elaborate pains to prevent his development. And the smaller the caliber of the white man the more frantically has he fought to prevent the intellectual and moral progress of the negro, for the simple but good reason that he has most to fear from such a result. He does not wish to see the negro approach the high moral standard of a man and gentleman.

Let me call your attention to a case in point. Some time since a well-dressed colored man was traveling from Augusta to Montgomery. The train on which he was stopped at a dinner-house. The crowd around the depot seeing him well dressed, fine-looking, and polite, concluded he must be a gentleman, (which was more than their righteous souls could stand,) and straightway they commenced to abuse him. And, sir, he had to go into the baggage-car, open his trunks, show his cards, faro-bank, dice, &c., before they would give him any peace; or, in other words, he was forced to give satisfactory evidence that he was not a man who was working to elevate the moral and intellectual standard of the negro before they would respect him. I have always found more prejudice existing in the breasts of men who have feeble minds and are conscious of it, than in the breasts of those who have towering intellects and are aware of it. Henry Ward Beecher reflected the feelings of the latter class when on a certain occasion he said: "Turn the negro loose; I am not afraid to run the race of life with him." He could afford to say this, all white men cannot; but what does the other class say? "Build a Chinese wall between the negro and the school-house, discourage in him pride of character and honest ambition, cut him off from every avenue that leads to the higher grounds of intelligence and usefulness, and then challenge him to a contest upon the highway of life to decide the question of superiority of race." By their acts, not by their words, the civilized world can and will judge how honest my opponents are in their declarations that I am naturally inferior to them. No one is surprised that this class opposes the passage of the civil-rights bill, for if the negro were allowed the same opportunities, the same rights of locomotion, the same rights to comfort in travel, how could they prove themselves better than the negro?

Mr. Speaker, it was said, I believe by the gentleman from Kentucky, [Mr. BECK,] that the people of the South, particularly his State, were willing to accord the colored man all the rights they believe him guaranteed by the Constitution. No one doubts this assertion. But the difficulty is they do not acknowledge that I am entitled to any rights under the organic law. I am forced to this conclusion by reading the platforms of the democratic party in the several States. Which one declares that that party believes in the constitutionality of the Reconstruction Acts or the several amendments? But upon the other hand, they question the constitutionality of every measure that is advanced to ameliorate the condition of the colored man; and so skeptical have the democracy become respecting the Constitution, brought about by their unsuccessful efforts to find constitutional objections to every step that is taken to elevate the negro, that now they begin to doubt the constitutionality of the Constitution itself. The most they have agreed to do, is to obey present laws bearing on manhood suffrage until they are repealed by Congress or decided to be unconstitutional by the Supreme Court.

Let me read what the platform of the democratic party in Alabama has to say on this point:

> The democratic and conservative party of the State of Alabama, in entering upon the contest for the redemption of the State government from the radical usurpers who now control it, adopt and declare as their platform—
>
> 1. That we stand ready to obey the Constitution of the United States and the laws passed in pursuance thereof, and the constitution and laws of the State of Alabama, so long as they remain in force and unrepealed.

I will, however, take the gentleman at his word; but must be allowed to ask if so why was it, even after the several amendments had been officially announced to be part of the Federal Constitution, that his State and others refused to allow the negro to testify in their courts against a white man? If they believed he should be educated (and surely this is a right) why was it that his school-houses were burned down, and the teachers who had gone down on errands of mercy to carry light into dark places driven off, and in some places killed? If they believe the negro should vote, (another right, as I understand the Constitution,) why was it that Ku-Klux Klans were organized to prevent him from exercising the right of an American citizen, namely, casting the ballot—the very thing they said he had a right to do?

The professed belief and practice are sadly at variance, and must be intelligently harmonized before I can be made to believe that they are willing to acknowledge that I have any rights under the Constitution or elsewhere. He boasts of the magnanimity of Kentucky in allowing the negro to vote without qualification, while to enjoy the same privilege in Massachusetts he is required to read the constitution of that State. He was very unhappy in this comparison. Why, sir, his State does not allow the negro to vote at all. When was the constitution of Kentucky amended so as to grant him the elective franchise? They vote there by virtue of the fifteenth amendment alone, independent of the laws and constitution of that Commonwealth; and they would to-day disfranchise him if it could be done without affecting her white population. The Old Bay State waited for no "act of Congress" to force her to do justice to all of her citizens, but in *ante bellum* days provided in her constitution that all male persons who could read and write should be entitled to suffrage. That was a case of equality before the law, and who had a right to complain? There is nothing now in the amended Federal Constitution to prevent Kentucky from adopting the same kind of clause in her constitution, when the convention meets to revise the organic law of that State, I venture the assertion that you will never hear a word about it; but it will not be out of any regard for her colored citizens, but the respect for that army of fifty-thousand ignorant white men she has within her borders, many of whom I see every time I pass through that State, standing around the several depots continually harping on the stereotyped phrase, "The damned negro won't work."

I would not be surprised though if she should do better in the future. I remember when a foreigner was just as unpopular in Kentucky as the negro is now; when the majority of the people of that State were opposed to according the foreigner the same rights they claimed for themselves; when that class of people were mobbed in the streets of her principal cities on account of their political faith, just as they have done the negro for the last seven years. But what do you see to-day? One of that then proscribed class is Kentucky's chief Representative upon this floor. Is not this an evidence of a returning sense of justice? If so, would it not be reasonable to predict that she will in the near future send one of her now proscribed class to aid him in representing her interests upon this floor?

Mr. Speaker, there is another member of this body who has opposed the passage of this bill very earnestly, whose position in the country and peculiar relations to the Government compel me to refer to him before I conclude. I allude to the gentleman from Georgia, [Mr. STEPHENS.] He returns to this House after an absence of many years with the same old ideas respecting State-rights that he carried away with him. He has not advanced a step; but unfortunately for him the American people have, and no longer consider him a fit expounder of our organic law. Following to its legitimate conclusion the doctrine of State-rights, (which of itself is secession,) he deserted the flag of his country, followed his State out of the Union, and a long and bloody war followed. With its results most men are acquainted and recognize; but he, Bourbon-like, comes back saying the very same things he used to say, and swearing by the same gods he swore by in other days. He seems not to know that the ideas which he so ably advanced for so many years were by the war swept away, along with that system of slavery which he intended should be the chief corner-stone, precious and elect, of the transitory kingdom over which he was second ruler.

Sir, the most of us have seen the play of Rip Van Winkle, who was said to have slept twenty years in the Katskill Mountains. On his return he found that the small trees had grown up to be large ones; the village of Falling Waters had improved beyond his recollection; the little children that used to play around his knees and ride into the village upon his back had grown up to be men and women and assumed the responsibilities of life; most of his friends, including Nick Vedder, had gone to that bourn whence no traveler returns; but, saddest of all, his child, "Mene," could not remember him. No one can see him in his efforts to recall the scenes of other days without being moved almost to tears. This, however, is fiction. The life and actions of the gentleman from Georgia most happily illustrate this character. This is a case where truth is stranger than fiction; and when he comes into these Halls advocating the same old ideas after an absence of so many years, during which time we have had a conflict of arms such as the world never saw, that revolutionized the entire body-politic, he stamps himself a living "Rip Van Winkle."

I reiterate, that the principles of "State-rights," for the recognition of which, he now contends, are the ones that were in controversy during our late civil strife. The arguments *pro* and *con* were heard in the roar of battle, amid the shrieks of the wounded, and the groans of the dying; and the decision was rendered amid shouts of victory by the Union soldiers. With it all appear to be familiar except him, and for his information I will state that upon this question an appeal was taken from the forum to the sword, the highest tribunal known to man, that it was then and there decided that National rights are paramount to State-rights, and that liberty and equality before the law should be coextensive with the jurisdiction of the Stars and Stripes. And I will further inform him that the bill now pending is simply to give practical effect to that decision.

I sympathize with him in his inability to understand this great change. When he left here the negro was a chattel, exposed for sale in the market places within a stone's throw of the Capitol; so near that the shadow of the Goddess of Liberty reflected by the rising sun would fall within the slave-pen as a forcible reminder that there was no hopeful day, nothing bright in the future, for the poor slave. Then no negro was allowed to enter these Halls and hear discussions on subjects that most interested him. The words of lofty cheer that fell from the lips of Wade, Giddings, Julian, and others were not allowed to fall upon his ear. Then, not more than three negroes were allowed to assemble at any place in the capital of the nation without special permission from the city authorities. But on his return he finds that the slave-pens have been torn down, and upon their ruins temples of learning have been erected; he finds that the Goddess of Liberty is no longer compelled to cover her radiant face while she weeps for our national shame, but looks with pride and satisfaction upon a free and regenerated land; he finds that the laws and regulations respecting the assembling of negroes are no longer in force, but on the contrary he can see on any public holiday the Butler Zouaves, a fine-looking company of colored men, on parade.

Imagine, if you can, what would have been the effect of such a sight in this city twelve years ago. Then one negro soldier would have caused utter consternation. Congress would have adjourned; the Cabinet would have sought protection elsewhere; the President would have declared martial law; troops and marines would have been ordered out; and I cannot tell all that would have happened; but now such a sight does not excite a ripple on the current of affairs; but over all, and worse to him than all, he finds the negro here, not only a listener but a participant in debate. While I sympathize with him in his inability to comprehend this marvelous change, I must say in all earnestness that one who cannot understand and adjust himself to the new order of things is poorly qualified to teach this nation the meaning of our amended Constitution. The tenacity with which he sticks to his purpose through all the vicissitudes of life is commendable, though his views be objectionable.

While the chief of the late confederacy is away in Europe fleeing the wrath to come in the shape of Joe Johnston's history of the war, his lieutenant, with a boldness that must challenge the admiration of the most impudent, comes into these Halls and seeks to commit the nation through Congress to the doctrine of State-rights, and thus save it from the general wreck that followed the collapse of the rebellion. He had no other business here. Read his speech on the pending bill; his argument was cunning, far more ingenious than ingenuous. He does not deny the need or justness of the measure, but claims that the several States have exclusive jurisdiction of the same. I am not so willing as some others to believe in the sincerity of his assertions concerning the rights of the colored man. If he were honest in this matter, why is it he never recommended such a measure to the Georgia Legislature? If the several States had secured to all classes within their borders the rights contemplated in this bill, we would have had no need to come here; but they having failed to do their duty, after having had ample opportunity, the General Government is called upon to exercise its right in the matter.

Mr. Speaker, time will not allow me to review the history of the American negro, but I must pause here long enough to say that he has not been properly treated by this nation; he has purchased and paid for all, and for more, than he has yet received. Whatever liberty he enjoys has been paid for over and over again by more than two hundred years of forced toil; and for such citizenship as is allowed him he paid the full measure of blood, the dearest price required at the hands of any citizen. In every contest, from the beginning of the revolutionary struggle down to the war between the States, has he been prominent. But we all remember in our late war when the Government was so hard pressed for troops to sustain the cause of the Union, when it was so difficult to fill up the ranks that had been so fearfully decimated by disease and the bullet; when every train that carried to the front a number of fresh soldiers brought back a corresponding number of wounded and sick ones; when grave doubts as to the success of the Union arms had seized upon the minds of some of the most sanguine friends of the Government; when strong men took counsel of their fears; when those who had all their lives received the fostering care of the nation were hesitating as to their duty in that trying hour, and others questioning if it were not better to allow the star of this Republic to go down and thus be blotted out from the great map of nations than to continue the bloodshed; when gloom and despair were wide-spread; when the last ray of hope had nearly sunk below our political horizon, how the negro then came forward and offered himself as a sacrifice in the place of the nation, made bare his breast to the steel, and in it received the thrusts of the bayonet that were aimed at the life of the nation by the soldiers of that government in which the gentleman from Georgia figured as second officer.

Sir, the valor of the colored soldier was tested on many a battlefield, and to-day his bones lie bleaching beside every hill and in every valley from the Potomac to the Gulf; whose mute eloquence in behalf of equal rights for all before the law, is and ought to be far more persuasive than any poor language I can command.

Mr. Speaker, nothing short of a complete acknowledgment of my manhood will satisfy me. I have no compromises to make, and shall unwillingly accept any. If I were to say that I would be content with less than any other member upon this floor I would forfeit whatever respect any one here might entertain for me, and would thereby furnish the best possible evidence that I do not and cannot appreciate the rights of a freeman. Just what I am charged with by my political enemies.

I cannot willingly accept anything less than my full measure of rights as a man, because I am unwilling to present myself as a candidate for the brand of inferiority, which will be as plain and lasting as the mark of Cain. If I am to be thus branded, the country must do it against my solemn protest.

Sir, in order that I might know something of the feelings of a freeman, a privilege denied me in the land of my birth, I left home last year and traveled six months in foreign lands, and the moment I put my foot upon the deck of a ship that unfurled a foreign flag from its mast-head, distinctions on account of my color ceased. I am not aware that my presence on board the steamer put her off her course. I believe we made the trip in the usual time. It was in other countries than my own that I was not a stranger, that I could approach a hotel without the fear that the door would be slammed in my face. Sir, I feel this humiliation very keenly; it dwarfs my manhood, and certainly it impairs my usefulness as a citizen.

The other day when the centennial bill was under discussion I would have been glad to say a word in its favor, but how could I? How would I appear at the centennial celebration of our national freedom, with my own galling chains of slavery hanging about me? I could no more rejoice on that occasion in my present condition than the Jews could sing in their wonted style as they sat as captives beside the Babylonish streams; but I look forward to the day when I shall be in the full enjoyment of the rights of a freeman, with the same hope they indulged, that they would again return to their native land. I can no more forget my manhood, than they could forget Jerusalem.

After all, this question resolves itself to this: either I am a man or I am not a man. If one, I am entitled to all the rights, privileges, and immunities common to any other class in this country; if not a man, I have no right to vote, no right to a seat here; if no right to vote, then 20 per cent. of the members on this floor have no right here, but, on the contrary, hold their seats *in violation of law*. If the negro has no right to vote, then one-eighth of your Senate consists of members who have no shadow of a claim to the places they occupy; and if no right to a vote, a half-dozen governors in the South figure as usurpers.

This is the legitimate conclusion of the argument, that the negro is not a man and is not entitled to all the public rights common to other men, and you cannot escape it. But when I press my claims I am asked, "Is it good policy?" My answer is, "Policy is out of the question; it has nothing to do with it; that you can have no policy in dealing with your citizens; that there must be one law for all; that in this case justice is the only standard to be used, and you can no more divide justice than you can divide Deity." On the other hand, I am told that I must respect the prejudices of others. Now, sir, no one respects reasonable and intelligent prejudices more than I. I respect religious prejudices, for example; these I can comprehend. But how can I have respect for the prejudices that prompt a man to turn up his nose at the males of a certain race, while at the same time he has a fondness for the females of the same race to the extent of cohabitation? Out of four poor unfortunate colored women who from poverty were forced to go to the lying-in branch of the Freedmen's Hospital here in the District last year three gave birth to children whose fathers were white men, and I venture to say that if they were members of this body, would vote against the civil-rights bill. Do you, can you wonder at my want of respect for this kind of prejudice? To make me feel uncomfortable appears to be the highest ambition of many white men. It is to them a positive luxury, which they seek to indulge at every opportunity.

I have never sought to compel any one, white or black to associate with me, and never shall; nor do I wish to be compelled to associate with any one. If a man do not wish to ride with me in the street-car I shall not object to his hiring a private conveyance; if he do not wish to ride with me from here to Baltimore, who shall complain if he charter a special train? For a man to carry out his prejudices in this way would be manly, and would leave no cause for complaint, but to crowd me out of the usual conveyance into an uncomfortable place with persons for whose manners I have a dislike, whose language is not fit for ears polite, is decidedly unmanly and cannot be submitted to tamely by any one who has a particle of self-respect.

Sir, this whole thing grows out of a desire to establish a system of "caste," an anti-republican principle, in our free country. In Europe they have princes, dukes, lords, &c., in contradistinction to the middle classes and peasants. Further East they have the brahmans or priests, who rank above the sudras or laborers. In those countries distinctions are based upon blood and position. Every one there understands the custom and no one complains. They, poor innocent creatures, pity our condition, look down upon us with a kind of royal compassion, because they think we have no tangible lines of distinction, and therefore speak of our society as being vulgar. But let not our friends beyond the seas lay the flattering unction to their souls that we are without distinctive lines; that we have no nobility; for we are blessed with both. Our distinction is color, (which would necessarily exclude the brahmans,) and our lines are much broader than anything they know of. Here a drunken white man is not only equal to a drunken negro, (as would be the case anywhere else,) but superior to the most sober and orderly one; here an ignorant white man is not only the equal of an unlettered negro, but is superior to the most cultivated; here our nobility cohabit with our female peasants, and then throw up their hands in holy horror when a male of the same class enters a restaurant to get a meal, and if he insist upon being accommodated our scion of royalty will leave and go to the arms of his colored mistress and there pour out his soul's complaint, tell her of the impudence of the "damned nigger" in coming to a table where a white man was sitting.

What poor, simple-minded creatures these foreigners are. They labor under the delusion that they monopolize the knowledge of the courtesies due from one gentleman to another. How I rejoice to know that it is a delusion. Sir, I wish some of them could have been present to hear the representative of the F. F. V.'s upon this floor (and I am told that that is the highest degree that society has yet reached in this country) address one of his peers, who dared ask him a question, in this style: "I am talking to white men." Suppose Mr. Gladstone— who knows no man but by merit—who in violation of our custom entertained the colored jubilee singers at his home last summer, or the Duke de Broglie, had been present and heard this eloquent remark drop from the lips of this classical and knightly member, would they not have hung their heads in shame at their ignorance of politeness, and would they not have returned home, repaired to their libraries, and betaken themselves to the study of Chesterfield on manners? With all these absurdities staring them in the face, who can wonder that foreigners laugh at our ideas of distinction?

Mr. Speaker, though there is not a line in this bill the democracy approve of, yet they made the most noise about the school clause. Dispatches are freely sent over the wires as to what will be done with the common-school system in the several Southern States in the event this bill becomes a law. I am not surprised at this, but, on the other hand, I looked for it. Now what is the force of that school clause? It simply provides that all the children in every State where there is a school system supported in whole or in part by general taxation shall have equal advantages of school privileges. So that if perfect and ample accommodations are not made convenient for all the children, then any child has the right to go to any school where they do exist. And that is all there is in this school clause. I want some one to tell me of any measure that was intended to benefit the negro that they have approved of. Of which one did they fail to predict evil? They declared if the negroes were emancipated that the country would be laid waste, and that in the end he would starve, because he could not take care of himself. But this was a mistake. When the reconstruction acts were passed and the colored men in my State were called upon to express through the ballot whether Alabama should return to the Union or not, white men threw up their hands in holy horror and declared if the negro voted that never again would they deposit another ballot. But how does the matter stand now? Some of those very men are in the republican ranks, and I have known them to grow hoarse in shouting for our platforms and candidates. They hurrah for our principles with all the enthusiasm of a new-born soul, and, sir, so zealous have they become that in looking at them I am amazed, and am often led to doubt my own faith and feel ashamed for my lukewarmness. And those who have not joined our party are doing their utmost to have the negro vote with them. I have met them in the cabins night and day where they were imploring him for the sake of old times to come up and vote with them.

I submit, Mr. Speaker, that political prejudices prompt the democracy to oppose this bill as much as anything else. In the campaign of 1868 Joe Williams, an uncouth and rather notorious colored man, was employed as a general democratic canvasser in the South. He was invited to Montgomery to enlighten us, and while there he stopped at one of the best hotels in the city, one that would not dare entertain me. He was introduced at the meeting by the chairman of the democratic executive committee as a learned and elegant, as well as eloquent gentleman. In North Alabama he was invited to speak at the Seymour and Blair barbecue, and did address one of the largest audiences, composed largely of ladies, that ever assembled in that part of the State. This I can prove by my simon-pure democratic colleague, Mr. SLOSS, for he was chairman of the committee of arrangements on that occasion, and I never saw him so radiant with good humor in all my life as when he had the honor of introducing "his friend," Mr. Williams. In that case they were extending their courtesies to a coarse, vulgar stranger, because he was a democrat, while at the same time they were hunting me down as the partridge on the mount, night and day, with their Ku-Klux Klan, simply because I was a republican and refused to bow at the foot of their Baal. I might enumerate many instances of this kind, but I forbear. But to come down to a later period, the Greeley campaign. The colored men who were employed to canvass North Carolina in the interest of the democratic party were received at all the hotels as other men and treated I am informed with marked distinction. And in the State of Louisiana a very prominent colored gentleman saw proper to espouse the Greeley cause, and when the fight was over and the McEnery government saw fit to send on a committee to Washington to present their case to the President, this colored gentleman was selected as one of that committee. On arriving in the city of New Orleans prior to his departure he was taken to the Saint Charles, the most aristocratic hotel in the South. When they started he occupied a berth in the sleeping-car; at every eating-house he was treated like the rest of them, no distinction whatever. And when they arrived at Montgomery I was at the depot, just starting for New York. Not only did the conductor refuse to allow me a berth in the sleeping-car, but I was also denied a seat in the first-class carriage. Now, what was the difference between us? Nothing but our political faith. To prove this I have only to say that just a few months before this happened, he, along with Frederick Douglass and others, was denied the same privileges he enjoyed in coming here. And now that he has returned to the right party again I can tell him that never more will he ride in another sleeping-car in the South unless this bill become law. There never was a truer saying than that circumstances alter cases.

Mr. Speaker, to call this land the asylum of the oppressed is a misnomer, for upon all sides I am treated as a pariah. I hold that the solution of this whole matter is to enact such laws and prescribe such penalties for their violation as will prevent any person from discriminating against another in public places on account of color. No one asks, no one seeks the passage of a law that will interfere with any one's private affairs. But I do ask the enactment of a law to secure me in the enjoyment of public privileges. But when I ask this I am told that I must wait for public opinion; that it is a matter that cannot be forced by law. While I admit that public opinion is a power, and in many cases is a law of itself, yet I cannot lose sight of the fact that both statute law, and the law of necessity manufacture public opinion. I remember, it was unpopular to enlist negro soldiers in our late war, and after they enlisted it was equally unpopular to have them fight in the same battles; but when it became a necessity in both cases public opinion soon came around to that point. No white father objected to the negro's becoming food for powder if thereby his son could be saved. No white woman objected to the negro marching in the same ranks and fighting in the same battles if by that her husband could escape burial in our savannas and return to her and her little ones.

Suppose there had been no reconstruction acts nor amendments to the Constitution, when would public opinion in the South have suggested the propriety of giving me the ballot? Unaided by law when would public opinion have prompted the Administration to appoint members of my race to represent this Government at foreign courts? It is said by some well-meaning men that the colored man has now every right under the common law; in reply I wish to say that that kind of law commands very little respect when applied to the rights of colored men in my portion of the country; the only law that we have any regard for is *uncommon law* of the most positive character. And I repeat, if you will place upon your statute-books laws that will protect me in my rights, that public opinion will speedily follow.

Mr. Speaker, I trust this bill will become law, because it is a necessity, and because it will put an end to all legislation on this subject. It does not and cannot contemplate any such idea as social equality; nor is there any man upon this floor so silly as to believe that there can be any law enacted or enforced that would compel one man to recognize another as his equal socially; if there be, he ought not to be here, and I have only to say that they have sent him to the wrong public building. I would oppose such a bill as earnestly as the gentleman from North Carolina, whose associations and cultivations have been of such a nature as to lead him to select the crow as his standard of grandeur and excellence in the place of the eagle, the hero of all birds and our national emblem of pride and power. I will tell him that I have seen many of his race to whose level I should object to being dragged.

Sir, it matters not how much men may differ upon the question of State and national rights; there is one class of rights, however, that we all agree upon, namely, individual rights, which includes the right of every man to select associates for himself and family, and to say who shall and who shall not visit at his house. This right is God-given and custom-sanctioned, and there is, and there can be no power overruling your decision in this matter. Let this bill become law and not only will it do much toward giving rest to this weary country on this subject, completing the manhood of my race and perfecting his citizenship, but it will take him from the political arena as a topic of discussion where he has done duty for the last fifty years, and thus freed from anxiety respecting his political standing, hundreds of us will abandon the political fields who are there from necessity, and not from choice and enter other and more pleasant ones; and thus relieved, it will be the aim of the colored man as well as his duty and interest, to become a good citizen, and to do all in his power to advance the interests of a common country.

June 9, 1874

William Lloyd Garrison
to the Boston Journal

To the Editors of The Boston Journal:

Authentic intelligence from various portions of the South reveals the pregnant fact that the old rebel element is again in the ascendant, slaughtering like dogs obnoxious loyal white and colored citizens, and inaugurating a new reign of terror as bloody and unrelenting as marked the scenes of 1860–61. If the tragedies that are daily occurring were simply murder or assassination to gratify personal revenge or to obtain a coveted booty, they might be left to the disposal of the local authorities, and no Governmental interference would be deemed desirable or necessary; but they are notably for disloyal ends, against the enjoyment of equal civil and political rights, and in the interest of that rebellious spirit which involved us in one of the bloodiest conflicts recorded in the annals of history, and which incomparably prefers to rule in hell rather than reign in heaven. They mean the suppression of freedom of speech, freedom of the press, the right peaceably to assemble together for redress of grievances, the independent exercise of the elective franchise in the hands of free men, and the overthrow of all the safeguards of personal security. They mean rebellion and war—an *imperium in imperio*, whereby American citizenship may be trampled upon with impunity. Of these, take as specimens the summary massacre, by a mob of masked assassins, of sixteen colored citizens in Gibson county, Tennessee, and the cold-blooded murder of six white Republican office-holders and seven colored men at one time in Red River Parish, Louisiana, by an armed band of "White Leaguers." In Garrard county, Kentucky, "a perfect reign of terror" is reported, United States troops having been fired upon, a number of negroes killed, and the residence of Hon. William Sellers (Republican) burned to the ground. Of course, the rebel justification for these horrible deeds is that the victims were conspiring for the destruction of the whites, or purposing some other evil device; but the accusation is manifestly that of the wolf in the fable against the lamb. In the end, it is always shown in such cases that the aggressors are the disloyal and degraded whites, whose tiger ferocity is untamable. The colored people of the South are the least inclined to bloodshed of any considerable portion of mankind; they forbear and forgive, and meekly endeavor to keep the peace in a manner that would be regarded as lack of manhood in white men; they know full well, moreover, that in any collision with their satanic enemies they would be the chief sufferers, and a circumspection, born of prolonged martyrdom, leads to all possible endurance on their part under the most cruel provocations. If in any case, goaded to desperation, any of their number arm in self-defence, or are nerved to pull a trigger, the act is magnified into a diabolical uprising of the blacks to exterminate the whites, whose passions are most easily "set on fire of hell."

Let it not be forgotten that the Southern dispatches to the Associated Press, concerning such thronging horrors, are sent over the wires by rebel hands or rebel instigation. In ninety-nine cases out of one hundred they are malignant fabrications; and the single exceptional case is enormously exaggerated. The object is to hoodwink the people of the North, and paralyze any patriotic action against rebel perfidy and oppression. And that object is measurably obtained by the readiness of Northern Democratic journals to accept these lying telegrams as entirely trustworthy, and to treat reliable statements of rebel outrages as Republican *canards*, started for electioneering purposes. It may be safely assumed that not one of them will venture to denounce any of those outrages, however undeniable or revolting; for the party of which they are the organs is still bitterly anti-negro and essentially Southern in all its leadings and aspirations. Its history is pre-eminently one of abject subserviency to the old slave oligarchy, and it is just as ready to sacrifice every principle of justice and every claim of humanity to secure their affiliation as in other days. Hence, in proportion to its success will be the chance of slaughtering loyal whites and blacks with impunity at the South, and subjecting the whole country to rebel domination.

One of our Boston dailies says: "The reports of outrages in the Southern States have a suspicious look. Is it not a little queer that these reports of outrages always come a little before the autumn elections?" It is just because of these elections that the whites "begin to form themselves into bands to persecute and intimidate the negroes," so that they may take forcible and absolute possession of the polls. This is the citadel they are bound to capture, and having done so, they will become masters of the situation. Union men and colored freemen, except protected by the presence of United States troops, will find themselves driven to the wall, and the ballots in their hands to be thrown at the peril of their lives!

This is a part of the dreadful inheritance bequeathed to us by chattel slavery—a part of the penalty we are to pay for having been accomplices in the crime of making man the property of man. And the end is not yet!

The real truth is that the South is still rebel in heart and purpose, devoid of all patriotic feeling, charged with deadly malignity toward all Northern residents on her soil who will not wear a padlock upon their lips, utterly anti-American, covered with gross ignorance and brutal demoralization like a pall, and closely allied to barbarism. That in Georgia alone, forty-eight militia companies refuse to carry the United States flag, while bearing United States arms drawn from the arsenals of the General Government, is symptomatic of her rotten condition generally. In vain has her bloody rebellion been more than magnanimously condoned by that Government, and not a single traitor executed for treason; in vain has the North charitably contributed millions of dollars to save the Southern people from the horrors of starvation, and millions more to spread the light of education among them; in vain have Northern capital, enterprise and industry sought to develop the locked-up resources of that thriftless and inert section of our land; in vain has every effort been made to "conciliate our Southern brethren" by divers ways and means not always commendable. Darkness has as much fellowship with light and Belial with Christ, as the South has with the North. All her sufferings are by her own infliction, and she is her one implacable enemy—besotted, desperate, insane.

Here is the venomous hiss of the Old Serpent of slavery and sedition, as aspirated by the Iuka (Miss.) *Herald*:

"We must act speedily and decidedly, no matter what it costs. Better lose the lives of half our citizens than see the whole outrageously trampled upon by an ignorant and savage negro mob. We suggest to our brethren the formation of White Leagues in every civil district in every county in the State. Let them meet in secret and be bound by the most solemn oaths, and let death be the penalty of any violations of the Order. Already, we have good reason to believe, such leagues have been formed in many counties, and the thing is becoming more and more popular every day of its existence. *This land is ours, by right and by inheritance*, and we must, we will control it, even at the expense of oceans of blood and millions of lives. The constant cry all over the South is, the negroes are threatening to burn this town and that; to murder the women and children in this place or the other. Let the hellish barbarian brutes go on; we will take a score of lives for every woman or child murdered; and when once we start, in fact not a damnable negro savage assassin will be left in the South. We accept the gauge."

With such a demoniacal spirit as this pervading the South, when it comes to the question of equal rights for whites and blacks alike, what but the most terrible scenes may be expected? "We tell you, now," says the Natchitoches *Vindicator*, menacingly addressing the colored voters, "and let it be distinctly remembered that you have fair warning, that we intend to carry the State of Louisiana in November next, or *she will be a military territory*."

See how divine retribution is meted out to such evil-doers!

Of Missouri the St. Louis *Globe* says—"A little more of the present rule of ignorance, brutality and outlawry, [not by 'Northern carpet-baggers,' but by those to the 'manner born,'] now witnessed in many of the counties of this State, and Missouri will be set back twenty years in her material prosperity."

Of the present condition of Kentucky, the Louisville *Courier-Journal* says:

"The law against the carrying of concealed weapons is a dead letter. There has scarcely been the conviction of a respectable, well-to-do man for murder or homicide the last twenty years. Every coward and bully goes armed. Every case of manslaughter goes unpunished. Every case of shooting with intent to kill passes by as an amusing episode, provided there be no funeral. Even the most atrocious, cold-blooded, deliberate, malignant, dastardly assassinations have left no mark on the statute books except the mark of acquittals purchased by money or intimidation. Red-handed murderers roam at large among respectable people. Red-handed murderers occupy places of responsibility and trust. The rule is that you may kill your man with impunity. There is no danger of the gallows or the prison for the assassin who has money and friends. A drink too many—a word too much—a pull at the trigger of a six-shooter, and a funeral, and a mock trial, and no thought for the widow and the orphan, no thought for the public peace, so the murderer be a good-natured fellow, who is sorry, and has enough to pay the piper. That's the way the law wags in Kentucky."

The same paper alleges that there are at this moment fifty cases of homicide on the criminal dockets of the State which ought to be recorded as murder cases, where the defendants are on bail with the least possible danger of an adverse result, and that there are five hundred cases of shooting with intent to kill, which will never come to trial.

Of the condition to which Virginia is reduced, the Richmond *Whig* makes a doleful recital; but it consolingly and maliciously tells the impecunious Virginians that "they must remember that their woes could have been, and would have been, a hundred-fold worse under the curses of Radicalism that have fallen upon those unfortunate Commonwealths where the negro (Banquo's ghost!) and the political allies of the negro are supreme." Whistling to keep its courage up, it declares that "there is a splendid day somewhere in the future for Virginia;" but that day no living person shall see, unless there be a radical change in the spirit and policy of the Old Dominion. "Ephraim is joined to his idols; let him alone. He feedeth on wind, and followeth after the east wind; the balances of deceit are in his hand; he *loveth to oppress*. He shall be desolate in the day of rebuke. . . . . . Ye have ploughed wickedness, ye have reaped iniquity; ye have eaten the fruit of lies. Sow to yourselves in righteousness, reap in mercy; break up your fallow ground; for it is time to seek the Lord, till he come and rain righteousness upon you."

In vain does the *Whig* boast of the advantages and attractions Virginia presents in her fertile soil, her fine forests, her rivers and roadsteads, her manufacturing facilities, her mineral riches, her healthful and charming climate! Has she not always been in possession of these? And with what beggarly results! What she and the entire South need are a new heart and a right spirit; then it will go well with them—and not till then. At present, "their works are works of iniquity, and the act of violence is in their hands. Their feet run to evil, and they make haste to shed innocent blood; wasting and destruction are in their paths; the way of peace they know not, and there is no judgment in their goings. They hatch cockatrice' eggs, and weave the spider's web; he that eateth of their eggs dieth, and that which is crushed breaketh out into a viper."

But the serious question is: What does the General Government intend to do for the protection of the loyal men of the South against a dominating band of assassins?

Yours for equal rights,

WM. LLOYD GARRISON.

P.S. Just as I am sealing this communication, an answer to my interrogation is found in the letter of President Grant to General Belknap, showing that he is not unmindful of his constitutional duties at such an alarming crisis.

Boston, Sept. 3, 1874.

Boston Journal, September 5, 1874

Eugene Lawrence to Harper's Weekly

NINE YEARS have passed since Louisiana, wasted, ruined, and depraved by slavery and by rebellion, came out from a contest in which, had only the guilty suffered, it had been punished not half so severely as it deserved. Its slave-traders had forced it among the earliest into revolt. The very thought of a limitation upon their dreadful traffic filled them with unreflecting rage. The election of LINCOLN seemed to menace the slave-trade on the Mississippi; the auction-blocks of New Orleans might no longer be supplied from Kentucky and Tennessee with human chattels; and the desperate leaders of the violent faction forced the small yet wealthy community to rise in arms against the government. With a population of perhaps seven hundred thousand, more than half of whom were colored, all Unionists in life and death, while of the whites it is not probable that a majority were ready for the mad measures of the slave-traders, the State soon felt the results of its folly, and fell again into the hands of the government. At the close of the rebellion Louisiana was impoverished with an excess of poverty to which not even South Carolina had reached. A large proportion of its white population were paupers, maintained by the alms of the national government. Its lucrative slave-trade was stopped forever; its colored people were free. There was no money to pay its taxes, no resources to maintain its levees; no hope of rescue from its fallen condition except the aid of the national government and the Northern capitalists. Of this, so generously offered, the State freely availed itself, and commerce once more began to revisit the deserted wharves of New Orleans. So fertile is its land, and so favorable the site of its metropolis, that a few years of peace would soon impart to Louisiana new elements of progress; and, as the centre of Western trade, and the home of Western merchants, New Orleans might rise to a high rank among the sea-ports of the world.

But this the fallen rebels were resolved to prevent. Malice ruled in their counsels of such a depth of depravity as could only be born of the poisonous remnants of slavery. They formed secret associations, not, as one might suppose, to restore agriculture, to enlarge trade, to preserve good order, and invite the commerce and emigration of the West, but to insult and terrify honest negro laborers, to drive off white settlers who were Republicans, and at last murder both; to hold the State in miserable poverty and force the people to live still on the alms of the government. The reports of the Ku-Klux Committee for 1871–72 show how successfully the White Leaguers of four or five years ago overawed or ill-treated their miserable fellow-citizens; how in 1868 scarcely a Republican ventured to vote in many parishes, and what perpetual bankruptcy and poverty ruled in the small community. Two thousand persons were murdered by the White Leaguers in a population not much larger than that of Brooklyn.

The fact that the Ku-Klux or the White League began its reign of terror in Louisiana immediately after the war, and has continued it ever since, until it rose into the recent rebellion, or that the Democratic leaders, M'ENERY and PENN, owe all their political strength to its prevalence, is what the chiefs of the lawless faction in the State would now willingly conceal. Having spread a deadly terror through all the Republican population, they are now satisfied, and they labor to hide from the Northern press and people by all their arts the means by which they hope to control all future elections. Yet it is plain to the whole Northern public that it is not any misgovernment on the part of the KELLOGG rule that brought the White League into existence, since it appeared at once upon the close of the rebellion; nor is it the fault of the Federal officials that the assassins have ravaged the State under the names of Knights of the White Camellia or of a White Man's Party for the past nine years. It is not the State but the Federal government against which the outrages have been aimed. It was the lingering fires of rebellion that blazed up anew in unlucky Louisiana; and it is certain that no government favorable to the Union would satisfy these supporters of M'ENERY and PENN. They will have nothing but an ascendency of the rebel interests.

Our White Leaguers who were only a few days ago urging that every one who opposed their rule in New Orleans should be "shot down like a dog," are now complaining of "misrepresentation" and of the harsh construction put upon their actions by the more observant part of the Northern press. We think their actions are not unworthy of their words, and that they are not unknown to the history of the times. Never did so small a community as Louisiana in so few years exhibit such a succession of horrors. In 1868 we have the raids on the negro voters detailed in the Ku-Klux reports, when the White Camellias dominated in the streets of New Orleans. In 1869–71 fear kept them in tolerable quiet. In 1872 they re-appear. In 1873 they burned or shot down sixty or seventy negroes at Grant Parish, and attempted an insurrection in New Orleans. In 1874 they have murdered the United States officials at Coushatta and a large number of negroes; they have risen in rebellion in New Orleans and shot thirty or forty Unionists in a deadly contest. They are still importing large quantities of arms, and are evidently preparing for further massacres whenever the eye of the law is withdrawn. That such men should complain that they are "misrepresented" is an excess of effrontery; that they should find any portion of the Northern Democracy willing to believe any thing they choose to affirm against the Republican government is not a little remarkable. It is ridiculous to suppose that the murderers and revolutionists of 1874 are in any way to be disconnected from those of 1868 or 1873, or that M'ENERY and PENN are not the chiefs of a band of assassins and outlaws of whom the white as well as the colored population of Louisiana would rejoice to be able to rid themselves.

There is evidently a strong desire entertained by the people of the whole country to bring back peace and prosperity to all the Southern States that are still suffering from the terrors of the White Man's League or the lingering penalties of the rebellion, and to lend aid to their merchants and farmers to rise from their temporary depression. They want capital and labor to extend their means of internal communication, and a large immigrant population to add to the value of their lands; they want public schools and churches, a free press, and liberty of speech and action to relieve them gradually from the influence of their dangerous classes, to diffuse knowledge, and increase the results of labor. But none of these can they hope to obtain in the midst of their civil convulsions. Insurrection is the most costly of political measures, and Louisiana is the most unlucky of all the States, because it has been tormented by a horde of traitors. While Charleston flourishes in peace and has become already an opulent sea-port, New Orleans is the scene of a lamentable decay. Galveston and Mobile draw away its commerce, and the Western merchants turn away in alarm from the home of the White Man's League. Even Florida, where peace has been maintained and the Ku-Klux apparently suppressed forever, has made a rapid progress, while Savannah languishes and Georgia is losing its population. If, therefore, the Northern and Western press are desirous of aiding in developing the natural advantages of the Southern States, it is plain that their first duty is to point out the causes that have led to their decay. Publicity and a perfect information of the real condition of the country are the earliest steps in its future advance. If there are outlaws in any of the States, or any reign of disorder, the truest friends of the South are those who expose and denounce them. Secrecy only increases the evil, and bad men hide their ill deeds in darkness.

The question is now fairly before the people, How can life and liberty be secured to all classes of our citizens in the Southern States, and those enormities prevented in the future that have made the name of Democracy in Tennessee and even Kentucky, in Alabama, Georgia, Louisiana, and Arkansas, odious to the instincts of civilization? Modern progress abhors the notion of murder and of inhumanity, and it would be well for our people to place the mark of their disapprobation upon the party that hopes to profit by these cruel measures at the South with so conclusive a condemnation as shall show how deeply they detest them.

It is quite certain that the Southern Democratic leaders have not begun as yet an era of peace. Every part of their section has shown traces of a war of intimidation against the Union party. It is only a short time ago that the Louisville papers related the outrages of the White Man's League almost in the suburbs of that city. Tennessee has recently been the scene of frightful massacres. The colored and white Republicans of the South, in many districts, vote with the fear of death before them. Their courage has been tested by nine years of perilous devotion to good order and peace. Will their countrymen now desert them?   EUGENE LAWRENCE.

Harper's Weekly, October 31, 1874

Isaac Loveless to Ulysses S. Grant

I take the opetunety of Writting you A few Lines to show you the condision that We collard People is in in tenn for votin the Republican ticket   We are With Bread or meet an With out help We Will Perish   We are all most Povity stricken to death Now an We ask you to Look at our condish an do some thing for us   We are dependin on you for help   We are here among demercrats an they say that they in tend to starve the dam negros out that vote the Radical ticket the Reason of that We say that We intend to Run you the third time for Presidency   Now dear sir if you are the friend of the colard men Pleas help us for if there Ever Was a need time now is the time   I Want you to Bring to your mine When I Was under your command at vicks Burg missip   you know how Bad you hated to see your men Without somthing to eat   it is With us now Like it Was With us in time of the War an if We Evr needed help We need it now dear sir I never throught When I Was in the armey that I ever Would come to this   now Sir you may think that We are Lazy But the Land holders say We shall not Work for them an you know that Put us in a Bad fix   Look at this Letter inquier aBout it an see for your self Whether I tell the truth or not   dear sir our chance is slender here an We ask you to Look for us a Little While for We need som one to Look for us now   dear sir if you can do us no Good Give us ease By Writting to us   I hope When you Get this that My name may sound in years as it did at the serender of vicks Burg Pleas Writ soon . . . if you think of us as you once did We know that you Will help us . . .

November 9, 1874

Ulysses S. Grant:
from Annual Message to Congress

YOUR ATTENTION will be drawn to the unsettled condition of affairs in some of the Southern States.

On the 14th of September last the governor of Louisiana called upon me, as provided by the Constitution and laws of the United States, to aid in suppressing domestic violence in that State. This call was made in view of a proclamation issued on that day by D. B. Penn, claiming that he was elected lieutenant-governor in 1872, and calling upon the militia of the State to arm, assemble, and drive from power the usurpers, as he designated the officers of the State government. On the next day I issued my proclamation commanding the insurgents to disperse within five days from the date thereof, and subsequently learned that on that day they had taken forcible possession of the statehouse. Steps were taken by me to support the existing and recognized State government, but before the expiration of the five days the insurrectionary movement was practically abandoned, and the officers of the State government, with some minor exceptions, resumed their powers and duties. Considering that the present State administration of Louisiana has been the only government in that State for nearly two years; that it has been tacitly acknowledged and acquiesced in as such by Congress, and more than once expressly recognized by me, I regarded it as my clear duty, when legally called upon for that purpose, to prevent its overthrow by an armed mob under pretense of fraud and irregularity in the election of 1872. I have heretofore called the attention of Congress to this subject, stating that on account of the frauds and forgeries committed at said election, and because it appears that the returns thereof were never legally canvassed, it was impossible to tell thereby who were chosen; but from the best sources of information at my command I have always believed that the present State officers received a majority of the legal votes actually cast at that election. I repeat what I said in my special message of February 23, 1873, that in the event of no action by Congress I must continue to recognize the government heretofore recognized by me.

I regret to say that with preparations for the late election decided indications appeared in some localities in the Southern States of a determination, by acts of violence and intimidation, to deprive citizens of the freedom of the ballot because of their political opinions. Bands of men, masked and armed, made their appearance; White Leagues and other societies were formed; large quantities of arms and ammunition were imported and distributed to these organizations; military drills, with menacing demonstrations, were held, and with all these murders enough were committed to spread terror among those whose political action was to be suppressed, if possible, by these intolerant and criminal proceedings. In some places colored laborers were compelled to vote according to the wishes of their employers, under threats of discharge if they acted otherwise; and there are too many instances in which, when these threats were disregarded, they were remorselessly executed by those who made them. I understand that the fifteenth amendment to the Constitution was made to prevent this and a like state of things, and the act of May 31, 1870, with amendments, was passed to enforce its provisions, the object of both being to guarantee to all citizens the right to vote and to protect them in the free enjoyment of that right. Enjoined by the Constitution "to take care that the laws be faithfully executed," and convinced by undoubted evidence that violations of said act had been committed and that a wide-spread and flagrant disregard of it was contemplated, the proper officers were instructed to prosecute the offenders, and troops were stationed at convenient points to aid these officers, if necessary, in the performance of their official duties. Complaints are made of this interference by Federal authority; but if said amendment and act do not provide for such interference under the circumstances as above stated, then they are without meaning, force, or effect, and the whole scheme of colored enfranchisement is worse than mockery and little better than a crime. Possibly Congress may find it due to truth and justice to ascertain, by means of a committee, whether the alleged wrongs to colored citizens for political purposes are real or the reports thereof were manufactured for the occasion.

The whole number of troops in the States of Louisiana, Alabama, Georgia, Florida, South Carolina, North Carolina, Kentucky, Tennessee, Arkansas, Mississippi, Maryland, and Virginia at the time of the election was 4,082. This embraces the garrisons of all the forts from the Delaware to the Gulf of Mexico.

Another trouble has arisen in Arkansas. Article 13 of the constitution of that State (which was adopted in 1868, and upon the approval of which by Congress the State was restored to representation as one of the States of the Union) provides in effect that before any amendments proposed to this constitution shall become a part thereof they shall be passed by two successive assemblies and then submitted to and ratified by a majority of the electors of the State voting thereon. On the 11th of May, 1874, the governor convened an extra session of the general assembly of the State, which on the 18th of the same month passed an act providing for a convention to frame a new constitution. Pursuant to this act, and at an election held on the 30th of June, 1874, the convention was approved, and delegates were chosen thereto, who assembled on the 14th of last July and framed a new constitution, the schedule of which provided for the election of an entire new set of State officers in a manner contrary to the then existing election laws of the State. On the 13th of October, 1874, this constitution, as therein provided, was submitted to the people for their approval or rejection, and according to the election returns was approved by a large majority of those qualified to vote thereon; and at the same election persons were chosen to fill all the State, county, and township offices. The governor elected in 1872 for the term of four years turned over his office to the governor chosen under the new constitution, whereupon the lieutenant-governor, also elected in 1872 for a term of four years, claiming to act as governor, and alleging that said proceedings by which the new constitution was made and a new set of officers elected were unconstitutional, illegal, and void, called upon me, as provided in section 4, Article IV, of the Constitution, to protect the State against domestic violence. As Congress is now investigating the political affairs of Arkansas, I have declined to interfere.

The whole subject of Executive interference with the affairs of a State is repugnant to public opinion, to the feelings of those who, from their official capacity, must be used in such interposition, and to him or those who must direct. Unless most clearly on the side of law, such interference becomes a crime; with the law to support it, it is condemned without a hearing. I desire, therefore, that all necessity for Executive direction in local affairs may become unnecessary and obsolete. I invite the attention, not of Congress, but of the people of the United States, to the causes and effects of these unhappy questions. Is there not a disposition on one side to magnify wrongs and outrages, and on the other side to belittle them or justify them? If public opinion could be directed to a correct survey of what is and to rebuking wrong and aiding the proper authorities in punishing it, a better state of feeling would be inculcated, and the sooner we would have that peace which would leave the States free indeed to regulate their own domestic affairs. I believe on the part of our citizens of the Southern States—the better part of them—there is a disposition to be law abiding, and to do no violence either to individuals or to the laws existing. But do they do right in ignoring the existence of violence and bloodshed in resistance to constituted authority? I sympathize with their prostrate condition, and would do all in my power to relieve them, acknowledging that in some instances they have had most trying governments to live under, and very oppressive ones in the way of taxation for nominal improvements, not giving benefits equal to the hardships imposed. But can they proclaim themselves entirely irresponsible for this condition? They can not. Violence has been rampant in some localities, and has either been justified or denied by those who could have prevented it. The theory is even raised that there is to be no further interference on the part of the General Government to protect citizens within a State where the State authorities fail to give protection. This is a great mistake. While I remain Executive all the laws of Congress and the provisions of the Constitution, including the recent amendments added thereto, will be enforced with rigor, but with regret that they should have added one jot or tittle to Executive duties or powers. Let there be fairness in the discussion of Southern questions, the advocates of both or all political parties giving honest, truthful reports of occurrences, condemning the wrong and upholding the right, and soon all

will be well. Under existing conditions the negro votes the Republican ticket because he knows his friends are of that party.
Many a good citizen votes the opposite, not because he agrees
with the great principles of state which separate parties, but
because, generally, he is opposed to negro rule. This is a most
delusive cry. Treat the negro as a citizen and a voter, as he is
and must remain, and soon parties will be divided, not on the
color line, but on principle. Then we shall have no complaint
of sectional interference.

December 7, 1874

Philip H. Sheridan to William W. Belknap

HEADQRS. MILITARY DIVISION OF THE MISSOURI,
NEW ORLEANS, LA., *January* 4, 1875.
The Hon. W. W. BELKNAP, *Sec'y of War, Washington:*

It is with deep regret that I have to announce to you the existence in this State of a spirit of defiance to all lawful authority; and an insecurity of life which is hardly realized by the General Government or the country at large. The lives of citizens have become so jeopardized, that unless something is done to give protection to the people, all security usually afforded by law will be overridden. Defiance to the laws and the murder of individuals seem to be looked upon by the community here from a stand-point which gives impunity to all who choose to indulge in either, and the civil government appears powerless to punish, or even arrest. I have to-night assumed control over the Department of the Gulf.

P. H. SHERIDAN, Lieutenant-General.

———————

HEADQRS. MILITARY DIVISION OF THE MISSOURI,
NEW ORLEANS, LA., *January* 5, 1875.
The Hon. W. W. BELKNAP, *Sec'y of War, Washington:*

I think the terrorism now existing in Louisiana, Mississippi, and Arkansas, could be entirely removed, and confidence and fair dealing established, by the arrest and trial of the ringleaders of the armed White Leagues. If Congress would pass a bill declaring them banditti, they could be tried by military commission. This banditti, who murdered men here on the 14th of last September, also more recently at Vicksburg, Miss., should, in justice to law and order, and the peace and prosperity of this Southern part of the country, be punished. It is possible that, if the President would issue a proclamation declaring them banditti, that no further action need be taken, except that which would devolve upon me.

P. H. SHERIDAN, Lieut.-General U. S. Army.

Carl Schurz: from Speech in the Senate on Louisiana

SIR, there is one thing which every free people living under a constitutional government watches with peculiar jealousy as the most essential safeguard of representative institutions. It is the absolute freedom of legislative bodies from interference on the part of executive power, especially by force. Therefore, in a truly constitutional government, may the proceedings of the Legislature be good or ever so bad, is such interference, especially as concerns the admission of its own members, most emphatically condemned and most carefully guarded against, whether it proceed from a governor or from a president or from a king, under whatever circumstances, on whatever pretexts. And whenever such interference is successfully carried out, it is always, and justly, looked upon as a sure sign of the decline of free institutions.

There is another thing which especially the American people hold sacred as the life element of their republican freedom: It is the right to govern and administer their local affairs independently through the exercise of that self-government which lives and has its being in the organism of the States; and therefore we find in the Constitution of the Republic the power of the National Government to interfere in State affairs most scrupulously limited to certain well-defined cases and the observance of certain strictly-prescribed forms; and if these limitations be arbitrarily disregarded by the national authority, and if such violation be permitted by the Congress of the United States, we shall surely have reason to say that our system of republican government is in danger.

We are by the recent events in Louisiana forced to inquire how the cause of local self-government and of legislative privilege stands in the United States to-day. Before laying their hands upon things so important, so sacred, the authorities should certainly have well assured themselves that they have the clearest, the most obvious, the most unequivocal, the most unquestionable warrant of law. Where, I ask, is that warrant? In the Constitution of the United States we find but one sentence referring to the subject. It says in the fourth section of the fourth article:

> The United States shall guarantee to every State in this Union a republican form of government, and shall protect each of them against invasion; and on application of the Legislature, or of the executive (when the Legislature cannot be convened) against domestic violence.

So far the Constitution. There are two statutes prescribing the mode in which this is to be done, one passed in 1795 and the other in 1807. The former provides that "in case of insurrection in any State against the government thereof, it shall be lawful for the President of the United States, on application of the Legislature of such State or of the executive (when the Legislature cannot be convened) to call upon the militia of other States to suppress the insurrection." The statute of 1807 authorizes the President to employ the regular Army and Navy for the same purpose, provided, however, that he "has first observed all the prerequisites of the law."

Had in this case the circumstances so described occurred, and were "all the prerequisites of the law" observed? There had been an insurrection in Louisiana on the 14th of September, 1874, an insurrection against the State government recognized by the President of the United States. That State government had been overthrown by the insurgents. The President, having been called upon by Acting Governor Kellogg, issued his proclamation commanding the insurgents to desist. They did so desist at once, and the Kellogg government was restored without a struggle, and has not been attacked since. The insurrection, as such, was totally ended. On the 4th of January nobody pretends that there was any insurrection. The State of Louisiana was quiet. The State-house was surrounded by the armed forces of Governor Kellogg. Those forces were not resisted; their services were not even called into requisition. There was certainly no demand upon the President for military interference by the Legislature; neither was there by the governor "in case the Legislature could not be convened," for the Legislature did convene without any obstruction at the time and in the place fixed by law, and was called to order by the officer designated by law. And yet, there being neither insurrection nor domestic violence, there being neither a call for military interference upon the President by the Legislature nor by the governor "in case the Legislature could not be convened," there being, therefore, not the faintest shadow of an observance of "all the prerequisites of the law" as defined in the statute, the troops of the United States proceeded, not against an insurrection, not against a body of men committing domestic violence, but against a legislative body sitting in the State-house; and the soldiers of the United States were used to execute an order from the governor determining what persons should sit in that Legislature as its members and what persons should be ejected. I solemnly ask what provision is there in the Constitution, what law is there on the statute-book furnishing a warrant for such a proceeding?

It is said in extenuation of the interference of the military power of the United States in Louisiana that the persons ejected from that Legislature by the Federal soldiers were not legally-elected members of that body. Suppose that had been so—but that is not the question. The question is where is the constitutional principle, where is the law authorizing United States soldiers, with muskets in their hands, to determine who is a legally-elected member of a State Legislature and who is not?

It is said that the mode of organizing that Legislature was not in accordance with the statutes of the State. Suppose that had been so; but that is not the question. The question is where is the constitutional or legal warrant for the bayonets of the Federal soldiery to interpret the statutes of a State as against the Legislature of that State, and to decide in and for the Legislature a point of parliamentary law?

It is said that the governor requested the aid of United States soldiers to purge the Legislature of members he styled illegal. That may be so; but that is not the question. The question is, where is the law authorizing United States soldiers to do the bidding of a State governor who presumes to decide what members sitting in a Legislature regularly convened at the time and place fixed by law are legally elected members?

It is said the trouble was threatening between contending parties in Louisiana. Suppose that had been so; but that is not the question. The question is, where is the law from which the National Government, in case of threatening trouble in a State, derives its power to invade the legislative body of that State by armed force, and to drag out persons seated there as members, that others may take their place? Where is that law, I ask? You will search the Constitution, you will search the statutes in vain.

I cannot, therefore, escape from the deliberate conviction, a conviction conscientiously formed, that the deed done on the 4th of January in the State-house of the State of Louisiana by the military forces of the United States constitutes a gross and manifest violation of the Constitution and the laws of this Republic. We have an act before us indicating a spirit in our Government which either ignores the Constitution and the laws, or so interprets them that they cease to be the safeguard of the independence of legislation and of the rights and liberties of our people. And that spirit shows itself in a shape more alarming still in the instrument the Executive has chosen to execute his behests.

Sir, no American citizen can have read without profound regret and equally profound apprehension the recent dispatch of General Sheridan to the Secretary of War, in which he suggests that a numerous class of citizens should by the wholesale be outlawed as banditti by a mere proclamation of the President, to be turned over to him as a military chief, to meet at his hands swift justice by the verdict of a military commission. Nobody respects General Sheridan more than I do for the brilliancy of his deeds on the field of battle; the nation has delighted to honor his name. But the same nation would sincerely deplore to see the hero of the ride of Winchester and of the charge at the Five Forks stain that name by an attempt to ride over the laws and the Constitution of the country, and to charge upon the liberties of his fellow-citizens. The policy he has proposed is so appalling, that every American citizen who loves his liberty stands aghast at the mere possibility of such a suggestion being addressed to the President of the United States by a high official of the Government. It is another illustration how great a man may be as a soldier, and how conspicuously unable to understand what civil law and what a constitution mean; how glorious in fighting for you, and how little fit to govern you!

And yet General Sheridan is not only kept in Louisiana as the instrument of the Executive will, but after all that has happened encouraged by the emphatic approval of the executive branch of this Government.

I repeat, sir, all these things have alarmed me, and it seems not me alone. In all parts of the country the press is giving voice to the same feeling, and what I learn by private information convinces me that the press is by no means exaggerating the alarm of the people. On all sides you can hear the question asked, "If this can be done in Louisiana, and if such things be sustained by Congress, how long will it be before it can be done in Massachusetts and in Ohio? How long before the constitutional rights of all the States and the self-government of all the people may be trampled under foot? How long before a general of the Army may sit in the chair you occupy, sir, to decide contested-election cases for the purpose of manufacturing a majority in the Senate? How long before a soldier may stalk into the national House of Representatives, and, pointing to the Speaker's mace, say, 'Take away that bauble?'"

Mr. President, these fears may appear wild and exaggerated, and perhaps they are; and yet these are the feelings you will hear expressed when the voice of the people penetrates to you. But I ask you, my associates in this body, in all soberness, can you tell me what will be impossible to-morrow if this was possible yesterday? Who is there among us who but three years ago would have expected to be called upon to justify the most gross and unjustifiable usurpation of Judge Durell and the President's enforcement of it as the legitimate and lawful origin of a State government? And who of you, when permitting that to be done, would have expected to see the United States soldiery marched into the hall of a State Legislature to decide its organization? Permit that to-day, and who of you can tell me what we shall be called upon, nay, what we may be forced to permit to-morrow?

Look at the condition of the Southern States. I well remember the time, not a great many years ago, when the State of Virginia was said to be in so alarming a condition—and I remember prominent republicans of that State hanging around this body to convince us of it—that in case the conservatives should obtain control of the State government the streets and fields of Virginia would run with blood. So it was predicted of North Carolina, and so of Georgia; and, indeed, I deny it not, there were very lamentable disorders in many of those States during the first years after the war. Now, sir, what was the remedy? You remember what policy was urged with regard to Georgia. It was to prolong the existence of Governor Bullock's legislature for two years beyond its constitutional term, to strengthen the power of that Governor Bullock, that champion plunderer of Georgia, who not long afterward had to run from the clutches of justice; and unless that were done it was loudly predicted upon this floor there would be a carnival of crime and a sea of blood!

Well, sir, it was not done. The people of those States gradually recovered the free exercise of their self-government, and what has been the result? Virginia is to-day as quiet and orderly a State as she ever was, I think fully as quiet and orderly as most other States, and every citizen is securely enjoying his rights. And who will deny that in North Carolina and Georgia an improvement has taken place, standing in most glaring contrast with the fearful predictions made by the advocates of Federal interference? And that most healthy improvement is sustained in those States under and by the self-government of the people thereof. This is a matter of history, unquestioned and unquestionable. And that improvement will proceed further under the same self-government of the people as society becomes more firmly settled in its new conditions and as it is by necessity led to recognize more clearly the dependence of its dearest interests on the maintenance of public order and safety. That is the natural development of things.

It will help the Senator from Indiana [Mr. MORTON] little to say that, with all this, the republican vote has greatly fallen off in Georgia, and that this fact is conclusive proof of a general system of intimidation practiced upon the negroes there. It is scarcely worth while that I should repeat here the unquestionably truthful statement which has been made, that the falling off of the negro vote is in a great measure accounted for by the non-payment of the colored people of the school tax upon which their right to vote depended. I might add that perhaps the same causes which brought forth a considerable falling off in the republican vote in a great many other States, such as Indiana and Massachusetts and New York, produced the same result in Georgia also, and that the same motives which produced a change in the political attitude of whites may have acted also upon the blacks. Is not this possible? Why not? But I ask you, sir, what kind of logic, what statesmanship is it we witness so frequently on this floor, which takes the statistics of population of a State in hand and then proceeds to reason thus: So many colored people, so many white, therefore so many colored votes and so many white votes; and therefore so many republican votes and so many democratic votes; and if an election does not show this exact proposition, it must be necessarily the result of fraud and intimidation and the National Government must interfere. When we have established the rule that election returns must be made or corrected according to the statistics of population, then we may decide elections beforehand by the United States census and last year's Tribune Almanac, and save ourselves the trouble of voting.

Intimidation of voters! I doubt not, sir, there has been much of it, very much. There has been much of it by terrorism, physical and moral, much by the discharge of employés from employment for political cause, but, I apprehend, not all on one side. I shall be the last man on earth to say a word of excuse for the southern ruffian who threatens a negro voter with violence to make him vote the conservative ticket. I know no language too severe to condemn his act. But I cannot forget, and it stands vividly in my recollection, that the only act of terrorism and intimidation I ever happened to witness with my own eyes was the cruel clubbing and stoning of a colored man in North Carolina in 1872 by men of his own race, because he had declared himself in favor of the conservatives; and if the whole story of the South were told it would be discovered that such a practice has by no means been infrequent.

But there was intimidation of another kind.

I cannot forget the spectacle of Marshal Packard, with the dragoons of the United States at the disposition of the chairman of the Kellogg campaign committee at the late election in Louisiana, riding through the State with a full assortment of warrants in his hands, arresting whomsoever he listed. I cannot forget that as to the discharge of laborers from employment for political cause a most seductive and demoralizing example is set by the very highest authority in the land. While we have a law on our statute-book declaring the intimidation of voters by threatened or actual discharge from employment a punishable offense, it is the notorious practice of the Government of the United States to discharge every one of its employés who dares to vote against the administration party; and that is done North and South, East and West, as far as the arm of that Government reaches. I have always condemned the intimidation of voters in every shape, and therefore I have been in favor of a genuine civil-service reform. But while your National Government is the chief intimidator in the land, you must not be surprised if partisans on both sides profit a little from its example.

Nor do I think that the intimidation which deters a colored man from voting with the opposition against the republican party is less detestable or less harmful to the colored men themselves than that which threatens him as a republican. I declare I shall hail the day as a most auspicious one for the colored race in the South, when they cease to stand as a solid mass under the control and discipline of one political organization, thus being arrayed as a race against another race; when they throw off the scandalous leadership of those adventurers who, taking advantage of their ignorance, make them the tools of their rapacity, and thus throw upon them the odium for their misdeeds; when they begin to see the identity of their own true interests with the interests of the white people among whom they have to live; when they begin to understand that they greatly injure those common interests by using the political power they possess for the elevation to office of men, black or white, whose ignorance or unscrupulousness unfits them for responsible trust; when freely, according to the best individual judgment of each man, they divide their votes between the different political parties and when thus giving to each party a chance to obtain their votes, they make it the interest and the natural policy of each party to protect their safety and respect their rights in order to win their votes. I repeat what I once said in another place: not in union is there safety, but in division. Whenever the colored voters shall have become an important element, not only in one, but in both political parties, then both parties under an impulse of self interest will rival in according them the fullest protection. I may speak here of my own peculiar experience, for they may learn a lesson from the history of the adopted citizens of this country. I remember the time when they stood in solid mass on the side of one party, and schemes dangerous to their rights were hatched upon the side of the other. When both parties obtained an important share of their votes, both hoping for more, both became equally their friends. This will be the development in the South, and a most fortunate one for the colored people. It has commenced in the States I have already mentioned, where self-government goes its way unimpeded, and I fervently hope the frantic partisan efforts to prevent it in others will not much longer prevail. I hope this as a sincere and devoted friend of the colored race.

But the Senator from Indiana may say that will bring about a still greater falling-off in the republican vote. Ah, sir, it may; but do you not profess to be sincerely solicitous for the safety and rights of the colored man? Are not some of you even willing to see the most essential principles of constitutional government invaded, to see State governments set up by judicial usurpation, and State Legislatures organized by Federal bayonets only that the colored man may be safe? Gentlemen, you can have that much cheaper if you let the colored man protect himself by the method I advise. The colored people will then be far safer than under a broken Constitution; the peace and order of society will be far more naturally and securely established than under the fitful interference of military force. And that can be accomplished by permitting the self-government of the people to have its course. But the republican vote may thus fall off. That is true. The party may suffer. Indeed it may. But, Senators, I, for my part, know of no party, whatever its name or fame, so sacred that its selfish advantage should be considered superior to the peace and order of society and good understanding among the people. I do not hesitate to say that I prefer the conservative government of Virginia to the republican government of Louisiana; and, if I mistake not, an overwhelming majority of the American people are of the same opinion.

January 11, 1875

William Lloyd Garrison to the Boston Journal

To the Editors of The Boston Journal:

It is to be expected that, let President Grant do what he may in the discharge of his official duties to uphold the recognized State Government of Louisiana against armed sedition, he will be basely vilified and ferociously assailed by the great body of conspirators who rose in rebellion for the dismemberment of the Union under the administration of President Lincoln; for, though they were put down by the strong arm of national power, in spirit (deny it who will) they are still as perfidious, as brutal, as law-despising, as disloyal as before their treasonable revolt. In any issue as to the enjoyment of equal rights with those whom they once owned as mere chattels, it is as impossible for them to speak the truth or to deal justly, as it is for wolves to abhor blood and become docile by the interposition of the shepherd for the safety of the sheepfold. As of old, they still devise wicked devices to destroy the poor with lying words. As of old, their feet run to evil, and they make haste to shed innocent blood. As of old, they hate him that rebuketh in the gate, and they abhor him that speaketh uprightly. As of old, they grope for the wall, there is no judgment in their goings, and THE WAY OF PEACE THEY KNOW NOT.

It cannot be otherwise, unless human nature among them is wholly unlike what it is in every other portion of the globe. The curse of negro slavery clings to them like leprosy, though the foul "institution" is abolished. It continues to feed their haughty pride, perpetuate their contempt of the lowly and helpless, disorder their reason, obscure their vision, bias their judgment, shape their policy, stimulate their love of dominion, nourish their disloyalty, poison their blood. It is true they have ceased to be slaveholders and traffickers in human flesh; but by no will or consent of their own; and to-morrow, if it were in their power, they would with one accord restore the slave system, with all its hideous accompaniments of slave-drivers, slave-hunters, slave-speculators—yokes, fetters, thumb-screws, gory whips, baying bloodhounds—the marriage institution overthrown, indiscriminate and forceful amalgamation universal, the sacred ties of relationship trampled upon, cradles plundered, slave auction blocks crowded with victims from infancy to old age to be sold in lots to the highest bidder, the Bible a prohibited volume, teaching a slave the alphabet at the risk of imprisonment or death, the very soil stained with the tears and blood of unrequited labor, a Fugitive Slave Law in active operation, a slave representation in Congress, and a SLAVE CODE more bloody than that of Draco's.

Fortunately, to re-enslave the millions set free is a task they can never accomplish; another St. Domingo tragedy, on a far more awful scale, would follow the attempt. It is the consciousness of this fact, and that their former chattels are now constitutionally enfranchised American citizens, that makes them writhe in agony, gnaw their tongues for pain, and in their madness resolve that the ballot in the hand of the negro shall be unavailing for his protection, and he reduced as near as possible to a state of serfdom; all loyal white men espousing his cause to be regarded and treated as having no rights that rebels at heart are bound to respect. At this hour the blood of thousands of unoffending colored persons—shot down like wild beasts—is upon their souls, crying to Heaven for that divine retribution from which the guilty may not hope to escape. Abject submission to their usurping sway is essential to personal safety, reciprocal social consideration, political preferment, official respect, business success and religious intercourse. With them the end sanctifies the means, however desperate and bloody; and that end is first, midst, last, and always, "A WHITE MAN'S GOVERNMENT"—tantamount to the old slaveholding oligarchic supremacy. In their lawless and defiant White League organizations they are accurately described by General Sheridan (himself no sentimentalist, and without any sympathetic leaning either toward negroes or Indians) as "a banditti."

This faithful but repulsive portraiture is drawn solely in the interest of liberty and equal rights, though painful the task; not to gratify personal, partisan or sectional ill-will. It no more implies an unkind or an uncharitable spirit, on the part of the limner, than when the ancient prophet declared—"This people hath a revolting and a rebellious heart; they are revolted and gone. They lay wait, as he that setteth snares, they set a trap, they catch men. As a cage is full of birds, so are their houses full of deceit; they overpass the deeds of the wicked. O foolish people, and without understanding; which have eyes, and see not; which have ears, and hear not. Woe is me now! for my soul is wearied because of murderers!"

That from such a class the wildest outcries and the fiercest threats should be heard against President Grant and General Sheridan for what they have done to maintain order in Louisiana, and to make it possible for a legitimate Republican form of Government to exist on its soil, is as inevitable a sequence as was the demoniacal cry of old, "Why hast thou come to torment us before the time?" As if the time had not fully come for the torment! Surely, that which instigates to mischief is to be held accountable for a breach of the peace; and not the power which seeks to preserve order.

Nor is it surprising that the Democratic organs and leaders at the North should re-echo the wrathful reproaches and defamatory accusations flung by their old Southern allies against Grant and Sheridan in this matter of Louisiana. To the extent of their daring they have always been the servile tools of "the lords of the lash," ready to sanction all their vile machinations for the perpetuation of negro slavery, and to go with them to the verge of rebellion. Nay, if when that outbreak came a Democratic Administration had been in power, Jefferson Davis and his myrmidons would have been allowed to succeed in their treasonable aims. Northern Democracy was never known to rejoice in any loyal victory: it opposed every measure essential to the preservation of the Federal and the overthrow of the Rebel Government, it contemplated the massacre at Fort Pillow and the horrors of Andersonville with iron-hearted indifference; it raved at the enlistment of colored soldiers and the act of emancipation; it opposed all constitutional amendments to make that act effective; and it was as vociferous and unprincipled in branding Abraham Lincoln as a tyrant and usurper, as it is now in applying the same libelous epithets to Ulysses S. Grant. In one of his latest and most solemnly recorded testimonies that noble patriot and lamented philanthropist, Gerrit Smith, said—and being dead, he yet speaketh:

"Better anything, better everything, than the ruin that would befall our country from the ascendency of that party which sympathized with the rebels in the late rebellion and with their malignant purpose to perpetuate slavery; and which still cherishes its traditional hatred of the black man. The slaughter of the innocent still going on at the South is due to this hatred, as was all Ku Kluxism, as was the negro murdering mob of 1863 in New York, and as was every one of the pro-slavery mobs that disgraced the North. Whether the outbreak against our colored brethren be at the North or at the South, the Democratic party is its inspiration, its soul and sustenance."

But, while neither truth nor fair dealing toward President Grant is to be looked for from such quarters, it is amazing to see what a "Bull Run panic" has seized upon the Republican party in consequence of such artful clamors, and to find in leading Republican journals the worst possible construction placed upon the action of the President, as though he were plotting for military dictatorship and, consequently, the overthrow of our free institutions! No worse impeachment of his motives and purposes has been made by any Southern rebel sheet. The man who conducted the nation to victory in the interest of Liberty and Union, wearing his laurels with the utmost modesty; whose magnanimity toward the conquered has no parallel in warfare; whose fidelity to his official trust was so conspicuous during his first term as to insure his renomination for the Presidency by acclamation of the National Republican Convention, and his election by the American people by an overwhelming vote; who has assiduously sought the repose and security of all classes at the South, using only the semblance of military power, and even then, with great reluctance and extreme circumspection; who, to avoid the heavy responsibility resting upon him, has in vain invoked the action of Congress, session after session, and therefore been compelled to act according to his best judgment by the oath exacted of him; who may or may not have erred in that judgment, as shall hereafter appear when all the facts are obtained; whose position has been one of the most trying conceivable, fairly entitling him, if not to commiseration, at least to a decent regard for his office, generous consideration and honorable treatment:—this man is now sweepingly denounced by Republican journals, in hot response to the allegations of White Leaguers and their Northern Democratic supporters, as guilty of the most high-handed usurpation, and as acting despotically in the organization of a State Legislature to the furtherance of his own ambitious ends. He has been hastily and impetuously condemned, without waiting to know the real state of the case or giving him a chance to be heard in self-defence. The version of the affair at New Orleans by the White Leaguers and their accomplices is accepted as truthful, and their malignant assault upon the President indorsed as truly patriotic. This is a strange mingling of injustice and infatuation. No fair-minded man, who has not for the time being lost his head, believes that either President Grant or Gen. Sheridan has intentionally usurped powers with which he is not entrusted, or that he has acted otherwise than as his official duty demanded for the general welfare, according to his most patriotic convictions under the most trying circumstances.

Be it so that both have seriously erred. "To err is human," but it is compatible with the noblest intentions; and where these dominate, flagrant designs against the rights of the few or the many are not to be imputed. Whatever blame is to be cast, let it rest upon Congress for not legislating for the government of Louisiana, as repeatedly urged by the President to do so.

> "The dangers of the days but newly gone,
>   (Whose memory is written on the earth
>   With yet appearing blood,) and the examples
>   Of every minute's instance, (present now,)
>   Have put us in these ill-beseeming arms:
>   Not to break peace, nor any branch of it;
>   But to establish here a peace indeed,
>   Concurring both in name and quality."

Yours, against all injustice, usurpation and tyranny,
                    WM. LLOYD GARRISON.

Boston, Jan. 12, 1875.

Boston Journal, January 13, 1875

Ulysses S. Grant: Message to the Senate on Louisiana

EXECUTIVE MANSION, *January 13, 1875.*
To the Senate of the United States:

I have the honor to make the following answer to a Senate resolution of the 8th instant, asking for information as to any interference by any military officer or any part of the Army of the United States with the organization or proceedings of the general assembly of the State of Louisiana, or either branch thereof; and also inquiring in regard to the existence of armed organizations in that State hostile to the government thereof and intent on overturning such government by force.

To say that lawlessness, turbulence, and bloodshed have characterized the political affairs of that State since its reorganization under the reconstruction acts is only to repeat what has become well known as a part of its unhappy history; but it may be proper here to refer to the election of 1868, by which the Republican vote of the State, through fraud and violence, was reduced to a few thousands, and the bloody riots of 1866 and 1868, to show that the disorders there are not due to any recent causes or to any late action of the Federal authorities.

Preparatory to the election of 1872 a shameful and undisguised conspiracy was formed to carry that election against the Republicans, without regard to law or right, and to that end the most glaring frauds and forgeries were committed in the returns, after many colored citizens had been denied registration and others deterred by fear from casting their ballots.

When the time came for a final canvass of the votes, in view of the foregoing facts William P. Kellogg, the Republican candidate for governor, brought suit upon the equity side of the United States circuit court for Louisiana, and against Warmoth and others, who had obtained possession of the returns of the election, representing that several thousand voters of the State had been deprived of the elective franchise on account of their color, and praying that steps might be taken to have said votes counted and for general relief. To enable the court to inquire as to the truth of these allegations, a temporary restraining order was issued against the defendants, which was at once wholly disregarded and treated with contempt by those to whom it was directed. These proceedings have been widely denounced as an unwarrantable interference by the Federal judiciary with the election of State officers; but it is to be remembered that by the fifteenth amendment to the Constitution of the United States the political equality of colored citizens is secured, and under the second section of that amendment, providing that Congress shall have power to enforce its provisions by appropriate legislation, an act was passed on the 31st of May, 1870, and amended in 1871, the object of which was to prevent the denial or abridgment of suffrage to citizens on account of race, color, or previous condition of servitude; and it has been held by all the Federal judges before whom the question has arisen, including Justice Strong, of the Supreme Court, that the protection afforded by this amendment and these acts extends to State as well as other elections. That it is the duty of the Federal courts to enforce the provisions of the Constitution of the United States and the laws passed in pursuance thereof is too clear for controversy.

Section 15 of said act, after numerous provisions therein to prevent an evasion of the fifteenth amendment, provides that the jurisdiction of the circuit court of the United States shall extend to all cases in law or equity arising under the provisions of said act and of the act amendatory thereof. Congress seems to have contemplated equitable as well as legal proceedings to prevent the denial of suffrage to colored citizens; and it may be safely asserted that if Kellogg's bill in the above-named case did not present a case for the equitable interposition of the court, that no such case can arise under the act. That the courts of the United States have the right to interfere in various ways with State elections so as to maintain political equality and rights therein, irrespective of race or color, is comparatively a new, and to some seems to be a startling, idea, but it results as clearly from the fifteenth amendment to the Constitution and the acts that have been passed to enforce that amendment as the abrogation of State laws upholding slavery results from the thirteenth amendment to the Constitution. While the jurisdiction of the court in the case of Kellogg *vs.* Warmoth and others is clear to my mind, it seems that some of the orders made by the judge in that and the kindred case of Antoine were illegal. But while they are so held and considered, it is not to be forgotten that the mandate of his court had been contemptuously defied, and they were made while wild scenes of anarchy were sweeping away all restraint of law and order. Doubtless the judge of this court made grave mistakes; but the law allows the chancellor great latitude, not only in punishing those who contemn his orders and injunctions, but in preventing the consummation of the wrong which he has judicially forbidden. Whatever may be said or thought of those matters, it was only made known to me that process of the United States court was resisted, and as said act especially provides for the use of the Army and Navy when necessary to enforce judicial process arising thereunder, I considered it my duty to see that such process was executed according to the judgment of the court.

Resulting from these proceedings, through various controversies and complications, a State administration was organized with William P. Kellogg as governor, which, in the discharge of my duty under section 4, Article IV, of the Constitution, I have recognized as the government of the State.

It has been bitterly and persistently alleged that Kellogg was not elected. Whether he was or not is not altogether certain, nor is it any more certain that his competitor, McEnery, was chosen. The election was a gigantic fraud, and there are no reliable returns of its result. Kellogg obtained possession of the office, and in my opinion has more right to it than his competitor.

On the 20th of February, 1873, the Committee on Privileges and Elections of the Senate made a report in which they say they were satisfied by testimony that the manipulation of the election machinery by Warmoth and others was equivalent to 20,000 votes; and they add that to recognize the McEnery government "would be recognizing a government based upon fraud, in defiance of the wishes and intention of the voters of the State." Assuming the correctness of the statements in this report (and they seem to have been generally accepted by the country), the great crime in Louisiana, about which so much has been said, is that one is holding the office of governor who was cheated out of 20,000 votes, against another whose title to the office is undoubtedly based on fraud and in defiance of the wishes and intentions of the voters of the State.

Misinformed and misjudging as to the nature and extent of this report, the supporters of McEnery proceeded to displace by force in some counties of the State the appointees of Governor Kellogg, and on the 13th of April, in an effort of that kind, a butchery of citizens was committed at Colfax, which in bloodthirstiness and barbarity is hardly surpassed by any acts of savage warfare.

To put this matter beyond controversy I quote from the charge of Judge Woods, of the United States circuit court, to the jury in the case of The United States *vs.* Cruikshank and others, in New Orleans in March, 1874. He said:

> In the case on trial there are many facts not in controversy. I proceed to state some of them in the presence and hearing of counsel on both sides; and if I state as a conceded fact any matter that is disputed, they can correct me.

After stating the origin of the difficulty, which grew out of an attempt of white persons to drive the parish judge and sheriff, appointees of Kellogg, from office, and their attempted protection by colored persons, which led to some fighting, in which quite a number of negroes were killed, the judge states:

> Most of those who were not killed were taken prisoners. Fifteen or sixteen of the blacks had lifted the boards and taken refuge under the floor of the court-house. They were all captured. About thirty-seven men were taken prisoners. The number is not definitely fixed. They were kept under guard until dark. They were led out, two by two, and shot. Most of the men were shot to death. A few were wounded, not mortally, and by pretending to be dead were afterwards, during the night, able to make their escape. Among them was the Levi Nelson named in the indictment.
>
> The dead bodies of the negroes killed in this affair were left unburied until Tuesday, April 15, when they were buried by a deputy marshal and an officer of the militia from New Orleans. These persons found fifty-nine dead bodies. They showed pistol-shot wounds, the great majority in the head, and most of them in the back of the head. In addition to the fifty-nine dead bodies found, some charred remains of dead bodies were discovered near the court-house. Six dead bodies were found

under a warehouse, all shot in the head but one or two, which were shot in the breast.

The only white men injured from the beginning of these troubles to their close were Hadnot and Harris. The court-house and its contents were entirely consumed.

There is no evidence that anyone in the crowd of whites bore any lawful warrant for the arrest of any of the blacks. There is no evidence that either Nash or Cazabat, after the affair, ever demanded their offices, to which they had set up claim, but Register continued to act as parish judge and Shaw as sheriff.

These are facts in this case as I understand them to be admitted.

To hold the people of Louisiana generally responsible for these atrocities would not be just, but it is a lamentable fact that insuperable obstructions were thrown in the way of punishing these murderers; and the so-called conservative papers of the State not only justified the massacre, but denounced as Federal tyranny and despotism the attempt of the United States officers to bring them to justice. Fierce denunciations ring through the country about office holding and election matters in Louisiana, while every one of the Colfax miscreants goes unwhipped of justice, and no way can be found in this boasted land of civilization and Christianity to punish the perpetrators of this bloody and monstrous crime.

Not unlike this was the massacre in August last. Several Northern young men of capital and enterprise had started the little and flourishing town of Coushatta. Some of them were Republicans and officeholders under Kellogg. They were therefore doomed to death. Six of them were seized and carried away from their homes and murdered in cold blood. No one has been punished, and the conservative press of the State denounced all efforts to that end and boldly justified the crime.

Many murders of a like character have been committed in individual cases, which can not here be detailed. For example, T. S. Crawford, judge, and P. H. Harris, district attorney, of the twelfth judicial district of the State, on their way to court were shot from their horses by men in ambush on the 8th of October, 1873; and the widow of the former, in a communication to the Department of Justice, tells a piteous tale of the persecutions of her husband because he was a Union man, and of the efforts made to screen those who had committed a crime which, to use her own language, "left two widows and nine orphans desolate."

To say that the murder of a negro or a white Republican is not considered a crime in Louisiana would probably be unjust to a great part of the people, but it is true that a great number of such murders have been committed and no one has been punished therefor; and manifestly, as to them, the spirit of hatred and violence is stronger than law.

Representations were made to me that the presence of troops in Louisiana was unnecessary and irritating to the people, and that there was no danger of public disturbance if they were taken away. Consequently early in last summer the troops were all withdrawn from the State, with the exception of a small garrison at New Orleans Barracks. It was claimed that a comparative state of quiet had supervened. Political excitement as to Louisiana affairs seemed to be dying out. But the November election was approaching, and it was necessary for party purposes that the flame should be rekindled.

Accordingly, on the 14th of September D. P. Penn, claiming that he was elected lieutenant-governor in 1872, issued an inflammatory proclamation calling upon the militia of the State to arm, assemble, and drive from power the usurpers, as he designated the officers of the State. The White Leagues, armed and ready for the conflict, promptly responded.

On the same day the governor made a formal requisition upon me, pursuant to the act of 1795 and section 4, Article IV, of the Constitution, to aid in suppressing domestic violence. On the next day I issued my proclamation commanding the insurgents to disperse within five days from the date thereof; but before the proclamation was published in New Orleans the organized and armed forces recognizing a usurping governor had taken forcible possession of the statehouse and temporarily subverted the government. Twenty or more people were killed, including a number of the police of the city. The streets of the city were stained with blood. All that was desired in the way of excitement had been accomplished, and, in view of the steps taken to repress it, the revolution is apparently, though it is believed not really, abandoned, and the cry of Federal usurpation and tyranny in Louisiana was renewed with redoubled energy. Troops had been sent to the State under this requisition of the governor, and as other disturbances seemed imminent they were allowed to remain there to render the executive such aid as might become necessary to enforce the laws of the State and repress the continued violence which seemed inevitable the moment Federal support should be withdrawn.

Prior to, and with a view to, the late election in Louisiana white men associated themselves together in armed bodies called "White Leagues," and at the same time threats were made in the Democratic journals of the State that the election should be carried against the Republicans at all hazards, which very naturally greatly alarmed the colored voters. By section 8 of the act of February 28, 1871, it is made the duty of United States marshals and their deputies at polls where votes are cast for Representatives in Congress to keep the peace and prevent any violations of the so-called enforcement acts and other offenses against the laws of the United States; and upon a requisition of the marshal of Louisiana, and in view of said armed organizations and other portentous circumstances, I caused detachments of troops to be stationed in various localities in the State, to aid him in the performance of his official duties. That there was intimidation of Republican voters at the election, notwithstanding these precautions, admits of no doubt. The following are specimens of the means used:

On the 14th of October eighty persons signed and published the following at Shreveport:

> We, the undersigned, merchants of the city of Shreveport, in obedience to a request of the Shreveport Campaign Club, agree to use every endeavor to get our employees to vote the People's ticket at the ensuing election, and in the event of their refusal so to do, or in case they vote the Radical ticket, to refuse to employ them at the expiration of their present contracts.

On the same day another large body of persons published in the same place a paper in which they used the following language:

> We, the undersigned, merchants of the city of Shreveport, alive to the great importance of securing good and honest government to the State, do agree and pledge ourselves not to advance any supplies or money to any planter the coming year who will give employment or rent lands to laborers who vote the Radical ticket in the coming election.

I have no information of the proceedings of the returning board for said election which may not be found in its report, which has been published; but it is a matter of public information that a great part of the time taken to canvass the votes was consumed by the arguments of lawyers, several of whom represented each party before the board. I have no evidence that the proceedings of this board were not in accordance with the law under which they acted. Whether in excluding from their count certain returns they were right or wrong is a question that depends upon the evidence they had before them; but it is very clear that the law gives them the power, if they choose to exercise it, of deciding that way, and, *prima facie*, the persons whom they return as elected are entitled to the offices for which they were candidates.

Respecting the alleged interference by the military with the organization of the legislature of Louisiana on the 4th instant, I have no knowledge or information which has not been received by me since that time and published. My first information was from the papers of the morning of the 5th of January. I did not know that any such thing was anticipated, and no orders nor suggestions were ever given to any military officer in that State upon that subject prior to the occurrence. I am well aware that any military interference by the officers or troops of the United States with the organization of the State legislature or any of its proceedings, or with any civil department of the Government, is repugnant to our ideas of government. I can conceive of no case, not involving rebellion or insurrection, where such interference by authority of the General Government ought to be permitted or can be justified. But there are circumstances connected with the late legislative imbroglio in Louisiana which seem to exempt the military from any intentional wrong in that matter. Knowing that they had been placed in Louisiana to prevent domestic violence and aid in the enforcement of the State laws, the officers and troops of the United States may well have supposed that it was their duty to act when called upon by the governor for that purpose.

Each branch of a legislative assembly is the judge of the election and qualifications of its own members; but if a mob or a body of unauthorized persons seize and hold the legislative hall in a tumultuous and riotous manner, and so prevent any organization by those legally returned as elected, it might become the duty of the State executive to interpose, if requested by a majority of the members elect, to suppress the disturbance and enable the persons elected to organize the house.

Any exercise of this power would only be justifiable under most extraordinary circumstances, and it would then be the duty of the governor to call upon the constabulary or, if necessary, the military force of the State. But with reference to Louisiana, it is to be borne in mind that any attempt by the governor to use the police force of that State at this time would have undoubtedly precipitated a bloody conflict with the White League, as it did on the 14th of September.

There is no doubt but that the presence of the United States troops upon that occasion prevented bloodshed and the loss of life. Both parties appear to have relied upon them as conservators of the public peace.

The first call was made by the Democrats, to remove persons obnoxious to them from the legislative halls; and the second was from the Republicans, to remove persons who had usurped seats in the legislature without legal certificates authorizing them to seats, and in sufficient number to change the majority.

Nobody was disturbed by the military who had a legal right at that time to occupy a seat in the legislature. That the Democratic minority of the house undertook to seize its organization by fraud and violence; that in this attempt they trampled under foot law; that they undertook to make persons not returned as elected members, so as to create a majority; that they acted under a preconcerted plan, and under false pretenses introduced into the hall a body of men to support their pretensions by force if necessary, and that conflict, disorder, and riotous proceedings followed are facts that seem to be well established; and I am credibly informed that these violent proceedings were a part of a premeditated plan to have the house organized in this way, recognize what has been called the McEnery senate, then to depose Governor Kellogg, and so revolutionize the State government.

Whether it was wrong for the governor, at the request of the majority of the members returned as elected to the house, to use such means as were in his power to defeat these lawless and revolutionary proceedings is perhaps a debatable question; but it is quite certain that there would have been no trouble if those who now complain of illegal interference had allowed the house to be organized in a lawful and regular manner. When those who inaugurate disorder and anarchy disavow such proceedings, it will be time enough to condemn those who by such means as they have prevent the success of their lawless and desperate schemes.

Lieutenant-General Sheridan was requested by me to go to Louisiana to observe and report the situation there, and, if in his opinion necessary, to assume the command, which he did on the 4th instant, after the legislative disturbances had occurred, at 9 o'clock P.M., a number of hours after the disturbances. No party motives nor prejudices can reasonably be imputed to him; but honestly convinced by what he has seen and heard there, he has characterized the leaders of the White Leagues in severe terms and suggested summary modes of procedure against them, which, though they can not be adopted, would, if legal, soon put an end to the troubles and disorders in that State. General Sheridan was looking at facts, and possibly, not thinking of proceedings which would be the only proper ones to pursue in time of peace, thought more of the utterly lawless condition of society surrounding him at the time of his dispatch and of what would prove a sure remedy. He never proposed to do an illegal act nor expressed determination to proceed beyond what the law in the future might authorize for the punishment of the atrocities which have been committed, and the commission of which can not be successfully denied. It is a deplorable fact that political crimes and murders have been committed in Louisiana which have gone unpunished, and which have been justified or apologized for, which must rest as a reproach upon the State and country long after the present generation has passed away.

I have no desire to have United States troops interfere in the domestic concerns of Louisiana or any other State.

On the 9th of December last Governor Kellogg telegraphed to me his apprehensions that the White League intended to make another attack upon the statehouse, to which, on the same day, I made the following answer, since which no communication has been sent to him:

> Your dispatch of this date just received. It is exceedingly unpalatable to use troops in anticipation of danger. Let the State

authorities be right, and then proceed with their duties without apprehension of danger. If they are then molested, the question will be determined whether the United States is able to maintain law and order within its limits or not.

I have deplored the necessity which seemed to make it my duty under the Constitution and laws to direct such interference. I have always refused except where it seemed to be my imperative duty to act in such a manner under the Constitution and laws of the United States. I have repeatedly and earnestly entreated the people of the South to live together in peace and obey the laws; and nothing would give me greater pleasure than to see reconciliation and tranquillity everywhere prevail, and thereby remove all necessity for the presence of troops among them. I regret, however, to say that this state of things does not exist, nor does its existence seem to be desired, in some localities; and as to those it may be proper for me to say that to the extent that Congress has conferred power upon me to prevent it neither Kuklux Klans, White Leagues, nor any other association using arms and violence to execute their unlawful purposes can be permitted in that way to govern any part of this country; nor can I see with indifference Union men or Republicans ostracized, persecuted, and murdered on account of their opinions, as they now are in some localities.

I have heretofore urged the case of Louisiana upon the attention of Congress, and I can not but think that its inaction has produced great evil.

To summarize: In September last an armed, organized body of men, in the support of candidates who had been put in nomination for the offices of governor and lieutenant-governor at the November election in 1872, and who had been declared not elected by the board of canvassers, recognized by all the courts to which the question had been submitted, undertook to subvert and overthrow the State government that had been recognized by me in accordance with previous precedents. The recognized governor was driven from the statehouse, and but for his finding shelter in the United States custom-house, in the capital of the State of which he was governor, it is scarcely to be doubted that he would have been killed.

From the statehouse, before he had been driven to the

custom-house, a call was made, in accordance with the fourth section, fourth article, of the Constitution of the United States, for the aid of the General Government to suppress domestic violence. Under those circumstances, and in accordance with my sworn duties, my proclamation of the 15th of September, 1874, was issued. This served to reinstate Governor Kellogg to his position nominally, but it can not be claimed that the insurgents have to this day surrendered to the State authorities the arms belonging to the State, or that they have in any sense disarmed. On the contrary, it is known that the same armed organizations that existed on the 14th of September, 1874, in opposition to the recognized State government, still retain their organization, equipments, and commanders, and can be called out at any hour to resist the State government. Under these circumstances the same military force has been continued in Louisiana as was sent there under the first call, and under the same general instructions. I repeat that the task assumed by the troops is not a pleasant one to them; that the Army is not composed of lawyers, capable of judging at a moment's notice of just how far they can go in the maintenance of law and order, and that it was impossible to give specific instructions providing for all possible contingencies that might arise. The troops were bound to act upon the judgment of the commanding officer upon each sudden contingency that arose, or wait instructions which could only reach them after the threatened wrongs had been committed which they were called on to prevent. It should be recollected, too, that upon my recognition of the Kellogg government I reported the fact, with the grounds of recognition, to Congress, and asked that body to take action in the matter; otherwise I should regard their silence as an acquiescence in my course. No action has been taken by that body, and I have maintained the position then marked out.

If error has been committed by the Army in these matters, it has always been on the side of the preservation of good order, the maintenance of law, and the protection of life. Their bearing reflects credit upon the soldiers, and if wrong has resulted the blame is with the turbulent element surrounding them.

I now earnestly ask that such action be taken by Congress as to leave my duties perfectly clear in dealing with the affairs of Louisiana, giving assurance at the same time that whatever may be done by that body in the premises will be executed according to the spirit and letter of the law, without fear or favor.

I herewith transmit copies of documents containing more specific information as to the subject-matter of the resolution.

U. S. GRANT.

John R. Lynch: from Speech in Congress on the Civil Rights Bill

CIVIL RIGHTS AND SOCIAL EQUALITY.

I WILL NOW endeavor to answer the arguments of those who have been contending that the passage of this bill is an effort to bring about social equality between the races. That the passage of this bill can in any manner affect the social status of any one seems to me to be absurd and ridiculous. I have never believed for a moment that social equality could be brought about even between persons of the same race. I have always believed that social distinctions existed among white people the same as among colored people. But those who contend that the passage of this bill will have a tendency to bring about social equality between the races virtually and substantially admit that there are no social distinctions among white people whatever, but that all white persons, regardless of their moral character, are the social equals of each other; for if by conferring upon colored people the same rights and privileges that are now exercised and enjoyed by whites indiscriminately will result in bringing about social equality between the races, then the same process of reasoning must necessarily bring us to the conclusion that there are no social distinctions among whites, because all white persons, regardless of their social standing, are permitted to enjoy these rights. See then how unreasonable, unjust, and false is the assertion that social equality is involved in this legislation. I cannot believe that gentlemen on the other side of the House mean what they say when they admit as they do, that the immoral, the ignorants and the degraded of their own race are the social equals of themselves, and their families. If they do, then I can only assure them that they do not put as high an estimate upon their own social standing as respectable and intelligent colored people place upon theirs; for there are hundreds and thousands of white people of both sexes whom I know to be the social inferiors of respectable and intelligent colored people. I can then assure that portion of my democratic friends on the other side of the House whom I regard as my social inferiors that if at any time I should meet any one of you at a hotel and occupy a seat at the same table with you, or the same seat in a car with you, do not think that I have thereby accepted you as my social equal. Not at all. But if any one should attempt to discriminate against you for no other reason than because you are identified with a particular race or religious sect, I would regard it as an outrage; as a violation of the principles of republicanism; and I would be in favor of protecting you in the exercise and enjoyment of your rights by suitable and appropriate legislation.

No, Mr. Speaker, it is not social rights that we desire. We have enough of that already. What we ask is protection in the enjoyment of *public* rights. Rights which are or should be accorded to every citizen alike. Under our present system of race distinctions a white woman of a questionable social standing, yea, I may say, of an admitted immoral character, can go to any public place or upon any public conveyance and be the recipient of the same treatment, the same courtesy, and the same respect that is usually accorded to the most refined and virtuous; but let an intelligent, modest, refined colored lady present herself and ask that the same privileges be accorded to her that have just been accorded to her social inferior of the white race, and in nine cases out of ten, except in certain portions of the country, she will not only be refused, but insulted for making the request.

Mr. Speaker, I ask the members of this House in all candor, is this right? I appeal to your sensitive feelings as husbands, fathers, and brothers, is this just? You who have affectionate companions, attractive daughters, and loving sisters, is this just? If you have any of the ingredients of manhood in your composition you will answer the question most emphatically, No! What a sad commentary upon our system of government, our religion, and our civilization! Think of it for a moment; here am I, a member of your honorable body, representing one of the largest and wealthiest districts in the State of Mississippi, and possibly in the South; a district composed of persons of different races, religions, and nationalities; and yet, when I leave my home to come to the capital of the nation, to take part in the deliberations of the House and to participate with

you in making laws for the government of this great Republic, in coming through the God-forsaken States of Kentucky
and Tennessee, if I come by the way of Louisville or Chattanooga, I am treated, not as an American citizen, but as a
brute. Forced to occupy a filthy smoking-car both night and
day, with drunkards, gamblers, and criminals; and for what?
Not that I am unable or unwilling to pay my way; not that I
am obnoxious in my personal appearance or disrespectful in
my conduct; but simply because I happen to be of a darker
complexion. If this treatment was confined to persons of our
own sex we could possibly afford to endure it. But such is not
the case. Our wives and our daughters, our sisters and our
mothers, are subjected to the same insults and to the same uncivilized treatment. You may ask why we do not institute civil
suits in the State courts. What a farce! Talk about instituting
a civil-rights suit in the State courts of Kentucky, for instance,
where the decision of the judge is virtually rendered before he
enters the court-house, and the verdict of the jury substantially
rendered before it is impaneled. The only moments of my life
when I am necessarily compelled to question my loyalty to my
Government or my devotion to the flag of my country is when
I read of outrages having been committed upon innocent colored people and the perpetrators go unwhipped of justice, and
when I leave my home to go traveling.

Mr. Speaker, if this unjust discrimination is to be longer tolerated by the American people, which I do not, cannot, and
will not believe until I am forced to do so, then I can only
say with sorrow and regret that our boasted civilization is a
fraud; our republican institutions a failure; our social system
a disgrace; and our religion a complete hypocrisy. But I have
an abiding confidence—(though I must confess that that confidence was seriously shaken a little over two months ago)—
but still I have an abiding confidence in the patriotism of this
people, in their devotion to the cause of human rights, and in
the stability of our republican institutions. I hope that I will
not be deceived. I love the land that gave me birth; I love the
Stars and Stripes. This country is where I intend to live, where
I expect to die. To preserve the honor of the national flag and
to maintain perpetually the Union of the States hundreds, and
I may say thousands, of noble, brave, and true-hearted colored

men have fought, bled, and died. And now, Mr. Speaker, I ask, can it be possible that that flag under which they fought is to be a shield and a protection to all races and classes of persons except the colored race? God forbid!

THE SCHOOL CLAUSE.

The enemies of this bill have been trying very hard to create the impression that it is the object of its advocates to bring about a compulsory system of mixed schools. It is not my intention at this time to enter into a discussion of the question as to the propriety or impropriety of mixed schools; as to whether or not such a system is essential to destroy race distinctions and break down race prejudices. I will leave these questions to be discussed by those who have given the subject a more thorough consideration. The question that now presents itself to our minds is, what will be the effect of this legislation on the public-school system of the country, and more especially in the South? It is to this question that I now propose to speak. I regard this school clause as the most harmless provision in the bill. If it were true that the passage of this bill with the school clause in it would tolerate the existence of none but a system of mixed free schools, then I would question very seriously the propriety of retaining such a clause; but such is not the case. If I understand the bill correctly, (and I think I do,) it simply confers upon all citizens, or rather recognizes the right which has already been conferred upon all citizens, to send their children to any public free school that is supported in whole or in part by taxation, the exercise of the right to remain a matter of option as it now is—nothing compulsory about it. That the passage of this bill can result in breaking up the public-school system in any State is absurd. The men who make these reckless assertions are very well aware of the fact, or else they are guilty of unpardonable ignorance, that every right and privilege that is enumerated in this bill has already been conferred upon all citizens alike in at least one-half of the States of this Union by State legislation. In every Southern State where the republican party is in power a civil-rights bill is in force that is more severe in its penalties than are the penalties in this bill. We find mixed-school clauses in some of their State constitutions. If, then, the passage of this bill, which does not confer upon the colored people of such States any rights that they do not possess already, will result in breaking up the public-school system in their respective States, why is it that State legislation has not broken them up? This proves very conclusively, I think, that there is nothing in the argument whatever, and that the school clause is the most harmless provision in the bill. My opinion is that the passage of this bill just as it passed the Senate will bring about mixed schools practically only in localities where one or the other of the two races is small in numbers, and that in localities where both races are large in numbers separate schools and separate institutions of learning will continue to exist, for a number of years at least.

I now ask the Clerk to read the following editorial, which appeared in a democratic paper in my own State when the bill was under discussion in the Senate. This is from the Jackson Clarion, the leading conservative paper in the State, the editor of which is known to be a moderate, reasonable, and sensible man.

The Clerk read as follows:

THE CIVIL-RIGHTS BILL AND OUR PUBLIC-SCHOOL SYSTEM.

The question has been asked what effect will the civil-rights bill have on the public-school system of our State if it should become a law? Our opinion is that it will have none at all. The provisions of the bill do not necessarily break up the separate-school system, unless the people interested choose that they shall do so; and there is no reason to believe that the colored people of this State are dissatisfied with the system as it is, or that they are not content to let well enough alone. As a people, they have not shown a disposition to thrust themselves where they are not wanted, or rather had no right to go. While they have been naturally tenacious of their newly acquired privileges, their general conduct will bear them witness that they have shown consideration for the feelings of the whites.

The race line in politics never would have been drawn if opposition had not been made to their enjoyment of equal privileges in the Government and under the laws after they were emancipated.

As to our public-school system, so far as it bears upon the races, we have heard no complaint whatever. It is not asserted that it is operated more advantageously to the whites than to the blacks. Its benefits are shared alike by all; and we do not believe the colored people, if left to the guidance of their own judgments, will consent to jeopardize these benefits in a vain attempt to acquire something better.

Mr. LYNCH.   The question may be asked, however, if the colored people in a majority of the States are entitled by State legislation to all of the rights and privileges enumerated in this bill, and if they will not insist upon mixing the children in the public schools in all localities, what is the necessity of retaining this clause? The reasons are numerous, but I will only mention a few of them. In the first place, it is contrary to our system of government to discriminate by law between persons on account of their race, their color, their religion, or the place of their birth. It is just as wrong and just as contrary to republicanism to provide by law for the education of children who may be identified with a certain race in separate schools to themselves, as to provide by law for the education of children who may be identified with a certain religious denomination in separate schools to themselves. The duty of the law-maker is to know no race, no color, no religion, no nationality, except to prevent distinctions on any of these grounds, so far as the law is concerned.

The colored people in asking the passage of this bill just as it passed the Senate do not thereby admit that their children can be better educated in white than in colored schools; nor that white teachers because they are white are better qualified to teach than colored ones. But they recognize the fact that the distinction when made and tolerated by law is an unjust and odious proscription; that you make their color a ground of objection, and consequently a crime. This is what we most earnestly protest against. Let us confer upon all citizens, then, the rights to which they are entitled under the Constitution; and then if they choose to have their children educated in separate schools, as they do in my own State, then both races will be satisfied, because they will know that the separation is their own voluntary act and not legislative compulsion.

Another reason why the school clause ought to be retained is because the negro question ought to be removed from the politics of the country. It has been a disturbing element in the country ever since the Declaration of Independence, and it will continue to be so long as the colored man is denied any right or privilege that is enjoyed by the white man. Pass this bill as it passed the Senate, and there will be nothing more for the colored people to ask or expect in the way of civil rights. Equal rights having been made an accomplished fact, opposition to the exercise thereof will gradually pass away, and the everlasting negro question will then be removed from the politics of the country for the first time since the existence of the Government. Let us, then, be just as well as generous. Let us confer upon the colored citizens equal rights, and, my word for it, they will exercise their rights with moderation and with wise discretion.

CONCLUSION.

In conclusion, Mr. Speaker, I say to the republican members of the House that the passage of this bill is expected of you. If any of our democratic friends will vote for it, we will be agreeably surprised. But if republicans should vote against it, we will be sorely disappointed; it will be to us a source of deep mortification as well as profound regret. We will feel as though we are deserted in the house of our friends. But I have no fears whatever in this respect. You have stood by the colored people of this country when it was more unpopular to do so than it is to pass this bill. You have fulfilled every promise thus far, and I have no reason to believe that you will not fulfill this one. Then give us this bill. The white man's government negro-hating democracy will, in my judgment, soon pass out of existence. The progressive spirit of the American people will not much longer tolerate the existence of an organization that lives upon the passions and prejudices of the hour. But when that party shall have passed away, the republican party of to-day will not be left in undisputed control of the Government; but a young, powerful, and more vigorous organization will rise up to take the place of the democracy of to-day. This organization may not have opposition to the negro the principal plank in its platform; it may take him by the right hand and concede him every right in good faith that is enjoyed by the whites; it may confer upon him honor and position. But if you, as leaders of the republican party, will remain true to the principles upon which the party came into power, as I am satisfied you will, then no other party, however just, liberal, or fair it may be, will ever be able to detach any considerable number of colored voters from the national organization. Of course, in matters pertaining to their local State affairs, they will divide up to some extent, as they sometimes should, whenever they can be assured that their rights and privileges are not involved in the contest. But in all national contests, I feel safe in predicting that they will remain true to the great party of freedom and equal rights.

I appeal to all the members of the House—republicans and democrats, conservatives and liberals—to join with us in the passage of this bill, which has for its object the protection of human rights. And when every man, woman, and child can feel and know that his, her, and their rights are fully protected by the strong arm of a generous and grateful Republic, then we can all truthfully say that this beautiful land of ours, over which the Star Spangled Banner so triumphantly waves, is, in truth and in fact, the "land of the free and the home of the brave."

February 3, 1875

Thomas Whitehead: from Speech in Congress on the Civil Rights Bill

Now, Mr. Speaker, I propose to examine a little into the exigency of this law. Well, who is to be benefited by this? The present father of this bill says the colored man is to be benefited by it. How is he to be benefited? What are you to do for him? I think the examination to which the manager of this bill was subjected by the gentleman from Indiana [Mr. NIBLACK] reduced him to one single point, to which I will advert after a little. Now the colored man is a citizen. He can vote. He can hold office. He can sue and be sued. He can be a witness. He can hold property. He can do in my State just what any other man can do, and if this is to give him equal rights with me I say he has them there now; and I say he has them in your State and in every other State. He has equal rights, he can hold property, he can hold office, he can sue and be sued, he can plead and be impleaded, and he can come to Congress, as a gentleman beside me suggests, and there are seventeen colored men who are now members of the Virginia Legislature.

Now, what is the object of this bill? They say it is to give the colored man something he has not got. Well, there has always been a longing on the part of the colored man to get something he did not have, and a longing on the part of his white brother, who has taken charge of him as his special ward, to pretend to give him something he did not have. In our country they had it that each colored man was to have forty acres of land and a mule. A man came down one day in my district and asked one of these colored men if he had got his forty acres. He said he had not. He had a square stick in his hand, and said he was employed by the Government to stake off lands, and wherever he stuck it down the forty acres were to be measured by that stick. He sold it for five dollars, and the old man to whom he sold it wanted a receipt, and he gave him this receipt: "As Moses lifted up the serpent in the wilderness, so I lifted the last five dollars of this old darky." What became of this traveling individual I do not know. His countenance was pious, but his baggage was light.

There has, however, been this longing on the part of the colored man, as I have said. But it will never be satisfied, in my opinion, because the Almighty has given him what he cannot get rid of—a black skin. Did you ever see one who believed in black angels? Did you ever hear of one who wanted a black doll-baby? You have not the power to make him white, and he never will be satisfied short of that. That is the trouble about the whole matter. His condition cannot be altered, and the best thing we can do is what we propose to do in our State—educate him, and take care of him, and do the best we can with him. My cradle was rocked by a colored woman; I was nursed in her arms, and she has had from that day to this not only my respect but my affection. You do not like the colored man half as well as I do.

But now, as I have said, what are you going to do in legislating for him? What are you going to give him? You are going to violate the Constitution and legislate for the States. You are going to pass a law of Congress to regulate hotels. Now, what will you effect by it? A colored man goes to a hotel and asks the hotel-keeper if he can accommodate him. He does not think he can. "Why can't you?" "I am not in the habit of telling people my business." What is a suit worth based on that? You cannot get even a colored jury to try and convict a man on that evidence. He would get nothing. How are you going to establish whether the man was refused the accommodation on account of race, color, or previous condition of servitude, religion, or anything else? How are you going to get at that? If a man keeps his mouth shut you cannot make him open it, and the law is inoperative.

Well, a colored man goes into a railroad car and one of the officers of the road says, "You cannot go into that car; it is a ladies' car." He rejects him because he is not a lady. Are you going to have the case brought up in the United States court, trying to prove that he is a lady? You might have a "rocky" time if you tried to prove that. Well, again, he wants to have his goods hauled, and the man owning the team says that he cannot haul them; and instantly the gentleman from Massachusetts asks you to bring that man into a United States court and have the case heard there. We had at one time a United States judge in the State of Virginia who might have made a decision of that kind; but that judge has gone, thank God, to his eternal account, and we have not an unjust judge in our borders. There may be some in the State of my friend from Mississippi, [Mr. LAMAR.]

Mr. LAMAR. I will say that the judge of the Federal court in the State of Mississippi is a man who has administered harsh and ungracious laws in a spirit of benignity and justice.

Mr. WHITEHEAD. Well, that is a good man, neither a ruffian, a horse-thief, nor an assassin.

Mr. LAMAR. No, sir.

Mr. WHITEHEAD. I am glad to hear of that coming from the State of Mississippi.

Now, the reason upon cross-examination by the manager of this bill why it should be passed was what I will presently state. He has said it—and I call upon every honest man on the other side of the House to listen to it—he has said that colored men, under the laws as now existing, have been made citizens and clothed with the rights of citizens, and have all the rights at common law and all the rights this bill proposes to give them, and are entitled to recover for any damage they may receive under the common law. Then why pass this bill; *cui bono?* Why pass this bill if he has these rights in the State courts and can recover for all the damages he may have received from his exclusion from theaters or hotels or cars? Why pass this law? Why pass this law against which the people have, as he says, some prejudice? Why pass this law which, as the people decided last fall, they did not want? Why pass this law which the men most interested in tell you will do harm? Why pass this law which the republicans in my State opposed last fall? Why pass a law which your own party tell you will do no good? Some of you gentlemen on the other side of the House were called upon to give an account of your stewardship last fall, and you will not be here in the next Congress to do it; but some of you will be here. Let those of you who will be here get ready to give an account of your stewardship, for the people will require it at your hands. They will want to know why you created this trouble and disturbance. I tell you that the people of the North, when they see clearly, and they are beginning to see clearly, that the administration, the passage of laws like this, is shaking the foundations not only of the rights of the States, but the integrity of the Government and the prosperity of the people, will rebuke you for your course. You have been told here from your own side of the House of the decrease in the industries of the country in some places, the falling off in the sale of those articles that you sold to us and by which you made money; you have been told of the destruction of your trade in New Orleans; and it is all the result of your own work and your own legislation, your own folly.

Well, as I said, the gentleman who controls this bill gives you one reason for its passage, and only one. He says that in the Southern States murder, assassination, and robbery prevail. I say here now that I have heard that statement a hundred times, and whenever an exception has been made taking out any State from that category, it has been done upon the call of somebody denying the statement. The statement is continually made broadly that within the Southern States murder, assassination, robbery, and every evil thing is going on. It is said that a negro cannot get justice in the courts in a Southern State if he brings suit before the circuit court there. In other words, he says that the circuit judges in the Southern States will forswear themselves, and having sworn to try cases according to the law, will try them according to the color of the man who is the suitor.

Now, sir, just here I, coming from one Southern State, undertake to say that whenever that statement is made it is deliberately untrue. There is not a circuit judge in the southern States who is not in every respect the equal, morally, mentally, physically, of the gentleman from Massachusetts, and they are all better looking than he is, every one of them. I appeal to you gentlemen on the other side because I know many of you personally. Are you going to stand by these wholesale charges against the southern judiciary without exception; are you going to say that the circuit judge of my district in Virginia would forswear himself? Sir, I have known him to do what you would not do in favor of a poor black man. A colored man had been brought before him for trial for an assault on another colored man, and excitement and white prejudice (if you choose) was against him; and I heard the judge refuse to imprison him till he paid the fine which strict law would have justified; and he said he would give him a chance to work and pay it. I heard a judge charge a jury that if any of them had any prejudice against a man merely on account of his color, he should not serve on that jury. Our judges have watched against any possible prejudice of jurors, and in their dealings with colored suitors and criminals have leaned to the side of mercy.

Now, I say that this wholesale charge that the judiciary of any State of the South is corrupt, that our judges will forswear themselves about this matter of color, is a slander on that people and proved so every day by you yourselves. Who are we here, the Representatives of the people of the different Southern States? Who is the gentleman from Mississippi [Mr. LAMAR] but a Representative of the people of Mississippi? There are men in his district in every respect as good as he is; there are men in all our districts as good as we are, men as correct in every respect. We are but the Representatives of people who are just like us. Now, I will just set up one of these gentlemen, and you on your side may set up the gentleman from Massachusetts, [Mr. BUTLER,] and then look at them both. Does the gentleman from Mississippi look like a robber? Do I look like an assassin? Is there anything in the appearance of any of these gentlemen representing the States where, it is said, murder is so rife, where there are assassins, thieves, and robbers—does anybody here look like a thief or a robber?

Now, what is the meaning of all this? What is the meaning of the assertion that the minority are robbers and assassins? The minority! Who are the minority in my State? They are all republicans. We have a majority of democrats down there. How is it in the State of my friend from North Carolina, [Mr. VANCE?] There is a mighty big majority down there on our side. Is it the minority in North Carolina and Virginia that are the robbers and assassins and horse-thieves? I do not think so. They are very good people in their way, though they do not know quite so much as they might know. Some of them cannot read or write, but they can make their mark. Some of them do not know much about constitutional law, but they are very good people and get along very well.

I take it there are some other things that people are to be judged by. I take it that this House will—and if you do not the people will—judge honestly and correctly in this matter, and say whether we here are the representatives of murderers, assassins, horse-thieves, and robbers. God Almighty made us all, and he made us very much alike. We show very much on the outside what we are inside, and I am willing to come up to a showing. I am willing to take myself as an example, and be set up on the one side, and have the gentleman from Massachusetts, who made this charge, set up on the other, and then let you judge between us. Did Dickens, that magnificent pen painter, when he drew the picture of Quilp, intend to present the picture of a saint or gentleman; or when he drew the picture of Uriah Heep rubbing his hands so smoothly and sleekly intend to draw the picture of a bold, brave man or of a hypocrite? I am willing to be judged by being looked squarely in the eye by any man on the other side, side by side with the man who has made this charge. Let any man look in the eye of each and then judge between us.

I call upon the gentlemen who have been serving with me in this House for a year past to say whether I have ever used a harsh word here against any section. I have not used an epithet toward a single gentleman in this House. I have made no charges against the people of any section, either in regard to their moral character or their behavior. I stand here, and I have the right to stand here, as a Representative from the State of Virginia, and repel and hurl back into the face of the gentleman from Massachusetts the charge that our judges are not as good as are any other judges; that they are not as honest or as high-toned as are other judges in his or any other State or court.

Then if our judges are honest, the colored man can get justice in the Southern States, and according to the gentleman's own argument there is no necessity for passing this law. So I think. Then what is the matter? Why pass this law? Why crack the party whip here? Why are caucuses held to arrange the means of getting this bill through the House against the resistance of some republican members who do not see much good in this thing? Why is this? I will tell you why.

We are expected to raise a row down South about it. That is one of the whys about it. These people in Louisiana are not half as smart as they ought to be. You cannot get a bayonet into the State of Virginia unless you send it there on your own hook. I tell you we are not going to kick up any row about the civil-rights bill. That will give a pretense for your military interference.

Let me tell you what we will do. About the time the "forty acres and a mule" notion got going through the South, a sergeant who was quartered down there said to a man who had a pretty big plantation, "What are you going to do about it when they divide up your land? There is going to be a big row down here. I heard one man say that he was going to sit down by his spring and shoot the children as they came for water. What are you going to do about it? Are you going to make a fuss about it?" The answer was, "Not in the least." "Well," said he, "suppose they divide up your nine or ten hundred acres and leave you only forty acres; what are you going to do?" "Why" the planter replied, "I am going to stay quietly on those forty acres, proceed with my business, and buy back the rest; I expect it will all be deeded back in a year. If the negro is smarter and more active than I am, he can have what he can make."

We are not going to have any bayonets down our way; you may as well understand that. I know that this bill is intended to stir up bad blood, to mix the two races in the schools, so that the children may first get to fighting and then the parents, and then instantly there will be a call for bayonets. But you will be mistaken in your expectation. You expect that some tavern-keeper, perhaps, may get angry and kick some fellow out, that then a fight will follow, and then will come the bayonet.

But, sir, we have tried that thing. We are a little smarter now than we were in 1861, when certain men wanted to take Washington City with gate-hinges and did not. But I will tell you what *you will do*. You will carry out what you are already doing. Slavery was no bone of contention in the Revolution. When George Washington left Virginia and the boys made a bee-line for Boston, there was then no row between Massachusetts men and Virginians about slavery. They thought alike on that subject. After awhile Massachusetts changed her opinion; and then by degrees she went on, until finally, against all precedent, she determined to set free all the negroes that we had and take glory to herself for having set at liberty a great mass of people. But to whom did they belong? Not to her; they did not cost her one cent. She took our money when she set them free, and then consoled her conscience by saying that it was a punishment upon us for having gone into the war. What was the cause of that war? The continual picking at that subject of slavery—a continual irritation of sections with that question—a continual interfering with other people's business, disturbing the country time and again, until an irritated people broke loose and said, as Abraham said to Lot, "Now, let us divide right here; if the land up there suits you, you go there; and if the land down here suits us, we will stay here." Did you do like Lot? Did you divide the land in that way? No; you said, "You shall not go out of this partnership; come right back." We did not come straight back, but after considerable trouble and noise we did come back. We came back very much like the prodigal son in some respects, but not in others. We did not come back very repentant for anything we had done; we did not hang upon anybody's neck; but we came back mighty near starved and hardly filled with the "husks that the swine did eat." We did not have much when we got back. Since we came back we have been trying to raise something; we have been trying to see whether we cannot get to be tolerably comfortable; but you have turned right around and commenced that same picking, and not having the slave to pick at, you pick at the free negro. You have started this thing; and whether gentlemen here personally believe it or not, it is in *somebody's* mind to keep up this disturbance, to keep up this difficulty, until it ends in somebody's political benefit—in somebody gaining political power. You persisted in irritating Louisiana until it broke out and you capture it. You are irritating Mississippi, by seizing a sheriff with the United States Army, so that Mississippi may break out. You are irritating Alabama until she may break out, and you may grab her. South Carolina has been irritated until you have captured her soul and body and lands and tenements. I suppose you will keep on stirring up North Carolina. My friend here [Mr. VANCE] is a good-natured man, and it will take a great deal to stir him up. Stir up North Carolina, stir up Virginia, stir up Tennessee and Kentucky, and Maryland and Missouri; arouse bad blood; get the people enraged with each other; possibly there may be some outbreak, and thus the republican party may be saved.

But, sir, no such thing will happen; there will be no outbreak—at least not down our way. If that is your hope, you are lost; if that is your hope, you may as well begin now to pick up stakes and leave Washington now. You will save a month's board by the operation. We do not intend to break the peace. But I will tell you what we do intend to do; I give it seriously as prophecy, and you may as well heed it now. If you think we are going to stand this thing quietly and tamely, you are very much mistaken. If you think we are going to be irritated in this way without doing anything, then you have hold of the wrong men. But we do not intend to shoot anybody. We are not ruffians—either "border ruffians" or any other sort; and we do not mean to steal anything; we want that expressly understood; that is not in our line. We do not intend to steal plate, or jewelry, or horses, or anything else. That is not our way of doing business. We do not expect to steal anything, either, from the Constitution. We are going to comply with the law. You ought to have found that out already. After the war we were under military rule until 1868; we had military governors and military judges and military everything else. A man almost had to get a pass to go to his own spring for water. Yet we stood that; and we elected a so-called republican governor—one Gilbert C. Walker—reconstructed ourselves, and by the by he will be here in Congress after the 4th of March—six feet three inches of good Virginia conservatism.

You had all this session to improve the currency for the benefit of our broken people, and you would not do it. I do not know whether it was for that reason or not, but from what has occurred I begin to suspect that it was. You attempted to put the bill through by main force, breaking down rules which were established for your protection in old times. You have changed the rules for the purpose of forcing this thing down our throats. Perhaps you wish to make somebody mad. You will not make me mad at least. I am in the finest humor I have been in since I have been a member upon this floor. I do not intend to get mad; I have not the least idea of getting mad. But there is no doubt you have been intending to force this down our throats for the purpose of raising bad blood between the sections. It will raise what will result in your discomfiture. It may result in our selling our last pound of tobacco and cotton abroad even if we do not get three-fourths of the price for it. O, ho! says the gentleman from Massachusetts, [Mr. WIL-LIAMS.] You did not say O, ho! when it occurred before. It resulted in the establishment of a gold basis down in Texas, where they still have gold and do not need any paper. They do not want paper when they have gold down there yet. We can do the same thing in Virginia. General Washington shipped his tobacco to and bought his goods in England. We can do the same thing again. I do not suppose we can be whipped because we do not buy of you. I do not suppose we are to be accused of sedition or of armed rebellion against the Government because we will not buy goods in Philadelphia, New York, or Boston, or anywhere else. You are driving us to that. We do not want to do it. We told you we were ruined, that we had nothing when we came out of the war except our naked land and some-times only the chimneys left of the houses which our fathers lived in. Still we were willing to shake hands across the bloody chasm and do the best we could if you would only give us a fair chance. You promised, but you broke your word. You told us to go back and we should be taken care of and have a fair chance; that we should have a chance to recruit; that we should have a chance to live again in peace; that after slavery was gone we should be no more disturbed. But that promise has not been kept. That old saint, Thad. Stevens, began to stir up bad blood. The balance of the Christian statesmen have been stir-ring it up ever since. They have all been attempting to make bad blood between the two sections and destroy any chance we had. They have attempted to prevent the shaking of hands across the bloody chasm of the men upon both sides who upon many battlefields won glorious renown for the American name.

Thus, Mr. Speaker, our people have been deceived. You fur-ther told us to reconstruct our State governments according to your demands. The State of Virginia was told to reconstruct as the Northern States proposed and we should come back on equal terms. We were told that all we had to do was to say in our constitution slavery was abolished, and no claim would ever be made for emancipated slaves. We were told to repudiate the confederate debt, which was worth something to our people. After we had done all this and our representatives knocked at the doors of Congress for admission, you sent them back. You sent back the men who were elected under that constitution to this House.

When we at last got in here you started again upon a mission in which there is nothing but bad blood, a mission in which there is a stirring up of bad feeling, in which there can be no good to the black man or to the white man. If I were to go to stir up the laboring men in the State of Massachusetts, what would you think of it? What would you think if I went to Pennsylvania to stir up the "Molly Maguires" against the men who own the coal-mines? What would you think if I went to the manufacturing towns in New England to stir up bad blood between the manufacturers and their employés? What would you think if I told the laboring men there that they had been cheated—that they had been cheated by the manufacturers out of the just profits of their labor? What would you think if I indulged in such demagogism throughout the country? Would you think me an intelligent, faithful, honest man? Yet that is what your party is doing in the South. You go into our States and tell these people that we have robbed them; that we have oppressed them; that we did these things for a long series of years, and that now you intend to give them the right to put the bottom rail on the top. It will soon get to the bottom again if it has not the brains to stay at the top. You cannot put a man up that way by force who ought to remain at the bottom. We cannot force them to do what they do not want to do.

We have been buying your goods ever since the war. We took your money gladly and bought your goods for the articles we raised—cotton and tobacco. Now, you are doing all this, and for no good. You are doing it when it can do no good to the black man. I believe you have not a laboring population in your State any better off than the black man is in Virginia. We have never had a riot. We have no lynching there. We have no cries of "bread or blood," or strikes, or anything of that sort there. The laboring man there has plenty to eat and dresses just as well as his former master used to do, and frequently a great deal better—at all events a good deal better on Sunday. We are in peace. We are in quiet. You are trying to throw a fire-brand in among us and to stir up one part of the population against the other; and God forgive you your imbecility if you do not know it is wrong.

This is the result of your bill. Who are driving you on in the South? Men who have reaped the advantage of all the wrongs that have been perpetrated there; men who came there to reap that advantage, and have got rich by it; and other men who have got into all the Federal offices that have been distributed all over the South for corrupting the few weak-kneed people who live there. Or you send strangers among us to rule us and make profit out of our taxation. This has been done, and yet you say you are a Christian people. And in the face of all this we are called "ruffians;" we are called hard names, bitter epithets are used against us; and you hug the pious delusion to your souls that you are doing God service in all this cruelty and all this wrong.

Well, there is an old man, an old client of mine down in Virginia, who had a way of drawing consolation from subjects in which to other eyes it seemed least likely to exist. He always drew some consolation from the result of any event no matter what it was, and, as a final result, "Thank God there is a hell." I am mighty near in this case now. I thought when I saw the republicans last winter voting upon this bill that you would say this: "There is no use in crowding these people any longer," even if it be but prejudice.

Prejudices exist everywhere. What was it but prejudice that caused the English nation to sacrifice thousands of men and millions of dollars in India? It was the prejudice which the sepoy had about putting mutton tallow on his cartridge instead of lard. This prejudice of his was nothing in itself, but it was so woven into his nature that he could not escape from it. And if we give you the power to say, if we are charitable enough to admit now that our opposition was from mere prejudice, you might be magnanimous enough, you might be bold and strong enough to say, when in the contest of arms from sheer weakness and exhaustion we went down, yet you had found us foemen worthy of your steel; when we went down you might have the magnanimity to say, "Now you are down we will not tread upon you or persecute you any longer." But am I to believe that the men who were brave enough to stand against the desperate charges and attacks we made against the northern troops from Manassas to Appomattox Court House are not men enough to stand up before the country and say, "We will not do this wicked and iniquitous thing against a brave and defenseless people?" Am I to believe the men whom I thought brave and chivalrous and strong and honorable have got in their hearts a spirit to persecute a man when the sword is out of his hand and his musket is thrown away?

February 3, 1875

Charles A. Eldredge: Speech in Congress on the Civil Rights Bill

Mr. ELDREDGE.   Mr. Speaker, I stand before the House at this time a specimen of the effects of the civil-rights bill. I can assure the House that if its effect on the administration of this Government is as disastrous——

The SPEAKER *pro tempore*, (Mr. GARFIELD in the chair.)   The gentleman will suspend until the House comes to order. The confusion is so great that nothing he says can be heard.

Mr. ELDREDGE, (after a pause.)   I remark in continuation of the sentence which I had commenced that if the effect of the administration of the civil-rights bill upon the country is as disastrous as resistance to its passage through the House has been to me and to my health, it would be a sufficient argument against its passage.

Mr. Speaker, in the remarks I have to make in opposition to the bill now before the House I intend little more than to enter my protest against further legislation upon the subject. I have heretofore and frequently discussed the principles involved in this bill, and in various forms of argument, as well as I was able, endeavored to present the constitutional objections, the impolicy, and the danger of this class of legislation. The convictions of the past have been confirmed and strengthened, and the dangers apprehended and pointed out more than realized in the experience of the results. Indeed, the legislation of Congress since the close of the war upon the negro question, and the effects of that legislation upon the Southern States and even upon the Union itself, stand a perpetual reproach to the party by whom it was enforced, and an ever-present remonstrance and protest against further enactments in the same direction.

It ought to be enough to "call a halt" that entire States, once proud and majestic commonwealths, are in ruins, lying prostrate before us, in the very struggle and article of death—the work of our legislation. Look at South Carolina; that once proud and prosperous State with her three hundred thousand property-holders, two hundred and ninety thousand of them white, including the intelligent, educated, refined men and women of the whole State, subjected by this kind of legislation to the control, domination, and *spoliation* of an uneducated, semi-barbarous African race just emancipated from the debasing and brutalizing bonds of slavery. Look at Mississippi, Arkansas, Alabama, and Louisiana, once the most genial and fairest portion of the Republic—grand, mighty States of the Union, marching rapidly and proudly forward in the outward and upward march of wealth and civilization, rent and torn by civil strife, ravaged, desolated, and destroyed by *actual war*—a war of races brought on and kept up by congressional legislation. This state of things is not the result of natural causes, but it is the result of the *unnatural relation* in which the two races have been placed to each other. It is the result of the conflict which may always be expected when it is attempted to subject men of culture, civilized men, men accustomed to freedom, to the domination and rule of brute force. The history of the world furnishes no instance of harmonious government brought about by the forced equality and commingling of such antagonistic forces, and certainly not by the subjugation of the intellectual to the physical. The white race, with its pride of blood, the memory of its achievements, the consciousness of its superiority and power, will never brook African equality or live under Africanized governments; and the sooner this truth is realized by American statesmen the sooner will the remedy for the evils that are upon us be devised.

Sir, this negro question is the mightiest problem of the age; none of half its magnitude, so far as the future of the Republic is concerned, confronts the statesman of this country to-day. It will not do longer to treat it as a mere partisan question or allow the passions evoked by the war to control legislation in regard to it. The excuses heretofore made for imposing African governments upon the southern white men will not do. Higher consideration must control. You cannot turn from this sickening reality and foul work of your hands with the flippant and senseless plea so often interposed, even if it were true, (which it is not,) that slavery embruted and unfitted the emancipated negro for the duties devolved upon him for the government of himself and those you have placed under him, and that it is only a just retribution upon his former master who had so long oppressed him.

This retort, which has been so successful in prejudicing the ignorant and thoughtless and so effectively used in persuading your partisan followers, will not avail at the bar of statesmanship. The very statement refutes itself. It matters not now who was or was not responsible for slavery, whom it injured, or how deep the degradation and wrong it wrought. The question for the statesman is and always was, in view of the facts, what are the demands of patriotism? So far as the freedmen were concerned in introducing them into the governing force of the country, as a part thereof, it was a question of their *fitness* for the duties imposed and no other consideration should have entered into its determination. No partisan consideration should have been allowed to divert the mind from the real question involved.

Are they according to the fundamental principles that under-lie our system, in the broad light of our civilization, qualified according to the requirement and experience of enlightened statesmanship to govern themselves as a race, as a people? Nay more, is it safe and wise, considering only the true interest of the Republic, to intrust them not only with the government of themselves, but with the government of their former mas-ters, their wives and children and all the vast and varied interests of state? None but the merest partisan and demagogue could *pretend* that by an act of legislation the negro race can be in-vested all at once with those high qualities of statesmanship, that self-control, that moderation of conduct, that consideration for individual rights, those sensibilities and refinements, that sense of reciprocal duties and obligations, and those exalted ideas of government which, whatever the white race now possesses, whatever it *now is*, have been the growth and accumulations of ages and have sprung *from* and are a part of our civilization.

In making these suggestions I would not disparage or dis-courage the negro race. I would not deprive them of any legal right. Nor would I throw any impediment in the way of their growth and development as men. They should have a fair field and an equal chance in the race of life—a full, free opportunity to overcome all natural or acquired prejudices against them, and to demonstrate if they can that they are capable of attaining to the high civilization of the white race. To put them in places of trust, of responsibility, and power without any qualification, without any preparation, is simply to do them the greatest possible injury and at the same time, whenever it is done, to endanger our system of republican government. This has been done already to the great detriment of both the black and white races.

No man or community of men, no race or people on the face of the earth, ever was thrust forward by any other people or race, so far as legislation can put them forward, so rapidly and so regardless of the welfare of both races as the white race has the negro of America. I do not believe there is a candid man, certainly no *statesman*, who will now deny that the investiture of the great mass of ignorant, stupid negroes with the power of government was a mistake. It would have been far better, in my judgment, for the black race, for its future as well as its present well-being, to have required some previous preparation, some educational qualification as a condition to the exercise of the right of suffrage. It would have been more in consonance with our system, the corner-stone of which we profess is the intelligence of the people, to have made intelligence the condition of the exercise of the exalted privilege and duty of governing in common with the white race. This, I believe, would have stimulated the black man to greater efforts and given him a better appreciation of the privilege itself. It would have modified his conceit and been an inducement to acquaint himself with the duties he would take upon himself; it would have moderated his demands for place and power by a better comprehension of the great responsibility imposed, and it would have made him far less offensive and obnoxious to those whose conviction and prejudice were against the equality the law conferred. In any and every view that can be taken of the subject it would have been better both for the negro and the white man, for the whole country, to have had some period of probation and preparation, some learning and knowledge of the science of government as a prerequisite to its administration, and as some assurance of his fidelity to and capability for the performance of the duties required.

Sir, I will not deny it must be admitted on all hands, that the negro has not been justly and fairly dealt by. He has not been sincerely and candidly treated by those who have made the greatest professions of being his friends. His present nor his future welfare nor any of his greatest interests as a man and a citizen of the Republic in his relations with the white race have been much considered in the legislation claimed to be in his interest and for his advantage. He has been made the sport and convenience of the republican party ever since his emancipation; he has been a sort of shuttlecock cast about for the amusement or *advantage* of those who have made him believe they were his special guardians and friends. The right or privilege of suffrage, for which so much is demanded of him by those who still for their own purposes champion his cause and claim to be *par excellence* his friends, was not conferred because of love for him or his race or any real advantage it was believed it would be to him, but because it was supposed it would add to and strengthen their political party and prolong their power. Herein was committed the grand error, mistake, blunder, or crime, whichever it should be called, upon the negro question. Both he and the State and all the most vital interests of both have been sacrificed and made subservient to the supposed interests of a mere political party.

The black man has been literally forced into his present attitude in relation to the white race; forced, too, without knowledge or any comprehension of what is to be the result. He is little to be blamed for the condition in which he now is or the circumstances that surround him. He has been and is being "ground as between the upper and the nether millstone" by two antagonistic and opposing forces. He is no longer loved by either except for the use that can be made of him, and his welfare is at all times sacrificed to the paramount interest of party. The pretended affection of the republican party has been his delusion and snare. It deluded him into faith in its friendship and into its support, and thereby into sharp and hostile antagonism with those among whom he was reared and must live, and with whom every interest of happiness and prosperity demands he should be friends. It deluded him into the giving up of a *real* for a *pretended* friendship, and caused him to sacrifice the toleration and encouragement of those whose interests were in common with his own for those who had nothing in common with him and who could never care for him except in so far as he strengthened them in the control of political and partisan power. It induced him to separate from and antagonize his natural ally and friend in an unnatural and partisan alliance with men who had no higher motive than to use him for their own selfish purposes, regardless of the consequences to him or his race.

Mr. Speaker, it would be interesting and instructive, if we had time, to commence at the beginning of the history of the republican party upon the negro question and note its development and progress step by step down to the present time. I think we should be able to see and comprehend the motive by which it has been actuated and controlled. We should see how at one time or another it has disavowed with indignant denial most or all of the measures it has afterward advocated and enforced. We should see that party exigencies and party considerations alone have controlled it in the most of what it has done. We would then see how little the welfare and advantage of the colored race had entered into the consideration or controlled its action in relation thereto.

In 1868 in its national platform upon which President Grant was first elected it denied the right of the Federal Government to control the suffrage of the loyal States, and declared as a fundamental principle that the control of it belonged exclusively to the people of the several States. Before the President was inaugurated, in January, 1869, a distinguished member of this House from the State of Massachusetts, afterward Secretary of the Treasury, and now a Senator of the United States in the Senate, reported by the direction of a majority of the Judiciary Committee of the House in favor of the enforcement of universal suffrage by the Federal Government. He enforced his views by a lengthy and impassioned speech, urging the conferring of suffrage upon the colored man almost upon party grounds alone. He assured the House and the country that it was "*the last of the series of great measures*" with which the "*republican party was charged*" for the pacification of the country and for the establishment of the institutions of the country upon the broadest possible basis of "*republican equality both State and national.*" And his main argument was based upon the fact that this measure would add *one hundred and fifty thousand votes to the republican party*—enumerating the number from the several States, and appealing to his party to know if they were going to decline the services of one hundred and fifty thousand men "*who are ready to battle for us at the ballot-box* in favor of human rights."

This is the sordid, selfish appeal that has been made upon this negro question from the beginning. Not *his interest*, not the *interest of the Republic*, not the great interest of *patriotism* and *humanity*, but the interest of the republican party.

One hundred and fifty thousand men stand ready to do battle for *us*, for *our party*, for the *republican party*; and can we decline the *tempting offer*? They may be ignorant of the first principles of government—unable to read, write, or even to speak and understand *any intelligible language*—unqualified in every respect according to the requirements of our system; they may endanger the Republic, jeopardize our most cherished institutions, drag down and degrade the white race, injure and destroy the colored race by bringing the two races into fatal collision; but it will add *one hundred and fifty thousand votes to our party*. These are the considerations, *the controlling* considerations of the past upon this subject, and such are the motives for further agitation for civil and social rights and social equality of the races. In these motives and in this spirit your civil-rights bills and all like measures have their origin and growth. They are the pandering of party to the ignorance, conceits, unreasoning ambitions, untrained and selfish instincts of the least advanced and spoiled portion of the negro race. The better class, the most thoughtful, those who are really capable of understanding some thing of the situation and condition of affairs, are beginning to see through these schemes and machinations of their pretended friends. They see the folly and danger of these measures—of pressing the demands of the lowest portion of the race for place and position without preparation, without qualification, and against the prejudice which is more because of this ignorance and unfitness than any other repugnance which may be felt. They comprehend the situation so far, at least, as to understand that the demand for further recognition and "*the protection of their civil rights*" comes from those the least competent to understand or appreciate what has been done for them or the rights they now may enjoy. They understand that the clamor for civil rights comes

from the most ignorant and dissolute, the dishonest, schem-
ing politician of their own race, instigated by the unprincipled
"carpet-bagger," "scalawag," and "pot-house" politician, who
would make merchandise of all the rights of the colored race
and of their bodies and souls, if thereby they could keep themselves in control of place and power. The most intelligent and
worthy of the black race are grateful and contented that so
much has been done for them, and that with so many favorable surroundings their destiny is in their own hands. They
have sense enough to comprehend, in some degree at least, the
solemnity and greatness of the work of self-government under
even the most favorable circumstances, and, knowing that immunities and privileges imply obligations and duties, would
not force themselves forward without preparation. The colored race in this country have opportunities such as no other
race or people in the history of the world ever had.

The chains of slavery wherewith they were bound are broken and removed, and the whole people placed at once, by
the race that held them in bondage, upon terms of perfect,
absolute equality with themselves. They are not only in the enjoyment of all that *freedom* itself can give, but the lights of the
highest civilization are shining upon them, and the examples
of refinement, education, patriotism, and progress—the development of centuries—are before and around them, to guide
and exalt their aspirations. If there be anything of them; if they
have in them the elements of growth, civilization, and greatness; if in the economy of the Almighty they are or *are* to be
capable of self-government and the comprehension and appreciation of the great principles of civil liberty and republican
government—nothing on earth is now in their way. They start
from vantage-ground—with everything to stimulate, inspire,
and guide them.

The law has done all it can accomplish for them. So far as the
law is concerned, the black man is in all respects the equal of
the white. He stands and may make the race of life upon terms
of perfect equality with the most favored citizen. There is no
right, privilege, or immunity secured to *any* citizen of the Republic that is not confirmed to the colored. There is no court,
no tribunal, no judicial jurisdiction, no remedy, no means of
any sort in the land, provided by law for the redress of wrongs

or the protection of the rights of life, liberty, or property of the white man that is not equally open and available to the black man. The broad panoply of the Constitution and the whole body of laws, civil and criminal, and every means provided for their enforcement, cover and extend to every American citizen, without regard to color or previous condition. The white man may with no more legal impunity trench upon or invade the dominion of the black man's rights than the black man may the white man's. The barriers of laws surrounding and protecting them are the same. There is no distinction, no exception, no immunity in favor of the white race. And let it never be forgotten that voluntarily, in the pride and majesty of its power, the white race has thus far *done it all*. With sublime indifference and disregard of all natural and conventional differences, if not with *sublime wisdom and discretion*, the LIBERATOR, the white race, decreed and proclaimed to the world that his *former slave, the negro race*, whatever he may have been or may become, is henceforth and forever shall be under the law of the Republic a co-citizen and an equal. He may compete for any office; he may contest any citizen; he may aspire to any position; he is eligible to the most exalted place in the Republic.

And, sir, what would gentlemen, what would the greatest patriot, the greatest philanthropist, have more? What would the intelligent negro, the man best capable of comprehending the wants, the necessities, the highest good of his own race, ask for more? The common-law rights of both are the same. Both are equal in its protection. White and black may alike invoke its interposition for the protection of rights and the redress of wrongs. If equality, exact and impartial equality, of legal rights and legal remedies is desired, it is now enjoyed alike by both. If you would not place one race above the other; if you would make no distinction "on account of race or color or previous condition;" if you would have the recent amendments to the Constitution impartially administered; if you would have the laws of the land throughout its length and breadth, in their application to the citizen, take no note of the color of his skin or the race from which he sprang, let the "common law" remain unchanged; let there not be one law for the white man and another for the black man. No change, no distinction in favor of the one or the other can fail to injure both.

To make the colored citizen feel that he is the pet, the especial favorite of the law, will only feed and pander to that conceit and self-consequence which is now his weakest and perhaps most offensive characteristic. If he be made to feel that extraordinary provisions of law are enacted in his favor because of his weakness or feebleness as a man, the very fact weakens and enfeebles him. The consciousness that there is necessity for such legislation and protection for him must necessarily humiliate and degrade him. Such laws, too, are a constant reminder to him that he is inferior to the white race. They not only remind him of his inferiority and the superiority of the white race in its not requiring these special enactments, but they naturally and necessarily awaken in him a feeling of bitterness and unfriendliness toward the white race. It is impossible that the negro race should live upon terms of mutual confidence and friendship with a race from whom it requires to be protected by a special code—against whose wrongs and oppressions he is not safe except those wrongs are denounced by extraordinary laws and penalties. There can be no peace, no harmony, no confidence, no mutual respect, no feeling of equality between two races living together and protected from the infringement of each other's rights by different laws and different penalties. It is useless to deprecate or deplore the natural or acquired prejudice of the races so long as the laws enacted for their government in their very nature necessarily awaken, keep alive, and foster them. And whether the prejudice be the plant of the Almighty or the growth of slavery, it cannot be removed by legislative enactments. It may be, as in my judgment it most certainly will be, increased and aggravated by such legislation as this, but it cannot be lessened. If the southern man believes, correctly or erroneously, that the negro race is an inferior race, this kind of legislation is certainly not calculated to remove that belief. This bill and all such bills go upon the ground that the colored race is inferior, feebler, and less capable of taking care of itself than the weakest and most inferior white man. *This* is the very predicate of this legislation. And whether he claims the natural equality of the races or not, it is an insult to every colored man in the Republic. It is an unnecessary exaggeration and parading of the distinction between them.

Sir, I have intimated already, and it has been illustrated and demonstrated in and by the effects of previous similar legislation, that the greatest danger now to be apprehended lies in the bringing of the two races into fatal antagonism of rights and interests. If there be natural prejudice, if there be antipathy, if there be antagonisms between the races, almost the entire legislation of Congress on the negro question has been and is calculated to increase and intensify them all. I have referred to some of the effects upon the colored race; but the effects upon the white race and its disposition toward the colored cannot be less deleterious. Born and reared with the idea that they were masters and the colored men slaves, it was not the work of a moment, or a small thing, to reconcile themselves to the changed condition. And yet, under all the circumstances, they may appeal with confidence to this House, the country, or the world that they have conducted themselves with commendable patience and forbearance. Have we not all been disappointed and surprised at their magnanimity and submission? Have they not commended themselves to our warmest sympathy and approbation? Have they not borne themselves under the greatest trials and the severest ordeals to which poor human nature can be subjected with a greatness and grandeur almost sublime?

Without malice, without resentment, without reproach, they have acquiesced in the emancipation of their slaves and their elevation to free and equal citizenship with themselves.

If there have been some factions, dissatisfied, and turbulent spirits, it was to have been expected. But the hostile collisions, strifes, and conflicts, I believe on my soul, are more to be attributed to the political and unwise legislation of Congress than to all other causes combined. But because they have thus far with almost broken spirits submitted, we must not forget there is a point beyond which Congress must not go. We must not from the past presume too much. We must not for political or partisan considerations seek to degrade or dishonor them. The white people of the Southern States are a proud, honorable, intelligent people. They are the depositaries of the civilization of many centuries. The negro race, possessed of all the natural capabilities the most enthusiastic African admirer can claim for it, even with the example of the white race constantly before it, must grow and develop rapidly for many, many years before it will attain to the same civilization.

Let us beware, then, how we create the means for irritation and strife between the whites and the blacks of the South. It can be no doubtful or uncertain struggle. Let party exigencies and party necessities be whatever they may seem, it is worse than madness, it is a crime without a name, to bring the two races by our legislation into collision. The white men of the South cannot be brought to submit to the domination of the black man. The attempt will bring ruin and destruction upon the black man or it will end in the extinction of both black and white. The black man *has been* a slave, *the white man never*. The black man has with submission and patience worn the yoke of bondage and threw it not off himself; the white man never did and never will submit to be ruled by any race but his own. He may and probably will for a time submit to the sword of the Federal power, but I pray gentlemen not to presume upon *that too far*. His ancestors long ago taught the Anglo-Saxon the idea of opposition to "*intolerable burdens*." And no Anglo-Saxon can bear dishonorable burdens, or burdens imposed upon him by other hands than his own, without seeking the first opportunity to throw them off. The pride of blood and race will never brook the rule of inferior men. The gentleman from Massachusetts [Mr. BUTLER] well said "social equality could not be brought about by legislation." Neither can you by legislation make the white man submit to the rule and domination of the black. I beg gentlemen, as I did in speaking upon this subject in 1868, to "hesitate long before they attempt to bring it about." It will, *it must* end in the overthrow and destruction of the weaker race.

February 4, 1875

James A. Garfield: from Speech in Congress on the Civil Rights Bill

Mr. GARFIELD.   Mr. Speaker, I concur with those gentlemen who have said that this is a solemn and an interesting occasion. It recalls to my mind a long series of steps which have been taken during the last twenty-five years in the greatest of all the great moral struggles this country has known; and the measure pending here to-day is confronted, in the last assault which has been made upon it, by the first argument that was raised against the anti-slavery movement in its first inception; I mean the charge that it is a sentimental abstraction rather than a measure of practical legislation.

The men who began this anti-slavery struggle forty years ago were denounced as dreamers, abstractionists, who were looking down to the bottom of society and attempting to see something good, something worthy the attention of American statesmen, something that the friend of human rights ought to support in the person of a negro slave. Every step since that first sentimental beginning has been assailed by precisely the same argument that we have heard to-day. I expressed the hope years ago, Mr. Speaker, that we had at last achieved a position on this great question where we could remit the black man to his own fate under the equal and exact laws of the United States. I have never asked for him one thing beyond this: that he should be placed under the equal protection of the laws, with the equal right to all the blessings which our laws confer; that as God's sun shines with equal light and blessing upon the lofty and the humble alike, so here the light of our liberty shall shine upon all alike; and that the negro, guaranteed an equal chance in the struggle of life, may work out for himself whatever fortune his own merit will win.

And now a word to our own people. The warnings uttered to-day are not new. During the last twelve years it has often been rung in our ears that by doing justice to the negro we shall pull down the pillars of our political temple and bury ourselves in its ruins.

I remember well when it was proposed to put arms in the hands of the black man to help us in the field. I remember in the Army of the Cumberland where there were twenty thousand Union men from Kentucky and Missouri and we were told that those men would throw down their arms and abandon our cause if we dared to make the negro a soldier. Nevertheless the men whose love of country was greater than their prejudice against color stood firm and fought side by side with the negro to save the Union.

When we were abolishing slavery by adopting the thirteenth amendment we were again warned that we were bringing measureless calamity upon the Republic. Did it come? Where are the Cassandras of that day who sang their song of ruin in this Hall when we passed that thirteenth amendment? Again when the fourteenth amendment was passed the same wail was heard, the wail of the fearful and unbelieving. Again when it was proposed to elevate the negro to citizenship, to give him the ballot as his weapon of self-defense, we were told the cup of our destruction was filled to its brim. But, sir, I have lived long enough to learn that in the long run it is safest for a nation, a political party, or an individual man to dare to do right, and let consequences take care of themselves, for he that loseth his life for the truth's sake shall find it. The recent disasters of the republican party have not sprung from any of the brave acts done in the effort to do justice to the negro. For these reasons I do not share in the fears we have heard expressed to-day, that this bill will bring disaster to those who shall make it a law. What is this bill? It is a declaration that every citizen of the United States shall be entitled to the equal enjoyment of all those public chartered privileges granted under State laws to the citizens of the several States. For this act of plain justice we are told that ruin is again staring us in the face! If ruin comes from this, I welcome ruin.

Mr. Speaker, the kind of cowardice which shrinks from the assertion of great principles has followed this grand anti-slavery movement from the beginning until now; but God taught us early in this fight that the fate of our own race was indissolubly linked with that of the black man on this continent—not so-cially, for none of us are linked by social ties except by our own consent, but politically in all the rights accorded under the law.

This truth was stated early by one of our revered poets when he said:

> We dare not share the negro's trust.
>   Nor yet his hope deny;
> We only know that God is just,
>   And every wrong shall die.
>
> Rude seems the song; each swarthy face,
>   Flame-lighted, ruder still;
> We start to think that hapless race
>   Must shape our good or ill;
>
> That laws of changeless justice bind
>   Oppressor with oppressed;
> And close as sin and suffering joined
>   We march to Fate abreast.

Their fate politically must be ours. Justice to them has always been safety for us. Let us not shrink now.

February 4, 1875

Hinds County Gazette:
How to Meet the Case

IN ALL past elections since the adventurers obtained control in Hinds county, only dishonest and rascally carpet-baggers have been able to obtain a hearing from the negroes. The carpet-baggers by deception and falsehood have kept the negroes from attending conservative meetings—they have refused to allow conservatives to speak at their meetings—and they have rejected all propositions for holding joint meetings for discussion. The object sought to be accomplished by the carpet-bag leaders in all this, has been fully understood, and is perfectly characteristic. Their tactics with, and their harangues to the unfortunate and ignorant negroes, have been base fabrications and lies—bold deceptions and falsehoods—infamous insinuations and innuendos—and all designed to array the blacks in a deadly hostility against the whites, and to keep the blacks in supreme ignorance of the true situation, of their practical interests, and the best interests of the country. By this means, the scoundrels, white and black, have obtained full control over the deluded and duped negroes, and have used them as tools—as the potter uses the clay in his hands—for the robbery of the people, for the exhaltation to office of thieves and rascals—and for the disgrace and ruin of the country.

There are those who think that the leaders of the Radical party have carried this system of fraud and falsehood just far enough in Hinds county, and that the time has come when it should be stopped—peaceably if possible, forcibly if necessary. And to this end, it is proposed that whenever a Radical pow-wow is to be held, the nearest anti-Radical club appoint a committee of ten discreet, intelligent and reputable citizens—fully identified with the interests of the neighborhood and well known as men of veracity—to attend as representatives of the tax-payers of the neighborhood and the county and true friends of the negroes assembled; and that whenever the Radical speakers proceed to mislead the negroes, and open with falsehoods, and deceptions, and misrepresentations, that the committee stop them right then and there, and compel them to tell the truth or quit the stand.

We know of no better way in which the falsehoods and frauds scattered by Ames' emissaries can be successfully met in the presence of the negroes, and we suggest that the practicability of this plan be discussed in the clubs. Really honest men of the Radical party, if there be such, cannot object to it. The professional liars and thieves will of course call it "intimidation," "force," and all that. Well, if men will not voluntarily cease telling lies about their neighbors and the people of the country, they ought to be forced to stop it.

Desperate cases require desperate remedies. We have a desperate case on hand. Nothing less than the recovery of Hinds county and the state of Mississippi—and all that our people hold dear on earth—from the hands of regularly organized bands of thieves and robbers and perjured scoundrels. We must use remedies equal to the emergency of the case, if we desire to arrest the disease.

Hinds County Gazette, August 4, 1875

Ulysses S. Grant to Edwards Pierrepont

Long Branch, N. J.
Sept. 13th/75

HON. EDWARDS PIERREPONT,
ATTY. GEN. U. S.
DEAR SIR:

Your report upon the Mississippi revolt, by Special Messenger, is received, and I have just read it. I am somewhat perplexed to know what directions to give in the matter. The whole public are tired out with these annual, autumnal outbreaks in the South, and there is so much unwholsome lying done by the press and people in regard to the cause & extent of these breaches of the peace that the great majority are ready now to condemn any interference on the part of the government. I heartily wish peace and good order might be restored without the issueing of a proclamation. But if it is not the proclamation must be issued; and if it is I shall instruct the Commander of the forces to have no childs play. If there is a necessity for Military interference there is justice in such interference as to deter evil doers.

I start to-morrow for Utica. If a proclamation becomes necessary it can be given to the press at once, and take date from its publication, and be sent to me there for signature. I believe this will be proper? If it is not the publication will have to await my signature.

I do not see how we are to evade the call of the governor, if made strictly within the Constitution and acts of Congress there under. If the Executive is to be the judge when such insurrection or invasion exists as to warrant federal interference the Constitutional provision refered to in your report may become a dead letter even under a well meaning but timid executive. The so called liberal and opposition press would then become the power to determine when, or whether, troops should be used for the maintanance of a republican form of government.

I think on the whole a proclamation had better be prepared

and sent to me for signature. It need not be published, nor the public made aware of its existence without telegraphic advice. In the mean time I would suggest the sending of a dispatch— or letter by private messenger—to Gen. Ames urging him to strengthen his position by exhausting his own resorces in restoring order before he receives govt. aid. He might accept the assistance offered by the citizens of Jackson and elsewhere. I am fully aware that the proffered assistance might prove dangerous. It might prove the offer of the wolf to the Shepherd to take charge of the sheepfold. But Governor Ames, and his advisors, can be made perfectly secure. As many of the troops now in Miss. as he deems necessary may be sent to Jackson. If he is betrayed by those who offer assistance he will be in a position to defeat their ends and punish them. I will wait to hear what you, and such members of the Cabinet as you may choose to consult, have to say to these suggestions. If you wish to send any dispatch to me that you do not wish opperators to read give it to Mr. Luckey and he will put it in Sipher.

Very Respectfully
your obt. svt.
U. S. GRANT

Edwards Pierrepont to Adelbert Ames

DEPARTMENT OF JUSTICE, ⎱
WASHINGTON, D. C., *September* 14, 1875. ⎰

To Governor AMES, *Jackson, Miss.*

This hour I have had dispatches from the President. I can best convey to you his ideas by extracts from his dispatches:

> The whole public are tired out with these annual autumnal outbreaks in the South, and the great majority are ready now to condemn any interference on the part of the Government. I heartily wish that peace and good order may be restored without issuing the proclamation, but if it is not the proclamation must be issued. But if it is, I shall instruct the commander of the forces to have no child's play. If there is a necessity for military interference there is justice in such interference, to deter evil-doers. I would suggest the sending of a dispatch or letter, by means of a private messenger, to Governor Ames, urging him to strengthen his own position by exhausting his own resources in restoring order before he receives Government aid. He might accept the assistance offered by the citizens of Jackson and elsewhere. Governor Ames and his advisers can be made perfectly secure, as many of the troops now in Mississippi as he deems necessary may be sent to Jackson. If he is betrayed by those who offer assistance he will be in a position to defeat their ends and punish them.

You see by this the mind of the President—with which I, and every member of the cabinet who has been consulted, are in full accord. You see the difficulties, you see the responsibilities which you assume. We cannot understand why you do not strengthen yourself in the way the President suggests. Nor do we see why you do not call the Legislature together and obtain from them whatever power, and money, and arms, you need. The Constitution is explicit that the Executive of the State can call upon the President for aid in suppressing domestic violence only when the Legislature cannot be convened, and the law expressly says, "In case of an insurrection in any State against the government thereof, it shall be lawful for the

President, on application of the Legislature of such State, or of the Executive when the Legislature cannot be convened," etc. It is plain that the meaning of the Constitution and laws, when taken together, is that the Executive of a State may call upon the President for military aid to quell domestic violence only in case of an insurrection in any State against the government thereof when the Legislature cannot be called together.

You make no suggestions, even, that there is any insurrection against the government of the State, or that the Legislature would not support you in any measures you might propose to preserve the public order. I suggest that you take all lawful means and all needed measures to preserve the peace by the forces in your own State, and let that country see that citizens of Mississippi, who are largely favorable to good order, and who are largely Republican, have the courage and the manhood to fight for their rights, and to destroy the bloody ruffians who murder the innocent and unoffending freedmen. Everything is in readiness. Be careful to bring yourself strictly within the Constitution and the laws, and if there is such resistance to your State authorities as you cannot by all the means at your command suppress, the President will quickly aid you in crushing these lawless traitors to human rights.

Telegraph me on receipt of this, and state explicitly what you need.

Very respectfully yours,

EDWARDS PIERREPONT.

Sarah A. Dickey to Ulysses S. Grant

Allow a humble woman to address your Excellence in behalf of the poor oppressed colored people of the Southern states and especially of this State. Seeing, as I do, that thousands of them are just on the eve of being sacrificed at the hand of the assassin, I cannot hold my peace. Whoever says to you that our troubles in Miss. are slight and that we do not need assistance from the Federal Government is an enemy to the colored people and sanctions their slaughter. I have been laboring in the capacity of an educator, either directly or indirectly, for the freedmen, in this State ever since Dec. 1863. Have been at Clinton nearly five years. During this time I have made the acquaintance of quite a number of the white people, and have learned their sentiments in reference to the colored people and the, so called, carpetbaggers. *I know* that they are a desperate people: *I know* their 'hearts are deceitful above all things.' I *know*, too, that the white people of this state, and I believe also of all the other Southern States, have united almost to a man to keep up this killing of colored men until they shall have succeeded in killing off all of the *leading* men, and as many others as possible. All they want is to see them dead on the ground. They will avail themselves of every apparent opportunity and make every pretext that they possibly can to commit these bloody deeds until they shall have satiated their thirst for the blood of these innocent people. I was at the republican mass meeting, held at this place (Clinton) on the 4th inst., myself. Was on the ground early and I saw enough with my own eyes to convince any honest person that the republicans went there for nothing but peace, profit and pleasure, and that the democrats, who were on the ground, went there for the express purpose of creating a disturbance and of killing as many as they could. The Southern white people are just as deceitful and as wily as men can be. I know that the Authorities of our Government are doing and will do all that they can, so far as they understand the necessities of the case, to stay the sheding of innocent blood: but I feel that with the certain knowledge which I have, it would be inhuman in me to remain quiet. I feel sure, I MAY be mistaken, yet I do feel very sure that to arm a militia of colored men is simply to usher them into the jaws of death. If a *war* of *races* or of *parties* should ensue then you would know just what course to take; but I fear that the white people would take a course which would be equally if not more disastrous to the colored people and which would be much harder to meet by the general government. I think they would only make it another pretext to slaughter colored men not only here but all over the State. . . . I know that these Southern people are simply carrying on a kind of gurrilla war and I know that they are planning to continue in this course until they shall have succeeded in killing thousands of colored men and of reducing the remnant to a condition of slavery. You hear a great deal about the massacre at Clinton, but you do not hear the worst. It cannot not be told. Hoping God's blessings may attend these earnest thoughts . . . P. S. Do not understand me to say that Gov. Ames is not doing all in his power to allay these difficulties. I believe he is.

September 23, 1875

Margaret Ann Caldwell: Testimony to the Select Senate Committee

MRS. CALDWELL—HINDS COUNTY.

JACKSON, MISS., *June* 20, 1876.

Mrs. MARGARET ANN CALDWELL (colored) sworn and examined.

By the CHAIRMAN:

THE WIDOW OF SENATOR CALDWELL.

Question. What is your name?   —Answer. Margaret Ann Caldwell.

Q. Where do you live?   —A. In Clinton, Hinds County.

Q. Was Mr. Caldwell, formerly senator, your husband?   —A. Yes, sir.

Q. What was his first name?   —A. Charles.

Q. When did he die?   —A. Thursday night, in the Christmas. Him and his brother was killed.

Q. You may state to the committee what you know of his death.   —A. I know when he left the house on the Thursday evening, in the Christmas, between dark and sundown. In the beginning of the day he was out on his fox-chase all day. The first commencement was an insult passed on his nephew, and he came out home.

STORY OF HIS ASSASSINATION.

Q. Who was that?   —A. David Washington; he is in Washington City now. He is there in business; watchman in the Treasury Department now; has been ever since October, I think. So they picked a fuss; Waddy Rice, in George Washington's blacksmith shop, in Clinton. They commenced talking this way: I think David said they asked, "How many did he kill on the day of the Moss Hill riot? Who did he shoot?" David said that he did not know as he shot anybody; said he didn't know that he shot anybody. They told him, he said, "he came there to kill the white people, and if he did, to do his work in the day, and not to be seeking their lives at night." David came immediately back to my house. His uncle was at the fox-chase. I said, "Don't go out any more. Probably they are trying to get up a fuss here."

His uncle sent him down town for something. He staid in the house until he came.

That was about four o'clock in the evening, and some one had told about the fuss picked with his nephew, and he walked down town to see about it, I suppose. He was down town a half hour, and came back and eat his dinner, and just between dark and sundown he goes back down town again. He went down town knocking about down there. I do not know what he was doing down there, until just nearly dusk, and a man, Madison Bell, a colored man, came and says, "Mrs. Caldwell you had better go down and see about Mr. Caldwell, I think the white folks will kill him; they are getting their guns and pistols, and you had better go and get your husband away from town."

I did not go myself; I did not want to go myself, but went to Professor Bell and said would he go and get him. Mr. Bell went, and he never came back at all until he came back under arrest.

I was at my room until just nearly dark.

The moon was quite young, and the chapel bell rang.

We live right by it. I knew the minute the bell tolled what it all meant.

And the young men that lived right across the street, when the bell tolled, they rushed right out; they went through the door and some slid down the window and over they sprang; some went over the fence. They all ran to the chapel and got their guns. There was 150 guns there to my own knowing; had been there since the riot, at the Baptist chapel. They all got their guns.

I went down town, and then all got ahead everywhere I went; and some of them wanted to know who I was, but I hid my face as well as I could. I just said "woman" and did not tell who I was.

As I got to town I went to go into Mr. Chilton's store and every store was closed just that quick, for it was early, about 6 o'clock. All the other stores were closed. Chilton's was lit up by a big chandelier, and as I went over the lumber-yard I saw a dead man. I stumbled over him, and I looked at him, but I did not know who it was, and I went into Chilton's, and as I put my foot up on the store steps, standing as close, maybe a few feet, (everything was engaged in it that day,) there was Judge Cabinis, who was a particular friend of my husband; a particular friend to him. He was standing in the center with a gun with a blue strap, in the center of the jam; and as I went to go in they cussed me and threatened to hurt me, and "make it damned hot for me," and the judge among the balance; but he said he didn't know me afterward. And they all stood; nobody would let me go in; they all stood there with their guns.

I know there was two dead men there, but I did not think it was my husband at the time.

I stood right there, and as I stood they said to me, "If you don't go away they would make it very damned hot for me;" and I did not say anything, and walked off, and walked right over the dead man. He was right in my path where I found the body. He was lying broadside on the street. I did not know who he was. I then stooped and tried to see who he was, and they were cursing at me to get out of the town, to get out.

Then I went up, and there was Mrs. Bates across the street, my next-door neighbor. I seed her little girl come up by us and she said, "Aunt Ann, did you see my uncle here?" I said, "I did not. I saw a dead body on the street; I did not see who he was." She said, "What in the world is going on down town?" Says I, "I don't know, only killing people there." She says, "Aaron Bates's hand is shot all to pieces, and Dr. Bangs is killed." He was not killed, but was shot in the leg; nobody killed but my husband and brother.

I went on over to the house, and went up stairs and back to my room and laid down a widow.

After I had been home I reckon three-quarters of an hour, nearly an hour, Parson Nelson came up—Preacher Nelson— and he called me. I was away up-stairs. He called several times, and I heard him call each time. He called three or four times, and says: "Answer; don't be afraid; nobody will hurt you." He says "Don't be afraid; answer me;" and after I had made up my mind to answer, I answered him what he wanted, and he said, "I have come to tell you the news, and it is sad news to you. Nobody told me to come, but I come up to tell you." I didn't say anything. "Your husband is dead," he said; "he is killed, and your brother, too, Sam."

I never said anything for a good while. He told me nobody would hurt me then; and when I did speak, says I, "Mr. Nelson, why did they kill him?" He says, "I don't know anything about it." He said just those words: "I don't know anything about it." He says, after that, "Have you any men folks about the place?" I says, "No." He says: "You shan't be hurt; don't be afraid of us; you shan't be hurt."

I never said anything whatever. He went off.

Sam's wife was there at the same time with three little children. Of course it raised great excitement.

After a length of time, Professor Hillman, of the Institute, the young ladies' school or college, he brought the bodies to the house; brought up my husband, him and Frank Martin. Professor Hillman and Mr. Nelson had charge of the dead bodies, and they brought them to the house; and when they brought them, they carried them in the bed-room, both of them, and put them there; they seed to having them laid out, and fixed up, and all that.

Mr. Nelson said in my presence, I listened at him, he said, "A braver life never had died than Charley Caldwell. He never saw a man died with a manlier spirit in his life."

He told me he had brought him out of the cellar.

You see when they had shot Sam, his brother, it was him who was lying there on the street. They shot him right through his head, off of his horse, when he was coming in from the country, and he fell on the street. He was the man I stumbled over twice. I did not know who he was. When they shot him, they said that they shot him for fear he would go out of town and bring in other people and raise a fuss. He found out, I suppose, that they had his brother in the cellar, so he just lay there dead; he that was never known to shoot a gun or pistol in his life—never knew how.

Mr. Nelson said that Buck Cabell carried him into the cellar; persuaded him to go out and drink; insisted upon his taking a drink with him, and him and Buck Cabell never knowed anything against each other in his life; never had no hard words. My husband told him no, he didn't want any Christmas. He said, "You must take a drink with me," and entreated him, and said, "You must take a drink." He then took him by the arm and told him to drink for a Christmas treat; that he must drink, and carried him into Chilton's cellar, and they jingled the glasses, and at the tap of the glasses, and while each one held the glass, while they were taking the glasses, somebody shot right through the back from the outside of the gate window, and he fell to the ground.

As they struck their glasses, that was the signal to shoot. They had him in the cellar, and shot him right there, and he fell on the ground.

When he was first shot, he called for Judge Cabinis, and called for Mr. Chilton; I don't know who else. They were all around, and nobody went to his relief; all them men standing around with their guns. Nobody went to the cellar, and he called for Preacher Nelson, called for him, and Preacher Nelson said that when he went to the cellar door he was afraid to go in, and called to him two or three times, "Don't shoot me," and Charles said, "Come in," he wouldn't hurt him, and "take him out of the cellar;" that he wanted to die in the open air, and did not want to die like a dog closed up.

When they taken him out, he was in a manner dead, just from that one shot; and they brings him out then, and he only asked one question, so Parson Nelson told me—to take him home and let him see his wife before he died; that he could not live long.

It was only a few steps to my house, and they would not do it, and some said this.

Nelson carried him to the middle of the street, and the men all hallooed, "we will save him while we've got him; dead men tell no tales." Preacher Nelson told me so. That is what they all cried, "We'll save him while we got him; dead men tell no tales."

Whether he stood up right there in the street while they riddled him with thirty or forty of their loads, of course, I do not know, but they shot him all that many times when he was in a manner dead. All those balls went in him.

I understood that a young gentleman told that they shot him as he lay on the ground until they turned him over. He said so. I did not hear him.

Mr. Nelson said when he asked them to let him see me they told him no, and he then said, taking both sides of his coat and bringing them up this way so, he said, "Remember when you kill me you kill a gentleman and a brave man. Never say you killed a coward. I want you to remember it when I am gone."

Nelson told me that, and he said that he never begged them, and that he never told them, but to see how a brave man could die.

They can find no cause; but some said they killed him because he carried the militia to Edwards, and they meant to kill him for that. The time the guns were sent there he was captain under Governor Ames, and they said they killed him for that; for obeying Governor Ames.

After the bodies were brought to my house, Professor Hillman and Martin all staid until one o'clock, and then at one o'clock the train came from Vicksburgh with the "Murdocs." They all marched up to my house and went into where the two dead bodies laid, and they cursed them, those dead bodies, there, and they danced and threw open the window, and sung all their songs, and challenged the dead body to get up and meet them, and they carried on there like a parcel of wild Indians over those dead bodies, these Vicksburgh "Murdocs." Just one or two colored folks were setting up in the room, and they carried on all that in my presence, danced and sung and done anything they could. Some said they even struck them; but I heard them curse and challenge them to get up and fight. The Vicksburgh Murdocs done that that night. Then they said they could not stay any longer.

Then the day after that Judge Cabinis asked me was there anything he could do, and I told him, I said, "Judge, you have already done too much for me." I told him he had murdered my husband, and I didn't want any of his friendship. Those were the words I told him the next day, and he swore he did not know me that time; but I saw Judge Cabinis with this crowd that killed my husband. I saw him right in the midst, and then he made his excuse. He said he did everything he could for Charles, and that he was crazy. Well, they could not tell anything he had done.

They said Aaron Page was shot during the fuss.

In the league that was held here in that town, that day my husband was buried, they all said that he did not shoot him.

They said that Aaron Page was shot accidentally; that my husband did not kill him. All started up from picking a fuss with his nephew.

As for any other cause I never knew; but only they intended to kill him because for carrying the militia to Edwards; for obeying Governor Ames; and that was all they had against him.

THE MODOCS AFTER THE CLINTON RIOT.

At the same time, when they had the Moss Hill riot, the day of the dinner in September, when they came over that day, they telegraphed for the Vicksburgh "Murdocs" to come out, and they came out at dark, and when they did come, about fifty came out to my house that night; and they were breaking the locks open on doors and trunks; whenever they would find it closed they would break the locks. And they taken from the house what guns they could find, and plundered and robbed the house. The captain of the Vicksburgh "Murdocs," his name is Tinney.

Q. What day was that?   —A. The day of the Moss Hill riot, in September.

THREATS AGAINST MR. CALDWELL
AFTER THE CLINTON RIOT.

Q. When; the Clinton riot?   —A. The 4th day of September. They came out, and Tinney staid there, and at daybreak they commenced to go, and he, among others, told me to tell my husband that the Clinton people sent for him to kill him, and he named them who they were to kill—all the leaders especially, and he says, "Tell him when I saw him"—he was gone that night; he fled to Jackson that evening with all the rest— "we are going to kill him if it is two years, or one year, or six; no difference; we are going to kill him anyhow. We have orders to kill him, and we are going to do it, because he belongs to this republican party, and sticks up for these negroes." Says he, "We are going to have the South back in our own charge, and no man that sticks by the republican party, and any man that sticks by the republican party, and is a leader, he has got to die." He told me that; and that the southern people are going to have the South back to ourselves, and no damned northern people and no republican party; and if your husband don't join us he has got to die. Tell him I said so." I told him what he said. I did not know Tinney at the time; and when I saw my husband enter I told him, and he knew him from what I said, and he saw him afterward and told him what I said. He just said that he said it for devilment. They carried on there until the next morning, one crowd after another. I had two wounded men. I brought them off the Moss Hill battle-field, and these men treated me very cruelly, and threatened to kill them, but they did not happen to kill them.

CLINTON RIOT.

Next morning, before sun up, they went to a house where there was an old black man, a feeble old man, named Bob Beasly, and they shot him all to pieces. And they went to Mr. Willis's and took out a man, named Gamaliel Brown, and shot him all to pieces. It was early in the morning; and they goes out to Sam. Jackson's, president of the club, and they shot him all to pieces. He hadn't even time to put on his clothes. And they went out to Alfred Hasting; Alfred saw them coming. And this was before sun up.

Q. This morning after the Clinton riot? —A. On the morning of the 5th, and they shot Alfred Hastings all to pieces, another man named Ben. Jackson, and then they goes out and shoots one or two further up on the Madison road; I don't know exactly; the name of one was Lewis Russell. He was shot, and Moses Hill. They were around that morning killing people before breakfast. I saw a young man from Vicksburgh that I knew, and I asked him what it all meant.

Q. Who was he? —A. Dr. Hardesty's son; and I asked him what did it mean, their killing black people that day? He says, "You all had a big dinner yesterday, and paraded around with your drums and flags. That was impudence to the white people. You have no right to do it. You have got to leave these damned negroes; leave them and come on to our side. You have got to join the democratic party. We are going to kill all the negroes. The negro men shall not live." And they didn't live; for every man they found they killed that morning, and did not allow any one to escape them, so he said. So he told me all they intended to do about the colored people for having their dinner and parading there, and having their banners; and intended to kill the white republicans the same. Didn't intend to leave any one alive they could catch, and they did try to get hold of them, and went down on Monday morning to kill the school-teacher down there, Haffa, but he escaped. Jo Stevens and his son Albert Stevens, I believe, was his name—they just murdered them right on through. These people staid there at the store and plundered it, and talked that they intended to kill them until they got satisfaction for three white people that was killed in that battle here. I can show who was the first white man that started the riot; and I can show you I have got his coat and pants, and I can show you how they shot him. They blamed all on my husband; and I asked what they killed Sam for; asked Dr. Alexander. They said they killed him because they were afraid he would tell about killing his brother. They killed my husband for obeying Governor Ames's orders, and they cannot find anything he did. He didn't do anything to be killed for. Then they have got his pistols there and they won't give them to me. I have asked I don't know how many times.

June 21, 1876

Albion W. Tourgée: Root, Hog, or Die

RECONSTRUCTION has been a failure. It is useless to deny this fact. It has not only been a failure, but one of so utter and ignominious a character that people are even disinclined to go back and inquire into its causes. Of course, by failure it is not meant to be said that the physical unity of the nation has not been restored, and the lately rebellious States rehabilitated with their former rights and privileges in the Federal Union. This, however, was the smallest and simplest part of the duty which devolved on the Government at the close of the war, and which was endeavored to be performed under the name and style of Reconstruction.

The word itself was one of ill-omen, in that it rushed back into the past for the type and model of what was to be in the future. By its very force it accustomed the people to the idea that the work which was to be done was but the patching up of an old garment; that it was an act of restoration rather than one of creation. It foreshadowed an attempt to put new wine into old bottles, which has been but too successfully carried into execution, with a result which can at present be inferred only from the rule in such cases prescribed and certain ominous events which have already appeared.

The duty which lay before the Government was not chiefly nor primarily to restore statal relations. That was a matter which could be done in ten minutes and by a single act of five lines. Its duty was to erect in the lately rebellious regions Republican governments, in which the rights of all should be secured, protected and maintained. Such governments had never existed here. Free speech, free thought, free labor, and free ballot, were strangers to the territory which fell a victim to secession. The very basic elements of Republican government were lacking here. Reconstruction hinted at going back to these husks. The duty of the nation was to tread them under foot, and sternly set its face to secure to every man in that new domain which its arms had just conquered from slavery, not only the rights of a freeman, but the protection and security of a freeman, and an unmistakable guarantee that he might transmit them to his children, and they to theirs in endless perpetuity.

This the nation has utterly and completely failed to do. In name, the colored man is a citizen. In theory, he has the rights of a freeman. In fact, he exercises those rights only by sufferance, and in all but two of the States he is hardly more of a citizen than when he was sold on the block, or driven a-field by those whom he served.

In this respect reconstruction is a failure in a wider and completer sense than most of those even who are subjected to its effects, at this time appreciate.

The cause of this failure is largely embraced in the philosophy set forth with more force than elegance by Mr. Greeley in the words of the subject of this article: "Root, hog, or die." Soon after the war he put this forth as the quintessence of his theory in regard to the southern blacks. He was willing that they should be clothed with the ballot, given equal rights and privileges with the whites, among whom they lived—no more and no less—and then he would leave them to stand or fall, sink or swim, survive or perish, as they might. He would have them preside over their own future, and make or mar their destiny for themselves. In enunciating this doctrine the *Tribune* philosopher was by no means putting forth any new or startling hypothesis. He was announcing no theory peculiar to himself, and evolved from the depths of his own consciousness. On the contrary, he was only giving a peculiarly striking illustration of that faculty of shrewd observation which enabled him during a long life, to keep on the crest of American public opinion without once falling into the trough, which was but a little way before or behind, even when the party—of which he was one of the leaders—was dashed on the rocks, it was too blind to see and avoid. He knew that the people of the North looked upon slavery as the sole cause of rebellion and supposed that treason must die for lack of nutriment when it was destroyed. He knew that the average American citizen drew a sigh of relief when the question of emancipation was decided, not so much on account of its giving freedom to the black as because it was thought by him to settle a most vexatious and troublesome question. It was thought that it would take the "nigger" out of politics. For half a century the curly locks and ebon integument of the African had obtruded on every platform and complicated every question. Saints could not pray and senators could not legislate in peace because of the ubiquitous "nigger." When the war was over and emancipation an accomplished fact, therefore, the average American gave a sigh of relief, and said, "Thank God, the nigger is dead! He is free now. Let him go to work and prove if he is as good as a white man." He was willing to give him a "white man's chance," and let him do a white man's work, if he could. It was, in the main, the idea of the ring and prize fighter, which we have brought from old England—"let the best man win." Greeley chose, however, to embody it in the more forcible and less elegant vulgarism of the Northwest: "Root, hog, or die."

Because this phrase exactly represented the feeling of ninetenths of the people of the North at that time in regard to the freedmen of the south, it became a general exponent of the nation's feeling, and unconsciously, no doubt, molded in no small degree the tone and character of the legislation which constituted the reconstruction code.

The idea which underlay all this legislation, was that if the freedmen were clothed with the same powers as the whites, had the same privileges and immunities, nothing more need be done in their behalf. Some said they would take care of themselves and their future; would rise and flourish, develop and grow strong and prosperous. Others, perhaps as many, said they never could rise; that they were a race imbecile in all the requisites of success and prosperity and predicted that they would fail and fall. But all agreed that whether they rose or fell, it should be of themselves. "Root, hog, or die," expressed the philosophy of both.

Right here occurred the errors which the few years which have elapsed since these governments were created and autonomic States erected on the ruins of the Confederacy, have shown so plainly that one can but wonder that their existence could have been overlooked. Two facts were neglected in this legislation which were fatal to its value:

1. That men who had come up from barbarism through two hundred and fifty years of slavery, could not make complete self-protecting, well-balanced, advancing freemen in a day.

2. That a party made up chiefly of these could never protect itself, nor the rights of its members, from the assaults of a party combining experience, culture and wealth, and animated by the keenest party spirit, the rancor of race prejudice, and the sting of defeat.

It was not giving the colored man a fair showing, though it professed to be based on that very idea. It was pitting ignorance against knowledge, poverty against wealth, ineptness against experience, the habit of deference against the habit of command, the weak against the powerful, and then saying to them: "Go on! take care of yourselves! root, hog, or die!"

The fruits of this error were states which were in the control of parties incompetent to their management or solidification, extravagance, corruption and all the vagaries naturally incident to ignorance and inexperience, suddenly entrusted with power. The next noticeable result is the rapid disappearance of this class as a ruling element, even where it is in the majority, and the rising of the recently master race above it, with renewed hatred and malevolence toward them. This is but a forerunner of the practical disfranchisement and de-citizenship of the colored man, until, by his own act, or by some favoring providence, he shall rise again provided with the freeman's only armor of proof—knowledge, education, experience; not because they are inferior to their brethren of lighter integuments in mental power or facility of culture, but because while they were yet babes, too weak to walk without a guiding and controlling hand, the nation said to them: "Root, hog, or die!"

The responsibility for this failure does not rest with the people of the South. No class of them urged the hasty and ill-considered legislation which characterized the period of reconstruction. The people of the North and hot-headed legislators who were ambitious to do all that was to be done in an instant must bear the blame. Neither understood the disease nor the remedy. They were willing to apply a nostrum without making a diagnosis. Who, but a people and a party who were intoxicated with success, would ever have dreamed of conferring the power of a State upon a party having not more than a tenth of the property, intelligence and experience in public affairs which was to be found in its limits? Who would expect such power to last, or the rights of the individual members of such a party to be secured from the encroachment of the compact, educated, wealthy minority? It was simply a fool's hazard. Milton said that one of the attributes of divinity is the power to compress eternity into an hour. The Congress of the United States thought for the moment that it had that power. It was mistaken, and the poor and weak of the South are reaping now the bitter fruits of its stupid error. Something more than emancipation was necessary to make the slave a self-protecting citizen. Something more than the election franchise was necessary to secure to the freedmen, the rights of the citizen. That something is intelligence, culture, development. If the nation had given freedmen of the Southern States thoroughly organized schools instead of the ballot; if it had given the stable and even-handed justice instead of Ku-Klux and white leagues; if it had waited until there was a right-minded, intelligent and loyal people, before it attempted to create loyal States; if it had waited until the freedman had grown used to liberty, and had learned something of its duties; until the master had become accustomed to yield to his late slave the rights and privileges of a citizen; until the traditions of the mart and the plantation had grown dim; if the nation had waited until these things had come to pass, there would have been no burlesque of statal organizations—mere hot-beds of future evils—scattered through the South today. The wards of the nation would be slowly and surely rising to the full stature of self-sustaining man-hood, and the bitterness of hereditary hostility would be fading out of the bosoms of the nation's recent foes under the warmth of material prosperity and national advancement. As it is, the State machinery which has been put in operation at the South is but a set of engines made ready for the hands of our enemies, by means of which the results of the war may be made value-less, the fruits of emancipation destroyed, and the future of the freedmen made one of darkness, doubt and struggle; and in all likelihood, one of tyranny, resistance and bloodshed. All this is the legitimate result of hasty legislation, based upon imperfect knowledge of its subject matter, and the weathercock philoso-phy, "Root, hog, or die."

c. 1876

John R. Lynch: Speech in Congress on Mississippi

Mr. LYNCH   I regret that it is necessary for me to make
any remarks upon this subject at all. I certainly would not have
done so but for some remarks that fell from the lips of my honorable colleague [Mr. SINGLETON] who reported this bill from
the committee; a gentleman, by the way, for whom I have the
highest regard, and in whose judgment, upon some things, I
have unlimited confidence. He is doubtless aware of the fact
that there is not a member upon this floor from whose views
upon any subject I dissent with more reluctance than his. I confess, Mr. Chairman, that I shall not confine myself to the subjects contained in this bill, but will endeavor to combat some of
the arguments that were so forcibly and eloquently presented by
my colleague in favor of the passage of this bill as reported from
the committee. I will ask the Clerk to read a short passage from
my colleague's speech to which it is my purpose to reply.

The Clerk read as follows:

> It may be proper, Mr. Chairman, to state the reasons why we
> considered it necessary to embark in the work of retrenchment.
> We cannot cast our eyes to any portion of this country and
> view the pecuniary circumstances and surroundings of our peo-
> ple without being fully convinced and understanding that it is
> necessary we should do something for the relief of an overbur-
> dened people. I do not know how it may be in other sections
> of the country except as I see by the reports in the newspapers,
> but for my own section I know the people there are so over-
> taxed and so overburdened with debt that it is almost impos-
> sible for them in many instances to obtain even the common
> necessaries of life.

And again:

> This is not all. There are other causes for our poverty and
> our distress. One of them is the fact that we have not had home
> rulers; that we have been governed and controlled by a set of
> men who, like the worthless drift-wood that lies rotting upon

the banks of a stream, at the flood-tide of reconstruction was gathered up and precipitated upon us. These men came among us for no other purpose than for spoils; and they were not scrupulous as to the means by which they obtained them. We have been controlled by them. They have manipulated the Legislatures of our States, because they have been in the ascendency in several of them; and the consequence has been that we were overburdened with taxes, our money extorted from us unjustly, and we are left in such condition that to-day we are scarcely able to meet the taxes levied upon our real estate.

Mr. LYNCH.   Now, Mr. Chairman, to give additional emphasis, doubtless, to the above, my colleague remarked that he is a southern man, every inch of him, from the crown of his head to the sole of his foot. To this I have no objection. I, too, am a southern man. I admit, however, that I am not in the ordinary acceptation of that term. That term, I am aware, in its ordinary acceptation, includes only that portion of the white people who resided south of Mason and Dixon's line anterior to the rebellion. But, to speak practically and not theoretically, I can say that I too am a southern man—by birth, education, inclination, and interest.

I will say, Mr. Chairman, that it is not my purpose, in discussing this subject, to attempt to revive any of the unpleasant feelings engendered by the war. Far from it. I am anxious to see the day come when all those unpleasant feelings that were created by that struggle, when everything in the nature of race prejudices will be buried in the grave of forgetfulness never again to be remembered. I am anxious to see the day come when the rights and privileges of all classes of citizens will be recognized and universally acquiesced in from one end of the country to the other, so that we all can gladly and truthfully say, this is our beloved country, with which we are well pleased.

I am not unmindful of the fact that I occupy a seat upon this floor to-day not by the votes of colored men alone, but by those of white men as well; not by the votes of those who fought the battles of the Union alone, but by the votes of a large number of those who fought bravely the battles of the confederacy as well; not by the votes of outspoken, pronounced republicans alone, but by the votes of a large number of those whom we are pleased to designate liberal and moderate conservatives as well. I hope therefore that my colleague will not object when I claim the right to speak not only for the colored people, not only for republicans, but for a large number of liberals and conservatives as well.

Now, sir, let us see something about what my colleague said in regard to the imposition of taxes by adventurers— by persons who have no interest in the soil. In speaking of carpet-baggers—those who have imposed heavy, oppressive, and unreasonable taxes upon the people of the South—I cannot believe that my colleague intended to include the State he has the honor so ably to represent in part upon this floor. I ask is he aware of the fact that nine-tenths of the offices in the State of Mississippi are now and have been ever since the re-admission of that State into the Union held by southern men—men who are to the manor born, many of whom fought bravely the battles of the confederacy, and who, according to what they say, are not ashamed of it?

Mr. SINGLETON. If you will allow me, I desire to say that I know exactly to the contrary.

Mr. LYNCH. I regret that my colleague is not better informed. [Laughter.] Why, sir, my colleague can say that a majority of them are held by republicans; but if he says they are held by carpet-baggers, it is a mistake. Some of them are, but about nine-tenths of them are held by southern men. And I ask him is he not aware of the fact that these men, representing a large percentage of the wealth, the intelligence, and the virtue of the people of that State—is he not aware of the fact that they are a class of men whom the democratic party were proud to acknowledge in days passed and gone as among their brightest intellects and their ablest leaders? Why, sir, when we speak of men who are holding offices in the South, and especially in the State of Mississippi, we will find a large majority of those offices held by this class of men. Although not identified with my colleague's party now, yet they upheld the cause of the South— that cause for which he no doubt fought, or at least with which he sympathized—as bravely as those who are identified with the political organization of which he is an honorable member.

I will say, Mr. Chairman, that I commend my colleague in his zeal to inaugurate economy, retrenchment, and reform. He has my cooperation and support as long as he confines himself within the bounds of reason and moderation. I am with him heart and soul to bring about economy, retrenchment, and reform wherever it can be effected. But when he comes forward and tells us that the passage of this bill is demanded in consequence of the heavy taxes under which the people of the South and Mississippi especially are laboring, this demands some little reply, some notice.

Now, sir, let us see what these taxes are of which my colleague so eloquently complained. Let us see why it is that he comes forward and asks that a large number of our important consulships shall be abolished and that the compensation of our foreign ministers shall be reduced in order to relieve the overburdened tax-payers of the South and of Mississippi especially. Let us see wherein that statement can be substantiated and sustained.

Now, Mr. Chairman, the taxes in the State of Mississippi levied for the support of her government are nine and a quarter mills, or $9.25 on each $1,000 worth of taxable property, four mills only of which are for the support of the State government, two mills for educational purposes, and the other three and a quarter mills to pay the interest on the public debt and to create a sinking fund for its liquidation.

Now my colleague says that this is a heavy burden, and appeals to the House to come to the relief of the tax-payers of the South, and especially of the State of Mississippi. He says that if you could stand where he stood, if you could see the anxious countenances of the taxpayers of Mississippi, when the tax-collector was crying off their property to the highest bidder, and see the tears falling down their pallid cheeks, you would sympathize with them, and reduce the pay of these officers for their relief. He says that the people of the South are suffering, and we must make these retrenchments, these reforms, even though it be done at the expense of the honor of this great nation, and I hope my friend from Virginia [Mr. TUCKER] will pardon me for using the word nation in this connection, but the word has become so familiar to me that I cannot help it.

But my colleague says that the people must be relieved, that these burdens must be taken off their shoulders, and that the way to do it is to abolish these important consulates and reduce the compensation of our foreign ministers. Now, sir, in fact the people of Mississippi pay directly comparatively nothing to support the General Government. I admit that, according to the theory of the gentleman from New York, [Mr. Cox]—and I do not wish to be understood as combating it—we pay doubtless a great deal indirectly, in consequence of the tariff imposed upon articles necessary for home consumption. We pay something in that way, but so far as direct taxes are concerned, I repeat, the people of Mississippi pay comparatively nothing. Still that is no reason why we should not be in favor of retrenchment; but that was not my colleague's line of argument. His argument was that it was local taxation imposed upon us by those who came there in the flood-tide of reconstruction, for the purpose of living upon the substance of the people. Now, for my colleague's benefit, I have had a little comparison made, a comparison of the tax system of Mississippi in 1865, when my colleague's party held undisputed control of the State government, and in 1875, when the party with which I am identified had control of it. In 1865 the total amount of taxes levied was about $2,634,000, as follows:

Upon realty and personalty	$184,000
Upon privileges	200,000
Upon incomes	200,000
Upon cotton	2,000,000
Upon polls	50,000

My colleague says that we can raise seven million bales of cotton in one part of the State alone, which is about three millions more than I suppose we could raise in the whole State; but I presume he is better posted on this subject than I am. In 1875 the total amount of taxes levied according to this comparison or estimate was about $1,711,500, distributed as follows:

Upon realty and personalty	$1,461,500
Upon privileges	200,000
Upon polls	50,000
Total amount levied in 1865	2,634,000
Total amount levied in 1875	1,711,500
Difference	922,500

Then, Mr. Chairman, the people of Mississippi paid in 1875 about $922,500 less than they did in 1865.

My colleague spoke of the public debt, the debt under which the people of the South are groaning and laboring, especially in Mississippi. Mr. Chairman, the public debt of my State is to-day less than half a million dollars exclusive of what is called the Chickasaw and common-school funds, and yet he asks us to go to work and relieve the burdens of the people of Mississippi by reducing the appropriations for the diplomatic and consular service of the Government.

Mr. Chairman, I wish to tell my colleague what I believe to be the true remedy for the evils complained of in the Southern States. The true remedy, I think, is for a public opinion to be inaugurated that will crush out mob law and violence and enforce obedience to the laws of the country. What we want in the South is a public opinion that will cause every man, wherever he may have been born, whatever may be his color, whatever his politics, to feel perfectly safe and secure in the exercise of his rights and privileges as an American citizen.

I can assure my colleague that what we want more than anything else is to have these political agitators, these instigators of strife, these promoters of confusion and disturbers of public peace, forced to take back seats. What we want is to bring about a public sentiment that will render impossible the existence of White Leagues, Ku-Klux Klans, and other dangerous, mischievous, and rebellious organizations. It is in consequence of an unsettled state of affairs, of an unhealthy public opinion that has tolerated the existence of these dangerous organizations and justified these crimes that have been committed upon the rights of private citizens, that the development of that portion of our country has been prevented.

You may make as many reductions in the appropriations as you please. But until there shall be brought about by a revolution in the public sentiment of the South a better condition of affairs, that part of our country will never prosper as it should. What we need is to have the people of that portion of our country, the tax-payers, those who are interested in the soil, to rise up in their might and to declare that these men who go about from place to place appealing to the passions and prejudices of race and riding into power upon the demerits of others and not upon any merits they may themselves possess shall be forced to that position which they deserve. That is what we want, and I hope my colleague agrees with me that we must have the good men of the South of both races unite so as to render impossible the elevation to power of a class of men who go about creating confusion, stirring up strife, and trying to keep the country all the time in an unsettled condition.

When this shall have been brought about, then and not until then will merit, honesty, capacity, efficiency, be made the test of political preferment, and not a man's capacity to appeal successfully to race prejudices and the baser instincts of mankind. I can assure my colleague that what we want is to have his party inaugurate a liberal, fair, generous, reasonable policy that will tolerate an honest difference of opinion upon political questions. We want his party to pursue a policy that will convince the colored voters that their identification as a mass with any one political organization is no longer a matter of necessity.

Sir, I express it as my honest opinion that the identification of the colored people as a mass with one political organization, especially so far as local matters are concerned, is not so much a matter of choice as it is, in consequence of democratic hostility to them as a race, a matter of necessity. The affiliation of the masses of the white people in the South with one political organization is not so much a matter of choice with them as it is the result of the existence of a public opinion which in some localities does not tolerate an honest difference of opinion upon political questions except at the sacrifice of social position and success in business.

These are the evils that must be removed. White men must be allowed to disagree upon political questions without being socially ostracised and destroyed in business. Colored men must be convinced that they too can divide in political matters without running the risk of losing their rights and privileges under the Government. When this can be done all will be well and the South will prosper, but not till then.

We hear a great deal about emigration to the South. But how can we get emigrants to go there; how can we get capital there, when men must know before they go that their status in society, their success in business will depend upon their political affiliations? How can you get them to go there when it is understood beforehand that a public expression of an honest political opinion, unless it happens to be in accordance with the popular views of the hour, means social ostracism and destruction in business? How can you get capitalists to invest in southern communities when they are informed beforehand that public opinion there will sustain and tolerate a class of men who make it their business to ignore the Constitution, disregard the laws, defy the decrees of courts, outrage the rights of private citizens, and revolutionize State, county, and municipal governments?

Sir, I say let us have peace, let us have toleration, let us have an honest difference of opinion without being socially ostracised and without being destroyed in business, and then the South will prosper as other sections of the country do, and not till then. These are the evils under which we are laboring and under which we are now struggling.

Now let me appeal to my colleague, [Mr. SINGLETON,] for he is aware of the fact that I look upon him as one of the best men in the House; that I have the highest respect and admiration for him; that I love him, [laughter;] I hate to disagree with him; it pains me to be compelled to dissent from him—let me appeal to him to endeavor to get his party leaders and party managers to re-adopt and faithfully adhere to that grand old democratic doctrine of former days "the Union, the Constitution, and the enforcement of the laws."

February 10, 1876

Ulysses S. Grant to Daniel H. Chamberlain

Washington, D. C. July 26th 1876—

DEAR SIR:

I am in receipt of your letter of the 22d of July—and all the enclosures enumerated therein—giving an account of the late barbarous massacre of innocent men at the town of Hamburg—South Carolina—The views which you express as to the duty you owe to your oath of office—and to the citizen—to secure to all, their civil rights, including the right to vote according to the dictates of their own consciences, and the further duty of the Executive of the nation to give all needful aid, when properly called on to do so, to enable you to insure this inalienable right, I fully concur in—The scene at Hamburg, as cruel, bloodthirsty, wanton, unprovoked, and as uncalled for as it was, is only a repitition of the course that has been pursued in other Southern States within the last few years—notably in Mississippi and Louisiana—Mississippi is governed to day by officials chosen through fraud and violence, such as would scarcely be accredited to savages, much less to a civilized and christian people—How long these things are to continue, or what is to be the final remedy, the Great Ruler of the Universe only knows—But I have an abiding faith that the remedy will come, and come speedily, and earnestly hope that it will come peacefully.—There has never been a desire on the part of the North to humiliate the South—nothing is claimed for one State that is not freely accorded to all the others, unless it may be the right to Kill negroes and republicans without fear of punishment, and without loss of caste or reputation—This has seemed to be a privilege claimed by a few States.—I repeat again that I fully agree with you as to the measure of your duties in the present emergency, and as to my duties—Go on, and let every Governor where the same dangers threaten the peace of his State, go on in the conscientious performance of his duties to the humblest as well as proudest citizen, and I will give every aid for which I can find law, or constitutional power.—Government that cannot give protection to the life, property and all guaranteed civil rights (in this country the greatest is an untrammeled ballot,) to the citizen, is in so far a failure, and every energy of the oppressed should be exerted, (always within the law and by constitutional means,) to regain lost privileges or protection—Too long denial of guaranteed rights is sure to lead to revolution, bloody revolution, where suffering must fall upon the guilty as well as the innocent—Expressing the hope that the better judgment and coopera- tion of the citizens of the State over which you have presided so ably, may enable you to secure a fair trial and punishment of all offenders, without distinction of "race, color, or previ- ous condition of servitude"—and without aid from the federal government—but with the promise of such aid on the condi- tions named in the foregoing—I subscribe myself

Very respectfully.
Your obedient servant—
U. S. GRANT

The Nation: *The South in the Canvass*

ONE OF the saddest features in the condition of the South just now is the part it plays in the political contests at the North. We do not think we are at all uncharitable when we say that, during the next three or four months, Mr. Chandler and Mr. Cornell, and their subordinates and assistants in the canvass, will look for outrages and murders of negroes in their paper every morning as the most welcome bits of news on which their eye could light. To hear that a negro in Georgia or Mississippi was taken into the woods and whipped will make them smile; but to hear that several negro houses were burnt down, and the occupants pushed back into the flames, or that twenty negroes, arrested on a charge of chicken-theft, were taken from the custody of the sheriff on the way to jail and butchered in cold blood, will make them laugh and clap their hands, and run lustily to the nearest stump to improve and spread the story. We do not say that the Democrats are incapable of experiencing under like circumstances the same unseemly joy; but, luckily for them, the best news they can hear from the South at present is the news of peace and order. It is for the interest of their party that the negroes should be prosperous and secure, and that, if anybody at the South is uncomfortable, it should be the whites. It is of no slight importance to a party to have its interests and those of society identical, and no slight misfortune to be even in a small degree dependent on public calamities for success. The Democrats have in fact had recent and dismal experience of the Republican state of mind, for during the four years of the war a Union defeat and disaster supplied them with almost all their political capital; they wept when their neighbors were glad, and made merry when they were sad. But they may now thank their stars that from this devilish temptation they have been at last delivered, and that the more peaceful the South is, the better for them and their cause.

We are led to make these observations by seeing the great importance which the Republican orators and editors evidently attach to the Hamburg affair. Some of them, in fact, talk of it with as much gusto as if it were likely to exert a decisive influence on the Presidential election, or, at all events, as if one more good, substantial slaughter of negroes would make Hayes's election sure. Now, no language can well be too strong in condemnation of the state of manners which makes such occurrences as that at Hamburg possible. Nothing the negroes had done or tried to do, according to any version of the affair, could make the shooting of the prisoners anything but a piece of atrocious savagery. It is ridiculous for a community in which such things are either sanctioned or tolerated to talk of itself as civilized. There is no use in being white in color if your conduct is that of an Ashantee, and the shooting of unarmed and suppliant prisoners is in all respects worthy of the society of Coomassie. In resorting to such modes of repressing negro excesses, the Southern men reach the lowest negro level. But then the atrocity of the affair, and of all such affairs, does not necessarily connect it with the general politics of the country. There is no sense in allowing it to determine how one will vote at the Presidential election if the vote is meant merely to be an expression of disapprobation. To vote for Hayes, for instance, without regard to other considerations, merely to show Southerners that we disapprove of such conduct, would be little short of folly. Southerners know already that the whole North, and the whole civilized world, disapprove of such conduct. They would not know it any better if we elected Hayes ten times over. Moreover, the election of Hayes would of itself not necessarily act as a deterrent from such acts. Stump orators and party organs talk as if it would, but they know it would *not*. Electing a Republican President, or keeping the Republican party in power, is not of itself sufficient to mend matters at the South. We have had a Republican President and a Republican House and Senate for eight years, and yet the South is, according to those who are most clamorous for a further trial of the remedy, in a terrible condition, as the Hamburg matter shows. Mr. Boutwell thought, only last year, that we were on the eve of another civil war; and Mr. Dawes, when stumping for Butler at the last election, assured us that all Southern negroes went to bed every night in confident expectation of arson or murder. Now, if this is the result of eight years of Republican legislation and administration in time of peace, it is useless to urge us to try four years more of it as a certain specific. Nor is it easy to see why matters should get any worse under a Democratic Administration, for the same prospect of impunity exists now which would exist then. As long as the State governors do not call for Federal interference, the President, whether Republican or Democratic, could do nothing for the protection of negro life and property, and of this call there is little chance anywhere now, except in South Carolina or Louisiana, and in a year more there will be none in Louisiana. Nor is there much likelihood that any President will be permanently armed, as under one of the late Force Acts, with the ordinary police duty of protecting life and property at the South, because this would involve a complete change in the structure of the Government.

In fact, when we lay aside rhetoric and think out the answer to the question, In what way is a Republican Administration such as we have had likely to be more beneficial to the colored people of the South than a Democratic one? we are driven to the conclusion that the only difference would be in the fact that Federal office-holders would probably be more friendly to them under the one than under the other, and that the vague dread which has lingered in the minds of Southerners since the war as to the extremes to which the North might go if roused, would die out more rapidly under a Tilden than under a Hayes—we say more rapidly, for die out it will under either. But then, it is hardly worth while for rational men to allow anything so important as a Presidential election to turn on considerations so vague and shadowy as these. Nor will it do to overlook the fact that there is nothing to which all the corrupt politicians of the Republican party cling so eagerly as to the theory that their dislodgment from power will in some mysterious manner be followed by undefined disasters at the South. It is this which constitutes almost their whole political capital at present; and so frantically do they cling to it that, even when detected in knavery, they try to escape by alleging that some of their accusers or the witnesses or bystanders served in the rebel army—reminding one of the American consul who fought on the Papal side at the battle of Mentana, and who, when called to account for it by Mr. Seward, made answer that the man who saw him fight and reported him to the State Department was an Englishman.

We are, however, very far from asserting or insinuating that the condition of the South ought not to enter into the calculations of a voter who is making up his mind on which side he ought to cast his ballot at the coming election. On the contrary, we think it ought to engage his attention as seriously as, if not more seriously than, any other topic. But we do say, with all the earnestness at our command, that he is not the friend but the enemy both of Southern blacks and Southern whites who votes for the continuance of, or with the design of continuing, that form of protection which General Grant has extended to them through Casey, and Packard, and Durell, and Kellogg, and Ames, and Scott, and Parker. If the success of the Republican ticket is going to perpetuate this shameful and demoralizing system, every honest and patriotic man ought to think twice before voting it; and if anybody infers from the occurrence of such incidents as the Hamburg tragedy that the system ought to be continued, he may be sure that his reasoning apparatus needs overhauling. The reason why we did not think Mr. Hayes's letter satisfactory touching the Southern question was that he was not sufficiently explicit as to the proper remedies for the Southern disease, but simply talked of his desire for peace and conciliation in general terms, such as pacificators of the Grant school have all along used, and which may cover almost any kind of policy. The statesmanlike view of the Southern difficulty is simple enough. It is that a slave society in a thinly-peopled agricultural country, at the close of sudden emancipation and a bloody civil war, is in a semi-barbarous condition, out of which nothing but the combination of the leading civilizing influences which have raised all other societies will raise it, such as education, growth of population, manufactures, and trade; and that even these influences, powerful and beneficent as they are, can do but little without the aid of the great healer and restorer, Time. The Carpet-Baggers' and Politicians' view of the case is also simple—viz., that here are six millions of "unrepentant rebels," who ought to be in all respects like the inhabitants of Massachusetts, and who only need to be literally treated with grape and canister and the penitentiary to make the whole South a pleasing reproduction, in the matter of free discussion, brotherly kindliness, and general culture, of the town of Concord in that State; and that when they attack negroes their case is exactly like that of a party of Bostonians who should abandon their workshops and warehouses and suddenly begin slaughtering the inhabitants of the next block. We were glad to see that Mr. Wheeler, in his letter of acceptance, gave in his adhesion to the nobler and more rational view of this great national affliction. We wish Mr. Hayes had been equally explicit, so that we might know that when he comes into power his reform of the civil service will consist, above all things, in the representation of the Administration at the South by the best and purest men it can find, so as to satisfy the whites that we are at least honest and worthy of respect, and the blacks that real liberty has no necessary connection with corruption and disorder or the exaltation of ignorance and the abasement of intelligence.

July 27, 1876

Robert G. Ingersoll: from
Speech at Indianapolis

LADIES AND GENTLEMEN, FELLOW CITIZENS AND CITIZEN SOLDIERS:—I am opposed to the Democratic party, and I will tell you why. Every State that seceded from the United States was a Democratic State. Every ordinance of secession that was drawn was drawn by a Democrat. Every man that endeavored to tear the old flag from the heaven that it enriches was a Democrat. Every man that tried to destroy this nation was a Democrat. Every enemy this great Republic has had for twenty years has been a Democrat. Every man that shot Union soldiers was a Democrat. Every man that denied to the Union prisoners even the worm-eaten crust of famine, and when some poor, emaciated Union patriot, driven to insanity by famine, saw in an insane dream the face of his mother, and she beckoned him and he followed, hoping to press her lips once again against his fevered face, and when he stepped one step beyond the dead line the wretch that put the bullet through his loving, throbbing heart was and is a Democrat.

Every man that loved slavery better than liberty was a Democrat. The man that assassinated Abraham Lincoln was a Democrat. Every man that sympathized with the assassin—every man glad that the noblest President ever elected was assassinated, was a Democrat. Every man that wanted the privilege of whipping another man to make him work for him for nothing and pay him with lashes on his naked back, was a Democrat. Every man that raised bloodhounds to pursue human beings was a Democrat. Every man that clutched from shrieking, shuddering, crouching mothers, babes from their breasts, and sold them into slavery, was a Democrat. Every man that impaired the credit of the United States, every man that swore we would never pay the bonds, every man that swore we would never redeem the greenbacks, every maligner of his country's credit, every calumniator of his country's honor, was a Democrat. Every man that resisted the draft, every man that hid in the bushes

and shot at Union men simply because they were endeavoring
to enforce the laws of their country, was a Democrat. Every
man that wept over the corpse of slavery was a Democrat. Every man that cursed Abraham Lincoln because he issued the
Proclamation of Emancipation—the grandest paper since the
Declaration of Independence—every one of them was a Democrat. Every man that denounced the soldiers that bared their
breasts to the storms of shot and shell for the honor of America
and for the sacred rights of man, was a Democrat. Every man
that wanted an uprising in the North, that wanted to release
the rebel prisoners that they might burn down the homes of
Union soldiers above the heads of their wives and children,
while the brave husbands, the heroic fathers, were in the front
fighting for the honor of the old flag, every one of them was
a Democrat. I am not through yet. Every man that believed
this glorious nation of ours is a confederacy, every man that
believed the old banner carried by our fathers over the fields of
the Revolution; the old flag carried by our fathers over the fields
of 1812; the glorious old banner carried by our brothers over
the plains of Mexico; the sacred banner carried by our brothers
over the cruel fields of the South, simply stood for a contract,
simply stood for an agreement, was a Democrat. Every man
who believed that any State could go out of the Union at its
pleasure, every man that believed the grand fabric of the American Government could be made to crumble instantly into dust
at the touch of treason, was a Democrat. Every man that helped
to burn orphan asylums in New York, was a Democrat; every
man that tried to fire the city of New York, although he knew
that thousands would perish, and knew that the great serpent of
flame leaping from buildings would clutch children from their
mothers' arms—every wretch that did it was a Democrat. Recollect it! Every man that tried to spread smallpox and yellow
fever in the North, as the instrumentalities of civilized war, was
a Democrat. Soldiers, every scar you have on your heroic bodies
was given you by a Democrat. Every scar, every arm that is lacking, every limb that is gone, is a souvenir of a Democrat. I want
you to recollect it. Every man that was the enemy of human
liberty in this country was a Democrat. Every man that wanted
the fruit of all the heroism of all the ages to turn to ashes upon
the lips—every one was a Democrat.

I am a Republican. I will tell you why: This is the only free Government in the world. The Republican party made it so. The Republican party took the chains from four millions of people. The Republican party, with the wand of progress, touched the auction-block and it became a schoolhouse. The Republican party put down the Rebellion, saved the nation, kept the old banner afloat in the air, and declared that slavery of every kind should be extirpated from the face of this continent. What more? I am a Republican because it is the only free party that ever existed. It is a party that has a platform as broad as humanity, a platform as broad as the human race, a party that says you shall have all the fruit of the labor of your hands, a party that says you may think for yourself, a party that says, no chains for the hands, no fetters for the soul.

I am a Republican because the Republican party says this country is a Nation, and not a confederacy. I am here in Indiana to speak, and I have as good a right to speak here as though I had been born on this stand—not because the State flag of Indiana waves over me—I would not know it if I should see it. You have the same right to speak in Illinois, not because the State flag of Illinois waves over you, but because that banner, rendered sacred by the blood of all the heroes, waves over you and me. I am in favor of this being a Nation. Think of a man gratifying his entire ambition in the State of Rhode Island. We want this to be a Nation, and you cannot have a great, grand, splendid people without a great, grand, splendid country. The great plains, the sublime mountains, the great rushing, roaring rivers, shores lashed by two oceans, and the grand anthem of Niagara, mingle and enter, into the character of every American citizen, and make him or tend to make him a great and grand character. I am for the Republican party because it says the Government has as much right, as much power, to protect its citizens at home as abroad. The Republican party does not say that you have to go away from home to get the protection of the Government. The Democratic party says the Government cannot march its troops into the South to protect the rights of the citizens. It is a lie. The Government claims the right, and it is conceded that the Government has the right, to go to your house, while you are sitting by your fireside with your wife and children

about you, and the old lady knitting, and the cat playing with
the yarn, and everybody happy and serene—the Government
claims the right to go to your fireside and take you by force
and put you into the army; take you down to the valley of
the shadow of hell, put you by the ruddy, roaring guns, and
make you fight for your flag. Now, that being so, when the
war is over and your country is victorious, and you go back
to your home, and a lot of Democrats want to trample upon
your rights, I want to know if the Government that took you
from your fireside and made you fight for it, I want to know
if it is not bound to fight for you. The flag that will not protect its protectors is a dirty rag that contaminates the air in
which it waves. The government that will not defend its defenders is a disgrace to the nations of the world. I am a Republican because the Republican party says, "We will protect
the rights of American citizens at home, and if necessary we
will march an army into any State to protect the rights of the
humblest American citizen in that State." I am a Republican
because that party allows me to be free—allows me to do my
own thinking in my own way. I am a Republican because it
is a party grand enough and splendid enough and sublime
enough to invite every human being in favor of liberty and
progress to fight shoulder to shoulder for the advancement of
mankind. It invites the Methodist, it invites the Catholic, it
invites the Presbyterian and every kind of sectarian; it invites
the Freethinker; it invites the infidel, provided he is in favor
of giving to every other human being every chance and every
right that he claims for himself. I am a Republican, I tell you.
There is room in the Republican air for every wing; there is
room on the Republican sea for every sail. Republicanism says
to every man: "Let your soul be like an eagle; fly out in the
great dome of thought, and question the stars for yourself."
But the Democratic party says; "Be blind owls, sit on the dry
limb of a dead tree, and hoot only when that party says hoot."

What is the next question? The next question is, will we protect the Union men in the South? I tell you the white Union
men have suffered enough. It is a crime in the Southern States

to be a Republican. It is a crime in every Southern State to love this country, to believe in the sacred rights of men.

The colored people have suffered enough. For more than two hundred years they have suffered the fabled torments of the damned; for more than two hundred years they worked and toiled without reward, bending, in the burning sun, their bleeding backs; for more than two hundred years, babes were torn from the breasts of mothers, wives from husbands, and every human tie broken by the cruel hand of greed; for more than two hundred years they were pursued by hounds, beaten with clubs, burned with fire, bound with chains; two hundred years of toil, of agony, of tears; two hundred years of hope deferred; two hundred years of gloom and shadow and darkness and blackness; two hundred years of supplication, of entreaty; two hundred years of infinite outrage, without a moment of revenge.

The colored people have suffered enough. They were and are our friends. They are the friends of this country, and, cost what it may, they must be protected.

There was not during the whole Rebellion a single negro that was not our friend. We are willing to be reconciled to our Southern brethren when they will treat our friends as men. When they will be just to the friends of this country; when they are in favor of allowing every American citizen to have his rights—then we are their friends. We are willing to trust them with the Nation when they are the friends of the Nation. We are willing to trust them with liberty when they believe in liberty. We are willing to trust them with the black man when they cease riding in the darkness of night, (those masked wretches,) to the hut of the freedman, and notwithstanding the prayers and supplications of his family, shoot him down; when they cease to consider the massacre of Hamburg as a Democratic triumph, then, I say, we will be their friends, and not before.

Now, my friends, thousands of the Southern people and thousands of the Northern Democrats are afraid that the negroes are going to pass them in the race of life. And, Mr. Democrat, he will do it unless you attend to your business. The simple fact that you are white cannot save you always. You have to be industrious, honest, to cultivate a sense of justice. If you do not the colored race will pass you, as sure as you live. I am for giving every man a chance. Anybody that can pass me is welcome.

I believe, my friends, that the intellectual domain of the future, as the land used to be in the State of Illinois, is open to pre-emption. The fellow that gets a fact first, that is his; that gets an idea first, that is his. Every round in the ladder of fame, from the one that touches the ground to the last one that leans against the shining summit of human ambition, belongs to the foot that gets upon it first.

Mr. Democrat, (I point down because they are nearly all on the first round of the ladder) if you can not climb, stand one side and let the deserving negro pass.

I must tell you one thing. I have told it so much, and you have all heard it fifty times, but I am going to tell it again because I like it. Suppose there was a great horse race here to-day, free to every horse in the world, and to all the mules, and all the scrubs, and all the donkeys.

At the tap of the drum they come to the line, and the judges say "it is a go." Let me ask you, what does the blooded horse, rushing ahead, with nostrils distended, drinking in the breath of his own swiftness, with his mane flying like a banner of victory, with his veins standing out all over him, as if a network of life had been cast upon him—with his thin neck, his high withers, his tremulous flanks—what does he care how many mules and donkeys run on that track? But the Democratic scrub, with his chuckle-head and lop-ears, with his tail full of cockle-burrs, jumping high and short, and digging in the ground when he feels the breath of the coming mule on his cockle-burr tail, he is the chap that jumps the track and says, "I am down on mule equality."

September 21, 1876

David Brundage to Ulysses S. Grant

ALLOW ME to inform you of the Stupendous frauds committed
at the Polls on wednesday the 4th inst—The Republicans could
undoubtedly carry the Elections in this part of the State, if protected even by the Law, but the Law is dormant, & not executed. On the day of Election, a crowd of white men Stood at
the Polls & knocked, kicked, pushed, pulled hair & Stuck pins
& Small bladed knives in the col. voters, and would not let a col
man vote unless he casted a Democratic ticket. The managers
of the Polls would throw down the Republican tickets openly,
or tear them up, & put in Democratic ones, and every Election
day in Milledgeville, the old State Capital (or Polls) is filled with
army Rifles & Shot Guns well charged. One time at the Polls,
a difficulty Started between the Sheriff & a col man, but Soon
Subsided. I happened to look up & Saw every window fairly
darkened with cocked guns. This is the case in this Section. The
Secession Democrats, are always the instigators, in every difficulty, and make it appear that it is the col man. I have known
col men to be murdered in cold blood, & nothing done in the
courts. Several col men have been Slaughtered outright by ku-
kluxism, and Still nothing done. Now the col people are trying
to assert their rights at the Ballot Box, which is about the only
priviledge they have, & the kuklux are threatening them with
death and the lash. At one time through this Section young
drunken and unprincipled white men commenced lashing
white men, and not long afterwards, the Roads were guarded
& Some of the kuklux, left for the Spiritual world, & the matter
Stoped, but threatened again. Tis true, I am Southern born but
proud to Say that my tender age prevented me from raising
arms against the United States Government. I have been acting
as a justice of the Peace for Several years, & always respected
my oath, regardless of color. Here recently a great many of the
white people & all the col in the counties Hancock Washington
& Baldwin, run me for Senator, & I fairly beat the race, but
cheated out of it. nearly all the white people turned against me

because the col people Supported me, & the managers of the Election changed tickets right before my eyes. I tried to get the Sheriff to Stop the Election but to no use. I had to Submit & If I commence a contest, my life is at Stake. Mr Peter O'Neal *c* run for Representative, & Mr Johnathan Norcross, for Governor & all treated in like manner. This is general evil through the recent Georgia Elections So far as I have heard. The Secession Democrats are So enraged that they openly declare to kill the man that the col people elect, & a man is in danger all the time. I do not See how matters can Stand under Such Circumstances. Some of the managers of the Polls are prominent church members, and dont Show any remorse of conscience, in Swearing to emphatical falsehoods. This is the State of matters without any exageration. About three years ago I wrote to you about kuklux depredations, but never heard from you, however if they Start again I will get Several to join me, & try to Stop them with powder & Ball. This the only thing that did Stop them. Unless the Polls are Supported by troops, at the Presidencial Election I do not See how the col man will make out. one third of them dont go to the Polls from fear, & a great many have to remain at home, because the white man will turn him off, to keep his crop, or wages. This is often the case, & no chance to gain any thing in the Courts. No chance for the poor col man. The poverty Striken white men are the most eager to raise difficulties with the col man, & Still cling to the Secession Democrats, as they did in the Rebellion. They will not hear reason, for their minds are inflated with poisonous Secession hatred. The col People as a universal thing, are obedient kind & industrious, and their complaint, which is true, they Cant get their wages even by Law—for the Courts will not do but little for them. A great many poor white men in this Country are more dependent than the col man, & yet they are So narrow minded, they will Sustain the Secession Democrats against their own interest. The recently elected men, threaten to Scale the Exemption Laws which will undoubtedly be the Case. Unless Hays & Wheeler are elected we poor class of people in the South are 'gone up.' I close. Please burn this. Write me a few words of advice.

October 14, 1876

Rutherford B. Hayes:
Diary, November 12, 1876

Sunday, November 12.—The news this morning is not con-clusive. The headlines of the morning papers are as follows:— The *News*, "Nip and Tuck"; "Tuck has it"; "The Mammoth National Doubt";—and the *Herald* heads its news column, "Which?" But to my mind the figures indicate that Florida has been carried by the Democrats. No doubt both fraud and violence intervened to produce the result. But the same is true in many Southern States.

We shall, the fair-minded men of the country will, history will hold that the Republicans were by fraud, violence, and intimidation, by a nullification of the Fifteenth Amendment, deprived of the victory which they fairly won. But we must, I now think, prepare ourselves to accept the inevitable. I do it with composure and cheerfulness. To me the result is no personal calamity.

I would like the opportunity to improve the civil service. It seems to me I could do more than any Democrat to put South-ern affairs on a sound basis. I do not apprehend any great or permanent injury to the financial affairs of the country by the victory of the Democrats. The hard-money wing of the party is at the helm. Supported, as they should be and will be, in all wise measures, by the great body of the Republican party, nothing can be done to impair the national credit or debase the national currency. On this, as on all important subjects, the Republicans will still hold a commanding position.

We are in a minority in the Electoral Colleges; we lose the Administration. But in the former free States—the States that were always loyal—we are still in a majority. We carry eigh-teen of the twenty-two and have two hundred thousand ma-jority of the popular vote. In the old slave States, if the recent Amendments were cheerfully obeyed, if there had been nei-ther violence nor intimidation nor other improper interference with the rights of the colored people, we should have carried enough Southern States to have held the country and to have secured a decided popular majority in the nation. Our adversaries are in power, but they are supported by a minority only of the lawful voters of the country. A fair election in the South would undoubtedly have given us a large majority of the electoral votes, and a decided preponderance of the popular vote.

I went to church and heard a good, strong, sensible sermon by Critchfield's son-in-law. After church and dinner I rode with General Mitchell and his children out to Alum Creek and around past the place of my old friend Albert Buttles. We talked of the Presidential question as settled, and found it in all respects well for me personally that I was not elected. On reaching home at Mitchell's, we found my son Webb with the following dispatch from Governor Dennison, a prudent and cautious gentleman, which seems to open it all up again:—

> WASHINGTON, D. C., November 12, 1876.
>   Received at Columbus 2:05 P. M.
> To GOVERNOR R. B. HAYES.
> You are undoubtedly elected next President of the United States. Desperate attempts are being made to defeat you in Louisiana, South Carolina, and Florida, but they will not succeed.
>   W. DENNISON.

In the evening I asked if there were objections to publishing this dispatch. About 10 P. M. reply came, "No objections."

Abram Hewitt: Memorandum of Conversation with Ulysses S. Grant

AFTER a few commonplace remarks, the President said that he longed for the day when he should be able to retire from office; That he counted the hours just as when he completed his terms at West Point during the last three months of his term he looked forward for the freedom which was in store for him: That for sixteen years he had consecrated his life to the public service without any interval of rest or any possibility of being free from great responsibility;—That while he was in the army, during the war, he was in the picket line, so to speak, for four years, and that if in any of the engagements where he had gained a victory, he had lost a battle, the whole cause of the Union would have been lost; That during Johnson's administration, he was the bulwark between Congress on the one hand, and the President on the other, and had been compelled to exercise greater powers, and discharge more complicated duties than any previous General-in-chief; That during his eight years of the Presidency, the most difficult questions had been presented, and had to be solved.—: That he was aware that at times, he had been misunderstood, but he believed that the great mass of the people were disposed to do him and his motives full justice, To which I remarked that I had no question of that fact; That his career formed the most memorable part of American history; That his fame was the property of the American people; That we all had a jealous regard for him, and, speaking for the Democratic party, I could assure him that they were disposed to do him full justice; and that they had a confidence that now, at the close of his administration, no act of his would tarnish the glory of his past achievements.—The President replied that the present House of Representatives had not given evidence of a desire to do him justice; That they had raked up petty accusations against him, and had brought back from Ireland a lunatic, who for a long time had followed him about, threatening vengeance, so that for six months, he had carried a heavy cane for protection.—I said to him that this matter had made so little impression on the public mind that I was not aware of such an investigation, and I begged that he would not attribute to a great party, the malice or blunders of a few individuals; That he was recognized by both parties, as the General who had brought the war to a close, and who had assured the continuance of the Union.—I then remarked that the present crisis was one in which he could render to the country even a greater service than any he had heretofore rendered, and that it seemed to me that it rested wholly with him whether the present complication should result in war, or in a peaceful solution.—He replied that if there was to be any fighting, he certainly would not begin it: That he would maintain order, as he was bound to do, but that he would not provoke any collision by the use of mere power, where it was not his duty to employ it.—I then referred to the recent use of troops in South Carolina.—He said that his orders to General Ruger directed him simply to preserve the peace, and that he had not been authorized to interfere in the organization of the legislature:—That General Ruger's report showed he issued orders in accordance with these instructions, but that the orders had been misconstrued by a young officer, and that members had been refused admission to the hall, but as soon as this fact had been brought to the notice of General Ruger, this obstruction was removed.—He referred to the statement signed by General Gordon and Wade Hampton, that notice had been sent by General Ruger to the members from Laurens and Edgefield counties, that they would be removed from the hall, unless they absented themselves, and he stated that this was an error; that General Ruger had not directed any such notice to be given, though it was probable that Governor Chamberlain had sent such notice.—As to the organization of the two houses, the President, after a conversation of some length, laid down this proposition.—That neither house had a quorum for the transaction of business, and was therefore, not properly constituted; That it required sixty-three members to make a quorum; That, the Republican house had fifty-nine members with certificates, and that the Democratic house had fifty-six members with certificates; That in case he should be called upon, as he might be, to recognize one or other of the houses; he should not recognize either, unless it had sixty-three members holding the original certificates of election. I called his attention to the fact that four members holding these original certificates of election, had been unseated by the Republican house, and other persons, having no certificates of election, had been put in their place. The President thought that this could not be the case, and I promised to inquire, and let him know the fact.—I have since inquired, and am told positively, that the four members from Barnwell, having regular certificates, have thus been unseated by the Republican house.—The President said if this was so, it could not be justified.—Then, coming to the Presidential question, he said he thought he had sufficient information to justify him in forming a judgment as to the situation, and he repeated a remark previously made, that he did not think any man could afford to take the place of President, unless the general judgment concurred in the belief that he was fairly elected; That so far as South-Carolina was concerned, he believed that the state had gone, on the face of the returns, for Hayes & Wheeler, throwing out entirely the counties of Edgefield and Laurens; that in these counties there had been really no election; that they had been overridden by companies of armed men from Georgia, and that the black population had been deterred from voting, and although he, the President, had nothing officially to do with the matter, as it was confined to the returning board alone, he thought that these counties had been properly thrown out, and that the state of South-Carolina should justly be counted for Hayes & Wheeler.—As to Florida, he said that the result was very close, but that on the face of the returns, he believed that Hayes & Wheeler had a majority of about forty, and that this was independent of the question of frauds, which, if allowed a fair weight, would probably increase the majority, as he was credibly informed.—I asked him from whom he got his information, and he said from Mr. Kasson, who had gone South at his request.—Up to this point, the President had enjoined no confidence, but coming to Louisiana, he remarked that what he should say to me must be in confidence.—He said that on the face of the returns, Tilden & Hendricks unquestionably had a majority of six to eight thousand votes: That there were six parishes in which there had been intimidation to such an extent, that he did not think there had been a fair election, and that they had to be thrown out; That he believed that when thrown out, there was still a majority for Tilden & Hendricks, to which I remarked that it was somewheres about two thousand,—and that this majority could only be overcome by assuming that the votes of five thousand naturalized citizens of New-Orleans were all Democratic, and that by throwing them out on account of some defect in the naturalization papers.— The President remarked that the returning-board in Louisiana was in very bad odor with the public; that the people had no confidence in it, and even if it did right, it would not be credited with honest intentions.—He believed that there had been no honest election in Louisiana since Slidell got control of its politics.—I suggested to him that, as a matter of fact, it was not possible to have a fair election in that state, and that it was a most serious blow to Republican government, that a state in which a fair election could not be had, should decide a Presidential contest.—The President replied that this was true, and that it would not be unreasonable that the vote of Louisiana should be thrown out, as it was in 1872, on account of irregularities of election, and the peculiar functions of the returning-board.—I remarked that this would give the election to Tilden; that he would then have a clear majority of all the electors appointed.—He said, 'no'; that it had been held in Lincoln's time that the President must have a majority of all the votes to which the states are legally entitled.—I replied that it had been so asserted, but that no tribunal had ever considered the question. The President answered 'certainly not, because Lincoln had the necessary majority.'—Whereupon I remarked that if a majority had belonged to the states in rebellion, it would not be held that the loyal states should go without a President, and he said; 'certainly not, they would have to do the best they could.'—However, assuming that Louisiana were thrown out, and that it was still necessary to have one hundred and eighty-five votes, this would throw the election into the House, who would then elect the President, and the Senate would elect the Vice President, which was one solution of the problem.—However, he said he did not expect there would be any serious trouble; that a solution would be reached, that would, in the main, be satisfactory to the people; That if one of the doubtful states should cast all or any part of its votes for Tilden, that would settle the question.—He would be inaugurated as quietly as he, General Grant, had been.—It was not, however, for him to decide the question, but it was the duty of Congress under the Constitution: That his duty would be to see that their decision was carried into effect.—I asked the President whether in the event of the two houses getting into conflict, and coming to blows, he would feel it his duty to use the military force of the Goverment to restore order.—To which he replied; 'certainly not,' but that if either side should call up an armed force or a mob, to its support, he would feel bound to protect the public property from its attack, and to repel them from the Capitol.—In conclusion, he said that his great desire was to retire from office with the country at peace, and generally satisfied with the conclusion which might be arrived at; and that he thought it rather hard that any one should suspect him, who had given his best years to preserve the country, of any design upon its liberties.—I assured the President of the great gratification I experienced in hearing such sentiments expressed; That I was confirmed in my faith in his patriotism, and that it should not be long before the whole country, and both parties, would do him and his motives full justice.—I omitted to say, in the proper place above, that, speaking of the Presidential election, the President said that it was a matter of substance, and not of technicalities; That any attempt to appropriate a vote in Vermont, or Rhode Island or Oregon, which had given a Republican majority, would be regarded only as a trick, just as any attempt to get a vote of Louisiana by fraud would be regarded as indefensible.—I assured the President that I heartily concurred in this view, and that if a vote from Oregon was really certified to the Democrats, I did not believe that any other use would be made of it than to get a fair hearing in the case of the other states, which, in the judgment of the Democratic party, might be improperly certified to Hayes; That neither Governor Tilden or his friends desired to have him succeed to the Presidency unless he had been honestly elected, and that in the event of there being so much doubt in regard to the real result, as to make it difficult for fair-minded men to say who was elected, I felt justified in saying that Governor Tilden and his friends, would cheerfully assent to a new election; That while he and they felt that they had a duty to perform, that they were not disposed to press an extreme issue in the face of a reasonable doubt. Incidentally, I mentioned to the President that the House would probably appoint committees to investigate and report upon the facts developed in the elections of South-Carolina, Florida and Louisiana.—He replied that he expected that they would do so, and thought it very proper, and that it would be a very desirable thing to get reports from committees properly constituted.—Incidentally, the President said that Mr. Anderson, on the Louisiana returning board, was a brother of Major Robert Anderson of Fort Sumter fame, and of Lars Anderson of Cincinnatti; He must, therefore, be an honest man, and that he would be inclined to believe any certificate he might sign, and to discredit any certificate he did not sign.—I since learn that the gentleman is not a brother of the gentleman named.

December 3, 1876

Chicago Tribune: *The Court of Arbitration*

THERE CAN be no mistaking the universal sentiment of the public with reference to the condition of political affairs at Washington. The public demand peace, and they demand this peace with sublime indifference as to its effect upon the hopes and prospects of the expectant Postmasters, Collectors, Gangers, and Tide-waiters. Every man in the land has an opinion of his own as to whether HAYES or TILDEN was legally and fairly elected. This opinion may be influenced by his previous political preferences; but, outside of the mob of office-seekers and office-holders, there are but few persons in either party who are not willing to accept any honest and fair decision of the case, no matter which candidate may by that decision be counted in.

The country suffered through the long campaign from May to November from the general disturbance, excitement, alarm, and distrust. On more than one occasion during that campaign the country was brought to the verge of civil war; and the President was compelled, in order to prevent a war of races, to station troops in several States to preserve the peace. The close of the polls on election-day without a war was accepted as a great relief; but that relief to the public mind was of short duration. The result of the election was for a time uncertain, and, when finally ascertained, was clouded with charges of fraud, violence, unfairness, and bribery. The worst passions of the previous campaign were again excited, and the country was brought to the contemplation of the fact that the 4th of March will see two persons proclaimed President, each organizing a Government, each claiming to be elected, and each supported by one of the Houses of Congress. The outcome of such a condition of affairs must be eventually the settlement of the conflicting claims by compromise and arbitration, or by war and the arbitrament of the sword. At this juncture, a joint committee of the two Houses of Congress have reported a scheme by which this settlement of all the questions by an arbitration

shall take place first, leaving revolution, war, and anarchy out
of the business altogether. Mr. LINCOLN told the Rebels that
even at the end of a war there would have to be a settlement,
and it would save years of distress and bloodshed to have the
settlement first, and omit the war. The suggestion is as timely
now as it was in 1861. Mr. HAYES' right to the office must be
determined by law or by arms: why not have the legal settlement now, and dispense with that of force?

There are four hundred thousand people in Chicago who
are directly affected by this threatened disturbance. The value
of property is depressed; the volume of business is decreased;
the employment of labor is arrested; industrial occupation is
restricted. The hoarding of money and its withdrawal from
business have been extensive, not only in Chicago but all over
the country. Capital is withdrawn from investment. No man
ventures into new business. The earnings of labor have been
largely reduced, and business and trade paralyzed, because of
the complications which threaten to produce the Mexican plan
of having two or more Governments always on hand, each
claiming to be the lawful one.

There is not a mechanic or a laborer in Chicago whose condition has not been seriously injured by the protracted disturbance of confidence caused by the violence of the Presidential
contest and its subsequent complications. There is not a stone-
cutter, mason, carpenter, painter, wheelwright, blacksmith,
shoemaker, harnessmaker, tanner, or iron or steel worker, or
any person engaged in mechanical or other labor, whose wages,
income, and even employment, have not been injured, and seriously, by the general paralysis of business produced by this
threatened conflict, involving the erection and maintenance of
rival claimants and rival Governments. When one man or ten
men lock up their money, withdraw it from use, it is lost to
general business, and the loss falls directly upon those who live
by their daily earnings.

Six months ago there was a decided improvement in general business. There were larger sales, larger production, more
employment, and more money distributed. That improvement
was delayed in becoming general because of the pending election. Everywhere, all over the land, preparations were made
for a grand revival of production that was to follow the close

of the Presidential election. But that election was not closed; the contest put on new shapes; the two Houses of Congress assumed irreconcilable attitudes; and the madness of party has since then threatened revolution and civil war.

The country demands peace; it cares nothing personally for HAYES or TILDEN, or this or that party; and when the means are offered for a prompt, final, and peaceful adjudication of the whole difficulty by a majority of the Judges of the Supreme Court, it will hold every man and every party guilty of a great national wrong who shall defeat such an adjudication. While the banks and the Boards of Trade all over the country are unanimous in favor of this peaceful settlement, they are not as deeply interested in it as are the vast armies of men who are members of the labor unions, whose means of support for themselves and families are cut off and destroyed by the general prostration, from which there can be no revival and no recovery until this question shall be settled.

With this question settled, the country will promptly recover. Our currency—paper, gold, and silver—waits only for peace to become equalized in values; our manufactures only wait for peace and national security to enter upon a production for export, to which the country has been a stranger since 1860. All things are ripe, with abundance of capital, for a general revival of trade, and of production, and general employment of labor, which has been so largely idle since 1873. The politicians, the placemen, strikers and blowers in office and out of office, stand in the way. They want office and plunder, and they prefer even war to a denial of their wants. Wo be unto those who overlook the suffering interests of the whole people and listen to the clamor of the howling mob of spoils-seekers.

Chicago Tribune, January 21, 1877

St. Louis Globe Democrat: *The Warning*

THE VERY strong temptation to call Mr. Phillips a Cassandra now is checked by the reflection that Mr. Phillips was called a Cassandra twenty years ago, and it is impossible not to remember that if we had listened to his sinister prophecies at a former period, we might not now be compelled against our will to listen to his new warnings against an old danger. Mr. Phillips is narrow, prejudiced, obstinate, fanatical; he refuses to see anything more than the negro side of any controversy in which the negro is involved, and he has no more hesitation in saying disagreeable things than politicians ordinarily have in repeating pleasant platitudes. But if the people of the United States are sensible, they will listen to Wendell Phillips' words with serious attention, for they are worthy of the serious attention of all, and they will not concern themselves about Phillips' personal peculiarities or past record, but will simply ask themselves whether his words are true, and whether his forecast of the political situation is reasonable.

His whole argument turns on a plain question of fact: Are the Southern Democrats willing to accord to the negro his civil and political rights without reservation or abridgment? If they are, then all of Wendell Phillips' eloquence is idle wind; his contest is merely with the phantoms of his own conjuring. But, if the Southern Democrats are not willing to accord civil and political rights to the negro as fully and as freely as they are accorded to the immigrants in New York or in Illinois, then his warnings are indeed those of a Cassandra foretelling worse than the fate of Troy; the war will have to be fought over again, or else all of its results will have to be surrendered. It follows as the night the day.

Is it worth while seriously to argue the question whether the White League Democrats of the South are in favor of negro equality? Thus far, out of some 8,000,000 of them, Wade Hampton is the only man who has ever committed himself to the doctrine, and he protests so much that we believe that even he would not call God to witness his sincerity so often if he did not have a fixed assurance that there was not the slightest danger of his being called on to make his professions good. Why, what reason should the White League have for its existence except an opposition based on color? Proscription of the negro, exclusion from the polls, the schools, the jury box, the witness stand, is the one plank in their platform, the one article of their creed, the one principle of their politics, their bond of union, their incentive to action, the source of their strength, and the purpose of their lives. The war is over, and they don't propose to renew it. They admit the authority of the Union in national affairs; but negro equality in local politics—do we need to give them a trial before making up our minds on that point?

The last vestige of Federal interference in local politics will probably disappear in a few days. The fates have been too strong to allow a further continuance of that method of securing republican governments; but do not let us be deceived about the consequences. Let us not delude ourselves by crying peace, when the only peace there is is the peace of Poland, the peace of death, the peace which reigned until the election of Lincoln came to disturb it. If we surrender, let us surrender with our eyes open; let us admit that the untiring hate of the Southerners has worn out our endurance, and that though we staked everything for freedom under the spur of the rebellion, we have not enough of principle about us to uphold the freedom, so dearly bought, against the persistent and effective opposition of the unrepentant and unchanged rebels. Whether we will ever again struggle to regain that supremacy of liberty which we are about to abdicate so basely, is a question to be discussed by itself; for the present, it suffices to say that the words of Phillips are less than the truth; that his bitter and burning eloquence fails to do justice to the situation, and that the day which sees the last Federal soldier evacuating the South in obedience to the demands of the White Leaguers, will also see the last of the liberty which we conquered for the negroes.

March 31, 1877

The Nation:
The Political South Hereafter

THE DISSOLUTION of the last sham government at the South—
an event which we have a right to believe cannot now be long
delayed—will place the Southern States, as regards the rest
of the nation, in a position which they have not before occupied for almost a generation. Heretofore, in the discussion of
nearly all national questions, the most embarrassing and vexatious element at any time to be considered, and frequently an
overwhelmingly important one, was "the South." This term
designated a number of contiguous States, bound together by
mutual interest in the maintenance of a social system which
was understood to be inimical to the feelings, at least, if not
to the welfare, of the inhabitants of all other States; and "the
South" was always, therefore, a more definite term than "the
West" or "the North." Slavery dominated every other interest,
and held the Southern States together in political unity. The
phrase "the solid South" was a legitimate one before, during,
and even after the war, and only recently has it become a political bugbear. But the threefold cord which bound the Southern
States together—the defence and perpetuation of slavery, the
struggle for the establishment of an independent confederacy,
and the trials of reconstruction—no longer exists, and nothing
has taken or can take its place. For a time, perhaps, traditions
of the dead "institution," war memories, and the possession
of a race of freedmen may together do something toward per-
petuating a united South, but the union will surely be mostly
in appearance, and any little reality which it may possess will
speedily give way before opposing and stronger forces.

We believe the proposition to be almost self-evident, indeed,
that hereafter there is to be no South; none, that is, in a distinctively political sense. The negro will disappear from the field
of national politics. Henceforth the nation, as a nation, will
have nothing more to do with him. He will undoubtedly play
a part, perhaps an important one, in the development of the

national civilization. The philanthropist will have still a great deal to do both with him and for him, and the sociological student will find him, curiously placed as he is in contact and competition with other races, an unfailing source of interest; but as a "ward" of the nation he can no longer be singled out for especial guardianship or peculiar treatment in preference to Irish laborers or Swedish immigrants. There is something distasteful, undeniably, in the idea of one who has played so important a part in our past political history making his final exit in the company of the Carpet-baggers; but for this unfortunate coincidence the negro is not to be blamed.

The disappearance of the factitious interest which made the South politically a unit will permit the rapid development of several natural and obvious disintegrating forces which, indeed, have been already in operation for some time, but the results of which have been obscured by the overshadowing interloper which has just been disposed of. Climate, soil, natural productions, diversity of pursuit, and varieties of race will certainly disintegrate politically the States of the South as well as the States of the North. The "sunny" South, of course, was a fiction, an agreeable convention only, for in the matter of climate the South presents variations comparable at least with any to be found in the North. St. Louis, St. Augustine, and New Orleans, for instance, are as diverse in climate as are any three cities which might be selected in the Northern States. The pecuniary ties, moreover, which unite some Southern States to the North are already stronger than any which bind them to their former political associates. Missouri, for instance, in its commercial relations and sympathies is a Northern State, as, in a modified sense, are Maryland and Delaware; and Florida apparently is set apart already as the winter home of wealthy and invalided Northern men, whose influence upon the tone of its politics begins to be perceptible notwithstanding the hubbub of its recent performances in counting electoral votes. Again, it is evident that the cotton, rice, tobacco, and cane-producing districts of the South will attract very different classes of people, and beget very different manners and opinions from those inevitably associated with mining and manufacturing communities. Thus, South Carolina will soon differ from Missouri even more than Vermont does from Pennsylvania or Minnesota from Massachusetts. Political disintegration at the South may show itself most plainly at first in connection with the discussion of economic questions. There is to-day throughout all the Southern States, probably, a traditional inclination towards free-trade, although the leaning is not a very decided one, and the change from this to an opposing attitude is a process which may be witnessed soon in several of them. Is it not possible, at least, that the cotton and rice States may increase their present leaning towards free-trade, while Louisiana, Virginia, and Kentucky demand protection against Cuban sugar and tobacco? Or, on the other hand, may not South Carolina yearn for Government aid in the establishment of manufactories, and New Orleans sigh for free-trade in Mississippi products? Will the present great poverty of the Southern States, again, incline them to give ear to the jingle of "silver" theories, and make "greenback" delusions easy of belief, or will the memory of their own once plentiful "scrip" be a sufficient protection against indulgence in financial heresies? And will the South look with longing eyes upon visions of canals and railroads until it heedlessly begins the cry for internal improvements at Government expense, or will it be warned by the ghosts of Crédit Mobilier and Northern Pacific? It is evident, we believe, without lengthening the list of these enumerations or suggestions, that the Southern States may soon be as divided upon the subjects of tariff, currency, *laissez-faire* or paternity in government, etc., as we have been and still are at the North, and if New Hampshire and North Carolina should happen to join hands in defence of some political theory in opposition (say) to Louisiana and New York, "the South" would soon become as vague an expression, from a political point of view, as "the West" is now.

The future of the freedman will be bound up undoubtedly with that of the white man, and does not now require separate consideration. Great numbers of negroes will certainly remain upon the cotton-fields, rice-swamps, and cane and tobacco plantations, and, being employed as field-hands, their political opinions for a long time to come will inevitably reflect those of their employers. Others will learn to work in factories or become mechanics and small farmers, and, generally, all over the South for a long time, negroes will find the places now filled at the North by Irish, German, and Chinese laborers. The political influence of the freedman, considered as distinct from that of the white man, will be almost imperceptible. His ultimate influence upon our civilization, as determined by the relative fecundity of the two races, and their action and reaction upon one another as the negro becomes better educated and more independent, is a subject which can be discussed more profitably a generation hence.

Generally speaking, while the political breaking up of the South will do away with a powerful barrier to national advancement, and will bring each State into closer sympathy with the national Government, nevertheless we hardly expect to receive any immediate and valuable aid from the South toward the solution of our present executive, judicial, and legislative problems. In this, however, we may happily be mistaken. It is true that the South has long been more "provincial" than the North, that it is far from possessing similar educational advantages, that it is now almost barren of literary productions or literary and scientific men, and that these facts would seem to indicate a natural soil for the germination and growth of all kinds of crude and coarse theories of society and government; but, on the other hand, it is not easy to imagine the South developing theories more crude than some now cherished in Indiana and Pennsylvania, and which find shelter even in New York and Massachusetts. We are inclined to believe, also, that the average man of the South is a more pliant and enthusiastic follower of his chosen leader than the average man of the North, and the Gordons, Hills, Lamars, and Hamptons may be depended upon to exert a widespread and, in the main, healthful influence. We cannot forget that it was the well-digested plan of a Southern Gordon with regard to the collection of revenue to which a Northern Morton could give no friendly reception and could make no better reply than a taunt and a sneer. But the important point to be remembered here is the fact that *all* political contributions of the South, of whatever character, will hereafter go towards the upbuilding of a national as distinguished from a "sectional" unity. For the first time in our history we are entitled to assert that there is no danger of national dissolution. Heretofore our chief attention has been given to the saving of national life, and only incidentally have we been able to consider its character or to decide upon the best methods of perfecting it. We can now devote ourselves to legitimate politics—that is, to studies of governmental science—with a fair prospect of being able to throw some light upon many of the unsolved problems of modern life.

The Nation, April 5, 1877

CODA
1879

❦

John Russell Young: from Around the World With General Grant

Frequently our conversation would turn to home affairs and politics. On these questions the General always speaks without reserve. "I have never," he said, "shared the resentment felt by so many Republicans toward Mr. Hayes on the ground of his policy of conciliation. At the same time I never thought it would last, because it was all on one side. There is nothing more natural than that a President, new to his office, should enter upon a policy of conciliation. He wants to make everybody friendly, to have all the world happy, to be the central figure of a contented and prosperous commonwealth. That is what occurs to every President, it is an emotion natural to the office. I can understand how a kindly, patriotic man like Hayes would be charmed by the prospect. I was as anxious for such a policy as Mr. Hayes. There has never been a moment since Lee surrendered that I would not have gone more than halfway to meet the Southern people in a spirit of conciliation. But they have never responded to it. They have not forgotten the war. A few shrewd leaders like Mr. Lamar and others have talked conciliation; but any one who knows Mr. Lamar knows that he meant this for effect, and that at least he was as much in favor of the old *régime* as Jefferson Davis. The pacification of the South rests entirely with the South. I do not see what the North can do that has not been done, unless we surrender the results of the war. I am afraid there is a large party in the North who would do that now. I have feared even that our soldiers would begin to apologize for their part in the war. On that point what a grand speech General Sherman made in New York on a recent Decoration Day. I felt proud of Sherman for that speech. It was what a soldier and the general of an army should say. The radical trouble with the Southern leaders is, that instead of frankly acting with the Republicans in the North, they have held together, hoping by an alliance with the Democrats to control the government. I think Republicans should go as far as possible in conciliation, but not far enough to lose self-respect. Nor can any one who values the freedom of suffrage be satisfied with election results like those in the last canvass for the presidency. I have no doubt, for instance, that Mr. Hayes carried North Carolina, and that it was taken from him. No one old enough to read and write can doubt that the Republican party with anything like a fair vote would have carried, and perhaps did carry, Arkansas, Alabama, and Mississippi. I never doubted that they carried Louisiana, South Carolina, and Florida. Whether it was wise or unwise to have given the negro suffrage, we have done so, and no one can look on satisfied and see it taken from him. The root of the whole difference lies in that.

"The South," continued the General, "has been in many ways a disappointment to me. I hoped a great deal from the South, but these hopes have been wrecked. I hoped that Northern capital would pour into the South, that Northern influence and Northern energy would soon repair all that war had wasted. But that never came. Northern capitalists saw that they could not go South without leaving self-respect at home, and they remained home. The very terms of the invitations you see in all the Southern papers show that. The editors say they are glad to have Northern men provided they do not take part in politics. Why shouldn't they take part in politics? They are made citizens for that. So long as this spirit prevails there will be no general emigration of Northern men to the South. I was disappointed, very much so. It would have been a great thing for the South if some of the streams of emigration from New England and the Middle States toward Iowa and Kansas had been diverted into the South. I hoped much from the poor white class. The war, I thought, would free them from a bondage in some respects even lower than slavery; it would revive their ambition; they would learn, what we in the North know so well, that labor is a dignity, not a degradation, and assert themselves and become an active Union element. But they have been as much under the thumb of the slave-holder as before the war. Andrew Johnson, one of the ablest of the poor white class, tried to assert some independence; but as soon as the slave-holders put their thumb upon him, even in the Presidency, he became their slave. It is very curious and very strange. I hoped for different results, and did all I could to bring them around, but it could not be done.

"Looking back," said the General, "over the whole policy of reconstruction, it seems to me that the wisest thing would have been to have continued for some time the military rule. Sensible Southern men see now that there was no government so frugal, so just, and fair as what they had under our generals. That would have enabled the Southern people to pull themselves together and repair material losses. As to depriving them, even for a time, of suffrage, that was our right as a conqueror, and it was a mild penalty for the stupendous crime of treason. Military rule would have been just to all, to the negro who wanted freedom, the white man who wanted protection, the Northern man who wanted Union. As State after State showed a willingness to come into the Union, not on their own terms but upon ours, I would have admitted them. This would have made universal suffrage unnecessary, and I think a mistake was made about suffrage. It was unjust to the negro to throw upon him the responsibilities of citizenship, and expect him to be on even terms with his white neighbor. It was unjust to the North. In giving the South negro suffrage, we have given the old slave-holders forty votes in the electoral college. They keep those votes, but disfranchise the negroes. That is one of the gravest mistakes in the policy of reconstruction. It looks like a political triumph for the South, but it is not. The Southern people have nothing to dread more than the political triumph of the men who led them into secession. That triumph was fatal to them in 1860. It would be no less now. The trouble about military rule in the South was that our people did not like it. It was not in accordance with our institutions. I am clear now that it would have been better for the North to have postponed suffrage, reconstruction, State governments, for ten years, and held the South in a territorial condition. It was due to the North that the men who had made war upon us should be powerless in a political sense forever. It would have avoided the scandals of the State governments, saved money, and enabled the Northern merchants, farmers, and laboring men to reorganize society in the South. But we made our scheme, and must do what we can with it. Suffrage once given can never be taken away, and all that remains for us now is to make good that gift by protecting those who have received it.

from Around the World With General Grant (1879)

Joseph H. Rainey: From Remarks in Congress on South Carolina Elections

MR. SPEAKER, much has been said on this floor regarding the presence of soldiers at or near the polls on election day, and on the fact that Governor Chamberlain requested military protection from the National Government during the campaign preceding the election. If the military had interfered to suppress the exercise of free speech during the campaign or a free ballot at the polls on election day by the democrats, there would be some propriety and pertinency in these complaints; but when it is so notorious that the military only protected from violence the republicans in the exercise of their right of free speech and free ballot, which the democrats endeavored to suppress by violence and intimidation, these complaints become absurd and unreasonable. All these objections to the presence of troops, when the reasons on which these objections are founded are wholly wanting, have, to say the least, a refreshing coolness; and when in addition it is so well known that their presence prevented the party complaining from carrying out their nefarious designs of depriving the party protected by them from the exercise of their political rights, it presents the most remarkable spectacle of the exact reversal of a political axiom otherwise sound and excellent. In a word, the presence of troops when they prevent the exercise of free speech and a free ballot is decidedly objectionable, but when they interfere to protect its exercise by both or either parties there can be no objection except by the party that seeks to suppress or prevent them. It is urged that the presence of soldiers in the State prevented contestant from being returned elected, by protecting, I suppose, those who gave me the majority of the votes.

This fact aroused his virtuous indignation; but the gentleman has no indignation to spare against the State militia forces that were so largely employed to defeat my re-election in 1878. The presence of the military at the Sumter meeting of October 12, 1878, when the artillery from Columbia united their forces with the infantry of Sumter County and loaded their cannon with bags of ten-penny nails to fire upon the unarmed republicans is now a matter of history. The conduct of the State military forces at this meeting was but a specimen of the manner in which they acted not only throughout my congressional district but in every other part of the State. From the above it is evident that the objection is not to a military force *per se*, but to the national arms. Where the State military force succeeds in accomplishing what the national force prevented, namely, suppression of free speech and free voting, there is no objection to their presence at election time. Can anything better prove the hollow mockery of these objections and the wisdom of Governor Chamberlain in asking for troops and of President Grant in sending them? What a contrast in 1876! We had comparatively a fair election, free from violence, but not free from democratic fraud. But in 1878 both fraud and violence united to crush out a legitimate republican majority in my district of about 6,000, and gave the democratic candidate a majority of 8,000. He could have been declared elected by a majority of 20,000 with as much legal propriety. I now come to the thought with which I desire to conclude these remarks.

It has been asserted and dwelt upon with force and emphasis on this floor that the corruption of the republican party was great. I have not denied that some pecuniary corruption existed during the first four years of republican rule in South Carolina, in the perpetration of which republicans and democrats were combined. Democrats outside the Legislature, who wanted special legislation enacted, were the first to corrupt the republicans. The briber, my moral philosophy teaches, is just as bad as the bribed. I notice there has been no word of condemnation for them, while the republicans have been assailed. The republican party in South Carolina was destroyed in 1876–77; not by desertion of thousands of them who went over to the democrats, as the gentleman from Louisiana asserted in the paragraph following:

> By the middle of October, 1876, the fortunes of the republican leaders in South Carolina had grown desperate. The colored voters were deserting them by thousands. They were flocking to democratic meetings; they were riding in democratic processions; they were joining democratic clubs. On this point there can be no doubt—

but for the want of a simple guarantee of protection in the exercise of their acquired rights. The Government that had bestowed the gift failed to sustain and protect them in the enjoyment of the same. Up to this time the democratic party has been in possession of the State for two years, and an important election has taken place during that period.

Now, let us compare the two governments of these two parties during that period and see if the ills complained of have not been cured by the substitution of greater and more fundamental evils. Republicans ruled under Governor Chamberlain from 1874 to 1876, and in the first two years of democratic rule under Governor Hampton, say from 1876 to 1878, no corruption has been charged much less proven against the former's administration. As compared with Governor Hampton's doubtless it was more extravagant; that I concede for sake of argument. Now let us see if economy has not been purchased at much too dear a rate. The democrats have had control for two years; what are the fruits of that power? While no individual corruption has been charged against those in power, the State to-day is an acknowledged repudiator in the exchanges of the world. After solemn pledges that the bonded debt should be held inviolate she refuses to pay the principal and interest of her bonds, and her public credit has been utterly ruined thereby. One of her own native-born judges says with stinging sarcasm, in deciding in favor of the validity of the bonds that the Legislature has repudiated, "that the State should certainly return money she has received and used from the sale of bonds before she repudiates them." Her bonds that could have readily been sold when the democrats were inducted into power are now begging purchasers at any price; public schools are closed nine months in the year.

Mr. Speaker, there are some things that are far more precious in the eye of the American citizen at least than all the wealth of the Indies, and those are human liberty and human rights. These are fundamental and much prized by my race; yes, sir, superior to all pecuniary consideration, as the soul is to the body. For their possession and their complete exercise men and nations have willingly laid down their lives in all ages. It is for this that even the uncivilized Zulus are fighting in Africa to-day. But to the point. Can the saving of a few thousand or hundreds of thousands of dollars compensate for the loss of the political heritage of American citizens? Must the will of the majority to rule, the very foundation and corner-stone of this Republic, be supplanted, suppressed, or crushed by armed mobs of one party destroying the ballots of the other by violence and fraud? The destruction of a free ballot by the democrats is an evil of greater magnitude than the extravagance of the republicans. The one will eventually destroy the Republic by sapping the foundation of its sacred institutions, while the other is but a comparatively slight and temporary evil, which ill can easily be repaired.

This is but the record of the respective parties for the past four years. I cannot believe there is a true American citizen on this continent, with that instinctive love of liberty which should characterize all such, that would hesitate for an instant in preferring the republican administration of Governor Chamberlain, with all its alleged extravagance, to the present administration in South Carolina, with its fatal and pernicious destruction of the rights and privileges of republicans. I have only to say, in conclusion, sir, that I heartily reciprocate and appreciate the kind personal sentiment that has been expressed toward me by my colleague. Our personal and official intercourse has been most agreeable, notwithstanding our wide political difference, and I assure him I shall always cherish a pleasant recollection of it.

March 3, 1879

Chronology
January 1865–April 1877

1865   U.S. House of Representatives approves Thirteenth Amendment to the Constitution abolishing slavery by 119–56 vote on January 31 (amendment was approved by the U.S. Senate, 38–6, on April 8, 1864). Congress establishes Bureau of Refugees, Freedmen, and Abandoned Lands within the War Department, March 3. (Staffed mainly by army officers, the Bureau will field about 900 assistant commissioners and agents throughout the South.) President Abraham Lincoln is inaugurated for a second term, March 4, and Andrew Johnson becomes vice president. Robert E. Lee surrenders his army to Ulysses S. Grant at Appomattox Court House, Virginia, April 9. Lincoln is shot in Washington, D.C., April 14, and dies on morning of April 15; the same day, Johnson is sworn in as president. Remaining Confederate forces surrender, April 26–June 2. Johnson issues amnesty proclamation, May 29, pardoning former Confederates who swear future loyalty to the United States and restoring their property, except slaves. The proclamation exempts from the general amnesty federal officials and military officers who joined the rebellion, Confederate civil and military leaders, and persons with more than $20,000 in taxable property, but allows them to apply for individual pardons. The same day, Johnson issues a second proclamation, appointing a provisional governor for North Carolina and directing that elections be held for delegates to a state constitutional convention; the proclamation restricts voting to those who take the amnesty oath and are qualified to vote under pre-secession state law, thus excluding black men from the franchise. Johnson issues similar proclamations for Mississippi, Georgia, Texas, Alabama, South Carolina, and Florida, June 13–July 13. (Wartime Reconstruction governments established in Virginia, Tennessee, Arkansas, and Louisiana by the Lincoln administration are recognized by Johnson.) Beginning in Mississippi, six states hold constitutional conventions, August 14–November 8, and elections to state offices, October 2–November 29. (Convention meets in

Texas, February 7–April 2, 1866, and elections are held on June 25.) Johnson directs the Freedmen's Bureau to issue order on September 12 restoring abandoned lands to owners who swear allegiance. Thirty-ninth Congress refuses to admit senators and representatives from any of the former Confederate states when it meets on December 4. Joint Committee on Reconstruction, made up of six senators and nine representatives (twelve Republicans and three Democrats), is appointed on December 13 to investigate conditions in the South and make recommendations concerning readmission. Ratification of the Thirteenth Amendment is declared complete, December 18. U.S. army has 111,000 men occupying the former Confederacy, including 23,000 in Texas.

1866   Grant issues order on January 12 protecting military personnel and Freedmen's Bureau agents in the South from civil prosecution for acts committed under military authority, southern Unionists from prosecution for resisting Confederate forces during the war, and blacks from being "charged with offenses for which white persons are not prosecuted or punished in the same manner and degree." Johnson vetoes bill extending life of the Freedmen's Bureau and expanding its powers, February 19. Senate fails to override veto, February 20. Johnson vetoes Civil Rights Bill, March 27, and issues proclamation declaring an end to the insurrection in every former Confederate state except Texas, April 2. Veto of civil rights bill is overridden by the Senate, April 6, and the House, April 9. Racial violence in Memphis, Tennessee, May 1–3, kills forty-six African Americans and three whites. Confederate veterans in Pulaski, Tennessee, form the Ku Klux (later known as the Ku Klux Klan), a secret society that soon spreads through the state. Fourteenth Amendment to the Constitution is approved by the Senate, 33–11, June 8, and by the House, 120–32, June 13. Majority report of the Joint Committee on Reconstruction, June 18, concludes that the former Confederate states are not yet entitled to congressional representation. Congress overrides Johnson's veto of revised Freedmen's Bureau Bill, July 16. Tennessee is readmitted to Congress, July 24, after it ratifies the Fourteenth Amendment. Mob attacks supporters of new state constitution in New Orleans, July 30, killing thirty-four black and three white persons. Johnson issues proclamation declaring insurrection at an end in Texas and throughout the United States,

August 20. Johnson makes controversial speaking tour ("The Swing Around the Circle") through the East and Midwest, August 28–September 15, in attempt to rally support for pro-administration congressional candidates. Republicans make major gains in fall elections.

1867   Congress overrides Johnson's veto and grants suffrage to black men in the District of Columbia, January 8, and passes bill, January 10, extending suffrage to black men in federal territorial elections (territorial bill becomes law without Johnson's signature). On March 2 Congress passes Reconstruction Act and Tenure of Office Act over the president's veto, as well as the Command of the Army Act, which Johnson signs under protest. Reconstruction Act declares that no legal state governments exist in the former Confederate states (except Tennessee), divides these states into five military districts, and sets conditions for their regaining congressional representation, including ratification of the Fourteenth Amendment and the adoption of state constitutions providing for black male suffrage. The Tenure of Office Act restricts the power of the president to remove certain government officials without the approval of the Senate, while the Command of the Army Act requires that all presidential orders to the army go through Grant and protects him from being removed as commander of the army against his will. (Army now has about 23,000 men on occupation duty in the former Confederacy; by October 1870 there are about 4,300 troops stationed in the South outside of Texas.) Supplementary Reconstruction Acts, passed over Johnson's veto on March 23 and July 19, strengthen power of military district commanders to supervise state constitutional conventions and remove civil officials. Ku Klux Klan groups begin forming throughout the South. Johnson suspends Secretary of War Edwin M. Stanton from office on August 12 and appoints Grant as secretary of war ad interim. Ballot measures extending suffrage to black men are defeated in Ohio, October 8, and Minnesota and Kansas, November 5; Kansas voters also reject separate measure granting suffrage to women. Democrats make gains in northern elections for state offices, including in New York, Pennsylvania, and Ohio.

1868   Senate votes 36–6 on January 13 not to concur in Stanton's suspension. Grant vacates office at War Department, January 14, and Stanton reoccupies it. Voters ratify new state constitutions and elect Republican governors in Alabama, Arkansas, Louisiana, South Carolina, Georgia, North

Carolina, and Florida, February 1–May 6. Ku Klux Klan becomes increasingly involved in terrorist violence against African Americans and white Republicans. Johnson dismisses Stanton on February 21 and appoints Lorenzo Thomas, the adjutant general of the army, secretary of war ad interim. House of Representatives votes 126–47 to impeach President Johnson, February 24, and approves eleven articles of impeachment, March 2–3. Congress passes fourth Reconstruction Act, March 11, making a majority of votes cast (as compared to a majority of registered voters) sufficient to ratify proposed state constitutions. House managers begin presenting the case against Johnson in the Senate, March 30. Senate acquits Johnson of the most comprehensive article of impeachment by one vote, 35–19, on May 16. Republican national convention meeting in Chicago unanimously nominates Grant for president on the first ballot, May 21, and nominates Schuyler Colfax of Indiana, the Speaker of the House, for vice president. Johnson is acquitted of two further articles of impeachment, 35–19, on May 26, and his trial is adjourned indefinitely. Congress overrides presidential vetoes of bills readmitting Arkansas, June 22, and Alabama, Florida, Georgia, Louisiana, North Carolina, and South Carolina, June 25. Democratic national convention meeting in New York nominates Horatio Seymour, former governor of New York, for president and Frank P. Blair, a former Missouri congressman who had served as a Union major general, for vice president, July 9. Congress passes bill on July 25 ending most operations of the Freedmen's Bureau on January 1, 1869. (Bureau continues to support schools through the summer of 1870, and ends all operations on June 30, 1872.) Ratification of the Fourteenth Amendment is declared, July 28. Georgia assembly expels twenty-five black legislators, September 3, claiming that the new state constitution does not explicitly permit them to serve. Grant defeats Seymour in presidential election, November 3, receiving 214 of 294 electoral votes and 52 percent of the popular vote; in the former Confederacy, Grant carries six states and Seymour two (no electors are chosen in Virginia, Mississippi, and Texas).

1869   Fifteenth Amendment to the Constitution is approved by the House, 144–44, February 25, and by the Senate, 39–13, February 26. Grant is inaugurated on March 4. House refuses to seat representatives from Georgia, March 5. Grant signs legislation on April 10 requiring Virginia, Mississippi, and Texas to ratify the Fifteenth Amendment as a condition for readmission; the law also provides for referendums to be held on the new Virginia and Mississippi state constitutions with separate votes taken on disqualification clauses barring many former Confederates from voting or holding office. In *Texas v. White*, decided April 12, the U.S. Supreme Court upholds 5–3 the constitutionality of the Reconstruction Acts. Virginia approves new constitution and rejects disqualification clauses, July 6; a moderate Republican supported by the state's Conservative Party is elected governor, and Conservatives win control of the state legislature. Conservatives win control of Tennessee legislature and elect a conservative Republican as governor, August 5, ending Radical Republican rule in the state. Texas and Mississippi approve new state constitutions and elect Republican governors, November 30; Mississippi voters also reject Confederate disqualification clause. Congress restores military rule in Georgia, December 22.

1870   Virginia is readmitted to Congress, January 26. Mississippi is readmitted, February 23. Hiram Revels of Mississippi becomes the first African American to sit in the Senate, February 25 (elected to fill the remainder of an unexpired term, Revels serves until March 3, 1871). Ratification of the Fifteenth Amendment is declared on March 30. The same day, Texas is readmitted. Enforcement Act, making the denial of suffrage on racial grounds through force, fraud, bribery, and intimidation a federal offense, is signed by Grant on May 31. North Carolina governor William W. Holden uses special state militia in attempt to suppress the Ku Klux Klan in Alamance and Caswell Counties, June–September; although about 100 suspected Klansmen are arrested, none are convicted. Grant signs legislation on June 22 establishing Department of Justice, increasing power of the federal government to enforce Reconstruction legislation. Georgia is readmitted to Congress, July 15. Joseph H. Rainey of South Carolina becomes the first African American to sit in the House of Representatives, December 12 (Rainey serves until March 3, 1879). Conservatives in the North Carolina assembly vote articles of impeachment against Governor William W. Holden, December 19, alleging that he had abused his authority in his attempt to suppress the Ku Klux Klan. In election marked by violence and intimidation against Republican voters, Democrats gain control of the Georgia legislature, December 20–22.

1871   Second Enforcement Act, establishing federal supervision over congressional elections in cities with more than 20,000 people, is signed into law on February 28. (Act is primarily aimed at election fraud in northern cities.) North Carolina state senate removes Holden from office, March 22. (Although Republicans will hold governorship through 1876, the Conservatives remain in control of the state.) Third Enforcement Act, also known as the Ku Klux Klan Act, is passed by the House, 93–74, and by the Senate, 36–13, on April 19 and is signed by Grant the next day. Act authorizes prosecution in federal court of individuals who conspire to deprive citizens of their rights under the Fourteenth and Fifteenth Amendments and gives the president the power to call out federal troops and to suspend the writ of habeas corpus. Federal attorneys begin prosecution of Klansmen, concentrating on cases in North and South Carolina and Mississippi. Grant suspends writ of habeas corpus in nine counties in South Carolina, October 17, and dispatches federal troops, resulting in arrests of hundreds of suspected Klansmen (several dozen defendants are eventually convicted). Rufus Bullock, the Republican governor of Georgia, resigns on October 23 to avoid impeachment by the Democratic legislature, and a Democrat is elected governor on December 19.

1872   Convention of Liberal Republicans opposed to the Grant administration meets in Cincinnati, May 1–3, and nominates Horace Greeley, editor of the *New-York Tribune,* for president and Benjamin Gratz Brown, governor of Missouri, for vice president. Grant signs Amnesty Act, May 22, which restores the right to vote and hold office to almost all of the former Confederates excluded under Section 3 of the Fourteenth Amendment. Republican convention meeting in Philadelphia, June 5–6, nominates Grant for president and Senator Henry Wilson of Massachusetts for vice president. Democratic convention endorses Greeley and Brown, July 9. Grant is reelected on November 5, winning 286 out of 352 electoral votes and more than 55 percent of the popular vote; in the former Confederacy, Grant carries six states, Greeley three. (Electoral votes from Louisiana and Arkansas are not counted by Congress because of conflicting election returns.) Republican William Pitt Kellogg and conservative Fusionist candidate John McEnery both claim victory in Louisiana gubernatorial election.

1873   Kellogg and McEnery both hold inauguration ceremonies on January 14 and establish rival state governments. Grant recognizes Kellogg as legitimate governor but does not attempt to disperse McEnery supporters. Grant is inaugurated for second term on March 4. Armed white supremacists attack black militia guarding courthouse in Colfax, Louisiana, on April 13, killing at least sixty-two and as many as eighty-one African Americans. U.S. Supreme Court issues 5–4 decision in the *Slaughterhouse Cases*, April 14, narrowly interpreting the privileges and immunities clause of the Fourteenth Amendment and limiting the rights of national citizenship. Grant sends troop reinforcements to Louisiana and issues proclamation on May 22 ordering pro-McEnery forces to disperse. Series of financial failures in New York City, September 8–18, leads to widespread panic and severe national economic depression. Democrats win gubernatorial election in Texas, December 2, ending Republican rule in the state.

1874   Dispute over outcome of 1872 gubernatorial election in Arkansas leads to armed confrontation in Little Rock between supporters of rival Republicans Joseph Brooks and Elisha Baxter, April 15. Grant recognizes Baxter as the legitimate governor, May 22. Supreme Court justice Joseph Bradley, sitting as circuit judge in New Orleans, overturns the convictions of three men found guilty of federal civil rights violations in connection with the Colfax massacre, June 27. Ruling in *U. S. v. Cruikshank* calls into question constitutionality of the Enforcement Acts and inhibits further federal prosecutions of terrorism cases in the South. White League militia murders three black and six white Republicans near Coushatta, Louisiana, August 29–30, as part of campaign to overthrow the Kellogg government and install McEnery as governor. On September 14 the White League defeats the New Orleans Metropolitan Police and seizes control of the city in street fighting that kills thirty-five people. Grant orders 5,000 troops sent to New Orleans, and Kellogg is restored as governor on September 19 after the White League forces disperse. Democrats win gubernatorial election in Arkansas, October 13. Fall elections give the Democrats a majority in the House of

Representatives and reduce the Republican majority in the Senate. Democrats gain control of the legislature and win governorship in Alabama, November 3, in election marked by widespread violence and intimidation. White Line militia kills at least twenty-nine African Americans in Vicksburg, Mississippi, in early December as part of campaign to seize control of the county government.

1875   Democrats attempt to gain control of Louisiana legislature on January 4 by forcibly installing five members in the state house of representatives. At Kellogg's request, federal troops eject the five Democrats from the statehouse; the action is widely denounced in Congress and in the northern press as an illegitimate military intervention in civil affairs. Civil Rights Act, forbidding racial discrimination in public accommodations, transportation, and jury service, is signed by Grant on March 1. (Act is declared unconstitutional by the Supreme Court in 1883.) In *Minor v. Happersett*, decided 9–0 on March 9, the Supreme Court rules that the Fourteenth Amendment does not give women citizens the right to vote. Mississippi governor Adelbert Ames requests federal troops on September 8 to suppress violence by White Line militia attempting to intimidate Republican voters in the state election. Attorney General Edwards Pierrepont forwards message to Grant at his summer home in Long Branch, New Jersey. Grant writes to Pierrepont on September 13 describing federal intervention in the South as unpopular but necessary and reluctantly agreeing to send troops. Pierrepont selectively quotes from the president's letter in his reply to Ames on September 14, encouraging Ames to suppress disorders with the state militia and promising federal intervention only in case of direct rebellion against the state government. Violence in Mississippi continues, and on November 2 the Democrats win control of the state legislature.

1876   Supreme Court overturns convictions of Colfax massacre defendants in *U. S. v. Cruikshank*, decided 9–0 on March 27. Along with *U. S. v. Reese*, a Kentucky voting rights case decided 8–1 the same day, the *Cruikshank* decision severely limits the power of the federal government to enforce the Fourteenth and Fifteenth Amendments. Adelbert Ames resigns as governor of Mississippi, March 29, to avoid impeachment and is succeeded by a Democrat. Republican national convention meets in Cincinnati, June 15–17, and nominates Ohio governor Rutherford B. Hayes for president and New York congressman William A. Wheeler for vice president. Democratic national convention, held in St. Louis June 27–29, nominates New York governor Samuel J. Tilden for president and Indiana governor Thomas A. Hendricks for vice president. Violence increases in South Carolina as white Democrats organize "rifle clubs" to intimidate Republican voters. Six black men are killed in Hamburg, July 8, and about thirty African Americans are killed in Ellenton, September 16–19. Grant sends troops to South Carolina and issues proclamation on October 17 calling on armed groups to disperse. Election on November 7 results in disputed electoral count caused by conflicting election returns in South Carolina, Florida, and Louisiana, and disqualification controversy over an Oregon elector. Democrats win Florida gubernatorial contest, while Republicans and Democrats establish rival state governments in South Carolina and Louisiana.

1877   Republicans introduce bill in Congress, January 10, to create fifteen-member electoral commission. Measure is approved by the Senate, 47–17, January 25, and by the House, 191–86, January 26, and is signed by Grant on January 29. Commission is made up of three Republican and two Democratic senators, three Democratic and two Republican representatives, and five associate justices of the Supreme Court. Commission begins deliberations on February 1, and in a series of 8–7 votes, awards all of the disputed electors to Hayes, giving him electoral majority of one, 185–184. Joint session of Congress declares Hayes the victor, March 2. Hayes privately takes oath of office, March 3, and is publicly inaugurated on March 5. On Hayes's orders federal troops are withdrawn from the South Carolina statehouse in Columbia, April 10, and Republican governor Daniel H. Chamberlain surrenders his office. Democrat Wade Hampton, a former Confederate lieutenant general, becomes governor of South Carolina on April 11. Federal troops are withdrawn from the statehouse in New Orleans, April 24. Stephen Packard, Kellogg's successor, leaves office and Francis T. Nicholls becomes governor of Louisiana on April 25, completing the "redemption" of the southern states from Republican rule.

Biographical Notes

Jourdon Anderson (December 1825–April 15, 1907) Born into slavery in Tennessee. Emancipated by the Union army in 1864. Moved in 1865 to Dayton, Ohio, where he lived for the rest of his life. Worked as a servant, janitor, coachman, and hostler before becoming a sexton in 1894, probably at the Wesleyan Methodist Church.

Sidney Andrews (October 7, 1835–April 10, 1880) Born in Sheffield, Massachusetts. Attended University of Michigan, 1856–59. Washington correspondent for the *Chicago Tribune* and the *Boston Advertiser*, 1864–69. Traveled in the Carolinas and Georgia, September–November 1865, writing dispatches collected in *The South Since the War* (1866). Published *The St. Thomas Treaty* (1869), pamphlet advocating the purchase of the islands of St. Thomas and St. John from Denmark. Joined staff of literary magazine *Every Saturday*, 1871. Private secretary to Massachusetts governor William Washburn, 1872–74. Secretary to Massachusetts Board of State Charities, 1874–79.

Susan B. Anthony (February 15, 1820–March 13, 1906) Born in Adams, Massachusetts. Began friendship with Elizabeth Cady Stanton in 1851 and became active in the women's rights movement. Served as agent for the American Anti-Slavery Society, 1856–61. Organized petition drive in support of the Thirteenth Amendment, 1863–64. Helped found the American Equal Rights Association in 1866. Published weekly newspaper *Revolution*, 1868–70. Served as an executive officer of the National Woman Suffrage Association, 1869–90. Arrested in Rochester, New York, for voting in the 1872 election and was fined $100. Edited *History of Woman Suffrage* (3 vols., 1881–86) with Stanton and Matilda Joslyn Gage. Served as vice president of the National American Woman Suffrage Association, 1890–92, and succeeded Stanton as its president, 1892–1900.

Francis Preston Blair (April 12, 1791–October 18, 1876) Born in Abingdon, Virginia. Served as clerk of the Franklin County, Kentucky, circuit court, 1812–30. Became editor of the Frankfort *Argus of Western America* in 1829. Moved to Washington, D.C., in 1830 to edit *The Globe*, a new newspaper founded to support the Jackson administration. Became a member of Andrew Jackson's "Kitchen Cabinet" of unofficial advisers. Cofounded the *Congressional Globe* in 1833 to report debates and proceedings in Congress. Gave up editorship of *The Globe* in 1845 due to differences with the new Polk administration.

Supported Free Soil Party in 1848 and helped organize first Republican national convention in 1856. Served as advisor to Abraham Lincoln; his son, Montgomery Blair, was postmaster general under Lincoln, 1861–64. Opposed Republican Reconstruction measures after Lincoln's death and returned to the Democratic Party.

Frank P. Blair (February 19, 1821–July 9, 1875) Born in Lexington, Kentucky, the son of Francis Preston Blair. Member of the Missouri house of representatives, 1852–56. Served in Congress as a Free Soil Democrat, 1857–59, and as a Republican, 1861–62 and 1863–64. Major general of volunteers in the Union army, 1862–65. Democratic candidate for vice president, 1868. Democratic senator from Missouri, 1871–73.

Benjamin Brim (born c. 1817) An emancipated slave working as a tenant farmer in Grant Parish, Louisiana, Brim was shot and seriously wounded in April 1873 during the Colfax Massacre. He testified for the prosecution in *U. S. v. Cruikshank* in 1874.

David Brundage Lived in Milledgeville, Georgia, in 1876, when he wrote to President Ulysses S. Grant about Democratic intimidation at the polls.

Richard Harvey Cain (April 12, 1825–January 18, 1887) Born to free parents in Greenbrier County, Virginia (now West Virginia). Moved to Ohio in 1831. Became minister in the African Methodist Episcopal Church and served as pastor in Brooklyn, New York, 1861–65. Sent by A.M.E. Church to Charleston, South Carolina, in 1865. Edited newspapers *South Carolina Leader*, 1866–68, and *Missionary Record*, 1868–78. Delegate to the South Carolina state constitutional convention, 1868. Member of the state senate, 1868–70. Served in Congress as a Republican, 1873–75 and 1877–79. Became bishop in the A.M.E. Church and served as president of Paul Quinn College in Waco, Texas, 1880–84.

Margaret Ann Caldwell A resident of Clinton, Mississippi, who testified before a Senate investigating committee in June 1876 about the murder by white supremacists of her husband, state senator Charles Caldwell, and her brother-in-law, Sam Caldwell, in December 1875.

Maria Carter (born March 4, 1844) Born in South Carolina, Carter was living in Haralson County, Georgia, in 1871 when she testified about the murder of John Walthall before a congressional committee investigating the Ku Klux Klan.

Maria F. Chandler A resident of West Liberty, West Virginia, who wrote to Thaddeus Stevens in 1866 about woman suffrage. In 1867 she wrote to Senator Charles Sumner seeking his support for women's rights, and in 1882, when Chandler was living in Meadville, Pennsylvania, she and four other persons sent a petition to the U.S. Senate calling for woman suffrage.

Salmon P. Chase (January 13, 1808–May 7, 1873) Born in Cornish, New Hampshire. Established law practice in Cincinnati, Ohio, in 1830. Free Soil Democratic senator from Ohio, 1849–55. Republican governor of Ohio, 1856–60. Secretary of the treasury, March 1861–June 1864. Appointed chief justice of the U.S. Supreme Court in December 1864, succeeding Roger B. Taney, and served until his death. Presided over the Senate impeachment trial of President Andrew Johnson in 1868.

Georges Clemenceau (September 28, 1841–November 24, 1929) Born in the Vendée region of northeastern France. Studied medicine in Paris, 1861–65. Became active in republican opposition to Napoleon III. Traveled to New York in summer of 1865 to observe American politics and began writing dispatches for Paris newspaper *Le Temps*. Taught French and riding at the Catherine Aitken Seminary, girls' school in Stamford, Connecticut. Married Mary Plummer, one of his students, in June 1869, then returned to France with her. (They separated in 1876 and were divorced in 1891.) Served on the Paris municipal council, 1871–76, in the chamber of deputies, 1876–93, and in the senate, 1902–10. Premier of France and minister of the interior, 1906–9; premier and minister of war, 1917–20.

Richard Henry Dana (August 1, 1815–January 6, 1882) Born in Cambridge, Massachusetts. Published travel narrative *Two Years Before the Mast* (1840). Established successful legal practice in Boston. Defended fugitive slaves Shadrach Minkins and Thomas Sims (1851) and Anthony Burns (1854), as well as several abolitionists charged for their involvement in the rescue of Shadrach Minkins. Helped found Massachusetts Republican Party in 1855. Served as U.S. attorney for Massachusetts, 1861–66. Appeared before the U.S. Supreme Court in 1863 as lead government attorney in the *Prize Cases* and argued for the legality of the Union blockade of Confederate ports; the Court subsequently ruled 5–4 for the government. Member of the Massachusetts house of representatives, 1867–68. Ran for Congress in 1868 as independent Republican but was overwhelmingly defeated by the Republican incumbent, Benjamin F. Butler. Appointed U.S. minister to Great Britain by President Grant in March 1876, but nomination was rejected by the Senate.

Sarah A. Dickey (April 25, 1838–January 23, 1904) Born near Dayton, Ohio. Began teaching in 1857. Joined the Church of the United

Brethren in Christ in 1858. Taught at school for freed people established by the United Brethren in Vicksburg, Mississippi, 1863–65. Graduated from the Mount Holyoke Female Seminary (now Mount Holyoke College) in 1869. Returned to Mississippi and taught school in Raymond, 1869–70, and Clinton, 1870–71. Enlisted support in Mississippi and the North for a new school for black women. Opened Mount Hermon Seminary for Colored Females in 1875 and served as its principal until her death. Ordained as minister in the United Brethren in 1896.

Frederick Douglass (February 1818–February 20, 1895) Born in Talbot County, Maryland. Escaped from slavery in Baltimore in 1838. Became lecturer for the American Anti-Slavery Society in 1841. Published *Narrative of the Life of Frederick Douglass, An American Slave* in 1845. Edited and published series of antislavery newspapers, 1847–63. Published *My Bondage and My Freedom* in 1855. Edited and published *The New National Era*, 1870–73. Served as U.S. marshal, 1877–81, and recorder of deeds, 1881–86, for the District of Columbia. Published *Life and Times of Frederick Douglass* in 1881. Served as minister to Haiti, 1889–91.

Charles A. Eldredge (February 27, 1820–October 26, 1896) Born in Bridport, Vermont. Admitted to bar in 1846. Member of the Wisconsin state senate, 1854–56. Served in Congress as a Democrat, 1863–75.

Robert Brown Elliott (August 11, 1842?–August 9, 1884) Born and educated in England. Moved to South Carolina in 1867. Delegate to the South Carolina constitutional convention in 1868. Served as a Republican in the state house of representatives, 1868–70. Admitted to the bar in 1868. Elected to Congress in 1870 and served, 1871–74. Speaker of the South Carolina house of representatives, 1874–76. Elected state attorney general in 1876, but was forced out of office in 1877. Worked as a treasury department inspector in Charleston, 1879–81, and New Orleans, 1881–82.

Joseph S. Fullerton (December 3, 1835–March 20, 1897) Born in Chillicothe, Ohio. Practiced law in St. Louis at outbreak of Civil War. Served as assistant adjutant general (staff officer) in the Union army, 1863–65. Adjutant to Major General Oliver O. Howard, commissioner of the Freedmen's Bureau, 1865. Served as acting assistant commissioner of the Freedmen's Bureau for Louisiana in the fall of 1865. At direction of President Johnson, made inspection tour of Freedmen's Bureau operations in the South with Major General James Steedman in spring and summer of 1866. Mustered out of army in September 1866. Postmaster of St. Louis, 1867–69. Chairman of the Chickamauga and Chattanooga National Park Commission, 1890–97.

James A. Garfield (November 19, 1831–September 19, 1881) Born in Orange, Ohio. Graduated from Williams College in 1856. Principal of the Western Reserve Eclectic Institute (now Hiram College), 1857–61. Admitted to bar, 1861. Served as officer in the Union army, 1861–63, and was promoted to major general of volunteers. Republican congressman from Ohio, 1863–80. Elected president of the United States, 1880. Fatally wounded by assassin in Washington, D.C., July 2, 1881, and died two months later.

William Lloyd Garrison (December 12, 1805–May 24, 1879) Born in Newburyport, Massachusetts. Coedited *The Genius of Universal Emancipation* in Baltimore with Benjamin Lundy, 1829–30. Convicted of libel for accusing a local merchant of involvement in the domestic slave trade and spent forty-nine days in the Baltimore jail. Founded abolitionist weekly *The Liberator* in Boston, 1831. Helped found the New England Anti-Slavery Society in 1832 and the American Anti-Slavery Society in 1833. Served as president of the American Anti-Slavery Society, 1843–65. Ended publication of *The Liberator* in December 1865 after the Thirteenth Amendment was ratified. Wrote public letters in support of the Fifteenth Amendment, women's suffrage, temperance, and the rights of Chinese immigrants.

Ulysses S. Grant (April 22, 1822–July 23, 1885) Born in Point Pleasant, Ohio. Graduated West Point in 1843. Fought in U.S.-Mexican War. Resigned from U.S. army in 1854. Served in Union army as colonel, 1861, brigadier general, 1861–62, and major general, 1862–64. Promoted to lieutenant general, 1864, and general, 1866; general-in-chief of the army, 1864–69. Secretary of war ad interim, August 1867–January 1868. Nominated for president by the Republican Party in 1868; defeated Democrat Horatio Seymour, and won reelection in 1872 by defeating Liberal Republican Horace Greeley. President of the United States, 1869–77. Made world tour, 1877–79. Wrote *Personal Memoirs of U. S. Grant*, published posthumously in 1885–86.

Horace Greeley (February 3, 1811–November 29, 1872) Born in Amherst, New Hampshire. Moved to New York City in 1831. Founded and edited literary weekly *New-Yorker*, 1834–41. Edited Whig newspapers *Jeffersonian*, 1838–39, and *Log Cabin*, 1840. Founded *New-York Tribune* in 1841 and edited the newspaper until his death. Served as Whig congressman, 1848–49. Nominated for president by the Liberal Republicans and the Democrats in 1872 but was defeated by Ulysses S. Grant.

Andrew J. Hamilton (January 28, 1815–April 11, 1875) Born in Huntsville, Alabama. Admitted to bar in 1841. Moved to Texas in 1846. Member of the Texas house of representatives, 1851–53. Served in

Congress as an Independent Democrat, 1859–61. Opposed secession. Fled to Mexico in 1862. Military governor of Texas, November 1862–June 1865. Provisional governor of Texas, June 1865–August 1866. Associate justice of the state supreme court, 1867–69. Delegate to the state constitutional convention, 1868–69. Unsuccessful moderate Republican candidate for governor, 1869.

Frances Ellen Watkins Harper (September 24, 1825–February 22, 1911) Born to free parents in Baltimore, Maryland. Taught school in Ohio and Pennsylvania. Published *Poems on Miscellaneous Subjects* (1854). Toured New England, Canada, and the western states as an antislavery lecturer, 1854–60. Married Fenton Harper in 1860, but was widowed in 1864. Resumed lecturing and made several tours of the South during Reconstruction. Published narrative poem *Moses: A Story of the Nile* (1869), *Poems* (1871), and poetry collection *Sketches of the South* (1872). Founded YMCA Sabbath School in Philadelphia, 1872. Active in temperance and women's suffrage movements. Published novel *Iola Leroy* (1892). Helped found National Association of Colored Women in 1896.

Lewis Hayden (c. 1811–April 7, 1889) Born into slavery in Kentucky. Lost contact with his first wife, Esther, and his child after they were sold by Henry Clay. Escaped from slavery in 1844 with his second wife, Harriet. Moved in 1846 to Boston, where the Haydens opened a clothing store and gave shelter to scores of fugitive slaves. A member of the Boston Vigilance Committee that resisted the Fugitive Slave Law, Hayden played a leading role in the rescue of Shadrach Minkins from the Suffolk County Courthouse in 1851 and the unsuccessful attempt to rescue Anthony Burns in 1854. Appointed messenger in the office of the Massachusetts secretary of state, 1858. Helped recruit black soldiers for the Massachusetts 54th and 55th Regiments during the Civil War. Elected to the Massachusetts house of representatives in 1873 and served a single one-year term.

Rutherford B. Hayes (October 4, 1822–January 13, 1893) Born in Delaware, Ohio. Admitted to bar in 1845. Served as officer in the Union army, 1861–65, and was promoted to brigadier general of volunteers. Republican congressman from Ohio, 1865–67. Governor of Ohio, 1868–72 and 1876–77. Republican candidate in disputed presidential election, 1876. President of the United States, 1877–81.

Abram Hewitt (July 31, 1822–January 18, 1903) Born in Haverstraw, New York. Became a successful iron manufacturer and philanthropist. Democratic congressman from New York, 1875–79 and 1881–86. Chairman of the Democratic National Committee, 1876–77. Mayor of New York City, 1887–88.

William W. Holden (November 24, 1818–March 1, 1892) Born near Hillsborough, North Carolina. Publisher and editor of the Raleigh *North Carolina Standard*, 1843–68. Opposed secession in 1861 until the outbreak of hostilities at Fort Sumter. Advocated negotiated peace with the Union in 1863. Ran for governor in 1864 as a peace candidate, but was defeated. Appointed provisional governor of North Carolina by President Johnson in May 1865. Defeated in November 1865 election. Helped found Republican Party in North Carolina and was elected governor in 1868. His use of state militia to suppress the Ku Klux Klan in 1870 led to his impeachment and removal from office by the state legislature in 1871. Served as postmaster of Raleigh, 1873–81.

Marcus S. Hopkins (November 18, 1840–March 4, 1918) Born near Berlin Heights, Ohio. Enlisted in 7th Ohio Infantry in 1861 and was commissioned as first lieutenant in 1862. Seriously wounded at Cedar Mountain and spent remainder of war on garrison duty. Served with Freedmen's Bureau in Virginia as officer in charge of Prince William County, Virginia, 1865–67, and Orange and Louisa Counties, 1867–68. Received law degree from Columbian College (now George Washington University), 1871. Served with Department of the Interior, 1871–75. Practiced law in Washington, D.C., from 1875 until his death. The diary he kept in 1868 while serving with the Freedmen's Bureau was published in *Virginia Magazine of History and Biography* (1978).

Oliver O. Howard (November 8, 1830–October 26, 1909) Born in Leeds, Maine. Graduated from West Point in 1854. Officer in U.S. army, 1854–61. Brigadier general of volunteers, 1861–62. Major general of volunteers, 1863–69. Commissioner of the Freedmen's Bureau, 1865–72. President of Howard University, 1869–74. Returned to active military service in 1872 and served as negotiator with the Apaches. Commanded troops during the Nez Percé War, 1877. Retired from army in 1894.

Robert G. Ingersoll (August 11, 1833–July 21, 1899) Born in Dresden, New York. Admitted to Illinois bar in 1854. Served as officer in Union army, 1861–62. Appointed attorney general of Illinois in 1867 and served until 1869. Campaigned for Republican candidates and became a popular orator and lecturer, known as the "Great Agnostic" for his advocacy of freethinking.

Harriet Jacobs (1813–March 7, 1897) Born in Edenton, North Carolina. Escaped from slavery in 1842. Published *Incidents in the Life of a Slave Girl, Written by Herself* under pseudonym in 1861. Engaged in Quaker-sponsored relief work among former slaves in Washington, D.C.; Alexandria, Virginia; and Savannah, Georgia, 1862–68.

Andrew Johnson (December 29, 1808–July 31, 1875) Born in Raleigh, North Carolina. Moved to Tennessee in 1826 and worked as tailor in Greenville. Served as a Democrat in Congress, 1843–53, and in the Senate, 1857–62. Military governor of Tennessee, 1862–65. Elected vice president of the United States on National Union ticket, 1864. Succeeded Abraham Lincoln as president of the United States, April 15, 1865, and served until 1869. Impeached in 1868 but was acquitted by the Senate. Elected to the Senate as a Democrat in 1875 and served until his death.

Eugene Lawrence (October 10, 1823–August 17, 1894) Contributed several articles on Reconstruction to *Harper's Weekly* during the 1870s, along with a series of nativist attacks on the Roman Catholic Church. Published several books, including *The Lives of British Historians* (1855), *Historical Studies* (1876), *The Jews and their persecutors* (1877), and *A Primer of American Literature* (1880).

Abraham Lincoln (February 12, 1809–April 15, 1865) Born near Hodgenville, Kentucky. Moved to Illinois in 1830. Served as a Whig in the state legislature, 1834–41, and in Congress, 1847–49. Helped found the Republican Party of Illinois in 1856. Campaigned unsuccessfully in 1858 for Senate seat held by Stephen A. Douglas. Received Republican presidential nomination in 1860 and won election in a four-way contest; his victory led to the secession of the southern states. Issued final emancipation proclamation on January 1, 1863. Won reelection in 1864 by defeating Democrat George B. McClellan. Died in Washington, D.C., after being shot by John Wilkes Booth.

Isaac Loveless A former soldier who had served in the 46th U.S. Colored Infantry, 1863–65, Loveless wrote to President Grant in 1874 from Somerville, Tennessee, protesting the intimidation of black voters by white Democrats.

John R. Lynch (September 10, 1847–November 2, 1939) Born in Concordia Parish, Louisiana, the son of an enslaved woman and a white plantation manager. Freed by the Union army in Mississippi in 1863. Studied photography and opened a studio in Natchez. Served as a Republican in the Mississippi house of representatives, 1869–73, and in Congress, 1873–77 and 1882–83. Treasury auditor in the navy department, 1889–93. Admitted to the bar, 1896. Served as an army paymaster, 1901–11, including postings in Cuba and the Philippines. Moved to Chicago in 1912. Published *The Facts of Reconstruction* (1913) and *Some Historical Errors of James Ford Rhodes* (1922). Autobiography *Reminiscences of an Active Life* appeared posthumously in 1970.

Christopher G. Memminger (January 9, 1803–March 7, 1888) Born in Nayhingen, Germany. Immigrated to Charleston, South Carolina, as a child. Served in the South Carolina house of representatives, 1836–52 and 1855–60. Delegate to the Confederate Provisional Congress, February 1861–February 1862. Secretary of the treasury in the Confederate government, February 1861–July 1864. Pardoned by President Johnson in 1866.

Oliver P. Morton (August 4, 1823–November 1, 1877) Born in Salisbury, Indiana. Admitted to bar in 1847. Served as circuit court judge in Indiana, 1852. Republican governor of Indiana, 1861–67. Served in the Senate as a Republican from 1867 until his death. Member of the commission that resolved the disputed 1877 presidential election.

Levi Nelson An emancipated slave working as a blacksmith in Grant Parish, Louisiana, Nelson was shot and seriously wounded in April 1873 during the Colfax Massacre. He testified for the prosecution in *U. S. v. Cruikshank* in 1874.

Joseph Noxon A Tennessee Unionist who wrote to President Andrew Johnson from New York City in 1865.

Wendell Phillips (November 29, 1811–February 2, 1884) Born in Boston. Admitted to Massachusetts bar in 1834. Began making antislavery speeches in 1837 and became an ally of William Lloyd Garrison. Advocated abolitionism, prohibition, women's rights, prison reform, and peaceful relations with American Indians while also giving popular lectures on nonpolitical subjects. Criticized Abraham Lincoln as lacking commitment to emancipation and equal rights, and broke with Garrison to oppose Lincoln's reelection in 1864. Succeeded Garrison as president of the American Anti-Slavery Society in 1865 and led the society until 1870, when it dissolved itself following the adoption of the Fifteenth Amendment. Ran for governor of Massachusetts in 1870 as the Labor Reform and Prohibition candidate.

Edwards Pierrepont (March 4, 1817–March 6, 1892) Born in North Haven, Connecticut. Admitted to the bar in 1840. Served as judge of the superior court of New York City, 1857–60. Member of the New York state constitutional convention, 1867–68. U.S. attorney for the Southern District of New York, 1869–70. Attorney general of the United States, May 1875–May 1876. Minister to Great Britain, May 1876–December 1877.

James S. Pike (September 8, 1811–November 29, 1882) Born in Calais, Maine. Edited the Calais *Gazette and Advertiser*, 1836–37. Engaged in successful land speculation. Washington correspondent for the *Boston Courier*, 1844–50, and the *New-York Tribune*, 1850–60.

Opposed Kansas-Nebraska Act and helped found Maine Republican Party. U.S. minister to the Netherlands, 1861–66. Resumed position as Washington correspondent for the *Tribune*, 1866. Visited South Carolina in the winter of 1873 and published series of articles that appeared in expanded form in *The Prostrate State: South Carolina Under Negro Government* (1873). Published *The New Puritan: New England Two Hundred Years Ago* (1879), a biography of his ancestor Robert Pike, and *The First Blows of the Civil War* (1879), collecting his articles and correspondence from the 1850s.

Joseph H. Rainey (June 21, 1832–August 2, 1887) Born into slavery in Georgetown, South Carolina. Father, a barber, was able to buy his family's freedom in the early 1840s. Learned father's trade and became successful barber in Charleston. Fled South Carolina in 1862 as steward on blockade runner and spent remainder of the war in Bermuda. Returned to Charleston in 1865. Delegate to the state constitutional convention in 1868. Elected to Congress as a Republican in 1870, becoming the first African American in the House of Representatives, and served from 1870 to 1879. Served as a collector of internal revenue in Charleston, 1879–81.

James T. Rapier (November 13, 1837–May 31, 1883) Born to free parents in Florence, Alabama. Educated in Canada. Returned to Alabama after the Civil War. Member of the state constitutional convention in 1867. Founded the *Republican State Sentinel*, the first black-owned newspaper in Alabama. Elected to Congress as a Republican and served 1873–75. Defeated for reelection in 1874 in campaign marked by white supremacist violence and intimidation. Unsuccessful candidate for Congress in 1876. Served as a collector of internal revenue in Alabama, 1878–83. Founded *Haynesville Times* in 1878 and used it to advocate black migration to the western states.

Carl Schurz (March 2, 1829–May 14, 1906) Born in Liblar-am-Rhein, Germany. Immigrated to the United States in 1852. U.S. minister to Spain, 1861–62. Served as officer in the Union army, 1862–65, and was promoted to major general of volunteers. Republican senator from Missouri, 1869–75. Helped lead the Liberal Republican movement in 1872. Secretary of the interior in the Rutherford B. Hayes administration, 1877–81. Editor of the *New York Evening Post*, 1881–84.

Robert K. Scott (July 8, 1826–August 12, 1900) Born in Armstrong County, Pennsylvania. Moved to Ohio after U.S.-Mexican War. Officer in Union army, 1861–65; appointed brigadier general of volunteers in 1865. Assistant commissioner of the Freedmen's Bureau for South Carolina, 1866–68. Republican governor of South Carolina, 1868–72. Returned to Ohio, 1877.

Philip H. Sheridan (March 6, 1831–August 6, 1881) Born in Albany, New York. Graduated from West Point in 1853. Served as officer in U.S. army, 1853–61. Promoted to brigadier general of volunteers, 1862, and major general, 1863–64, commissioned major general in regular army, 1864. Commanded occupation forces in Louisiana and Texas, 1865–67. Directed campaigns against southern Plains Indians, 1867–69. Commanded army west of the Mississippi, 1869–83. Commanding general of the army from 1883 until his death.

Charles C. Soule (June 25, 1842–January 7, 1913) Born in Boston. Graduated from Harvard College, 1862. Served as lieutenant in the 44th Massachusetts Infantry, 1862–63, and as a captain in the 55th Massachusetts Infantry, commanding black soldiers, 1863–65. Assigned to the Freedmen's Bureau in South Carolina until August 1865, when he was mustered out of the army. Established successful business selling law books in Boston, 1881.

Elizabeth Cady Stanton (November 12, 1815–October 26, 1902) Born in Johnstown, New York. Helped organize the women's rights convention held in Seneca Falls, New York, in July 1848 and drafted its "Declaration of Rights and Sentiments." President of the Woman's State Temperance Society, 1852–53. Advocated women's rights in appearances before the New York legislature in 1854 and 1860. Organized petition drive with Susan B. Anthony in support of the Thirteenth Amendment, 1863–64. First vice president of the American Equal Rights Association, 1866–68. Edited weekly newspaper *Revolution*, 1868–70. President of the National Woman Suffrage Association, 1869–70 and 1877–90, and of its successor, the National American Woman Suffrage Association, 1890–92. Edited *History of Woman Suffrage* (3 vols., 1881–86) with Anthony and Matilda Joslyn Gage.

George L. Stearns (January 8, 1809–April 9, 1867) Born in Medford, Massachusetts. Established successful business manufacturing lead pipe, 1841. Financial supporter of the Free Soil Party in 1848 and helped found Republican Party in Massachusetts. Purchased arms for free-state settlers in Kansas and secretly supported John Brown's plan for a slave uprising in Virginia. Helped recruit black troops for the Union army. Published *The Right Way*, weekly newspaper that supported black manhood suffrage, 1865–67.

Thaddeus Stevens (April 4, 1792–August 11, 1868) Born in Danville, Vermont. Moved to Pennsylvania in 1815 and was admitted to the bar in 1816. Served in Congress as an antislavery Whig, 1849–53, and as a Republican from 1859 until his death. Chairman of the managers chosen by the House of Representatives to present the case against President Andrew Johnson at his impeachment trial in 1868.

George Stoneman (August 22, 1822–September 5, 1894) Born in Busti, New York. Graduated from West Point in 1846. Served as officer in the U.S. army, 1846–61, as brigadier general in Union army, 1861–62, and as major general, 1862–66. Mustered out of volunteer service in 1866 and became colonel in postwar army. Served as Reconstruction military commander in Virginia, June 1868–March 1869. Retired from army in 1871 after being relieved of his command in Arizona by President Grant for failing to prevent massacre of Apaches under military protection at Camp Grant. Democratic governor of California, 1883–87.

Charles Sumner (January 6, 1811–March 11, 1874) Born in Boston, Massachusetts. Graduated from Harvard College in 1830 and Harvard Law School in 1833. Elected to the U.S. Senate as a Free Soiler in 1851. Badly beaten with a cane on the Senate floor by South Carolina congressman Preston Brooks on May 22, 1856, two days after delivering his antislavery speech "The Crime Against Kansas." Reelected as a Republican in 1857, but did not return to his seat in the Senate until December 1859. Reelected in 1863 and 1869 and served until his death. Joined Liberal Republicans in opposing the reelection of President Grant in 1872.

Albion W. Tourgée (May 2, 1838–May 21, 1905) Born in Williamsfield, Ohio. Enlisted in 27th New York Infantry in 1861. Suffered serious spinal injury during retreat from Bull Run. Served as lieutenant in the 105th Ohio Infantry, 1862–63; fought at Perryville and Chickamauga. Resigned commission after reinjuring back. Moved to Greensboro, North Carolina, in 1865 and opened law practice. Delegate to Southern Loyalist Convention held in Philadelphia, 1866. Edited weekly newspaper *Greensboro Union Register*, 1866–67. Delegate to the state constitutional conventions in 1868 and 1875. Elected as a state superior court judge in 1868 and served until 1874. Published novel *Tionette* (1874). Served as federal pension agent, 1875–77. Unsuccessful Republican candidate for Congress, 1878. Left North Carolina in 1879 and eventually settled in Maysville, New York. Published novels *A Fool's Errand* (1879) and *Bricks Without Straw* (1880), set in North Carolina during Reconstruction, and *The Invisible Empire* (1880), a documentary account of the Ku Klux Klan. Edited literary weekly *Our Continent*, 1881–84. Continued to publish novels and essays, including *An Appeal to Caesar* (1884), an examination of American race relations. Advocated racial equality, national support for public schools, and antilynching legislation in weekly column for the Chicago *Daily Inter-Ocean*, 1888–98. Served as lead attorney for Homer Plessy in Louisiana railroad segregation case *Plessy v. Ferguson*, decided by the U.S. Supreme Court in 1896. Appointed U.S. consul in Bordeaux, France, in 1897 and served until his death.

Cynthia Townsend A freed woman who testified in 1866 before a congressional investigating committee about the recent Memphis massacre.

Mark Twain (November 30, 1835–April 21, 1910) Born Samuel Langhorne Clemens in Florida, Missouri. Worked as typesetter and occasional writer for newspapers in Missouri, New York, Iowa, and Ohio, 1851–56. Riverboat pilot on the Mississippi, 1857–61. Wrote for newspapers in Nevada, 1862–64, and California, 1864–66. Visited Europe and the Holy Land, 1867. Owned one-third interest in the *Buffalo Express*, 1869–72. Published numerous travel narratives and novels, including *The Innocents Abroad* (1869), *Roughing It* (1872), *The Adventures of Tom Sawyer* (1876), *Adventures of Huckleberry Finn* (1885), *A Connecticut Yankee in King Arthur's Court* (1889), and *Puddn'head Wilson* (1894).

Elihu B. Washburne (September 23, 1816–October 23, 1887) Born in Livermore, Maine. Admitted to bar in 1840 and began legal practice in Galena, Illinois. Served in Congress as a Whig, and then as a Republican, 1853–69. Served as secretary of state for eleven days at the beginning of the Grant administration, March 1869. U.S. minister to France, 1869–77.

Thomas Whitehead (December 27, 1825–July 1, 1901) Born in Lovingston, Virginia. Admitted to the bar in 1849. Served in Confederate army as an officer in the 2nd Virginia Cavalry, 1861–65. Elected commonwealth attorney of Amherst County, Virginia, 1866; removed from office by military governor, 1868; reelected in 1869 and served until 1873. Elected to Congress as a Conservative (Democrat) and served, 1873–75. Virginia commissioner of agriculture, 1888–1901.

Sarah J. C. Whittlesey (1825–1896) Born in Williamston, North Carolina. Moved to Alexandria, Virginia, in 1848. Published poetry, stories, and novels, including *Heart-Drops from Memory's Urn* (1852), *The Stranger's Stratagem, or, The Double Deceit, and other stories* (1860), *Bertha, the Beauty: A Story of the Southern Revolution* (1871), and *Spring Buds and Summer Blossoms* (1889).

J. A. Williamson A landowner in Fayette County, Tennessee, who wrote to the Freedmen's Bureau in 1865 regarding the freed people in his county.

John Russell Young (November 20, 1840–January 17, 1899) Born in County Tyrone, Ireland. Immigrated to the United States in 1841. Began working for the *Philadelphia Press* in 1857. Reported on the Civil War in Virginia, 1861–62. Served as managing editor of the *Press* and the *Washington Chronicle*, 1862–65. Managing editor of the *New-York*

Tribune, 1866–69. Editor of the *New York Standard*, 1870–72. Became European correspondent for the *New York Herald* in 1872. Accompanied Ulysses S. Grant on his world tour, 1877–79, and published *Around the World with General Grant* (1879). U.S. minister to China, 1882–85. Served as Librarian of Congress, 1897–99.

Note on the Texts

This volume collects nineteenth-century American writing about Reconstruction, bringing together speeches, public and private letters, messages, addresses, government reports, petitions, interviews, congressional resolutions, testimony given in court and before congressional committees, newspaper and magazine articles, diary entries, memoranda, and excerpts from travel narratives written by participants and observers and dealing with events in the period from 1865 to 1879. Some of these documents were not written for publication, and some of them existed only in manuscript form during the lifetimes of the persons who wrote them. With one exception, the texts presented in this volume are taken from printed sources. In cases where there is only one printed source for a document, the text offered here comes from that source. Where there is more than one printed source for a document, the text printed in this volume is taken from the source that appears to contain the fewest editorial alterations in the spelling, capitalization, paragraphing, and punctuation of the original. In one instance where no printed source was available, the text in this volume is printed from a manuscript.

This volume prints texts as they appear in the sources listed below, but with a few alterations in editorial procedure. The bracketed conjectural readings of editors, in cases where original manuscripts or printed texts were damaged or difficult to read, are accepted without brackets in this volume. In cases where an obvious slip of the pen in a manuscript was marked by earlier editors with "[*sic*]," the present volume omits the "[*sic*]" and corrects the slip of the pen. In instances where earlier editors supplied in brackets letters or words that were omitted from the source text by an obvious slip of the pen or printer's error, this volume removes the brackets and accepts the editorial emendation. Bracketed editorial insertions used in the source texts to identify persons, or to supply dates and locations, have been deleted in this volume. In instances where canceled, but still legible, words were printed in the source texts with lines through the deleted material, or where canceled words were printed within angled brackets, this volume omits the canceled words.

The text of the editorial on amnesty by Horace Greeley printed in the *New-York Tribune* on March 16, 1871, placed quotation marks at the beginning of every line of a quoted passage as well as at its beginning and end. This volume provides quotation marks only at the beginning and ending of a quoted passage.

Three typesetting errors that appeared in the printed source texts are corrected in this volume: at 26.35, "as those were who" becomes "as those who were"; at 423.21, "tell him right down" becomes "tell him write down"; at 433.40, "our fears our groundless" becomes "our fears are groundless." Two slips of the pen in the document printed from manuscript are also corrected: at 71.29, "will be recieved" becomes "will be received," and at 72.31, "other wrongs to numerous" becomes "other wrongs too numerous." Four errors in the letter written by Charles C. Soule to Oliver O. Howard on June 12, 1865, and in the enclosed address to the freed people of the Orangeburg District, are treated as slips of the pen and corrected in this volume, even though they were not corrected in *Freedom: A Documentary History of Emancipation, 1861–1867, Series 3, Volume 1: Land and Labor, 1865*: at 37.20, "away with. Some well" becomes "away with, some well"; at 37.24–25, "done in theory. the system" becomes "done in theory, the system"; at 39.29, "waiting too much" becomes "wanting too much"; at 40.5, "for his family. and" becomes "for his family, and."

The following is a list of the documents included in this volume, in the order of their appearance, giving the source of each text. The most common sources are indicated by these abbreviations:

Advice   *Advice After Appomattox: Letters to Andrew Johnson, 1865–1866*, ed. Brooks D. Simpson, Leroy P. Graf, and John Muldowny (Knoxville: The University of Tennessee Press, 1987). Copyright © 1987 by The University of Tennessee Press.

PAJ   *The Papers of Andrew Johnson*, ed. LeRoy P. Graf, Ralph W. Haskins, and Paul H. Bergeron (16 vols., Knoxville: The University of Tennessee Press, 1967–2000). Volume 8 (1989), Volume 9 (1991), Volume 10 (1992), Volume 11 (1994), ed. Paul H. Bergeron. Copyright © 1989, 1991, 1992, 1994 by The University of Tennessee Press.

PUSG   *The Papers of Ulysses S. Grant*, ed. John Y. Simon and John F. Marszalek (32 vols. to date, Carbondale: Southern Illinois University Press, 1967–2012). Volume 20 (1995), Volume 25 (2003), Volume 26 (2003), Volume 27 (2005), Volume 28 (2005), ed. John Y. Simon. Copyright © 1995, 2003, 2005 by the Ulysses S. Grant Association. Reprinted with the permission of the Ulysses S. Grant Association.

Richardson   *A Compilation of the Messages and Papers of the Presidents, 1789–1902*, ed. James D. Richardson (11 vols., New

York: Bureau of National Literature and Art, 1902–4).
Volume VI (1903), Volume VII (1903).

SPTS   *The Selected Papers of Thaddeus Stevens*, ed. Beverly Wilson Palmer and Holly Byers Ochoa (2 vols., University of Pittsburgh Press, 1997–98). Volume 2 (1998). Copyright © 1998 by University of Pittsburgh Press.

Tourgée   *Undaunted Radical: The Selected Writings and Speeches of Albion W. Tourgée*, ed. Mark Elliott and John David Smith (Baton Rouge: Louisiana State University Press, 2010). Copyright © 2010 by Louisiana State University Press. Reprinted with permission.

PRESIDENTIAL RECONSTRUCTION, 1865–1866

Frederick Douglass: What the Black Man Wants, January 26, 1865. *Equality of all men before the law claimed and defended; in speeches by Hon. William D. Kelley, Wendell Phillips, and Frederick Douglass, and letters from Elizur Wright and Wm. Heighton* (Boston: Press of Geo. C. Rand & Avery, 1865), 36–39.

Abraham Lincoln: Speech on Reconstruction, Washington, DC, April 11, 1865. *Abraham Lincoln: Speeches and Writings, 1859–1865*, ed. Don E. Fehrenbacher (New York: Library of America, 1989), 697–701. Copyright © 1953 by The Abraham Lincoln Association. Reprinted with permission.

Springfield Republican: Restoration of the Union, April 20, 1865. *The Frankfort Commonwealth*, April 21, 1865.

Andrew Johnson: Interview with Pennsylvania Delegation, May 3, 1865. *PAJ*, vol. 8, 21–23.

Colored Men of North Carolina to Andrew Johnson, May 10, 1865. *PAJ*, vol. 8, 57–58.

Andrew Johnson: Reply to a Delegation of Colored Ministers, May 11, 1865. *PAJ*, vol. 8, 61–62.

Salmon P. Chase to Andrew Johnson, May 12, 1865. *Advice*, 23–25.

Joseph Noxon to Andrew Johnson, May 27, 1865. *PAJ*, vol. 8, 119.

Delegation of Kentucky Colored People to Andrew Johnson, June 9, 1865. *PAJ*, vol. 8, 203–5.

Charles C. Soule and Oliver O. Howard: An Exchange, June 12 and 21, 1865. *Freedom: A Documentary History of Emancipation, 1861–1867. Series 3, Volume 1: Land and Labor, 1865*, ed. Steve Hahn, Steven F. Miller, Susan E. O'Donovan, John C. Rodrigue, and Leslie S. Rowland (Chapel Hill: The University of North Carolina Press, 2008), 215–22. Copyright © 2008 by The University of North Carolina Press. Reprinted with permission of The University of North Carolina Press, www.uncpress.unc.edu.

Richard Henry Dana: Speech at Boston, June 21, 1865. *Speech of Richard H. Dana, Jr., at a meeting of citizens held in Faneuil Hall: June 21, 1865, to consider the subject of re-organization of the rebel states* (Boston, MA: 1865), 1–4.

Charles Sumner to Gideon Welles, July 4, 1865. *The Selected Letters of Charles Sumner*, Volume II, ed. Beverly Wilson Palmer (Boston: Northeastern University Press, 1990), 313–15. Copyright © 1990 by Beverly Wilson Palmer; copyright © 1990 by University Press of New England, Lebanon, NH.

Wendell Phillips to the *National Anti-Slavery Standard*. *National Anti-Slavery Standard*, July 8, 1865.

Francis Preston Blair to Andrew Johnson, August 1, 1865. *PAJ*, vol. 8, 516–23.

Colored People of Mobile to Andrew J. Smith, August 2, 1865. Records of the Assistant Commissioner for Alabama, Bureau of Refugees, Freedmen, and Abandoned Lands, 1865–1870, RG 105, National Archives Microfilm Publication M809, Roll 23 (Washington, DC: National Archives and Records Administration, 1969).

Jourdon Anderson to P. H. Anderson, August 7, 1865. *New-York Daily Tribune*, August 22, 1865.

Carl Schurz to Andrew Johnson, August 29, 1865. *Advice*, 106–15.

Christopher Memminger to Andrew Johnson, September 4, 1865. *PAJ*, vol. 9, 22–25.

Thaddeus Stevens: Speech at Lancaster, Pennsylvania, September 6, 1865. *SPTS*, vol. 2, 12–25.

Georges Clemenceau to *Le Temps*, September 28, 1865. Georges Clemenceau, *American Reconstruction 1865–1870, and the Impeachment of President Johnson*, ed. Fernand Baldensperger, translated by Margaret MacVeagh (New York: The Dial Press, 1928), 35–42. Copyright © 1928 by The Dial Press, Inc.

Andrew Johnson: Interview with George L. Stearns, October 3, 1865. *PAJ*, vol. 9, 178–81.

Andrew Johnson: Speech to the 1st U.S. Colored Infantry, Washington, DC, October 10, 1865. *PAJ*, vol. 9, 219–23.

Sarah Whittlesey to Andrew Johnson, October 12, 1865. *PAJ*, vol. 9, 232–34.

Edisto Island Freedmen to Andrew Johnson, October 28, 1865. *PAJ*, vol. 9, 296–97.

J. A. Williamson to Nathan A. M. Dudley, October 30, 1865. *Freedom: A Documentary History of Emancipation, 1861–1867. Series 3, Volume 1: Land and Labor, 1865*, ed. Steve Hahn, Steven F. Miller, Susan E. O'Donovan, John C. Rodrigue, and Leslie S. Rowland (Chapel Hill, NC: The University of North Carolina Press, 2008), 833–34. Copyright © 2008 by The University of North Carolina Press.

Reprinted with permission of The University of North Carolina Press, www.uncpress.unc.edu.

Address of the Colored State Convention to the People of South Carolina, November 24, 1865. *Proceedings of the Colored People's Convention of the State of South Carolina, held in Zion Church, Charleston, November, 1865* (Charleston: South Carolina Leader Office, 1865), 23–26.

Andrew J. Hamilton to Andrew Johnson, November 27, 1865. *PAJ*, vol. 9, 436–39.

Sidney Andrews: from *The South Since the War*. Sidney Andrews, *The South Since the War: as shown by fourteen weeks of travel and observation in Georgia and the Carolinas* (Boston: Ticknor and Fields, 1866), 383–400.

Carl Schurz: from Report on the States of South Carolina, Georgia, Alabama, Mississippi, and Louisiana, December 18, 1865. *Senate Executive Document No. 2*, 39th Congress, 1st Session (Washington, DC: 1866), 16–17, 41–42, 45–46.

Ulysses S. Grant to Andrew Johnson, December 18, 1865. *Advice*, 212–14.

Lewis Hayden: from *Caste among Masons*. Lewis Hayden, *Caste among Masons: Address before Prince Hall Grand Lodge of Free and Accepted Masons of the State of Massachusetts, at the Festival of St. John the Evangelist, December 27, 1865* (Boston: Edward S. Coombs & Company, 1866), 7–10.

Harriet Jacobs to *The Freedman*, January 9 and 19, 1866. *The Harriet Jacobs Family Papers*, vol. II, ed. Jean Fagan Yellin (Chapel Hill: The University of North Carolina Press, 2008), 655–57. Copyright © 2008 Jean Fagan Yellin. Used by permission of the publisher. Reprinted with permission of The University of North Carolina Press, www.uncpress.unc.edu.

Marcus S. Hopkins to James Johnson, January 15, 1866. *Freedom: A Documentary History of Emancipation, 1861–1867. Series II: The Black Military Experience*, ed. Ira Berlin (Cambridge and New York: Cambridge University Press, 1982), 800–801. Copyright © 2010 by Cambridge University Press. Reprinted with permission of Cambridge University Press.

Andrew Johnson: Exchange with Frederick Douglass, February 7, 1866; Response of Colored Delegation to President Johnson, February 7, 1866. *PAJ*, vol. 10, 41–48, 53–54.

Joseph S. Fullerton to Andrew Johnson, February 9, 1866. *PAJ*, vol. 10, 64–69.

Andrew Johnson: Veto of the Freedmen's Bureau Bill, February 19, 1866. *PAJ*, vol. 10, 120–27.

Andrew Johnson: Speech in Washington, DC, February 22, 1866. *PAJ*, vol. 10, 145–57.

Andrew Johnson: Veto of the Civil Rights Bill, March 27, 1866. *Richardson*, vol. VI, 405–13.

CONGRESSIONAL RECONSTRUCTION, 1866–1869

Maria F. Chandler to Thaddeus Stephens, April 1, 1866. *SPTS*, vol. 2, 116–17.

Harper's Weekly: Radicalism and Conservatism. *Harper's Weekly*, April 21, 1866.

Thaddeus Stevens: Speech in Congress on the Fourteenth Amendment, Washington, DC, May 8, 1866. *SPTS*, vol. 2, 131–36.

Frances Ellen Watkins Harper: Speech at the National Woman's Rights Convention, New York City, May 10, 1866. *Proceedings of the eleventh National Woman's Rights Convention, held at the Church of the Puritans, New York, May 10, 1866* (New York: Robert J. Johnston, 1866), 45–48.

George Stoneman to Ulysses S. Grant, May 12, 1866. *House Executive Documents, No. 122*, 39th Congress, 1st Session, 1–3.

The New York Times: An Hour With Gen. Grant. *The New York Times*, May 24, 1866.

Elihu B. Washburne to Thaddeus Stevens, May 24, 1866. *SPTS*, vol. 2, 150–51.

Cynthia Townsend: Testimony to House Select Committee, Memphis, Tennessee, May 30, 1866. *House Report No. 101*, 39th Congress, 1st Session (Washington, DC: 1866), 162–64.

Joint Resolution Proposing the Fourteenth Amendment, June 13, 1866. *The Statutes at Large, Treaties, and Proclamations, of the United States of America from December, 1865, to March, 1867*, ed. George P. Sanger (Boston: Little, Brown, and Company, 1868), 358–59.

Oliver P. Morton: from Speech at Indianapolis, June 20, 1866. *Speech of Gov. Oliver P. Morton: delivered at Masonic Hall, Tuesday evening, June 20, 1866* (Indianapolis, IN: 1866), 1–3, 7–8.

Philip H. Sheridan to Ulysses S. Grant, August 1 and 2, 1866. *House Executive Documents, No. 68*, 39th Congress, 2nd Session, 9, 11.

Harper's Weekly: The Massacre in New Orleans. *Harper's Weekly*, August 18, 1866.

Andrew Johnson: Speech at St. Louis, September 8, 1866. *PAJ*, vol. 11, 192–201.

Thaddeus Stevens: Speech at Lancaster, Pennsylvania, September 27, 1866. *SPTS*, vol. 2, 196–201.

Frederick Douglass: Reconstruction. *The Atlantic Monthly*, December 1866.

Thaddeus Stevens: Speech in Congress on Reconstruction, Washington, DC, January 3, 1867. *SPTS*, vol. 2, 211–21.

Mobile Daily Advertiser and Register: No Amendment—Stand Firm. *Mobile Daily Advertiser and Register*, January 9, 1867.

Albion W. Tourgée: To the Voters of Guilford, October 21, 1867. *Tourgée*, 25–27.

Harper's Weekly: Impeachment. *Harper's Weekly*, December 14, 1867.

Albion W. Tourgée: The Reaction. *National Anti-Slavery Standard*, January 4, 1868.

New-York Tribune: The President Must Be Impeached. *New-York Tribune*, February 24, 1868.

Thaddeus Stevens: Speech in Congress on Impeachment, Washington, DC, February 24, 1868. *SPTS*, vol. 2, 352–58.

Bossier Banner: White Men to the Rescue! *Bossier Banner* (Bellevue, LA), March 28, 1868.

The Nation: The Result of the Trial. *The Nation*, May 21, 1868.

Frank P. Blair to James O. Broadhead, June 30, 1868. Edward McPherson, *The Political History of the United States of America During the Period of Reconstruction* (Washington, DC: Philp & Solomons, 1871), 380–81.

Frederick Douglass: The Work Before Us. *The Independent*, August 27, 1868.

Elizabeth Cady Stanton: Gerrit Smith on Petitions. *The Revolution*, January 14, 1869.

Joint Resolution Proposing the Fifteenth Amendment, February 27, 1869. *The Statutes at Large, Treaties, and Proclamations, of the United States of America from December 1867 to March 1869*, ed. George P. Sanger (Boston: Little, Brown, and Company, 1869), 346.

"LET US HAVE PEACE," 1869–1873

Ulysses S. Grant: First Inaugural Address, March 4, 1869. *Richardson*, vol. VII, 6–8.

Frederick Douglass and Susan B. Anthony: Exchange on Suffrage, May 12, 1869. Remarks by Douglass: *New York World*, May 13, 1869; remarks by Anthony: *The Selected Papers of Elizabeth Cady Stanton and Susan B. Anthony, Volume II: Against an Aristocracy of Sex, 1866 to 1873*, ed. Ann D. Gordon (New Brunswick, NJ: Rutgers University Press, 2000), 238–41. Copyright © 2000 by Rutgers, the State University of New Jersey. Reprinted with permission of Rutgers University Press.

Mark Twain: Only a Nigger. *The Buffalo Express*, August 26, 1869.

Georges Clemenceau to *Le Temps*, November 3, 1869. Georges Clemenceau, *American Reconstruction 1865–1870, and the Impeachment of President Johnson*, ed. Fernand Baldensperger, translated by Margaret MacVeagh (New York: The Dial Press, 1928), 297–99. Copyright © 1928 by The Dial Press, Inc.

The New York Times: Reconstruction Nationalized. *The New York Times*, February 21, 1870.

William W. Holden to Ulysses S. Grant, March 10, 1870. *Senate Executive Documents, No. 16, Pt. 2*, 41st Congress, 3rd Session (Washington, DC: 1871), 41.

Ulysses S. Grant: Message to Congress, March 30, 1870. *Richardson*, vol. VII, 55–56.

Albion W. Tourgée to Joseph C. Abbott, May 24, 1870. *Tourgée*, 47–51.

Robert K. Scott to Ulysses S. Grant, October 22, 1870. *PUSG*, vol. 20, 249–50.

Horace Greeley and Robert Brown Elliott: Exchange on Amnesty, March 16–17, 1871. *New-York Tribune*, March 16 and 21, 1871.

Joseph H. Rainey: Speech in Congress on the Enforcement Bill, Washington, DC, April 1, 1871. *Congressional Globe*, 42nd Congress, 1st Session, 393–95.

James A. Garfield: from Speech in Congress on the Enforcement Bill, Washington, DC, April 4, 1871. *Congressional Globe Appendix*, 42nd Congress, 1st Session, 149, 153, 154–55.

Maria Carter: Testimony to the Joint Select Committee, Atlanta, Georgia, October 21, 1871. *Testimony taken by the Joint Select Committee to inquire into the condition of affairs in the late insurrectionary states, Georgia, volume I* (Washington, DC: Government Printing Office, 1872), 411–14.

Horace Greeley: Reply to Committee of the Liberal Republican Convention, May 20, 1872. *Proceedings of the Liberal Republican Convention, in Cincinnati, May 1st, 2d and 3d, 1872* (New York: Baker & Godwin, Printers, 1872), 38–40.

Frederick Douglass: Speech in New York City, September 25, 1872. *The New York Times*, September 26, 1872.

James S. Pike: South Carolina Prostrate. *New-York Tribune*, March 29, 1873.

Ulysses S. Grant: Second Inaugural Address, Washington, DC, March 4, 1873. *Richardson*, vol. VII, 221–23.

THE END OF RECONSTRUCTION, 1873–1877

Levi Nelson and Benjamin Brim: Testimony in the Colfax Massacre Trial, New Orleans, February 27 and March 3, 1874. *New Orleans*

Republican, February 28, 1874 (Nelson testimony) and March 4, 1874 (Brim testimony).

Robert Brown Elliott: Speech in Congress on the Civil Rights Bill, Washington, DC, January 6, 1874. *Congressional Record*, 43rd Congress, 1st Session, 407–10.

New York Herald: General Grant's New Departure. *New York Herald*, January 20, 1874.

Richard Harvey Cain: Speech in Congress on the Civil Rights Bill, Washington, DC, January 24, 1874. *Congressional Record*, 43rd Congress, 1st Session, 901–3.

James T. Rapier: Speech in Congress on the Civil Rights Bill, Washington, DC, June 9, 1874. *Congressional Record*, 43rd Congress, 1st Session, 4782–86.

William Lloyd Garrison to the *Boston Journal*, September 3, 1874. *The Letters of William Lloyd Garrison, Volume VI: To Rouse the Slumbering Land, 1868–1879*, ed. Walter M. Merrill and Louis Ruchames (Cambridge, MA: The Belknap Press of Harvard University Press, 1981), 345–350. Copyright © 1981 by the President and Fellows of Harvard College. Reprinted with permission.

Eugene Lawrence to *Harper's Weekly*. *Harper's Weekly*, October 31, 1874.

Isaac Loveless to Ulysses S. Grant, November 9, 1874. *PUSG*, vol. 25, 192–93.

Ulysses S. Grant: from Annual Message to Congress, December 7, 1874. *Richardson*, vol. VII, 296–99.

Philip H. Sheridan to William W. Belknap, January 4 and 5, 1875. *The American Annual Cyclopædia and Register of Important Events of the Year 1874* (New York: D. Appleton and Company, 1875), 498–99.

Carl Schurz: from Speech in the Senate on Louisiana, Washington, DC, January 11, 1875. *Congressional Record*, 43rd Congress, 2nd Session, 366–67, 369–70.

William Lloyd Garrison to the *Boston Journal*, January 12, 1875. *The Letters of William Lloyd Garrison, Volume VI: To Rouse the Slumbering Land, 1868–1879*, ed. Walter M. Merrill and Louis Ruchames (Cambridge, MA: The Belknap Press of Harvard University Press, 1981), 360–64. Copyright © 1981 by the President and Fellows of Harvard College. Reprinted with permission.

Ulysses S. Grant: Message to the Senate on Louisiana, January 13, 1875. *Richardson*, vol. VII, 305–14.

John R. Lynch: from Speech in Congress on the Civil Rights Bill, Washington, DC, February 3, 1875. *Congressional Record*, 43rd Congress, 2nd Session, 944–45, 947.

Thomas Whitehead: from Speech in Congress on the Civil Rights Bill, Washington, DC, February 3, 1875. *Congressional Record*, 43rd Congress, 2nd Session, 952–55.

Charles A. Eldredge: Speech in Congress on the Civil Rights Bill, Washington, DC, February 3, 1875. *Congressional Record*, 43rd Congress, 2nd Session, 982–85.

James A. Garfield: from Speech in Congress on the Civil Rights Bill, Washington, DC, February 4, 1875. *Congressional Record*, 43rd Congress, 2nd Session, 1004, 1005.

Hinds County Gazette: How to Meet the Case. *Hinds County Gazette* (Raymond, MS), August 4, 1875.

Ulysses S. Grant to Edwards Pierrepont, September 13, 1875. *PUSG*, vol. 26, 312–13.

Edwards Pierrepont to Adelbert Ames, September 14, 1875. *Appleton's Annual Cyclopædia and Register of Important Events of the Year 1875* (New York: D. Appleton and Company, 1876), 516.

Sarah A. Dickey to Ulysses S. Grant, September 23, 1875. *PUSG*, vol. 26, 298.

Margaret Ann Caldwell: Testimony to the Select Senate Committee, June 20, 1876. *Mississippi in 1875: Report of the Select Committee to inquire into the Mississippi Election of 1875, with the testimony and documentary evidence*, vol. I (Washington, DC: Government Printing Office, 1876), 435–40.

Albion W. Tourgée: Root, Hog, or Die, c. 1876. *Tourgée*, 58–62.

John R. Lynch: Speech in Congress, Washington, DC, February 10, 1876. *Congressional Record*, 44th Congress, 1st Session, 1005–7.

Ulysses S. Grant to Daniel H. Chamberlain, July 26, 1876. *PUSG*, vol. 27, 199–200.

The Nation: The South in the Canvass. *The Nation*, July 27, 1876.

Robert G. Ingersoll: from Speech in Indianapolis, September 21, 1876. *The Works of Robert G. Ingersoll*, volume IX (New York: The Dresden Publishing Co., 1908), 157–64, 179–82.

David Brundage to Ulysses S. Grant, October 14, 1876. *PUSG*, vol. 27, 214–15.

Rutherford B. Hayes: Diary, November 12, 1876. *Diary and Letters of Rutherford Birchard Hayes, Nineteenth President of the United States*, volume III, ed. Charles Richard Williams (Columbus: The Ohio State Archæological and Historical Society, 1924), 377–78. Copyright 1924 by Ohio State Archæological and Historical Society.

Abram Hewitt: Memorandum of Conversation with Ulysses S. Grant, December 3, 1876. *PUSG*, vol. 28, 78–81.

Chicago Tribune: The Court of Arbitration. *Chicago Tribune*, January 21, 1877.

St. Louis Globe Democrat: The Warning. *St. Louis Globe Democrat*, March 31, 1877.

The Nation: The Political South Hereafter. *The Nation*, April 5, 1877.

CODA, 1879

John Russell Young: from *Around the World With General Grant.*
John Russell Young, *Around the World With General Grant: A
Narrative of the Visit of General U.S. Grant, Ex-President of the
United States, to various Countries in Europe, Asia, and Africa, in
1877, 1878, 1879, to which are added certain conversations with General
Grant on questions connected with American politics and history,* vol-
ume II (New York: Subscription Book Department, The American
News Company, 1879), 359–63.

Joseph H. Rainey: from Remarks in Congress on South Carolina
Elections, Washington, DC, March 3, 1879. *Appendix to the Congressional Record,* 45th Congress, 3rd Session, 267.

This volume presents the texts of the printings and the one manuscript
chosen as sources here but does not attempt to reproduce features
of their typographic design or physical layout. The texts are printed
without alteration except for the changes previously discussed and for
the correction of typographical errors. Spelling, punctuation, and capitalization are often expressive features, and they are not altered, even
when inconsistent or irregular. The following is a list of typographical
errors corrected, cited by page and line number: 39.29, waiting; 41.21,
yourselves; 42.39, my; 45.5, condemnation.; 47.30, [Applause]; 48.15,
before?; 49.28, socíciety; 54.3, [Great applause].; 54.37, it, We; 55.9, ex-
ecise; 62.3, adulturation; 72.39, Alabama that; 75.25, negroos; 137.20, to
some,; 151.26, whereever; 155.26, years; 172.9, deal talk; 173.19, did'nt;
182.11, So; 183.31, State; 185.25, i.e; 198.10, complimentary; 198.21, that
any; 203.15, affected; 204.19, Toombes,; 206.33, inuendoes; 230.7, an
duties; 232.34, 38 to; 247.38–39, ascertained I; 250.33, JOHNSON; 255.14,
him; 263.37, devlish; 268.17, had'nt; 281.1, Fredmen's; 282.21, perilled;
285.18, Goverment; 288.33. to that; 316.22, alter; 322.34, Brobdignang-
ian; 325.25–26, as said; 350.5, BRODHEAD.; 358.19, supprise; 358.23, ju-
dical; 358.37, to day; 359.13, O'Connel; 359.33, party, measure; 361.20,
wive's; 361.36, Philips; 392.31, attrocities; 420.29, him, They; 429.36,
maintainance; 432.37, applause. It; 450.8, the set; 450.15, among the the;
460.31, Louisana; 491.34, Cardoza,; 504.30, asked; 553.31, themselve,;
565.13, Misissippi; 580.33, preparation without; 589.13, this;; 589.17, inu-
endos; 608.28, could not rise;; 633.25, Secssion; 636.8, WestPoint.

Notes

In the notes below, the reference numbers denote page and line of this volume (the line count includes headings, but not rule lines). No note is made for material included in the eleventh edition of *Merriam-Webster's Collegiate Dictionary*. Biblical references are keyed to the King James Version. Quotations from Shakespeare are keyed to *The Riverside Shakespeare*, ed. G. Blakemore Evans (Boston: Houghton, Mifflin, 1974). Footnotes and bracketed editorial notes within the text were in the originals. For further historical and biographical background, and references to other studies, see Eric Foner, *Reconstruction: America's Unfinished Revolution, 1863–1877*, Updated Edition (New York: Harper Collins Publishers Inc., 2014); Brooks D. Simpson, *The Reconstruction Presidents* (Lawrence: University Press of Kansas, 1998); *Reconstruction: A Historical Encyclopedia of the American Mosaic*, ed. Richard Zuczek (Santa Barbara, CA: Greenwood, 2016); and Richard White, *The Republic for Which It Stands: The United States During Reconstruction and the Gilded Age, 1865–1896* (New York: Oxford University Press, 2017).

PRESIDENTIAL RECONSTRUCTION, 1865–1866

5.8–9 the meetings of this society] Douglass spoke at the thirty-second annual meeting of the Massachusetts Anti-Slavery Society, held in Boston on January 26, 1865.

5.17–18 I have lived out West] In Rochester, New York, where Douglass lived from 1848 to 1870.

5.31 Mr. Phillips] Wendell Phillips; see Biographical Notes.

5.32 Gen. Banks . . . policy.] Major General Nathaniel P. Banks (1816–1894), a former Republican governor of Massachusetts, was the Union military commander in Louisiana, 1862–64. Banks had instituted a contract labor system that bound freed people to work on plantations for one-year terms in return for wages, food, and shelter.

8.10–11 Toombses and Stephenses] Robert Toombs (1810–1885) was a congressman, 1845–53, and senator, 1853–61, from Georgia who had commanded a brigade in the Confederate army and served as inspector general of Georgia militia in 1864; Alexander H. Stephens (1812–1883), congressman from Georgia, 1843–59, and vice president of the Confederacy, 1861–65.

11.1–3 "What doth it . . . his own soul?"] Cf. Matthew 16:26, Mark 8:36.

11.36   eleven States . . . old thirteen.] In 1787 black men were explicitly enfranchised in New York, New Jersey, Pennsylvania, and North Carolina, and
were prohibited from voting in Virginia, Georgia, and South Carolina. Maryland permitted voting by men who had been freed before 1783, while the laws
in Massachusetts, New Hampshire, Connecticut, Rhode Island, and Delaware
did not explicitly address the question.

11.37–38   In 1812 Gen. Jackson . . . citizens] Andrew Jackson published an
address to the free people of color in Louisiana in 1814, asking them to help
defend the state against British invasion.

13.24   Mr. Quincy] Edmund Quincy (1808–1877), an abolitionist who served
as vice president of the Massachusetts Anti-Slavery Society, 1848–60.

14.2   *Speech on Reconstruction*] Lincoln delivered this speech, his last public
address, from a window in the White House. John Wilkes Booth was in the
audience with his co-conspirator Lewis Powell, who later recalled that Booth
told him: "That is the last speech he will ever make."

14.12   I myself, was near the front] Lincoln visited Ulysses S. Grant's headquarters in City Point, Virginia, from March 24 to April 8, 1865, and toured
Richmond after its evacuation by Confederate forces.

15.7   One of them] Salmon P. Chase; see Biographical Notes.

15.15   new constitution of Louisiana] A new state constitution was approved
by white Unionist voters on September 5, 1864.

19.2   Springfield Republican] Published and edited by Samuel Bowles (1826–
1878), the *Springfield Republican* was one of the most influential newspapers
in Massachusetts.

19.26   the President's plan] President Lincoln had used his annual message to
Congress in December 1863 and an accompanying proclamation to outline a
plan for restoring loyal governments in the insurrectionary states. Under his
proposal, a new state government committed to the abolition of slavery could
be established after 10 percent of the state's voters had sworn future allegiance
to the Union.

20.1–2   theories of reconstruction . . . into territories] Some Radical Republicans, including Massachusetts senator Charles Sumner, had advanced the
theory that the Confederate states had lost their sovereignty and reverted to
the status of federal territories.

21.2–3   *Interview with Pennsylvania Delegation*] The text of Johnson's remarks printed here appeared in the *New York Herald*, May 4, 1865.

21.5   MR. CHAIRMAN] Simon Cameron (1799–1889), a former senator from
Pennsylvania who had served as secretary of war, March 1861–January 1862,
and as minister to Russia, 1862–63.

24.29   Fort Wagner and Port Hudson] Black troops took part in the Union assaults on Fort Wagner, South Carolina, July 18, 1863, and Port Hudson, Louisiana, May 27, 1863.

25.5–6   you were . . . North Carolina] Andrew Johnson was born in Raleigh, North Carolina, in 1808 and lived in the state until 1826, when he moved to Tennessee.

26.2–3   *Reply to a Delegation of Colored Ministers*] Johnson met with a delegation from the National Theological Institute for Colored Ministers, founded in Washington, D.C., in 1865 by the Baptist minister Edmund Tunney (1816–1872). His remarks are taken from the *Washington Morning Chronicle*, May 12, 1865.

26.14   I have owned slaves] Johnson purchased his first slave, a young woman named Dolly, in 1842. He was recorded in the 1860 census as owning five slaves, who worked primarily as domestic servants. The Johnson family freed their slaves in August 1863.

26.32–34   I was the first . . . Tennessee were free] On October 24, 1864, Johnson addressed a crowd of African Americans who had held a torchlight parade in Nashville in support of the Lincoln-Johnson ticket. Speaking from the steps of the state capitol, Johnson reminded the marchers that Tennessee had been exempted from the Emancipation Proclamation, then said that "with the past history of the State to witness, the present condition to guide, and its future to encourage me, I, Andrew Johnson, do hereby proclaim freedom to every man in Tennessee!" He later expressed the wish that "a Moses might arise" who would lead the freed people to safety. When voices in the crowd shouted "You are our Moses," Johnson replied: "Well, then, humble and unworthy as I am, if no other better shall be found, I will indeed be your Moses, and lead you through the Red Sea of war and bondage, to a fairer future of liberty and peace." Slavery remained legal in Tennessee until February 22, 1865, when loyal white voters approved an abolition amendment to the state constitution.

28.3   *Salmon P. Chase*] Chief Justice Salmon P. Chase met with President Johnson several times in April 1865 and advised him to enfranchise black men in the South. On May 1 Chase left Washington on an inspection tour of the South, ostensibly undertaken for the purpose of reopening the federal district courts in the region. As the chief justice traveled along the Atlantic seaboard from Virginia to Florida he wrote seven letters to Johnson, reporting on his conversations with southerners and Union officers and offering his advice on Reconstruction. When Chase reached Mobile, Alabama, in early June, he learned that Johnson had instituted a Reconstruction policy for North Carolina without providing for black suffrage (see Chronology, May 29, 1865). Chase continued on his tour, but stopped writing to the president.

28.7   General Dodge] George S. Dodge (1838–1881), the chief army quartermaster at Wilmington.

28.8–9   Hawley . . . Abbot] Brigadier General Joseph R. Hawley (1826–1905), commander of the Wilmington district, was born in North Carolina and lived there until 1837, when he moved to Connecticut. Brevet Brigadier General Joseph C. Abbott (1825–1881), a lawyer and journalist from New Hampshire, moved to North Carolina after leaving the army and served in the U.S. Senate as a Republican, 1868–71.

28.28 Mr. Moore] Bartholomew F. Moore (1801–1878) served as attorney general of North Carolina, 1848–51, and was a delegate to the state constitutional convention held in October 1865.

30.13–16 New York Herald . . . general suffrage.] The *New York Herald*, founded and edited by James Gordon Bennett (1795–1872), had urged President Johnson on May 3, 1865, to give "the emancipated negroes of the rebel States, the right to vote along with the whites." In an editorial titled "Chief Justice Chase, the Great Negro-Worshipper," that appeared on May 24, the *Herald* changed its position: "According to the constitution the question of negro suffrage is left to the several States, and there we are content to leave it." The newspaper denounced Chase's southern tour as an exercise of his presidential ambitions, and warned that his advocacy of black suffrage was "provoking a new social war between the races of the South."

30.19–21 The spokesman . . . in Philadelphia] Jonathan C. Gibbs (1827–1874), ordained as a Presbyterian minister in 1852, was an active abolitionist who also campaigned against racial discrimination in New York and Pennsylvania. Gibbs later moved to Florida, where he served as secretary of state, 1868–72, and as superintendent of public education, 1872–74.

32.17 rebels will re-elect . . . Virginia.] In a proclamation issued on May 9, 1865, Johnson had recognized the Unionist "restored government" of Virginia established in Alexandria in 1863 by Governor Francis H. Pierpont. After six counties along the eastern shore of Virginia held elections for the state legislature on May 25, the *New-York Daily Tribune* reported on May 27 that "the Disunionists" had "swept the State, as far as the returns have come in."

33.12 Strong arm of Millitary power] Lincoln had declared martial law and suspended the writ of habeas corpus in Kentucky on July 5, 1864, in response to the guerrilla warfare in the state.

33.32 *Genl. Palmer*] Major General John M. Palmer (1817–1900) commanded the Department of Kentucky, February 1865–April 1866.

34.1 you will not Remove Marshall Law] Johnson would issue a proclamation ending martial law in Kentucky on October 12, 1865.

34.17 sold a slave] Slavery remained legal in Kentucky until the ratification of the Thirteenth Amendment.

34.34–37 Chas A. Roxborough . . . Wm. F. Butler] In Louisville city directories from 1866–71, Charles A. Roxborough is listed as a steward, Richard M. Johnson as a dry goods merchant, Henry H. White as a laborer, and William F. Butler as a steamboat steward.

35.31–32 Brevet Brigadier General Hartwell] Alfred S. Hartwell (1836–1912) had commanded the black 55th Massachusetts Infantry Regiment, 1863–64, before becoming a brigade commander.

35.34 Brig. Gen'l. Hatch's] John P. Hatch (1822–1901) commanded the Northern District of the Department of the South.

43.24–25 Genl Saxton is the Asst Commissioner for S.C.] Brigadier General Rufus Saxton (1824–1908) was the wartime Union commander in the South Carolina Sea Islands. Saxton served as assistant commissioner of the Freedmen's Bureau for South Carolina from May 1865 to January 1866. He was relieved on Johnson's orders for opposing the return of the abandoned coastal plantations reserved in January 1865 for settlement by freed people.

44.32–33 the Supreme Court . . . unanimous decision] In the *Prize Cases*, decided 5–4 on March 10, 1863, the majority ruled that Lincoln's proclamation of April 19, 1861, had imposed a legal blockade on southern ports, while the dissenters held that a lawful state of civil war did not begin until July 13, 1861, when Congress authorized the declaration of a state of insurrection. Dana, the U.S. district attorney for Massachusetts, had appeared before the Court in the *Prize Cases* as lead counsel for the government.

45.20–21 sinking the Alabama . . . Channel] The USS *Kearsarge* sank the Confederate commerce raider CSS *Alabama* off Cherbourg, France, on June 19, 1864.

47.29–30 New Jersey . . . proposition of amendment] New Jersey rejected the Thirteenth Amendment on March 16, 1865, then ratified it on January 23, 1866, a month after it was declared in effect. In 1784 Thomas Jefferson proposed a plan of government for the western territory ceded to Congress under the Articles of Confederation. His plan included a proviso prohibiting slavery after 1800 in any new state formed out of the ceded territory, but his antislavery measure failed to win the required majority of seven states because of the illness of a New Jersey delegate.

47.35–36 Louisiana . . . Kentucky] Louisiana ratified the Thirteenth Amendment on February 17, 1865; Kentucky rejected the amendment on February 24, 1865, and did not ratify it until March 18, 1976.

50.32–33 Prof. Parsons] Theophilus Parsons (1797–1882), the Dane Professor of Law at Harvard, 1848–70.

51.29–30 "Every turf . . . soldier's sepulchre."] Cf. lines 31–32 of "Hohenlinden" (1802) by Thomas Campbell (1777–1844).

52.12–14 President Johnson . . . North Carolina] See Chronology, May 29, 1865.

54.13–14 sown the wind . . . reap the whirlwind?] See Hosea 8:7.

56.2 *Gideon Welles*] A former journalist from Connecticut, Welles (1802–1878) served as secretary of the navy in the Lincoln and Johnson administrations, 1861–69.

56.7   Mr Hooper] Samuel Hooper (1808–1875), a successful merchant, was a Republican congressman from Massachusetts, 1861–75. Sumner would marry Alice Mason Hooper (1838–1913), the widow of William Sturgis Hooper, Samuel Hooper's son, in October 1866, but they separated in June 1867 and divorced in 1873.

56.8   What you say . . . the Administration] Welles had written to Sumner on June 30, 1865, defending Johnson's Reconstruction policy as being "within constitutional limitations" and arguing that the former Confederate states had not "forfeited their civil, territorial, or political rights," including the right to determine their own suffrage qualifications.

56.33   requirements of a republican govt.] Article IV, Section 4, of the Constitution provides that the "United States shall guarantee to every State in this Union a Republican Form of Government."

57.18–19   Burke, "to turn . . . the Constitution,"] Cf. Edmund Burke (1729–1797), in his speech in the House of Commons on American taxation, April 19, 1774: "are we to turn to them the shameful parts of our constitution?"

57.28–29   oath of office . . . Congress] On July 2, 1862, Congress passed legislation requiring all federal civil and military officers to take the so-called Ironclad Oath and swear that they had never voluntarily supported or aided the rebellion.

60.14–15   the CLERK OF THE HOUSE OF REPRESENTATIVES.] A former newspaper editor, Edward McPherson (1830–1895) was a Republican congressman from Pennsylvania, 1859–63. Defeated for reelection in 1862, McPherson served as clerk of the House from December 1863 until December 1875. When the Thirty-ninth Congress met on December 4, 1865, McPherson, acting according to a plan devised by Representative Thaddeus Stevens, omitted the names of the representatives from the former Confederate states while calling the roll and refused to hear any Democratic objections. The Republican majority then elected Schulyer Colfax of Indiana as Speaker.

61.22–23   potentates of Europe . . . our Continent] Napoleon III invaded Mexico in 1862 and installed the Austrian archduke Maximilian (1832–1867) as emperor in 1864. Maximilian was overthrown and executed by the republican forces of Benito Juárez (1806–1872) soon after the withdrawal of the last French troops in 1867.

62.12   marked servitude . . . days of Ham.] See Genesis 9:18–25. The "curse of Ham" was often used to justify enslaving black people because African peoples were listed among Ham's descendants in Genesis 10:6–20.

63.1   Faneuil Hall appeal] The public meeting in Boston that Richard Henry Dana addressed on June 21, 1865 (see pp. 44–55 in this volume) adopted several resolutions, including the following: "Resolved, That in reorganizing the rebel States, the safety of loyal citizens in those States, the stability of our government, and the claims of justice, require that none shall be allowed to vote who are not loyal, and that none should be expelled from voting because of their race or color."

64.18–19 Mr. Chase to say . . . worth fighting for."] Montgomery Blair (1813–1883), the eldest son of Francis Preston Blair, had served as postmaster general from 1861 until 1864. In a speech delivered at Clarksville, Maryland, on August 26, 1865, Montgomery Blair alleged that during a cabinet meeting held in March 1861 to discuss whether Fort Sumter should be resupplied, Chase had said: "Let the South go; it is not worth fighting for."

64.22 Essex Junto] A faction of conservative Massachusetts Federalists who opposed the presidential policies of both John Adams and Thomas Jefferson.

64.26–29 carried a bill through congress . . . appealed to the people] On July 2, 1864, Congress passed a Reconstruction bill, sponsored by Ohio senator Benjamin F. Wade and Maryland congressman Henry Winter Davis, that required a majority of a state's white male voters to swear allegiance before elections could be held for a new state constitutional convention. Suffrage in the new elections would be restricted to voters who took the "Ironclad Oath" swearing that they had never voluntarily supported or aided the Confederacy. After Lincoln pocket vetoed the bill, Wade and Davis published a manifesto denouncing the president on August 5, 1864.

65.39–40 "out upon . . . fellowship"] *1 Henry IV*, I.iii.208.

71.2 *Andrew J. Smith*] Major General Andrew J. Smith (1815–1897), the senior army occupation commander in Alabama.

71.26 ocupation of Mobile] Union troops occupied Mobile on April 12, 1865.

71.33 C. C. Andrews] Brigadier General Christopher C. Andrews (1829–1922).

71.34 Mayor Slough] Robert H. Slough (1820–1872) was the mayor of Mobile, 1861–65. On August 4, 1865, Major General Noah Swayne (1834–1902), the assistant commissioner of the Freedmen's Bureau for Alabama, ordered the civil courts in Alabama to accept the testimony of African Americans; failure to comply would result in cases being tried in military courts. After Lewis Parsons, the provisional governor appointed by President Johnson, issued a proclamation urging compliance with Swayne's order, Slough resigned as mayor on August 14, 1865.

72.28–30 the Methodists South . . . of their Zion] Before the war the black Zion Church congregation in Mobile had vested the title to its church building with white trustees due to legal restrictions on black property ownership. The trustees unsuccessfully attempted to take possession of the church in 1865.

74.2 *P. H. Anderson*] A merchant and farmer, Patrick Henry Anderson (1823–1890), was listed in the 1860 census as the owner of thirty-two slaves.

74.3 LETTER FROM . . . OLD MASTER.] The letter first appeared in the *Cincinnati Commercial* and was reprinted in the *New-York Daily Tribune* on August 22, 1865. It was included by Lydia Maria Child in *The Freedmen's Book* (1865), a collection of stories, speeches, and poems intended for use as a reader in schools for freed people.

74.28   Mandy] Amanda McGregor Anderson (1828–1913), who had married Jordan Anderson in 1848.

75.18   V. Winters] Valentine Winters (1807–1890), a successful banker who had helped Jordan Anderson and his family settle in Dayton. It is possible that Winters collaborated with Anderson in writing the letter to P. H. Anderson.

76.3   *Carl Schurz to Andrew Johnson*] From July to September 1865 Schurz made an extensive inspection tour of the South on behalf of President Johnson, traveling through South Carolina, Georgia, Alabama, Mississippi, and Louisiana. During his trip Schurz sent thirteen letters and telegrams to the president, as well as five dispatches to the *Boston Daily Advertiser*.

76.23–24   report . . . the Provost Marshal at Selma] In his report, Major John P. Houston of the 5th Minnesota Infantry cited twelve cases in which whites had murdered blacks and characterized the killings as "but a small part of those that have actually been perpetrated." Houston concluded that "the country is filled with desperadoes and banditti who rob and plunder on every side" and "is emphatically in a condition of anarchy."

76.28–29   Capt. A. C. Haptonstall] Captain Abram C. Haptonstall of the 47th Illinois Infantry.

77.1   Maj. Genl. Woods] Major General Charles R. Woods (1827–1885) commanded the Department of Alabama, June 1865–May 1866.

77.7   Gov. Parsons] Lewis E. Parsons (1817–1895), a successful lawyer and Unionist, was appointed provisional governor of Alabama by Johnson on June 21, 1865. Parsons served as governor until December 20, 1865, when the legislature elected him to the U.S. Senate. The exclusion of the former Confederate states from the Thirty-ninth Congress prevented him from taking his seat.

77.11–12   Governor Parson's own proclamation] In a proclamation issued on August 9, 1865, Parsons enjoined the citizens of Alabama to cease the widespread stealing of horses and cotton.

77.29   adjournment of the Convention.] The Mississippi state constitutional convention met from August 14 to 24, 1865.

78.3   Amos R. Johnson] Amos R. Johnston (1810–1879) was a lawyer and the editor of the *Jackson Standard*.

78.6–8   "If we do . . . Black Republicans."] In fact, Johnston made these remarks during the convention debate over abolishing slavery, not the debate over repeal of the secession ordinance.

78.19–20   second section of the Amendment] The second section of the

Thirteenth Amendment stated: "Congress shall have the power to enforce this article by appropriate legislation."

78.21–22   action of the Convention . . . abolition of slavery] On August 21, 1865, the convention adopted an article that read: "The institution of slavery having been destroyed in the State of Mississippi, neither slavery nor involuntary servitude otherwise than in the punishment of crimes, whereof the party shall have been duly convicted, shall hereafter exist in this State; and the Legislature at its next session and thereafter as the public welfare may require, shall provide by law for the protection and security of the persons and property of the freedmen of the State, and guard them and the State against any evils that may arise from their sudden emancipation."

79.22–23   Genl. Osterhaus] Major General Peter Osterhaus (1823–1917) commanded the Northern District of Mississippi, June 1865–January 1866.

80.13–14   Gov. Sharkey's . . . militia of the State] William L. Sharkey (1797–1873), a former state judge who had opposed secession, was appointed provisional governor of Mississippi by Johnson on June 13, 1865, and served until December 25, 1865. On August 19 Sharkey issued a proclamation calling for the raising of militia in Hinds and Madison Counties.

80.17   Gen'l. Osterhaus' correspondence with Gov. Sharkey] Osterhaus told Sharkey on August 21 that no military organization not commanded by U.S. army officers could be permitted in the state.

80.19   Genl. Slocum's Genl. Order No. 22] Major General Henry W. Slocum (1827–1894), commander of the Department of Mississippi, issued an order on August 24 revoking Sharkey's militia proclamation.

82.9   Secretary of State] James R. Yerger (1840–1891).

82.17–21   Gen. Dana . . . Gen. McPherson] Major General Napoleon Dana (1822–1905) served on occupation duty in Mississippi, August 1864–May 1865. Major General James B. McPherson (1828–1864) was a corps commander under Grant during the Vicksburg campaign, 1862–63.

83.16–17   Genl. Slocum's order . . . not be sustained] President Johnson overruled Slocum on September 2 and ordered him to let Sharkey form a militia.

87.24–25   Russia has just started] Serfdom was abolished in Russia in 1861 by Czar Alexander II (1818–1881).

92.3   *Speech at Lancaster*] Stevens had lived in Lancaster since 1842. The text of the speech is taken from the *Lancaster Evening Express*, September 8, 1865.

94.5   Semmes] Raphael Semmes (1809–1877) commanded the Confederate commerce raider *Alabama*, 1862–64.

94.29–31   "*by an impartial . . . by law.*"] From the Sixth Amendment.

95.2–3 Lord Russell] William Russell, Lord Russell (1639–1683), was convicted of treason and executed for his alleged involvement in the Rye House plot to assassinate Charles II and his brother James.

95.18–19 the court in the prize cases] See note 44.32–33.

97.7 Halleck . . . Hautefeuille] Henry Halleck (1814–1872), *International Law, or, Rules Regulating the Intercourse of States in Peace and War* (1861); Laurent-Basile Hautefeuille (1805–1875), French writer on international maritime law.

97.11 Vattel] Emerich de Vattel (1714–1767), *The Law of Nations, Or, Principles of the Law of Nature, Applied to the Conduct and Affairs of Nations and Sovereigns* (1760, originally published in French in 1758).

97.24 Capt. Wirz] Captain Henry H. Wirz (1823–1865) was the commandant of the Confederate prisoner of war camp at Andersonville, Georgia, from April 1864 until his arrest in May 1865. He was tried on multiple charges, including murder, and was hanged on November 10, 1865, the only Confederate officer to be executed for war crimes.

98.17–18 Fort Pillow and Fort Wagner] Confederate troops captured the Union outpost at Fort Pillow, Tennessee, on April 12, 1864, and killed hundreds of black soldiers trying to surrender. Black soldiers captured at Fort Wagner, South Carolina, on July 18, 1863, were threatened with possible execution or enslavement by Confederate authorities.

98.18–19 Sixty thousand . . . starved to death] About 30,000 Union prisoners died in Confederate prisons and camps.

98.22 corner-stone should be slavery,"] In a speech delivered at Savannah, Georgia, on March 21, 1861, Alexander Stephens (1812–1883), the Confederate vice president, said that the "corner-stone" of the new Confederacy "rests upon the great truth, that the negro is not equal to the white man; that slavery—subordination to the superior race—is his natural and normal condition."

99.3 six millions of freedmen] The 1860 census recorded 3,950,528 slaves living in the United States, so the figure of "four millions," used by Stevens at 104.34, is more accurate.

101.10–12 Grotius . . . Phillimore.] Hugo Grotius (1583–1645), Dutch writer on international law; Samuel von Pufendorf (1632–1694), German legal philosopher; Thomas Rutherford (1712–1771), British moral philosopher and legal scholar; Sir Robert Joseph Phillimore (1810–1885), British jurist and author of *Commentaries on International Law* (4 vols., 1854–61).

101.17 Theophilus Parsons . . . public speech] Parsons (see note 50.32–33) spoke at the meeting held at Faneuil Hall, Boston, on June 21, 1865.

102.22–23 Gen. Smith conquered . . . proclamation!] Brigadier General Alexander Smyth (1765–1830) issued a proclamation to his army in upstate

New York on November 17, 1812, declaring that his forces would soon conquer Canada. His attempt to cross the Niagara River on December 1 failed because of poor preparation, and Smyth was relieved of his command.

102.27–30   Mr. Bancroft . . . feudal principles.] The historian George Bancroft (1800–1891) made this argument in his memorial oration for President Lincoln, delivered in New York City on April 25, 1865.

104.17   Milesians] Irish immigrants, from the mythic ancestors of the Celtic population of Ireland.

104.36   the Blairs] Francis Preston Blair (see Biographical Notes) and his sons Montgomery (see note 64.18–19) and Frank (see Biographical Notes).

104.37–38   a single experiment] President Lincoln had signed a contract on December 31, 1862, with Bernard Kock, a cotton trader who proposed to transport 5,000 freed slaves to Île à Vache, a small uninhabited island off the southwest coast of Haiti. In April 1863 a ship carried 453 former slaves from Fort Monroe, Virginia, to the island, where attempts to establish a cotton plantation failed. Of the colonists, 88 died of hunger and disease, 73 fled to the Haitian mainland, and 292 returned to the United States on the relief ship *Marcia Day*, which docked at Alexandria, Virginia, on March 20, 1864.

105.12–13   say, as Mr. Lincoln . . . HAS COME!"] Lincoln replaced Montgomery Blair as postmaster general with William Dennison on September 23, 1864, as a conciliatory gesture to Radical Republicans.

106.3   "cold obstruction, and to death."] Cf. *Measure for Measure*, III.i.118.

106.11   the Dorr case] *Luther v. Borden*, decided 8–1 on January 3, 1849, arose from the 1842 Dorr Rebellion in Rhode Island that led to the establishment of rival "People's" and "Freeholder's" state governments. The Supreme Court rejected the plaintiff's challenge to the legitimacy of the Freeholder's government, ruling that it was a political question to be decided by Congress and not the judiciary.

108.8–9   Both parties . . . Albany, New York] The New York Democratic state convention was held in Albany on September 7, 1865, while the Republican state convention met in Syracuse on September 20.

108.11   "Dionysius the Tyrant,"] Dionysius (c. 430–367 B.C.E.) ruled Syracuse as a tyrant, 405–367.

108.12   murder of Mrs. Surratt] Mary Surratt (1823–1865) was convicted by a military commission of conspiring to assassinate President Lincoln and hanged on July 7, 1865, after President Johnson refused to grant clemency. She was the first woman ever to be executed by the federal government.

109.9–10   on October 2 . . . in Wisconsin.] State constitutional amendments extending suffrage were defeated on October 2, 1865, in Connecticut, 33,489–27,217, and on November 7 in Minnesota, 14,480–12,170, and in

Wisconsin, 55,591–46,388. In Iowa, where the Republican platform called for amending the state constitution to permit black male suffrage, the Republican ticket carried the state on October 10, but with a significantly reduced majority.

109.33–34 convention of Massachusetts Republicans . . . Worcester.] The convention met on September 14, 1865.

111.31–34 Senator Hunter . . . Fort Monroe] Robert M. T. Hunter (1809–1887) was a congressman from Virginia, 1837–43 and 1845–47, and a senator, 1847–61. Hunter served as the Confederate secretary of state, 1861–62, and in the Confederate senate, 1862–65, and was one of the three peace commissioners who met with Lincoln at Hampton Roads, Virginia, on February 3, 1865. Imprisoned in Fort Pulaski outside of Savannah, Georgia, Hunter was granted a parole by Johnson on September 6, 1865. Clement Clay (1816–1882) was a senator from Alabama, 1853–61. Clay served in the Confederate senate, 1862–64, and as a Confederate agent in Canada, 1864–65. Accused of complicity in the assassination of President Lincoln, he was imprisoned in Fort Monroe, Virginia, until his release on April 18, 1866. An exiled Irish nationalist who supported the Confederacy, John Mitchel (1815–1875) edited the *Richmond Enquirer*, 1863–65. Mitchel moved to New York City after the fall of Richmond and became the editor of the pro-Confederate *New York Daily News*. He was arrested by the military on May 14 for aiding the rebellion and was imprisoned in Fort Monroe until his release on October 30, 1865.

111.35 Jefferson Davis's trial has been delayed] Davis was eventually released on bail on May 13, 1867, while under indictment for treason. His trial was repeatedly postponed, and on December 25, 1868, Johnson issued a general amnesty proclamation that covered Davis, ending the case.

111.39–40 in 1862 . . . Chandler] Lieutenant Colonel Daniel T. Chandler (1820–1877) submitted an inspection report on Andersonville to the Confederate war department on August 5, 1864.

112.4 thousands . . . died at Andersonville] About 13,000 Union prisoners died in the camp.

112.7 General Lee . . . a college] Washington College (now Washington and Lee University) in Lexington, Virginia.

112.9–10 Magruder . . . Maury] Former Confederate officers Major General John B. Magruder (1807–1871), Major General Sterling Price (1805–1867), Brigadier General Trusten Polk (1811–1876), and Commander Matthew F. Maury (1806–1873). All four men returned to the United States by 1868.

113.4 *Interview with President Johnson*] The interview appeared in *The New York Times* on October 23, 1865.

117.2–3 *1st U.S. Colored Infantry*] Organized in the District of Columbia and mustered in on June 30, 1863, the regiment saw action in the fighting around Petersburg and Richmond, June–December 1864, and in North Carolina, January–April 1865. It lost four officers and 67 men killed or mortally wounded in battle; one officer and 113 men died of disease.

122.5–6 an order . . . Major General commanding] The order was issued by a provost judge acting under the authority of Major General Alfred H. Terry (1827–1890), the commander of the Department of Virginia, June 1865–August 1866. It sought to protect the rights of African Americans charged with violating a local curfew.

122.32–34 "clothed with a little . . . the angels weep!"] Cf. *Measure for Measure*, II.ii.118, 121–22.

122.37 father and brother] Lunar Whittlesey (b. 1795), a tutor, and Oscar Whittlesey (b. 1826), a lawyer.

125.9–10 restoring these lands to the former owners.] On January 16, 1865, Major General William T. Sherman issued Special Field Orders No. 15, reserving a coastal strip of abandoned and confiscated lands thirty miles wide from Charleston, South Carolina, to the St. John's River in Florida for settlement by freed people. By the summer of 1865 about 40,000 former slaves were living on the 400,000 acres of land set apart by the order. (Some of the settlers worked their 40-acre plots with surplus mules provided by the Union army, possibly giving rise to the phrase "forty acres and a mule.") In October of 1865 Johnson directed Oliver O. Howard, the commissioner of the Freedmen's Bureau, to begin restoring the land covered by Special Field Orders No. 15 to owners who had taken the oath of allegiance. Howard visited Edisto Island on October 19 and told the freed people that their land would be returned. A committee of three men—Henry Bram, Ishmael Moultrie, and Yates Sampson—replied to Howard a few days later. Referring to Howard's loss of his right arm at Fair Oaks, Virginia, in 1862, they wrote: "You ask us to forgive the land owners of our Island, *You* only lost your right arm. In war and might forgive them. The man who tied me to a tree & gave me 39 lashes & who stripped and flogged my mother & my sister & who will not let me stay In His empty Hut except I will do His planting & be Satisfied with His price & who combines with others to keep away land from me well knowing I would not Have any thing to do with Him If I Had land of my own.—that man, I cannot well forgive. Does It look as If He Has forgiven me, seeing How He tries to keep me In a condition of Helplessness." The committee also wrote to President Johnson on October 28.

127.3 *Nathan A. M. Dudley*] Brevet Brigadier General Nathan A. M. Dudley (1825–1910) was superintendent of the Freedmen's Bureau for the Memphis subdistrict.

129.3–4 *Address . . . South Carolina*] The convention met in Charleston, November 20–25, 1865, and was attended by more than fifty delegates. Its address was drafted by Richard Harvey Cain (see Biographical Notes).

130.32–37   Breathes there . . . foreign strand?] Walter Scott (1771–1832), "Lay of the Last Minstrel" (1805), canto VI.

131.16   Convention and Legislature] The South Carolina state constitutional convention was held in Columbia, September 13–27, and the new legislature convened on October 25, 1865.

132.28   "a man's a man for a' that."] From "Is There for Honest Poverty," song (1795) by Robert Burns (1759–1796).

135.37   my Secretary of State.] An opponent of secession, James H. Bell (1825–1892) was an associate justice of the Texas supreme court, 1858–64, and secretary of state in the Texas provisional government, 1865–66.

136.6   address to the freedmen] Hamilton issued the address on November 17, 1865.

136.39   Rio Grande . . . for obvious reasons] Hamilton refers to the ongoing conflict in Mexico; see note 61.22–23.

138.3–4   *Sidney Andrews* . . . Since the War] In early September 1865 Sidney Andrews, a Washington correspondent for the *Chicago Tribune* and the *Boston Advertiser*, landed in Charleston, South Carolina. Andrews traveled through the Carolinas and Georgia until the beginning of December, then sailed north from Savannah. *The South Since the War* was published in the spring of 1866.

140.18–19   Mr. Wendell Phillips . . . "The South Victorious."] Phillips first gave "The South Victorious" in Boston on October 17, 1865, and then repeated the speech in several New England cities. The speech attacked both Johnson and the Republicans in Congress for failing to push for black suffrage.

141.29–30   "Do men gather . . . figs of thistles?"] Matthew 7:16.

142.28–29   Howell Cobb] Cobb (1815–1868) was a congressman from Georgia, 1843–51 and 1855–57, governor of Georgia, 1851–53, secretary of the treasury, 1857–60, president of the Provisional Confederate Congress, 1861–62, and commander of Georgia state troops, 1863–65.

144.36–37   apples of Sodom] In the *History of the Jewish War* (c. 75), book IV, chapter VIII, Flavius Josephus (c. 37–c. 100) describes fruits growing near the burned land of Sodom that "have a colour, as if they were fit to be eaten; but if you pluck them with your hands, they dissolve into smoke, and ashes" (translated by William Whiston).

145.9–10   Wade Hampton] A wealthy plantation owner, Hampton (1818–1902) had served in the Confederate army throughout the war and risen to the rank of lieutenant general. In the election for governor held on October 18, 1865, Hampton had been narrowly defeated by James L. Orr, 9,928–9,185. He later served as governor of South Carolina, 1877–79, and in the Senate, 1879–91.

145.12–13   letter . . . people of the State] The letter was printed in the *Columbia Daily Phoenix*, November 15, 1865.

152.26–28 "All men's . . . across the land,"] Alfred, Lord Tennyson (1809–1892), "The Golden Year" (1846).

153.3–4 *Carl Schurz* . . . of the South] Schurz returned to his home in Bethlehem, Pennsylvania, in October 1865 and began writing an extensive report on his southern tour. He submitted the document to President Johnson on November 22 and asked permission to publish it, but apparently received no reply. When the Senate reconvened in December, Charles Sumner, aware that Schurz's report was highly critical of the president's policy, called for its release. On December 18 Johnson sent the report to the Senate, along with a much shorter letter from General Ulysses S. Grant (see pp. 158–61 in this volume). Schurz's report ran to forty-five printed pages and was accompanied by forty-four documents, most of them written by army officers on occupation duty. Printed by order of the Senate, the report circulated in tens of thousands of copies.

158.3 *Ulysses S. Grant to Andrew Johnson*] In the fall of 1865 President Johnson urged Grant to make an inspection tour of the South. Grant left Washington on November 27 and visited Virginia, North Carolina, South Carolina, Georgia, and Tennessee before returning to the capital on December 11. Johnson then asked him to submit a report on his trip, hoping that it would offset the critical appraisal of southern conditions contained in the Schurz report. On December 18, 1865, Johnson sent both documents to the Senate, along with a message in which the president expressed satisfaction with the prospects for "a harmonious restoration" of the Union. "The people throughout the entire south evince a laudable desire to renew their allegiance to the government," Johnson wrote, "and to repair the devastations of war by a prompt and cheerful return to peaceful pursuits."

158.10 resolution of the 12th instant] The resolution, introduced by Charles Sumner, asked the president to transmit the Schurz report to the Senate.

162.3 *Lewis Hayden* . . . Masons] In the summer and fall of 1865 Hayden had traveled to Virginia and the Carolinas to help establish Masonic lodges. He reported on his trip in a speech given to the Prince Hall Grand Lodge in Boston on December 27, 1865.

162.10–11 Ishmael . . . against them] See Genesis 16:11–12.

163.3–6 "Truth, crushed . . . his worshippers."] William Cullen Bryant (1794–1878), "The Battle-Field" (1839), lines 33–36.

163.23–24 Andrew Johnson . . . our Moses] See note 26.32–34.

163.32 Pittsburg Landing] Northern name for the battle of Shiloh, April 6–7, 1862.

163.33 Milliken's Bend] Black troops helped defend the Union supply depot at Milliken's Bend, Louisiana, against a Confederate attack on June 7, 1863.

164.2–3 make treason . . . punish the traitor.] Speaking to a delegation from Illinois on April 18, 1865, Johnson said: "The American people must be taught—if they do not already feel—that treason is a crime and must be punished; that the government will not always bear with its enemies; that it is strong not only to protect, but to punish."

165.6   Your letter] Jacobs was answering a letter sent by the New York Society of Friends.

165.13   the Bluff] Yamacraw Bluff, on the south bank of the Savannah River.

166.24   Ham Island] An island in the Savannah River.

166.33   Colonel Sickles] Colonel Hiram F. Sickles (1818–1892), the subassistant commissioner of the Freedmen's Bureau at Savannah.

167.3   *James Johnson*] Major James Johnson was the Freedmen's Bureau superintendent for the tenth district of Virginia.

169.3–6   *Andrew Johnson . . . Colored Delegation*] Johnson met in the White House on February 7, 1866, with a "delegation of colored representatives from different States of the country, now in Washington to urge the interests of the colored people before the Government." The account of their meeting, and the delegation's written reply to the president, appeared in the *Washington Morning Chronicle* on February 8, 1866.

169.8   George T. Downing] A successful entrepreneur and active abolitionist, George T. Downing (1819–1903) owned a restaurant and hotel in Newport, Rhode Island, and a catering business in Providence. From 1855 to 1866 Downing led an ultimately successful campaign to desegregate the public schools in Rhode Island.

178.25–26   The President . . . what is right.] On February 8, 1866, Philip Ripley (c. 1827–1896), a correspondent for the *New York World*, spoke with one of Johnson's private secretaries about the previous day's meeting. In a letter written the same day to Manton Marble (1834–1917), the editor of the *World*, Ripley quoted the unnamed secretary as saying: "The President no more expected that darkey delegation yesterday than he did the cholera." Ripley then wrote that after the meeting, Johnson had told the secretary: "Those d—d sons of b—s thought they had me in a trap! I know that d—d Douglass; he's just like any other nigger, & he would sooner cut a white man's throat than not."

178.33   the undersigned] The letter was signed by George T. Downing, John Jones, William Whipper, Frederick Douglass, Lewis H. Douglass, and "others." Jones (1817–1879) was a successful tailor in Chicago who had campaigned against the discriminatory "Black Laws" in Illinois; Whipper (1804–1876) was a Pennsylvania lumber merchant and moral reformer; Lewis H. Douglass (1840–1908), the oldest son of Frederick Douglass, had served as the sergeant major of the 54th Massachusetts Infantry.

181.7   Act now before Congress] The Freedmen's Bureau bill was drafted by Illinois Republican Lyman Trumbull (1813–1896), the chairman of the Senate judiciary committee. It was passed by the Senate, 37–10, on January 25, 1866, and by the House, 136–33, on February 6.

184.31 Asst. Commr. . . . North Carolina] Brevet Brigadier General Elipha-let Whittlesey (1821–1909) was the Freedmen's Bureau assistant commissioner for North Carolina, July 1865–May 1866.

188.2–3 *Veto of the Freedmen's Bureau Bill*] In preparing his veto message, Johnson used drafts written by Secretary of State William H. Seward, Secretary of the Navy Gideon Welles, Senator James R. Doolittle (1815–1897), a Republi-can from Wisconsin, and Senator Edgar Cowan (1815–1885), a Republican from Pennsylvania, as well as the letter sent to him by Joseph Fullerton on February 9, 1866 (pp. 181–87 in this volume).

188.15–18 The act to establish . . . not yet expired.] The Freedmen's Bu-reau Act, passed on March 3, 1865, provided that the Bureau would "continue during the present war of rebellion, and for one year afterward."

190.35–36 the rebellion is in fact at an end.] Johnson would issue a procla-mation on April 2, 1866, declaring a formal end to the insurrection in all of the former Confederate states except Texas. A second proclamation, issued on August 20, 1866, declared an end to the insurrection in Texas and stated that "peace, order, tranquillity, and civil authority now exist in and throughout the whole of the United States of America."

197.14–15 I return the bill to the Senate] The Senate failed to override the veto in a 30–18 vote on February 20. A revised version of the bill, which ex-tended the operations of the Freedmen's Bureau for two years instead of in-definitely, was passed by Congress on July 3, 1866. Johnson vetoed the bill on July 16, but his veto was overridden the same day by the House, 103–33, and by the Senate, 33–12.

198.2–3 *Speech on Washington's Birthday*] The text printed here is taken from *The New York Times*, February 23, 1866.

198.8–10 your Committee . . . city to-day.] A public meeting held in Wash-ington on February 22, 1866, adopted a series of resolutions supporting the readmission of the southern states to Congress, opposing black suffrage, and endorsing Johnson's veto of the Freedmen's Bureau bill.

198.37 completion of the monument] Construction of the Washington Mon-ument began in 1848 but was halted in 1854 by a lack of funds. In 1876 Con-gress made the monument a public project, and construction was completed in 1884 by the U.S. Army Corps of Engineers.

199.16 since 1796] The year Tennessee became a state.

199.24–25 illustrious JACKSON . . . be preserved."] The toast offered by President Andrew Jackson at a banquet held in Washington on April 13, 1830, to celebrate Thomas Jefferson's birthday.

199.36–39 In 1833 . . . crushed the serpent] A South Carolina convention passed a nullification ordinance on November 24, 1832, prohibiting the collection of the federal tariffs authorized in 1828 and 1832 and threatening secession if the federal government responded with force. Jackson issued a proclamation on December 10 asserting federal supremacy and denouncing nullification as illegal. On March 2, 1833, he signed a force bill, authorizing the military to enforce the revenue laws, as well as a compromise tariff law lowering rates. The South Carolina convention then met on March 11 and rescinded the nullification ordinance, ending the crisis.

203.21–22   a committee] The Congressional Joint Committee on Reconstruction; see Chronology, December 13, 1865.

204.19   Slidells] John Slidell (1793–1871) was a congressman from Louisiana, 1843–45, a senator, 1853–61, and a Confederate envoy to France, 1861–65.

204.40   Forney."] John W. Forney (1817–1881), publisher and editor of the *Philadelphia Press* and the *Washington Chronicle*, served as secretary of the U.S. Senate, July 1861–June 1868. Forney initially supported the Johnson administration, but broke with the president when he vetoed the Freedmen's Bureau bill. In a letter published in the *Philadelphia Press* on February 20, Forney described Johnson as "callous and treacherous" and criticized his "ill-digested, incoherent and illogical harangues."

205.17–19   a conversation . . . amendments to the Constitution] On January 22, 1866, Thaddeus Stevens introduced in the House of Representatives a proposed constitutional amendment, framed by the Joint Committee on Reconstruction, that apportioned representation in the House among the states "according to their respective numbers, counting the whole number of persons in each State." Under its provisions, if any state "denied or abridged" the elective franchise "on account of race or color, all persons therein of such race or color shall be excluded from the basis of representation." While the House was considering the amendment, Johnson met at the White House on January 28 with Senator James Dixon (1814–1873), a conservative Republican from Connecticut who supported the administration. An account of their conversation appeared in the *Washington Chronicle* the next day, in which Dixon was referred to as "a distinguished Senator." It reported that Johnson opposed making further amendments to the Constitution, and that if an amendment were to be adopted to change the basis for representation, it should apportion representation among the states according to the number of qualified voters. Johnson was also quoted as opposing "agitation on the negro franchise question," which he predicted would lead to a war between the races. The House approved the proposed amendment, 120–46, on January 31, but it was rejected by the Senate, 25–22, on March 9, 1866.

205.25–26   it was charged . . . a king his head] During a debate on the representation amendment in the House on January 31, 1866, Thaddeus Stevens referred to the *Washington Chronicle* story as "the command" of the president, "made, in my judgment, in violation of the privileges of this House; made in such a way that centuries ago, had it been made to Parliament by a British king, it would have cost him his head."

206.17–18   I have been denounced for "whitewashing."] In remarks made in the Senate on December 19, 1865, Charles Sumner compared the message transmitted by President Johnson the previous day (see note 158.3) to "the whitewashing message" on the civil strife in Kansas Territory sent to Congress by President Franklin Pierce on January 24, 1856.

207.6–7   I am not afraid . . . attack another?] In the text of the speech printed in the *New-York Daily Tribune* on February 24, 1866, this sentence read: "No, no, I am not afraid of assassins attacking me where a brave and courageous man would attack another."

207.10   "willing to wound yet afraid to strike."] Alexander Pope (1688–1744), *Epistle to Dr. Arbuthnot* (1735).

207.18–19   the blood of . . . seed of the Church.] Tertullian (c. 155–c. 225), *Apologeticus* (197).

207.27–28   I had a conversation with Mr. LINCOLN] No evidence has been found corroborating the conversation described by Johnson.

214.2   *Veto of the Civil Rights Bill*] Johnson prepared this veto message using drafts written by William H. Seward, Gideon Welles, and Henry Stanbery (1803–1881), an attorney from Ohio who later served as attorney general in the Johnson administration, July 1866–March 1868, and as lead defense counsel in the president's Senate impeachment trial.

214.5–7   the bill . . . their civil rights] The bill, drafted by Illinois senator Lyman Trumbull, was passed by the Senate, 33–5, on February 2, 1866, and by the House, 111–38, on March 13.

215.37–40   "of good moral . . . happiness of the same."] From the Naturalization Act of 1795.

216.20–26   Chancellor Kent . . . public decorum.] James Kent (1763–1847), *Commentaries on American Law*, volume II, part IV, lecture XXXII (1832 edition). Kent served as chief justice of the New York Supreme Court of Judicature, 1804–14, and as chancellor of New York, 1814–23.

224.30   return the bill to the Senate] Johnson's veto was overridden in the Senate, 33–15, on April 6, and in the House, 122–41, April 9, 1866.

CONGRESSIONAL RECONSTRUCTION, 1866–1869

229.21   your advocacy of Woman Suffrage in Congress.] During a debate in the House on January 31, 1866, Ohio Republican Robert Schenck (1809–1890) suggested changing the proposed representation amendment (see note 205.17–19) so as to make the number of qualified male voters over twenty-one in each state the basis for apportioning representatives. Stevens objected on several grounds, and at one point asked: "Why has he put in that word 'male?' It was never in the Constitution of the United States before. Why make a crusade against women in the Constitution of the nation?"

229.22–23 "Keep back no . . . thy speech."] James Russell Lowell (1819–1891), "Above and Below" (1848).

231.10–11 Dr. JOHNSON . . . EDMUND BURKE] Samuel Johnson (1709–1784) defended the American policy of Lord North's government in his pamphlet *Taxation No Tyranny*, published in March 1775. Edmund Burke criticized the government in his speeches in Parliament on American taxation, April 19, 1774, and on conciliation with the colonies, March 11, 1775.

232.30 National Union party] The name adopted by the coalition of Republicans and War Democrats who met in Baltimore in June 1864 to nominate Lincoln for a second term.

234.32–36 words of ANDREW JOHNSON . . . for all time."] From a speech Johnson made in Nashville on June 10, 1864, after his nomination for vice president by the National Union Convention in Baltimore.

235.3–4 *Speech . . . Fourteenth Amendment*] The proposed amendment was framed by the Joint Committee on Reconstruction on April 28, 1866, and reported to the House by Stevens two days later.

237.2 rebel vice president and the commander-in-chief] Alexander H. Stephens testified before the Joint Committee on April 11, 1866, and Robert E. Lee on February 17, 1866.

237.12–13 amendment repudiating the rebel debt] The amendment was passed by the House, 151–11, on December 19, 1865, but was never acted upon by the Senate.

237.21–26 it was denounced . . . whole African race;"] Stevens quotes or paraphrases from a speech made by Charles Sumner in the Senate on March 7, 1866, opposing the representation amendment.

237.30 Lindley Murray] Born in Pennsylvania, Murray (1745–1826) was a successful English author of books on grammar and spelling.

238.2 fought the beasts at Ephesus] 1 Corinthians 15:38.

238.6–10 The first section . . . of the laws.] The first section was drafted by Congressman John Bingham (1815–1900), an Ohio Republican who served on the Joint Committee on Reconstruction. At the time of Stevens's speech, the section did not include the definition of United States citizenship subsequently added in the Senate by Michigan Republican Jacob M. Howard (1805–1871).

239.8 The second section] In the version of the amendment reported to the House on April 30, 1866, the section read: "Representatives shall be apportioned among the several States which may be included within this Union, according to their respective numbers, counting the whole number of persons in each State, excluding Indians not taxed. But whenever, in any State, the elective franchise shall be denied to any portion of its male citizens not less than twenty-one years of age, or in any way abridged except for participation in rebellion or other crime, the basis of representation in such State shall be reduced in the proportion which the number of such male citizens shall bear to the whole number of male citizens not less than twenty-one years of age."

240.13   The third section] As reported on April 30, the third section read: "Until the 4th day of July, in the year 1870, all persons who voluntarily adhered to the late insurrection, giving it aid and comfort, shall be excluded from the right to vote for representatives in Congress and for electors for president and Vice-President of the United States."

240.36   the fourth section] In the version of the amendment reported on April 30, the fourth section read: "Neither the United States nor any State shall assume or pay any debt or obligation already incurred, or which may hereafter be incurred, in aid of insurrection or of war against the United States, or any claim for compensation for loss of involuntary service or labor." The clause securing the validity of the public debt of the United States was added in the Senate.

241.2–3   "all these things . . . unto you."] Matthew 6:33.

241.4   I move to recommit] Under the rules of the House, the motion to recommit allowed the debate to continue. On May 10, 1866, the House approved the joint resolution, 128–37.

242.4   *National Woman's Rights Convention*] The eleventh National Woman's Rights Convention was held at the Church of the Puritans on Union Square, New York City, on May 10, 1866.

242.11   My husband] Fenton Harper (1822–1864).

243.32   situation of Ishmael] See Genesis 16:11–12.

244.27–28   Judge Taney . . . my race] In his opinion in *Scott v. Sandford* (1857), Chief Justice Roger B. Taney (1777–1864) wrote: "They had for more than a century before been regarded as beings of an inferior order, and altogether unfit to associate with the white race either in social or political relations, and so far inferior that they had no rights which the white man was bound to respect, and that the negro might justly and lawfully be reduced to slavery for his benefit."

244.31   Louisiana Second] Two regiments of the black Louisiana Native Guards, the 1st and the 3rd, took part in the unsuccessful Union assault on the Confederate lines at Port Hudson, Louisiana, on May 27, 1863. The combined strength of the two regiments before the attack has been estimated at 1,080 men, and their reported losses in the battle were thirty-six killed and 133 wounded. Contemporary press accounts in the North incorrectly reported that the 2nd Louisiana Native Guards had participated in the attack and lost 600 men.

244.33–35 Olustee . . . Col. Hallowell] The black 54th Massachusetts Infantry, under the command of Colonel Edward N. Hallowell (1837–1871),
helped cover the Union retreat following the Confederate victory at Olustee,
Florida, on February 20, 1864.

244.38 a woman in our country] Harriet Tubman (c. 1820–1913), an abolitionist and guide on the Underground Railroad who served as a Union nurse
and scout in South Carolina.

245.3–4 one of Montgomery's most successful expeditions] A friend of John
Brown, Colonel James Montgomery (1814–1871) led the black 2nd South Carolina Volunteers on a raid up the Combahee River in June 1863 that freed more
than 700 slaves. Tubman is credited with gathering intelligence for the raid
and served on the expedition.

245.6 conflict with a brutal conductor] Tubman suffered a serious injury to
her left arm while traveling through New Jersey on the Camden and South
Amboy Railroad in October 1865 when a conductor and two other men
dragged her from a regular car into the smoking car.

248.18 John Creighton, recorder of the city] An elected position, the city
recorder served as the judge of the city criminal court. Creighton (1834–1868),
an Irish immigrant, held the position, 1863–64 and 1865–66.

249.5 editor of the Lewiston Falls *Journal*] Nelson Dingley Jr. (1832–1899),
a Republican who later served as governor of Maine, 1874–76, and in Congress, 1881–99.

249.6–7 Maine artist SIMMONS] The sculptor Franklin Simmons (1839–1913)
made a bust of Grant in 1866. His standing sculpture of Grant in his general's
uniform was placed in the rotunda of the U.S. Capitol in 1900.

249.19–20 Mr. SWINTON . . . a history] *Campaigns of the Army of the Potomac* (1866) by William Swinton (1833–1892), a correspondent for *The New
York Times*.

249.36–37 failure to capture Petersburg . . . mine explosion.] Union
troops failed to break through the Petersburg defenses after crossing the James
River, June 15–18, 1864, and after the explosion of a mine under the Confederate lines on July 30.

250.33 JOHNSTON and DICK TAYLOR] General Joseph Johnston (1807–1891)
and Lieutenant General Richard Taylor (1826–1879), son of President Zachary
Taylor. Johnston had signed the surrender agreement for Confederate forces
in the Carolinas, Georgia, and Florida on April 26, 1865, while Taylor signed
the surrender for Alabama, Mississippi, and eastern Louisiana on May 4.

252.3 *Elihu B. Washburne to Thaddeus Stevens*] On May 14, 1866, the House
appointed a three-member select committee to investigate the violence in
Memphis. The committee, chaired by Washburne, heard testimony from 164
witnesses in Memphis from May 22 to June 6, and issued two reports on July

25, 1866. The majority report, signed by Washburne and his Republican colleague John M. Brownall, described the riot as "an organized and bloody massacre of the colored people" caused by racial prejudice and hostility toward the federal government. George S. Shanklin, the Democratic member of the committee, concluded that future violence could best be avoided by restoring the political rights of former Confederates and abolishing the Freedmen's Bureau.

252.19–20 no steps . . . murderers to justice.] No one was ever prosecuted by either the civil or military authorities for crimes committed during the riot.

253.10–11 they took this place.] The Union army occupied Memphis on June 6, 1862.

254.1–2 girl Rachael . . . how old] Rachel Hatcher was fourteen. She attended a Freedmen's Bureau school that was burned during the riot.

254.37 Dickerson] Fayette Dickerson, a forty-year-old freedman and former Union soldier, died of his wounds a week after being shot.

255.33 name of Harriet] Harriet Armour, who testified on May 31 that "Mr. Dunn" and another man had raped her in her home. She was one of five black women identified as victims of rape in the select committee's report.

256.18 Mr. BROOMALL] John M. Broomall (1816–1894) was a Republican congressman from Pennsylvania, 1863–69.

256.24 Mr. SHANKLIN] George S. Shanklin (1807–1883) was a Democratic congressman from Kentucky, 1865–67.

257.7–8 killed . . . the policeman?] John Stevens, the policeman fatally wounded in the initial confrontation on May 1, 1866, had accidentally shot himself in the leg.

258.2–3 *Joint Resolution . . . Fourteenth Amendment*] The final version of the amendment was approved by the Senate, 33–11, on June 8, and by the House, 120–32, on June 13. Ratification of the amendment was declared on July 28, 1868.

260.5 improvement of my health] Morton had suffered a stroke on October 11, 1865, that partially paralyzed his legs. He left Indianapolis on November 17, 1865, and traveled to Paris to seek medical treatment, returning Indiana on April 12, 1866.

260.15 this stage] Morton spoke in the Masonic Hall in Indianapolis.

262.20 seizing the military power of the State] The Democrats tried to force the governor to share control of the state militia with a committee of state officers, but were unable to pass the necessary legislation because the Republican minority bolted, preventing the general assembly from achieving a quorum.

262.26–27 locking up the public treasure] The general assembly failed to pass an appropriations bill in the 1863 session, which the Democrats believed would force Governor Morton to call a special session that would then pass the militia bill. Instead, Morton financed state operations by obtaining loans from banks, Republican county commissions, and the War Department in Washington. In the 1864 elections the Republicans regained control of the new general assembly that met in January 1865.

262.37–38   decided by the Supreme Court against the credit] In June 1863 the Indiana supreme court ruled that the state auditor could not pay interest on the state debt without an appropriation by the general assembly. Morton was eventually able to meet the interest payments by obtaining an advance from a New York bank.

263.17   Camp Morton] A Union prisoner of war camp in Indianapolis.

264.22–23   Convention in Chicago . . . a failure] The Democratic national convention met in Chicago on August 30, 1864, and adopted a platform calling for an immediate armistice after "four years of failure to restore the Union by the experiment of war."

265.14–15   Bowles, Milligan . . . Humphreys] William A. Bowles (1799–1873), Lambdin Milligan (1824–1899), John C. Walker (1828–1883), Harrison H. Dodd (1824–1906), Stephen Horsey (1823–1898), and Andrew Humphreys (1821–1904) were antiwar Indiana Democrats accused of involvement in an aborted plot to stage an insurrection in Indianapolis on August 16, 1864 (see pp. 262.39–263.19 in this volume). Walker avoided prosecution by seeking refuge in Canada, while Dodd also fled to Canada after escaping from custody. Bowles, Milligan, Horsey, and Humphreys were tried by a military commission in Indianapolis and convicted in December 1864. While Humphreys was found guilty of lesser charges and eventually paroled, Bowles, Milligan, and Horsey were convicted of treason and sentenced to hang. President Johnson commuted their sentences to life imprisonment at hard labor in May 1865. The defendants appealed their conviction to the U.S. Supreme Court, which ordered their release in April 1866. On December 17, 1866, the Court released its opinions in *Ex parte Milligan*, in which a majority of five justices ruled that military trials of civilians were impermissible where the civil courts remain open. The four dissenting justices agreed with overturning the verdicts in the Milligan case, but held that Congress could authorize military trials for civilians in time of war.

265.18–19   John Morgan . . . Booth] Brigadier General John Hunt Morgan (1825–1864), Confederate cavalry commander who led raids through Kentucky, Indiana, and Ohio before being killed by Union troops in Greenville, Tennessee, on September 4, 1864; Jerome Clark (1844–1865), known as "Sue Mundy," Confederate guerrilla in Kentucky who was hanged in Louisville on March 15, 1865; Champ Ferguson (1821–1865), Confederate guerrilla in Kentucky and Tennessee who was hanged in Nashville on October 20, 1865; Henry Wirz (see note 97.24); Lewis Powell alias Payne (1844–1865), co-conspirator of John Wilkes Booth and attempted assassin of William H. Seward, who was hanged in Washington, D.C., on July 7, 1865; John Wilkes Booth (1838–1865), assassin of Abraham Lincoln, who was killed by Union troops near Port Royal,

Virginia, on April 26, 1865. Clark, Ferguson, and Powell were all tried by military courts.

265.37–38   New York rioter . . . colored asylums] The Colored Orphan Asylum in New York City was evacuated by its staff before it was burned by draft rioters on July 13, 1863. At least 105 people were killed during the riot, including at least eleven black men who were lynched by white mobs.

267.6–7   Lyon . . . Hackleman.] Brigadier General Nathaniel Lyon (1818–1861), killed at Wilson's Creek, Missouri, August 10, 1861; Brigadier General Philip Kearny (1815–1862), killed at Chantilly, Virginia, September 1, 1862; Major General James B. McPherson (1828–1864), killed at Atlanta, Georgia, July 22, 1864; Brigadier General Pleasant A. Hackleman (1814–1862), a lawyer and newspaper editor from Indiana, killed at Corinth, Mississippi, October 3, 1862.

267.7–8   fictitious sufferings of Jeff Davis] Davis was kept in solitary confinement during his initial incarceration at Fort Monroe, Virginia, and had his ankles manacled for a period of five days in late May 1865.

268.14–16   the Devil offered . . . worship him] See Matthew 4:8–9.

270.9–10   political body . . . convention of 1864] A provision adopted by the convention that framed the 1864 Louisiana state constitution allowed for it to be reconvened at a future date. A group of former delegates to the 1864 convention met at the Mechanics Institute in New Orleans on July 30, 1866, in an attempt to adopt a new constitution providing for black male suffrage.

270.24   About forty whites and blacks] The army later reported that at least thirty-four black and three white supporters of the convention had been killed, along with one white bystander who was struck by a stray bullet.

271.9   Fort Pillow] See note 98.17–18.

271.13   this bad man.] John T. Monroe (1822–1871) was elected mayor of New Orleans in 1860 and served until 1862, when he was removed and imprisoned by the Union occupation authorities. Monroe was reelected in March 1866 and served until March 1867, when Sheridan used his powers as district commander under the Reconstruction Act to remove him from office.

272.6–7   slavery shot Lovejoy] Elijah P. Lovejoy (1802–1837), a Presbyterian minister, was killed by a mob in Alton, Illinois, on November 7, 1837, while attempting to defend the press of his antislavery newspaper.

273.13–14   Fenians attempted . . . peaceful neighbor] About 800 members of the Fenian Brotherhood crossed the Niagara River into Canada on June 1, 1866, and fought 850 Canadian militiamen at Ridgeway the next day, an engagement in which ten Fenians and nine Canadians were killed. The Fenians returned on June 3 to the United States, where they were arrested and then released. A second Fenian force crossed the border at St. Albans, Vermont, on June 7 and occupied three Quebec villages for two days before retreating to American territory.

273.29–31   "on application . . . be convened."] From Article IV, Section 4, of the U.S. Constitution.

274.10   he telegraphed to the Attorney-General] On July 28, 1866, Albert Voorhies (1829–1913), the lieutenant governor of Louisiana, and Andrew Herron (1823–1882), the state attorney general, informed Johnson in a telegram that they planned to have the members of the convention arrested under a court order, and asked him if the army would interfere. Johnson replied the same day that the military would "sustain" court proceedings against the convention.

274.17–20   Mayor's proclamation . . . the President."] The proclamation issued by Monroe on July 30, 1866, read: "Whereas the extinct convention of 1864 proposes meeting this day; and whereas intelligence has reached me that the peace and good order of the city might be disturbed: Now, therefore, I, John T. Monroe, mayor of the city of New Orleans, do issue this my proclamation calling upon the good people of the city to avoid with care all disturbance and collision; and I do particularly call upon the younger members of the community to act with such calmness and propriety as that the good name of the city may not be tarnished, and the enemies of the reconstruction policy of President Johnson be not afforded an opportunity, so much courted by them, of creating a breach of the peace and of falsifying facts to the great injury of the city and State; and I do further enjoin upon all good citizens to refrain from gathering in or about the place of meeting of said extinct convention, satisfied from recent despatches from Washington that the deliberations of the members thereof will receive no countenance from the President, and that he will sustain the agents of the present civil government and vindicate its laws and acts to the satisfaction of the good people of the city and State."

274.29–31   President telegraphed . . . not be tolerated"] On July 30, 1866, after learning that a riot had broken out in New Orleans, Johnson sent a telegram to Andrew Herron, the state attorney general: "You will call on General Sheridan, or whoever may be in command, for sufficient force to sustain the civil authority in suppressing all illegal or unlawful assemblies which usurp or assume to exercise any power or authority without first having obtained the consent of the people of the State. If there is to be a convention, let it be composed of delegates chosen from the people of the whole State. The people must be first consulted in reference to changing the organic law of a State. Usurpation will not be tolerated. The law and the Constitution must be sustained, and thereby peace and order."

274.37–38   "Why did you . . . of the people?"] Johnson had telegraphed James Madison Wells (1808–1899), the governor of Louisiana, on July 28, 1866: "I have been advised that you have issued a proclamation convening the convention elected in 1864. Please inform me under and by what authority this has been done, and by what authority this convention can assume to represent the whole people of the State of Louisiana." (The president had been misinformed; while Wells supported the recall of the 1864 convention, he had not issued a proclamation reconvening it.)

276.2 *Speech at St. Louis*] Johnson made this speech as part of his "Swing Around the Circle" (see Chronology, August 28–September 15, 1866). The text is taken from the St. Louis *Missouri Democrat*, September 10, 1866.

276.27–28 cries for Seward] Secretary of State William H. Seward accompanied Johnson on the tour.

278.3 shed is upon their skirts] See Jeremiah 2:34.

279.4 Fletcher] Thomas C. Fletcher (1827–1899), the National Union (Republican) governor of Missouri, 1865–69.

281.30–31 neutrality law . . . faithfully executed.] In a proclamation issued on June 6, 1866, Johnson warned that "certain evil-designed persons" were plotting to violate U.S. and international law, and authorized the army and navy to take measures to prevent future raids.

281.34 introduced a bill] Massachusetts congressman Nathaniel P. Banks, the chairman of the foreign affairs committee, reported to the House on July 25, 1866, that the existing Neutrality Act of 1818 "disregards the inalienable rights of all nations" and serves British interests. Banks introduced a new neutrality bill that was passed unanimously the next day, but which was never acted upon by the Senate.

282.1 the heels of the session] The first session of the Thirty-ninth Congress adjourned on July 28, 1866.

282.24 can get $4,000 extra pay.] On July 28, 1866, Congress raised the annual pay of senators and representatives from $3,000 to $5,000, effective December 4, 1865.

284.6 Drake's Constitution?"] Charles D. Drake (1811–1892), a lawyer from St. Louis, was the principal drafter of the 1865 Missouri constitution that abolished slavery in the state and required all voters, jurors, public officeholders, lawyers, teachers, and clergy to swear an "ironclad oath" that they had never committed any disloyal act during the rebellion. The constitution was approved by the voters, 43,670–41,808, on June 6, 1865.

285.4–6 Judge Chase . . . try him?] Jefferson Davis had been indicted for treason in Virginia on May 8, 1866. If his case had gone to trial, it would have been heard in the U.S. circuit court in Richmond, with Chief Justice Chase presiding along with John C. Underwood (1809–1873), the judge for the Eastern District of Virginia.

288.3 *Speech at Lancaster*] Stevens spoke at a Republican rally. The text is taken from the *Lancaster Evening Express*, September 29, 1866.

288.23 Dan Rice] Rice (1823–1900) was a celebrated American circus clown, impresario, and humorist.

288.31–32 celebrated general . . . eminent naval officer] Ulysses S. Grant and Admiral David G. Farragut (1801–1870).

289.6   Senator, Doolittle] James R. Doolittle (1815–1897), a Republican senator from Wisconsin, 1857–69.

289.9   Judge Kimmel] Francis M. Kimmel (1816–1900), a lawyer in Chambersburg, Pennsylvania, had served as the president judge of the court of common pleas in Somerset, Bedford, Fulton, and Franklin Counties, 1850–60.

289.14–16   elder clown . . . neck broken almost] Secretary of State Seward broke his jaw and right arm and injured his neck in a carriage accident in Washington, D.C., on April 5, 1865, nine days before he was attacked in his home by Lewis Powell.

289.31   Colonel Forney's *Chronicle*] See note 204.40.

291.38–292.1   I introduced a bill . . . form loyal governments.] Stevens introduced the bill on May 28, 1866, and reintroduced it in a speech he gave on July 28, the day Congress adjourned.

292.20–21   Governor Hamilton to Governor Holden] Andrew J. Hamilton and William W. Holden; see Biographical Notes.

292.34–35   The noble men . . . traitors' convention] A coalition of Democrats and conservative Republicans met in Philadelphia as the National Union Convention, August 14–16, 1866, and adopted resolutions endorsing Johnson's Reconstruction policies. The Southern Unionists Convention, also known as the Southern Loyalists Convention, met in Philadelphia, September 3–7, and endorsed the enfranchising of black men in the southern states.

293.13   Pennsylvania Convention] The Pennsylvania constitutional convention of 1837–38.

294.3–4   Second Session of the Thirty-ninth Congress] The second session began on December 3, 1866.

294.15   Earl Russell] Lord John Russell, 1st Earl Russell (1792–1878), a Whig, served as foreign secretary, 1859–65, and as prime minister, 1865–66.

297.23–24   walked by faith . . . by sight.] See 2 Corinthians 5:7.

301.5–6   this bill] The bill provided for forming new state governments in the South; see note 291.38–292.1.

301.10   late decision of the Supreme Court] *Ex parte Milligan*; see note 265.14–15.

302.17–23   Watson . . . shot him dead] Dr. James L. Watson fatally wounded William Medley in Rockbridge County, Virginia, on November 14, 1866. Although Watson confessed to the shooting, he was released from custody by the Lexington magistrates court. Brigadier General John M. Schofield (1831–1906), the assistant commissioner for Virginia in the Freedmen's Bureau, ordered Watson's arrest and trial by a military commission, and refused to honor a writ of habeas corpus issued for Watson by the Virginia circuit court in Richmond. On December 21, President Johnson ordered that the commission be dissolved after receiving an opinion by Attorney General Henry Stanbery that cited the Supreme Court's decision in *Ex parte Milligan*.

306.10   "*de lunatico inquirendo*."] A writ ordering that the person named in the writ be examined for insanity.

308.10   Rickety Weirze] Henry Wirz.

309.27–28   "like clay . . . the potter,"] Cf. Romans 9:21.

309.29–30   law of last session . . . Territories] The House passed a bill, 79–43, on May 10, 1866, prohibiting the denial of suffrage in territorial elections on the grounds of race or color. Similar legislation passed the Senate, 24–8, on January 10, 1867, and was agreed to by the House; the bill then became law without President Johnson's signature.

310.9–10   convention of southern loyalists,] See note 292.34–35.

311.40   "devils were . . . the houses."] When Martin Luther was warned not to attend the Diet of Worms in 1521, he is reported to have replied: "Were there as many devils in Worms as tiles upon the roofs of the houses, still would I enter."

314.8–9   Alabama . . . signs of flinching] Robert M. Patton (1809–1885), governor of Alabama, 1865–68, sent a special message to the state legislature on December 7, 1866, in which he recommended that the legislature ratify the Fourteenth Amendment so that the state could be readmitted to Congress. The amendment was rejected by the senate, 27–2, and by the house of representatives, 69–8.

314.28   President's late message] Johnson's second annual message to Congress, December 3, 1866.

315.6   the Constitutional Convention] The election for delegates to the North Carolina constitutional convention of 1868 was held November 19–20. Of the 120 delegates chosen, 107 were Republicans, including fifteen African Americans. The convention met in Raleigh, January 14–March 17, 1868, and the new constitution was approved by the voters, 93,086–74,016, April 21–23.

317.10   Great is Diana!"] Acts 19:28.

318.3–4   REPORT of the majority . . . impeachment of the President] The House Judiciary Committee approved a resolution calling for impeachment, 5–4, on November 25, 1867, and submitted a majority and two minority reports.

318.8   two months since, we said] In an editorial published in *Harper's Weekly* on October 5, 1867.

318.10–11   he had issued . . . which forbade him.] Johnson issued an amnesty proclamation on September 7, 1867, that extended his proclamation of May 29, 1865. In January 1867 Congress had repealed the section of the 1862

Confiscation Act that authorized the president to issue proclamations extending pardon and amnesty to persons engaged in the rebellion.

318.18–19   his removal of SHERIDAN and SICKLES] Johnson removed Major General Philip H. Sheridan as commander of the Fifth Military District, consisting of Louisiana and Texas, on August 17, 1867, and Major General Daniel E. Sickles (1819–1914) as commander of the Second Military District, made up of North and South Carolina, on August 26.

319.6–7   the Reconstruction bill] See Chronology, March 2, 1867.

322.12–17   a man who . . . most feasible candidate] Ulysses S. Grant.

323.19   the elections] The fall 1867 elections; see Chronology.

326.26   the Howard Amendment] The Fourteenth Amendment, which was introduced in its final form in the Senate on May 29, 1866, by Jacob M. Howard, a Republican from Michigan.

328.11   WINEGAR] Tourgée's middle name, which he used to sign a series of letters that he contributed to the *National Anti-Slavery Standard* in 1867–68.

329.3–4   *Tribune* . . . Be Impeached] This editorial was written by the managing editor of the *New-York Tribune*, John Russell Young (see Biographical Notes), while Horace Greeley was away from New York City on a lecture tour.

329.22   Warren Hastings] Hastings (1732–1818), governor-general of British India, 1772–85, was impeached for misconduct after his return to England. His trial before the House of Lords extended, with long intervals, from 1788 to 1795 and ended in his acquittal on all charges.

330.38–39   Lorenzo Thomas] Brigadier General Lorenzo Thomas (1804–1875) was adjutant general of the U.S. Army, 1861–69; see Chronology, February 1868.

331.1–2   Mr. Coyle . . . Gen. Hancock] John Francis Coyle (c. 1820–1905) was the co-owner of the Washington *National Intelligencer*, 1865–69, and a supporter of Johnson. Major General Winfield S. Hancock (1824–1886) had replaced Sheridan as commander of the Fifth Military District in August 1867 (see note 318.19–20).

333.9   Philadelphia Convention] The pro-administration National Union Convention, held in Philadelphia, August 14–16, 1866.

333.33–34   last annual message] Johnson sent his third annual message to Congress on December 3, 1867.

334.4   Mr. Belmont] New York financier August Belmont (1813–1890) was chairman of the Democratic National Committee, 1860–72.

335.30   the dead Douglas] Johnson attended the dedication of a memorial to Senator Stephen A. Douglas (1813–1861) in Chicago, September 6, 1866, during his "Swing Around the Circle" speaking tour.

337.3–4   *Thaddeus Stevens . . . Impeachment*] Stevens was ill and requested that Edward McPherson, the clerk of the House (see note 60.14–15), read his speech for him.

337.34   *malum in se*] Wrong in itself.

337.35   gentleman from Pennsylvania] George W. Woodward (1809–1875) served as a Democratic congressman from Pennsylvania, 1867–71.

338.26–27   Story's Commentaries . . . the Constitution] *Commentaries on the Constitution of the United States*, first published in 1833 by Joseph Story (1779–1845), an associate justice of the Supreme Court, 1811–45; *History of the Origin, Formation, and Adoption of the Constitution of the United States* (1854–58) by the historian and legal writer George Ticknor Curtis (1812–1894).

339.31–32   question of veracity, rather angrily discussed] Grant and Johnson exchanged a series of letters from January 24 to February 11, 1868, regarding Grant's refusal to continue serving as secretary of war ad interim. The correspondence was made public and resulted in a final break between the two men.

340.11–13   annual message . . . Congress are unconstitutional] In his message of December 3, 1867, Johnson described the three Reconstruction Acts passed by Congress, March 2–July 19, 1867, as unconstitutional.

341.4–5   Andrew Johnson . . . misprision of bribery] This charge was not included in the articles of impeachment voted by the House, March 2–3, 1868.

343.5   the proposed Constitution] Elections were held in Louisiana for a state constitutional convention, September 27–28, 1867, that met in the Mechanics' Institute in New Orleans from November 23, 1867, to March 9, 1868. The convention adopted a constitution that enfranchised black men, abolished property qualifications for office holding, established racially integrated public schools, and prohibited racial discrimination in public conveyances and accommodations. It was ratified by the voters, 51,737–39,076, April 17–18, 1868.

343.7   slubberdegullions] Slobbering, dirty fellows.

345.24   a lawyer] Benjamin F. Butler (1818–1893) was a major general in the Union army, 1861–65, and a Republican congressman from Massachusetts, 1867–75 and 1877–79. Elected governor of Massachusetts as a Democrat, he served a one-year term in 1883, and was the presidential candidate of the Greenback and Anti-Monopolist Parties in 1884.

345.30   the Managers were overmatched] Besides Butler, the House managers were John Bingham (1815–1900), a Republican congressman from Ohio, 1855–63 and 1865–73, and U.S. minister to Japan, 1873–85; George S. Boutwell (1818–1905), a Republican congressman from Massachusetts, 1863–69, secretary of the treasury, 1869–73, and a Republican senator from Massachusetts, 1873–77; John A. Logan (1826–1886), a Democratic congressman from Illinois, 1859–62, a major general in the Union army, 1862–65, a Republican congressman from Illinois, 1867–71, and a senator, 1871–77 and 1879–86; Thaddeus Stevens (see

Biographical Notes); Thomas Williams (1806–1872), a Republican congressman from Pennsylvania, 1863–69; and James F. Wilson (1828–1895), a Republican congressman from Iowa, 1861–69, and a senator, 1883–95. Johnson was defended by Henry Stanbery (1803–1881), who served as attorney general, July 1866–March 1868; William M. Evarts (1818–1901), who served as attorney general, July 1868–March 1869, as secretary of state, 1877–81, and as a Republican senator from New York, 1885–91; Benjamin R. Curtis (1809–1874), who served as an associate justice of the U.S. Supreme Court, 1851–57; Thomas A. R. Nelson (1812–1873), an Opposition congressman from Tennessee, 1859–61, and wartime Unionist; and William S. Groesbeck (1815–97), a Democratic congressman from Ohio, 1857–59.

346.25–26 Trumbull . . . Van Winkle] Lyman Trumbull (1813–1896), senator from Illinois, 1855–73; William Pitt Fessenden (1806–1869), senator from Maine, 1854–64 and 1865–69, and secretary of the treasury, 1864–65; James Grimes (1816–1872), governor of Iowa, 1854–58, and a senator, 1859–69; John B. Henderson (1826–1913), senator from Missouri, 1862–69; Joseph Fowler (1820–1902), senator from Tennessee, 1866–71; and Peter Van Winkle (1808–1872), senator from West Virginia, 1863–69. All six senators were Republicans who had opposed Johnson's policies, but nevertheless broke with their party and voted to acquit him.

346.38–39 other charges . . . bad language in 1866] The tenth article of impeachment accused Johnson of attempting "to bring into disgrace, ridicule, hatred, contempt and reproach, the Congress of the United States" by making "certain intemperate, inflammatory and scandalous harangues." After quoting passages from speeches the president gave in Washington, D.C., on August 12, Cleveland on September 3, and St. Louis on September 8, 1866, the article declared that Johnson had "brought the high office of the President of the United States into contempt, ridicule and disgrace," and was thereby "guilty of a high misdemeanor in office."

347.1 trying to seduce General Emory] The ninth article charged Johnson with attempting on February 22, 1868, to give direct orders to Brevet Major General William H. Emory (1811–1887), the commander of the Department of Washington, in violation of the Command of the Army Act, which required that all orders to the army go through Grant (see Chronology, March 2, 1867).

347.13 his declaration . . . year and a half previously] In a speech Johnson gave in Washington, D.C., on August 12, 1866.

348.15 the second and third] The second and third articles accused Johnson of violating the Tenure of Office Act by attempting to appoint Lorenzo Thomas as secretary of war ad interim on February 21, 1868.

348.28 Caius Verres] Gaius Verres (c. 114 B.C.E.–43), the Roman proconsul of Sicily, 73–71, was prosecuted for corruption by Cicero in 70 B.C.E. The trial ended when Gaius fled Rome and went into exile in Massilia (Marseilles).

348.32   Ross] Edmund G. Ross (1826–1907), Republican senator from Kansas, 1866–71, who voted to acquit Johnson. James Dixon (1814–1873) of Connecticut, James R. Doolittle (1815–1897) of Wisconsin, and Daniel Norton (1829–1870) of Minnesota, three conservative Republicans who supported Johnson's policies, also voted to acquit the president.

350.3   *Frank P. Blair to James O. Broadhead*] An attorney in St. Louis, Broadhead (1819–1898) served as U.S. attorney for the Eastern District of Missouri, 1861–62, and as provost marshal general for the Department of Missouri, 1863–64. Blair's letter was printed, with his approval, in the *New York Herald* on July 3, 1868.

350.8–9   my name . . . the Democratic Convention] Broadhead nominated Frank P. Blair for president on July 9, 1868, after the convention had held eighteen ballots without result (under the rules, a two-thirds majority was required to win the nomination). Blair received thirteen and a half votes on the nineteenth ballot. After Horatio Seymour was nominated on the twenty-second ballot, Blair was unanimously chosen as the vice presidential candidate.

352.19–21   Lord Granby's character . . . without observation.] See *Letters of Junius* (1769–72), letter VII, March 3, 1769. John Manners, marquess of Granby (1721–1770), served as commander-in-chief of the forces, 1766–70. "Junius" may have been the pseudonym of Sir Philip Francis (1740–1818), a senior clerk in the war office.

352.28–29   Governor Seymour . . . resist the drafts] Horatio Seymour (1810–1886), the Democratic governor of New York, 1863–64, had repeatedly criticized the wartime draft as unconstitutional.

353.22–23   little effort . . . Mr. Chase] Chief Justice Chase sought the Democratic presidential nomination in 1868 and gained tentative support from several leading New York Democrats before the convention met, but received no more than four votes during the balloting.

355.1–2   Cardinal Granville] Antoine Perrenot de Granvelle (1517–1586), a French bishop in the service of Philip II of Spain, was chief counselor to Margaret of Parma (1522–1586), the Spanish regent in the Netherlands, 1560–64. He was removed by Philip after leading Dutch nobles protested against his influence.

355.21–22   Henry A. Wise . . . Beauregard.] Wise (1806–1876) was governor of Virginia, 1856–60, and a brigadier general in the Confederate army, 1861–65; Wade Hampton, see note 145.9–10; Robert Toombs, see note 8:10–11; Howell Cobb, see note 142.28–29. Nathan Bedford Forrest (1821–1877), a Tennessee planter and slave trader before the war, served as a Confederate cavalry commander, 1861–65, and was promoted to lieutenant general; after the war he became the first grand wizard of the Ku Klux Klan, 1867–69. Pierre G. T. Beauregard (1818–1893) was a Confederate general, 1861–65. Both Hampton and Forrest were delegates to the 1868 Democratic national convention.

355.22–23   evil spirits cast . . . herd of swine.] See Matthew 8:28–34, Mark 5:1–20, and Luke 8:26–39.

356.4   Arlington Heights] The Union army occupied the estate on Arlington Heights, which Mary Custis Lee (1808–1873) had inherited from her father, on May 24, 1861, and established a national cemetery on its grounds in 1864.

356.21   Colfax] Schuyler Colfax (1823–1885) was a Republican congressman from Indiana, 1855–69, Speaker of the House, 1863–69, and vice president of the United States, 1869–73.

357.3   *Gerrit Smith*] A wealthy New York landowner, Smith (1797–1874) was a philanthropist, social reformer, and abolitionist who helped found the anti-slavery Liberty Party in 1840 and was its presidential candidate in 1848, 1856, and 1860. Stanton and Smith were first cousins.

357.27   read the signs of the times] See Matthew 16:3.

359.12   Being in Ireland] Stanton visited Ireland in 1840.

359.14   Repeal of the Union] Repeal of the Act of Union of 1800, which had abolished the Irish parliament in Dublin.

359.25–26   defeated "negro suffrage" in Kansas.] On November 5, 1867, voters in Kansas defeated a proposed constitutional amendment extending suffrage to black men, 19,421–10,483. In a separate referendum, an amendment enfranchising women was defeated, 19,857–9,070. Stanton and Susan B. Anthony had canvassed the state on behalf of the women's suffrage initiative in the late summer and fall.

360.21–23   cruel and unjust laws . . . wives and daughters.] From 1854 to 1860 Stanton and Anthony had campaigned for the reform of the marital property and inheritance laws in New York State.

360.30   Snake Hill] A hill in what is now Secaucus, New Jersey.

361.12–13   Hester Vaughan . . . sentence of death] Vaughan had immigrated to the United States from England in 1863 intending to marry her suitor, only to discover that he already had a wife and child. While working as a servant near Philadelphia she was allegedly raped by a member of the household and then dismissed after she became pregnant. In February 1868 Vaughan was discovered lying next to a dead newborn child in a Philadelphia boardinghouse. After she was convicted of murder in July and sentenced to death, her case was taken up by a number of women, including the physicians Susan A. Smith (1818–1883) and Clemence Lozier (1813–1888), the journalist Eleanor Kirk (1831–1908), the popular lecturer Anna Dickinson (1842–1932), and Stanton and Anthony, who protested against her trial by an all-male court. John W. Geary (1819–1873), the governor of Pennsylvania, pardoned Vaughan in May 1869 on the condition that she immediately return to England.

361.20–21   Generals Cole and Sickles . . . paramours dead] Brevet Major General George W. Cole (1827–1875), a businessman from Syracuse, New York, shot and killed his longtime neighbor and attorney, L. Harris Hiscock (1824–1867), in the lobby of an Albany hotel on June 4, 1867, shortly after learning that Hiscock had "dishonored" his wife, Mary Barto Cole (1832–1910). After his first trial ended in a hung jury, Cole was acquitted on December 7, 1868, by a jury that professed doubt as to his sanity at the moment of the shooting. Daniel E. Sickles (1819–1914), a Democratic congressman from New York, 1857–61, shot and killed Philip Barton Key (1818–1859), U.S. attorney for Washington and the son of Francis Scott Key, on February 25, 1859, shortly after learning that Key was having an affair with his wife, Teresa Bagioli Sickles (1836–1867). Sickles was acquitted of murder in April 1859, becoming the first defendant to successfully use the defense of temporary insanity in an American court. He later became a major general in the Union army, lost a leg at Gettysburg, and served in the Carolinas during Reconstruction (see note 318.19–20).

362.37–38   elections of '67 . . . against Negro Suffrage] See Chronology, October–November 1867.

364.2–3   *Joint Resolution Proposing the Fifteenth Amendment*] The final version of the resolution was approved by the House, 144–44, on February 25, 1869, and by the Senate, 39–13, on February 26. An earlier version of the amendment, prohibiting the denial of suffrage on account of "race, color, nativity, property, education, or creed," was approved by the Senate, 31–27, but was rejected by the House, 133–37.

"LET US HAVE PEACE," 1869–1873

372.3–4   *Frederick Douglass . . . on Suffrage*] Douglass and Anthony spoke on the first day of the third annual meeting of the American Equal Rights Association, held at Steinway Hall in New York City on May 12, 1869. The AERA had been founded in May 1866 for the purpose of securing "equal rights to all American citizens, especially the right of suffrage, irrespective of race, color, or sex." The remarks made by Douglass are taken from the *New York World*, while Anthony's remarks are taken from a shorthand reporter's transcription preserved in the Susan B. Anthony Papers in the Library of Congress.

372.11–12   Rev. Mr. Frothingham . . . the President.] Octavius Brooks Frothingham (1822–1895), a former Unitarian minister, was the founder of the Independent Liberal Church in New York City. In the absence of Lucretia Mott (1793–1880), the president of the AERA since its founding, the meeting was presided over by Elizabeth Cady Stanton, the first vice president of the Association. In her address, Stanton referred to "the daughters of Adams, Jefferson, and Patrick Henry"; protested against making American women "the political inferiors of unlettered and unwashed ditch-diggers, boot-blacks, butchers and barbers, fresh from the slave plantations of the South"; and said: "Think of Patrick and Sambo and Hans and Yung Tung, who do not know the difference between a monarchy and a republic, who cannot read the Declaration of Independence or Webster's spelling book, making laws for Lucretia Mott, Ernestine L. Rose, Susan B. Anthony or Anna E. Dickinson."

372.24–25 fifteen States of the Union.] The fifteen states where slavery existed at the beginning of the Civil War.

373.2 convention in Boston] The women's rights convention held in Boston, November 18–19, 1868, that founded the New England Woman Suffrage Association. Howe was chosen as the Association's first president.

373.26–27 Tilton, Powell, & Phillips] Theodore Tilton (1835–1907), editor of the New York weekly newspaper *The Independent*; Aaron Macy Powell (1832–1899), editor of the *National Anti-Slavery Standard*; and Wendell Phillips.

373.28 the Constitutional Convention] The New York constitutional convention, held in Albany, June 1867–February 1868.

374.22–24 Alexander Hamilton . . . whole being."] Cf. *The Federalist No. 79*, May 28, 1788: "In the general course of human nature, *a power over a man's subsistence amounts to a power over his will.*"

375.5 our working women's meetings] The Working Women's Association, founded by Anthony in September 1868.

375.7 Mr Croly] David Goodman Croly (1829–1899), managing editor of the *New York World*.

375.28–29 the business of this association] Anthony and Stanton broke away from the American Equal Rights Association in May 1869 and founded the National Woman Suffrage Association, which opposed ratification of the Fifteenth Amendment. The AERA dissolved, and in November 1869 Lucy Stone, Julia Ward Howe, and Henry Brown Blackwell (1825–1909) founded the American Woman Suffrage Association, which supported the Fifteenth Amendment. The two organizations merged in 1890 to form the National American Woman Suffrage Association.

377.4 *November 3, 1869.*] Clemenceau wrote this article after his return to France from the United States.

381.8–9 my proclamation . . . the reasons] The proclamation referred to several recent crimes committed in Alamance County, including the murder in Graham of Wyatt Outlaw (c. 1820–1870). A carpenter, former Union soldier, active Republican, and the first African American to serve as the town constable, Outlaw was taken from his home on the night of February 26, 1870, by several dozen Klansmen and hanged from a tree near the county courthouse. In December 1871 Judge Albion W. Tourgée convened a grand jury that indicted eighteen men for Outlaw's murder, but the indictments were dismissed after the state legislature passed a bill in 1873 extending amnesty to all crimes committed by members of secret organizations.

381.36–37 commanding general of this department] Brigadier General Edward R. S. Canby (1817–1873) commanded the Department of Virginia, April

1869–April 1870. At the direction of Secretary of War William W. Belknap (1829–1890), Canby sent two infantry companies to Alamance County, where they remained until May 1870.

382.4   the State law] The law gave the governor the power to proclaim a state of insurrection, summon the militia, and request federal assistance. It was passed on January 29, 1870.

382.5–7   pamphlet . . . Lenoir County prisoners] *Testimony of the witnesses in the preliminary examination of the Lenoir County prisoners: the secrets of the Ku-Klux-Klan, &c., &c., &c.* (1869) recorded the testimony given in New Bern, North Carolina, August 31–September 3, 1869, by several Klansmen charged with murder, arson, and conspiracy.

383.16–20   "at the time . . . bound to respect"] A paraphrase of Chief Justice Taney's opinion in the Dred Scott case.

383.33   The Father . . . Farewell Address] President Washington published his farewell address on September 19, 1796.

384.3–4   first annual message . . . eighth message.] Washington delivered his first annual message to Congress on January 8, 1790, and his eighth on December 7, 1796.

385.2   *Albion W. Tourgée to Joseph C. Abbott*] For Abbott, see note 28.8–9. Tourgée's letter was printed in the *New-York Tribune* on August 3, 1870.

385.5–6   John W. Stephens] A native of North Carolina, Stephens (1834–1870) was a tobacco trader who had briefly served in the Confederate army. He later became an agent for the Freedmen's Bureau, joined the Republican Party, and was elected to the North Carolina senate in 1868.

385.7–8   the Court House] The Caswell County Courthouse in Yanceyville, North Carolina.

385.17   stabbed . . . hanged on a hook] John G. Lea (1843–1935), a former Klansman, confessed to his role in Stephens' murder in a document signed and witnessed on July 2, 1919. His statement, made at the request of the North Carolina Historical Commission, was made public only after Lea's death in 1935. Lea described how Stephens was lured to his death by Frank Wiley (c. 1825–1888), a Democrat who had served as county sheriff before the Civil War: "A democratic convention was in session in the court room on the second floor of the courthouse in Yanceyville, to nominate county officers and members of the Legislature. Mr. Wiley, who was in the convention, brought Stevens down to a rear room on the ground floor, then used for the storage of wood for the courthouse. I had ordered all the Ku Klux Klan in the county to meet at Yanceyville that day, with their uniforms under their saddles, and they were present. Mr. Wiley came to me and suggested that it would be a better plan, as Stevens had approached him to run on the republican ticket for sheriff and he had told him that he would let him know that day, to fool him down stairs, and so just before the convention closed, Wiley beckoned to Stevens and carried him down stairs, and Captain

Mitchell, James Denny and Joe Fowler went into the room and Wiley came out. Mitchell proceeded to disarm him (he had three pistols on his body). He soon came out and left Jim Denny with a pistol at his head and went to Wiley and told him that he couldn't kill him himself. Wiley came to me and said, 'You must do something; I am exposed unless you do.' Immediately I rushed into the room with eight or ten men, found him sitting flat on the floor. He arose and approached me and we went and sat down where the wood had been taken away, in an opening in the wood on the wood-pile, and he asked me not to let them kill him. Captain Mitchell rushed at him with a rope, drew it around his neck, put his feet against his chest and by that time about a half dozen men rushed up: Tom Oliver, Pink Morgan, Dr. Richmond and Joe Fowler. Stevens was then stabbed in the breast and also in the neck by Tom Oliver, and the knife was thrown at his feet and the rope left around his neck. We all came out, closed the door and locked it on the outside and took the key and threw it into County Line Creek."

385.32 election in August next] The election, held on August 4, 1870, resulted in the Conservative Party winning control of the state legislature.

387.39 Four thousand or 5,000 houses] Tourgée later asserted that this figure appeared in the *Tribune* in error, and that in his original letter he had estimated that the Klan had broken into four or five hundred houses.

389.21 *en masque*] In disguise.

391.4 an Election] In the election held in South Carolina on October 19, 1870, the Republicans reelected Governor Scott, retained control of the state legislature, and were victorious in all four congressional races.

392.34–35 Senator Robertson and Col Patterson] A native of the state, Thomas J. Robertson (1823–1897) was a Republican senator from South Carolina, 1868–77. Born in Pennsylvania, John J. Patterson (1830–1912) moved to South Carolina in 1869 and served as a Republican senator, 1873–79. Patterson was indicted for bribery and corruption in 1877, but the charges were later dropped.

394.23 Tuesday] Tuesday, March 14, 1871.

395.15 Gen. Farnsworth] John F. Farnsworth (1820–1897) was a Republican congressman from Illinois, 1857–61 and 1863–73. He served as an officer in the Union army, 1861–63, and was promoted to brigadier general.

395.35–36 Mr. Beck of Kentucky] James B. Beck (1822–1890) was a Democratic congressman from Kentucky, 1867–75, and a senator, 1877–90.

398.10–11 "A hunted seeker . . . sake."] John Greenleaf Whittier (1807–1892), "The Exiles" (1840), lines 39–40.

403.3–4 possible chance of the doctor's recovery.] John Winsmith (1802–1888) recovered and testified on July 11, 1871, in Spartanburg, South Carolina, before a select congressional committee investigating Klan violence.

403.11 represented the people in the Legislature] Winsmith served in the state legislature 1830–32, 1852–62, and 1865–66.

404.11–12 "A tale unfold . . . thy soul."] *Hamlet*, I.v.15–16.

405.30 Mr. SHELLABARGER] Samuel Shellabarger (1817–1896) was a Republican congressman from Ohio, 1861–63, 1865–69, and 1871–73. He had introduced the proposed enforcement bill on March 28, 1871.

408.9 "we are not . . . not stone,"] Cf. *Julius Caesar*, III.ii.142.

408.17 "Bloody treason . . . us."] *Julius Caesar*, III.ii.192.

408.18–19 "and if we perish, we perish!"] See 2 Kings 7:4.

409.26–31 Madison . . . in war."] The passage Garfield cites is an observation regarding the United Netherlands, the subject of *The Federalist No. 20*, published on December 11, 1787. Madison examined the history of the Amphictyonic and Achæan Leagues in *The Federalist No. 18*, December 7, 1787.

410.17 Sedan] Napoleon III surrendered to the Prussian army at Sedan on September 2, 1870, and was deposed on September 4 when the revolutionary Government of National Defense assumed power in Paris.

410.24–25 fearful reaction from despotism.] An insurrection in Paris on March 18, 1871, led to the formation of the revolutionary Commune on March 28.

412.5 President . . . recent message] Grant sent a special message to Congress on March 23, 1871, asking for the passage of legislation that would "effectually secure life, liberty, and property and the enforcement of law in all parts of the United States."

415.32 Judge Advocate General] Joseph Holt (1807–1894), judge advocate general of the U.S. Army, 1862–75.

415.38–416.1 Petition of Right . . . Charles II.] The Habeas Corpus Act of 1679.

416.1–3 lord chief justice . . . a grand jury] In 1865 Edward Eyre (1815–1901), the British governor of Jamaica, brutally repressed a rebellion by black farm laborers in Morant Bay. Eyre believed that George William Gordon (1820–65), a mixed-race member of the colonial assembly, had planned the uprising, and ordered that Gordon be arrested in Kingston, where martial law was not in effect, and taken to Morant Bay, where he was tried for high treason before a military tribunal and hanged. An attempt to prosecute Eyre for abuse of office failed in 1868 when a grand jury refused to indict him after being charged by Sir Colin Blackburn (1813–1896), a justice of the Queen's Bench. In June 1868 Sir Alexander Cockburn (1802–1880), the lord chief justice of England, 1859–1880, publicly disagreed with the interpretation of the law presented to the grand jury by Blackburn.

416.5–6 same judge . . . Queen vs. Nelson] Cockburn had charged a grand jury in *Regina v. Nelson and Brand*, an attempt in 1867 to prosecute Colonel Alexander Nelson, who had established the tribunal that tried

George William Gordon, and Lieutenant Herbert Brand, the naval officer who had presided over the tribunal. The grand jury declined to indict either officer.

416.9–10   The Nation . . . Mr. Mulford] *The Nation: The Foundations of Civil Order and Political Life in the United States* (1871) by Elisha Mulford (1833–1885), an Episcopal priest. Mulford later published *The Republic of God, an Institute of Theology* (1881).

416.34   Mr. Justice Davis] David Davis (1815–1886) was an Illinois circuit judge, 1848–62, an associate justice of the U.S. Supreme Court, 1862–77, and an independent senator from Illinois, 1877–83.

417.32   The Chief Justice] Salmon P. Chase.

418.16   "cry havoc . . . dogs of war?"] *Julius Caesar*, III.i.273.

418.28   House will grant general amnesty] On April 10, 1871, the House approved, 134–45, an amnesty bill similar to the one eventually enacted in 1872; see note 425.34–36.

418.34–36   called upon . . . actual necessity] Congressman Shellabarger modified the bill to meet the objections of Republican moderates such as Garfield, and an amended version was approved by the House, 118–91, on April 6. The final version was passed on April 19 by the House, 93–74, with Garfield voting in favor, and by the Senate, 36–13. As enacted, the law did not authorize the president to declare martial law, and his power to suspend the writ of habeas corpus expired with the end of the next session of Congress (in effect, in June 1872). The second section of the Enforcement Act of 1871 was struck down by the U.S. Supreme Court in *United States v. Harris* (1883), which ruled that while the federal government could protect citizens against the denial of their constitutional rights by state action, it lacked the power to punish the denial of rights by private individuals.

419.6   the CHAIRMAN] The Joint Select Committee on the Condition of Affairs in the Late Insurrectionary States was formed by Congress on April 20, 1871, to investigate the activities of the Ku Klux Klan. The committee submitted its majority and minority reports on February 19, 1872, along with twelve volumes of testimony taken in North and South Carolina, Georgia, Florida, Alabama, and Mississippi. Horace Maynard (1814–1882), a Republican from Tennessee, was the chairman of the subcommittee that examined witnesses in Georgia in the fall of 1871. Maynard served in Congress, 1857–63 and 1866–75, as attorney general of Tennessee, 1863–65, as minister to Turkey, 1875–80, and as postmaster general, 1880–81.

419.16   John Walthall] Maria Carter was one of several witnesses who testified about the murder of John Walthall, including his widow, Tilda Walthall, and her husband, Jasper Carter.

422.14   Mr. BAYARD] Thomas F. Bayard (1828–1898) was a Democratic senator from Delaware, 1869–85, who later served as secretary of state, 1885–89, and ambassador to Great Britain, 1893–97.

425.2–3   *Horace Greeley . . . Liberal Republican Convention*] See Chronology, May 1–3, 1872.

425.34–36   political rights and franchises . . . reestablished] The House had passed a general amnesty bill on May 13, 1872, that removed the disabilities imposed by Section 3 of the Fourteenth Amendment from all persons, "except Senators and Representatives of the Thirty-Sixth and Thirty-Seventh Congresses, officers in the judicial, military, and naval service of the United States, heads of Departments, and foreign ministers of the United States." The bill was passed by the Senate on May 21, 1872, and signed into law the next day.

428.3–4   *Frederick Douglass . . . New York City*] Douglass gave this speech at a Republican campaign meeting held at the Cooper Institute on September 25, 1872.

429.7   writing to Mr. Sumner] On July 11, 1872, twenty-four "citizens of color" wrote to Senator Charles Sumner from Washington, D.C., and asked "the purest and best friend of our race" for his opinion on the presidential election. Sumner, already known for his harsh public denunciations of Grant, replied on July 29 in an open letter addressed to "Colored Citizens" in which he endorsed Greeley for the first time.

429.18–19   colored citizens . . . Faneuil Hall] Douglass had addressed a meeting of black voters held in Faneuil Hall in Boston on September 5, 1872.

430.38–39   words of the leading traitor] Edwards Pierrepont (see Biographical Notes), an earlier speaker at the meeting, had quoted from a speech made by Jefferson Davis at Augusta, Georgia, on May 26, 1872, in which Davis said: "You know me only as the representative of your cause. That cause is dear to me—more precious even than life, and I glory in its remembrance."

431.9–10   three thousand . . . Pentecost.] See Acts 2:1–41.

431.17   Prodigal Son] See Luke 15:11–32.

433.24   Mr. Black] Jeremiah S. Black (1810–1883) was a justice of the Pennsylvania supreme court, 1851–57, attorney general, March 1857–December 1860, and secretary of state, December 1860–March 1861. Black appeared before the U.S. Supreme Court as a private attorney in numerous cases, including *Ex parte Milligan* and the *Slaughterhouse Cases*, and drafted President Johnson's veto of the first Reconstruction Act.

434.33   The Chairman] Luther R. Marsh (1813–1902) was a successful New York attorney and occasional orator.

435.3   *James S. Pike: South Carolina Prostrate*] This was the first in a series of six reports from South Carolina that Pike published in the *New-York Tribune* in 1873; the remaining articles appeared on April 8, 10, 11, 12, and 19. The series was collected in *The Prostrate State: South Carolina Under Negro Government* (1874).

436.7–8   George McDuffie and Robert Y. Hayne] McDuffie (1790–1851) was a congressman from South Carolina, 1821–34, governor, 1834–36, and a senator, 1842–46. Hayne (1791–1839) was a senator from South Carolina, 1823–32, and governor, 1832–34.

436.10–11 Jefferson . . . God is just."] Cf. *Notes on the State of Virginia* (1787), Query XVIII, "Manners": "Indeed I tremble for my country when I reflect that God is just."

439.6–7 famous schooner Wanderer] The *Wanderer* illegally landed four hundred African slaves on the Georgia coast in November 1858.

441.20 rejected constitutionally] The Senate failed to ratify the Santo Domingo annexation treaty by a vote of 28–28 on June 30, 1870.

THE END OF RECONSTRUCTION, 1873–1877

449.2–3 *Levi Nelson . . . Colfax Massacre*] Levi Nelson and Benjamin Brim testified at the trial of nine white men facing federal conspiracy charges for their role in a massacre committed in Grant Parish, Louisiana, on Easter Sunday in 1873. Grant Parish was formed in north-central Louisiana in 1869 out of portions of two existing parishes. It was named after the newly inaugurated president, and Colfax, the parish seat, was named after the new vice president. The 1872 elections in Louisiana, which produced rival governors, lieutenant governors, and legislatures at the state level, also resulted in rival claimants to local offices in Grant Parish. On March 25, 1873, the Republican parish judge and sheriff took possession of the courthouse in Colfax, which was soon guarded by an improvised militia of black residents. Christopher Columbus Nash (1838–1922), the Fusionist sheriff, formed a posse to seize the courthouse, and entered Colfax on April 13, 1873, with about 140 men, about half of them Confederate veterans. Equipped with superior firearms and a small cannon, the white posse drove about 150 poorly armed black militiamen from their defensive positions, set fire to the courthouse, and began killing prisoners. At least sixty-two, and possibly as many as eighty-one, African Americans were killed in the fighting and subsequent massacre. Three members of the white posse were killed in the fighting; two of them may have been fatally wounded by fire from their own side. James R. Beckwith (1838–1912), the U.S. attorney for Louisiana, brought nine defendants—William Cruikshank, Austin P. Gibbons, John Hadnot, Tom Hickman, Bill Irwin, Alfred Lewis, Donas and Prudhomme Lemoine, and Clement Penn—to trial in New Orleans on February 23, 1874, charged with conspiring to violate the Enforcement Act of 1870. The trial ended on March 16, with the acquittal of Lewis and a hung jury regarding the remaining defendants. Beckwith retried the case from May 18 to June 10, and won convictions against Cruikshank, Hadnot, and Irwin, who faced possible sentences of ten years in prison. William B. Woods (1824–1887), the federal circuit court judge who tried the case, rejected motions for a new trial on June 27, but the same day Joseph P. Bradley (1813–1892), the supreme court justice assigned to the Fifth Circuit, overturned the verdicts. The case went on appeal to the U.S. Supreme Court, which unanimously upheld

Bradley's decision on March 27, 1876. In his opinion for the Court, Chief Justice Morrison R. Waite (1816–1888) severely limited the reach of the Enforcement Act by ruling that the Fourteenth Amendment did not protect the right to assemble, to bear arms, or to vote, nor did it protect citizens against the criminal acts of private individuals.

449.12 old man Hadnot] James Hadnot (1821–73), the state representative from Grant Parish, was fatally wounded on April 13, 1873, possibly by gunfire from his own side. His nephew, John Hadnot, was one of the Colfax defendants.

451.9 A. Tillman] Alexander Tillman (1843–1873), a black farmer, was one of the leaders of the courthouse defenders.

452.20–21 Jesse McKinney] McKinney (1834–1873), a black farmer in Grant Parish, was shot by white men on horseback in front of his wife and six-year-old son on April 5, 1873. His murder caused hundreds of African American men, women, and children to seek safety at the Colfax courthouse.

455.4 Shaw] Daniel Wesley Shaw, the white Republican sheriff of Grant Parish, had testified as a defense witness. Shaw claimed that he had been held prisoner by the black defenders of the courthouse and denied that he had authorized them to act as a posse.

456.4 *Speech . . . Civil Rights Bill*] Charles Sumner had introduced a new civil rights bill in 1870, but was unable to advance it through the Senate. In December 1873 Massachusetts congressman Benjamin F. Butler (see note 345.24) introduced a version of Sumner's bill in the House. The bill reported by Butler prohibited racial discrimination in public schools, public accommodations, public conveyances, places of amusement, and cemeteries, and allowed plaintiffs to seek damages in the federal courts.

456.22–23 grateful State . . . Fort Griswold] Fort Griswold was captured by Benedict Arnold during his raid on New London, Connecticut, on September 6, 1781.

456.36 among the black people] Elliott quotes from the text of Greene's letter printed in *History of the Republic of the United States* (7 vols., 1857–64) by John Church Hamilton (1792–1882), Alexander Hamilton's son. In the text printed in *The Papers of Alexander Hamilton* (1961), edited by Harold C. Syrett, this phrase appears as "among the back people."

457.6–7 his dispatch] Jackson's report to Secretary of War James Monroe, January 9, 1815.

457.8 Mr. BECK] See note 395.35–36.

457.26–28 a State . . . declaring her neutrality] Beriah Magoffin (1815–1885), the Democratic governor of Kentucky, 1859–62, proclaimed his state's neutrality on May 20, 1861. His neutrality policy collapsed in early September 1861 when both Confederate and Union troops entered the state.

457.36 Mr. STEPHENS] Stephens (see note 8.10–11) served in Congress as a Democrat from Georgia, 1873–82.

458.12–13 *Lieber on Civil Liberty*] Francis Lieber (1800–1872), *On Civil Liberty and Self-Government* (1853).

458.17–20 Natural liberty . . . *American Republic*] The quotation from Alexander Hamilton's pamphlet *The Farmer Refuted* (1775) appears in *History of the Republic of the United States* (1857–64) by John Church Hamilton (1792–1882).

458.37–459.4 Is it . . . maintained?] From a speech by Hamilton in the constitutional convention on June 29, 1787, as recorded by Robert Yates.

459.5–10 "the sacred . . . mortal power."] From *The Farmer Refuted* (1775).

459.11 the Slaughter-house cases!] The cases were decided 5–4 by the Supreme Court on April 14, 1873.

461.16 Chancellor Kent] See note 216.20–26.

461.26–27 Associate Justice Miller] Samuel Miller (1816–1890) served as an associate justice of the Supreme Court, 1862–90.

467.25 Mr. DAWES] Henry L. Dawes (1816–1903) was a Republican congressman from Massachusetts, 1857–75, and a senator, 1875–93.

468.3–5 Massachusetts in 1857 . . . constitution] The amendment adopted in 1857 required that new voters be able to read the Massachusetts constitution in English and write their own name.

470.20 harmless speculations in his study] Stephens was the author of *A Constitutional View of the Late War Between the States* (2 vols., 1868–70).

470.37–39 that gentleman shocked . . . corner-stone.] See note 98.22.

471.21–24 Mr. HARRIS . . . white men alone] John T. Harris (1823–1899) was a Democratic congressman from Virginia, 1859–61 and 1871–81. During the previous day's debate on the civil rights bill, Harris had said: "And I say there is not one gentleman upon this floor who can honestly say he really believes that the colored man is created his equal." When Alonzo J. Ransier (1834–1882), a black congressman from South Carolina, responded by saying, "I can," Harris replied: "Of course you can; but I am speaking to the white men of the House; and, Mr. Speaker, I do not wish to be interrupted again by him." Later, Harris asked "every gentleman on the other side of the House" to admit they were bound to respect the prejudice "that the colored man was inferior to the white." Ransier again objected, saying "I deny that," and Harris responded: "I do not allow you to interrupt me. Sit down; I am talking to white men; I am talking to gentlemen."

474.28–30 "reaped down . . . Sabaoth,"] James 5:4.

474.34–39   "Entreat me . . . and me."] Ruth 1:16–17.

475.7   Friday last] Friday, January 16, 1874.

475.28–29   when Grant . . . on his works"] Grant successfully demanded the "unconditional and immediate surrender" of the Confederate garrison at Fort Donelson, Tennessee, on February 16, 1862.

476.38   Credit Mobilier] Crédit Mobilier, a finance company organized to pay for the construction of the Union Pacific Railroad, had sold stock at a discount to several senators and congressmen in 1867. An exposé by the *New York Sun* in 1872 led to a growing scandal that had implicated James A. Garfield, House Speaker James G. Blaine, and Vice President Schuyler Colfax.

477.36   a Chief Justice] In December 1873 Grant nominated Attorney General George H. Williams (1823–1910) to succeed Chief Justice Salmon P. Chase, who had died in May. Williams encountered opposition in the Senate, in part because of the use of government funds to purchase a carriage for his wife, and Grant withdrew his nomination on January 8, 1874. The next day he nominated Caleb Cushing (1800–1879), a Massachusetts attorney who had served as attorney general in the Pierce administration, 1853–57. Cushing drew opposition due to his age, and when a letter Cushing had written to Jefferson Davis in March 1861, recommending a former clerk for a position in the Confederate government, was made public, his nomination was withdrawn. On January 19 Grant nominated Morrison R. Waite (1816–1888), an Ohio attorney who was unanimously confirmed by the Senate on January 21.

479.20–21   answer . . . Mr. VANCE] Robert B. Vance (1828–1899), a Democratic congressman from North Carolina, 1873–85, had spoken against the bill on January 10, 1874.

479.25   Mr. ROBBINS] William M. Robbins (1828–1905) was a Democratic congressman from North Carolina, 1873–79.

481.4–5   Charleston . . . Richmond] Black regiments were among the Union troops that occupied Charleston, South Carolina, on February 18, 1865, and that entered Richmond on April 3, 1865.

482.12   Missa Douglas] Margaret Crittenden Douglass (b. 1822), a white woman born in Washington, D.C., and raised in South Carolina, opened a school for free black children in Norfolk, Virginia, in June 1852. Douglass was arrested in May 1853 and charged with violating the state law against assembling African Americans, free or enslaved, for the purpose of teaching them to read and write. She denied having abolitionist sympathies and told the court that her motive was a wish that black children be able to read the Bible. In January 1854 Douglass was sentenced to one month in jail. She moved to Philadelphia after her release and published *Educational Laws of Virginia: The Personal Narrative of Mrs. Margaret Douglass* (1854).

484.25–26   The gentleman . . . our brave eagle.] In his speech on January

24, 1874, Robbins denounced "the leveling spirit" of "so-called universal equality men" and sarcastically suggested that the eagle be replaced as the national emblem by the crow, whose "plumage is of the favorite color, so popular with the dominant party."

487.22–23   the warriors . . . hair's breadth;"] See Judges 20:16.

489.19   Mr. Cox] Samuel S. Cox (1824–1889) was a Democratic congressman from Ohio, 1857–65, and from New York, 1869–1873 and 1873–85.

490.6–7   civil-rights bill . . . seven years] Sumner described his bill as a supplementary measure to the Civil Rights Act of 1866.

491.34   Cardozo] Francis L. Cardozo (1836–1903), the son of a free black woman and a white man, served as secretary of state of South Carolina, 1868–72, and as state treasurer, 1872–77.

492.30   gentleman from Tennessee] Roderick R. Butler (1827–1902) was a Republican congressman from Tennessee, 1867–75 and 1887–89. In his speech on the civil rights bill on June 5, 1874, Butler said: "As to hotels, the laws regulate them much better than Congress can. The colored people do not want to eat and sleep with the whites; they want, if a hotel-keeper charges them as much as he charges the white guests, to have as good bed and as good diet, and that certainly is just and right. And I have heard of no complaint in my State. I find in traveling along the railroads that when the trains stop at the eating-houses a table is provided for the colored passengers, supplied with the same eatables and served by the same servants as the whites, and they all pay the same price, and both seem content."

493.3–11   Mr. Brightly's . . . or otherwise."] Frederick C. Brightly (1812–1888), *An Analytical Digest of the Laws of the United States* (1858). The passage quoted by Rapier is taken from *Corfield v. Coryell* (1823), an opinion written by U.S. Supreme Court Justice Bushrod Washington (1762–1829) while sitting as a circuit judge in the Eastern District of Pennsylvania.

497.40   Kentucky's chief Representative] James B. Beck (see note 395.35–36) immigrated to the United States from Scotland in 1838.

499.27   Wade, Giddings, Julian] Benjamin F. Wade (1800–1878), senator from Ohio, 1851–69; Joshua R. Giddings (1795–1864), congressman from Ohio, 1838–42 and 1842–59; George W. Julian (1817–1899), congressman from Indiana, 1849–51 and 1861–71.

500.16–18   the chief . . . history of the war] Jefferson Davis sailed for Great Britain and France on January 25, 1874, and returned on June 16. His departure came shortly before the publication of Joseph E. Johnston's *Narrative of Military Operations*, in which the former Confederate general strongly criticized Davis's conduct of the war.

502.23–24   Jews could sing . . . streams] See Psalm 137.

504.28   F. F. V.'s] First Families of Virginia.

504.30–31 address one . . . white men."] See note 471.21–22.

504.34 Duke de Broglie] Jacques Victor Albert, duc de Broglie (1821–1901), premier and foreign minister of France, 1873–74.

506.11 Mr. SLOSS] Joseph H. Sloss (1826–1911), Democratic congressman from Alabama, 1871–75.

506.25–26 very prominent colored gentleman] Born in North Carolina, J. Sella Martin (1832–1876) escaped from slavery in 1856. An active abolitionist and campaigner for equal rights, he served as the pastor of the Joy Street Baptist Church in Boston and of the Fifteenth Street Presbyterian Church in Washington, D.C., before moving to Louisiana in 1870.

506.27–29 McEnery government . . . the President] See Chronology, November 1872–January 1873. The committee met with Grant on December 19, 1872.

507.33–34 appoint members . . . foreign courts] In 1869 Grant appointed Ebenezer Don Carlos Bassett (1833–1908), the principal of the Philadelphia Institute for Colored Youth, as American minister to Haiti. Bassett, the first African American to hold a diplomatic post, served until 1877.

509.19–20 rule in hell . . . heaven.] Cf. John Milton, *Paradise Lost*, Book I, line 263.

509.25 *imperium in imperio*] A sovereignty within a sovereignty.

509.27–28 summary massacre . . . Gibson county, Tennessee] A white mob broke into the county jail in Trenton, Tennessee, on August 26, 1874, re-moved sixteen black men who had been accused of plotting an armed uprising against the local white population, and murdered at least five of them. Federal prosecutors later charged fourteen men in connection with the killings, but were unable to secure any convictions.

509.29–31 cold-blooded murder . . . "White Leaguers."] Members of the White League murdered six white Republicans, including a parish tax collec-tor, registrar, and justice of the peace, near Coushatta, Louisiana, on August 30, 1874. The White League also murdered at least five black men in and around Coushatta, August 25–31.

509.31–35 Garrard county, Kentucky . . . burned] On August 19, 1874, fighting broke out in Lancaster, Kentucky, between supporters of the Demo-cratic and Republican candidates in the recent county elections. The house of William Sellers, a Republican member of the state house of representatives, was burned on August 22, and at least two men, one white and one black, were killed in the rioting.

510.16 "set on fire of hell."] James 3:6.

510.38 our Boston dailies] The *Boston Post*, in "An Administrative War," Sep-tember 2, 1874.

512.20 "We tell you . . . Natchitoches *Vindicator*] In "To Our Colored Citizens," July 18, 1874.

512.31–32 Louisville *Courier-Journal* says] In an editorial titled "The Pistol in Kentucky," August 13, 1874.

513.28–36 "Ephraim is joined . . . upon you."] Hosea 4:17, 12:1, 7, 5:9, 10:13, 12.

514.3–4 a new heart and a right spirit] Cf. Ezekiel 18:31.

514.5–11 "their works . . . into a viper."] Isaiah 59:6–8, 5.

514.18–19 President Grant to General Belknap] On September 2, 1874, Grant wrote to Secretary of War William W. Belknap: "The recent atrocities in the South, particularly in Louisiana, Alabama, and South Carolina, show a disregard for law, civil rights and personal protection that ought not to be tolerated in any civilized government." The president directed Belknap to consult with Attorney General Williams and to "order troops as to be available in cases of necessity."

516.19 M'ENERY and PENN] John McEnery (1833–1891), a lawyer from Monroe who had served as a Confederate officer, was nominated for governor of Louisiana in 1872 by a Fusion alliance of Democrats, Liberal Republicans, and Reformers (see Chronology, 1872–74). Davidson B. Penn (1836–1902), a New Orleans businessman and former Confederate officer, was the Fusion candidate for lieutenant governor in 1872.

516.27 KELLOGG] William Pitt Kellogg (1830–1918), a lawyer from Illinois who had served as a Union officer, was collector of the port of New Orleans, 1865–68, a Republican senator from Louisiana, 1868–72, and governor, 1873–77. Kellogg returned to the Senate as a Republican, 1877–83, and served in Congress, 1883–85.

522.15 the governor] Elisha Baxter (1827–1899), a wartime Unionist, was the Republican governor of Arkansas, 1873–74.

522.30 the governor chosen] Augustus H. Garland (1832–1899), a Democrat, was governor of Arkansas, 1874–77, a senator, 1877–85, and attorney general in the first Cleveland administration, 1885–89.

522.31 the lieutenant-governor] Volney V. Smith (1841–1897) was the Republican lieutenant governor of Arkansas, 1873–74. His challenge to Garland won little support, and he fled the state after the new governor obtained a warrant for his arrest. In 1875 Grant appointed Smith consul to St. Thomas, a position he held until the election of Grover Cleveland in 1884. Smith returned to Arkansas in 1888 and died in the state mental asylum.

522.37–38 Congress is now . . . I have declined] On February 6, 1875, the congressional committee investigating Arkansas affairs recommended accepting the new state government. Grant disagreed and suggested replacing Garland with Joseph Brooks, the Reform Republican candidate in 1872 (see Chronology, April–May 1874). The House rejected the president's recommendation and voted, 150–81, on March 2 to recognize the Garland government as legitimate, a decision Grant accepted.

525.27–28   murdered men . . . Vicksburg, Miss.] See Chronology, December 1874.

528.7–13   the troops . . . be ejected.] See Chronology, January 1875.

529.30–31   ride of Winchester . . . Five Forks] At dawn on October 19, 1864, Confederate troops surprised Union forces at Cedar Creek, Virginia, and drove them from their positions. Sheridan, who was returning to his command from a conference in Washington, learned of the attack in Winchester and rode to the front, rallying stragglers and directing a successful counterattack. Union troops led by Sheridan broke through the Confederate lines at Five Forks, Virginia, on April 1, 1865, turning the western flank of the Confederate defenses at Petersburg.

530.27   usurpation of Judge Durell] Edward H. Durell (1810–1887) was a federal district court judge in Louisiana, 1863–74. When the 1872 Louisiana state election resulted in conflicting sets of returns, Durell ruled in favor of the Republicans, at one point ordering the U.S. marshal to seize the statehouse in New Orleans. He resigned from the bench in December 1874 after the House Judiciary Committee recommended his impeachment for exceeding his authority during the election dispute and for alleged corruption in his handling of bankruptcy cases.

531.9–10   prolong the existence . . . two years] On April 14, 1870, the Senate had rejected, 25–24, an amendment to the bill readmitting Georgia that would have postponed the elections for the next general assembly from November 1870 to November 1872. (The legislative elections were held in December 1870; see Chronology.)

531.11   Governor Bullock] Rufus Bullock (1834–1907) was the Republican governor of Georgia from July 1868 to October 1871, when he resigned and fled the state to avoid impeachment and possible criminal prosecution on corruption charges.

531.32   Mr. MORTON] Oliver P. Morton; see Biographical Notes.

532.36   Marshal Packard] A former Union army officer from Maine, Stephen B. Packard (1839–1922) was the U.S. marshal for Louisiana, 1871–76, and had served as chairman of the 1872 Kellogg campaign.

532.38   the late election] The 1874 election.

535.19–25   As of old . . . KNOW NOT.] Cf. Isaiah 32:7; Proverbs 1:16; Amos 5:10; Isaiah 59:10, 59:8.

536.13   St. Domingo] Saint-Domingue, the French colonial name for Haiti.

536.40–537.7   "This people hath . . . of murderers!"] Cf. Jeremiah 5:23, 26–28, 21, 4:31.

537.13–14   "Why hast . . . before the time?"] Cf. Matthew 8:29.

537.39   Gerrit Smith] See note 357.3.

537.39–40   and being dead, he yet speaketh] Cf. Hebrews 11:4.

538.14   "Bull Run panic"] The first battle of Bull Run, fought near Manassas Junction, Virginia, on July 21, 1861, ended in a Union retreat that turned into a rout.

539.19   "To err is human,"] Alexander Pope (1688–1744), *Essay on Criticism* (1711), part II.

539.25–32   "The dangers . . . name and quality."] *2 Henry IV*, IV.i.80–87.

540.20–21   bloody riots . . . 1868] A congressional investigating committee in 1869 reported that 1,081 persons were killed in incidents of political violence in Louisiana from April to November 1868; a majority of the victims were black.

540.32   Warmoth] Henry C. Warmoth (1842–1931), the Republican governor of Louisiana, 1868–72, supported the Fusion ticket headed by John McEnery in the 1872 election.

541.16   Justice Strong] William Strong (1802–1895) served as an associate justice of the U.S. Supreme Court, 1870–80.

542.1   the judge] Edward H. Durell; see note 530.27. (Under the existing law, district court judges could hear cases in the circuit court.)

542.2   Antoine] Caesar Antoine (1836–1921), an African American from New Orleans, was the Republican lieutenant governor of Louisiana, 1873–77.

543.11   Judge Woods] William B. Woods (1824–1887) was a federal circuit court judge, 1869–80, and an associate justice of the U.S. Supreme Court, 1880–87.

544.4   Harris] Sidney Harris was fatally wounded on April 13, 1873, possibly by gunfire from his own side.

544.8   Cazabat] Alphonse Cazabat, the Fusion candidate who claimed the office of Grant Parish judge after the 1872 election.

544.10   Register] Robert C. Register, the white Republican who claimed the office of Grant Parish judge in 1873.

546.17–18   marshal of Louisiana] See note 532.36.

551.38   such action be taken by Congress] In March 1875 William A. Wheeler (1819–1887), a Republican congressman from New York, 1861–63 and 1869–77, fashioned a compromise that gave the Democrats control of the state house of representatives, the Republicans control of the state senate, and allowed Kellogg to remain as governor. The compromise was implemented on April 14, 1875.

553.3–4 *Lynch . . . Civil Rights Bill*] An amended version of Sumner's civil rights bill was passed by the Senate, 29–16, on May 22, 1874, two months after his death from a heart attack. The version of the bill before the House on February 3, 1875, no longer prohibited discrimination by cemeteries, and its school provision now allowed authorities to "establish and maintain separate schools and institutions, giving equal educational advantages in all respects, for different classes of persons." A section had also been added forbidding the disqualification of citizens from federal or state jury service on racial grounds.

561.7 father of this bill] Benjamin F. Butler.

561.10 Mr. NIBLACK] William E. Niblack (1822–1893) was a Democratic congressman from Indiana, 1857–61 and 1865–75.

561.28–29 forty acres . . . a mule.] See note 125.9–10.

561.36 Moses lifted . . . wilderness] See Numbers 21:9.

563.1–2 United States judge . . . Virginia] Probably a reference to John C. Underwood (1809–1873), a federal district judge in Virginia, 1863–73. A Radical Republican, Underwood presided over the 1867–68 Virginia constitutional convention.

563.6 Mr. LAMAR] Lucius Quintus Cincinnatus Lamar (1825–1893) served in Congress as a Democrat from Mississippi, 1857–60 and 1873–77, as a senator, 1877–85, as secretary of the interior, 1885–88, and as an associate justice of the U.S. Supreme Court, 1888–93.

563.7–8 judge . . . Mississippi] Robert A. Hill (1811–1900) served as the federal district judge for Mississippi, 1866–91.

563.11 a horse-thief, nor an assassin.] Earlier in the day Niblack had asked Butler why black citizens who were discriminated against could not pursue common-law actions in the state courts. Butler replied that "in certain portions of our country, under our flag, the judges of the local courts have to run away by night to save their lives from assassination," and added: "If bad men are in the majority; if murderers, lawless men, banditti; if horse-thieves are in the majority—men who ride at night in uniform and murder negroes—I think that if the State courts are powerless to punish, jurisdiction should be given to the Federal courts."

565.27 the minority . . . assassins] When William P. McLean (1836–1925), a Democrat from Texas, asked Butler if he was calling "the people in the South horse-thieves and murderers," Butler replied: "O, no; I said a minority."

565.31–32 Mr. VANCE] See note 479.20–21.

566.10–12 Quilp . . . Uriah Heep] Daniel Quilp, the villain of Charles Dickens's *The Old Curiosity Shop* (1841); Uriah Heep, a villainous hypocrite in *David Copperfield* (1849–50).

568.9–11 Abraham said . . . stay here."] See Genesis 13:5–9.

568.19–20 "husks . . . did eat."] Luke 15:16.

569.14 "border ruffians"] Term for proslavery Missouri militia who fought with free-soil settlers in Kansas Territory during the 1850s.

569.24–25 Gilbert C. Walker] Born in Pennsylvania, Walker (1833–1885) practiced law in New York and Chicago before moving to Norfolk, Virginia, in 1864. He was elected governor of Virginia in July 1869 as a "True Republican" supported by a coalition of Conservatives and moderate Republicans, and served from September 1869 to January 1874. Walker aligned himself with the Conservatives during his term as governor, and later served in Congress as a Democrat, 1875–79.

569.34 changed the rules] On February 1, 1875, the Republicans amended the House rules in order to prevent the Democrats from using delaying motions to block the consideration of the civil rights bill and other measures during the lame-duck session.

570.5–6 Mr. WILLIAMS] John M. S. Williams (1818–1886), a Republican congressman from Massachusetts, 1873–75.

571.12 "Molly Maguires"] A secret society of Irish coal miners who engaged in violence against mine owners and operators in the coal region of northeastern Pennsylvania in the 1860s and 1870s.

572.28–30 sepoy . . . lard.] The refusal of soldiers of the East India Company to bite on rifle cartridges greased with cow or pig fat was the immediate cause of a series of mutinies in 1857 that led to a widespread rebellion against British rule across much of northern India.

572.37 foemen worthy of your steel] Cf. Walter Scott, *The Lady of the Lake* (1810), canto V, stanza 10.

579.25–27 a distinguished member . . . a Senator] George S. Boutwell; see note 345.30.

579.31 lengthy and impassioned speech] Boutwell spoke in the House on January 23, 1869.

585.25–26 "hesitate long . . . it about."] From a speech Eldredge made in the House on March 28, 1868, opposing a bill setting conditions for the readmission of Alabama.

586.3–4 *Garfield . . . Civil Rights Bill*] Shortly after Garfield finished his speech, the House voted against keeping the schools clause in the bill, 148–113, and then approved a final version, 162–100. The Senate adopted the House bill, 38–26, on February 27, and it was signed by Grant on March 1, 1875. In the *Civil Rights Cases*, decided on October 15, 1883, the provisions regarding public accommodations, conveyances, and places of amusement were declared unconstitutional by the U.S. Supreme Court in an 8–1 decision. In his majority opinion, Justice Joseph P. Bradley ruled that the power given to Congress by the Fourteenth Amendment to correct racially discriminatory actions by the states did not extend to discriminatory acts by private individuals. Bradley also declared that racial discrimination by individuals was not a "badge of servitude" prohibited by the Thirteenth Amendment. In his dissent, Justice John Marshall Harlan (1833–1911) wrote that racially discriminatory acts by accommodation, transportation, and amusement facilities operating under state licenses were public, not private, actions and therefore subject to congressional prohibition under the Fourteenth Amendment. Harlan also asserted that since slavery was based upon the supposed racial inferiority of black people, acts of racial discrimination were clearly "badges of servitude" prohibited by the Thirteenth Amendment.

587.25–26 loseth his life . . . shall find it.] Cf. Matthew 10:39.

588.6–17 "We dare not . . . Fate abreast."] John Greenleaf Whittier (1807–1892), "Song of the Negro Boatmen" (1862).

589.3 Hinds County Gazette] Published in Raymond, Mississippi, the *Gazette* was owned and edited by George W. Harper (1824–94), a prominent local Democrat.

589.5 past elections] The next state elections were to be held on November 2, 1875.

589.6 Hinds county] The county included Jackson, the state capital, and the towns of Clinton and Raymond.

590.5 Ames'] A West Point graduate from Maine, Adelbert Ames (1835–1933) commanded a division in the Union army as a brigadier general. He served as the appointed provisional governor of Mississippi, 1868–70, as a Republican senator, 1870–74, and as the elected governor, 1874–76. In 1870 Ames married Blanche Butler (1847–1939), the daughter of Benjamin F. Butler.

591.9 Mississippi revolt] A Republican political rally and barbecue held in Clinton, Mississippi, on September 4, 1875, was attended by about 2,000 African Americans and about seventy-five whites, including eighteen Democrats from Raymond. When the Democrats tried to disrupt the rally, an altercation began and gunfire broke out. Three white men and at least five black persons were killed as hundreds of families fled the scene. Over the next two days several hundred members of the "White Line" militia moved through Hinds County and murdered between thirty and fifty African Americans. Governor Ames wrote to Grant on September 8 asking for federal assistance in suppressing the violence. Pierrepont responded by asking Ames if the "insurrection" could be put down with state forces. On September 11 Ames replied that attempting to use white militia against the "White Liners" would be ineffectual, while organizing a black militia risked "a war of races" that would spread through the South. Pierrepont forwarded his correspondence with Ames to Grant, along with several dispatches from Mississippi, including a message from James Z. George (1826–1897), the chairman of the Democratic-Conservative state committee, in which George claimed that "perfect peace prevails throughout the State."

591.23   Utica] Grant attended a reunion of veterans of the Army of the Cumberland in Utica, New York, September 15–16, 1875.

592.7   assistance offered . . . Jackson and elsewhere.] Among the messages forwarded to Grant by Pierrepont was a telegram from Henry R. Pease (1835–1907), a Republican who had served in the Senate from Mississippi, 1874–75. Pease wrote that a "civil posse composed of good citizens of all political parties and of sufficient force to protect life and property can be had in any county in the State," and warned that federal intervention would be "unwise, impolitic, and will only tend to aggravate existing difficulties."

592.18   Mr. Luckey] Levi P. Luckey (1842–1884), private secretary to Grant.

594.11–12   you take all . . . needed measures] Ames reluctantly began to organize and deploy black militia companies, then agreed to hold a "peace conference" with James Z. George and other Democratic leaders on October 13. At the meeting Ames agreed to stand down the militia in return for a promise by George that White Line violence would cease. On election day many black voters stayed away from the polls, and the Democrats gained control of both houses of the legislature. Ames resigned as governor on March 29, 1876, to avoid impeachment and left the state.

595.18   'hearts are . . . all things.'] Cf. Jeremiah 17:9.

597.4   Select Senate Committee] The five-member Select Committee to Inquire into the Mississippi Election of 1875 was appointed on May 31, 1876, and its majority and minority reports were submitted on August 7, 1876.

597.9   the CHAIRMAN] George S. Boutwell; see note 345.30.

597.10   SENATOR CALDWELL] Charles Caldwell (1831/32–1875), a freedman, was a successful blacksmith in Clinton. Caldwell was elected as a delegate to the Mississippi constitutional convention in 1868, served in the state senate, 1870–75, and was a supporter of the school for black women established by Sarah A. Dickey (see Biographical Notes).

597.17–18   Thursday night, in the Christmas.] Thursday, December 30, 1875.

597.32   Moss Hill] An abandoned plantation in Clinton, the scene of the political meeting held on September 4, 1875.

599.5   Judge Cabinis] Edwin W. Cabaniss, chancery judge of Hinds County.

600.3   your brother, too, Sam."] Sam Caldwell was Margaret Ann Caldwell's brother-in-law.

600.14   Professor Hillman] Walter Hillman (1829–1894), president of the Central Female Institute, a school for white women in Clinton.

602.10   he carried the militia to Edwards] Caldwell had commanded a company of black militiamen that transported a shipment of weapons from Jackson to Edwards on October 9, 1875.

602.16   "Murdocs."] White men who named themselves after the Modoc Indians, who had fought the U.S. Army in northern California and southern Oregon, 1872–73. The Modoc leader known as Captain Jack was notorious for having killed Brigadier General Edward R. S. Canby (see note 381.36–37) during a truce meeting held on April 11, 1873.

604.16   the club] A Republican club.

605.5   Haffa] William P. Haffa, a white schoolteacher from Pennsylvania who served as a justice of the peace, was murdered on September 6, 1875.

606.3–4   *Tourgée: Root, Hog, or Die*] The text of this essay is taken from an undated newspaper clipping in the Albion Winegar Tourgée Papers, Chautauqua County Historical Society, Westfield, New York. It was dated c. 1876 by Mark Elliott and John David Smith, the editors of *Undaunted Radical: The Selected Writings and Speeches of Albion W. Tourgée* (2010).

611.8   Mr. SINGLETON . . . this bill] Otho R. Singleton (1814–1889) was a Democratic congressman from Mississippi, 1853–55, 1857–61, and 1875–87. He reported an appropriations bill for the consular and diplomatic service to the House on February 3, 1876.

614.33–34   Mr. TUCKER . . . the word nation] John Randolph Tucker (1823–1887) served as attorney general of Virginia, 1857–65, and as a Democratic congressman, 1875–87. In a speech in the House on January 19, 1876, opposing the appropriation of $1.5 million for the Philadelphia Centennial Exhibition, Tucker noted that the word "national" did not appear in the text of the Constitution.

615.2   Mr. COX] Samuel S. Cox; see note 489.19.

616.3   Chickasaw and common-school funds] Funds for public schools in Mississippi derived from the sale of lands ceded by the Chickasaw Nation in 1832.

619.3   *Daniel H. Chamberlain*] A former Union officer from Massachusetts, Chamberlain (1835–1907) moved to South Carolina in 1866. He was a delegate to the state constitutional convention in 1868, the state attorney general, 1868–72, and governor, 1874–77.

619.6   your letter of the 22d of July] Chamberlain wrote that "most Republicans here" believed the recent killing in Hamburg "foreshadows a campaign of blood and violence" conducted "on the 'Mississippi plan.'" He asked Grant to make troop deployments that would make possible federal intervention "prompt and effective," but did not request immediate aid.

619.8   massacre of innocent men . . . Hamburg] A dispute over the right-of-way arose in the town of Hamburg, South Carolina, on July 4, 1876, between two white men in a carriage and a company of black state militia marching in the street. On July 8 two to three hundred armed white men gathered in Hamburg and demanded that the militia company surrender its arms. When they refused, the white gunmen laid siege to the militia armory and used a small cannon to force its evacuation. One white man and six African Americans were killed in the incident, including five black militiamen who were shot after they surrendered.

621.8   Mr. Chandler and Mr. Cornell] Zachariah Chandler (1813–1879) was a Republican senator from Michigan, 1857–75 and 1879, secretary of the interior, 1875–77, and chairman of the Republican National Committee in 1876. Alonzo B. Cornell (1832–1904) was vice president of the Western Union telegraph company and chairman of the New York Republican state committee. He later served as governor of New York, 1880–82.

622.15   Coomassie] Kumasi, now in Ghana, was the capital of the Ashanti empire. It was captured by the British in 1874 during the Third Anglo-Ashanti War.

622.37   Mr. Dawes] Henry L. Dawes (1816–1903) was a Republican congressman from Massachusetts, 1857–1875, and a senator, 1875–93.

623.24   Tilden] A wealthy lawyer, Samuel J. Tilden (1814–1886) was governor of New York, 1875–76, and the Democratic presidential nominee in 1876.

623.37–38   American consul . . . battle of Mentana] Edwin C. Cushman (1838–1909) was the U.S. consul in Rome, 1865–69. French and Papal forces defeated Italian volunteers led by Giuseppe Garibaldi (1807–1882) in the battle of Mentana, fought north of Rome on November 3, 1867.

624.11   Casey] James F. Casey (1830–1888), collector of customs at New Orleans, 1869–77, and brother-in-law of Julia Dent Grant.

624.12   Parker] Probably John M. G. Parker, postmaster at New Orleans, 1875–78.

624.19   Mr. Hayes's letter] Hayes formally accepted the Republican nomination in a letter dated July 8, 1876.

625.4–6   Mr. Wheeler . . . national affliction] William A. Wheeler (see note 551.38) wrote on July 15, 1876: "We of the North delude ourselves in expecting that the masses of the South, so far behind in many of the attributes of enlightened improvement and civilization, are, in the brief period of ten or fifteen years, to be transformed into our model Northern communities. That can only come through a long course of patient waiting to which no one can now set certain bounds."

626.3–4   *Ingersoll . . . Indianapolis*] Ingersoll spoke at the Soldiers' and Sailors' Reunion held in Indianapolis, September 20–21, 1876.

627.28   tried to fire the city of New York] A team of Confederate operatives set fire to several hotel rooms in New York City on November 25, 1864,
but failed to cause widespread destruction. Most of the arsonists escaped to
Canada, but one Confederate officer, Robert Cobb Kennedy (1835–1865), was
captured, tried by a military commission, and hanged.

627.32–33   tried to spread . . . yellow fever] In May 1865 a former Confederate agent testified at the trial of the Lincoln conspirators that in 1864 Dr. Lucas
P. Blackburn (1816–1887) had traveled twice to Bermuda, where he collected
clothes and bedding from yellow fever victims and arranged for their shipment
to several cities in the United States in an attempt to spread the disease. Blackburn was never prosecuted by American authorities, and he later served as the
Democratic governor of Kentucky, 1879–83.

632.5   Polls on wednesday the 4th] Elections for state offices and the U.S.
House of Representatives were held in Georgia on October 4, 1876.

633.4–5   Mr Peter O'Neal *c* run for Representative] O'Neal was an unsuccessful candidate for the Georgia House of Representatives. The letter "*c*" stands
for "colored."

633.5–6   Mr Johnathan Norcross, for Governor] Jonathan Norcross (1808–
1898), a successful businessman and antebellum mayor of Atlanta, was defeated
by Alfred H. Colquitt (1824–1894), the Democratic candidate, 111,297–33,443.

634.6–7   News . . . Herald] The Columbus, Ohio, *Sunday Morning News*
and the *Columbus Herald*, another weekly newspaper.

634.30–32   former free States . . . the twenty-two] Tilden carried New
York, Connecticut, New Jersey, and Indiana.

635.8   General Mitchell] John G. Mitchell (1838–1894), a lawyer in Columbus, had served as a brigadier general in the Union army. He was married to
Laura Platt Mitchell (1842–1916), Hayes's niece.

635.12   my son Webb] Webb Cook Hayes (1856–1934). A White House
secretary during his father's presidency, Webb Hayes later fought in the
Spanish-American War and the Philippines.

635.13   Governor Dennison] William Dennison (1815–1882) was the Republican governor of Ohio, 1860–62, and postmaster general, 1864–66.

637.17   General Ruger] Brevet Major General Thomas H. Ruger (1833–1907)
commanded the Department of the South, 1876–78.

637.20–23   Ruger's report . . . refused admission] In a dispatch sent to
Washington on November 30, 1876, Ruger reported that one of his officers
had temporarily excluded Democrats from the hall of the house of representatives in the South Carolina statehouse.

637.26   General Gordon] John B. Gordon (1832–1904), a former major general in the Confederate army, served as a Democratic senator from Georgia,

1873–80 and 1891–97, and as governor, 1886–90. Gordon reputedly organized and led the Ku Klux Klan in Georgia, a charge he denied before a congressional investigating committee in 1871.

638.34   Mr. Kasson] John A. Kasson (1822–1910) served as a Republican congressman from Iowa, 1873–77 and 1881–84, as U.S. minister to Austria-Hungary, 1877–81, and as minister to Germany, 1884–85.

638.38   Hendricks] Thomas A. Hendricks (1819–1885), the Democratic vice presidential nominee in 1876, was a congressman from Indiana, 1851–55, a senator, 1863–69, governor, 1873–77, and vice president of the United States, 1884–85.

639.13   Slidell] See note 204.19.

639.19–20   vote of Louisiana . . . in 1872] See Chronology, November 1872.

640.7–8   two houses . . . conflict] In the Forty-fourth Congress, 1875–77, the Republicans controlled the Senate while the Democrats held the majority in the House.

640.30–31   vote from Oregon] See Chronology, November 1876.

641.11–12   Major Robert Anderson] Anderson (1805–1871) commanded the Union garrison in Charleston harbor from November 1860 until the surrender of Fort Sumter on April 14, 1861.

642.9   Tide-waiters] A customs officer who inspects the landing of goods.

642.35–36   joint committee . . . a scheme] See Chronology, January 1877.

645.15   Wendell Phillips' words] In a speech given in Philadelphia on March 26, 1877, Phillips had denounced the southern policy of the new Hayes administration. "Half of what Grant gained for us at Appomattox, Hayes surrendered in Washington on the 5th of March," Phillips said. Referring to promises made by Wade Hampton and Francis T. Nicholls, the Democratic claimant to the Louisiana governorship, that they would "keep the peace and protect" black citizens, Phillips warned: "To trust a Southern promise would be fair evidence of insanity."

649.22   Crédit Mobilier and Northern Pacific] Crédit Mobilier, see note 476.38. The failure of Jay Cooke & Company to market Northern Pacific railroad bonds caused the firm to go bankrupt on September 18, 1873, setting off the Panic of 1873.

650.28   Hills] Benjamin H. Hill (1823–1882) was a Democratic congressman from Georgia, 1875–77, and a senator, 1877–82.

650.31–32   Southern Gordon . . . Northern Morton] In a speech in the Senate on March 9, 1876, John B. Gordon proposed civil service reforms to fight corruption in the collection of excise taxes on whiskey. Oliver P. Morton responded by noting that the excise taxes had been reimposed during the Civil

War, and said that "those who made the war are the last persons who have a right to complain of its consequences."

CODA, 1879

655.30–31 grand speech General Sherman] In his speech of May 30, 1878, Sherman said: "We claim that, in the great civil war, we of the National Union Army were right, and our adversaries were wrong; and no special pleading, no excuses, no personal motives, however pure and specious, can change this verdict of the war."

658.2–4 *Rainey . . . South Carolina Elections*] Rainey had won reelection in 1876, defeating the Democratic candidate John S. Richardson, 18,180–16,661. Richardson (1828–1894) challenged the results, claiming that voters had been intimidated by the presence of federal troops at the polls and the actions of black militia units and Republican political clubs. The House Committee on Elections recommended on May 18, 1878, that Rainey's seat be declared vacant, but the House took no action. On November 5, 1878, Richardson defeated Rainey, 22,707–14,096. Rainey obtained leave from the House on March 3, 1879, the final day of his congressional career, to have his remarks on his election case printed in the record.

658.6 election day] November 7, 1876.

659.33–34 gentleman from Louisiana . . . following] Ezekiel J. Ellis (1840–1889), a Democratic congressman from Louisiana, 1875–85, in the majority report of the Committee on Elections, May 18, 1878.

660.39 Zulus . . . Africa to-day.] In the Anglo-Zulu War, January–July 1879, which ended in the defeat of the Zulus.

661.21 my colleague] John H. Evins (1830–1884), a Democratic congressman from South Carolina, 1877–84.

Index

*This book is set in 10 point ITC Galliard, a face
designed for digital composition by Matthew Carter and based
on the sixteenth-century face Granjon. The paper is acid-free
lightweight opaque that will not turn yellow or brittle with age.
The binding is sewn, which allows the book to open easily and lie flat.
The binding board is covered in Brillianta, a woven rayon cloth
made by Van Heek–Scholco Textielfabrieken, Holland.
Composition by Dedicated Book Services.
Printing and binding by Edwards Brothers Malloy, Ann Arbor.
Designed by Bruce Campbell.*

THE LIBRARY OF AMERICA SERIES

Library of America fosters appreciation of America's literary heritage by publishing, and keeping permanently in print, authoritative editions of America's best and most significant writing. An independent nonprofit organization, it was founded in 1979 with seed funding from the National Endowment for the Humanities and the Ford Foundation.

In that dire extremity the members of the race which I have the honor in part to represent... the race which pleads for justice at your hands to-day, forgetful of their inhuman and brutal... in the swamps and in the rice-field, their valor on the land and on the sea, is a part of the...

ABRAHAM LINCOLN
THE MAN FOR THE DOLLAR
APRIL 6. 1859.

"I shall not attempt to retract or modify the Emancipation Proclamation, nor shall I return to slavery any person who is free by the terms of that Proclamation or by any acts of Congress."
ABRAHAM LINCOLN. *From the Annual Message, December 8, 1863.*

L I B E R T Y

ARMY

HON. ROB...
OF S...
DELIVERING HIS GREAT SPEECH ON CIVIL RI...

Of those who were slaves at the beginning of the rebellion full one hundred thousand are now in the U. S. Service.

J U R Y &

AMERICAN SLAVE LABOUR IS OF THE PAST — FREE LABOUR IS OF THE PRES...

The rights contended for in this bill are among the sacred rights of mankind which are not to be rummaged for among old parchments or musty records, they are written as with a sunbeam in the who...

THE SHACKLE BROKEN —